W9-BHH-117

Colin Wilson was born in Leicester in 1931. He left school at sixteen and spent several years working in a wool warehouse, a laboratory, a plastics factory and a coffee bar before *The Outsider* was published in 1956 to immense critical acclaim.

Since then he has written many books on crime, philosophy, the occult and sexual deviance, as well as a number of successful novels. His work includes *Encyclopaedia of Murder* (with Patricia Pitman), *A Casebook of Murder, Order of Assassins: The Psychology of Murder* and *A Criminal History of Mankind*.

Colin Wilson is well known as a lecturer and as a radio and television personality.

The Mammoth Book of
TRUE CRIME

By the same author

NON-FICTION
The Outsider
Religion and the Rebel
The Age of Defeat
Encyclopaedia of Murder (with Patricia Pitman)
Origins of the Sexual Impulse
Beyond the Outsider: The Philosophy of the Future
Voyage to a Beginning (autobiography)
A Casebook of Murder
The Occult
Order of Assassins: The Psychology of Murder
Strange Powers
Mysterious Powers
The Craft of the Novel
The Geller Phenomenon
Science Fiction as Existentialism
The Search for the Real Arthur
Starseekers
The Quest for Wilhelm Reich
Lord of the Underworld: Jung and the Twentieth Century
A Criminal History of Mankind
The Misfits
The Book of Great Mysteries (Ed.)

FICTION
Ritual in the Dark
The World of Violence
Necessary Doubt
The Glass Cage
The Killer
The Schoolgirl Murder Case
The Janus Murder Case
The Mind Parasites
The Space Vampires
Spider world

The Mammoth Book of
TRUE CRIME

Colin Wilson

Carroll & Graf Publishers, Inc.
New York

Text copyright Macdonald & Co. (Publishers) Ltd., © 1973/4/5/6
Introduction copyright Howard F. Dossor, © 1988
Selection copyright Robinson Publishing, © 1988

First published in collection form in Great Britain 1988
First Carroll & Graf edition 1988
Reprinted 1988

Carroll & Graf Publishers, Inc.
260 Fifth Avenue
New York, NY 10001

ISBN: 0–88184–411–X

All rights reserved.

Printed by Wm. Collins & Sons Ltd., Glasgow, Scotland

CONTENTS

Introduction ix
Acquittals 1
Alibis 10
Air Crimes 18
Arson 27
Artists' Crimes 36
Assassination 44
Bandits 53
Betrayal 61
Blackmail 70
Cannibalism 78
Chance in a Million 86
Children Who Kill 95
Con Men 104
Cop Killers 111
Country Killings 119
Crimes of Passion 127
Doctors of Death 134
Dominance 142
Drugs 150
Dual Personality 159
Families of Death 167
Female Murderers 175
Forgery 183

Gallows Cheats   191
Gangsters   202
Gentlemen Crooks   210
Greed   219
Gun Deaths   227
Headless Corpses   235
High Society Murder   243
Hired Killers   251
Homosexual Murder   260
Houses of Death   269
Husband Killers   278
Impostors   287
Inheritance Crime   296
Intolerance   308
Justice Delayed   317
Kidnappers   326
Killer Couples   334
Lady-killers   343
Left-luggage Murders   352
Lethal Lawyers   361
Libel   370
Lonely Hearts Killers   378
Manic Messiahs   387
Martyrs   396
Mass Murderers   405
Military Murders   414
Monsters   422
Motiveless Murder   430
Murderous Millionaires   437
Occult Detection   445
Office Crimes   452
Parent Killers   460
Perverts   468

Poisoners 476
Police Corruption 485
Protection Rackets 493
Robber Barons 502
Sabotage 512
Servants Who Murder 521
Sleep-walking Slayers 530
Stick-up Men 540
Stranglers 548
Suicide 556
Super-thieves 565
Train Murders 573
Underworlds 581
Unwanted Lovers 589
Vicious Triangles 597
Victims 605
Vital Clues 614
War Crimes 623

INTRODUCTION

Colin Wilson has had a long term interest in crime in general and in the phenomenon of murder in particular. Well before he was ten years old, he was reading copies of the magazines *True Detective* and *Modern Murder* after they were handed down to him by his mother and other members of his family. Nor was his interest morbid or prurient. As he read these tales of violent passion, he understood intuitively that they had something important to say to the human condition. They served to represent one side of the human psyche, the other side of which was represented by stories of great human achievement and individual self-fulfilment.

In 1956, Wilson wrote a long essay entitled *The Outsider as Murderer* for inclusion in his first published book, *The Outsider*. A problem with the length of the book meant that the essay was set aside for the time being but a fragment of it was published later as an appendix to *An Encyclopedia of Murder*, which Wilson wrote with Pat Pitman. The essay makes it clear that a genuine understanding of Wilson's criminology – for his theory amounts to nothing less than this – depends upon a comprehension of what he meant by the term 'Outsider'.

The Outsider is a person who perceives that much of what we call civilization is a denial of the finest of human values. He has an instinctive understanding that life is infinitely more than it appears to be: that our condition is a parody of our potential. He experiences a deep sense of alienation from both himself and his society. He knows that he is internally divided, but he also knows that the struggle to regain unity within himself is the most urgent task to which he can commit himself.

Because he cannot feel at home in the world, the Outsider closes in on himself; he crosses what Wilson has called 'the Indifference Threshold'. This is a state of dull insensitivity that often expresses itself as boredom. And boredom begets boredom

– that is, boredom creates a chain of negative reaction which heightens the boredom until it becomes intolerable. Thus, for the Outsider, life is not so much a stimulating encounter with experience as a senseless drifting.

Wilson saw that much of our living is done for us. We are taken over by what he calls 'the Robot', who drives our car for us so that we can recall turning the ignition key and then discovering ourselves at our destination, without having any recollection of the journey itself. It is the Robot who presses the keys on our typewriter while our minds concentrate on what we want to commit to paper. Obviously, the Robot is an efficient machine and it renders us a valuable service. But the Robot can take too much control over our lives. Wilson admits that he has even caught his Robot making love to his wife!

What happens when we cross the Indifference Threshold or allow the Robot to assume too much authority in our lives, is that we lose all sense of intensity: we neutralize the sense of purpose which normally sustains a forward thrust in our living. This is the Outsider's problem. He is like a child for whom a day has become like a week. Wilson provides another powerful analogy: the Outsider is like a grandfather clock being driven by a watch spring – and in this sense there is a measure of the Outsider in all of us.

By way of direct contrast with the negative dimensions of the Outsider's character, Wilson points to Abraham Maslow's notion of the 'self-actualising' man. According to Maslow, man has an ascending order of primary values. The first of these is the need for food. Once this is satisfied, a need for shelter manifests itself. Satisfy that and the need for love emerges – the need for a sense of belonging in both a society and a warm one-to-one relationship. Where this need is satisfied, a fourth emerges; the need for self-esteem. Then, at the apex of the pyramid, there is a need for self-actualization – the full realization of one's individual potential.

From one point of view, the entire life and work – now consisting of over seventy volumes – of Colin Wilson, could be described as a quest for a full comprehension of the laws governing self-actualization. His interest in murder and in the psychology of the murderer must always be considered in this context.

For Wilson,

murder is the meaninglessness of life become dynamic: a dramatization of the hidden futility of life. It is the human act, with all its inherent values, placed under the microscope slide where it cannot dissolve into the featureless landscape of all other human acts. The study of murder is not the study of abnormal human nature; it is the study of human nature stained by an act that makes it visible on the microscope slide.

Wilson has identified a variety of distinct classes of murder. First there is murder which occurs as a result of a frustrated vitality, although these are comparatively rare. A second class has its origin in sheer brutality; a total insensitivity to pain and suffering. Most murders in this class are committed by gangsters. By far the largest group of murders are those that are conceived in the narrowness and lack of imagination in the murderer's mind. A fourth class is of much more recent origin. It is murder for self-esteem; the criminal act through which the murderer makes his statement of identity to the world. Another class is the product of sheer boredom.

In the nineteenth century, the majority of murders were associated with robbery. Economic deprivation drove men to acts of violence against each other, with murder often the outcome. Today it is clear that many murders are related to sex. Improved living standards have made robbery less prevalent but these very improved living standards have brought other problems in their train. Today there is more neurosis and personality disorder. There is also more leisure time and thus a greater challenge to our imagination to make creative use of our freedom. Unfortunately, we have not trained ourselves sufficiently in the use of freedom and the not infrequent result is that we put it to the basest use. Wilson has written:

It seems possible that crimes of violence and sex crimes are one of the prices we pay for our high level of civilization. Few people feel 'at home' in a complex society but most people manage to bear it with the help of a psychiatrist or alcohol or some other means of periodic escape. The men who manage to bear it best are those with a sense of social purpose and an enthusiasm for organization. But the subnormal men, the weaklings, find it impossible to accept it on any terms and become social problems. They can be said to live 'in' society in the sense that a maggot lives in cheese; their role is wholly parasitic. Many such men are not even habitual criminals. They simply possess no sense of social responsibility and will take whatever offers itself.

The bigger and more centralized a society becomes, the more of these socially irresponsible individuals it creates. The impersonality of society produces either revolt or contemptuous indifference. Hence, the age of centralization is the age of the juvenile delinquent and the sex maniac.

For Wilson, the crimes of Jack the Ripper represent a turning point in the history of murder for they were the first of what may truly be called sex murders. In his recent, penetrating study of the mind of the Ripper, in *Jack the Ripper: Summing Up and Verdict*, written with Robin Odell, Wilson argues that he was not a demented doctor or clergyman, not a moral reformer but an introverted, unattractive little man whose lack of normal sex outlet had embittered him until his desire could only be exorcised by stabbing and slashing. But whoever he was, Jack the Ripper ushered in a new age of violent crime which has not yet come to an end.

One of the most important contributions made by Wilson to the study of murder is the notion of the *Violent Man* or the *Right Man*. Following on the research of the science fiction writer, A.E. Van Vogt, Wilson points to a certain personality type which is prone to violence. The type is characterized by an absolute obsession about being 'in the right'. It is virtually incapable of self-criticism and cannot tolerate even implied criticism of its behaviour. In a marriage, the Right Man will insist on total obeisance from his spouse and will apply a double standard to the relationship. While he may do as he pleases, his wife must work at preserving the marriage at all costs. Any act which challenges his authority or which attempts to confront him with his own inadequacies will almost certainly produce a violent reaction.

The notion of the Right Man has been translated into fiction by Wilson in his novel, *The Killer* – titled *Lingard* in the United States. This work should be read as a part of a trilogy of novels dealing with murder, the other two being *Ritual in the Dark* and *The Glass Cage*. *The Killer* is a composite of many real-life murderers including Peter Kürten, Williams Heirens and Peter Manuel. It also draws on the psychiatry of Medard Boss, Ludwig Binswanger and Paul J. Reiter Jr. In a sense it is a non-fictional novel, akin to Truman Capote's *In Cold Blood*. Commenting on *The Killer*, Wilson writes:

In Arthur Lingard I have tried to show the development of a Right Man who is also an Outsider in my sense: that is, who, in certain respects, *is* more imaginative and talented than those around him; who *does* possess more will and drive than they do. His life is not tragic in the Greek sense of inexorable doom but only in the sense of wrong choices, made freely, that end by frustrating his creative potential . . . Most criminals are not Right Men but the worst criminals are: a Kürten, a Manuel, a Haigh.

It is interesting to note that the only passage relating to criminology to be published in *The Essential Colin Wilson* – the contents of which were selected by Wilson himself – is the chapter on the Right Man that appeared in *The Criminal History of Mankind*. Clearly, Wilson considers the insight of profound importance.

Before leaving Wilson's fiction, it might be useful to note that his Saltfleet novels, *The Schoolgirl Murder Case* and *The Janus Murder Case*, are much more than light reading in the detective genre. The former is an important study in the link between sex and murder while the latter has a very valuable postscript on the multiple personality which may, indeed, lie at the centre of many murders.

Another important contribution made by Wilson to the science of criminology is his evaluation of the work of Dan MacDougald. In the mid-Fifties, MacDougald, in dealing with a group of Federal authorities in the United States, noted that they seemed strangely unable to hear the case he was putting to them. He concluded that this was because they had chosen to focus only on what they wanted to hear. MacDougald's suspicion was reinforced when he read that our five senses pick up ten thousand 'units of information' every second but our brain makes use of only about seven of them. In other words, the brain is a filter which screens out thousands of impulses and concentrates on whatever it selects as being important. MacDougald applied this insight and information to a group of prisoners in a local prison. He soon discovered that the criminal is very likely to be a person who has cut himself off from all positive stimuli and who has focussed on a very narrow range of negative feelings. He becomes emotionally insensitive to all the impulses that contradict his negative view of the world.

In an attempt to utilize these insights in the rehabilitation of prison inmates, MacDougald reasoned that the key to a man's attitudes lies in his understanding of words. He found that, for the criminals, words such as 'love', 'neighbour', 'responsibility' and 'hope' were either incompletely understood or were understood in a manner that contradicted their usual meanings. He set out to show them that the blame for their criminal behaviour lay in their own muddled and negative attitudes. In one incident, a prisoner who had an iron bar hidden in his clothes was discovered before he had an opportunity to use it on his intended victim, a fellow inmate. MacDougald took him aside and discussed the notion of 'forgiveness' with him. The result was that the prisoner bought his would-be victim coffee and they talked their dispute through. The two men eventually became friends.

Wilson warns that it would be a mistake to treat Mac-Dougald's work as trite or simplistic. It may well represent one of the most important breakthroughs in our understanding of what happens in the criminal mind. And it is more than just a diagnostic tool. It is a means of altering the basic attitudes of a personality type in which the need to evolve has been frustrated to the point where it explodes into violence. With these negative attitudes out of the way, it can resume its movement forward and the need for violence disappears.

It was Wilson who made a most important discovery in relation to couples who murder. As was the case with Brady and Hindley and with Leopold and Loeb, Wilson noted that with couples who kill, there is usually one dominant and one submissive person. Wilson's general theory of dominance suggests that five per cent of the human population is dominant and assertive. It constitutes, as it were, the avant-garde of the race. Most of the great artists will emerge from within this five per cent: so too will most of the major murderers of our age. It is as if the dominant five per cent are anxious to take the next step on the evolutionary pilgrimage and are frustrated because they do not know in which direction they should move. Their frustration frequently expresses itself in a bold, creative act such as the painting of a picture or the writing of a symphony – or in a cold-blooded act of murder.

In 1956, Wilson wrote that capital punishment was a gross folly because it robbed society of the opportunity to assess the criminal mentality more closely. When a murderer is apprehended, he argued, the best available psychiatrists and psychologists should make him the subject of an intense study. More recently, in a private conversation, Wilson admitted to having changed his mind on the matter. He is not, now, opposed to capital punishment. I suspect that his essential motive for this shift is humanitarian. Lifelong imprisonment, under the close scrutiny of a clinical team, is not a lifestyle that commends itself. For Colin Wilson, crime is a mistaken solution to the predicament in which humanity finds itself. It is a mistaken response to our need to evolve. It must be admitted that, in terms of our own development, we are all making constant mistakes but the criminal, particularly the murderer, goes further than anyone else in making the wrong response. The result is that we can see in the criminal something of our own stupidity; something of the inadequacy of our own response to life. This is the basis for Wilson's interest in murder. Essentially, his interest is philosophical. He says:

> I see murder as a response to a certain problem of human freedom; not as a social problem or a psychological problem, or even a moral problem but as an *existential* problem.
>
> In moments of crisis, man becomes aware that he possesses a far higher degree of freedom than he ever realized. In a sense, the problem of murder is implicit in Auden's lines:
>
> > Life remains a blessing
> > Although you cannot bless
>
> We are all subject to the great mystery of human boredom, which is the most common form of eclipse of the 'blessing'. But on the point of being shot, Graham Greene's whisky-priest suddenly realizes that 'it would have been so easy to be a saint.' Raskolnikov realizes that if he had to stand on a narrow ledge for ever, in eternal darkness and tempest, he would still prefer to do this rather than die at once. Even the American gangster, Charley Birger remarked, as he stood on the scaffold: 'It is a beautiful world, isn't it?' We deny this freedom during every moment of our lives, except in brief flashes of vision. But it is by far the most interesting possibility that human beings possess. And this recognition is the basis of my own philosophical vision, the central problem of all my work. We are like poverty-stricken Indians whose land is rich in oil; one day, someone is going to learn the technique of sinking wells. It will be the most important thing that has happened in human history.
>
> Murder interests me because it is the most extreme form of the denial of this human potentiality. Life devaluation has become a commonplace of our century. We talk glibly about social disintegration, about our moral bankruptcy, about the depth of our sense of defeat, and existentialist philosophers have been the chief exponents of this kind of pessimism. It may therefore sound absurd to say that every time I contemplate murder, I feel an odd spark of optimism. But is it so? We can accept boredom and philosophical pessimism as somehow inevitable, like the weather; but we cannot take this causal attitude towards murder. It arouses in us the same kind of morbid interest that the thought of fornication arouses in a puritanical old

maid. If the old maid were at all analytical, she would see this morbid interest as a proof that sex cannot really be dismissed as nasty and disgusting; we do not feel morbid interest in a beggar covered with sores, or the carcass of a dead rat. Her morbid interest is an inverted form of the recognition that sex can be man's most vital insight into his secret potentialities. And if a murder case arouses this same sick curiosity, it is because we instinctively recognize it as a denial of these secret potentialities of freedom. Our interest in murder is a form of stirring in our sleep.

Through the ongoing enunciation of his philosophy, Colin Wilson has made an invaluable contribution to our understanding of the human condition. He has taken us to the heart of pessimism and despair. But he has provided us with a return ticket for he has understood that to see real misery, real Hell, is to recognize that there *must* be a more noble lifestyle available to us. This volume is best read with this conviction in mind.

Howard F. Dossor
1988

ACQUITTALS

Every writer on crime has at some time puzzled over the question of why certain cases capture the public imagination. Why were the Victorians so fascinated by the murder of Maria Marten in the Red Barn? And what did they find so interesting about that utterly commonplace murder of Mr. William Weare by Thurtell and Hunt? Why do we still find Jack the Ripper's crimes more interesting than many more recent cases of mass murder – Dean Corll's sadistic killing of thirty boys near Houston, Texas, for example?

The answer, surely, is that although most people are incapable of murder, they nevertheless derive a kind of morbid pleasure from 'identifying' with the murderer, and feeling glad they're not in his shoes. The strange thing is that the reader does not identify with the victim – Maria Marten being shot, or William Weare having his brains battered out and his throat cut – but with the killer. And when he has read about the execution of William Corder or James Thurtell, he experiences the same kind of pleasure you get when you wake from a nightmare and find yourself in your own bed.

This explains the otherwise baffling fact that the public seems to get as much pleasure from reading about famous acquittals as from cases that ended on the gallows. The Green Bicycle case, the Peasenhall mystery, the Gorse Hall murder, turn up in anthologies of famous crimes with the same frequency as Crippen and Landru. Obviously, the reader enjoys the sensation of walking into the shadow of the gallows and then being allowed to escape.

Certainly no man ever came closer to the hangman's rope than William Gardiner, who stood trial for the murder of a servant girl called Rose Harsent in 1902. The reason was not his obvious guilt, but a certain sexual detail that scandalized the respectable British jury that tried him.

June 1, 1902, was a bright, sunny morning after a night of storm. William Harsent, a carter, walked through the peaceful Suffolk village of Peasenhall, on his way to take clean linen to his daughter Rose. He walked through the wet garden of Providence House, where the girl was in service, and pushed open the back door. What he saw made him drop the linen. Rose Harsent lay, half naked, at the foot of the stairs. Her throat was cut from ear to ear, and deep gashes covered her bare shoulders. She had been wearing a nightdress, but this had been partly torn from her, and partly burnt away. A broken medicine bottle lay on the floor beside the body.

The local policeman arrived, followed by the doctor. The policeman discovered that the broken medicine bottle had contained paraffin – which had apparently been used in the attempt to burn her. The girl's bed had not been slept in, but there were three letters in the room, one of which made an appointment to come and see her at midnight.

She had been pregnant

The signature made it clear that the author was William Gardiner, a young foreman carpenter who lived nearby; he had a wife and six children, and was known as a devout Methodist. Medical examination revealed that Rose Harsent had been dead at least four hours, and that she had been pregnant.

No one had any doubt that the father of the unborn child was William Gardiner, for in the previous year he and Rose had been the subject of scandal in Peasenhall. Two youths had seen them walking towards an empty cottage known as the 'Doctor's Chapel', which stood alone in a field. The youths had hidden behind a hedge until the two had gone inside, then crept closer. They were unable to see what was happening, but the sounds made it clear. There was a rustling of clothes, then the girl gasped 'Oh, oh.'

The silence that followed seemed to suggest a state of mutual satisfaction. Gardiner was heard to ask her what she was thinking. She answered: 'What you were reading last Sunday.' He asked her what he had been reading, and she replied: 'About what we are doing now.' She then went on to quote the verses from Genesis, chapter 38, about how Onan 'spilled his seed on the ground'.

When the story was repeated in Peasenhall, the villagers, who knew their Bible, had no doubt that Gardiner and Rose Harsent had either been engaged in extremely intimate 'petting', or that the youths had overheard an act of *coitus interruptus*. Gardiner was a Sunday School teacher; Rose Harsent was one of his choir girls.

The scandal was so great that an enquiry had been conducted by the Rev. John Grey; Gardiner had denied the story, saying that he had been in the 'chapel' with the girl only to help her move a stiff door. Gardiner had been told 'Let this be a warning to you for life', and had appeared to be suitably chastened. Yet although he promised to have nothing further to do with the girl, it was plain to people who observed them closely that they were still on intimate terms.

The day after Rose Harsent's body was found, a superintendent of police called on Gardiner, and asked him if the handwriting on one of the letters was his; Gardiner denied it. The policeman asked if the envelope in which a certain letter was contained was not identical with those used by Gardiner's building firm; again he denied it. But the next day, he was arrested and charged with Rose's murder.

Cutting up rabbits

Certainly, the case against him looked black. His clasp knife was found to be stained with blood, although he claimed he had been cutting up rabbits: in 1902, there was no way of testing whether a bloodstain was from a human being or an animal; Paul Uhlenhuth *had* discovered the basic principle in 1900, but it had never been used outside Germany.

Various witnesses said that they saw a large fire burning at the back of Gardiner's house on the morning after the murder; the prosecution argued that this explained why no bloodstained clothing was found in the house; Gardiner's wife testified that there had been a fire, but that it was only the usual fire they lit on Sundays; but she did not explain why they needed a fire on a hot June morning.

Gardiner's defence was an alibi, supported by his wife; he said he had been at home all evening, and been in bed beside his wife all night. Gardiner was lucky. In those days the jury's verdict in a murder trial had to be unanimous, and one member of the jury stubbornly refused to be convinced of his guilt. The judge had to order a retrial, and once again the jury failed to agree.

Gardiner should have been tried a third time; but the authorities decided he had been through enough, and entered a *nolle prosequi* – which meant no further prosecution would take place. It was equivalent to the Scottish verdict of 'Not Proven'.

Gardiner and his wife moved to a London suburb, where they opened a shop. Whether they prospered or not has never been recorded.

Was Gardiner guilty? We can never know. Certainly, Gardiner was not the only man who might have made Rose pregnant. Highly indecent verses were found in her room, and proved to have been written by the youth next door, who was in love with her. She was no blushing wallflower, but a forthright country girl who had no objection to keeping obscene verses. She may well have had other lovers beside Gardiner – a solution adopted by Brian Cooper in *Genesis 38* his novel about the murder, which suggests that the dissenting jury man who saved Gardiner's neck at the first trial knew the identity of the real murderer.

Only one thing is clear: Gardiner came close to the gallows, not because the evidence against him was particularly strong, but because the jury found it hard to forget that this Sunday School teacher had misbehaved himself on the floor of a disused cottage with one of his choir girls.

The age of sex crime

In the case of the Green Bicycle mystery, a man escaped the gallows because no possible motive could be found for the murder of a pretty 21-year-old girl. Nowadays, juries would have no difficulty imagining a motive; but in the year 1919, the age of sex crime had not yet arrived, and the accused was given the full benefit of the doubt.

It was on Saturday, July 5, 1919, that a farmer, driving his cattle along a quiet country road in Leicestershire, saw the body of a young girl lying in the road. Her bicycle lay nearby, and her head was surrounded by a pool of blood. A doctor who was called decided that she had met with some accident, but the local police constable was not satisfied. He returned to the spot the next morning, carefully searched the ground, and found a bullet that had been trodden into the road by a horse's hoof. The doctor now re-examined the girl, and discovered what he should have noticed on the previous day – that she had a bullet hole below the left eye.

She was identified as 21-year-old Bella Wright, a factory girl who lived in a cottage with her parents at Stoughton, a nearby village; her father was a farm labourer. On the previous day, she had set out on her bicycle to post a letter, afterwards paying a visit to an uncle who lived in the village of Gaulby. She had cycled into Gaulby accompanied by a man on a green bicycle. Questioned by her uncle about the man's identity, she said she didn't know him – he had spoken to her on the road. During the hour she spent with her uncle, the man wandered round the village; then she came out, and they cycled off together. It was an hour later when her body was found.

No clue to the man's identity was uncovered, the coroner's jury gave a verdict of 'murder by persons unknown', and there matters rested until the February of the following year. A bargeman was leading his horse at a leisurely amble along the canal bank when the tow rope caught on something. The man heaved at it, and pulled a green bicycle frame to the surface. It slipped back immediately; but he recalled the Bella Wright case, and reported the incident to the police. They dragged the canal, and recovered the frame. It was a green B.S.A. bicycle, and the number on the frame enabled the police to trace it to the shop that sold it in Derby; the shop had a record of the purchaser, a young man named Ronald Light.

The evidence looked black

Light proved to be an ex-army officer who was now an assistant master at a Cheltenham school. He had been invalided out of the army suffering from shellshock. He admitted to being the owner of the bicycle, and also to being the man who had been with Bella Wright shortly before her death. He agreed that he had disposed of the bicycle because he was afraid of being identified as the man on the green bicycle; he had also sold the clothes he was wearing at the time. He also threw into the canal a revolver holster, and bullets.

Light claimed that he had a slow puncture on the day he met Bella Wright, and that not long after they had left Gaulby together, it had become so bad that he decided he would have to walk home, whereupon, he said, they had separated at a cross-road; he heard later that she had been found shot. He also admitted to having owned a revolver at one time, but claimed that he had lost it during the last days of the war in France. Lack of motive certainly told in his favour; also, perhaps the fact that he was an ex-army officer. The trial lasted only three days and when the foreman of the jury announced the verdict as 'Not guilty', there were cheers in court.

Today, the prosecution would probably be more realistic, and suggest something along the line that Light picked up Bella with the hope of sexual intercourse, that he shot her during a struggle, then panicked and rode away, leaving her sexually unmolested. This view could have been supported by the evidence of two schoolgirls, who said that when they were out riding, they were accosted by a man on a green bicycle, who followed them for some distance.

But there *could* be another explanation of Bella Wright's death. In a nearby field, a dead crow was found, lying in a pool of blood. Did some farm hand, out looking for rabbits, take a shot at the crow, kill it – and also kill Bella Wright, who was in the line of fire? A gunsmith who gave evidence agreed that the bullet *could* have been fired from a rifle . . . .

Both the Gardiner and the Light cases continue to fascinate criminologists because the killer's identity remains a question mark. In the equally baffling Gorse Hall mystery, the killer was not only seen by several people, but actually overpowered and locked up, and still the case remains unsolved.

George Henry Storrs was a wealthy millowner who lived in a mansion near Dukinfeld, Yorkshire. On September 10, 1909, Storrs was drinking tea with his wife and a friend when someone from outside the window called 'Hold up your hands or I'll shoot'. Then a shot was fired, breaking the window, and a gun was jammed in. The blinds were drawn, but Storrs pulled them aside, and saw the gun barrel. He was about to rush outside and tackle the 'burglar', but his wife begged him not to, and apparently the man went away. The police investigated the matter, placed a guard on the hall for a few weeks, then allowed the case to drop. But six weeks later, on November 1, the cook ran into the sitting room saying: 'There's a man in the kitchen.'

Scullery window broken

Storrs rushed out, and saw a small, slightly built man with a blond moustache, who had a revolver. They struggled; Mrs. Storrs was about to hit the man with a shillelagh when he shouted: 'I won't shoot.' They snatched his revolver, and locked him in the scullery. Storrs then went into the kitchen, while his niece, a Miss Lindley, left the house and ran for help. Suddenly, there was a smashing of glass; the man had broken the scullery window and climbed out. He came back into the kitchen, and this time attacked Storrs with a knife.

When Mrs. Storrs and the servants reached the scene, Storrs was dying of several stab wounds, and the man had fled. Someone bent over the wounded man and asked him if he knew the identity of his attacker; Storrs shook his head and groaned

'No.' The mystery was baffling, but the police had a few leads. If the same man had broken the window in September, and twice attacked Storrs on the night of the murder, then he was a man with a grudge. After the September incident, Storrs had said that he knew of no one with a grudge against him – certainly not one of his own workers.

There was, however, a poor branch of the family, named Howard. Two weeks after the murder, Storrs' cousin, Cornelius Howard, was arrested and charged with the crime. He had a criminal record, and both Miss Lindley and Mrs. Storrs identified him as the attacker. Howard had no moustache in court, but a barber gave evidence that he had shaved it off the day after the murder: the evidence against Howard was certainly overwhelming. Only one question puzzled the prosecution – there was no apparent motive, and, of course, Storrs knew his cousin and should have recognized him.

Howard's alibi was that he had been playing dominoes with the landlord of the Ring o' Bells in Huddersfield. The landlord corroborated this; but he was an alcoholic whose memory was poor, and it was strongly suggested by the prosecution that the evening on which Howard had played dominoes was the one *before* the murder.

Howard was certainly a bad character, who had been arrested many times for burglary. He was not uneducated – and Miss Lindley had described the murderer as being a 'superior type of workman'. Is it possible that, whoever he was, he was one of those working-class socialists, followers of William Morris and Bernard Shaw, who decided to strike a direct blow at the 'exploiting class' by killing the wealthy millowner? We shall never know.

Howard was acquitted; so was another man who was put on trial for the murder at a later date, and the mystery of the killer who was seen by several people remains unsolved.

But perhaps the most remarkable of all cases of acquittal is one that took place in Bridgeport, Connecticut, in 1924. The fact that it has been turned into a film and a play testifies to its dramatic quality.

On a bitterly cold February evening, the Rev. Hubert Dahme, the popular priest of St. Joseph's Church, Bridgeport, was shot down in front of a crowd of people on the corner of Main Street. The killer simply walked off. The police were baffled, for the kindly old priest had no enemies, and they could think of no motive for the killing. Then, two weeks later, the police of the neighbouring town of Norwalk made an arrest. The accused was a 28-year-old alcoholic named Harold Israel. Under long, non-stop police questioning, he broke down and confessed. He had been broke, starving and exhausted on that evening of February 4, he said. He had been unable to find a job for months. As he walked down the street, uncontrollable hatred seethed up in him; he pulled out his revolver, and shot the first man he saw – the old priest – and then he ran away. A waitress in a nearby coffee bar came forward to say that she had seen Israel passing the window shortly before the murder, and had waved.

The State Attorney, a brilliant young man named Homer Cummings, seemed to have an open and shut case. But he was far from happy. It just didn't make sense. Why should Israel have been starving when he had a revolver worth $5 in any pawnshop? If he shot the first person he met, then why had the priest been shot in the back of the head, not the face? Cummings went to interview Israel, and his suspicions were confirmed. Under long questioning, the alcoholic's shaky nerve had broken, and he had confessed merely to be left alone. He insisted to Cummings that he was in a cinema at the time of the murder.

This left the evidence of the waitress. Cummings went to the hash house with his deputies at eight o'clock one evening, and asked the waitress where she was standing when she saw Israel. She showed him. Cummings looked out of the window – and could see nothing through the steam, and the bright lights of the street refracted in the glass. He sent some of his men to walk up and down outside; at a few feet, they were unrecognizable. Cummings himself went outside, and told the waitress to wave to him as he went past. She waved twice to the wrong man, but failed to recognize Cummings.

Strange moral

When she admitted that she had applied for the reward, Cummings knew her evidence was worthless. In court, he summarized what he had learned, and asked for the case to be dropped. Israel walked out of court a free man, sobbing. The shock had the effect of sobering him; he married and became a prosperous timber merchant. The young attorney later became Roosevelt's Attorney General, but the murder of Father Dahme remains unsolved to this day.

The moral of these famous cases of acquittal is a strange one.

The murderer who stands most chance of escape is not the careful planner, who broods on alibis and concealment, but the incompetent who kills without forethought. An odd conclusion, equally unsatisfying to the policeman, the criminologist, and the reader of crime stories.

ALIBIS

A case that would have taxed the ingenuity of Sherlock Holmes took place in Montana in September 1901. The body of an old man named Dotson was found in his cabin, near Helmsville, with a bullet in the heart. On the opposite wall, a gun had been rigged up in a wooden frame, with the muzzle pointing at the dead man. A string ran from the dead man's head, through a metal ring in the wall, to the trigger of the gun. It looked like a clear case of suicide. A note beside the body seemed to confirm this. It read: 'It warnt my son Clint done that Cullinane murder. Clint lide to save me. I done it.' It was signed Oliver Dotson, and friends verified that it was in his handwriting.

The 'Cullinane murder' had taken place on August 5, 1899. A prospector named Gene Cullinane had been found shot dead in his cabin, not far from Dotson's place. A few days later, sheriff's officers arrested Clint Dotson, and two other men named Oliver Benson and Ellis Persinger. Benson and Persinger admitted robbing Gene Cullinane, but alleged that it was Clint Dotson who had shot the prospector twice in the heart. Benson and Persinger were sentenced to ten years in prison; Clint Dotson received life.

Now it looked as if Dotson might have been innocent after all. He had what amounted to a double alibi. He was behind bars at the time of his father's death, so there could be no question that he might have forced his father to sign a false confession. Old Man Dotson seemed to be offering his son a kind of post-humous alibi for the time of the murder . . .

A strange problem

Undersheriff John Robinson, the man who had sent Clint Dotson to jail, went to interview Persinger and Benson. Were they quite sure it was Clint who had killed the prospector? They insisted they were absolutely certain; they had *seen* him do it.

10

That left the undersheriff with a strange problem. Why had the old man confessed to a crime he did not commit? He was certainly an alcoholic; but had never been weak in the head.

He checked with the prison governor at Deer Lodge jail, where Dotson was serving his sentence, and learned that one of Dotson's closest friends, a robber named Jim Fleming, had been released from prison only a few weeks earlier. Sheriff Robinson decided he had to talk to Fleming. But first he adopted one of Sherlock Holmes's favourite expedients, and put on the worst fitting clothes he could find.

Then he made his way to the distant ranch, fifty miles from Helena, where Fleming's girlfriend lived. He introduced himself as an ex-convict from Deer Lodge, and explained that he was looking for his old friend Jim Fleming. The girl believed him. She told him that Fleming would be back in a few days, and invited him to have a cup of coffee. They had a friendly talk, and soon she mentioned a matter of $50,000 that Clint Dotson had got when he robbed Union Pacific. It seemed that she was expecting a share of the money.

This is what Sheriff Robinson wanted to know. Now he had his motive for murder. He rode back to Helena, and made intensive inquiries to find out if Jim Fleming had been seen with old man Dotson at any time; soon he found what he wanted – someone who had seen them together just before the old man's death. Robinson went back to the ranch, lay in wait for Jim Fleming, and arrested him.

Incredible viciousness

The sheriff had nothing to go on but guesses; nevertheless, he played his suspect as a skilful angler plays a big fish. He told him that he had been talking to Clint Dotson in jail. He spoke as if he knew all about the Union Pacific robbery. 'Clint didn't do that stick up. He didn't have anything to do with it. There ain't no fifty thousand dollars.' And then he hinted casually that he knew Fleming had been drinking with old man Dotson just before his death. He knew because Clint had told him. . . Suddenly, Fleming saw himself surrounded by pitfalls of treachery. So when Robinson said: 'Would you like to make a statement?' Fleming said: 'Yes, I sure would.' The story he told revealed such incredible viciousness that even the veteran sheriff was shocked.

Clint Dotson had deliberately planned the murder of his own father, in order to clear himself of the murder of Gene Cullinane. With promises of a share of the $50,000 he had persuaded

Fleming to go to the old man's cabin, and get him drunk. When the old man was drunk, it was easy to persuade him to do anything; that was how Fleming had got the note. The old man did it 'for a joke'. Later, when Oliver Dotson was stupefied with the raw whiskey, Fleming shot him through the heart, and rigged up the shotgun to make it look like an accident.

Fleming was hanged on September 6, 1902, Dotson in April 1904; and the double alibi murder has come to rank as one of the strangest cases in modern criminal history. Yet if you had asked Clint Dotson if he had an alibi for the murder of Gene Cullinane, he would not have known what you were talking about. It is only in recent years, since the rise of the detective story and the TV thriller, that the word has passed into the language.

The Latin word 'alibi' actually means 'elsewhere', so it is incorrect to say: 'The prisoner has an alibi'; it should be 'The prisoner was alibi'. Oddly enough, it is only in the past fifty years or so that the criminal has given serious thought to the problem of alibis. In less sophisticated days, he committed his murder, and then did his best to be elsewhere when the crime was discovered. The modern criminal has discovered the advantage of persuading the police that he was already 'alibi' at the time the crime was committed.

On the whole, most of these attempts have been fairly crude. In *The Three Musketeers*, D'Artagnan puts back the clock half an hour, then draws the attention of his regimental commander to it, to establish that he could not possibly have been present at a certain fight. Real-life alibis have sometimes been as obvious — and absurd. George Joseph Smith, the 'Brides in the Bath' murderer, moved into rooms in Highgate, London, on December 17, 1914, accompanied by his new wife, a clergyman's daughter named Margaret Lofty.

The following day, the landlady heard sounds of splashing coming from the bathroom, and hands slapping the sides of the bath — then silence. This was broken by the sound of the organ playing in the sitting room; John Lloyd — alias George Smith — was establishing his alibi. A few minutes later, the front door slammed loudly; then he came back saying 'I've brought some tomatoes for Mrs. Lloyd's supper'. At this point, the landlady noticed water leaking through the ceiling. Lloyd rushed upstairs, burst into the bathroom, and shouted: 'My wife can't speak to me — go for a doctor.' Predictably, 'Mrs. Lloyd' was drowned.

But Smith might well have got away with it, if a newspaper report of the death had not been seen by a relative of one of Smith's previous victims. And when George Smith finally appeared in court, and the story of that evening was told by the prosecutor, Sir Archibald Bodkin, the killer found out that a poor alibi is worse than no alibi at all . . . .

Far more brilliant and elaborate alibis than George Smith's have proved just as ineffective. The classic American case – with all those features so dear to the heart of the lover of detective stories – took place just one year after the execution of the 'Brides in the Bath' killer. Frederick Small was an unsuccessful grocer of Portland, Maine, whose matrimonial affairs were pursued by misfortune.

His first wife died in childbirth; his second wife ran off with the president of a baseball team. Small was granted $10,000 damages. In 1911, when he was approaching the age of 45, Small married a third time, Florence Arlene Curry, a girl nearly 15 years his junior. The marriage was not happy; Small seems to have been a coarse and bullying man, who often beat his wife.

In 1914, Small decided that it was time to retire; they moved to a cottage near Mountainview, New Hampshire. It was on the edge of Lake Ossipee, and Small spent much of his time fishing. The Smalls were not poor, but neither were they as well off as the husband thought they deserved to be. In early 1916, he insured his wife's life for $20,000, and his cottage for a further $3,000. The outlay – $1,000 or so – was large, for Small's total fortune was less than $5,000. But he had plans for re-couping his losses.

The man who had sold him the life insurance was Edwin Conner, who was also principal of the local school. Unlike most of the residents of Mountainview, Conner seemed to find Small pleasant enough, and Small went out of his way to be nice to Conner. They even agreed to take a trip to Boston together, partly to look into some further insurance business, but mainly for pleasure.

On the morning of September 28, 1916, Small phoned his friend and asked him if he could make the Boston trip that day. This was short notice; Conner said it would be difficult. Small insisted. Finally, Conner said he would see what he could do. At two o'clock, a local wagon driver named Kennett was asked if he would collect Small at three-thirty, in time for the four o'clock train to Boston. Kennett deliberately arrived early, because on previous occasions Small had invited him in for a tot of rye whiskey. But this time he found Small all ready, waiting on the back porch. Small opened the door, shouted 'Goodbye' to his wife, and they drove off.

Everyone was sympathetic

The two men took the afternoon train, arriving in Boston at eight. There they checked into a hotel, and went to see a play; afterwards they ate supper, and returned to the hotel. The desk clerk was waiting with a message for Small. There had been a fire back at Mountainview, and he was to ring the local hotel. A few minutes later a distraught Frederick Small asked Conner to take the phone and confirm the message. His house was in flames, said the hotel keeper, and he had better hire a car and return immediately; Small's grief seemed enormous and genuine. Everyone was sympathetic.

Back home, as the dawn was rising over the lake, Small viewed the smouldering ashes of his cottage. In a choking voice, he asked the local doctor if someone could search the ruins for his wife's body. An hour later, the doctor rang Small at the hotel. 'We've found the body. What do you want us to do with it?' For a moment, Small was nonplussed; then he asked with amazement: 'You mean there's enough to be buried?'

There was indeed. For the body had collapsed through the floor of the sitting room, into the basement, and there were several inches of water in the basement. Mrs. Small still had a cord knotted tightly around her throat. She had a bullet wound in the skull, and the head had been bludgeoned.

Frederick Small was promptly placed under arrest. He insisted that his wife had been alive when he left the house, and asked Mr. Kennett to verify that she had come out on the back porch to say goodbye. The wagon driver replied that, as far as he could recollect, Small had called goodbye, but there had been no reply. The police found other evidence to indicate that the murder had been carefully planned. In the wreckage there was an alarm clock with wires and spark plugs attached to it. There could be no doubt that it was a timing device.

Small had been too clever. In order to make sure that his wife's body was completely consumed, he used a quantity of a substance known as thermite, a powder made of aluminium filings, metallic oxides and magnesium. It is used in welding, because it produces such an intense heat. The heat was intended to incinerate Mrs. Small's corpse; instead, it burned a hole in the floor, and the corpse fell into the water in the basement.

The evidence suggests that Small killed his wife accidentally, or in a fit of rage. Various witnesses described his violent temper. It is just possible that he might have escaped the gallows with a plea of second degree murder; as it was, he was hanged on January 15, 1918.

It is an interesting question whether Small's ingenuity inspired another fire murder in 1933. On October 25 of that year, Richard Budde, a middle-aged lumberjack of Eagle River, Wisconsin, arrived home from work at six in the evening, and found the doors all locked. As he shouted his wife's name, neighbours came over to see what was the matter. They forced their way in, and immediately smelled smoke; there had been a fire in the bedroom closet – a large wooden cupboard. It had burned through the floor, and the closet door had fallen through into the basement. So had the body of Virginia Budde, which had also been in the closet.

The door was unlocked

This was a baffling problem for Sheriff Thomas McGregor. Why had Mrs. Budde shut herself in the closet and set fire to it? Or was it possible that she had been *put* in there and set alight? On the other hand, the key was still in the lock of the closet door – on the outside – and the door was unlocked. The theory of the coroner was that Mrs. Budde, who had recently been ill, had gone into the closet and committed suicide by setting herself on fire. Burning oneself to death is, oddly enough, a fairly common form of suicide.

Budde had a watertight alibi. He had left for work at eight in the morning – neighbours not only heard him calling goodbye to his wife, but also something about bringing a loaf and some sausages home with him. The local fire chief estimated that the fire must have started about two in the afternoon. *If* Budde had killed his wife, he must have returned home to do so. That was just possible – he worked alone in the woods. But a check on the amount of wood he had chopped revealed that he had done an exceptionally hard day's work; there would have been no time to rush home and kill his wife – a process that would have taken two hours. Besides, the neighbours would most certainly have seen him.

The pathologist's report seemed to establish Budde's innocence beyond all doubt. Presence of smoke in the lungs proved that Mrs. Budde had been alive when she entered the closet. The fact that the door was unlocked seemed to clinch it. If she had been alive and conscious, she would have simply walked out. The coroner's jury saw no reason to doubt Budde's innocence. His wife's death brought him no advantage; she had not been insured, and there was no rumour of another woman. It was true that the Buddes often fought, but that was nothing unusual. A verdict of death through causes unknown was returned.

At which point – as in the Small case – fate took a hand. The coroner, P.J. Gaffney, was sitting alone in his office after the inquest, with various items of evidence on his desk – Mrs. Budde's half burnt shoes, fragments of clothing, and the lock from the closet door. By some chance, the lock fell off the desk.

Startled, Gaffney jumped up and picked it up. He noticed that the fall had made the lock spring out. He dropped it again. The lock went back. He tried it several times. Through some peculiar fault, each impact caused it to either lock or unlock. He sat down again, and began to think deeply. This didn't prove anything, of course. But if the closet door, complete with lock had fallen through into the basement, shouldn't it have been *locked* when it was found? The fact that it was unlocked suggested that it had been locked before it fell.

But if Budde had put his wife in the closet, how had he set fire to her six hours after he left for work? There was no evidence of a timing device. The coroner was a painstaking man. He bought wood, and constructed a closet of exactly the same size and design as the one in which Mrs. Budde had died. He lined it with a flame resistant material of the same kind that had lined Budde's closet. He allowed the same quarter inch air gap at the bottom of the door. He filled it with old clothes, set them alight, and closed the door. The fire that began at eight in the morning took more than twelve hours to burn through the floor. The fire chief had made a mistake. Richard Budde *could* have started the fire before he left for work.

With this much evidence, Gaffney decided on an autopsy. It confirmed all his suspicions: strychnine was found in Mrs. Budde's stomach. It had been a murder of atrocious cruelty. Budde had given his wife the poison – a large dose, enough to make her unconscious after considerable suffering. Then he had placed her in the cupboard, set fire to her, and then left her to suffocate. There was not enough of the body left to allow the coroner to estimate time of death.

Budde was tried, but there was one thing that the coroner had not been able to establish: a motive. The jury decided that Mrs.

Budde could have taken the strychnine herself. They acquitted Budde, who proceeded to drink himself to death. A few months later, in a fit of delirium tremens, he also took poison, in the bedroom where his wife had died. He left a note confessing to the murder. There were many people in Eagle River who said that it was his wife's ghost who drove him to kill himself. Gaffney was not entirely sceptical. He always claimed that the lock had been in the middle of his desk.

In the long run, the most effective alibis are probably the simplest. Perhaps the most effective method of all is to get someone else to provide it: preferably a wife, who cannot give evidence against her husband in court. Raymond Morris, the English sex murderer, persuaded seven-year-old Christine Darby to get into his car on August 19, 1967; her naked and misused body was found in nearby woods near Cannock Chase, Staffordshire. Morris was among those questioned by the police, because his car fitted the description of the murderer's car.

Morris's wife told the police that her husband had been at home at the time the murder was committed. She had no suspicion he was the killer; she only wanted to 'save him trouble'. In the following year, Morris tried to drag a ten-year-old girl into his car; a woman noted the number, and he was arrested; his wife's well-meant loyalty almost led to another murder.

This whole matter of alibis has undoubtedly been exaggerated by the rise of the detective story. Could *you* remember what you were doing on the evening of August 10 last year? Of course not. Fortunately most criminals are too stupid to realize that nothing makes a detective so suspicious as a 'watertight alibi'.

AIR CRIMES

Twenty-five-mile-an-hour winds lashed across the beach at Kitty Hawk on the morning of December 17, 1903, when Orville Wright clambered between the two wings of his clumsy, kite-like monstrosity and lay flat on his stomach. He slipped the rope that held back the 'kite', and the machine surged forward, lurched heavily, then suddenly swooped 10 feet into the air. For the next 10 seconds it wobbled up and down as Orville tried to control the rudder; then the nose pointed down, and it crashed into the sand. Orville jumped off, unhurt. The first motor driven aeroplane had carried a human being just over 100 yards, and the twentieth century had really arrived.

Even today, when we are thoroughly blasé about monster jets that can carry hundreds of passengers at more than 1,000 miles an hour, the story of those early days of flying makes some of the most exciting reading in the world. It had to happen, of course, once man had noticed that a box kite could sail for long distances through the air, and when Otto invented the internal combustion engine in 1877 it was inevitable that some genius would think of combining the engine with the box kite to make an aeroplane.

Vast ransoms

The great pioneer Otto Lilienthal stood on a hilltop in 1891 and leapt into the air, suspended from a kind of kite that made him look like an enormous bat; he planed smoothly down to the bottom of the hill, steering the kite by means of rudders. The two Wright brothers, Orville and Wilbur – who ran a cycle business in Dayton, Ohio – read about Lilienthal's gliding feats in 1896 and were feverishly excited. Lilienthal broke his neck in his 'glider'; so did the great English pioneer, Percy S. Pilcher. Undeterred, the Wright brothers worked on the problem of how to combine a glider and an engine, and they solved it that morning of December 17, 1903 – surely one of the great days in human history.

Every major technical advance has brought its own kind of crime. The horse was first used by Mongol hordes to prey on peaceful rural communities; sea-faring brought sea raiders like the Vikings and the pirates of the Mediterranean; and the railways inspired Jesse James to invent train robbery. The aeroplane, in its turn, has led to the development of a wide and peculiar variety of crimes, from international air-smuggling to the form of air piracy known as sky-jacking. Bank robbers have escaped in aeroplanes, murderers have thrown bodies from aeroplanes, and sky-jackers have parachuted from aeroplanes, carrying vast ransoms for the lives of the passengers. It is becoming increasingly clear that, if air crime is not to become one of the most serious problems of the future, there will have to be firm and concerted action by every civilized country in the world.

Yet even half a century ago such a thought would have been inconceivable Five years after the Wright brothers made their first flight, the prophet of science, H.G. Wells, wrote a novel called *The War in the Air* in which he described aerial 'dog fights', and bombing from an aeroplane. But no one took this seriously; it was just another example of Wells's grotesque imagination. Even well-informed people believed that the aeroplane would never be anything more than a scientific toy, like Edison's phonograph. Even Blériot's cross-Channel flight in 1909 did little to change that view. It was the dirigible balloon that was regarded as the great aerial hope of the future, at least until the First World War. Then it was the aeroplanes that did the real damage and helped to change the course of the war.

Futility

The war ended; the jazz age came and went, and it seemed that the underworld had overlooked the aeroplane as a potential instrument of crime. But one imaginative young American, Harry Crosby, saw it as a spectacular means of suicide. Rich, good looking and cultured, Crosby had no reason to want to die. But he had seen many of his friends die in the war, and he had more money than was good for him. Living in Paris during that period of futility and boredom described by Hemingway in *The Sun Also Rises*, Harry and his beautiful wife Caresse decided that they would commit suicide by aeroplane on a predetermined date, October 31, 1942.

They would do this by taking the aircraft up over the jungles of Brazil and flying it straight into the sun until they ran out of fuel. Crosby was obsessed by the sun. But when he actually committed suicide, on December 10, 1929, it was in a less original manner. He and his mistress – a society woman, Mrs. Josephine Bigelow – went to a studio in the Hotel des Artistes in New York, and there both died by shooting themselves through the head. So Crosby lost the chance of becoming the world's first air suicide.

That distinction probably goes to the first Japanese 'kamikaze' pilot, Admiral Musubumi Arima, who, on October 15, 1944, crashed his Zero fighter into the U.S.S. *Franklin* off the Philippine island of Luzon. Arima's action started a virtual epidemic of suicide by kamikaze pilots, whose reckless bravery came close to turning the war in the Pacific in favour of Japan.

But for a time there was another possible candidate for the doubtful honour of being the world's first aerial suicide. This was the ex-R.A.F. officer Bill Lancaster, whose strange disappearance was preceded by his trial on a charge of murder. Bill Lancaster, born in 1898 near Birmingham, England, entered the R.A.F. towards the end of the 1918 war, and left the service in 1926. He decided to try for a long distance flying record to Australia in a new light plane, the Avro Avian.

In love

Three weeks before the flight he met a pretty Australian journalist, Mrs. 'Chubbie' Miller, who begged him to allow her to go with him. They set out in October 1927. Bad weather forced a crash landing in Sumatra, and they arrived in Port Darwin in March 1928. Another pilot, Bert Hinkler, had passed them in another Avro Avian, so the Lancaster-Miller team failed to gain their record for the longest flight in a light plane. But they had one consolation: they were in love.

Their affair continued for the next four years, during which time Lancaster worked in America as a freelance flier. And although he remained in love with Chubbie, she had ceased to love him. In March 1932 Bill and Chubbie were living together in Miami, Florida, and Lancaster went away on a flying trip, leaving Chubbie together with a young airman-journalist named Haden Clarke, who was collaborating with her on her autobiography. Clarke was a weakling and a neurotic, and – like Lancaster – he aroused protective feelings in Chubbie. Soon they were having a love affair. She wrote to Lancaster to tell him that she had decided to marry Clarke.

Whitest man

Lancaster was shattered, although he did his best to behave like a gentleman. He telegraphed them, asking them to delay the wedding 'until he could come and be best man', and got home as soon as he could. It was April 20, 1932. The three had not been together long when Lancaster told Haden Clarke that he had betrayed his trust. Clarke blustered furiously. Finally, Chubbie and Clarke agreed to postpone their marriage for a month, to give them time to think it over.

Lancaster and Clarke slept in camp beds on the verandah. Lancaster said later that they made up their differences; Clarke, reportedly, volunteering: 'You're the whitest man I know.' In the middle of the night there was the sound of a shot, and Lancaster banged on Chubbie's door. Clarke, he said, had shot himself – and, worse still, had used a gun that he, Lancaster, had bought in St. Louis just before flying back to Miami.

There were two suicide notes, both typewritten, but signed by Clarke, but handwriting experts were doubtful about the author of the suicide notes. The inquest was postponed indefinitely.

Bill Lancaster and Mrs. Miller were detained for questioning after the death. Lancaster admitted forging the suicide notes, but he insisted that Clarke's death had been suicide, all the same.

Bigamous wife

The case against Lancaster looked black. His story was that he had woken up and found Clarke dying from the gun-shot wound in his head. Realizing he might be accused of murder, he had rushed out, typed the suicide notes, and tried to get the dying Clarke to sign them. Clarke was too weak, and Lancaster had done it.

When the defence counsel began to investigate Haden Clarke's background, however, they unearthed evidence that made the suicide seem altogether more likely. Clarke was not only married already, but had also a second – bigamous – wife. He was something of a confidence man, and was a drug addict. The dead man's skull was produced in court, and powder burns were pointed out near the wound. This suggested that the shot was self-inflicted; a wound-be killer would not risk waking his victim by pressing the gun against his head. Finally, Lancaster was found not guilty.

But he was fully aware that his career was probably ruined; many people thought him guilty. His relationship with Chubbie had not apparently survived the trial; he decided that there was only one way to get back into flying: to break a world record. This time he decided to try to break the speed record from England to the Cape; it had formerly been held by Jim Mollison, but had been broken by Amy Johnson, who was now a universal heroine. If he could break *her* record it would mean certain fame . . .

Mummified body

The flight was financed by his father. When he set out on April 11, 1933, he also had the comfort of knowing that Chubbie was prepared to make another effort to live with him when he returned. His task was to try to fly the 6,500 miles in less than four days and seven hours. Nearly 36 hours later he took off from Gao in Africa. Then he vanished.

A wide search was mounted. Many people were of the opinion that this was suicide. He was hours behind Amy Johnson, and there was no chance of beating her record. He had been heard to say that, if he failed, he had nothing to live for. If he *was* guilty of Clarke's murder, this was an additional reason for ending it all in a final crash-dive.

It was nearly 30 years later that the truth finally became known. The French had established an atomic station at Reggan, in the Sahara desert, and in February 1962 a motorized patrol 170 miles south of Reggan found the wrecked aeroplane, and a man's mummified body beside it. Lancaster's diary told the story of engine failure nearly two hours after leaving Reggan. The plane crashed, but he survived for eight days. At one point he saw the flare of a searching aeroplane and fired off one of his own flares. But although he spent the night in a state of euphoric hope, no rescue came. Finally, Bill Lancaster died of thirst. An odd coincidence adds mystery to the event. His death was within hours of the anniversary of Clarke's 'suicide'.

It was the Second World War that brought the age of air crime altogether closer, and in 1949 Brian Donald Hume, a petty crook who specialized in selling stolen cars, and who had learned to fly in the R.A.F., murdered Stanley Setty, the dealer who supplied them, and hacked his body in several pieces. On October 5, 1949, Hume hired an Auster aeroplane at Elstree and scattered parts of the body over the English Channel.

The next day he threw the torso out of an aeroplane, but it was washed ashore. Hume was traced through one of the five-pound notes used in Setty's last business transaction, but Hume insisted that he had disposed of the body at the insistence of three gangsters. He was found not guilty of murder, but guilty of being an accessory, and sentenced to 12 years in prison. When he came out in 1958 he wrote a confession of the murder for a Sunday newspaper.

But the priority in aerial murder undoubtedly goes to the French-Canadian Joseph Guay, who, on September 9, 1949, waved goodbye to his wife Rita as she boarded a Dakota of Canadian Pacific Airlines at Quebec. By the time the plane took off, Guay was sweating heavily. He had reason to. Five minutes later, the Dakota exploded in mid air, killing everyone on board. Guay was one of many relatives of passengers who streamed to the airport two hours later. He was apparently shattered by the news of the explosion, and broke down so convincingly that kindly onlookers drove him to a hotel. His five-year-old daughter was with him.

Seared metal

The plane had exploded over a dense forest near Sault-au-Cochon. Witnesses on the ground had noted that the plane's engines continued running after the explosion; this proved that the engines were not at fault. Twenty-three bodies were recovered from the wreckage. In the luggage compartment the searchers discovered seared metal that indicated that this was where the explosion had taken place, and chemical analysis revealed it was due to dynamite.

The police carefully checked the passenger list, and the list of baggage. One item intrigued them: a crate containing 'religious statuary', weighing 26 lbs. No statue had been found in the wreckage. An appeal by the police brought forward a taxi driver who had picked up a woman with a wooden crate on the day of the disaster and driven her to the airport. He was able to give her address.

When the police checked there, they discovered that Marie Petre was in hospital recovering from an overdose of sleeping tablets. When they called to see her, almost her first words were: 'He made me do it.' 'He' was the jeweller Albert Guay, who had also been her lover – before he discovered a younger and prettier mistress, Marie-Ange Robitaille. She admitted that Guay had asked her to buy dynamite for him, and that her brother, a cripple named Generaux, had made a timing mechanism to detonate it.

Wildly infatuated

Slowly, the incredible story became clear. Guay was a man who could never be contented with one woman. For years, Marie Petre

– who worked as a waitress – had been his mistress, and he supported her in a flat. Then, three years earlier, he had met the beautiful 16-year-old Marie-Ange – who preferred to be called Angel Mary – in a nightclub, where she worked as a cigarette girl. He became wildly infatuated with her, and she became his mistress.

When Guay's wife found out, she went to see Marie-Ange's father. As a consequence, Marie-Ange moved out, and Guay installed her in his other mistress's flat. After a few months of torment, the bitterly jealous Marie Petre moved out. Guay now became moody and savage, and Marie-Ange tried to leave him. He caught her on the train and dragged her back to the flat.

Impossible task

It was probably then that he began to brood on how he might gain a legal hold over her by marrying her. A friend of Guay's, named Lucien Carreau, told how Guay had once offered him 100 dollars to administer poisoned cherry brandy to Rita Guay. He had refused. After the air crash, Guay had called on him and offered him 500 dollars if he would promise to say nothing about the earlier offer – Guay could afford it; his wife had been insured for $10,000. Now thoroughly afraid, Carreau again refused. Guay, who did not like to be crossed, flew into a wild temper: 'He was like an animal' – and stormed out.

Guay's trial opened in March 1950. At first there was a certain amount of public sympathy for Marie Petre, who told how Guay called on her after the explosion, told her she was responsible, and dwelt sadistically on how they would hang her. However, when the crippled Generaux Ruest vanished, and had to be found and kept under police supervision to get him into court, there were many who wondered if the brother and sister were less innocent than they seemed.

As far as Guay was concerned, it was an open and shut case; the defence had an impossible task. They tried to insist that a timing mechanism made from an alarm clock would not work; an explosives expert disproved it by constructing one in court from an old alarm clock and making it blow a fuse in front of the jury. When he added that 10 lbs of dynamite would be enough to destroy any aeroplane. Guay's last hope vanished. He was found guilty and hanged in January 1952. Eighteen months later, Marie Petre and her brother also went to the gallows – new evidence revealed that they had quite willingly participated in the plot to blow up the aeroplane. Guay's gruesome descriptions of hanging, which had frightened Marie Petre into attempting suicide, proved to be true after all.

It is not entirely accurate to say that the age of air crime began with the Guay explosion and Hume's flight over the Channel. Ever since the end of the war international gangs had used aeroplanes for smuggling and other criminal operations. The book *Airline Detective* by ex-etective Donald Fish became a bestseller, and formed the basis of the popular television series *Zero One*; it is a brilliant description of the many forms of crime encountered by an airport security man.

Iron bar

The world's first sky-jacking took place as early as 1947. On July 16 of that year a Chinaman named Wong Yu, together with three other desperadoes, Chiu Tok, Chiu Choi and Chiu Cheng, tried to take over a Catalina flying boat of Cathay Pacific Airlines, flying from Macao to Hong Kong. The intention was straight air-piracy; the flying boat would be taken to a remote place on the Pearl River, the passengers robbed, and some held for ransom. But from the moment the four men flourished guns and ordered the pilots to change course, things went wrong. The co-pilot, a Scotsman named McDuff, grabbed an iron bar and began swiping at the gunmen. Wong Yu fired and killed the pilot, and the plane went into a dive and plunged into the river. Ironically, the only survivor was Wong Yu. In hospital he confided the story of the hijack to another patient – who was intensely interested, because he happened to be a police officer. Just two weeks after the world's first sky-jack, Wong Yu signed a confession and was executed.

It was in the late 1960s that sky-jacking suddenly became a real menace to world airline safety. Most of the early cases were of planes bound for Miami, Florida, which were ordered by left wing hijackers to fly to Cuba. One man, Raymond Anthony, a middle aged alcoholic, forced a plane from Baltimore to land in Cuba by threatening the pilot with a pen-knife, and by that time non-resistance had become so much a part of the airline pilots' policy that he succeeded. However, Cuba expelled him, and he was arrested and sentenced to 15 years in jail. American sky-jacking has become less popular only as it has become clear that Castro is intensely embarrassed by it, and would prefer not to give refuge to 'political exiles' – who are mostly cranks with a desire to get 'away from it all'.

Similarly, Arab terrorist sky-jacking has diminished as Middle Eastern countries have showed the same reluctance to allow refuge to the terrorists. It is impossible to doubt that *this* is the only genuine solution to the problem. And, somehow, it is appropriate that the terrorist menace should be creating some kind of unity between all the governments of our divided world.

ARSON

'During the firing of the haystacks, the thought that human beings might be burnt added to the sensations that I experienced. I always watched the fires, usually from near at hand, so near in fact that I have been asked to give a helping hand . . . . The shouting of the people and the glare of the fire pleased me. During big fires, I always had an orgasm. If you see in my confession sometimes several arsons in one night, then I had no success with the first or the second. I also had an orgasm when I fired the woods. It was a lovely sight when one pine after another was consumed in the flames fanned by a sharp east wind . . . that was wonderful.'

This extract is from the confessions of the arch sexual-pervert, Peter Kürten, the monster of Düsseldorf. And it introduces us to the most baffling of all sexual abnormalities: pyromania. Even today, little is known of this frightening urge. It is pointedly ignored in most textbooks of clinical psychiatry. Perhaps this is understandable. Anybody can understand a rapist or even a sadist, because there is a fragment of them in every one of us. But how can a normal human being understand someone who obtains sexual satisfaction from watching a fire?

We can obtain some insight into this complex process from a confession quoted by Dr. Melvin Reinhardt, in his classic study *Sex Perversions and Sex Crimes*. He cites the case of a 14-year-old boy who, with three other boys, was smoking cigarettes in a hay barn. Someone unintentionally tossed a cigarette butt into the hay; the barn caught fire, and all four ran away. The boy felt an odd compulsion to stop and watch; he stayed behind bushes, and observed the arrival of police and firemen. This *could*, of course, have been normal curiosity – most people like seeing a fire. But he also noted that he had vague sexual thrills from the sight of the flames. As he read about the blaze in the newspaper the next day, he again experienced the same excitement, and a compulsion to go and start another fire. This time the thrill was even stronger. Finally, by the time he was watching his fourth fire, the intensity was so great that he masturbated. He was caught and sent to a reformatory.

There *are* other psychological elements here that we can recognize: for example, his delight as he read the newspaper headlines, and thought that no one but he knew who was responsible. This is straightforward ego-satisfaction, and it undoubtedly plays a part in pyromania. The psychiatrist Dr. Wilhelm Stekel has commented that most pyromaniacs are unhappy, drifting individuals, who feel themselves rejected by society. They often suffer from strong feelings of inferiority. Even so, this fails to explain how or why fire is associated with sexual feeling.

It becomes somewhat clearer in another case cited by Reinhardt, involving an extraordinary, complex web of sexual emotions. The father of a family of three girls, all in their teens, had ceased to have sexual relations with his wife. His sexual desires became fixated on the 14-year-old daughter. One day, he met her out of school, drove her to a quiet lane, and had intercourse with her. The girl admitted in her statement to the police: 'For two or three times, Daddy removed my panties . . . then I began liking it.' Like many young girls, she was infatuated with her father.

For the next three years they continued to have sexual intercourse two or three times a week, and he also encouraged her to stimulate him orally. One night, the mother heard her daughter going to the father's bed. There was a violent quarrel, and she threatened to report him to the police. It was after this that he began to brood on killing his wife and one of the other daughters. (The third was away from home.) He then enlisted the aid of the incestuous daughter, who alleged: 'He said he wouldn't interfere with me any more if I helped to pour gasoline on the floor.'

On the afternoon of the murder, he met his youngest daughter, Ruth (age 13), in the kitchen and hit her violently in the stomach, knocking her unconscious. When his wife came in, he also struck her with his fists; he was obviously a powerful man, for three blows laid her out, too. The eldest daughter then came in; they both soaked the kitchen (and the unconscious wife and daughter) in paraffin. As they left, the man tossed a match into the room. As the place burst into flames, he drove off, went shopping, went for a swim, and then returned home, and found the fire engines there and the house burnt out. The empty paraffin cans gave the police the clue to the fire.

In this case, it would seem as if the fire was started as an attempt to cover up the crime. Understandably, no policeman of 50 years ago would have assumed there was any sexual element in the case. On the other hand, there is one highly significant point. In a carefully planned murder, the killer does not leave empty paraffin cans to suggest that the fire was started deliberately. However, every criminologist has observed that there are many cases of murder in which the killer seems to *want* to get caught. He does something that will provide an obvious clue: for example, parks his car near the scene of a murder, or leaves some article of clothing behind. This desire to expiate guilt happens most frequently in cases of sex murder.

It appeared to apply to the present case, and was undoubtedly the reason that led Dr. Reinhardt to classify it with other examples of pyromania. After three years of sexual intercourse with his daughter, the father felt a burden of guilt, and the fire was a strange, twisted attempt to *burn away* the guilt. This could well resolve the otherwise inexplicable relation between sex and fire. Fire is a symbol of purity, and the self-divided pyromaniac simultaneously longs for purity and is sexually excited by it. This is confirmed by another curious observation made by many criminologists: that the pyromaniac often feels the need either to urinate or empty his bowels when he sees the flames.

In *The Sexual Criminal*, Dr. Paul de River mentions two female pyromaniacs – middle-aged, sexually frigid women – who felt a compulsion to stoop down and urinate as they watched the fires they had started, and a burglar who had to hide in bushes and empty his bowels after he had watched a fire. In all these cases, the criminal confessed to an immense feeling of relief *and purification* after the act – all of which seems to suggest the psychological explanation of this mystery.

Most people know what it's like to feel thoroughly oppressed by their everyday life, and to want to simply run away from problems. The inadequate personality feels like that *all* the time – which explains why, as Stekel says, he is often a drifter; he keeps on running away. There is an exhilarating finality about a fire; for example, if you burn old love letters or diaries, it is like watching your own past go up in flames. In a weak, vacillating person, flames may become associated with a feeling of delight and relief – just as the Russian physiologist Pavlov taught dogs to salivate when he rang a bell, because they *associated* it with dinner.

So the pyromaniac starts fires because each one brings this sense of relief, of a new start – as well as satisfying a basic resentment against the civilization that oppresses him. (The pyromaniac burglar cited by de River did not *always* set fire to the apartment; sometimes he only lowered his trousers and defecated on the carpet; this seems to prove the association between fire and resentment.) Finally, it is easy to understand how two completely different forms of relief – fire and sex – can become associated, in the same 'Pavlovian' way.

This, then, is probably the basic psychology of the pyromaniac. There is evidence to suggest that, to some extent, it applies to *all* criminals who use fire as their 'final solution'. For some deep, atavistic reason, human beings have the feeling that fire can solve any problem whose solution seems to demand total destruction. This explains why witches and heretics were burned, and why the Nazis constructed ovens in their death camps. We can also see the same psychology at work in the case of Alfred Rouse, the English burning car murderer, and of the aptly named Samuel Furnace, whose crime was probably inspired by Rouse.

Numerous clues

In January 1933, Furnace, a builder of Camden Town, north London, killed a rent collector named Spatchett, stole £40 he was carrying, and then incinerated the body by setting fire to a shed that served him as an office. The corpse was assumed to be that of Furnace – until the pathologist noticed that it had been shot in the back of the head. A nationwise murder hunt for Furnace followed.

He wrote a letter to his brother-in-law, asking him to meet him in Southend-on-Sea, near London, and the brother-in-law informed the police. In prison, Furnace managed to poison himself by drinking a bottle of hydrochloric acid that he had sewn into the lining of his coat. A detailed study of the case reveals that Furnace was undoubtedly an 'inadequate personality'. To begin with, he was not (like Rouse) heavily in debt – only to the extent of £90. And his suicide revealed the same basic failure to face up to the consequences of his own actions.

The 'psychology of inadequacy' can be seen in an otherwise somewhat commonplace murder that took place in Ypsilanti, Michigan, in 1931. Three ex-convicts had been drinking moonshine whisky, and then decided to go out and rob someone. They found four 16-year-olds in a car in a lovers' lane, held them up, and robbed them of two dollars. One of the girls was then dragged out of the car and raped. The others resisted, and all were battered to death or shot. The robbers next set the car on fire. Because of numerous clues they left behind, they were placed under arrest within a few hours. A court tried the case and sentenced them to life imprisonment in record time – there was a howling mob outside the courthouse, hoping to lynch the men.

A more recent American case makes the link between incendiarism and inadequacy even plainer. Gerry Cornwell was a 32-year-old mechanic, who lived in Oakland, California. Until a few weeks before Christmas, 1955, he had lived with his mistress, an ex-waitress, Alice Franklin, who was three years older than himself. Then Alice transferred her affections to a 27-year-old steelworker, Robert Hand. Cornwell quietly moved out of the apartment. He actually remained on fairly good terms with his ex-mistress and her lover, and on the night of the murder had been at a party with them.

He was drunk, and followed them back home to 5955 Telegraph Avenue; hiding outside the bedroom window, he watched them make love, then fall into an alcoholic slumber. He went to a nearby garage, bought three gallons of petrol, then walked into the bedroom – where the lovers snored on – and drenched the bed in petrol. As he went out, the pilot light of the stove ignited the petrol fumes. Firemen rushed the victims to hospital, but both died a few hours later. The police had no difficulty in locating Cornwell, who confessed. An interesting legal point arose at the trial – whether Cornwell could be charged with murder when he had not actually struck the match that ignited the petrol. The judge, however, pointed out that it was undoubtedly his intention to kill his mistress and her lover, and he was found guilty and sentenced to life imprisonment. Cornwell's inadequacy appears throughout: handing over the apartment to his rival, remaining friendly with the lovers, following them back to the apartment to watch them make love – a strong touch of masochism here – and the blind rage that is so typical of the inadequate personality when pushed too far.

No account of fire-raisers would be complete without some account of 'the German Rouse cases' – although, in many ways, they fail to fit into the general pattern of pyromania. The first case actually took place a year before Rouse murdered an unknown tramp on the Northampton road. Kurt Erich Tetzner was also a commercial traveller, but in 1929 business was poor.

One day, his mother-in-law told him she had cancer, and that her only hope was an operation; her chances of surviving it were only 50/50. Tetzner dissuaded her – for just long enough to insure her life for the equivalent of £500. (Because of her cancer, he was unable to make it more.)

Then he persuaded her to have the operation after all. His gamble paid off; she died three days later. Tetzner was amazed and charmed at the ease with which one could get money out of the insurance companies. He discussed with his wife how they could repeat the *coup*. She suggested a plan that was virtually the same as Rouse's: to get a body from a graveyard and burn it in his own car. Tetzner disagreed about the graveyard. 'There must be blood around,' he said.

He tried advertizing for a 'travelling companion'. A young man applied, but something in Tetzner's manner made him suspicious, and he changed his mind. Next, Tetzner picked up a hitchhiker on the road to Munich. The man's name was Alois Ortner, and he was an out-of-work mechanic. In a town called Hof, Tetzner gave him money to have a shave and buy himself a collar and tie. Then, outside the town, he asked the mechanic to check an oil leak under the car.

As soon as the man disappeared, Tetzner seized a hammer and an ether pad. If he had waited until Ortner's head appeared, and then hit him, while he was still under the car, Tetzner might have succeeded. But in his excitement, he allowed Ortner to emerge before he attacked him. The mechanic fought back fiercely, then ran away into the woods. But apparently he failed to report the incident.

On November 25, 1929, Tetzner picked up another hitchhiker, a thinly clad youth of 21, whose name Tetzner never found out. The youth complained of being cold, so Tetzner wrapped him in the travelling rug. When his arms were tightly pinioned, he grabbed a piece of rope and strangled the youth. Near Ettershausen, he crashed the car into a tree, put the body in the driving seat, and sprinkled it with petrol. Then he laid a trail of petrol back to the car and set it on fire.

Phone calls from Strasbourg

Tetzner was more fortunate than Rouse; he was not seen as he ran away. The burnt-out car was found; his wife identified the corpse as that of her husband, and it was buried. She now applied to the insurance company for the 145,000 marks for which Tetzner had insured his life (more than £13,000 in present-day terms).

However, the insurance officials were suspicious; to begin with, the slightly built corpse was not really like Tetzner. They contacted the Leipzig police, who kept a man on permanent duty watching Frau Tetzner. During the next few days, she was twice called to the telephone in a neighbour's flat. The neighbour told the police that the call was from Strasbourg and that the caller identified himself as 'Herr Stranelli'.

The police then asked their Strasbourg colleagues to check on a Herr Stranelli, who was probably thick-set, and had a pudgy face with pig-like eyes. When a detective from Leipzig arrived, the Strasbourg police already had 'Stranelli' in custody. It was, as they had suspected, Tetzner.

Tetzner at first confessed to the murder, then withdrew the confession. His story in court was that he had accidentally knocked down the young man and killed him. He had placed the corpse in the boot of his car, and gone for supper. During the meal, he suddenly realized he could now carry out his plan to disappear . . . . A forensic expert from Leipzig University supported his story, saying that injuries to the body suggested it had been run over. But the jury disbelieved it, and Tetzner was condemned to death. He was executed at Regenburg on May 2, 1931.

A young man named Fritz Saffran read about Tetzner's crime with great interest. He was manager of a large furniture store, Platz and Co., in Rastenburg. To all appearances, the store appeared to be prosperous. In fact, it was nearly bankrupt. Saffran had been selling the furniture on hire purchase, and during the depression his customers were simply not paying. Herr Platz, the owner, was perfectly happy to leave the management of the store in the hands of the brilliant young manager, for Saffran not only paid him a generous pension, but was also his son-in-law.

In fact, Saffran was having an affair with the girl who kept the accounts, a strong-minded young woman named Ella Augustin, and was planning on disappearing with her. He had also taken into his confidence the chief clerk, Erich Kipnik. The plan was to insure Saffran's life heavily, plant a body in the store, and set the store on fire. The problem was, where to obtain a body? Their original plan – of digging one up from a grave – was rejected. The three of them then set up camp in the Nicolai forest, and every morning Kipnik and Saffran would each drive off in his car, looking for a victim.

At their trial it transpired that they had made several unsuccessful attempts. One man who got into the car with all three of them said he had six children, so they let him go. On another occasion, Ella lost her nerve while Kipnik was pounding a man with a life preserver, and allowed the person to go alive and free. Finally, they found a suitable victim, a young man on a bicycle – Saffran later said Kipnik had got out of the car and shot him, while Kipnik blamed Saffran. The corpse was duly taken to the store. For some reason, the conspirators delayed starting the fire.

The dead man – a dairyman named Dahl – was killed on September 12, 1930. But it was not until the evening of the 15th that a tremendous explosion shook the store. Many employees who were inside miraculously escaped safely. Kipnik, apparently in hysterics, declared that Saffran had rushed into the flames to try to save the account books. Later, a charred body was found.

Two weeks after the fire, a chauffeur named Reck was asked by Ella to call at her house and drive her mother to Königsberg. A man came out of the house, and the chauffeur recognized Saffran. He talked about this, and his gossip came to the ears of the police.

Their enquiries soon revealed the motive for the crime – that the store was nearly bankrupt. The manhunt for Saffran began. He was hiding in Berlin, with a relation of Ella Augustin's, a poor carpenter. In early November he stole the carpenter's identity papers, and boarded a train for Hamburg – from where he hoped to escape to America.

However, an old army acquaintance recognized him at the Spandau station, and notified the police. Saffran was arrested, and he, Kipnik, and Ella Augustin appeared in the same dock in Bartenstein, East Prussia, in March 1931. They pleaded for sympathy, begged the victim's wife tearfully for forgiveness, and tried to blame one another. The two men were sent to prison for life; Ella received five years.

A rare crime
Today, electronic fire alarms, fire-proof building materials, and automatic sprinklers are making arson one of the rarest of crimes. There is no reason why, in a civilized society, fire should not be stamped out like the bubonic plague. We may hope that the curious perversion known as pyromania may one day disappear of its own accord.

One thing, however, that is not in doubt is that when

Prometheus, in Greek mythology, stole fire from the Gods and brought it to earth, he did not live up to his name – which meant Forethinker. He literally did not know the conflagration he was starting, and for his crime he was riveted to a rock by Zeus, who daily sent an eagle to tear out the prisoner's liver – which was renewed each night. A cruel, but, in mythological terms, just punishment.

ARTISTS' CRIMES

It was a chilly, grey September morning in the year 1598 when two men faced one another with murder in their minds in Hogsden Fields, Shoreditch. In those far off-days of the first Queen Elizabeth, Shoreditch was not a slum on the edge of London's East End; it was an area of open fields to the north of the city wall. One of the two duellists was an actor called Gabriel Spencer; the other was a writer: Ben Jonson. Jonson was a powerful, stockily built man in his mid-thirties. His opponent was taller, stronger, and younger, and his rapier was 10 inches longer than Jonson's.

At a signal, they crossed swords and began to fight. Spencer attacked violently, and within a few minutes had wounded Jonson in the arm. Jonson lowered his sword; his second thought he was going to concede defeat. Then, with a burst of savage energy, he fought on, driving Spencer back by sheer physical weight. A sudden quick thrust, and Spencer staggered, dropped his rapier, and slowly crumbled. He was dead before he hit the ground, pierced in the right side. And Ben Jonson, one of England's greatest playwrights, joined the small company of men of genius who have deprived fellow human beings of life.

It would have been a pity if Jonson had lost the fight. Only two days before, he had become famous. His play *Every Man in His Humour* was presented at the Curtain Theatre in Shoreditch by a company called the Chamberlain's Men. Its chief actor was another young playwright whose name appears on the bill as Will. Shakespeare. He was already the successful author of plays like *The Merchant of Venice* and *Henry IV*, but Jonson's triumph temporarily eclipsed him. And it was this that led to the duel. Jonson was a member of a rival group of players, the Admiral's Company, who regarded him as just a hack writer. So he offered the play he knew to be a masterpiece to the Chamberlain's Men, perhaps urged on by his old friend Shakespeare.

The success angered Gabriel Spencer, a notoriously fiery actor who had already killed a man in a fight, and he made loud and sneering remarks about 'base fellows who betrayed their master to rival houses'.

That was enough for Jonson, who also had a quick temper. Fortunately, he won, but, even so, the duel almost cost him his life. He was thrown into Newgate Jail, accused of murder, then had to appear in court in a street called Old Bailey. The jury lost no time in finding him guilty, and the sentence would have been death. At this point, Jonson pleaded 'benefit of clergy'. He was not, of course, a clergyman; but in the Middle Ages only the clergy could read, so anybody who was able to read could call themselves a clergyman and demand to be tried by an ecclesiastical court.

By Jonson's time it had become a convenient way of avoiding the death sentence. Jonson was handed a book, to prove that he could read, then sentenced to be branded with a T (for Tyburn, the place where felons were hanged) on his left thumb. He went on to write some of the greatest comedies in the English language, and, according to legend, he was the indirect cause of the death of Shakespeare. He called on his old friend at Stratford in 1616 and the two went out drinking – after which they fell into drunken slumbers under an apple tree. Shakespeare caught a chill and died; Jonson lived on for more than 20 years.

There are very few men of genius who have been guilty of murder – or even, like Jonson, manslaughter. This may seem to be mere chance; after all, both murderers and men of genius form a fairly small portion of the population, so it is hardly surprising if the two categories seldom coincide. But the real reason lies deeper. It is hinted at by George Bernard Shaw, when he comments that we judge an artist by his highest moments, a criminal by his lowest.

The characteristic of the man of genius is a certain patience and far-sightedness. He knows he may not succeed tomorrow, or next month, or even next year; but he has to keep on. Even when he *has* achieved success, his next work may be so advanced and difficult that his admirers may reject it as incomprehensible – like Beethoven's last, and deeply religious, quartets. What he needs to keep going is a certain faith, the knowledge that what he is doing is right.

The criminal, on the other hand, lacks this kind of deep patience. His motto is: 'I want it now.' If he wants sex, his natural impulse is to seize a girl and rape her. If he wants to be rid of his wife, his natural impulse is to kill her. If he wants money, he reaches out and tries to grab it. To satisfy his desire, he is willing to turn his back on the community and commit an anti-social act. Yet, paradoxically, he also wants to be accepted by society, to be liked and respected. This is why the Kray brothers took every opportunity to be photographed with celebrities.

Artistic killers

It follows that the basic psychology of genius – the patience, the intuition, the ability to listen to an inner voice – is the exact opposite of that of the criminal. The German novelist Thomas Mann always insisted that the artist and the criminal have a great deal in common, and wrote a delightful novel, *Felix Krull, Confidence Man*, to illustrate his assertion. But Felix is just a charming rogue who never does anything truly wicked; the novel only proves that Mann knew very little about the psychology of a real criminal. He could have learned about it by studying the career of one of the few 'artistic killers' known to criminal history, Pierre-François Lacenaire, executed in January 1836 for murder.

Lacenaire's famous *Memoirs* represent him as a ruthless enemy of society who wrote that, after his first crime, 'I no longer belonged to myself but to cold steel' (i.e. to the guillotine). The truth is that Lacenaire was a third-rate poet and a hopelessly incompetent criminal. His most ambitious 'job' was an attempt to murder and rob a bank messenger, which he bungled. His motive for becoming a criminal was not heroic defiance of a corrupt society, but self-pity because his parents preferred his elder brother. He started by believing – perhaps correctly – that his parents owed him love; he ended by believing – incorrectly – that society owed him a living and a position. The *Memoirs* reek of self-pity. Perhaps the most significant words in the book are his comment that he had decided that his life would be 'a form of slow suicide'.

The *Memoirs* of Lacenaire had an important influence on another great writer who was fascinated by crime: the Russian Fyodor Dostoevsky. When he was the editor of a magazine, Dostoevsky deliberately published the *Memoirs* to increase circulation. And the author of *The House of the Dead* was deeply interested in this notion of a man of talent who considers himself at war with a corrupt society. He translated it onto an altogether higher level in *Crime and Punishment*, in which

Raskolnikov, a young and talented student, feels that his hopeless poverty prevents him from achieving anything worthwhile, and decides to give himself 'a start in life' by killing and robbing an old woman pawnbroker.

In fact, following the double murder (he is forced to kill the woman's sister as well), Raskolnikov realizes that he has destroyed something in himself; he is further away than ever from being able to give expression to his 'genius'. He surrenders to the police and undergoes the purgatory of imprisonment in Siberia before he can escape the consequences of his crime. It sounds like a typical piece of moralistic propaganda; but Dostoevsky had understood something profoundly important about the creative process. It is the very opposite of the destructiveness of the criminal. There have been many writers who have written violent and negative books: the Marquis de Sade, for example. But it is significant that de Sade never murdered anyone; in fact, the only people he 'tortured' were prostitutes whom he paid.

The fact is that, in spite of their sickening violence, de Sade's books are too intelligent, too creative, for their author to have actually killed or tortured anyone. It happens to be a simple fact of literary history that *no* great writer — not even a less-than-great writer — has ever committed cold-blooded murder. Perhaps the only known case of a man of genius committing murder is that of the Italian composer Gesualdo, who caught his wife in bed with a lover in the year 1590, and despatched both with his sword. He also murdered the second child of the marriage, in case he was not the father.

No modern court would find him guilty of first-degree murder; it was obviously a *crime passionnel*. Added to which, Gesualdo was undoubtedly mentally unbalanced; his strange, neurotic madrigals have gained a new popularity in the twentieth century because they sound so 'modern', so unlike the balanced, harmonious music of his contemporaries like Monteverdi.

Dostoevsky himself is believed to have committed a crime, although there is no definite evidence. In two of his novels, characters are haunted by memories of having raped a 10-year-old girl. The internal evidence of his works suggests that Dostoevsky may have done so, although most of his biographers are agreed that *if* it actually happened (and was not a figment of his masochistic imagination) then the girl was 'procured' for him by a corrupt governess or brothel-keeper, and that therefore his crime was not, technically speaking, rape, but carnal knowledge of a minor.

Mass murderer

There is always at least one major exception to a rule; the exception to the rule that artists are never killers appeared in modern Japan. It was at mid-afternoon on January 26, 1948, that a man walked into the Shiinimaki branch of Tokyo's Imperial Bank and introduced himself as Dr. Jiro Yamaguchi of the Welfare Department. The bank was about to close, and the last customer had already left; Yamaguchi was shown into the manager's office. The doctor – a neatly dressed man with a mole on his cheek and a scar on his chin – explained that the American occupation forces, under General MacArthur, were concerned about a dysentery epidemic, and that every employee in the bank would have to take a dose of preventative medicine.

The manager, Mr. Yoshida, called 14 clerks into the office and introduced the doctor. He told them to fetch their teacups, and carefully poured into each a quantity of liquid from a bottle, telling them to swallow it quickly. They all did. Some began coughing and complained that it burned. The doctor poured them another 'medicine' and told them to swallow it like the first. Some employees went to get water to gargle. Then they began collapsing. The 'doctor' had given them a solution of the deadliest of poisons, potassium cyanide. The fake doctor helped himself to the cash that was lying around – a mere $400 or so – and walked out, leaving 12 dead people lying on the floor of the bank. Three others, including the manager, were still alive. Stomach pumps saved their lives.

Inspector Ohori, of the Tokyo police department, was astounded to discover that this was not the first time a fake doctor had tried to administer 'medicine' to bank employees. It had happened the previous October at the Ebara branch of the Yasuda bank – when 18 clerks had been severely ill after drinking a poison given by a 'Welfare Department official'; the cyanide had not been strong enough to kill them, and the man had fled. Just over a week before the murders, a bank manager had become suspicious of a 'doctor' who tried to administer 'medicine' against dysentery, and the man had run away. Yet neither of these cases had been reported to the Tokyo police – only to local district police.

The day after the mass murder a man cashed a cheque stolen from the bank, but again escaped unnoticed. No 'Dr. Yamaguchi' could be located. However, the man who had administered poison at the Ebara bank had left a card with the name 'Dr. Shigeru Matsui'. There *was* a doctor of that name in

Sendai, and he recognized that the bandit had used one of his own cards. This gave the police a lead. How had the bandit obtained it? In March 1947 Dr. Matsui had attended a medical meeting; and had handed out no less than 96 cards – it is a Japanese custom – to other doctors. The recipients had, in turn, given Dr. Matsui *their* cards, and the doctor, in his methodical Japanese way, had kept all of these.

The police set about tracking down the 96 men. They were not all doctors. One of them was an artist named Sadimacha Hirasawa. His description corresponded closely with that of the wanted bandit; he had a mole on his left cheek and a scar under his chin. Otherwise, Hirasawa seemed at first an unlikely suspect: a respectable painter, head of a national art association. He had met Dr. Matsui on a ferry, and Dr. Matsui had been impressed because Hirasawa mentioned that he was taking a picture to present to the Crown Prince.

Closer examination, however, revealed reasons for believing that Hirasawa could be their man. He had given his wife 80,000 yen just after the robbery (about $150), and deposited another 44,400 yen in his bank. Yet a few days earlier he had been trying to borrow money. Hirasawa claimed the cash had come from selling pictures and from 'patrons', but no sales – or patrons – could be traced. One industrialist admitted buying a painting for about $5, which seems to indicate that the artist was not making a fortune. Employees at the banks identified Hirasawa as the robber, although others were unsure. Hirasawa insisted that he had received most of the money from the president of an industrial corporation. But when the police discovered that the president had been dead at the time he was supposed to have paid the money, Hirasawa suddenly confessed: 'You are right. No one can obtain money from a dead man. I am the man.'

Even so, the trial aroused great controversy, many people refusing to believe that an artist could be responsible for a mass murder. Hirasawa later withdrew the confession, claiming it had been extorted by police brutality. Although he was sentenced to death, the sentence was not carried out, and Hirasawa was, in effect, sentenced to life imprisonment.

If indeed Hirasawa were guilty – and there are still many who believe he is a victim of a miscarriage of justice – then he would be the only example of an artist who had killed calculatedly and in cold blood. Even Lacenaire's murders – at least two – were spur-of-the-moment affairs, done in the course of robbery.

Artists are often capable of violence, for talent almost invariably involves high dominance, and most dominant people are prone to impatience and sudden fits of anger. The painter Van Gogh tried to stab Gauguin with a knife when they were sharing a house in Arles; but when Gauguin turned round, Van Gogh went back to his room and cut off his own ear with the knife. The attack on Gauguin was the outcome of artistic frustration – the frustration that finally led him to suicide.

The list of artists, composers, and writers who have been victims of violence is altogether longer and more varied. Another of Ben Jonson's contemporaries, the dramatist Christopher Marlowe, was killed under mysterious circumstances. On Wednesday, May 30, 1593, Marlowe was dining with three companions in a tavern at Deptford, south London. They had been drinking all afternoon, and at nine in the evening Marlowe and a man called Ingram Frizer had some dispute about the bill, Marlowe was lying on a bed behind Frizer's chair, when, according to the others, he suddenly seized Frizer's dagger and struck at him. Frizer snatched back the dagger and struck back; the weapon entered above the right eye, killing Marlowe instantly.

It sounds like a simple case of manslaughter – except that two of the three men present were rather dubious characters. One was a spy, the other a cut-purse, while the third, Frizer himself, was employed by Sir Thomas Walsingham, the Queen's spymaster, and Marlowe's lover (the poet was homosexual). At the time, Marlowe was about to be tried for possessing blasphemous writings denying the divinity of Jesus.

One theory has it that he was killed on Walsingham's instructions, to avoid scandals and revelations. A modern writer, the American Calvin Hoffmann, had advanced the extraordinary theory that Marlowe did not really die. His death was faked – another man was killed in his place. Marlowe escaped abroad and continued to write great dramas – under the name of William Shakespeare. Hoffmann's book, *Murder of the Man Called Shakespeare*, is a fascinating piece of detection, but not convincing.

There are many people who believe that Mozart's early death – at the age of 36 – was murder. The Vienna of that period – the late eighteenth century – was awash with petty rivalries, and one of the men who plotted against Mozart was another composer, Antonio Salieri. Mozart became ill in 1791 and was convinced that he was being poisoned. His death certificate stated that the cause of death was 'severe miliary fever', which causes a rash with small lumps. Other contemporary accounts say he died of a 'deposit in his head', 'a violent grippe', 'a dropsy of the heart' and 'kidney failure'. More than 30 years later a Vienna newspaper reported that Salieri had confessed to murdering Mozart by poison, and had then attempted to commit suicide by cutting his throat. Salieri died two years later, after a long illness, and the Press again reported that his 'confession' was in a church archive. It has never been found, and there is no proof that he ever made such a confession – or, if he did, that it was true.

Creative geniuses

However, there can be no doubt whatsoever concerning the death of the composer Anton Webern, who died with three bullets in him on September 15, 1945. Webern, born in Austria in 1883, became a pupil of the controversial 'abstract' composer Schoenberg – most of whose music is severely intellectual and totally lacking in melody. Webern began composing according to Schoenberg's 'twelve tone system'. His works are extremely terse and 'difficult', and there are often long silences between the notes. In the 1930s Schoenberg had to flee to America; Webern, being non-Jewish, had nothing to fear from the Nazis, but his jagged, youth-oriented music was regarded as anti-German.

In 1945 he left his home at Mödling, and went to live with his son-in-law, a man named Mattl, at Mittersill. Mattl was highly unpopular with the American occupying forces because he ran a black-market in currency. On September 15, the American forces began to tighten up security regulations. A strict curfew had been imposed, and Mattl was deliberately not told. American soldiers surrounded his house. Webern strolled out in the dusk for a smoke, and an American soldier fired, hitting him three times. Webern died shortly afterwards. The American soldier alleged that he had fired in self-defence, because Webern had attacked him with an iron bar; Webern's wife was refused a pension or damages.

Fortunately, most artists, even if prone to self-pity, are not born victims; so cases like Webern's are almost as rare as cases like Lacenaire and Hirasawa. For humanity, this is just as well; the world may not always love its creative geniuses, but they are the people we can spare the least.

ASSASSINATION

It was October, in the year 1092, and the Grand Vizier of Turkey, Nizam-al-Mulk, was holding an audience in his tent. Guards armed with scimitars surrounded him: for he was one of the most powerful men in the Middle East, and many people wished him dead. The audience came to an end, Nizam climbed into his litter, and signalled the slaves to carry him out. At the door, a half-naked holy man – a Sufi – came forward to kiss Nizam's hand. The guards stood aside to allow him to approach. Suddenly, the holy man drew a knife from his trousers, and stabbed Nizam to the heart.

The guards leapt forward, and within seconds, the holy man had been cut to pieces. But he had carried out his instructions – instructions that came from his chief, known as The Old Man of the Mountain. And Nizam-al-Mulk had just become the first victim of the Assassins.

Impregnable fortress

The real name of the Old Man of the Mountain was Hasan ibn-al-Sabbah. He lived in an impregnable fortress, high in the Elburz mountains of Persia, and had the frightening distinction of having invented the art of political assassination. He was also the head of a sect called the Ismailis – the Moslem equivalent of Protestants. His followers believed he could guarantee them an eternity in paradise.

The traveller Marco Polo has a strange story to tell about the fortress of the Assassins (which was known as Alamut – Eagle's Nest). Polo claimed that the Old Man of the Mountain had a beautiful garden laid in the green valley behind the castle. He filled it with fruit trees, fountains and pavilions. When the Old Man wanted an enemy murdered he would ask for volunteers. The men who stepped forward would be given drugged wine; when they woke up, they would find themselves in 'paradise'; beautiful girls, or houris, were there to attend to all their needs.

After a few days of sensual delight, they were again drugged, and taken back to the fortress. The Old Man would tell them that he had allowed them a glimpse of the paradise that would be theirs forever if they died for him. This, said Polo, was why there was no shortage of volunteers. They were so eager to die – and become part of the life eternal – that the Old Man would sometimes order them to jump out of high windows, just to impress visitors.

Hasan ibn-al-Sabbah's aim was power: to make himself master of the Moslem world, and its religious leader. If he was to achieve this, he had to conquer the Turks, who ruled most of the Middle East, and who supported the orthodox Moslems. But how could a religious leader, with only a few hundred followers, conquer a great nation? Hasan had his answer: murder – carefully planned political murder. He reasoned that the best way to win a war is to slay your enemy's leader.

To begin with, his plan succeeded brilliantly. Nizam-al-Mulk's son, Fakhri, swore revenge. One day, in the street of Naishapur, he was accosted by an old beggar, who moaned: 'The true Moslems are no more and there is none left to take the hand of the afflicted'. Touched, Fakhri reached into his robe for money – and was stabbed to the heart.

Enraged, Nizam's other son, Ahmed, set out to avenge his father and brother. His army besieged the castle of the Old Man – and discovered, to its cost, that it was impregnable. Not long after he had abandoned the siege, Ahmed was also stabbed by an Assassin. He was luckier than his father and brother, and eventually recovered from the wound.

A knife and a note

Another Sheik who set out to fight the Old Man woke up one morning to find a knife embedded in the ground near his pillow, and a note: 'This knife could just as easily have been in your heart.' That convinced him; he made a truce with the Old Man instead.

Oddly enough, it was Hasan's very efficiency in the art of murder that finally defeated him. When people thought of the Old Man of the Mountain, they shuddered; he seemed like a poisonous black spider, brooding in his mountain retreat. A really successful leader needs friends and allies; Hasan ibn-al-Sabbah mainly inspired horror. When he died – still in his lair – at the age of 90, he was an embittered old man, who had achieved none of his great ambitions.

The Order of Assassins survived his death for another hundred years, and there were more Old Men of the Mountain. But their day was over, and they were finally stamped out by their enemies. The breakaway sect called the Ismailis still exists today. Its leader is called the Aga Khan, and in sporting circles he is perhaps better known as the owner of race horses.

Although the Assassins disappeared, there is a curious possibility – which has never been investigated by historians – that they may only have moved elsewhere. When the British became masters of India, in the mid-eighteenth century, they noticed that the roads were infested with brigands, and that hundreds of people disappeared each year.

At the time they didn't attach much significance to this fact. Then, in 1812, a young British doctor named Robert Sherwood, stationed with the army in Madras, suddenly entertained a horrible suspicion: that all the disappearances were not just casual murders by bandits, but carefully planned *religious sacrifices*.

He questioned some of the 'robbers' who had been caught, and induced them to talk to him frankly. They admitted that they belonged to a sect called the 'Thugs' (pronounced 'Tugs'), and that for one month a year, they took to the roads, and murdered countless travellers.

Strangling noose

Their method was almost foolproof. Looking like harmless travellers – sometimes religious pilgrims – they would find a party of wayfarers and ask if they could join them. As the days went by, more Thugs would join the band, until Thugs outnumbered the genuine travellers. At a given signal, a Thug would attack each traveller from behind, throwing a strangling noose around his neck, while another Thug tripped him and held him down.

When all the travellers were dead, they would be tossed into a mass grave, their bodies mutilated to aid decomposition. The Thugs would then hold a religious ceremony near the grave, offering the dead as sacrifices to their goddess Kali – the goddess of destruction and creation – and keeping their victims' money and valuables for themselves.

The British were horrified by these revelations; this was carrying a religion too far. William Sleeman was appointed to stamp out Thuggee, and he succeeded so well that by 1850, more than 4,000 Thugs had been tried, and most of them executed. Some betrayed other Thugs in exchange for their lives.

The Thugs were one of the biggest murder organizations in history; there was nothing like it until Hitler's death camps. Sleeman reckoned that they had committed over a million murders in the nineteenth century alone. But the mystery remains: who were they, and where did they come from?

There are a few clues. When the Assassins fled from the Middle East towards the end of the thirteenth century, one of the countries they went to was India. India still has an enormous number of Ismailis (although it should be noted that the Assassins were only one single branch of the Ismailis). Sleeman was puzzled that the Thugs worshipped the goddess Kali – a Hindu goddess – for they were not Hindus, but Moslems.

One captured Thug told Sleeman that Kali was another name for Fatima, the daughter of Mahomet. And Fatima was the head of a breakaway sect that later became the Ismailis . . . Altogether, it seems possible that the Thugs were the descendants of the Assassins of the Old Man of the Mountain.

The word 'assassin' was derived from 'hashishim' – a taker of hashish (or pot). This was how the Europeans explained to themselves the frightening self-sacrifice of Hasan's Ismailis. Gradually, the word passed into most languages. (In France, an *assassin* simply means a murderer.) In Europe, assassination lost its religious overtones, and became purely political. But since most Europeans lack the fanatical temperament, it remained relatively rare.

Two notable assassinations were those of Henry III of France, who was stabbed to death in 1589 by a Dominican Friar who disliked the king's Protestant sympathies – and the French King Henry IV, murdered in 1610 by a Catholic fanatic who thought he intended to make war on the Pope.

An insane grudge

Then came the Age of Reason; religious fervour cooled. There were still occasional attempts on the lives of kings and leading statesmen, but they were usually made by cranks, or men with an insane grudge. In 1757, an idiot called Robert François Damiens made a half-hearted attempt to murder Louis XV of France with a blunt knife, and was horribly executed, torn into four quarters while still alive by four horses. But less than a century later, the world had become more humane.

When a lunatic named Daniel McNaghten shot and killed the secretary of the Prime Minister of England, he was recognized as insane, and confined in an asylum. That was in 1843, and the result was the famous McNaghten rules, which saved many murderers from the gallows.

Yet, strangely enough, the great second age of assassination was now about to begin. It was signalled by the shot that rang out in a box at Ford's Theatre, in Washington, on the evening of April 14, 1865. Abraham Lincoln fell forward, shot in the back of the head. His assassin, John Wilkes Booth, leapt on to the stage. But he was wearing spurs, and one of them caught in the curtain; he fell fourteen feet, breaking his shin. It was the begining of the bad luck that lasted until he was killed, 12 days later, in a barn in Virginia. The sergeant who shot him said he had orders from the Almighty.

In December 1870, as Juan Prim, the Prime Minister of Spain, was leaving the government chamber in Madrid he was shot down by an unknown assassin. Prim was a liberal who was hated by the reactionary Right wingers. The murderer was never caught — one of the very few assassinations in which the killer escaped. But in the rest of Europe, it was not the Liberals who were becoming the target for assassins: it was the Establishment, the very notion of law and order.

The ideas of socialists such as the French social reformer Charles Fourier, Pierre Joseph Proudhon, and the German Karl Marx, had taken root. Men like Prince Peter Kropotkin and Enrico Malatesta were preaching an even more sinister doctrine called Anarchism — the belief that all men are naturally good, and that if only we could get rid of *all* authority, society would become a kind of Garden of Eden.

The strange thing was that these kindly idealists should become identified with slaughter and violence. The politician and economist Proudhon invented the word An-archy — meaning 'No government'. He would have been amazed if someone had told him that it would soon arouse as much horror as the word Assassin had eight centuries earlier.

The thunder of anarchist bombs began in 1879. The Czar of Russia, Alexander II, had survived several attempts on his life by bullets; on one occasion, the pistol blew up and shattered the would be assassin's arm. Then a terrorist called Zhelyabov swore he would blow the Czar sky high. He planted an immense charge of nitroglycerine on a railway line, so the explosion would blast the Czar's train into a ravine. It was a spectacular idea, but it failed when a passing cart cut the wire.

His next attempt *was* successful — but the Czar wasn't on the train. In February 1880, anarchists succeeded in planting a charge of dynamite in the dining room chimney of the Czar's Winter Palace, timed to go off as he ate his supper. A guest was late and the Czar delayed going into the room – which was demolished by the blast.

Home-made bombs

But Alexander's luck was beginning to run out. On March 1, 1881, he had been inspecting his troops, and was returning by carriage. Anarchists with home-made bombs – nitroglycerine in glass balls – were stationed along several possible routes in St Petersburgh. The Czar may have been feeling slightly more secure than usual, because Zhelyabov had been arrested the day before.

Suddenly, there was an explosion behind the carriage, shattering its door, and wounding a Cossack and a boy. The Czar made the mistake of getting out to offer his sympathies. Another anarchist threw a bomb, and this time the blast killed the assassin and 20 bystanders, and smashed windows for 180 yards.

The Czar's legs were mangled, and he died a few hours later in his palace, surrounded by his weeping family. The murder triggered a violent wave of reprisals against all known leftists. Political repression came down like a shutter of lead. In 1887 a student leader named Alexander Ulyanov was hanged, with four fellow students, for an unsuccessful attempt on the life of Alexander III. His younger brother Vladimir vowed to avenge the death, and 30 years later, he did so. By then he had changed his name to Lenin.

Now the anarchists were inspired by an ideal that amounted to a religion, and for the next quarter of a century, the bombs exploded and the blood flowed.

On May Day 1892 a workers' demonstration led by anarchists was broken up by mounted police in the Paris suburb of Clichy. Five anarchists were brutally beaten by the police. At their trial, an indignant prosecutor demanded the death penalty, but no one was now *that* angry or bitter; one defendant was acquitted, the other two given three and five year sentencess respectively.

Man with a scar

Six months later, the home of the judge, M. Benoist, was destroyed by a bomb, and two weeks after that, another bomb destroyed the home of the prosecutor who had demanded the death penalty. The police wanted to interview a young man with a scar on his hand. A café waiter named Lherot noticed such a mark on the hand of a voluble young customer, and called the police.

It took ten men to subdue the man, who called himself Ravachol. He proudly admitted the bombings, saying that his aim had been to avenge the Clichy anarchists. For a while, he was an anarchist hero – until the police discovered he had committed several murders in the course of robbery.

The police declared he was a common criminal, and the anarchists were inclined to agree. Just before his trial opened, another bomb exploded in the restaurant where he had been arrested, killing the proprietor.

When the trial opened, the Palais de Justice was surrounded by troops, anticipating more anarchist outrages. Ravachol was sentenced to death – so inciting further violence. 'I know I shall be revenged,' he said, and died shouting 'Long live Anarchy!'

Four months later, a bomb was planted in the Paris office of a mining company who were engaged in a struggle with strikers. It was discovered, and a policeman carried it off to his police station – where it exploded, killing six men.

In March 1893, a workman named August Vaillant, whose family was starving, manufactured a bomb out of a saucepan, gunpowder and nails, and hurled it in the Chamber of Deputies. It was intended to be a protest, not to kill anyone – only a few deputies were scratched with nails – but the government was now thoroughly alarmed, and Vaillant was speedily executed.

The anarchist cause had another martyr. A week later, a bomb exploded in a boulevard café, killing one man and wounding twenty. And bombs went off in other parts of Paris – four explosions in a few weeks. One of them killed the anarchist who was carrying the bomb, and he proved to be responsible for two of the explosions.

In another explosion, a writer named Laurent Tailhade lost an eye. He had made headlines some time before when asked his opinion of the Vaillant explosion; he had replied grandly: 'What do the victims matter if it's a fine gesture?'

Now he knew.

The avenger strikes

An anarchist named Emile Henry was arrested for the café explosion, and explained proudly that he had intended to kill as many of the 'bourgeoisie' – i.e. middle-class citizens who could afford to drink in cafés – as possible.

Henry was executed in May 1874. And the following month, as President Sadi-Carnot was driving through Lyon in his carriage, a young man stepped forward holding a bunch of flowers. The police let him approach. He drew a knife, and stabbed Sadi-Carnot to the heart.

The day after the murder of Sadi-Carnot, his widow received a letter – posted before the attack – containing a photograph of Ravachol, with the words: 'He is avenged.'

France was not the only country that resounded to the crash of anarchist bombs and pistols. In May 1885, police charged into Haymarket Square in Chicago to break up a demonstration of strikers. Someone hurled a bomb into the police ranks, killing seven officers.

As a result of this, eight anarchists were arrested arbitrarily and sentenced to death. One managed to blow himself up on the night before his execution; three were pardoned; the other four were hanged.

With so many people dying in want, or slaving for starvation wages, the United States was ideal soil for an anarchist movement. In June, 1892, there was a strike of steelworkers at Homestead, Pennsylvania, when strikers attacked and killed 'blacklegs', and the Governor sent in the militia to repress them.

A young Russian anarchist named Alexander Berkman managed to bluff his way into the office of the steelworks. There he drew a pistol, and shot the manager, Henry Clay Frick, twice, then stabbed him seven times. Miraculously, Frick survived; Berkman was sentenced to 16 years in gaol, and the United States broke into an uproar of condemnation or support for Berkman. As propaganda for anarchism, Berkman's act was totally successful.

Eight years later, in 1900, an Italian-American weaver called Gaetano Bresci, sailed from Paterson, New Jersey, intending to assassinate King Humbert I of Italy. He succeeded on July 29, shooting the king as he was distributing prizes at Monza, near Milan. In the United States, a Polish-American named Leon Czolgosz was fascinated by the newspaper account of the killing, and decided to earn himself a similar fame.

Since Lincoln's death, another American President had fallen at the hands of a killer. In 1881, President Garfield had been shot by a vain little coxcomb of a man, Charles Guiteau, who was suffering from delusions; Guiteau was executed, having gained the notoriety he craved.

Czolgosz also bought a revolver, and on September 6, 1901, joined a queue of people waiting to shake hands with President

William McKinley, who was visiting the Pan-American Exposition in Buffalo. As the President held out his hand, Czolgosz shot him in the chest and abdomen.

At his trial, Czolgosz refused to speak to anyone; he was the first assassin to die by electrocution. After his death, sulphuric acid was poured into his coffin to destroy the body.

In Russia, the bombs and pistols continued to explode, killing government ministers, chiefs of police, even the prime minister, Stolypin. In Serbia, King Alexander I and Queen Draga were slaughtered in their palace in Belgrade by army officers on June 10, 1903. And on February 1, 1908, the unpopular King Carlos I of Portugal was shot down, together with his son, Crown Prince Luis, in the corner of the Praça in Lisbon by revolutionaries.

Archduke murdered

But the shot that put an end to revolutionary slaughter exploded on Sunday, June 28, 1914. It killed Archduke Franz Ferdinand of Austria as he drove in his carriage in Sarajevo, in Serbia. It was fired by Gavrilo Princip. A second shot killed the Archduchess.

In a sense, Princip achieved more than any other revolutionary. His two shots brought about World War I, and the Russian Revolution of 1917. After more than a quarter of a century of bullets, bombs and blood, the anarchists had achieved their aim, and the second great age of assassination was over.

BANDITS

DYNAMITE BANDITS SLAY FAMILY OF THREE read the headline of the St. Louis newspaper. It was January, 1973. The men had walked into the home of Robert Kitterman, a bank manager of Grandin, Missouri, and forced Kitterman, his wife and his daughter to nearby woods. Kitterman was ordered to drive to his bank and empty the safe; dynamite, with a radio detonating device, was strapped to his chest. When he returned to the woods, the armed men took the money, then shot all three Kittermans through the head. A few days later, police arrested an ex-convict, Dallas Delay, and two accomplices, charging them with the murder of the Kitterman family.

The killers of the Kittermans were undoubtedly 'hoodlums' – a word that originated in San Francisco around 1870 to describe vicious young rowdies and criminals. But to describe them as 'bandits' is not entirely accurate; a bandit is not simply a member of a criminal band. When first used in Italy, it meant someone who was proscribed or 'banned' – that is to say, an outlaw.

Noble freedom fighters

These men were forced to live by robbery, but they were not necessarily robbers by choice, for many of them had been thrown off their land by grasping rulers – like Robin Hood and his outlaws of Sherwood Forest. In the case of the bandits – or noble 'klefts' – of Greece, they were forced to take to the mountains by the invasion of the Turks in the 15th century, and they regarded themselves as freedom fighters.

When the Turks left, the politicians found a new use for the brigands – as election agents. A village that refused to vote for the candidate supported by the bandit chief might find itself invaded at midnight, and the inhabitants subjected to mutilation and torture.

Italy was another country that was usually in a state of violent political upheaval. Men were forced to flee for their lives and became *banditi*, who regarded themselves as patriots – although travellers who fell into their hands had a less charitable word for it.

But perhaps the most bandit-ridden country of all was Corsica – that island of broken crags, stoney soil and black forests of cedars and pines. Centuries of oppression by Italians, Spaniards, Frenchmen, the Catholic Church and the Bank of San Gorgio – a Genoese bank that took over the island in 1511 and governed with murderous cruelty and ruthlessness – made the Corsicans fierce, violent and unforgiving. They brooded on their wrongs. This is a characteristic of the southern temperament – the tendency to hold grudges, to inflate emotions until they are out of all proportion to their original cause.

Sartre used the word 'magic' to describe the way in which such emotions completely overrule logic, until the world is seen through a sort of distorting mirror. *This* is the real key to the history of banditry. It is not natural for men to live as outlaws; all human beings have a strong 'territorial' instinct that makes them long for a home, a secure and peaceful existence. But the impetuous southerner often gets trapped in a whirlpool of violent emotion that cancels out these natural instincts for a short time, and by the time he recovers his senses it is too late.

The story of Nonce Romanetti may be taken as typical. It belongs to the early twentieth century, but could well have taken place in any century since 1500. Romanetti was a well-to-do cattle breeder and wine grower in the village of Calcatoggio in Corsica. Some kind of misunderstanding arose with another breeder, who accused Romanetti of killing and selling one of his cows without paying.

Gendarmes arrived at Romanetti's house at dawn; instead of accompanying them to the police station to clear up the misunderstanding, he leapt out of a window and hid in the *macchia*, the bush. According to his own version – which he gave to the writer Ashton-Wolfe – he contacted the breeder and offered to meet him and pay for the cow.

Generosity and honesty

Then he sent a friend to the meeting, while he himself kept watch from outside the village. When Romanetti saw gendarmes spring out to arrest his friend – believing him to be Romanetti – the latter sent a message to the breeder: 'Tell that black traitor that he will not hear the shot that kills him.' A few days later, a shot rang out from behind a tree, and the breeder fell dead. Romanetti vanished into the mountains and became a bandit.

Like many famous bandits, he acquired a reputation for bravery, generosity and fearless honesty within his own code. 'We have many murderers but not a single thief,' said one Corsican bandit proudly; robbing rich farmers or holding travellers for ransom was not considered thieving.

Romanetti became a kind of Public Enemy Number One because of the number of gendarmes who tried to trap him – and who died in the attempt. Eventually, he was lured into an ambush and riddled with bullets. His was a pointless life and a pointless death, like those of so many Corsicans who became *banditi* because of vendettas and blood feuds.

Romanetti was killed because he became careless – tired of the life of an outlaw. Other bandits were luckier; some managed to negotiate a pardon with the authorities that enabled them to return to their native villages and live in peace. As we have seen, the outlaw life is not natural to human beings. If continued too long, it seems to induce a sense of futility, a certain weariness with life.

In Italy, the bandits found another solution to this problem. In the first half of the 19th century, they began to create a criminal network that extended through society, an instrument of extortion and intimidation. In the Naples area it was called the Camorra, and in Sicily, the Mafia. As in Corsica, this kind of lawlessness flourished only because it was difficult to get justice through ordinary channels.

The Camorra and the Mafia kept their own kind of law and order; landowners and farmers payed them taxes, later to be called 'protection'. What had happened was that the outlaws had ceased to be outside society; *they* had turned society inside out. In the early part of this century, the leader of the Sicilian Mafia, Don Vito Cascio Ferro, was not a bandit with a price on his head, but a respectable and influential man who was treated with respect by civic officials.

Ferro is suspected of being the evil genius who organized the deliberate importation into America of the Mafia, as well as the Camorra and 'The Black Hand' gang. In America, Police Lieutenant Joseph Petrosino became the leading expert on those Italian secret societies which extorted money from hard working immigrants, and in 1907, Petrosino went to Sicily to see for himself where the whole thing originated. The Mafia had been warned.

A matter of prestige

At 8.45 on the evening of March 12, 1907, Petrosino was walking back to his hotel. Few people were about at that time, when suddenly four shots rang out. Petrosino was shot dead. Several people were arrested, including Don Vito Cascio Ferro. He was released later for lack of evidence against him, but he did afterwards confess to the crime, and confirmed this in his recently published official biography. He had demonstrated the superiority of a Trade Union of Criminals over the disorganised bandits of Corsica and Greece.

By the time Petrosino was killed, America's own outlaw tradition was already nearly sixty years old. It may be said to have started on January 24, 1848, when a carpenter named James Marshall strolled down to look at a mill-race he had constructed at Coloma, California.

He had closed a sluice gate that admitted water from the river, and was looking down at the debris in the bottom of the empty channel when he noticed something shining. He picked up several lumps of the coppery metal, and decided to show them to his boss, John Sutter. It didn't take Sutter long to recognize that the three ounces of heavy nuggets were gold — twenty-three carat gold.

Sutter and Marshall tried to keep their discovery secret, but Marshall had already told workmen at the sawmill. When they realized they could dig out gold with their pocket knives instead of working for a dollar a day, Sutter saw no more of them. It was hard luck on Sutter, who had brought men to California to staff his flour mill and sawmill; instead, they all vanished in search of gold.

As the news spread, men flooded into California from all over America — the 'forty-eighters' and 'forty-niners' — and with them, they brought ex-convicts and professional crooks who realized that the quickest way to get gold was to take it from the men who had panned it. The gold rush became a crime rush.

According to the historian John Rollin Ridge, one of the most famous of these bandits, a man named Joaquin Murieta, was driven to a career of crime in much the same manner as the earlier bandits of Greece and Corsica. Murieta, who earned himself the nickname 'Terror of the Stanislaus' — a California river which became a gold mining centre — came to California from Sonora, Mexico, in 1850 — until 1848, California had belonged to Mexico.

One day six roughnecks told him that 'greasers' were not allowed to mine on American soil. His wife Rosita tried to avert a fight, but Murieta was beaten unconscious; then his wife was raped. Twice more, the patient Mexican was driven from claims. Finally, he began to make a success as a small trader, but luck was still against him; riding into town on a horse borrowed from his brother-in-law, he was accused of stealing the horse.

An angry mob dragged him to his brother-in-law's ranch, lynched the brother-in-law, and flogged Murieta unconscious with a horse whip. 'From that hour,' says Ridge, 'he was the implacable foe of every American.' Joaquin vanished from the ranch, and soon afterwards one of the men who had taken part in the whipping was found dead. Like a Corsican outlaw, Joaquin was carrying out a vendetta.

He proved to be a born leader, and soon had an outlaw gang – mainly composed of Mexicans who were sick of being treated as third-class citizens by louts and roughnecks. A member of the gang who was captured at Los Muertos in February 1853 and hanged told his captors that no member of the gang was respected until he had killed a man. The members had to swear an oath, and traitors were hunted down remorselessly – again suggesting the traditions of the Corsican bandits.

On May 17, 1853, the legislature of California passed an act authorizing a skilled frontiersman, Harry Love, to lead a band of twenty rangers until they had tracked down and killed – or captured – Murieta. A girl who had deserted Murieta gave Love some useful leads. In July, 1853, Love came upon a group of men camping near the Tejon Pass. He did not know Murieta by sight, but he became suspicious when various members of the band told contradictory stories about their destination.

Good-looking hothead

Then a lieutenant who knew Murieta rode up; Joaquin leapt onto his horse and rode off in a hail of bullets. He was thrown off the horse, and shot down by his pursuers. Joaquin's head, and that of his lieutenant, 'Three Fingered Jack', were sawed off and taken to San Francisco pickled in spirits, for purposes of identification. Murieta's head was put on exhibition at Stockton, California, on June 24, 1853.

Later historians of the West accused John Rollin Ridge of inventing Murieta, but this was unfair. Joseph Jackson, a more conscientious historian, investigated the matter, and discovered that there *was* a Joaquin Murieta, a bandit who preyed on miners between 1851 and 1853, that he *had* been killed by Captain Harry Love and his rangers, and that his head had been brought back to San Francisco. Love had obtained the $1,000 reward.

Most of the Western outlaws who went to California in the fifties met the same fate as Murieta; Western justice was rough but remarkably efficient. Henry Plummer, a good-looking, hot-headed young man of Nevada City, California, spent some time in jail for killing the husband of a woman with whom he was having an affair. Released, he reached Montana, by way of Idaho, in 1861, and organized one of the largest and most efficient gangs of robbers the West had seen. The gang's members called themselves 'The Innocents'.

Anticipating the methods of later American politicians. Plummer gave lavish bribes to all who might be of use; stage coach officials actually saved him the trouble of holding up unprofitable coaches by chalking special symbols on coaches carrying bullion or payrolls. Vigilantes decided it was time these depredations ceased; they organized large posses, and hanged twenty-six of the gang in a period of six weeks; Plummer himself was one of the first to go.

But while determined law enforcement officers were wiping out the Murietas and Plummers, politicians in Washington were preparing to launch America into its great era of banditry. For this *was* one of the major effects of the Civil War that broke out between south and north in 1861. It had taken Italy, Corsica and Greece several hundreds of years to develop their tradition of banditry; America did the same thing in four with the infamous James brothers, and the fast-shooting Billy the Kid.

However, it was in southern Europe that banditry most flourished. In Italy, during the nineteenth century, it was not uncommon for whole villages to be taken over by brigands. In return for money and protection, the villagers would provide food, lodging – and silence.

One such village was Sonnino, a borough of Frosinone in the province of Rome, which established a reputation for lawlessness sufficiently disturbing for the authorities to contemplate the deportation or extermination of its entire population. The idea was, of course, rejected, and the village survived to furnish the history of banditry with one of its most colourful figures: Antonio Gasperoni.

As so often with outlaws, Gasperoni began his career as a bandit almost by mistake. He started his working life as a lowly cowherd and spent his time peacefully tending cattle in the fields surrounding his birthplace. He gave no sign of his future as a notorious outlaw until, as a young man, he fell passionately in love with a pretty country girl, Maria. Unfortunately, she was betrothed to another suitor of slightly higher social position, called Claudio. The latter was unquestionably the more violent of the two and, one night in August 1814, he attempted to stab Gasperoni with a stiletto.

Band of desperadoes

In the scuffle that followed, Gasperoni managed to grab the knife and succeeded in killing his would-be murderer. It was, for him, the beginning of a rampage of rape and slaughter that was to last for nearly ten years.

Gasperoni soon revealed that he was no ordinary peasant. He gathered around him a sizeable band of desperadoes and marshalled them with all the skill and organizational ability of a general. The band lived, in the traditional fashion, by kidnapping eminent political and ecclesiastical figures, and members of wealthy families, and holding them for ransom.

Occasionally, to convince reluctant relatives that the kidnapped man was really in danger of his life, they would cut off an ear or perhaps a hand and send it by messenger to the victim's home. The ransom was quickly paid up. It is a trick which has not been forgotten by present-day Italian bandits as the kidnapping of the young Paul Getty in 1973 savagely demonstrated.

There is no doubt that, to some extent, Gasperoni lived up to the popular myths about bandits. Though he ruthlessly slaughtered anyone, rich or poor, who interfered with his wishes, he was, nonetheless, capable of great acts of generosity towards many of the peasants who, willingly or otherwise, assisted him in his continuing battle with the law. At the same time his exploits against wealthy landowners and merchants created a core of sympathy amongst the oppressed and poverty-stricken of Italy.

The capture of this legendary figure and his band is an interesting reflection on the mentality of the peasant bandit. Though he appeared to have no scruples about taking human life, Gasperoni had an acute sense of sin about his 'unlawful' sexual relations with his favourite mistress. His religious principles demanded marriage and it was at his own marriage ceremony that the gang was captured. The local priest had ordered them to disarm before entering the church, and they walked out afterwards straight into the arms of waiting soldiers. The priest had betrayed them.

Gasperoni was imprisoned for life in the dungeons of Civita Castellana, the notorious Rome prison. But he suffered little hardship. His fame had become so widespread that tourists and travellers constantly demanded to see him and he was transferred to a 'luxury' cell where he could entertain his visitors – for a large fee – with romantic tales of brigandage based upon his experiences.

The truth seems to be that the bandit – the man who lives outside society, fighting injustice – is a basic figure of world folklore. It is essential to the legend that such men are fundamentally decent and brave, driven to banditry by bad luck, hunted down and finally destroyed by the cold, inexorable machinery of justice. There are few real-life bandits whose careers fit this idealized picture; so the facts are distorted until they can be made to fit. The legends of the great bandits tell us very little about human psychology or behaviour, but they do tell us a great deal about human dreams and aspirations. And perhaps, in the long run, this is just as important.

BETRAYAL

'What, you again?' said Monsieur Henri, chief of the criminal department of the Paris police. 'I told you that if I saw you again you'd go back to the galleys.'

The man who stood between two gendarmes was short, powerfully built, with a scarred face and a jaw like a lion. His name was Eugène-François Vidocq, and he was 34 years old. When Vidocq had last visited M. Henri's office, a few months earlier, it had been to make the police chief an offer. Vidocq had been in trouble all his life. He had escaped from prison half a dozen times, and for the past 10 years had been running an old-clothes business in Paris. But he had been recognized by former associates, and now they were blackmailing him. His offer: to betray half a dozen wanted criminals in exchange for immunity from the police.

Henri had refused the offer. Yet he had allowed Vidocq to walk out of his office a free man. He knew Vidocq would be back sooner or later – and that he would be able to drive a harder bargain. It happened on the morning of July 1, 1809; Vidocq had been betrayed to the police by his in-laws, and had been on the run for two months. Henri told the gendarmes to wait outside. Then he leaned forward.

'You offered to help us. Very well, you can help us.'

Vidocq tried not to show his delight. 'You mean I can go free?'

'No. You must go to prison – to the Bicêtre . . .' And he explained his needs. A burglar called Barthélemy Lacour, known as Coco, was in the Bicêtre. He had stolen a large quantity of silver. The silver had been recovered, and Coco was now awaiting trial. But there was no evidence against him. What Henri wanted was for Vidocq to get the evidence.

It sounded a fairly unimportant task. But Vidocq was not taken in. He knew that, once he had provided Henri with his evidence, that would not be the end. Henri wanted a police spy to work among the prisoners of the Bicêtre – one of the most dangerous of all tasks. If a prisoner was even suspected of being a spy he would be found dead the next morning. Few criminals were willing to take the risk. But Vidocq realized he had no choice, for he was at the end of his tether.

And this is a matter that requires some explanation. There are many criminals who would be glad of a chance to become honest citizens, but crime has trapped them, like an octopus, and if they free themselves from one tentacle another winds around the wrist or ankle; Vidocq was in this situation. He had never committed a serious crime. He had simply been a daring and violent young man, who landed in jail for the first time on a charge of being a public nuisance – he had caught his mistress with an officer, and had beaten them both up.

Because he had felt the sentence was unjust, he had been an intractable prisoner and got into more trouble. He escaped, was forced to steal, and was recaptured. He escaped again, and became famous for escaping. During one of his periods of freedom he became involved with a gang known as the Chauffeurs – the 'warmers'.

Torture by fire

These men made a habit of bursting into lonely farms at night and torturing the inhabitants to make them confess the whereabouts of their valuables. They often hung their victims upside down over a fire – hence the nickname. Vidocq may well have become a member, although he always insisted that he merely slept with the mistress of one of the Chauffeurs, and that she helped him to obtain false papers.

The pattern is familiar; we can see it in the career of the mass murderer Carl Panzram, executed in 1931, whose journal *Killer* is one of the most horrific documents in the history of criminology. Panzram was a highly dominant man; his reaction to prison and ill-treatment was wild rage, resulting in more crimes – murders committed to 'get his own back on society'. Yet it is possible to pity Panzram; given his temperament, and the forces against him, he never stood a chance. There are thousands of criminals in his position, and a few of them see the one possible road leading to escape from the downward spiral – the road Vidocq saw: to become a police spy.

Vidocq went into the Bicêtre, and his reputation as an escaper made him into a hero. He actually saved the life of the man he was there to betray: Coco was suspected of being a police spy, and it was Vidocq who vouched for him to the other prisoners. After that, the grateful Coco felt Vidocq was an intimate friend. He told him the story of the stolen silver, and confided that the police had no evidence against him. The only man who had seen him with the stolen property was a porter in the Rue Dauphine. At his trial, Coco was astounded when the porter appeared in court to give evidence against him. He was sentenced to the maximum term of imprisonment.

By that time Vidocq had already betrayed innumerable other criminals to justice. His powerful physique and his reputation as an escaper made him popular among the prisoners. They were all delighted when, nearly two years later, Vidocq escaped yet again, on his way to court. No one guessed that this time the police had contrived his escape.

Vidocq was lucky in more ways than one. A career of betrayal and double-dealing is an unpleasant existence which is likely to induce the kind of carelessness that no police spy can afford. But Vidocq was a born detective. His nostrils twitched with pleasure when 'the game was afoot'. Faced with a problem that the police had been unable to solve, Vidocq worked at it with a savage persistence that usually brought results.

Wiry counterfeiter

For example, the police wanted to get hold of a forger named Watrin, who had escaped from them some time before. Through patient enquiry at rooming houses Vidocq discovered that a man answering Watrin's description had left some of his possessions in a rented room. Vidocq and his mistress moved into the room next door. Weeks later they heard someone in the next room — Watrin had returned, also with a mistress. Vidocq burst in, but the wiry counterfeiter managed to dodge past him and out into the night. By means of bloodcurdling threats Vidocq persuaded the abandoned mistress to give him her regular address.

Vidocq was there within minutes and saw a shadowy figure dodge back into the house: Watrin. He chased Watrin up the stairs, and the forger turned and — with the skill of an apache — dealt Vidocq a tremendous kick in the chest. Then he locked himself in a room. Vidocq decided to try cunning. In a loud voice he ordered his mistress, Annette, to go for the police; then he clattered down the stairs himself, removed his shoes and tiptoed back up. When Watrin eased his head cautiously round the door he was seized by the hair and dragged to the nearest gendarmerie.

One more example of multiple betrayal will suffice to give an idea of the way Vidocq became Paris's most successful man-hunter. One day, in 1811, Vidocq was approached by a thief named Hotot, whom he had helped to arrest some time before. Hotot said he wanted to become a police spy, and he advised Vidocq that certain wanted pickpockets would be at the Fête de Saint-Cloud the following evening.

When Vidocq arrived with some police agents, Hotot appeared and told him regretfully that several thieves had recognized him and fled. The next morning Vidocq learned that a number of thefts had been committed on the other side of the Saint-Cloud area. Vidocq had contributed to the success of the robbery by borrowing local police to help him arrest the non-existent pickpockets. He realized that Hotot had betrayed him, but he said nothing and bided his time; in fact, he appeared to become very friendly towards Hotot.

One day some weeks later, returning from an all-night vigil with another agent, Vidocq passed Hotot's room. He decided to drop in casually. Hotot was still in bed. Vidocq produced a bottle, and all three had a drink. When he reported to M. Henri later in the day, Henri told him there had been a big lead robbery in the night; four men had stolen a quantity of lead from a half built house. 'I know one of them,' said Vidocq. He had noticed that Hotot's shoes were muddy, and that his clothes were damp; obviously he had been out all night.

Vidocq bought a cold chicken and called on Hotot again, announcing that he had come to lunch. They ate the meal sitting on the bed – Hotot was still not dressed. Vidocq casually dropped his hat on Hotot's shoes, then asked his assistant if he would mind slipping out with a message. The assistant departed with Hotot's spiked shoes concealed under his coat. Hotot had no desire to get up; he and Vidocq were halfway through a bottle of brandy, and when they were alone, Hotot said he could betray three men who had committed a big lead robbery the night before.

Hotot was proposing to betray his three associates. Moreoever, if he did so, he would probably escape trial for aiding the police. Vidocq was determined that this should not happen, so he asked Hotot if he would help him spy on a certain prisoner in the local jail. Hotot, eager to ingratiate himself, agreed, and so Vidocq was able to leave him safely locked in a prison cell while he went to round up the other thieves.

Two mistresses

He had no idea where to find them; but he had another piece of useful information. Hotot had two mistresses. Vidocq found one of them in a bar, and he bought her a drink. Then he mentioned that he had just left Hotot with the other mistress. Within half an hour she had not only told him many incriminating things about Hotot, she had led him to the rooms of the three other thieves. Vidocq picked them up, and told them that Hotot had intended to betray them. They immediately declared that it was Hotot who had planned the robbery. When all four thieves appeared in the same dock, Vidocq had his revenge on Hotot for the double-cross at Saint-Cloud.

Vidocq was so spectacularly successful that he was soon given his own police department; it was called the Sûreté. And for more than 20 years Vidocq ran the Sûreté in his own inimitable way, using his intimate knowledge of the underworld, and relying heavily on a complex net of informers, all known to one another. He was the founder of a method that has become a basic part of modern police work.

When he left the Sûreté in 1883 – due to political intrigues – Vidocq scored another 'first' when he became a private enquiry agent, the first private detective in Europe. He also became a close friend of the novelist Balzac, supplying ideas for Balzac's plots; Balzac repaid him by turning Vidocq into one of his most powerful creations: the master criminal Vautrin. Vidocq died in 1857 at the age of 82 – one of the few criminals who managed to free himself from the tentacles of the underworld and achieve a less dubious kind of celebrity.

The story of Vidocq demonstrates an adage known to every policeman: that there is no 'honour among thieves'. The thief is basically a 'chancer', a man who is in the business because he holds the naive belief that life ought to give him something for nothing. If he thinks he can get away with something, he will try. His criterion is success, not honour. That is one reason that the police never seem to have difficulty in finding informers – also known as 'narks', 'snouts' and 'grasses' – in spite of the danger of the profession.

Outcast teenager

The nark is not well paid – he may be lucky if he receives £20 for a tip-off that might cost him his life – but he has the satisfaction of feeling that he is not wholly an outcast, a member of the underworld; and this is, psychologically speaking, the most interesting aspect of the informer. When a man is young, crime comes more easily to him. A child is always wanting things it cannot have, and its desires are so strong that it doesn't greatly care by what means they are satisfied.

A teenager feels an outcast from society anyway; he is expected to start playing a responsible role in a world he did nothing to create, and his basic feeling about this world is usually one of rejection – what Marx called 'alienation'. He also begins to experience powerful sexual urges, an undiscriminating desire to undress and possess every pretty girl he sees, and if he happens to be goodlooking and charming, he may be able to play the successful Don Juan.

Yet although his seductions are perfectly legal – provided the girl is above the age of consent – he is still basically *stealing* what he wants, because he is taking it without any thought of return. Most rapists are under the age of 20, and rapists above the age of 30 are rare. Those few are psychopaths or near psychopaths. The reason for all this is that after the age of 20 or so the adult human being starts to experience a certain feeling of 'one-ness' with the community. If he is married, he probably goes out with other couples and invites them back to his house or flat, and the world ceases to be 'alien'.

He may still have a highly flexible morality; he may think nothing of buying a pair of tyres he knows to be stolen, or seducing his wife's best friend. But he begins to feel himself a part of society, and if he has a reasonable job and a home, he enters the stage of development that Abraham Maslow calls the 'self-esteem stage'. He wants to be liked and respected by other people. It *is* possible for a criminal to be liked and accepted – particularly if he happens to be an Al Capone or Reggie Kray – but it is not easy.

Suicidal tendencies

Generally speaking, it is true that crime comes 'naturally' only to the young. As a man approaches 30 he begins to dream of a solid, comfortable future, for, paradoxically, what he now wants mostly is the *protection* of society. A criminal who, because of an inborn tendency to violence or because he cannot break the habit of crime, continues to feel himself an 'outcast' as he approaches middle age also begins to develop suicidal tendencies, a sense of futility.

Many 'old lags' commit crimes that are so stupid that they seem to *want* to be caught. Carl Panzram, who had spent most of his life in and out of prisons, committed a murder in jail, and then firmly blocked all attempts to get him a reprieve; he wanted to die.

The informer, then, is trying to re-establish his link with society, to escape the vicious circle. This aspect of the psychology of the 'nark' has never been adequately recognized by criminal psychologists. There is, of course, a simpler – and less familiar – form of criminal betrayal: when 'thieves fall out'.

Dominant relationship

This usually seems to happen when the relation between thieves – or murderers – is one of dominance. It happened in the case of Burke and Hare, the infamous 'body snatchers'. Burke, the 'dancing master', was the brains of the pair, and he dominated the tall, cadaverous Hare. But when they were finally caught, almost red-handed, after the murder of a beggar woman called Docherty, it was Hare who turned King's Evidence and thus saved his own neck; Burke alone was hanged in 1829.

Hare went to the Midlands, and there is a story that when fellow-workers in a lime-kiln discovered his identity they threw lime in his eyes, blinding him. He certainly died as a blind old beggar in London. In the equally famous – or infamous – case in which Mr. William Weare was murdered near Elstree, all the three accomplices tried to pass the blame from one to the other. Weare was a gambler who had won a large sum of money from the well-known sportsman John Thurtell.

Thurtell, and two associates called Joseph Hunt and William Probert, took Weare to a cottage in Gills Hill Lane, where Thurtell murdered him by shooting him and then cutting his throat with a penknife. The next morning local labourers became suspicious when they saw two strange-looking characters searching the undergrowth near the cottage, and when Thurtell and Hunt had gone back indoors the labourers found the blood-stained knife and pistol lying on top of a wall. They reported the find to a magistrate, and the body of William Weare was soon discovered in the nearby pond.

The case caused a nationwide sensation, out of all proportion to its interest. Probert and Hunt both tried to turn King's Evidence, but Probert beat Hunt to it, and finally only Thurtell and Hunt were tried. Hunt's speech in his own defence was mostly a whine about having been promised immunity if he co-operated with the law. As to Thurtell, he made an impressive speech, declaring that he was a gentleman and incapable of murder, and that the real murderer was Hunt. This was undoubtedly a lie. Thurtell was hanged in front of the largest crowd that had ever gathered to watch a man being 'turned off', while Hunt was reprieved, and transported to Australia, where he lived to a ripe old age.

The Son of Man

Of more recent cases involving betrayal, the most psychologically interesting is certainly that of the Manson family. The followers of Charles Manson regarded him as a 'saviour', and often pointed out that his name meant the Son of Man. Consequently there is an element of ritual drama in his betrayal by one of his mistresses, Susan Atkins. The betrayal was not entirely deliberate. The 'family' was under arrest for car-stealing and no one suspected that they might be the killers of Sharon Tate and the La-Biancas.

Apparently out of boredom or a desire to impress, Susan Atkins began to drop hints about the murders to her cell-mate, who passed it on to another prisoner, who informed the police. At the subsequent trial she was undoubtedly regarded as the central figure, next to Manson himself. The rest of the family certainly regarded her as a Judas.

It seems clear that her 'unintentional' betrayal of Manson was less accidental than it looked; she had been feeling rebellious about him for some time before the arrest. It has been suggested that she felt he 'needed' a Judas to enable him to fulfil his destiny as a victim of society, but this is probably placing too complicated a construction on her motive.

One interesting comparison emerges with the Thurtell case. Many contemporaries declared that Thurtell's eloquence was deeply moving, and obviously felt that he should not have been executed. Similarly, many commentators in the West Coast 'underground' press seemed to feel that Manson was being unfairly treated. His murders were a protest against the establishment, and he was, in some arcane sense, innocent.

The fact remains that Thurtell's 'moving' speech consisted mostly of lies, as did Manson's own defence. What is so interesting is that many apparently decent, sane people should take the side of a murderer. And the explanation is that, although in practical terms they may be law-abiding citizens, there is an element of social immaturity about them that makes them take the side of the lonely but criminal, individual against 'society'. The lesson to be drawn is that there is a great deal of muddled thinking – and muddled feeling – in our society about crime. Educationists might include a history of murder in every school curriculum.

BLACKMAIL

'Do you feel a creeping, shrinking sensation, Watson, when you stand before the serpents in the Zoo, and see the slithery, gliding, venomous creatures, with their deadly eyes and wicked, flattened faces? Well, that's how Milverton impresses me. I've had to do with fifty murderers, but the worst of them never gave me the repulsion which I have for this fellow.'

The speaker is, of course, Sherlock Holmes, and the man he is referring to is the blackmailer, Charles Augustus Milverton, 'the worst man in London'. The story of Milverton was first published in *Collier's Magazine* in 1904. The date is interesting because the slithery Milverton was probably the first blackmailer ever to make his appearance in fiction.

In fact, the crime itself was relatively new; a law against 'threatening to publish with intent to extort money' was not passed until 1893, though the word 'blackmail' dates back to the time of Queen Elizabeth I, when certain free-booting Scottish chieftains used to extort money from farmers along the Scottish border. This 'protection money' was called black-mail, or black-rent, to distinguish it from the rent the farmer paid to his proper landlord.

This was not actually a crime – the law taking the view that if a farmer chose to pay black-rent, that was his own business. It was not until 1873 that the British parliament decided that 'demanding money with menaces' was just as unlawful as pointing a gun at somebody's head and taking his wallet.

Medium dominance
It may seem curious that English law – and this also applies to America – took so long to take account of blackmail, but the reason can be seen in *Charles Augustus Milverton*. Milverton makes a living by buying up 'compromising letters' written by ladies and gentlemen in high society, and threatening to send

them to the husband or wife of the imprudent writer. Holmes is engaged to try to recover certain indiscreet letters written by a young lady to a penniless country squire; now she is about to marry an Earl, and the blackmailer threatens to send the letters to the future husband.

And, in fact, real life Milvertons *were* making money in exactly this way. A century earlier, it would have been absurd; people in high society took mistresses – or lovers – all the time, and nobody gave a damn. Then Queen Victoria came to the throne, married a serious and religious German prince named Albert, and all that changed; in England, high society took its tone from the royal family. The Age of Respectability had arrived, and there were suddenly dozens of things that were just Not Done.

The 'breath of scandal' could ruin a man – and totally destroy a woman; Queen Victoria turned violently and passionately against her own son when she heard he was having an affair with an actress, whereas her predecessors on the throne of England would have thought there was something seriously wrong with a son who *didn't* fornicate with actresses, chambermaids and ladies-in-waiting. But the First Lady of England, being a woman of only 'medium dominance', was a romantic, one-man woman, who thought sex was rather dirty, and high society had to live up to her standards – or else.

The case that made the Victorians aware of the curious legal problems involved in blackmail took place in 1872. The lady in the case was called Lady Twiss; the blackmailer was a London solicitor named Alexander Chaffers. Lady Twiss was the wife of Sir Travers Twiss, a well-known Victorian advocate, and pro-fessor of International Law at King's College, London. She was regarded as thoroughly respectable – she had even been presented at Court to Queen Victoria. And now, to the horrified incredulity of British high society, she was accused by Mr. Chaffers of being a common prostitute.

Sir Travers Twiss had been a highly successful man of fifty when he had met a pretty Polish girl at his mother's house in 1859. Her name was Marie Van Lynseele, and she was the daughter of a Polish Major-General. Three years later, Sir Travers was in Dresden, and again met the pretty Pole. They fell in love, and married at the British Legation. On their return to England, Lady Twiss was presented first to the Prince of Wales, then to Queen Victoria.

One day, when she and her husband were walking in Kew Gardens, a man suddenly raised his hat and said hello. Lady

Twiss introduced him to her husband as a solicitor, Alexander Chaffers. Chaffers congratulated her on her marriage, and not long after, Lady Twiss received a bill for £46 from Mr. Chaffers 'for services rendered'. She ignored it. He sent another letter, this time asking for £150. Lady Twiss showed it to her husband, and explained that she really owed Chaffers some money for legal work he had once done for a maid in her employment. Whereupon Sir Travers Twiss arranged a meeting with Chaffers, and paid him £50, asking for a receipt. This was marked 'in full discharge'.

But Chaffers was apparently not satisfied. He continued to ask Lady Twiss for money. He wrote a letter to the Lord Chamberlain – the Court official responsible for vetting the list of people who would be received by the Queen – telling him that Lady Twiss had been, to put it crudely, a French whore who had managed to worm her way into high society.

The Lord Chamberlain was baffled. Short of hiring a private detective, he couldn't think of any way of investigating the story, so he decided to treat it as a hoax and forget it. But he told Lord and Lady Twiss about the accusations. They were horrified, and confirmed his opinion that Chaffers was a madman. Chaffers certainly had the persistence of a madman. He had a writ for libel served on Sir Travers, claiming that Lady Twiss had been spreading all kinds of slanders about him, and then went to the Chief Magistrate at Bow Street to make a sworn statement of 'the truth about Lady Twiss'.

Made public

This statement declared that she was actually a prostitute named Marie Gelas, and that she had been intimate with Chaffers on several occasions in certain houses of ill-fame in Belgium. Now, as much as he disliked the idea, Sir Travers Twiss had to take action. In May, 1871, Mr. Chaffers appeared at Southwark Police Court, charged with having 'published' various slanders against Sir Travers and Lady Twiss – in legal terminology, 'published' means simply 'made public'. Mr. Chaffers's defence was that the 'libels' were true.

Marie Van Lynseele claimed to be the daughter of a deceased Major-General, and that she had been brought up in Poland and Belgium as the adopted daughter of a Monsieur Jastrenski. Marie admitted that she *knew* someone called Marie Gelas; according to her, Marie Gelas had been her chaperone when she had first met Sir Travers.

During that visit, Marie Van Lynseele had fallen seriously ill, and Marie Gelas had decided that her employer ought to make a will; she therefore sent for Mr. Chaffers, whom she already knew, and got him to draw up a suitable document. This, said Lady Twiss, was the full extent of her acquaintance with Mr. Chaffers, and he had been paid his £50 professional fee after the meeting in Kew Gardens.

Mr. Chaffers replied that there never *had* been a 'chaperone' called Marie Gelas. Lady Twiss *was* Marie Gelas, and he had slept with her several times before she 'struck it rich'. Nowadays, this would be an open and shut case. Mr. Chaffers was admitting that he had tried to blackmail Lady Twiss by telling her husband about her past, and then, when that didn't work, trying to blackmail them both. But in 1872 there was no law against blackmail: only against libel.

Lady Twiss's problem was to prove that she was Marie Van Lynseele, daughter of a Major-General, not Marie Gelas. She called various witnesses to testify about her past, including a maid who swore on oath that Chaffers had tried to bribe her to support slanders against her mistress. Obviously Chaffers was a very nasty piece of work, and the judge made no attempt to hide his distaste.

Unsolved mystery

And then, quite unexpectedly, Lady Twiss surrendered. On the eighth day of the trial she decided she had had enough. Her counsel appeared in court to tell the judge that his client had left London, and decided not to continue the case. The judge had no alternative but to discharge Alexander Chaffers. He told him that for the rest of his life he would be 'an object of contempt to all honest and well-thinking men'; but the fact remained that Chaffers had won.

A week later, Sir Travers Twiss resigned from all his various distinguished posts. His wife had vanished to the Continent, and, as far as we know, he never saw her again. The *London Gazette* published a paragraph saying that Lady Twiss's presentation to the Queen – which had taken place three years earlier – had been 'cancelled' – which was the Victorian way of saying that it hadn't really happened at all, and the case remains an apparently unsolved mystery.

But it is easy enough to read between the lines: If Lady Twiss *had* been Marie Van Lynseele, she would presumably have fought to the last ditch. The court was already inclined heavily in her favour. Her foster-father, M. Jastrenski, had testified that she *was* Marie Van Lynseele, and many other witnesses had declared on oath that they knew Marie Gelas, and that she was *not* Marie Van Lynseele. It was a foregone conclusion that Chaffers would be found guilty and sent for trial.

What probably happened is that Marie Van Lynseele – or Gelas – had bribed various people to appear in her favour, but that she realized a trial would be a more serious matter; perhaps her witnesses refused to testify at a criminal trial, because they were afraid of the penalty for perjury. She decided the game was up, and vanished. If she was innocent, why did she tell her husband that she owed Chaffers the £50 for legal fees contracted on behalf of a maid, when she later testified in court that it was *her* will that Chaffers drew up?

Homosexual brothel
On the other hand, there remains the other possibility: that, persecuted by Chaffers, realizing that she had ruined her husband, no matter what the outcome of the case, Lady Twiss's nerve snapped and she fled. The case made upper-class Victorians aware how vulnerable they were to blackmail. A man like Chaffers didn't need any *evidence* that Lady Twiss was a prostitute. He only had to say so in court, and even if he was found guilty of libel, her reputation would never recover from the scandal.

It also made the Victorians aware that they needed a law to prevent people like Chaffers extorting money by threats: hence the statute of 1873 against 'demanding money with menaces'. It cost Sir Travers Twiss his career, but his case had changed the law.

Unfortunately, a change in the law was not quite the answer. When a crime suddenly attracts public attention, criminals everywhere wonder whether this is not a new source of income. The Victorian poor had always been the prey of rich debauchees; there were few working-class girls who could refuse the offer of five shillings for the use of their bodies. Now the poor began to retaliate by exerting blackmail on the seducers.

Oscar Wilde was blackmailed by some of the working class youths he slept with; when a homosexual brother in Cleveland Street was raided by the police in 1889, the whole affair was quickly hushed up when they realized that one of the chief clients was the Duke of Clarence, the grandson of Queen Victoria. 'Eddie' – as the Duke was known – was packed off on a world cruise, and endless possibilities of blackmail were averted.

But it was not only the lower classes who indulged in blackmail. Aristocrats could play the game just as ruthlessly. One of the most famous – and notorious – of Victorian aristocrats was Lady Warwick, known universally as Daisy – the song 'Daisy, Daisy' was written with her in mind. The ravishingly beautiful Daisy married the future Earl of Warwick in 1881 and became mistress of Warwick Castle and a huge fortune. She soon found her husband's passion for hunting and fishing a bore, and began to take lovers.

Sexual promiscuity

For several years she conducted a passionate affair with the dashing Lord Charles Beresford – in the Victorian age there was nothing to stop you having love affairs provided you were discreet about it, and avoided 'scandal'. When Lord Charles finally broke it off she went to his closest friend, the Prince of Wales, to beg him to help her get back a certain compromising letter.

Edward, Prince of Wales, was the son who had alienated Queen Victoria through his affair with an actress, and ever since that time he had devoted his life to sexual promiscuity with the energy of a Casanova. He took one look at Daisy, and dragged her towards the nearest bed. Daisy was willing enough; for although the Prince was no longer young or handsome – he was fat and inclined to wheeze – she saw he was a valuable ally. As to Prince Edward, he was genuinely in love with the delicious Daisy.

In 1893 her father-in-law died, and Daisy became mistress of a fortune. She immediately had Warwick Castle relandscaped, filled it with expensive carpets and furniture, and gave huge weekend parties that were famous for their extravagance. The socialist press attacked her for wasting so much money when the poor were starving; as a result she went to see the famous left-wing editor, W.T. Stead, and immediately became converted to socialism. She had the double pleasure of being immensely rich and being known as the defender of the poor.

As the years went by, Daisy's beauty faded and her fortune dwindled. In 1912 she realized that she was close to bankruptcy. And then she had her inspiration. She would write her memoirs, make sure they were scandalously frank, and sell them to a publisher for some huge sum – £100,000 was her first estimate. In 1914, she contacted a journalist and writer named Frank Harris – now known chiefly as the author of the semi-pornographic *My Life and Loves*.

Harris was not only an editor, a novelist and a Don Juan; he was a completely unscrupulous blackmailer, and he instantly saw the enormous possibilities of her scheme. All she had to do was to make sure she included the love letters of the Prince of Wales – later King Edward VII, who had died in 1910 – and then ask the Palace how much it was worth to suppress the book.

Two years earlier a Tory Member of Parliament, Charles du Cros, had lent Daisy £16,000, and he now wanted his interest on the sum. Daisy also happened to know that he wanted a knighthood, and that he had an attitude verging on adoration for King George V, Edward's son. She sent for du Cros, told him about the memoirs, and mentioned that she had letters from the late King in which, among more intimate and scandalous matters, he had given his frank opinion of such people as the Kaiser and the Tsar of Russia.

Du Cros rushed to see Georve V's A.D.C. and his solicitor. The solictor suggested that he had better ask Daisy how much she would take to suppress the book. Daisy said £85,000 – but told du Cros that he would have to see her 'partner', Frank Harris. Harris had fled to Paris, escaping his creditors; du Cros saw him at the Ritz Hotel, and was told that they would settle for a mere £125,000.

But the Establishment had its own way of dealing with blackmail. Instead of paying up, George V's solicitor asked for a court injunction to prevent Daisy publishing the late King's letters. Daisy at first found it incredible – to drag the affair into open court; but there she was mistaken. The Establishment co-operated admirably. The case was heard in chambers – a closed court. Edward VII's name was not mentioned; it was simply a matter of preventing the publication of 'certain letters'. The letters had to be handed over to the court. The injunction was granted, and the court also ordered that the letters were to be destroyed.

Two-way mirrors

This was not quite the end of the story. Before the letters were handed over, Frank Harris went to stay with Daisy Warwick at her house, Easton Lodge – she had been forced by debts to move out of Warwick Castle. He asked to see the letters – and when Harris left for America, the letters went with him. In order to get them back, Daisy had to pay Harris for them. She was the loser all round … Her only consolation was that du Cros, feeling sorry for her, took over £50,000 worth of her debts.

Since Daisy's time the art of blackmail has been turned into an exact science particularly by the espionage and counter-espionage services of all the major countries. In the West, we hear a great deal about the techniques of the Russian secret service, the K.G.B. – for example, how they blackmailed the American army sergeant James Harris, who appeared in the Rudolph Abel case, or of the pressure they brought to bear on the homosexual naval clerk, Vassall. But there can be no doubt that the C.I.A. and Britain's M.I.5. are just as skilled in its uses.

A favourite technique with both sides is to lure a diplomat – or member of the government – into a sexually compromising position. The Russians are credited with the discovery of the use of two-way mirrors for this purpose – the English and American method was cruder, using a picture or photograph with tiny holes in it, usually in the pupils of the eyes, with the camera concealed behind it.

The invention of transistors enabled the C.I.A. to perfect a whole new range of 'bugging devices'. One of these was a tiny pill that emitted a radio signal. The girl who has been chosen as the decoy swallows a pill that makes a 'bleep' noise. Another pill – which emits a 'bloop' – is concealed in the food of the victim, so he swallows it. Agents are then able to follow the couple with radio receivers, and when their receivers pick up simultaneous bloops and bleeps, they can assume that the bellies of both parties are in sufficiently close contact to warrant a sudden intrusion.

Blackmail is the least documented of all crimes for an obvious reason: if a blackmailer is caught by the police, it is in everybody's interests to make sure that the case receives no publicity. And in most civilized countries, it is generally agreed that when a victim reports blackmail to the police, he will not lay himself open to criminal charges, even if he is being blackmailed for a crime he has committed. Although this is a convention, not a law, it is seldom broken – the only exception being in cases involving treason. Slowly, very slowly, society is learning to combat the blackmailer. The day may yet come when blackmail, like piracy, is no more than a relic of the past.

CANNIBALISM

'I've got a problem,' said the full-bearded young hippie. 'I'm a cannibal.' The policeman who had just arrested him looked at him incredulously. The man reached into his pocket and pulled out a number of small bones. 'These aren't chicken bones. They're human fingers.'

The conversation sounds like something out of a bad horror movie, but it took place on the afternoon of July 13, 1970, near Lucia, California, and the speaker was 23-year-old Stanley Dean Baker.

The case had started two days earlier, when a fisherman saw a human body caught in the reeds of the Yellowstone River, north of the Yellowstone National Park in Montana. When police waded into the river to recover the body, they realized this was no case of drowning. The corpse was clad only in underpants, and it had neither head nor arms. The legs had been severed at the knees. Where the heart should have been there was an ugly hole in the chest. Later in the day a coroner established that the man had been stabbed 25 times.

The absence of the heart suggested disturbing possibilities. Ever since the Manson case in 1969 California had been plagued with a rash of 'ritual murders' – drug-ridden devil worship cults that offered human sacrifices in the manner of the ancient Incas and Aztecs. On Monday morning the police received a missing person report on Peter Schlosser, 22, who had driven off on Friday afternoon to camp in Yellowstone Park. He had been in a yellow sports car. This sounded as if it might be the victim. The police put out an alarm call for a 1969 Opel Kadett car.

In fact the car was involved in an accident at about the time alarm went out. Taking a corner on a dirt road too fast, it ran headlong into a pickup truck. The pickup was dented, but the sports car was almost a write off. The driver of the pickup suggested they should drive to the nearest garage and send for a tow. The two hippies who had been in the sports car went with him; but while he was in the telephone booth, they disappeared, running towards the nearest woods.

Half an hour later it was established that the damaged sports car belonged to the murdered man. The hunt was on, and it ended quickly and anticlimactically when a patrolman saw two bearded hippies on a dirt road, ordered them to bend over his car with their hands on it, and radioed for help. It was as they were driving into the Monterey police station that one of the men remarked: 'I have a problem. I'm a cannibal,' and confided that he had had a curious longing to eat human flesh ever since he received electric shock treatment for nervous disorder at the age of 17.

According to Stanley Dean Baker, his companion, Harry Stroup, had not been involved in the murder. He had been alone, he said, when Schlosser had offered him a lift on the previous Friday. All camping sites in the Yellowstone Park had been full, so they drove a few miles north and camped on the banks of the Yellowstone River. Schlosser had no suspicion that his companion was a homicidal maniac and a 'devil worshipper'.

In the middle of the night Baker shot his companion twice in the head with a .22 then stabbed him again and again with a hunting knife. He then cut up the body into six parts, severing the head, the arms and the legs. Baker alleged that he cut out the heart and ate it. Then, dropping a few severed fingers into his pocket, Baker threw the parts of the body into the river and drove off in the dead man's car.

In his possession when he was arrested was a paperback book, *The Satanic Bible*, a handbook of devil worship. Baker also stated that he had been on an 'acid trip' shortly before the murder, having taken 65 doses of LSD. The murder brings to mind the case of the 'Sydney mutilator', William MacDonald – the homosexual sadist who killed at least four down-and-outs in the early 1960s; MacDonald also described getting up in the middle of the night and stabbing a sleeping man in a frenzy, and MacDonald attributed his fits of insane violence to a severe emotional shock in his teens – in this case, a homosexual rape.

But MacDonald – who was found to be insane – did not eat any part of his victims. His frenzy of destruction did not carry him that far. What is suggested by a comparison of the two cases – is that cannibalism is a form of 'ultimate destruction' of the victim. When head-hunting tribes in New Guinea eat their conquered enemies, the act symbolizes total conquest, total contempt; the enemy is not only defeated, he is digested and then excreted. It seems possible that the motive for the Yellowstone murder was Baker's hatred of the thoroughly 'square' and respectable young man – Schlosser was an employee of the Mussel County Welfare Department at Roundup – the college graduate with his sports car, his horn-rimmed glasses, and his elaborate camping equipment. If this is true, it underlines one of the most disturbing trends in American crime in the 1970s, a trend that may be said to have started with the Manson 'family' murders: the tendency of groups who feel themselves to be 'social rejects' to lash out violently – and irrationally – at the 'respectable' members of society.

The civilized response to cannibalism is always one of violent disgust; Alfred Packer and the *Mignonette* survivors aroused a public reaction of horrified fascination that was out of all proportion to the crimes committed. And this could well be because the thought of cannibalism stirs up deep, atavistic memories in human beings. There can be little doubt that our remote, cave-man ancestors were cannibals. In 1927 anthropologists discovered remains of Pekin Man, half a million years old, near Choukoutien, in China; they also discovered humanoid skulls that had been split open, and the brains extracted – suggesting that Pekin Man was a cannibal.

Similar evidence has revealed that Neanderthal Man and Cro-Magnon Man, *homo sapiens*, was also at times a cannibal. And in fact this is logical enough. Unlike the great apes, man has always been a flesh eater, and one of his earliest discoveries was how to wield a bone club to crack the skulls of his enemies. Since all food had to be hunted, what is more natural than that our ancestors should have eaten their enemies? Later on, when tribal customs and superstitions developed, men began to entertain a magical belief that to eat any living creature was one way of absorbing its qualities.

Teeth marks

So, in many tribes, old people were eaten – rather than simply buried – because their children wanted to inherit their wisdom. The Greek historian Strabo declares that the tribes of Ireland practised cannibalism, while St. Jerome reports cannibalism in Scotland as late as the fourth century A.D. So we could say that it is only in fairly recent years that civilized man has given up the practice of eating his fellow men.

It is quite conceivable, therefore, that the explanation of Stanley Baker's cannibalism is not that black magic and LSD had driven him insane, but that they *released* some primitive, long-suppressed urge from his unconscious mind. The horror we feel when we read of cannibalism may be recognition that we are all capable of it.

This must be immediately qualified by stating that one form of cannibalism is purely sexual in origin. The Wisconsin necrophile, Ed Gein, arrested in 1957, was a sexually frustrated man who had for years been digging up newly buried female corpses, using them to satisfy his sexual needs and eating parts of them. The normal male sexual urge is, to some extent, a 'sadistic' urge: that is to say, it is a desire to penetrate, to violate, the female. When a sexually aroused male presses the female violently against him, all his actions are basically aggressive.

'Cannibal rapist'
In May 1971, 24-year-old Wayne Boden was arrested near Calgary, Canada, and charged with a series of rape murders. The first three victims were killed in Montreal; in each case there were teeth marks all over the breasts. The fourth victim, a schoolteacher, was found in Calgary, 2,500 miles away, on May 18, 1971. The odd feature of the case was that in three of the four murders the victim had been 'dating' her killer.

This was no case of a sex-starved psychopath grabbing a girl in a dark street, or bursting into her apartment; Boden was a good-looking, well-dressed, charming young man who would probably have had no difficulty in persuading most girls to satisfy normal sexual desires. But his desire was to use his teeth on the breasts and neck. Some of the Canadian newspapers dubbed Boden – sentenced to four terms of life imprisonment – the 'Vampire rapist', but it would undoubtedly have been more accurate to call him the 'Cannibal rapist'.

And in the cases of Ed Gein and Albert Fish this 'cannibal' element was taken to an extreme. It is an extension of the normal male desire to 'wholly possess' a girl, and is a common feature of cases of sexual assault. Jack the Ripper claimed to have eaten a kidney taken from one of his victims. In *The Sexual Criminal*, Dr. Paul de River describes the case of a rapist who, after repeatedly violating his victim, also bit off her nipples and swallowed them. He also cites the case of a necrophiliac mortuary attendant who had for years been violating the corpses of young women.

This man frequently inserted a catheter into the bladder in order to drink the urine. He was finally caught because his sexual frenzy led him one day to bite the buttocks of a corpse so violently that the marks were observed by the embalmer. If, like Albert Fish, he had been able to continue to give outlet to his perverse desires, he might well have ended by committing murder and eating the body.

Half dead

America's most famous 'cannibal' was Alfred Packer, the prospector who killed and ate four of his companions. In the autumn of 1873 Packer was one of a party of 20 men who set out from Salt Lake City, Utah, hoping to find gold in the mountains of San Juan. As the winter drew on, they came close to starvation, and were saved only by a tribe of friendly Indians. Ten returned to civilization; another 10 – with Packer as leader – pressed on. When Packer suggested that they should make for the source of the Rio Grande, four of the men declined to continue with him. These four later regretted their decision; caught in the winter snowstorms, two of them died, and the remaining two dragged themselves, half dead, into the Los Pinos Agency in February 1874.

In fact they had no reason to envy the others. All but Packer also met their deaths in the wilderness. A month after the two survivors had staggered into Los Pinos, another traveller came to the door, begging for food. It was Alfred Packer, and although he was obviously suffering from exhaustion, he looked fairly well fed. Packer's story was that the other five men had deserted him when he was ill. The men at the agency had no reason to doubt his story. Ten days later, Packer went on to Saquache, and began to drink heavily.

Headless corpse

He seemed to have plenty of money. The stories he told of his ordeal varied so much that people began to suspect foul play. He was arrested by General Adams, from the Agency, and held on suspicion. On April 2 two excited Indians rushed into the Agency holding strips of flesh which they said they had found outside. They said it was 'human meat'. Packer fainted. When he recovered, he told a strange story of cannibalism. They had been starving in the mountains and were living on roots. One day, when he had been out gathering firewood, he returned to the camp to find that the oldest man in the party, Israel Swan, had been murdered with a blow on the head, and the others were engaged in cutting up the body to eat it.

Swan's money – $2,000 – was divided equally. Packer ate part of Swan. When this food ran out, a man called Miller was killed with a sudden blow with a hatchet – he was the fattest. After Miller was eaten it was the turn of a man called Humphrey; then Noon. This only left Packer and a companion named Bell; they agreed not to try to kill one another. But one day, said Packer, Bell had attacked him in a frenzy, and he had been forced to kill him with a hatchet. He cut strips of flesh from the body, and continued his journey until he saw the Agency ahead – and then threw away the flesh.

The next day Packer led a party back into the mountains; but he claimed he was unable to remember the scene of the murder. That night he tried to kill the man to whom he was handcuffed and escape, but he was detected in time.

The five corpses were found in June, near the shores of Lake Christoval. It was immediately clear that Packer had lied. Four of the five had been shot in the back of the head. Miller's corpse was headless, but when the head was found, it was seen that he had been killed with a violent blow from the butt of a rifle. The ribs of all the dead men were exposed; evidently Packer's preference had been for the flesh of the breast. Blankets were found in a nearby cabin; Packer had lived there after the murders, making trips back to the frozen bodies for meat.

Packer's second attempt to escape was successful, and he was not caught again until January 29, 1883, nine years later. He had been recognized at Cheyenne, Wyoming; he was suspected of being a member of a gang of outlaws. He was tried for the murder of only one of the men, Israel Swan, and sentenced to death. However, at a retrial he was charged only with manslaughter, and sentenced to 40 years in jail. He received a pardon 18 years later, and died near Denver in 1907.

Packer undoubtedly murdered his five companions, and the crime *is* horrifying. Yet the charge of manslaughter suggests that the prosecution found it impossible to believe that anyone would eat human flesh for pleasure. Packer undoubtedly decided that they would all die of cold and starvation, and that if he hastened their deaths he alone might survive. This has been the motive in most of the cases of cannibalism by civilized human beings.

Certainly the most moving and remarkable of these was one that took place in the winter of 1972, when a planeload of survivors lived for 10 weeks in the Andes on the flesh of their companions. The Uruguayan plane, en route to Chile, crashed in the Andes with 45 people on board. After 10 days, the survivors reluctantly decided that their only chance of survival was to eat their dead companions. When they heard on the plane radio that the rescue search had been called off, there seemed no alternative to starving to death or eating their companions in order to live.

Exposure

Three of the men climbed higher up the mountain, and concluded that the wreck of their plane could not be seen from the air. One by one the badly injured died, until there were 27 of the original 45 left. A landslide of snow half-buried the plane and suffocated eight more of the party, including Liliana Methol, the last woman survivor – her husband, Javier Methol, was one of the few to get back to civilization. One of the 19 survivors recalled the words of a taxi-driver, that the snow stops and the summer starts in the Andes on November 15; this was October 31, and the thought gave them hope.

Occasionally they cooked the human flesh; but they had too little fuel to indulge in this luxury frequently. It was near the end of the first week of December that birds circled above their camp, and they realized that spring was at last approaching. Three more deaths from exposure decided three of the men to make an attempt to reach civilization and bring rescuers. Roberto Canessa, Nando Parado and Antonio Vizintin set off to climb the mountain – the first steps of a westward route – using cushions as snow shoes. It took them most of three days to reach the summit; and when Parrado reached it he saw nothing but snow-capped mountains ahead.

Sausage-meat

However, far to the west there were two mountain peaks that were not covered with snow. They had only enough food for 10 days, and the mountains looked as if they were at least two months' march away. They decided that Vizintin should return to the plane. Then the other two plodded on. For another week they continued, down the mountain and along a river valley, and finally the sight of a rusty horseshoe and a soup can told them they were close to civilization.

On December 20, 10 days after setting out, they saw three men on horseback on the other side of the river – peasants. The next day a poor peasant rode up to them, gave them cheese – and went on up the valley to inspect his cows. Later, they returned with him to his wooden hut – and finally, after 10 weeks, ate a normal meal. It was December 21. A Chilean airforce helicopter rescued the remaining 13 survivors on the following day. Of the original 45, only 16 returned to civilization. They had survived largely on the bodies of the other 29.

From the strictly criminal point of view there have been few notable cases involving cannibalism. Fish, Gein and Stanley Baker were all undoubtedly insane, and it could therefore be argued that they should be regarded as madmen rather than criminals. But four other cases should be noted briefly. In 1897 Adolph Leutgart, a sausage manufacturer of Chicago, murdered his second wife, Louise, and dumped her body in a vat he used for boiling sausage meat.

Many Chicagoans still refer to Leutgart as the man who turned his wife into sausages. In fact, this is untrue; he poured caustic potash on the body and boiled it. After a few days all that remained of his wife were two gold rings in the bottom of the vat. However, this was enough to convict Leutgart, who died in prison before he could be executed. He explained the murder by saying he was 'possessed by the devil'.

Pickled bodies

Fritz Haarmann, the Hanover butcher who killed youths and sold their bodies for meat, had two remarkable German contemporaries, Karl Denke, of Münsterberg, and George Grossmann, of Berlin. Both killers were caught – Grossmann in August 1921 and Denke in December 1924 – when sounds of a struggle led other tenants to investigate their rooms. Denke was in the process of killing a young journeyman; Grossmann had already killed a girl.

Denke's house was found to contain two large tubs of brine, in which various parts of male bodies were pickled. Denke had kept a detailed record of 30 victims, mostly down-and-outs, whom he had killed and partly eaten. Grossmann, who specialized in picking up young girls – preferably fat – at the railway station, had killed a dozen women and sold their bodies for meat, as well as eating parts himself. Both hanged themselves in prison before they could be executed.

Daylight

We may regard cannibalism as a terrible, dark survival of man's animal past, lurking like some sinister monster in the depths of the subconscious. But a healthier view is put by the anthropologist A.I. Hopkins, who points out that directly a primitive tribe comes into contact with civilization, cannibalism disappears of its own accord. 'Directly daylight falls on the habit, it withers away.' Study of the history of cannibalism suggests that these sane, balanced words come closer to the basic truth about human nature.

CHANCE IN A MILLION

Chance is that unplanned occurrence which alters the shape of events. To the murderer it is the break which permits him to avoid detection, to the pursuer it is the equally unexpected opportunity to ensnare his quarry. In all human affairs it is what John Milton called '*That power which erring men call chance*'.

The mathematical likelihood of things happening by chance is defined by the theory of probability, and 'chance' events are those which are not influenced by known causes. They are random eventualities – fate, risk and accident – for chance is like a blindfolded person taking a card from a pack.

The chance of a certain outcome taking place can be defined where the possibilities are limited. The chances of selecting a certain playing card are determined by the number of cards in the pack and also by the number of suits. For example, the chance of drawing a Heart is 13 out of 52 or $3\frac{1}{4}$ times more probable than selecting a King, of which there are only four in the pack.

Mathematical formulae can be used to work out the probability of a certain event happening. Prize-winning chances on one-arm bandits are carefully calculated, and insurance firms use probability tables when calculating life insurance premiums. There is no way of knowing in advance the life expectation of any particular individual. But experience of the risks inherent in different occupations added to information about health can reduce the areas of uncertainty. Each year a certain number of men within a prescribed age range and occupation die of heart disease. These are repeatable situations which are statistically reliable.

The criminal has no probability tables and no reliable statistics with which to plan his enterprises. The intending assassin could work out the chances of his gun jamming or of the transmission failing in his getaway car if he stopped to think about it. They are predictable occurrences against which he can take reasonable safeguards by servicing car and gun. But it is the million other possibilities – a fingerprint, a length of hair, a chip of paint, the workings of time – which provide the materials of chance. Conceiving of murder is a secret, hostile business, but its commission is public because murder cannot be done in a vacuum; the chance appearance of a passer-by has spelled disaster to many a murderer's plan.

Chance in the hostile world of the murderer is like some pathogenic organism; it lurks unseen, dangerous and challenging. As one of Ray Bradbury's characters discovered, it cannot be eliminated absolutely. A man, having committed murder, decides to eliminate all traces of his presence at the murder scene. He wipes the telephone he has used, the table he has touched, the door handle he has turned. He becomes obsessed, cleaning everything in an effort to remove all traces of his presence. In a frenzy he cleans the furniture, the walls, the floor, the ceiling, not once, but many times. Exhaustion and madness result.

The power of chance is its unpredictability. On May 22, 1924, the dead body of a boy was found in a culvert by a railroad near Chicago. Fourteen-year-old Bobbie Franks was found by maintenance men. He had been severely beaten about the head. Close by, an observant workman discovered a pair of horn-rimmed spectacles.

A Chicago optical firm identified the spectacles as having special frames which had been supplied to three customers. On their third call, the police found Nathan Leopold Jr., a 19-year-old amateur bird watcher and a student at Chicago University. He admitted the spectacles were his. Leopold said he must have lost the spectacles weeks previously while out bird watching. Questioned further about his activities, he said that he had been out with some girls and his friend, fellow student Richard Loeb.

Leob broke down under questioning and admitted to the crime. Leopold's confession was not long in following. The workings of chance had contrived to place Leopold at the scene of the murder. Those spectacles which slipped from his coat pocket ruined the 'perfect murder' which he and Loeb had master-minded.

Of all the items which might have been dropped at the scene, fate decreed it should be an easily identified personal article. Thus was ended the infamous experiment in murder of Leopold and Leob – two 'supermen' were undone by chance. A question

remains. Was Nathan Leopold careless in dropping his spectacles at the murder scene, or was he, as some psychiatrists have
suggested, acting from a subconscious wish to be found out?

The calculating murderer will consider the degree of risk
which his plan involves. He will safeguard against the workings
of chance in the same way that politicians, businessmen, and
militarists hedge their decisions. The commission of his crime is
a professional business. The carelessness induced by impulse is
ruled out, every conceivable contingency is taken into account.
But fate is there to play its hand in some freakish, million-to-one
chance of detection.

Such a freak occurrence was the Shark Arm incident in
Australia in 1935. Albert Hobson was fishing out at sea from
Coogee Beach near Sydney when he hooked a shark. While
hauling it in, his small catch was swallowed by a 14-foot tiger
shark. Realizing he had an exhibit for his brother's Coogee
Beach aquarium, Hobson called for some help to haul in the big
shark. In due course the captive tiger shark was displayed live to
the paying public.

On Anzac Day, April 25, 1935, seven days after being hooked,
the shark disgorged the contents of its stomach. Among the
regurgitated collection of half-digested material was the unmistakable shape of a human arm. The dismembered limb was
taken from the water by flabbergasted acquarium officials, and
the police were sent for. The arm had a rope knotted around the
wrist, and a tattoo of two boxers on the forearm.

Tin trunk

With the aid of the tattoo and finger prints, the limb was
identified as belonging to James Smith, a 40-year-old ex-
amateur boxer. Smith, who was employed by Reg Holmes, a
Sydney boat-builder, had been missing for over two weeks.
Police enquiries revealed that Smith had spent some time at a
rented holiday cottage at Cronulla on the coast. Patrick Brady, a
friend, had been with him. Brady, aged 42, was well known to
the police as a forger and, at the time, was lying low while
awaiting trial for forging cheques. The police could find no
bloodstains at the cottage, but there was one curious fact – a tin
trunk on the cottage's inventory had disappeared and had been
replaced with a new one.

Brady was arrested on a holding charge, but there was no
doubt that the police viewed him as the Number One suspect
regarding the disappearance and probable murder of James

Smith. Brady made a statement in which he denied killing his friend, but he implicated Smith's employer, Reg Holmes, in dealings with forged cheques. On May 17 Patrick Brady was formally charged with Smith's murder.

Bullet wounds

The millionth chance discovery of the tattooed arm triggered off an amazing sequence of events. Holmes denied even knowing Brady let alone being mixed up with forgery. Three days after making this denial Holmes was seen careering around Sydney Harbour in a speedboat – he had a gunshot wound in the head and smelled strongly of alcohol.

Holmes's injury turned out to be only a surface wound and he was soon discharged from hospital. He now changed his story to the police, telling them that Brady had admitted to him that he killed Smith and disposed of the body at sea in a tin trunk. If Brady was suspect No. 1, Holmes was now the key witness. However, on the eve of the coroner's inquest into the death of Jim Smith, the key witness was shot dead. Holmes was found in his car near a Sydney fishing wharf – he had three bullet wounds in his body inflicted by a .32 revolver.

At the inquest, Holmes's wife said that Smith had called on her husband asking for money and saying that he was in fear for his life. She also said that days later Brady arrived at her home. He was dirty and unkempt and was carrying a leather bag. The implication was that the bag contained the tattooed arm and was proof to Holmes that Smith was dead.

Doctors who had examined the arm agreed that the limb seemed to have been severed at the shoulder with a sharp knife. It did not appear likely that it had been bitten off by a shark. It was estimated that the arm had been in the water only a few weeks and there were erudite discussions by experts on the digestive processes of sharks.

On the important question of whether the arm came from a living or a dead person, the doctors could not be sure. They thought it unlikely that a man could remove his own arm in this way, but there were precedents of people surviving the accidental severance of a limb.

Brady's counsel challenged the authority of the Coroner to hold an inquest without a body. He was overruled on this occasion, but tried the same tactic when the case was heard at Sydney's Central Police Court. Counsel wanted to know how much of a body was a body? He used the novel argument that different parts of the same body might be found in four different areas under the jurisdiction of different authorities. In consequence, verdicts of manslaughter, suicide, an open verdict and murder could be arrived at on the same body. Despite the power of this argument, Brady was committed for trial.

The judge would not allow Holmes's statement as evidence. That was a blow to the prosecution, who had to rely on the admitted association of Brady and Smith – particulary during the last days that Smith was seen alive. But the police had been unable to find a single witness to testify to ill-feeling between the two.

Tragic deaths

Two days were sufficient for the trial judge to conclude that the evidence was circumstantial. He directed an acquittal. No sooner was Patrick Brady freed than he was re-arrested on a forgery charge.

Although he was acquitted of murder, Brady was dogged by publicity about the case. It appeared that Reg Holmes had been murdered (Brady was safely in custody at the time) for fear of what he might say when he went into the witness box. Even without Holmes, there were strong undercurrents of violence, drug smuggling, forgery, and fraud.

In 1935 Sir Sydney Smith, the famous forensic expert, visited Australia and was invited by the Sydney Criminal Investigation Branch to examine the tattooed arm. He concluded that Smith's body had been cut up on a mattress on the floor of the cottage at Cronulla. The parts of the body were put in the tin trunk which, when filled, still left an arm over. Unable to get the arm in the trunk, the murderer severed it from the shoulder and tied it to the outside of the trunk with rope.

Sir Sydney supposed that the trunk and its contents, together with the blood stained mattress, were taken out to sea and dumped. The arm worked loose and was eventually swallowed by Albert Hobson's shark.

The tattooed arm given up by the sea in such an incredible manner brought little luck to those swept up in the whirl of events. Brady lived the rest of his life in the shadow of the Shark Arm case, Holmes forfeited his life, and two others involved in the affair met tragic deaths.

The infamous arm was not preserved. All that remains of an incredible clue are the police reports, fingerprints, photographs, and a lot of questions.

Big ideas

The Shark Arm case shows that chance is double-edged. No doubt, when the tattooed arm made its weird appearance, the murderer cursed his bad luck. If only he had bought a tin trunk large enough to accommodate the whole body of his victim, tattooed arm and all. As it turned out, the arm alone was not enough to betray him – but that too was chance.

A woman who chanced to dream provided detectives with the clue they needed to locate a murder victim. At the end of the First World War two young army officers decided to form a business partnership. Twenty-five-year old Eric Tombe and 27-year-old Ernest Dyer started a motor business.

Tombe had £3,000 in the bank. Dyer had big ideas of motoring and horse racing. The first business failed and a second motoring venture also collapsed. In 1920 Tombe and Dyer decided to buy a racing stable and stud farm called 'The Welcomes' at Kenley in Surrey. Tombe put up most of the money. Dyer moved into the farmhouse at 'The Welcomes' with his wife and three children.

One night in April 1921 the farmhouse burnt down. No one was injured. Dyer swiftly lodged an insurance claim. The property had cost £3,000 to purchase, but Dyer had insured it for £12,000. The insurance company was suspicious and Dyer did not press the claim.

Dyer had expensive tastes. He indulged in fast women and slow horses. He borrowed money from Eric Tombe, then he forged his partner's signature on some cheques. This led to bitter accusations and quarrelling.

Several months went by with no improvement in the business prospects at 'The Welcomes'. Then Eric Tombe suddenly disappeared. He wrote a letter dated April 17 to his elderly parents in Kent: 'I shall be coming to see you on Saturday (21 April)' He never arrived.

Tombe's parents fretted over their son's disappearance. With the weeks dragging into months, the Reverend Tombe put advertisements in the personal columns of newspapers. He also searched some of his son's old haunts in London's West End. All his questions met with blank looks.

Then there came the first breakthrough. Reverend Tombe went to a barber in the Haymarket whose shop his son had frequented. Eric Tombe had not been there for a long time, but he had introduced a friend – 'Ernest Dyer, "The Welcomes", Kenley.'

The name Dyer meant nothing to the old clergyman, but he lost no time in visiting 'The Welcomes'. Although Dyer was not at home, his wife was. The only information she was able to give was the address of one of Eric Tombe's women friends. Reverend Tombe learned that his son had arranged to meet Dyer and two girls at Euston Station on April 25. The four planned a trip to Paris. But when they met in London Dyer was on his own. He showed the girls a telegram which he said Eric had sent. It read, 'Sorry to disappoint. Have been called overseas.'

Next Reverend Tombe went to see his son's bank manager. The manager listened sympathetically to the elderly clergyman's story. 'I don't think you need to worry about your son, Mr. Tombe,' he said. 'We have a letter here which was written by him only last month.'

The clergyman inspected the letter dated July 22, 1922. 'That is not my son's signature. This letter is a forgery,' he declared. The startled bank manager looked up Eric Tombe's file. It told a revealing story. In April 1922 Tombe had a credit balance of £2,570. The same month he instructed the bank to transfer £1,350 to a Paris bank for the use of Ernest Dyer. In July there was a letter giving power of attorney to Dyer. In August the account was heavily overdrawn.

Reverend Tombe was now convinced that Ernest Dyer had fleeced his son and probably murdered him. But where was Dyer, and, for that matter, where was Eric Tombe? The first part of the question was answered three months later by a stroke of chance. A man by the name of Fitzsimmons had advertised in the local papers at Scarborough, Yorkshire, for men 'of the highest integrity' to contact him regarding employment with exceptional prospects. All that was required was a substantial cash deposit. Mr. Fitzsimmons was about to initiate one of the oldest con tricks in the world – the police decided to ask him a few questions.

Nightmares

On November 16, 1922, a detective arrived at the Bar Hotel, Scarborough. He asked to see Mr. Fitzsimmons, who took him upstairs to his room. As the two men reached the upper landing Fitzsimmons made a furtive movement towards his pocket. Thinking that the man was intent on destroying some incriminating evidence, the detective seized hold of him. There was a struggle. Both men fell to the floor. There was a roar as a gun went off and Fitzsimmons went limp. He was dead, killed by a bullet from his own gun which he had kept concealed in his pocket.

Fitzsimmons's hotel room contained a treasure of incriminating evidence. There was a suitcase bearing the initials E.T. There was Eric Tombe's passport and a hundred cheques – on each of which was pencilled Tombe's forced signature. James Fitzsimmons, alias Ernest Dyer, had run true to form in his desperate efforts to make money.

Dyer's attempted con trick through the newspapers gave him away to the vigilant Scarborough police. But the workings of chance had spotlighted more than a conman. Dyer had a good deal to hide, and it seemed that the whereabouts of Eric Tombe would remain his secret.

It was another facet of that power which men call chance which led to the discovery of Eric Tombe. His mother chanced to dream – not of castles in the air, but of death. Night after night, she had the single recurrent, terrifying nightmare – she saw her son's dead body lying at the foot of a well.

Ten months after Dyer had been shot dead, the Reverend Tombe called at Scotland Yard. Superintendent Francis Carlin listened politely as the old man told his story and spoke passionately of his wife's nightmares. Carlin, a hardheaded policeman used to dealing with facts, nevertheless was struck by the ring of conviction in the Reverend Tombe's voice. 'We'll look into the matter,' he said.

Within a day or two, Carlin took some men down to 'The Welcomes'. The story of Mrs. Tombe's dream took on immediate reality, for in the grounds of the farm they found five disused wells. Carlin's men began to dig. The first well revealed nothing to reward their labours. The second was the same. But, after digging away at the bottom of the third well, they found a human foot sticking out of the mud. Hours later a body was dug out and taken to the mortuary. There, in a broken voice, the Reverend Tombe identified the corpse. 'Yes', he said, 'that is my dear boy.'

Pathologists found a gunshot wound at the back of the victim's head which had probably been caused by a shot gun fired at close range. What led up to Eric Tombe's death at 'The Welcomes' could only be surmised. It was assumed that Dyer and Tombe quarrelled, that Dyer shot his partner and then disposed of the body down the well.

Questioned by the police, Mrs. Dyer recalled a night when she was alone at 'The Welcomes' – her husband was in France on business. At about 11.0 p.m. she heard a noise in the yard. It sounded like stones dropping against a drainpipe. She called her dog and peered out into the yard. The animal, barking loudly, ran towards a disused shed. A figure emerged – to her utter astonishment Mrs. Dyer saw her husband whom she thought was miles away. The noise which had disturbed her was the sound made by the rocks dropped into the well by Dyer to seal in Tombe's body.

Hostile world

The part played by chance in the Tombe case was remarkable. No doubt thinking he was perfectly safe, Dyer promoted his newspaper con trick only to be outsmarted by the police. It was a reasonable risk that did not pay off. But Mrs. Tombe's dream about the location of her dead son's body was an incredible glimpse into the beyond.

Chance operates in all human affairs, but it seems to exert a special influence over erring men. The murderer sets himself above society – he alienates himself from the majority view which holds life in high regard. His business is secret and his task is to protect himself from a million chances of detection.

CHILDREN WHO KILL

The picture in the American newspaper shows a boy of about 11, his hands stuck in the pockets of his Levis, his hair neatly brushed. He doesn't look in the least like a juvenile delinquent, but the caption says: 'Earl Wear, of Pritchett, Colorado, stands solemnly before shelves of law books after relating that he shot his father, Leonard, with a .22 calibre hunting rifle while the father slept. "I was mad at him for making me go to school," Earl told the sheriff. Sanity examinations are scheduled for the boy.'

Cases like this turn up in American newspapers with appalling frequency: children who kill playmates in a burst of rage, children who shoot parents to avenge some imagined wrong. Is there something wrong with the American educational system? Or are American kids simply more aggressive than their European counterparts?

No. We have to face the fact that *most* children are capable of murder. Is there any adult who cannot recall having fantasies of revenge about some domineering schoolteacher, or at times hating his parents so much that he could kill them? It never lasts long, and in a normal, well-regulated society the gap between fantasy and action is too wide for a child to bridge. But supposing a loaded gun was actually lying there . . .? Or supposing there was a bottle of poison within a few feet of the cup of coffee the offending adult was about to drink?

The three brains
Children are more spontaneous creatures than adults. When they are hurt, they cry; when they are angry, they hit out; when they want something, they grab it. And it is this spontaneity that can turn a child into a killer. Anybody who really wants to understand the mind of the murderer would do well to begin by studying children who kill.

We now know that there is a part of the brain that controls aggression; it is called the amygdala, or amygdaloid nucleus. This is a part of what we might call man's 'old brain'. For, as strange as this sounds, man has *three brains*. Some four hundred million years ago the only life on earth was to be found in the sea, and these creatures, man's earliest ancestors, possessed only a primitive brain – a part which now forms the core of our brain.

It contains the apparatus for breathing, digestion, sex and aggression. When some of these fish-like creatures crawled ashore, some three hundred million years ago, they began to develop another brain *outside* the animal brain, and when these early amphibians turned into reptiles, these early crocodiles and lizards had two brains. The new 'outer brain', or cortex, permitted learning and intelligent behaviour. Finally, as primitive ape-like creatures developed into man, a third brain came into being: the thinking brain.

The truth seems to be that nature has made rather a mess of the evolution of the brain. Imagine a peasant who has lived in a small cottage, who one day makes enough money to build himself something bigger – and who builds a larger house *around* the old cottage. Then imagine, still further, that he is appointed ruler of the country, and decides to build himself a palace – which he has built *around* the other two buildings. This gives a rough idea of the structure of the human brain.

Now every human being starts as a kind of fish in his mother's womb, and slowly develops into something like an early reptile, then into an animal, and eventually into a human foetus. When we are born, we are regulated largely by the 'old brain'. The third brain, the human brain, is hardly developed at all. Young children are little animals. They remain basically very close to the animal – as far as their instincts and impulses go – until puberty. Then, and only then, does the really human part of the brain begin to actively develop.

There is another question that has to be considered before we can understand the child murderer: the question of dominance. We tend to regard aggression as being bad; but the truth is that a certain amount of aggression is essential, both for society and the individual. Think of Shakespeare, Milton, William Blake; all were, in their way, highly aggressive individuals. Some men of genius have actually been murderers, including Shakespeare's friend – and fellow playwright – Ben Jonson. Many a moody, impatient boy grows up to be an important writer.

To some extent, dominance is based on a *high energy output*. Faced with a challenge, the dominant person becomes a dynamo of energy; hormones rush into his bloodstream and he becomes a kind of juggernaut. And what happens when a man possesses this dynamo, but lacks the intelligence to make proper use of it? He becomes impatient, bad-tempered, a bully. He is liable to explosions of violence. The *third* brain, our specifically human brain, is not sufficiently developed to make use of his drive and will-power.

This explains what happens in the case of many children who kill. Peter Kürten, the sadist of Düsseldorf, during whose 'reign of terror' eight people were murdered and innumerable others stabbed or battered, confessed that he committed his first two murders at the age of nine.

He was playing on a raft on the banks of the Rhine with two boys. He pushed one of them into the water; the boy could not swim, and began to struggle. The other boy, who could swim, dived in to help him. Kürten managed to push him under the raft. Both were drowned, and since there were no witnesses, no one suspected Kürten.

Kürten's later crimes were committed out of sadism: he experienced a sexual orgasm as he stabbed or throttled a victim. But the sadism was a later development. He himself said so to the psychiatrist who examined him, Professor Berg – and Kürten proved to be an exceptionally honest witness on the subject of his psychopathic urges. He almost certainly pushed the boy off the raft in a burst of sudden rage. Probably there was no intention of killing – even when he thrust the other boy under the raft. He was still in the grip of his anger, and the aggression came easily.

Vain monster

Berg's classic book *The Sadist* reveals that Kürten was a strange and complex man. He was intelligent, and unusually honest. (He told lies mainly to try to get witnesses into trouble – another manifestation of his sadism.) He did not strike his workmates as violent; on the contrary, they found him a quiet man and a hard worker; they at first refused to believe that he could be 'the Monster'. His chief character defect was his vanity about his appearance; he always dressed with great care, and would spend long periods carefully inspecting himself in the mirror.

From Berg's book we discover that Kürten's father was a typical 'violent man', in the sense described by the writer A.E. Van Vogt: 'the examining magistrate described him as a man who scarcely knew any moral restraints, yet demanded for himself every sort of respect, nor did he suffer contradiction or any challenge to his will'. He was an alcoholic, and also a stupid man. His son Peter inherited some of his dominance and drive, but was more intelligent. He was also, like his father, a 'sex maniac' from an early age – he made his first attempt at rape at 16. It was the 'violent man' in him that made him kill his two playmates at the age of nine.

Of course, bad environment played an important part in creating the future killer. A dominant and intelligent child, who has seen his father screaming with rage, smashing windows, and raping his mother and eldest sister (a crime for which Kürten senior received 18 months in prison) is bound to develop a bitter and contemptuous attitude towards the world. When Kürten's own sexual drives became violent – in his early teens – they combined with the dominance and aggression to turn him into a sadist.

But the part played by environment is not necessarily vital in such cases. In many American instances of children who kill – like 11-year-old Earl Wear – the environment is as comfortable as a good income can make it. This can also be seen in a case that occurred in England in 1847: the poisoning of Samuel Nelme, Deputy Chairman of the Hackney Board of Guardians, by his grandson William Allnutt, aged 12. William, a sickly child who was often in trouble with his teachers, had seven brothers and sisters.

Five were away at boarding school, and at the time of the murder, two were staying with friends in the country – an indication that the household was fairly well off. Samuel Nelme was a dominant individual, and he was often impatient with his grandson, who was a dishonest child. (Not long before the murder, he stole a watch and 10 sovereigns – fairly ambitious booty for such a young boy.)

Boiling rage

On October 20, 1847, grandfather Nelme lost his temper with William, gave him a violent blow that knocked him down, and banged his head against the wall. In a boiling rage, William waited until his grandfather had gone to the wine cellar. Then he took a packet of arsenic – used to poison rats – out of a drawer in the bureau, and poured this into a bowl of sugar on the dining room table – a bowl used mainly by old Mr. Nelme, who had a sweet tooth. The next day, the sugar bowl was refilled.

William was clearly a vindictive child. He had had time to get over his rage; but he made no attempt to get ride of the arsenic. It stayed in the sugar bowl almost a week, and several members of the family were ill when they used it, including William's mother (who was a widow). William was apparently willing to poison the whole family in revenge.

Finally, a week after the arsenic had been placed in the sugar bowl, Samuel Nelme died in agony. It was not until nine days later, when the watch and 10 sovereigns were found to be missing, that William was questioned, and then arrested for theft. When an inquest revealed arsenic in Samuel Nelme's stomach, William confessed. (It is a characteristic of most child-criminals that they confess easily.) A letter he sent to his mother, admitting the crime, sounds genuinely repentant. At his trial, it was revealed that his father had been a 'right man', given to violent fits of temper, and also to epileptic attacks. He was also, like Kürten's father, an alcoholic.

So, again, it would seem that the father's dominance and violence was passed on to the child. William's defence was insanity, but the jury rejected it. He was sentenced to death, then reprieved, and sent to prison – where he apparently spent the remainder of his life. In those days, treatment of juvenile offenders was savage. (This continued well into the twentieth century. In 1924, 15-year-old Roland McDonald, of Amhurst, Maine, was found guilty of the shotgun killing of a young schoolmistress, Louise Gerrish. He was still in prison 34 years later, and when a lie detector test suggested he was not guilty of the murder, a request for parole was rejected.)

In the great majority of cases of murder of children by other children, the motive is usually some deep-seated resentment based upon jealously – the Mary Bell case is typical of this. There *are* exceptions; but most of these could be classified almost as 'motiveless murder'.

These usually occur in slums. There was Alfred Dancey, a 14-year-old boy of Bedminster, Gloucestershire, who in 1850 was bullied by two older boys. He pulled out a loaded pistol and shot one of his persecutors dead. He was sentenced to 10 years' transportation. Then there was Alfred Fitz, aged 9, a slum boy from Liverpool, who lost his temper with a playmate, James Fleeson, and killed him with a half brick. He and another boy threw James into the canal. Found guilty of manslaughter in August 1855, both were sentenced to 12 months in Liverpool Prison.

Perhaps the most famous – or infamous – of all juvenile killers was Jesse Pomeroy, who holds roughly the same place among children who kill as Jack the Ripper among adult murderers. Pomeroy has become a figure of legend; if he had not been caught at the age of 14, he would undoubtedly have become the American equivalent of Peter Kürten.

Insane resentment

Pomeroy was a tall, gangling youth with a harelip; one of his eyes was completely white. He was sadistic, and almost certainly homosexual. In 1871 and 1872, Boston parents became anxious about an unknown youth who seemed to have an insane resentment of younger children.

On December 22, 1871, a boy named Paine was tied to a beam and beaten unconscious; this took place at Powder Horn Hill. The same thing happened again in February 1872; a child named Tracy Hayden was enticed to the spot, stripped naked, beaten unconscious with a rope, and struck in the face so violently with a board that his nose was broken and several teeth knocked out. In July, a boy named Johnny Blach was taken to the same place and beaten; afterwards, his assailant moved him to a nearby creek and washed his wounds in salt water. In September, Robert Gould was tied to a telegraph pole near the Hartford and Erie railroad track, and was beaten and cut with a knife. Three more cases occurred in quick succession; in each, the boy was seven or eight years of age. All the victims were lured to a lonely place, stripped naked, beaten, and then stabbed or tortured with pins.

Pomeroy's description was so unusual that it was not long before he was arrested on suspicion. His victims identified him. He was sentenced to a period in the West Borough Reform School. He was 12 years old at the time. Eighteen months later, in February 1874, he was paroled and allowed to return home. His mother, according to one account, kept a grocery store. A month later, 10-year-old Mary Curran disappeared. Four weeks after that on April 22, the mutilated body of a 4-year-old boy, Horace Mullen, was found near Dorchester, a Boston suburb; he had 31 knife wounds, and his head was almost severed from the body.

Bloodstained knife

Jesse Pomeroy immediately came under suspicion. A bloodstained knife was found in his room, and the mud on his shoes was similar to that of the marsh where the child had been found. Pomeroy soon confessed to the murder. Shortly afterwards his mother had to move house – probably because of the scandal. The new tenant decided to enlarge the cellar. Labourers digging in the earth floor discovered the decomposed body of a young girl. Mary Curran's parents were able to identity their daughter from her clothes. Pomeroy also confessed to this murder.

He was sentenced to be hanged on December 10, 1874, but was reprieved because of his youth — he was then 14. His sentence was commuted — somewhat inhumanely — to solitary confinement for life. Subsequently, he made several attempts to escape from prison. One of them suggests that he had become suicidal.

In 1883, he succeeded in puncturing a gas pipe, waited until he was almost overcome with the fumes, then struck a match. The explosion blew out the door of his cell, but it also blew up Jesse Pomeroy. Three other convicts were burned to death. He was quickly moved to another jail — Charleston — and spent the next 41 years there. Towards the end of his life — he died at the age of 72 — he was moved to the Bridgewater State Farm for the criminally insane — the prison from which the alleged Boston Strangler, Albert de Salvo, later escaped.

Pomeroy has become a legend of horror — one highly unreliable account credits him with 27 murders, giving circumstantial — and totally untrue — details. On the other hand, none of the accounts states whether Pomeroy sexually assaulted his victims, and whether Mary Curran was raped. In spite of this, it seems clear that Pomeroy's motives were sexual.

There is no fundamental difference between the youthful killer and the homicidal adult. In the young criminal, impulses are translated directly into action — as they are in such mentally defective killers as Straffen, the child strangler. The youngster may be suffering from an 'hereditary taint', or may simply be violent and sullen by nature.

In 1886, a 12-year-old girl named Marie Schneider was tried in Berlin. She had taken a 3-year-old girl to a second-storey window, sat her on the window sill, and deliberately pushed her out — after stealing the child's earrings. She intended to sell the earrings to buy sweets. She was known as a sadistic and dishonest child, who never lost an opportunity to bully and torture younger children. She was sent to prison for eight years.

A 10-year-old boy named William York appears to be another example of 'hereditary taint'. He lived in the workhouse at the village of Eyke, near Bury St. Edmunds, England, and shared a bed with a 5-year-old girl, Susan Mayhew. One morning, when Susan had fouled the bed, William York took her into the yard, and methodically cut her wrist down to the bone, all the way round; he did the same to the elbow and her other arm, then slashed her thigh open. In 1748, he was sentenced to death, but was finally reprieved on condition he joined the navy – where, presumably, he would be brutalized by ill-treatment and sexual attacks.

In modern times, there is an increasing tendency for the 'young offender' to be an 'outsider' figure, alienated from his family and background. Graham Young, the English mass poisoner, sentenced to life imprisonment in 1972, is typical of this new phenomenon. His father, a machine setter, was a widower, and he married again when Graham was three. The family lived in Neasden, London. Graham was an 'odd' boy, fascinated by chemistry and by poisons, and – like Moors murderer Ian Brady – an admirer of Hitler. He felt an intense dislike of the commonplace. His sister Winifred tells a typical anecdote. On a bus with their cousin Sandra, they saw a friend, and Sandra remarked: 'That's Jacqueline's boyfriend, Jim.' Young repeated mockingly: 'Oh, is that Jacqueline's boyfriend, Jim?', and kept repeating variations on the sentence all the way home. Obviously, the 'ordinariness' of it made him unhinged and verbally sadistic.

He began trying out various poisons on his family when he was 13. His sister Winifred tasted a cup of tea one morning and threw it away – it had a bitter flavour. On the way to work, she felt things advancing and receding. Her employer sent her to hospital, where she was told she was suffering from Belladonna poisoning – her pupils were enormously enlarged. Taxed with this, Graham explained he had put it in her tea 'by mistake'.

The rest of the family continued to have bouts of sickness; so did a schoolfriend. During Easter 1962, his stepmother Molly, died, and was cremated. Then his father became seriously ill. Hospital tests showed he was suffering from arsenic and antimony poisoning. There had been friction between Graham and his father; every time his father admonished him, Graham gave him another dose of poison.

The Frankenstein

Sentenced to Broadmoor, Young was released after 9 years. He immediately found a job at John Hadland's (Photographic) Ltd., at Bovingdon, Herts. And the man who referred to himself as 'your friendly neighbourhood Frankenstein' immediately went back to his favourite hobby of poisoning. Before he was arrested, in November 1971, two workmates had died of thallium poisoning, and two more became seriously ill. Young may have started administering poison out of curiosity and resentment; unfortunately, it then became a habit.

Children are more malleable than adults, and therefore more easily treated. The problem of the juvenile criminal – the young murderer – is still a long way from a solution; but recent advances in psychiatry make the prospects of an answer more hopeful than they have ever been before. As the child is father to the man, so he can also be the sire to the killer. It is up to the parents and adults in society to watch for this immature monster, to spot him before he has time to fully develop, and to see that he gets the correct – and humane – treatment necessary to make his (or her) life happy, and to make the lives of others safe.

CON MEN

Would you believe that a car could be run on water instead of gasoline? Before you answer No, consider the incredible case of the inventor Louis Enricht. In the year 1916, the world was gripped by an oil crisis. One April morning, New York's reporters were invited to call at a house in Farmingdale, Long Island, to witness a demonstration which, they were assured, would be spectacular. The few reporters who turned up found a big, grey haired man with an impressive face and a foreign accent, who introduced himself as Louis Enricht, and explained that he had invented a cheap substitute for gasoline. The reporters yawned, and looked bored.

Enricht led them to a small European car, pointed out that the gas tank was empty, and asked the reporters to examine it closely to see that there was no supplementary fuel tank. They weren't experts, but it certainly didn't look as if Enricht was deceiving them. Enricht then asked a reporter to fill a bucket at the tap. When the man returned with the water, the inventor produced a bottle full of a green liquid. He told the man to empty it into the bucket – warning him that the stuff was deadly poison.

The reporter poured the bucket into the gas tank, and Enricht asked the driver to try the engine. After a few splutters, it started, and a smell of almonds pervaded the air. Enricht offered each of the reporters a ride around Farmingdale. If there *was* a concealed gas tank – which is the obvious hypothesis – then it must have been large, for the car trips went on for at least an hour.

The next day, the story made the front pages, and Enricht was besieged with letters, phone calls and reporters. He declined to see them. A Harvard professor declared sourly that no possible combination of chemicals could turn water into a combustible fuel, but Enricht declined to comment. His next visitor was Henry Ford himself. Ford examined the car carefully, and since

104

he was one of the world's leading experts, he was pretty thorough. He watched Enricht mix his green liquid with water, and then went for a ride in the car.

Enricht admitted that the smell was cyanide, but said it had been put in to conceal another smell. His process was absurdly simple, he said, and until his lawyer had devised a way to patent it, he wasn't dropping any hints.

Ford was so impressed that, even when the *Tribune* printed a story revealing that Enricht had been a fake company promoter, Ford ignored it. The evidence of his own eyes assured him that the car had run on water, and he gave Enricht a cheque for $10,000 on account.

When this news was leaked to the papers – by Enricht – Hiram P. Maxim, son of the inventor of the Maxim gun, offered Enricht a million dollars, and offered to build him a laboratory for further research. In fact, Enricht received only $100,000; he was to receive the rest when he handed over the formula – which, Maxim agreed, should not be until he had patented his discovery.

Penny-a-gallon fuel

Ford was infuriated, but since Enricht had returned his cheque, there was nothing much he could do. Then America came into the First World War, and Maxim was so busy making munitions that he agreed to call off the whole thing; he had more than recovered his investment in the upward turn taken by his company's shares when his deal with Enricht was announced.

The man who decided to take over from Maxim was a rich banker named Yoakum. He also gave Enricht $100,000, accepting a sealed envelope which was supposed to contain the formula. Yoakum told President Wilson that he intended to present the secret of penny-a-gallon fuel to the American people, and Wilson was delighted. But Enricht launched delaying tactics, and Yoakum hired the Pinkerton detective agency to investigate him.

He was flabbergasted to discover that Enricht had been seen consorting with Von Papen, the German military attaché, before the outbreak of war, and that the 'inventor' was suspected of being a German spy. Then Yoakum opened the envelope that was supposed to contain the formula – and found only a few liberty bonds. But there was no way to get Enricht into a court of law.

Yoakum had broken his own undertaking by opening the envelope. Talk about trying Enricht for treason dragged on until Yoakum died, and Enricht was once again in the clear.

At the age of 75 Enricht was still a man of restless imagination. In 1920, he announced that his continued experiments in
the manufacture of gasoline had led him to conclude that the
easiest and cheapest way was to distil it from peat. Such was the
magic of his name that investors again rushed to thrust cheques
into his hand, and he may have received as much as a quarter of
a million dollars.

But the Nassau County District Attorney decided it was time
someone brought Enricht's career to an end. The D.A. examined
Enricht's bank accounts until he found a cheque for $2,000,
handed over by an investor and promptly endorsed to pay a
bookmaker. That was fraud, since he was a limited company
and all money was supposed to benefit other investors. At the
age of 77, Enricht received seven years in gaol for grand larceny.
Paroled after a few years, he died at the age of 79 without
revealing to anyone the secret of his formula for cheap gasoline.

The formula

How did he do it? The answer may lie in a formula discovered by
Thomas Edison. He found that a mixture of acetone and liquid
acetylene *will* drive a car if mixed with water. If cyanide is
added, it hides the very distinctive nail-varnish smell of acetone.
The mixture costs more to make than gasoline, and it also had
the disadvantage of corroding the engine after a while. But this is
probably the answer to the enigma.

Undoubtedly, the most remarkable conman of them all was
the Scotsman, John Law. Born in Edinburgh in 1671, Law had
no need to work: his father, a successful goldsmith and
moneylender, left him two estates. But Law was immensely
ambitious. Besides, he was driven by another itch that char-
acterizes many of the great con men: the passion for beautiful
women. At 23 he went to London where his success in love
became as legendary as his success at cards. He packed more
experience into the next five years than most men in a lifetime.
Then his luck turned: he killed a man in a duel, was tried and
fled to the Continent.

There he continued to gamble and seduce: but he also became
a fascinated student of high finance. It seemed to him that the
secret of wealth was a perfectly simple one. All businesses run on
credit, and the more money they make, the more they borrow in
order to expand. But in those days, money was made of gold or
silver, and there was a limited amount of it to go round. The
answer, said Law, was to print paper money instead – which

could be instantly redeemed for gold merely by walking into a bank.

But so long as the customers trusted their paper money, why should they demand gold instead? And in that case, the government could issue any amount of paper money, and use it to increase trade. So long as there was no sudden panic, it was a foolproof way of increasing credit and prosperity.

Law returned to Scotland – which at the time had its own government, so that he was safe from arrest – and tried hard to persuade his fellow countrymen of the value of a national bank that would issue paper money. He was ignored. And when Scotland discussed union with England, he decided it was time to return to the Continent. In 1708 he went to Paris, and found it the most exciting capital in Europe. Everyone gambled. Soon Law was known in the most exclusive drawing-rooms in Paris, and the size of his stakes made him famous.

He met the Duc d'Orleans, and convinced him of his financial genius; for a while it looked as if he would get his opportunity to print paper money. Then the police began investigating him; D'Argenson, lieutenant of the Paris police, had received hundreds of complaints from losers who doubted Law's honesty. Law was driven out of France.

In 1715, Louis XIV died. Law could hardly believe his luck when he heard that his old friend the Duc d'Orleans had been appointed Regent of the young king, and was virtually dictator of France. He hurried back to Paris, and this time the Duke allowed him to put his schemes into effect.

To begin with, he gave Law permission to open a private bank and to print his own money. Law had built up a fortune of eighty thousand pounds, so he had the gold to back his notes – to begin with. He started out cautiously, aiming to create confidence. He lost money, but people came to feel that his notes were as safe as gold.

By 1718, Law's bank was making so much money that the Duke transformed it into a Royal Bank. Law could print as much money as he liked.

Now obviously, this was a very dangerous game. It is true that money makes money. But if there is a slump or sudden panic, a bank must have enough money to change all its notes into gold – or collapse. In theory, Law had all the money he needed; it was now time to use it to make more money: real money. The answer lay across the Atlantic, in Louisiana – which belonged to the French.

Louisiana consisted of thousands of square miles of swamps and uncultivated land; Law set himself to persuade the French people that it was full of gold, silk and valuable minerals, and that all they had to do to double their money was to invest it in Louisiana bonds. The money flowed in, Law cornered the Canadian fur market, and made huge profits.

But he was now aware of the dangers of this incredible game of confidence. As the money poured in, share prices rose; speculators could make fortunes overnight. Everything went faster and faster – and Law had to keep running faster than anybody, always making sure he had the gold to meet all demands. If Louisiana was to make money, he had to persuade emigrants to go there. Law hired men to go throughout France, telling stories of the wealth of Louisiana.

From the government he purchased the right to collect taxes, and made a vast fortune that way. He bought trading companies in the Far East. He cornered Virginia tobacco. The money kept flooding in. His office in the narrow Rue Quincampoix was besieged by crowds day and night; any shares he deigned to sell could be resold within minutes for twice their price. Money-lenders nearby lent money at one per cent *per hour*, and their customers still made a fortune.

Soon there wasn't enough gold to go round; the Duc d'Orleans had to be persuaded to pass laws forbidding goldsmiths to make gold articles weighing more than a few ounces. Confidence slumped, and the rush came. At first the bank would only cash one hundred livre note per person; soon this was reduced to ten livres. And In December 1720, two years after he had become head of the Compagnie de l'Occidente, Law decided it would be safer to flee the country.

For the next few years he lived quietly in London. His old skill as a gambler had not deserted him; when he had only a thousand pounds left, he staked it all on a bet that he could throw six double sixes one after the other: he won. But his luck turned – perhaps due to the curses of thousands of Frenchmen whom he had ruined. He remained on friendly terms with the Duc d'Orleans to the end; the Duke had remedied the bankruptcy by the simple expedient of burning every paper connected with the Royal Bank. But when Law finally died in Venice, in 1729, he was again a pauper.

In the year of the collapse of Law's Compagnie de l'Occidente, England was having its own grave financial crisis, the bursting of the South Sea Bubble. The full details of the dealings of the

South Sea Company are even more complex than those of Law's Royal Bank; but the parallels are otherwise very close. Law needed the permission of the Regent to start his company; the directors of the South Sea Company got their permission for their vast dealings by offering to take on the English National Debt – the money the government owes investors in government stocks.

Their equivalent of Louisiana was Peru and the South Seas. Between 1711 and 1720, millions of pounds changed hands, and fortunes were made. All kinds of other schemes swept to success on the tail of the South Seas comet: a scheme for making a 'wheel of perpetual motion', a scheme for making a soft metal out of mercury. One speculator even launched a scheme 'for great advantage, but nobody to know what it is', and made two thousand pounds in one morning.

The South Sea directors had to take legal action against these other companies, and in doing so, they started the panic slide that led to the crash. In this case, some investors got back at least some of their money, for the government seized part of the assets of the directors of the Company.

The Eiffel Tower

The classic 'con' case of modern times is undoubtedly that of Count Victor Lustig's sale of the Eiffel Tower – not once, but twice. Like John Law, Lustig came from a respectable middle-class family, and he too loved gambling and women. Some time before the First World War, he left his home in Czechoslovakia and moved to Paris. Lustig was only one of two dozen aliases that he used at different times; he learned the techniques of confidence trickery from the gambler Nicky Arnstein.

Lustig was in Paris when he saw a newspaper item reporting that repairs to the Eiffel Tower would cost thousands of francs. Some days later, several rich financiers received letters from a government department inviting them to a secret conference at the Hotel Crillon. The 'director deputy-general' who received them was actually Victor Lustig. He began by assuring them that this business was classified as top secret – hence the hotel suite instead of his office.

The government has decided, he told them, that the Eiffel Tower is too expensive to maintain; it is to be sold for scrap metal . . . They gaped. 'Would you gentlemen care to submit your bids to me?' He had already noted the man who was the obvious 'mark', Andre Poisson, a man who clearly felt socially inferior to the others. A few days later, Lustig rang him and told him that his bid was the highest – several million francs – and that if he would bring a certified cheque to the hotel, the deal could be concluded. Poisson was not entirely happy – until Lustig apologetically asked for a bribe, to ensure that negotiations would go smoothly.

That convinced Poisson that this was a genuine government official; he handed over the cash. And later, when it became clear he had been swindled, he was too ashamed to go to the police and make himself the laughing stock of France. The result was that Lustig was able to repeat the same trick a few years later.

The second part of Lustig's life was an anticlimax – an observation that applies to most confidence tricksters. In America in the early 1930s, he turned to the distribution of counterfeit money; the F.B.I. finally caught up with him, and he was sentenced to twenty years in gaol, dying in Alcatraz in 1947. The Federal agent mainly responsible for his capture, James P. Johnson, wrote the classic book on his career under the title *The Man Who Sold the Eiffel Tower*.

It is a saddening book, for it underlines the strange romanticism that leads brilliant and imaginative men to become confidence swindlers.

COP KILLERS

The London Metropolitan Police Force came into being in the year 1829. It was the brainchild of the Home Secretary, Sir Robert Peel; consequently, the new policemen became known as 'bobbies'. The nickname was not totally affectionate, however, for the people of London hated them. The old watchmen and parish constables who had kept order were just public employees, like rat-catchers and street-sweepers. These uniformed men were 'officials', whose business was to smell out offences against the law and put the offenders in jail; as a consequence, it was a risky job to be a policeman in the 1830s.

On June 29, 1830, Police Constable Grantham saw two drunken Irishmen quarrelling over a woman in Somers Town, north London. He tried to separate them and the men *and* the woman turned on him and knocked him down; the men 'put in the boot', kicking him brutally on the temple. He died shortly afterwards, thus becoming the first English policeman to die in the course of execution of his duty. The murderers walked off and were never brought to justice.

Six weeks later there was an incident that must have confirmed the London poor in their view that they were better off without the police. On August 16, Police Constable John Long accosted three suspicious-looking characters in Mecklenburgh Square, Grays Inn Road. One of them pulled a knife and stabbed Long to death. There was a hue and cry. A police constable who came on the scene saw a man running and grabbed him; the man protested that *he* was chasing one of the murderers.

A youth who was sitting on a doorstep was arrested by a police inspector; the youth protested that he was waiting for a friend, whereupon the police arrested the friend too. All three were taken into court, but the magistrate, reasoning that it was unlikely that a murderer would be sitting on a doorstep, discharged two of the defendants. But a tradesman's boy and a prostitute identified the remaining man as one of the policeman's assailants. No one asked the boy why, at an earlier stage, he had admitted that he had not even seen the murder. The accused man – almost certainly innocent – was hanged. One has a feeling that the early police force felt it was better to hang the wrong man than nobody at all.

In May, 1833, a rather mildly revolutionary group called the National Political Union called for a public meeting of 'anarchists and revolutionists' in Coldbath Fields, not far from the site of Constable Long's murder. Their 'revolutionary' programme was hardly extreme; they simply wanted votes for the working man. The Home Secretary didn't like the idea; he told the Commissioner of Police to ban the meeting. The ban was ignored; a crowd gathered, and a speaker on a soap box asked the crowd to be orderly and peaceable.

Revolution and sedition

They had little alternative, being surrounded by about 800 policemen and troops. Other speeches were made, and a police spy slipped away to report that revolution and sedition was being preached. The man in charge of the police, Lieut. Col. Charles Rowan, who had fought at Waterloo, ordered his men to advance slowly, holding their truncheons, and to halt frequently to allow 'innocent' bystanders to get away. The police advanced – and were booed and pelted with stones.

This angered the Force, and they began hitting out wildly, knocking down women and children as well as men. Police Constable Robert Culley tried to capture one of the anarchist's banners, and hit the man with a truncheon. The man drew a knife, and stabbed Culley in the chest; he staggered a few yards and fell dead. Culley was a married man of 27 whose wife was about to have a baby.

The Coroner's jury that met to consider how Culley met his death were not disposed to sympathize with the police; they were mostly respectable tradesmen, and they felt that the police should have minded their own business, and permitted the traditional British right of free speech. They asked the police witnesses impertinent questions; then, when they were sent out to reach a verdict, told the Coroner they were unable to agree.

The Coroner did what was quite common in those days – told them that they would stay in the room without food or drink until they *did* agree. The result was that the angry jury produced a verdict that enraged the police and delighted the British public: that the man who had killed Constable Culley — and who had never been caught — was only guilty of justifiable homicide. The spectators in the court cheered. The jury were treated as heroes, and found themselves wined and dined for their defiance of the 'bobbies'.

This raises again the fundamental question: were the public simply protesting against this frightening new innovation, a police force? Or was it rather the expression of something deeper — that idealistic anarchism which is perhaps a profound and permanent part of human nature? For it is not only, for instance, 'primitive' and peaceable societies such as the South Sea islanders who feel they have no need for civil authority. Slum dwellers in London's East End and country dwellers in tiny rural villages feel the same. The poor may fight among themselves; but they also help one another.

'Kill them like dogs'

In the poverty of Whitechapel and the Ratcliffe Highway there was a strong community spirit, which could be seen occasionally when a whole street hired a horse bus for an expedition to the country, or families went hop-picking to the fields of Kent, sleeping rough under hedges. As to country people, anyone who has ever moved from a city into a quiet country district has noticed the friendliness and warmth, and how a total stranger may go out of his way to offer help.

This is what had convinced nineteenth century 'peaceful anarchists' such as the Russians Kropotkin and Malatesta that men are good at heart, and that to subject them to the harsh processes of the law is an indignity to human nature. To some extent, it is undoubtedly the modern commercial metropolis, with its fairly well-to-do inhabitants living in flats, that has eroded this spirit of co-operation among ordinary people. No doubt Kropotkin, Bakunin, Proudhon and the rest were being absurdly idealistic when they imagined that a whole modern state could be run without the police, army or government. Yet they had grasped something about human nature that many people have lost sight of: that man is basically gregarious and prepared to help his fellow creatures, because he needs help from them.

This explains some of the deep and widespread hostility to the police that persists even in our crime-ridden society. It is, of course, due partly to a kind of stupidity, to the confused reasoning of socially immature individuals, but it is more than that. There is also the obscure longing for a more innocent form of society, where the brotherhood of man is a reality. Many anarchists would agree that society needs law and order, because there are always people who may commit violent crimes.

But the answer, according to them, is to have police purely as guardians of the peace, like the sheriff of an old Wild Western town, whose business was to chase rustlers and stop visiting cowboys from shooting up the local saloon – not to go around looking for people who have parked their horse on double yellow lines.

This view actually offers a ray of hope in a society where the killing of policemen has become an increasing problem. (In America, more police are killed every year than have been killed in England since the beginning of the century.)

If the police killing is pure anti-social viciousness, then this is a reason for gloom. But if it also springs from some distorted impulse of defiance and human dignity, then a little intelligent thinking may provide some of the answers.

The outline of some of these answers can be seen in the subsequent history of the police force. In America, on the continent of Europe, and especially in Russia, the police continued to be regarded by most ordinary people as an instrument of oppression. 'Police and militia, the bloodhounds of capitalism, are willing to murder!' declared a headline in the *Arbeiter-Zeitung*, the Chicago German language anarchist daily.

On May 4, 1885, police moved in to break up a strikers' meeting in the Haymarket Square when someone threw a bomb into the police ranks. The explosion was terrific, and when the bleeding and screaming confusion died down, seven policemen were lying dead. In the following year, eight anarchists – arrested at random from the crowd – were sentenced to death for the killings.

It started a chain reaction of shootings, explosions, strike-breaking and the deliberate starvation of workers and their families, and the violence continued intermittently for nearly half a century. The execution of Sacco and Vanzetti in 1927 marked the end of this phase of militant anarchism in America.

Shot through the neck

On May Day, 1891, French anarchists were dragged into the police station at Clichy and beaten viciously. At their trial, one of them shouted: 'If the police come, do not hesitate to kill them like the dogs they are . . .' On November 8, 1892, a bomb exploded in the police station in the Avenue de l'Opéra, Paris, blowing six policemen to fragments, including the one who had been rash enough to carry it, and once again there were explosions, assassinations, executions that continued for decades.

In 1922, anarchists robbed a train travelling from Paris to Lyons, and one of them murdered an army officer who resisted. A few days later police arrested an anarchist called Jacques Mecislav Charrier, who had been overheard boasting of the robbery in a bar. Seven days after the robbery, acting on information forced from Charrier, police ambushed two men in the Rue des Ternes, Paris. Both men were killed; so was a police inspector.

Charrier declared in court: 'I am a desperate enemy of society and I defy you to take my head.' And although he screamed and pleaded for mercy as he was dragged to the gulliotine, other French anarchists felt that the great war against the 'bloodhounds of capitalism' was going on.

In England, however, the situation had changed in favour of the police. To begin with, the English have always been traditionally lenient towards political offenders; when Karl Marx fled to England in 1850, he was amazed that the English police were unarmed, and that the authorities did not seem particularly concerned about the 'dangerous revolutionaries' in their midst. Anarchist and socialist clubs met openly, yet no one seemed worried. Jack the Ripper actually committed one of his murders – of Elizabeth Stride – in the backyard of one of these revolutionary clubs for foreign immigrants in 1888.

Marx was also astonished to find himself in a country where people seemed quite to like their policemen. The British bobby was usually an easy-going, kindly sort of man, and although there were still plenty of streets in London's East End where a policeman would never venture alone, no one actually regarded them as 'capitalist bullies'. Anybody who *wanted* to express that opinion was welcome to stand up on a soap box in Hyde Park and say so, while several bobbies looked benevolently on in case the crowd felt like attacking the speaker.

Two-hour chase
A number of violent incidents actually caused wide sympathy and support for the police. For example, there was the Tottenham outrage of 1909, when two young anarchists from the Baltic states tried to take a payroll from the men delivering it to

Schurmann's rubber factory. The wages clerk struggled; shots were fired, and the two men fled. Unarmed policemen chased them. The first victim of the gunmen was a small boy, who fell dead. Next, a policeman named Tyler was shot through the neck and killed. The chase pounded on through back gardens and across allotments; more policemen were wounded.

In the Chingford Road, the men leapt on to a passing tram, and forced the conductor to drive it. An elderly passenger lost his nerve, and was shot in the throat. As the gunmen leapt off the tram, a milkman who ran towards them was shot in the chest. The men stopped a horsedrawn grocer's van and ordered the teenage driver to whip up the horse. Policemen on bicycles – one of them carrying a cutlass – hurtled after them.

Passing a policeman, one of the men fired, hitting him in the foot; the policeman blew his whistle and despite his wound joined in the chase. The anarchists leapt out of the van as their pursuers gained ground, and raced across fields again; at a fence, one of them fell. Before the police could reach him, he had shot himself through the brain, and he died later in hospital. Finally, the police cornered the other man in a cottage; two policemen burst into the child's bedroom where he was hiding, and shot him through the head. The chase had lasted two hours, and covered six miles; a policeman and a child had been killed, seven more policemen shot, and fourteen other people injured.

It was this kind of incident that rallied warm support around the British police. So did the shootings in Houndsditch a year later, when three policemen were killed and four more injured by a gang of foreign burglars; and when the Houndsditch affair culminated in the famous Siege of Sidney Street, everyone in England was delighted that the foreign desperadoes had been trapped. On the whole, the British public had decided that its police force was to be trusted.

Climate of violence

The situation in America is different. The high incidence of police murders is due less to public hostility than to the general climate of violence, and the permissive American gun laws. Two typical cases of 1971 – one in England, one in America – will serve to underline the difference between the two countries.

On the evening of June 27, 1971, Detective Constable Ian Coward, 29, was driving through Reading when he noticed a white Morris that was swinging across the road in a manner that suggested the driver was drunk. When the car stopped in front of a restaurant, he got out and approached it. There were two men inside. He asked the driver for his identification and the driver, a young, unshaven man, got out to look for it. Coward went back to his own car, got into the driver's seat, and told the man to get in beside him.

At this moment, the other man approached the police car, pulled a gun, and fired nine bullets into Coward. As the policeman fell across the seat and through the open passenger door, the other man kicked him. Then both ran back to their car and drove off. Incredibly, Coward was still alive. He was rushed to hospital; but on July 23 he died.

Witnesses to the shooting were able to pick out the two men from the 'rogue's gallery' of mug-shots; they were identified as Arthur Skingle, 25, and Peter Sparrow, 28. Both had criminal records, and Skingle, the gunman, had been released from prison – where he had served a sentence for robbery with violence – only ten days earlier. The men drove the white Morris to a spot a few miles away, and set it on fire with petrol. It was a routine matter for the police to pick up the murderers, who were both sentenced to full life terms.

On November 29, 1971, Sergeant Mike McNeil of Albany, New York, pulled in a car driver for questioning; his driver's licence did not correspond to the car's registration number. While the driver was being interrogated, at the section house, his three companions, who were waiting outside in the car, escaped.

Shot by a woman

McNeil went after them, caught them up a block away, and ordered them into his car. Before they climbed in, he frisked them. Even so, he missed a revolver in the pocket of Joseph Guerin, and when McNeil climbed into the driving seat Guerin shot him several times in the back of the head.

The killer ran off; the other two – a man and a woman – remained, and were able to give the police a lead that eventually led to Guerin's arrest. It was then discovered that Sergeant McNeil's killer was also wanted for grand larceny and robbery. He was sentenced to 'life'.

McNeil was the second Albany officer to die in three days. On the 26 November, Patrolman Edward Stevens was detailed to collect a woman and escort her to a mental home – where a court had ordered her to have treatment. As he knocked on her door, she fired through it with both barrels of a shotgun, killing him instantly.

So little suspicion

The contrast between the two countries is immediately obvious. The British policeman had so little suspicion of the men he had stopped that he invited one of them to get into his car while he was sitting down. McNeil did it the right way, frisking Guerin before climbing into the car himself; but he still died. What strikes the reader about so many American crimes involving policemen is their *casualness*. Obviously, the war between police and criminals is on an altogether deadlier level than in England.

Most sociologists would agree that, to some extent, Rousseau, Diderot, Kropotkin and the rest were right. To get the best out of human beings, you need to give them a chance to exercise their freedom. Perhaps the situation needs to be 'defused' with sympathy and understanding. But it is also obvious that England has fewer police murders because it has fewer guns.

The police are not armed; neither are most criminals. It follows that the first step in solving America's problem could be simple; to pass logical and civilized gun laws.

COUNTRY KILLINGS

In her fascinating study *Murder and its Motives*, British writer F. Tennyson Jesse lists the half dozen commonest reasons for murder: money, revenge, jealousy, sadism, elimination, and conviction (i.e. political murder). However, she has missed out one of the most important: boredom – which is often the ultimate cause rather than the immediate motive for certain killings. Why did William Corder kill Maria Marten and bury her body in the Red Barn? Because he was bored with her. Why did he get involved with her in the first place? Because he was bored with his dull life in the wilds of the English countryside.

This despairing action is a basic recurring pattern in country style murders. The dullness leads to boredom; the boredom leads to sex; and the sex can lead to anything – from women tearing one another's hair out on the village green to a corpse in a ditch. Sophisticated city dwellers can hardly realize how much sex goes on in country areas, how much wife swapping and husband swapping, and even more dubious practices.

A horrifying example of this occurred in Cornwall, in the St. Austell area, when the body of a 10-year-old schoolgirl was found in 1969. Signs of sexual molestation led to alarm in the area and fear of a sex maniac. But a few days later, the victim's step-father was arrested and charged with the murder; at his trial, it was revealed that he had been her lover for years.

The city newspapers take care not to print the details of such cases – and of dozens of others involving incest, rape, and bestiality that are horribly familiar to every circuit judge in remote country areas. The fact appears to be that when human beings have nothing else to think about, their thoughts turn to sex. And that is the key to the great majority of murders in rural areas.

Pregnant girl

In many such murders, the details are so commonplace that they can only be found in local newspapers of the period. For example, the Maria Marten situation – a pregnant girl murdered by a lover who wants to avoid marrying her – has occurred dozens of times in the annals of crime in England alone. One such is recorded in the *Newgate Calendar*; it took place in 1700 in Lichfield, Staffordshire – which in those days was little more than a country village.

Elizabeth Price had already been seduced by an Army officer and had borne a child when she met Dr. George Caddell, a surgeon and a widower. 'A pregnancy was shortly the consequence of their intimacy,' says the *Newgate Calendar* primly. The girl pressed for marriage, but Dr. Caddell had meanwhile become engaged to the daughter of a professional colleague. One Saturday afternoon they went out for a long walk in the fields; then they sat under a hedge, and Caddell produced a knife and cut her throat.

He was so shocked and confused at the time that he left his case of instruments by the body; so when she was found the next day, no one had any difficulty in identifying the murderer. The girl's landlady also mentioned that she had left to take a walk with Dr. Caddell. It was an open and shut case; Caddell was hanged in July 1700.

What is interesting about this case is the way the *Newgate Calendar* presents it. In the days when it was first published (1774), all murdered girls were beautiful and, of course, innocent; all murderers were 'dastardly'. It explains that Caddell intended to murder Elizabeth Price before he met her that Saturday afternoon. It does not explain why, in that case, he spent the whole afternoon walking around with her before finally cutting her throat or why a premeditated murder should have been bungled so absurdly. But it offers enough facts to suggest the truth about the case.

It admits that 'innocent' Miss Price threatened to expose Dr. Caddell if he refused to marry her. What seems likely is that Caddell met her to try to persuade her to let him alone, or to submit to an abortion. When she refused, he probably lost his temper, seized a surgical knife and cut her throat. There is no evidence that he premeditated the crime; but there *is* a suggestion that Miss Price had a vengeful side to her nature which could have led him to lose his temper and kill her. The *Newgate Calendar* concludes:

Fatal catastrophe

'From this story the young officers of our army may learn a useful lesson: for if Miss Price had not been debauched by one of that profession, the fatal catastrophe had never happened.' Presumably every officer who read this made up his mind never to seduce a country girl again.

One of the most puzzling rape murders of the nineteenth century is remembered today only because it raised a peculiar point of law, and led to the abolition of a statute that dated back to Anglo-Saxon times. On the morning of May 27, 1817, a man climbed over a stile near the hamlet of Erdington (near Birmingham), and saw a bonnet, a folded dress, and a pair of ladies' shoes lying near a pond. On the damp grass nearby, there were definite signs that two people had been running. The pond was dragged – which brought to light the fully clothed body of a 20-year-old girl, Mary Ashford. Medical examination revealed that she had lost her virginity shortly before death, and that she had drowned.

On the previous evening, Mary had attended a dance, with a friend called Hannah Cox. She had gone to Hannah's in her ordinary clothes, changed into the dance frock there, and then spent most of the evening in constant demand from the local menfolk. The man she danced with most frequently was Abraham Thornton, a farmer's son. Thornton found her desirable; he told a friend that he was going to 'have' her before the night was over.

Neat and cheerful
He and Mary left the dance around midnight, and between then and four in the morning, she seems to have been with Thornton. At 4 a.m. she returned to Hannah Cox's and changed back into her ordinary clothes, bundling up the dance frock. She appeared cheerful, and her clothes were still neat and orderly. She left half an hour later, and was seen by a man who said good morning to her. What happened in the next hour and a half is a mystery. By six o'clock she was dead. And she had lost her virginity so violently that her skirt and stockings were covered with blood.

The obvious suspect was Thornton. But he behaved like an innocent man. He seemed amazed to hear of her death, and said openly: 'I was with her till four this morning.' He also admitted that he had seduced her – with her consent. Nevertheless, he was tried for her murder. And it was soon clear that there was no evidence to convict him. Three witnesses had seen him on his way home at about half past four, several miles from the pond where Mary's body was found. The jury took only six minutes to find him not guilty.

At this point, Mary's brother, as her heir-at-law, lodged an 'appeal of murder', a demand that Thornton should be tried a second time – a notion foreign to our modern sense of justice. When the judge asked Thornton whether he was guilty or not guilty, Thornton replied: 'Not guilty. And I am ready to defend the same with my body.' At this, his counsel handed him a pair of buckskin gloves; he put one on his left hand and threw the other on the ground in front of his accuser. He was invoking an even older principle – that of 'proving' his innocence in combat. Mary's brother William was prevented from picking up the glove – the case was complicated enough already without a duel in which someone might get killed. And once again, Thornton was found not guilty.

Armchair detectives

The case is the kind which delights armchair detectives. One solution would be that Mary fell into the pond accidentally – it had a steep bank, and was referred to as a 'pit' in the evidence. But if so, surely her dress and shoes would have gone in with her, not have been left neatly at the top of the slope?

Another possibility is that Thornton was unsuccessful in seducing her during the four hours they spent together – possibly because she was afraid of staining her dance frock. So he waited until she had changed her clothes, then made another attempt. She fought him, or tried to run away (hence the trampled grass); he raped her and pushed her into the pond. But there is a clear objection to that. The dance frock and the white stockings she wore at the dance were spotted with blood too.

Is it possible, then, that she yielded voluntarily to Thornton before changing her dress, and was raped by someone else on her way home? Taking into account all the facts, this seems as likely an explanation as any.

There is one other possibility: that she removed her dance frock while yielding to Thornton – hence the lack of grass stains on it when she changed at Hannah Cox's. Then, on the way home, she suddenly began to bleed heavily. She placed the dance frock and shoes at the top of the slope, and walked down towards the pond, intending to wash off the blood before she went home; she slipped and fell in . . .

At first sight, this seems to be the likeliest explanation – although this is one of those baffling cases where no explanation exactly fits. But Mary Ashford's death had one small effect on English law. The 'Appeal of Murder' and 'Wager of Battel' were abolished shortly after Thornton's trial.

Another tear-jerker

Throughout the nineteenth century, the melodrama *Maria Marten, or Murder in the Red Barn* played to packed houses all over England. (A spoof version of it is still popular.) But equally famous was another tear-jerker called *The Colleen Bawn* by Dion Boucicault, based on a now almost forgotten murder case. The colleen bawn (it means white girl), was a pretty schoolgirl called Ellie Hanley, who lived in the small village of Ballycahane, near Limerick, with her uncle – a ropemaker named Connery. Like Maria Marten, 15-year-old Ellie was the belle of the village; unlike Maria, she had an unblemished reputation.

In nearby Ballycahane Castle – actually a farm – lived the local squire, 26-year-old John Scanlan, an ex-army officer who had fought against Napoleon.

Scanlan attempted to seduce her, but Ellie was shy, inexperienced, and a good Roman Catholic. The virtue, however, only seems to have been skin deep; for when Scanlan persuaded her to elope with him and make an 'honest woman' of her, she decided to take her uncle's life savings – £120. They ran away in June 1819, and were married by a defrocked priest. Scanlan thought the marriage was not legal.

Defrocked priest

He was shocked to learn shortly afterwards that even a defrocked priest has the power to perform a ceremony of marriage, and that Ellie was therefore his wife. By the time he made this upsetting discovery, he had achieved his object – the taking of Ellie's virginity – and was thoroughly bored with her.

His servant Stephen Sullivan – his old army batman – was equally dismayed. He was entirely in favour of his master seducing a village girl; but he preferred to be the servant of a gay bachelor.

Scanlan had taken Ellie to the village of Glin – on the Shannon – for their honeymoon. The village was dull, and after a few days they moved to an island in the river. Both Scanlan and Sullivan wanted to get back to Castle Ballycahane, and the dogs and horses. But how could that be done? Ellie had spent a great deal of the stolen money on silk dresses. Her uncle wouldn't take her back. Besides, she was now in Scanlan's charge. In his boredom and desperation, the former officer and gentleman saw only one way out: to murder her.

Sullivan agreed to this solution. One moonlit night, they rowed out on the river; at a signal from Scanlan, Sullivan raised his club. Ellie thought it was a joke, and laughed. Sullivan was so unnerved by this that he dropped the club, and Ellie was rowed back home – unaware that she had been so near to death. The next attempt, however, was successful. This time, Sullivan was persuaded to do it alone. He drank a bottle of whiskey, then took Ellie out for another moonlight row. She fell asleep; Sullivan raised his gun, and brought it down with all his force. He missed and hit her shoulder; she woke up; but a few second later, another blow shattered her skull.

Next Sullivan removed her clothes – with the exception of the bodice, which would take too long to unlace – tied her knees against her chin, weighted the body with a stone, and threw her overboard.

Her body was cast ashore near Glin eight weeks later, on September 6, 1819. An arm was missing; a leg was broken in several places – from Sullivan's frantic blows – and the teeth were also missing. The skull was fleshless, but she could be identified from the large sockets of her prominent incisor teeth. A coroner's jury brought in a verdict of murder against John Scanlan and Stephen Sullivan. And the search for them began.

No one seemed to have seen the fugitives since July. But in September, someone thought he spotted John Scanlan near Ballycahane Castle. Troops surrounded it. A long search failed to reveal Scanlan – until a dragoon was about to drive his bayonet into a heap of straw in the barn, when there was a piercing yell, and Scanlan leaped to his feet.

Immediate execution

The famous lawyer Daniel O'Connell was engaged for the defence, and he tried to put the blame entirely on Sullivan, who was still missing. But to no effect. Scanlan was found guilty, and the judge ordered his immediate execution, in case family influence secured a reprieve. As the carriage taking Scanlan to the gallows was about to cross Ball Bridge in Limerick, the horses stopped, and refused to go forward. Scanlan had to dismount from the carriage and walk to the gallows on Gallows Green. The crowd saw in this an omen of his innocence; but he was executed all the same.

At about the time his master was being hanged, the actual murderer was being married to an heiress, in the village of Scartaglen, 30 miles away. But Sullivan's luck did not hold. The following March, he was accused – wrongly – of passing forged money; in Tralee jail, he was recognized and informed upon by a fellow prisoner. Sullivan stood trial in Limerick in July 1820, in the same dock in which Scanlan had stood. He was also hanged on the same gallows on July 27. Before he died, he admitted that he committed the murder, but added, 'It was Mr. Scanlan who put me up to it.'

In its time, the colleen brawn case achieved even more fame than that of Maria Marten. Not only did it become a play, but Sir Julius Benedict turned it into an opera, the *Lily of Killarney*, and Gerald Griffin wrote a best selling novel about it called *The Collegians*. All these versions emphasized Ellie's beauty and virtue; none of them pointed out that she had stolen her uncle's life savings and spent a large part of it on dresses.

Social interest

It can be seen why, from the criminologist's point of view, most 'country murders' are of great social interest. The motives usually spring from the banal rural background, and the details are mostly lurid. In cities, the style of murder changes from century to century; in the country, it tends to remain much the same. In 1936, the Scottish crime historian William Roughhead recorded a recent case that may be taken as typical. It happened in the Cuddies Strip, a lover's lane near Perth in Scotland.

In the August of the previous year a young couple were walking home at dusk in Cuddies Strip. Suddenly, there was a shot. They both turned round. There was another shot, and the boy, Danny Kerrigan, fell to the ground dying.

As his girlfriend, 17-year-old Marjory Fenwick bent over him, she found a man standing above her – small, squat, very powerful. 'Stay with him while I go for help!' exclaimed Marjory – and ran back towards the town. The man followed her until they reached a stile – where he threw her on the ground, dragged her into the bushes, stripped and raped her.

The rapist had bound the girl's wrists with a handkerchief. Through a laundry mark, the police were able to trace this to a nearby house, which had recently been burgled. The handkerchief had a smell of woodsmoke – which led the police to suspect that the assailant was camping somewhere. They quickly located a tent; it was occupied by an Irish tinker, John M'Guigan, 24, who was short, swarthy, and powerful. He was known locally as a Peeping Tom – and a telescope was found in his tent. M'Guigan was soon identified as the burglar who had stolen the handkerchief (among other things); he had left a fingerprint on a window. At the trial (at which William Roughhead was present), the defence claimed that Marjory Fenwick was lying.

M'Guigan was cleared of murder ... but jailed for 10 years for rape.

Even though this case was not strictly murder country style, it certainly typifies the kind of rural case in which the element of sexual assault, leading to violent death, is present.

Against this there *have* been notable 'country murders' in which the motive was not sexual. There was Ronald Harries, a 24-year-old farm worker, who murdered his aunt and uncle in October 1953, to take over their farm in Carmarthenshire, Wales.

In the same county a Polish Farmer, Michael Onufrejczyc murdered his partner, Stanislav Sykut, and concealed the body so well that it was never found.

There was also the famous murder of a cheat and gambler named William Weare by three villains called Thurtle, Hunt, and Probert in 1823. They lured him to a lonely field, and cut his throat and crushed his skull; for some odd reason, this fairly commonplace murder fascinated the British public as much as that of Maria Marten and Ellie Hanley.

These exceptions only emphasize the rule that most country murders arise out of sex and boredom, and achieve and maintain their interest by their trappings of lust, rape, self-disgust, and guilt.

CRIMES OF PASSION

Crime passionnel – the crime of passion. The words conjure up dark-skinned Latins like Rudolph Valentino, and sultry girls with daggers concealed in their stockings. 'The passion killer is characterized by emotional immaturity and a simplistic moral outlook,' said Dr. Magnus Hirschfeld, an expert on sex crime. Perhaps this explains why criminologists have paid so little attention to the *crime passionnel*. It seems *too* simple, too straightforward. A hot-tempered man strangles his flirtatious mistress, or a jealous woman stabs her unfaithful lover. What is there in that to exercise the ingenuity of a psychologist?

A great deal more than appears on the surface. It *is* true that southerners are more prone to commit crimes of passion than northerners. We say this because northerners are more cerebral and calculating, while southerners are more hot-blooded and emotional. But in that case, why is the rate of sex crime higher in northern countries? A man who commits murder for the satisfaction of a momentary physical impulse cannot really be called cooler or more calculating than a man who plans the murder of his mistress's husband.

Sexual maturity earlier

The real explanation is more complicated and altogether more interesting. In the northern countries, with their cold and difficult conditions, men and women have tended to develop as equals. They work hard together; and the women, muffled in their winter clothes, do not draw so much attention to their physical attractions – perhaps this explains why the Eskimos, according to early travellers, used to offer their wives to guests.

In warmer countries, the difference between male and female is more obvious. The sun bronzed peasant of Italy or Spain wears her brightly coloured skirt and off the shoulder blouse. Sexual maturity comes earlier in the warmer climate. The consequence is that southern men and women see one another as two separate races, almost separate species.

When this happens, their view of one another becomes strangely intermingled with illusions and idealizations. The Russian writer Maxim Gorky has caught this with great psychological accuracy to his story *Twenty-six Men and a Girl*. The men are bakers' assistants, confined all day in a damp cellar, and they are all in love with a girl called Tanya who calls there every day. One day, a swaggering soldier tells them that he could seduce Tanya – and he does it. Suddenly, the twenty-six men hate her; they turn on her and scream insults at her. And Tanya haughtily walks off, never to return. *She* is the realist. The soldier may have treated her like a whore, but he has given her pleasure. These men treat her like an angel, and then abuse her when she fails to live up to her image.

This tradition – of regarding Woman as a romantic goddess – has its roots deep in the southern cultural tradition. The 'troubadours' were poets who flourished in southern France and northern Italy as early as the eleventh century, and they invented the tradition of 'courtly love'. The troubadour's 'lady' was his absolute ruler; at a word from her, he would ride off round the world. The stories of King Arthur and his knights of the round table were first written in French, by poets who were inspired by the troubadours and their attitude to women. Scholars believe that the whole tradition of troubadour love originated among the Arabs in north Africa.

There is another – and less pleasant – side to the romantic view of Woman. She is supposed to be quiet, obedient and infinitely yielding; the fourteenth-century Italian poet Petrarch tells a story that remained popular for centuries. A nobleman who distrusts women finally marries a poor peasant girl called Griseldis. Then he proceeds to 'test' her to see how obedient she is. First, he takes her children from her as soon as they are born, then he announces that he intends to divorce her to marry another woman. Patient Griseldis agrees to everything – even attending his wedding and praising the beauty of the bride to be. Finally, overcome by her gentleness and patience, the nobleman admits he has merely been testing her; he takes her back, and 'they live happily ever after'.

Three bullets in him

Even if it *is* only a story, it captures the mediaeval attitude to women in a country like Spain or Italy. To modern ears, it sounds sadistic and slightly insane. Surely the nobleman could *tell* that she was a sweet, obedient girl without subjecting her to such humiliations? But that would not have satisfied Petrarch's readers, male or female. For Griseldis was supposed to be their idea of a perfect woman – beautiful, obedient, long-suffering, entirely dependent on Man, her master.

It is because these deep-rooted attitudes still persist in the southern temperament that southerners are prone to commit crimes of passion. The women who swooned over Rudolph Valentino or John Boles had no idea of what it would really be like to be married to a Sheik. The rape in the desert might be exciting but the rest could be hell – as Marguerite Laurent discovered when she married Prince Ali Kamel Bey Fahmy. But at least it was Prince Fahmy who ended with three bullets in him; in so many parallel cases, it is the woman who dies.

In 1972, Francisco Pineda, a car mechanic of Guadalajara, Mexico, walked into the bedroom of his employer, Fernando Ortega, a 32-year-old hunchback. His employer lay stretched on the floor in his pyjamas, dead. Francisco's pretty step-daughter, Maria Pineda, lay dead on the bed, her skirt around her thighs. Police discovered that both had died of cyanide poisoning; Ortega had forced her to drink cyanide at knife point, then drank it himself.

Ortega was suffering from tuberculosis; Maria had been acting as his nurse, administering injections. Ortega fell violently in love with her, but she was not attracted to the hunchback. She may have thought that the drink he forced on her contained knockout drops, and that his intention was simply to rape her.

In fact, in spite of the position of her dress, Maria had not been sexually molested. Ortega *could* have raped her before he killed himself, but that was not what he wanted. He loved her, and wanted to join her in death. The tragedy was stupid, pathetic – and typical of the southern temperament; and we can clearly see the southern attitude to women. Ortega adored her, she was his goddess. But she also had to pay with her life for the sin of disobedience to the male.

To the northern, pragmatic way of thinking, there is something absurd about such 'crimes of passion'. What the Anglo-Saxon fails to understand about the southern temperament is the way in which it can *blind* itself with emotion. How is it possible to deceive yourself without actually being insane? The French philosopher Jean Paul Sartre devoted some time to his problem, and in a work called *A Sketch of a Theory of the Emotions* produced some important ideas. He makes the strange and revolutionary suggestion that *all* emotion should be regarded as a kind of wishful thinking – or, as he prefers to call it, 'magic'.

He is not using the word in its occult sense. When an ostrich buries its head in the sand at the approach of an enemy, it is hoping to make the enemy disappear 'by magic'. If a girl faints as she is about to be attacked, says Sartre, this is not just a physical reaction; on the subconscious level it is also an attempt to make the rapist ago away 'by magic'.

All emotion, says Sartre, is a *substitute* for action. Take the case of a man who falls in love with a girl. If she also finds him attractive, they fall into one another's arms, and he releases his desire for her in lovemaking. If she rejects him – as Maria Pineda rejected Ortega – the desire goes on building up, encouraged by his brooding, until he is wildly, passionately in love with her, entirely possessed by an emotion which is a *substitute* for lovemaking. In the same way, a man who gets angry and represses it builds up tremendous inner rage, *out of all proportion to its object*; the man who lets out his rage by shouting or fighting ceases to feel anger.

The Moors murderer

All this may be dismissed as a clever but superficial theory – and indeed, there are few psychologists who would accept it entirely; but where crime is concerned, it is of immense importance. It suddenly reveals the answer to problems that otherwise baffled 'normal' people: for example, how *could* Ian Brady, the Moors murderer, kill innocent children; how could Manson and his followers slaughter people who had done them no harm? According the Sartre, *all* emotion is out of proportion to its object. Why do children never enjoy Christmas as much as they expect to? Because they build up an emotion of expectation which is untrue – wishful thinking or 'magic'.

The ideal way for a child to enjoy Christmas is not to know it was coming until it actually arrived, so it could simply *act out* its pleasure. Consider a murderer like the Düsseldorf sadist, Peter Kürten. In long periods of solitary confinement, he built up such a loathing of society that *no action could ever discharge it*. He might murder men, women and children, set barns on fire; but, like the child at Christmas, he had built up an expectation that could never be satisfied. The same is true of killers like Manson and Brady.

But it is when this theory is applied to the passion killers that we begin to recognize its frightening accuracy. Sometimes the whole crime is wrapped up in such a miasma of emotion that it seems unreal, like a crime committed in a nightmare.

France's classic *crime passionnel* of the early 1950s revealed more than just an element of fantasy – it also contained a subconscious wish for self-destruction. When a middle-aged mother and French woman named Yvonne Chevallier landed by plane at the penal settlements in New Guinea she had arrived to pay penance for the murder of her husband, Pierre, winner of the Légion d'Honneur, on the day he was made a minister in the newly formed French government of 1951.

Pierre was a promising young doctor when he first met Yvonne – then a midwife – in Orléans hospital in 1935. They were a contrasting couple – he from an old and distinguished local family; she of peasant stock. Their love and passion for each other overcame their social differences, and they married four years later when Pierre had joined the army in the fight against Hitler. The first of their two sons was born in 1940, and the second in 1945 (both boys were with Yvonne when she came to punish herself in the penal camps).

Resistance hero
Still not accepted by the Chevallier family ('They regarded me as one of the mistakes of Pierre's youth,' she later told her trial judge bitterly) she came to worship her gallant husband even more when he returned to Orléans and became one of the heroes of the local Resistance movement. At the end of hostilities he was easily the most popular man in the community, and it was but a short step for him to enter the battleground of politics. He no longer concentrated on his career as a doctor, and Yvonne found herself even more out of place as the wife of an ambitious politician.

Awkward, gauche, and conversationally clumsy, she did not fit into the social life that Pierre was obliged to lead in Paris – the headquarters of French politics. As he spent more and more time in the capital, and she was left alone but for her children in her Orléans home, Yvonne was deprived of both emotional and physical love. She resorted to drugs – veronal and maxiton – to get her through the long days and the even longer nights. Then came the day – the day she dreaded and knew to be inevitable – when she found a love letter in the pocket of one of Pierre's suits.

It was from a woman named 'Jeanette' and it appeared that she was not – surprisingly enough – a Parisian social beauty. She came from the Orléans area and Yvonne suspected that she was Jeanne Perreau – the beautiful, intelligent and ultra-presentable wife of the owner of one of the city's main department stores. Also she was 15 years younger than Yvonne – who felt more than ever like the plain little countrywoman, whose place in her husband's affections and bed had been taken by the sort of woman that he *should* have married.

After staging a typically jealous and acrimonious scene with the red-headed Madame Perreau (and gaining no satisfaction in any direction), Yvonne turned her hatred full upon her husband. After arguing with him, fighting with him, pleading with him – but not loving with him – she took the children away from Orléans on a long seaside holiday. Without sparing words or feelings, Pierre had told her that he no longer wished to sleep with her, and that he wanted a divorce. He believed his flourishing career could stand the publicity of a divorce action – but he had not bargained on the effect it would have upon Yvonne. She tried to commit suicide. Then, when that failed, she went to the nearest police station and took out a licence for a gun.

She was immediately given a gun certificate on the grounds that as the wife of a rising political figure (Pierre was now the Mayor of Orléans) she might need to protect herself from his rivals or enemies. She next obtained a 7.65 mm Mab automatic, took it home, and hid it in the upstairs linen closet. A short while later she had yet another row with Pierre – when he again threatened to divorce her, and this time added that he had another woman in mind whom he would marry. This, for Yvonne, was the final insult, the last threat.

Five times she shot . . .

She hurried out of the bedroom, took out the gun, returned, and pointed it not at Pierre, but at herself. 'If you leave me for another woman – any woman – I'll kill myself!' she screamed. Pierre – who was undressing and was down to his underwear – was still jubilant about his appointment that day to the French government. His name was in all the papers, and his new job as a minister was the talking point of Orléans.

But all this meant nothing to Yvonne. When he mocked her and told her to go ahead and shoot herself – 'As soon as I'm out of the room' – she turned the automatic upon him. Four times she shot – rapidly and with deadly aim. With a cry of pain and terror, Pierre fell to the floor with bullets in the chest, the forearm, the thigh, the chin – and fifth bullet fired minutes later which entered his back.

As soon as she had recovered her wits – and realized what it was she had done ('the gun went off by accident' she claimed later) – she picked up the telephone and rang the Orléans police station. She spoke to a friend of hers and Pierre's, Commissaire Gazano, and said simply: 'Please come here at once. My husband needs you urgently.' Within two hours – dressed in widow's weeds – she was placed in Orléans jail, and her trial for her crime of passion murder was held in November 1952.

It was then stated by the Presiding Judge, Mr. Raymond Jadin, that she had 'an animal passion' for her husband. 'You should have conquered it and have realized that you have no right to take the life of another person. This passion overwhelmed your whole way of life – without your attempting to control it. I understand your Calvary, but do not condone it.' A doctor who gave evidence stated that Yvonne had 'retained the mentality of a teenager in love with a student'. Stressing her feelings of inferiority – socially, physically, and intellectually – he concluded that she suffered from 'physical depreciation because her husband refused to make love to her. She despaired of ever being the equal of the man whom she had never stopped loving.' That was her state of mind at the time she killed him.

It only took Madame Jeane Perreau – 34 and, she said, 'of no profession' – to admit to the court that she became Pierre Chevallier's mistress in 1950 for the jury to feel sympathy for Yvonne. Her lawyer asked with emotion whether her two sons were to 'grow up alone in the world', and the jurors answered with an unequivocal No. They found Madame Chevallier 'not guilty' and on her acquittal there were few people in the packed courtroom – gendarmes included – who did not show their relief.

Her self-punishment in New Guinea – a sentence she awarded herself after receiving absolution from the Church for her crime – was a telling example of the guilt felt by those who commit crimes of passion. Most such murders are committed not out of genuine hatred, but out of spurned love. If affection is freely given and generously returned, crimes of passion would be removed from the criminal calendar. It is up to the man – or woman – in a relationship to ensure that if a break has to come, then it is made gently, with tact and kindness. In that way will they be protecting and lengthening their own lives.

DOCTORS OF DEATH

The nine-year-old girl was sobbing so violently that her father could not understand a word she said. He shook her impatiently: 'Where is Juliette?' The girl controlled herself for a moment. 'She's asleep, and the doctor says he's going to die.' The father, Jules Deitsch, rushed through the streets to the house where Doctor Etienne Deschamps was lodging. The door of his room was locked. Deitsch ran to the police station, and begged the police to help him break in. 'I think my twelve-year-old daughter is in there.' She was. When the police entered the room, Juliette was lying naked, on the bed. Beside her, also naked, lay a great hairy man with a beard. Blood was streaming from wounds in his chest, but he was still alive. The little girl was dead.

It was the beginning of one of the most sensational murder trials in the history of New Orleans. For when the body of Juliette Deitsch was examined, it was discovered that she was no longer a virgin, and that she had been carnally abused in other ways. There were even love bites on her body. And, as the evidence made clear, this had not happened just once, but dozens of times over the course of six months or so. Dr. Deschamps was obviously the worst kind of pervert.

How had the respectable carpenter, Jules Deitsch, come to allow his daughter to fall into the hands of the monster? Deitsch had met Dr. Deschamps in 1888, when Deschamps had told him that he was an adept in the occult. He possessed hypnotic powers, and he intended to use them to discover the lost treasure of the pirate Jean Lafitte. All he needed, he said, was the help of a pure young girl to act as a medium.

Deitsch was so impressed by the fifty-year-old doctor that he had no hesitation in entrusting Juliette to his care – in fact, both his daughters – for Juliette's young sister Laurence was fascinated by the doctor, and didn't want to be left out.

Later, Laurence described the 'experiments'. Juliette would be

134

told to undress and to climb into bed. She was an unusually well-developed child for her age, although she had not yet reached puberty. The doctor would also undress, and climb in beside her. He would soak a clean handkerchief in chloroform, and place it over her face.

The doctor always made them promise not to tell their father what had happened. So things had continued until that afternoon of January 30, 1889, when Deschamps had suddenly begun to sob in French: 'My God, what have I done?' Then Laurence, who was terrified, was told to run home and tell her father that the doctor was going to die. But the doctor did not die. The stab wounds he inflicted on his chest were too superficial to endanger his life.

It was obvious to everybody that Juliette's death was accidental – to everybody, at least, but the prosecutor. He alleged that Deschamps had deliberately killed the girl because he knew that his sexual abuses would soon be discovered. This was obviously absurd, since killing her was the sure way to discovery. On the other hand, Deschamps was more cunning and calculating than he tried to make out. The police found letters in his room, written by Juliette and signed 'Your love forever', and 'your little mistress'.

Covering his tracks

Juliette, however, was a backward child, and could not have composed them. Deschamps had written them, and got her to copy them out, so that he could claim she had been willing to be seduced. But if she was willing, why chloroform her, as he had on every occasion? Besides, the letters also mentioned a jeweller in the neighbourhood called Charlie, and implied that he had been the man who had originally taken Juliette's virginity. But 'Charlie' was proved to be innocent. Again, Deschamps was covering his tracks. Why should he, argued the prosecutor, unless he meant to kill her?

The Deschamps case – which ended with the doctor being hanged – gained nationwide coverage in the American press. This was not simply because of the sensational nature of the crime: it was because Deschamps was a doctor. It is a curious fact of criminal history that doctors who commit murder excite more interest than almost any other type of criminal. The usual explanation for this is that doctors are supposed to save life, not take it. But that supposes that the public are more interested in morality than they actually are. The true explanation is that the doctor is a symbol of middle-class respectability.

In earlier centuries, people felt the same morbid interest in priests who committed crimes – hence the excitement aroused by the trial of Father Urbain Grandier, burned alive in 1634 on a charge of having seduced and bewitched a convent full of nuns.

The great age of medicine was the nineteenth century. It was also the great age of the medical murderer. Yet the company of killers had one distinguished predecessor of the eighteenth century: Dr. Levi Weil, whose strange story helps to explain why the medical murderer was such a latecomer on the criminal scene. Dr. Weil, a Dutch Jew, came to London from Holland in the 1760's – the London of Dr. Johnson, the actor David Garrick and the statesman Edmund Burke.

London then was full of disease, and most doctors were constantly busy. But this Jewish doctor with a foreign accent encountered a certain amount of prejudice, and his practice remained small.

Brother's gang

One day, a merchant asked Weil if he would travel out to Enfield, outside London, to attend to his sister – the regular doctor was ill. Weil drove to the village, attended the old lady – with some success – and then ate supper with her brother, who paid him in cash.

All the way home Weil thought about the house full of money and jewellery and determined to take some of it for himself. In the City, he said goodbye to the merchant – and promptly made his way back to Enfield. When he finally reached home at daylight, he was exhausted, but some £90 richer – more money than he had made in months.

Ironically, Weil's practice began to improve as his income from burglary soared to £500 a month. He kept his surgery open, knowing it was his best disguise. He entered the houses of wealthy patients, 'cased the joint', and passed on the information to a gang run by his brother. On one occasion, he heard that an old caretaker who lived near St. Paul's Cathedral had his life's savings hidden in the room.

Other burglars had already broken in, but although they had prised up every floorboard and ripped plaster off the walls, they had been unable to locate the money. Weil was called to the old man's bedside when he was ill. He tried to persuade the caretaker to go into hospital; the vehemence with which the idea was rejected convinced Weil that the money was hidden in his room.

The floor and the walls had been explored – so it had to be the ceiling. A great beam crossed the room. Weil examined it when the caretaker was asleep, and found a cavity. Two nights later, as the old man slept heavily from one of the doctor's sedatives, Asher Weil and an accomplice took nearly £3,000 from the hiding place in the beam. The old man never discovered the robbery. He died a few days later. This may have been Weil's first murder.

By then, the gang had swelled to eight. One of the members, a German Jew named Isaacs, tried to conceal more than his share of the booty, and was dismissed. That was Weil's first mistake. Not long after, he made his second.

In the autumn of 1771, the gang – including Weil himself – waited until after dark in the vicinity of a house in Chelsea Fields – in those days, Chelsea was a village outside London. When all the lights were out, they knocked loudly.

The servant who opened the door was overpowered. The lady of the house, a Mrs. Hutchings, fought strenuously, but was tied with her petticoats over her head. In the upper part of the house the gang burst into a bedroom, and two servants who had been asleep started up, alarmed. One was knocked out; the other, as he struggled, was shot with a pistol.

After that, the gang flew with their loot. Unfortunately for them, the servant, John Slow, died. Now the authorities decided to offer a reward for the gang, and Isaacs, the man who had been dismissed, saw his opportunity for revenge.

He knew that if he turned King's Evidence, he would be safe. Weil was planning his most ambitious robbery so far – of a diamond merchant expecting a consignment of £40,000 worth of jewels – when he was placed under arrest by the Bow Street runners. Six of the gang were tried; two were acquitted for lack of evidence – a proof that, even in those days, justice was impartial. But Weil and his brother were among those executed at Tyburn on December 9, 1771.

The next notable name in the roll of medical infamy is that of Dr. Edmé Castaing of Paris. At the age of 27, Dr. Castaing enjoyed the good life, and did not look forward to the lifetime of drudgery of a general practitioner. One of his patients was a wealthy man named Hippolyte Ballet, who had tuberculosis. Castaing became friendly with Hippolyte's younger brother Auguste, and learned that the brothers were on bad terms – so bad that Hippolyte had excluded his brother from his will. One evening, as they drank together, Auguste hinted that Castaing might hasten his brother's death, and gain possession of the will.

So, on October 22, 1822, Hippolyte quite suddenly died, to the astonishment of other doctors who had occasionally attended him. A month later, Castaing paid off all his debts, and lent his mother 300,000 francs. The following year, on June 2, Castaing and Auguste Ballet went for a drive in the country, and stopped at a hotel in St. Cloud, where they ate and drank. Then Auguste was suddenly taken ill, and soon died, attended by his friend Castaing and two other doctors. The other G.P.s recognized the signs of morphine poisoning and they discovered that, even after Ballet had started to vomit, Castaing had gone to a local chemist and bought more morphine. When it was discovered that Ballet had made a will in Castaing's favour, the doctor was arrested.

Castaing was relying on the fact that morphine was very difficult to detect. And he was proved to be right. Although the doctors agreed that Auguste Ballet had shown all the signs of morphine poisoning — vomiting, diarrhoea, heavy breathing, contraction of the pupils — no trace of morphine could be detected in his stomach. The prosecutor asked indignantly if all murderers who used morphine should be allowed to go free, just because medical science was unable to detect its presence. That swung the jury. Castaing was sentenced to death, and executed in December 1823, protesting his innocence.

The next medical murder of any note took place in the peaceful environment of Harvard University, in Cambridge, Massachusetts, more than a quarter of a century later. Like so many medical murderers, Professor John Webster, aged 56, was given to living beyond his means. He frequently borrowed money from a wealthy friend, Dr. George Parkman. But Parkman ceased to be friendly when he learned that Webster's famous mineral collection, which Webster had pledged to him as security for a loan, had also been pledged to another creditor. The angry Parkman threatened exposure. On November 23, 1849, Parkman failed to return home for lunch, and the river was dredged in case he had drowned.

In fact, Parkman had called on Webster in his laboratory, and as he turned to go out, Webster had struck him such a tremendous blow on the back of the head — with a piece of wood — that he died. Later on, Webster alleged that Parkman had been so insulting that he had hit him in a blind rage; but all the evidence indicates a cool head and careful planning. Later the same day, he told an agent who collected his lecture fees that he had repaid Parkman. And that night, behind locked doors, he proceeded to dismember the body and to burn it in his medical furnace.

Two days after Parkman's disappearance, Webster called on his family, and told them that he had repaid Parkman a few hours before his disappearance. Surely this proved that Parkman had been killed by a robber who had concealed the body . . .? Unfortunately for Webster, the caretaker at the medical school, Littlefield, detested him. Littlefield wondered why the doctor worked all night in his laboratory, and kept his furnace burning all the time. Whenever Webster left the laboratory, he took care to double lock the door; but Littlefield had a plan. The furnace was built against a wall, and there was a passageway on the other side. With his wife standing guard, Littlefield broke through the wall with a crowbar, shone his torch through – and saw a bone which he recognized as a human pelvis.

At his trial, which lasted eleven days – and got national press coverage – Webster pleaded not guilty. He contended that the bones in the furnace were not Parkman's at all – just the remains of a body they had been using for dissection. But a dentist positively identified the false teeth as Parkman's, and Webster's defence collapsed. Before he was hanged, in August 1850, he confessed to killing Parkman 'in a fit of rage'.

Weak characters
The murder of Parkman was the beginning of what might be called the great age of medical murderers. It lasted for about a hundred years – from approximately 1855, the year in which Dr. William Palmer of Rugely poisoned his racetrack associate John Cook, to 1954, when Dr. Sam Sheppard of Ohio was found guilty of murdering his wife. Studying the killers, an interesting point emerges. A great majority of the medical murderers were weak characters, given to lying or boasting, and to living beyond their means. And this implies that many of them were drawn to the medical profession to satisfy vanity – the self-esteem urge.

This was perhaps most obvious in the case of the Glasgow poisoner, Dr. Edward William Pritchard. In photographs, he looks a typical Victorian *paterfamilias*, with his frock coat and bushy beard, surrounded by a respectable-looking family. In fact, he was an utterly weak character, a joke among his colleagues because of his incredible boasting and lying. He claimed to be a friend of the Italian patriot Guiseppe Garibaldi, although they had certainly never met.

A typical narcissist, he was fond of presenting people with photographs of himself – he even handed one to a stranger he met on the train. He gave lectures – mostly invented – in which he described himself as an intrepid traveller and hunter. He also regarded himself as a great lover, and seduced servant girls and anyone else who would have him. In 1863, when he was 38, a fire broke out in the room of the servant girl in his house; she was found dead, and it seemed clear that she had made no attempt to leave her bed during the fire. Pritchard was widely suspected, but he nevertheless won a claim from an insurance company.

In 1864, he made another servant girl – aged 15 – pregnant, but performed an abortion. And it may have been desire to marry her that led him to start poisoning his wife Mary, to whom he had been married for nearly twenty years. In November, 1864, she became ill, vomiting and dizzy. A doctor called in by Pritchard suspected she was being poisoned, and wrote to Mary Pritchard's brother, suggesting she should be moved into hospital. The result was that Mary Pritchard's mother, Mrs. Taylor, decided to come and nurse her daughter. Soon, Mrs. Taylor was suffering from the same symptoms. She died on February 24, 1865, and Mrs. Pritchard followed her a month later.

Pritchard provided both death certificates, stating that Mrs. Taylor died of apoplexy, and his wife of gastric fever. Someone wrote an anonymous letter to the police, and Pritchard was arrested. When the bodies were exhumed, both were found to be saturated with antimony, which Pritchard was proved to have bought.

Since the 1880s, England has produced her fair quota of medical murderers, while America has produced many more.

Test tube diseases

There was Dr. Milton Bowers, of San Francisco, who almost certainly poisoned three of his wives, but who succeeded in persuading a jury to acquit him in 1888, and lived happily (with another wife) until 1905.

Most ambitious of all was Dr. Clarke Hyde, of Kansas City, who decided in 1909 to poison no less than seven relatives who stood between him and the fortune of Thomas Swope, the millionaire founder of Kansas City. Hyde was married to Swope's niece Frances. In October that year, Swope and his financial adviser James Hunton died – apparently from natural causes. Shortly afterwards, Hyde procured several test tubes of diphtheria and typhoid germs, claiming he intended to take up the study of bacteriology. Five assorted brothers- and sisters-in-law then fell ill, and Hyde told them it was typhoid fever. Chrisman Swope died after Hyde administered a capsule, and other members of the family showed symptoms of typhoid fever.

When Hyde left on a trip to New York, all the patients improved considerably — which confirmed the suspicion of the nurses that the doctor was responsible for their illness. Hyde then made a curious mistake; walking along a lamplit street, he took something out of his pocket, and stamped it into the snow. One of the brothers-in-law saw him, and investigated; he picked up a broken capsule, and recognized the odour as potassium cyanide. The body of old Thomas Swope was exhumed, and cyanide and strychnine were found in it. Hyde was tried and found guilty; but he had money enough to appeal to a whole series of higher courts. In 1917 he was freed,

Since the trial of Sam Sheppard in 1954, there have been no more medical murders in the United States — or, if there have been, they have gone undiscovered. Nowadays, when there is almost no poison or drug that cannot be detected even in the smallest quantities, it looks as if the great epoch of the medical murderer — who mostly killed out of greed and for gain — is over.

DOMINANCE

The scene is your local barroom any night after work. You and some of the boys have got together for a few quick ones before going home. There are four or five of you sitting at a table sipping beer, exchanging anecdotes, telling jokes. Suddenly someone you all know – let's call him Dennis – walks in from the street and strides up to the counter. He orders his drink and stands eyeing your party as if he were thinking of making a bid for you. Then, without being told to or being able to stop yourselves, you all find yourselves on your feet. You hurry over to Dennis, ask him how he's keeping, what sort of a day he's had, what his drink is.

He did not come and sit down with you. You stood up and went collectively to join him. What has just happened, whether you realize it or not, is a case of dominance. Dennis the Dominator has asserted his power, his influence upon you. You don't know why it happened, or how it happened – it just did. That is what dominance is all about.

The human animal has reacted as though compelled, brainwashed, or, in some mysterious way, hypnotized. In order to understand and recognize this social phenomenon, it is first of all necessary to examine the way in which dominance operates among birds and animals. Everyone who has ever kept chickens has noticed the existence of the 'pecking order.' It is as if each chicken carried a number around its neck. Number ten is allowed to peck number eleven – or any higher number – but has to submit quietly if number nine chooses to deliver an admonishing peck. And the 'pecking order' appears to be a law of nature that appears to most tribes of wild animals.

A television film made by the naturalist Jane Goodall on the wild dogs of Africa showed that the leader need not necessarily be a male. The pack was led by a female who exercised complete authority over dogs of both sexes.

142

Will to succeed

But what is perhaps the most important 'discovery' about dominance was not made by any single naturalist; it has simply emerged quietly until it is now generally recognized. It is this: that among *all* animal groups, the number of highly dominant ones seems to be the same – an average of 5 per cent.

The explorer Sir Henry Stanley knew about it at the turn of the century. For when Bernard Shaw asked him how many men could lead his party, if he himself became ill, Stanley replied promptly; 'One in twenty.' When Shaw asked if this was exact or approximate, Stanley replied: 'Exact.' He was referring to the will to power, to dominate, to succeed – which tallied with Shaw's own frequently expressed theory of the Life Force; the inner drive which leads us (or the more dominant among us) to success in our jobs and professions.

It was Robert Ardrey, the American author of *African Genesis*, who first gave publicity to the 'one in twenty' theory. Ardrey's research showed him that one of the most closely guarded secrets of the Korean War was that no escapes were made by American prisoners. This was because their Chinese captors had discovered an infallible method of preventing breakouts. They observed the prisoners carefully for a while, then removed the 'dominant' ones – the 5 per cent who were leader figures – and put them in a separate compound under heavy guard. Once the leaders were removed, the other prisoners became far easier to handle – in fact, they could be left with almost no guard at all. The Chinese observed that the number of dominant prisoners was always exactly one in twenty.

The Nazis recognized the significance of this when, during World War II, they placed all the most incorrigible escapers together in 'escape-proof' prisons like Colditz. More recently, in Britain, the 1966 commission into prison reform headed by Lord Louis Mountbatten recommended that the more dangerous convicts were not split up among a large number of prisons – but were kept together.

Frustration factor

So far, however, no zoologist has conducted careful research to establish why the dominant minority appears to be 5 per cent. A study should be made of leading surgeons, ministers, politicians, sportsmen, and pop stars to ascertain whether or not they form 5 per cent of their profession, or, indeed, separate 5 per cents of the population. Obviously it is not only criminals who are dominant, and Ardrey defines dominance as occurring when 'two or more animals (or humans) pursue the same activity.' The view is also held that crooks only become crooks because their will-power is frustrated or denied in some way – thus rechannell-ing their efforts to succeed into antisocial areas. One of the few countries where official figures are available is Russia, where the Communist Party of the Soviet Union contains approximately 5 per cent of all the people – 14½ million members out of a population of 242 million.

In the U.S. scientific probes have been made into the whole question of dominance, and the researches of John B. Calhoun – at the National Institute of Mental Health at Bethseda, Maryland – threw up one of the most disturbing observations on the subject of power over others. Calhoun wanted to observe the behaviour of rats under conditions of overcrowding.

A large number of rats were placed in three interconnecting cages. The 'king rat' took over the central cage for himself and his harem; the other rats were forced into the other two cages, so they were now grossly overcrowded. *And the dominant 5 per cent quickly became a criminal 5 per cent.* These 'criminal rats' did things that are never seem among rats in nature. Rats have an elaborate and self-protecting courting ritual; but these rodents wandered around in gangs, raping any spare females they chanced upon. They also became cannibals, eating the baby rats.

Here, then, it seems, we have an immediate explanation of the high crime rate in the slum areas of our great cities. Overcrowd-ing produces a kind of violent opportunism among the dominant 5 per cent. One of the Kray twins – the brothers who, in the 1960's, ruled over the crime kingdom of London's East End – said that in their environment crime was the only way to 'get somewhere'.

Pointless brutality

The state of mind produced by overcrowding leads to an attitude of desperation, which, in turn, leads the weaker members of the society to become even weaker and so disappear or go under (female rats, for example, tend to abort), while the dominant ones became more violent, grabbing at whatever food or sex they wanted. Under these conditions all sense of leisure vanishes. Crimes become brutal, and pointless. The dominant children may also become criminals.

An item in the world press for November 1972 stated briefly that two boys, aged 11 and 12, had been arrested in New York for raping a seven-year-old girl and then throwing her to her death from the roof of the tenement in which they lived. It was the overcrowded rat syndrome seen in human terms.

From the point of view of the emerging 'new criminology' it makes no difference whether the dominant minority is 5 per cent or 4 per cent or 6 per cent. All that is important is to recognize that, in any society, there is a small group whose dominance is definitely higher than that of the others. And that, under conditions of stress, this dominance may express itself in crime.

A graphic example of this occurred on a warm June evening in 1956, when the chief forester of Büderich, a village near Düsseldorf, was out patrolling some woods in which a number of courting couples had recently been attacked and murdered. Suddenly he came across a man crouching in the bushes, holding a revolver. In a clearing a few yards away, two lovers were kissing in a parked car. The forester, who was armed, succeeded in arresting the Peeping Tom and then took him to Büderich Police Station.

There the prisoner identified himself as Werner Boost, a 28 year-old mechanic from Düsseldorf. It was while Criminal Commissioner Eynck was interviewing Boost that his secretary rang to say that a man named Franz Lorbach wanted to see him. Lorbach was a small, pale man with a weak chin. And what he wanted to report was that Werner Boost was a mass murderer. Eynck quotes him as saying: 'He's a monster, an ogre. I'm in his power – hypnotized by him. He forces me to do things I don't want to . . .'

He told Eynck that for more than three years, Boost had been preying on courting couples in the woods. At first, he only robbed them, while Lorbach looked on. Then he began forcing the couples to take drugs that would stupefy them, and he and Lorbach would rape the women. One car they approached in January 1953, contained two men – although Boost did not realize this until he had wrenched open the driver's door, and shot the driver, a Dr. Servé, through the head. He ordered Lorbach to kill the other man, but Lorbach couldn't do it; he whispered to the man to lie down and sham dead, and then struck him with the butt of his gun.

In November 1955 and February 1956, there were two more murders of courting couples in the Düsseldorf area. Friedhelm Behre and Thea Kurmann were battered unconscious; the girl was raped; then the car was pushed into a disused quarry filled with water, where they drowned. Peter Falkenberg and Hildegard Klassing were killed more elaborately; he was shot, and she was given an injection of cyanide; then their car was driven into a haystack and burned.

Boost denied everything; but ballistic evidence proved that he was the killer of Dr. Servé, and he was sentenced to life imprisonment. If Lorbach's account of Boost's crimes is even half true, then Werner Boost is Germany's most spectacular criminal since Peter Kürten, the Düsseldorf sadist and mass murderer who was executed in 1931.

Strange relationship

In retrospect, this relationship with Lorbach is the strangest aspect of the case. Boost was a loner – a man, according to Lorbach, possessed by feelings of malevolence towards the human race. 'To him, killing a human being is no different to slaughtering an animal.' He didn't need an accomplice, and even if he did, Lorbach was the worst choice he could have made. Lorbach was a coward and an incompetent; once, when he'd failed to kill a female cashier on Boost's orders, he paid Boost about 600 marks 'as compensation'.

Eynck describes Lorbach as having a face like a rabbit. Boost bound Lorbach to him by giving him drugs, which may help to explain Lorbach's unwilling slavery. But it does not explain why Boost wanted such a companion. The evidence seems to indicate that, in some odd way, Boost needed Lorbach as much as Lorbach needed Boost; more, perhaps, since Lorbach hated his servitude and wanted to escape.

It was this kind of strange and seemingly inexplicable relationship that, in 1936, fascinated a young Jewish psychologist called Abraham Maslow. Maslow spent hours watching the monkeys in the Bronx Zoo, New York. Their behaviour puzzled him. To begin with, they seemed to think of nothing but sex – 'the screwing went on all the time' said Maslow. But that was more or less explainable to a Freudian. After all, Freud had asserted that sex is the basic impulse in all animals. What baffled Maslow in this simian Sodom and Gomorrah was that male apes mounted other males, females mounted other females, and on occasion, females even mounted males. Were they all 'wantons'? And then, one day, the answer struck him. It was always the highly dominant apes that mounted the less dominant ones, and it made no difference whether they were male or female. He was witnessing the ape equivalent of 'pecking order'.

This made Maslow interested in the whole phenomenon of dominance. Maybe Freud was wrong about the importance of sex.

The logical thing, Maslow decided, was to study dominance in women – the naturally undominant sex. Between 1937 and the early 40's, he made careful case studies of nearly 200 women. The results, when he published them, were so startling that psychologists did not know what to make of them.

Sexual experiments

What was so remarkable was that the women seemed to fall quite clearly into *three* groups, which Maslow labelled High Dominance, Medium Dominance, and Low Dominance. High dominance women tended to be highly sexed. Most of them masturbated without feeling guilt; they enjoyed sexual experimentation; they were promiscuous. Many had had lesbian experience. In order to achieve full sexual satisfaction, these women needed a highly dominant male. One highly dominant woman was a nymphomaniac who could have an orgasm just by looking at a man; yet with one male, she had not been able to achieve a climax because 'I just couldn't respect him.'

Medium dominance women tended to be gentle souls, altogether less experimental. They wanted to marry 'Mr. Right', and they looked for a kind, thoughtful man who would be a good home-builder. In courtship, they liked soft music and soft lights and romance; highly dominant males frightened them, and struck them as brutal.

Low dominance women did not really like sex at all; they thought it was dirty, to be indulged in only for the purpose of producing children. They considered the male sex organ to be crude and ugly. (High dominance women found it beautiful.) they wanted the kind of man who would admire them from a distance.

One interesting point to emerge was that *all* women preferred a man of slightly higher dominance than themselves – not *too* domineering or he frightened them. In keeping with this, high dominance males tended to find medium dominance females sentimental and sloppy; as to low dominance woman, they might take them to bed, given the chance, but they would never experience much personal involvement.

A couple in history who appeared to have shared the right and mutually satisfying 'domination relationship' were the Duke and Duchess of Marlborough. The Duke was a professional soldier renowned for his brilliant use of mobility and fire-power. He gained a number of famous victories, the most notable being his defeat of the French and Bavarians at the Bavarian village of

Blenheim in 1704. On returning home from these triumphs, he found that dominance and sex went together as naturally as powder and shot. And his wife the Duchess contentedly recorded in her diary: 'My lord returned from the war today and pleasured me twice in his top boots.'

In the sphere of crime, dominance-based partnerships are usually of a lethal and destructive nature. When a high dominance personality, with criminal tendencies, decides to form an alliance with a medium dominance personality – simply for the pleasure of having a slave and disciple – the result can be highly explosive. For crime *is* a way of asserting dominance, and the submissiveness of the slave leads the Master to seek out new ways of expressing his power. The history of crime is full of these relationships between high and medium dominance personalities.

Apart from two cases dealt with in this book, 'Granite Woman' Ruth Snyder and her corset salesman lover, Judd Gray; and Ian Brady and Myra Hindley, the British Moors murderers – there are many examples of a warped relationship between a highly dominant criminal and a mainly undominant accomplice. The partnership of Martha Beck and Raymond Fernandez – a petty confidence swindler who specialized in swindling love-hungry American widows out of their savings – became internationally known as 'The Lonely Hearts Killers'. Martha, a fat and oversexed nurse, was also a dominant and unpleasant personality – she had been deprived of the custody of her children for ill-treating them – but not a criminal. And it was Martha who decided to join Fernandez in his swindling activities – and who also decided that the victims should die so they couldn't complain.

But the Manson case is certainly the most bizarre example of dominance murder. When Charles Manson came to San Francisco in 1967, he was 33 years old, and had spent most of his adult life in jail for petty crimes. Later publicity portrayed him as a demonic, Svengali-like figure with smouldering eyes; in fact, he attracted followers by his gentleness, charm, and intelligence. There was something of the Charlie Chaplin tramp about him, the slightly comic man-of-sorrows, permanently bullied by the world.

Like Brady and Loeb, he preached a superman philosophy, derived mainly from a science fiction novel by the American author Robert Heinlein, *Stranger in a Strange Lane*. The disciples gathered round, and Manson (whose name, as one of his girls pointed out, meant Man's Son) led them around California like a new messiah, preaching universal love and the innocence of the senses.

As he became accustomed to this new role, Manson began to dream of fame; he wanted to 'be somebody', an influence like Bob Dylan or the Maharishi, the Indian mystic who, for a time, influenced and guided the Beatles. But all his efforts to become a singing star and launch long-playing records came to nothing.

He began to preach revolution, the overthrow of society, the destruction of the 'pigs' and capitalists. He was the 'leader'; his 'family' accepted him almost as a kind of god; he had to *do* something to prove himself worthy of their devotion. And so he ordered his followers to commit murder – of the pop musician Gary Hinman, of the film star Sharon Tate and her house guests, of the supermarket owner Leno LaBianca and his wife.

Desire for thrills

In the second half of the twentieth century, the pattern of murder seems to be changing. The Leopold and Loeb 'superman' murder – in which the two young Chicago students went out and killed 14-year-old Bobbie Franks for 'kicks' – was labelled 'the crime of the century' by journalists of the 1920's. They found the case unique and without apparent motive. The killers came from wealthy families and had no obvious reasons for frustration.

But, seen in the light of Loeb's dominance over his more intellectual but less prepossessing partner, the crime – and its motive – becomes comparatively easy to comprehend. Curiosity, the desire for 'thrills', the need to prove themselves 'better' and less 'bourgeois' than their friends and relatives drove them to murder. Without Loeb's nagging, jeering and ever-present 'superiority' over him – it is doubtful if Leopold would ever have been anything more dangerous than a scholar too bright and insufficiently creative for his own – and other people's – good. The yearning to act in a criminal way would have been there; but he would never have acted alone.

Our problem today, then, is to ensure, as far as possible, that the dominant one and the one who wishes to be dominated are kept apart. Until that is done, partnerships as deadly as those of Leopold and Loeb, Snyder and Gray, Brady and Hindley, will be a menace in our midst – a menace that could strike at any of us, anywhere and at any time.

DRUGS

One night in 1957, a 17-year-old chemist named Humphry Davy was heating a mixture of damp iron filing and nitric acid. Cautiously, he bent forward to sniff the retort. The gas smelt sweetish, and seemed to have no ill-effect – which surprised him, since he had been warned it could kill. He sniffed more deeply, and was suddenly filled with a sensation of lightness. There was a buzzing noise in his ears, and objects in the room seemed to be getting bigger and falling towards him. Oddly enough, he was not alarmed; on the contrary, he felt a tremendous gaiety, and burst out laughing. Then he passed out. When he woke up, he exclaimed: 'What a wonderful discovery! Laughing gas.'

When he published the discovery four years later – in a book called *Medicinal Gases* – it launched him on the road to fame. Laughing gas – or 'nitrous air', as its discoverer, Joseph Priestley, had called it – became a craze. The apparatus was cheap, the chemicals easily obtainable. Unfortunately, they were often impure: the nitrous oxide gas became contaminated with the deadly nitrogen peroxide. Many people were poisoned; some died. And the gas-sniffing craze ended as suddenly as it had begun. Humphry Davy didn't know it, but he had inaugurated the Age of Drugs.

Opium mixture

It is true that the world had known about drugs for a long time – alcohol, opium, hashish, tobacco. But no one thought of them as particularly harmful. For example, a mixture of opium and alcohol could be bought in any apothecary's shop; it was called laudanum, and parents gave it to their children to make them sleep. A few years after the publication of Davy's book, a young writer suffering from toothache bought laudanum at a druggist's in London's Oxford Street. Its effect on him was a revelation.

'What a resurrection! . . . what an apocalypse . . . That my pains had vanished was now a trifle in my eyes; this negative effect was swallowed up by the immensity of those positive effects which had opened before me, in the abyss of divine enjoyment thus suddenly revealed.'

His name was Thomas De Quincey; and he was to discover – to his cost – that these excursions into the 'abyss of divine enjoyment' left behind a feeling of dullness and languor. Although he lived to be 74, and wrote the celebrated *Murder Considered as one of the Fine Arts*, most of his work was in short reviews and essays. Laudanum robbed the famous 'English opium eater' of the stamina to write the great books he dreamed of. And despite his *Confessions of an English Opium Eater*, no one considered opium as any more dangerous than alcohol.

In 1803, at about the same time that De Quincey was taking his first dose of laudanum, a young German chemist's assistant named Friedrich Wilhelm Sertürner was experimenting with opium in an attempt to isolate its 'sleep-giving' component. One day, he poured ammonia over the opium, and was startled to see white crystals forming in the liquid. He tried this white powder on his dog, and it fell asleep. He then invited three friends to join him in an experiment; they sat around a table, and each took half a grain of the powder. It produced a sense of warmth and delight. A second half a grain made them feel deliciously sleepy and happy; a third half a grain put them into a deep sleep, from which they woke up vomiting. They had taken an overdose of morphine – for this was the name that Sertürner gave to his drug, from the Greek word 'morpheus' – sleep.

So, for the first time, men became aware of the deadly nature of the magical painkiller. Those who took repeated quantities built up a resistance to it, and needed larger doses. If withdrawn from it, they went through agonies; and if they continued feeding themselves increasingly larger doses, they degenerated and died.

In the 1850's, there were sudden hopes of a solution to the problem of morphine addiction. A German doctor called Scherzer came back from Peru with some leaves of a plant called 'coca'; the Indians of Peru would chew this, and could then endure the most severe fatigues. Dr. Albert Niemann isolated its basic constituent in the laboratory, and gave it the name cocaine. American doctors tried using the drug on morphine addicts – and it seemed to free them of the craving for morphine. Until they realized that it did this by setting up a new addiction to cocaine. . . .

Greatest killer

In 1898, another German chemist finally isolated the most dangerous of the alkaloids derived from opium – heroin – which proved to be the greatest killer of all. By this time, everyone realized that the real problem was not the drug, but the people who trafficked in it. And the world's chief drug trafficker was, unfortunately, also its most powerful seagoing nation – Britain.

The British discovered opium when they invaded India. Its use had been known since the days of Homer (who refers to it), but the Indians, with their misery and poverty, were the first to make large scale use of it. By 1830, the East India Company had a monopoly on Indian opium. Having discovered that India was so profitable, the British wanted to trade with China. But the Chinese were traditionally isolationist; with their rigid hierarchies and ancient customs, they didn't want anything to do with the white man.

So, with typical cunning, the natives of 'Perfidious Albion' used opium as a lever to open the door into China. Their ships sailed to Macao, and traded their opium for tea. The opium went up river to the sacred city of Canton, where no white man was allowed to set foot. Soon, the Cantonese were so hooked on opium that the British had to supply it in bulk.

A wealthy group of Cantonese called the Hong merchants became the go-betweens. The British (and American) ships would anchor down river at Macao. The Hong merchants would go on board and do their business, then hordes of junks would take the chests of opium – weighing more than a hundredweight each – back to Canton. They would bring tea in exchange. The ships would then set sail, duly chased by vessels of the Chinese navy, which fired salvoes after them.

This was strictly a game – in fact, the British ships lagged to give the Chinese a chance to send their shots whistling near their bows. The Hong merchants then reported to the Emperor that once again the wicked foreigners had been repelled by the imperial navy. All would be peaceful until the next year, when the British returned with another four or five million pounds' worth of opium.

For years this comedy was played out, to the mutual satisfaction of both sides. Then, in 1838, The Emperor appointed a rigidly honest official called Lin Tsê-hsü to stop the traffic. This was a major mistake. Lin seized more than a thousand tons of opium and dumped it in the river. The enraged British government sent in the Royal Navy. It went up and down the coast, bombarding Chinese towns, and captured the island of Chusan. The Chinese troops, with their bows and arrows, were mown down. The humiliated Emperor had to backpedal. He paid the British six million dollars in compensation for the destroyed opium, and gave them the port of Hong Kong. When the first 'Opium War' ended in 1842, the Chinese also had to pay another twenty-one million dollars compensation. They now had opium on the doorstep – flooding in through Hong Kong.

At first, the Chinese mixed their opium with tobacco; later, they invented the opium pipe. Like the Indians, they proved to be highly susceptible to this new drug. The reason, quite simply, was poverty. When any nation has widespread poverty, and some cheap drug that is easy to obtain, the result is bound to be widespread addiction. The same thing happened in London in the 1690's with the introduction of gin. By 1914, about a half of the population of China used opium. The new opium derivative, heroin, was also entering in vast quantities – one Dutch firm alone was shipping in 4,600 pounds a year. (At present day prices worth half a *billion* dollars.)

Foreign devils

No wonder, therefore, the Chinese felt that the 'foreign devils' were sapping their lifeblood, and periodically rebelled and slaughtered every white man they could lay their hands on. It is a typical irony of history that the heroin which is now proving such a menace to the civilizations of Europe and America should be flooding in from the East – through the 'Asiatic connection'.

In 1853, Dr. Alexander Wood invented one more aid to the 'decline of the West' – a hypodermic syringe for the injection of morphine. By the 1880's, the most famous fictional detective of all time, Sherlock Holmes, was injecting himself with doses of morphine and cocaine, and explaining to the horrified Dr. Watson that it saved him from boredom. Even at that late date, the average European and American failed to recognize the gravity of the drug menace.

It took America until 1914 to pass legislation – the Harrison Act – against the illegal flow of narcotics into the country. By that time, addiction was already widespread – *one American in every four hundred was an addict*. The act had the effect of lowering this to one in every four thousand. Harry J. Anslinger, then head of the Bureau of Narcotics, described how, as a child (around 1904), he was sent to urgently buy morphine at the local druggist's; a female addict was screaming with agony in the upstairs room of a farmhouse. The druggist handed the morphine to the 12-year-old boy without question.

In 1930 – when Anslinger became a Commissioner of Narcotics in the newly formed Federal Bureau of Narcotics – the Chinese were still the chief opium traders in the United States, and there were opium dens in just about every large city. In those days, in spite of the example of Al Capone, the average American still thought of the typical underworld gangster as a sinister Chinaman with a dragon tattooed on his arm.

It was the world of Fu Manchu. The 'tongs' had started in the gold fields in the 1850's, and spread to New York, San Francisco, and every other city with a Chinese quarter. The word made people shudder. The 'hatchet men' of the tongs had a reputation for sadistic brutality; a man who offended them, or refused to pay protection money, might be found staked out in his own sitting room, bleeding from a thousand cuts.

Anslinger started by raiding the 30 or so opium dens in Washington, D.C. The Chinese found it unbelievable; they had been operating for so long they couldn't imagine being closed down. Even though the word got around that the police were acting, the dens stayed open, and were in full operation when detectives marched in.

One of the chief spurs to Anslinger's assault on the opium dens was sexual scandal involving white girls – many of them teenagers of good families. The roaring twenties, with their speakeasies and bootleg gin, had liberated them. They found visits to Chinatown thrilling, and their first experiences of opium smoking delightful. As soon as they were hooked, they were persuaded to take part in sexual orgies.

Pretty white girls

The Chinese, according to Anslinger, put a high premium on pretty, cultured, white girls, the kind who would normally get engaged to a husky college boy from an upper-class family. Many of the girls were unconscious when they lost their virginity. If their new way of life worried them, they were soothed and relaxed by special capsules handed out by Joe Sing, the Chinaman in whose apartment the Washington orgies took place. The capsules contained heroin. As soon as the victims became dependent, they were sent to 'parties' with other girls, at which their 'clients' were Chinese.

It was not too difficult to put the clamps on the Chinese opium dens. But the effects were not wholly desirable. The bootleg era was coming to an end, and the Irish and Italian mobsters were growing unpopular with the American public; events like the St. Valentine's Day Massacre in Chicago had made them too notorious. When Capone was arrested for carrying a gun in 1929, the gangs saw that the bad old days were over. The original Mafia (or Black Hand) was controlled by Italian gangsters who believed in looking out for themselves – 'Mustache Petes', the new generation called them.

Riddled with bullets

One of the up and coming young men was a Sicilian named Salvatore Luciano – later better known as Lucky Luciano; he believed it was a mistake to be a loner. His boss, Joe Masseria – the man who had given him his underworld training – took the opposite view. One night, after a large meal with Luciano, Masseria was riddled with bullets. (Luciano was out washing his hands at the time.) And Lucky's views found many converts at that dinner on September 11, 1931.

Between 30 and 40 Mustache Petes were murdered across America, in anticipation of Hitler's 'night of the long knives'. The old Mafia vanished; a new organization – sometimes known as the Syndicate, sometimes as Murder Incorporated, sometimes as the Unione Siciliano – sprang up across the United States. Gangsterism ceased to be a matter of public scandal; it became quietly 'legal' and mobs throughout the country co-operated.

Many of the old Mustache Petes had refused to touch drugs. Luciano, however, had always trafficked in drugs, although his main interest was prostitution – using the drugs to hook recruits. But now the Volstead Act was repealed and prohibition was no longer in force, the mobsters had to find other ways of making money. There were various forms of 'protection' – in the docks, in the garment industry. There was gambling. And there was heroin. Luciano, in partnership with Louis Buchalter (known as Lepke), operated in all these lucrative fields.

The drugs operation became big business in 1935 – when three racketeers living in the Bronx grew tired of the drudgery involved in processing their own heroin with homemade equipment, and asked Lepke to join them in smuggling heroin from China. Lepke knew how to go about it. He bribed two customs officials to supply him with the stamps used to indicate that a piece of luggage has been inspected. A trunk packed with heroin would then be unloaded at the dock. Its owner would casually sit down on it for a moment. When he moved away, the appropriate customs stamp would be in place, and a porter would then take the trunk to a waiting vehicle.

A resentful ex-ladyfriend 'squealed' on Lepke. Anslinger's men moved in and made arrests. Lepke himself disappeared – and then proceeded to cover his tracks by a campaign of mass murder. He had the money to pay Murder Incorporated assassins to kill potential witnesses against him. An equally effective method, with family men, was to kill one of their children, with the threat that the same would happen to the others. As the Narcotics operatives felt Lepke slipping through their fingers, they turned the full heat on the underworld; a campaign of nonstop raids and harassments.

It worked. The gang bosses, tired of all this activity, sent messages to Lepke that if he didn't give himself up, they would see to it that his corpse was delivered to Anslinger. Accordingly, he surrendered. It took Anslinger until 1944 to see justice done, but he finally had the satisfaction of seeing Lepke go to the electric chair.

Luciano was also removed from the mobs' scene in 1936 – charged with organizing prostitution on a grand scale. He went to jail for a 50-year term, but was released in 1945, on payment of a large donation to the Republican Party funds and deported to Sicily. (He had also organized an effective anti-sabotage campaign – from inside prison – which had substantially aided the American war effort.) But the removal of Luciano and Lepke made no difference to the drugs racket. For even in these early days it brought in larger sums of money than gambling or protection. A consignment of heroin that cost $100,000 could be resold in 1936 for $5,000,000. (Nowadays, with the price at $100,000 a kilo, it would fetch $500,000,000.)

The 'China connection' was by no means the most important. In the 1920's, before the authorities were fully aware of the dangers of heroin, an international businessman named Elias Eliopoulos had large quantities of opium shipped from China to France – where it was processed, quite legally, in French drugs factories. When the government finally decided to make this illegal, Eliopoulos persuaded the factories to move to Istanbul, Turkey, where the trade flourished.

The new ruler of Turkey, Kemal Ataturk, closed these factories at Christmas 1931. But Turkey was a poor country; opium was big business. The factories moved to remoter parts of the country, where they were no longer under the eye of Kemal, and the fields of Turkey began to produce vast quantities of poppies.

In the late 1960's, the Turkish government finally began to respond to U.S. pressure to clamp down on opium. But by then it was too late – far too late. World production of opium was up to 1,200 tons a year, and in the United States, drug addiction was back to its old 1914 level – one addict in every four hundred people. (But the population has more than doubled since 1914.) Nearly 60 per cent of the world's opium production came from the 'drugs triangle' in the highlands of Burma, Thailand and Laos.

In fact, during the Vietnam war, the American forces actively encouraged the production of opium in these remote areas, because it brought prosperity and kept the peasants anti-Communist. Ironically, there is very little heroin addiction in Turkey, or south-east Asia – possibly because the pressures of modern life have not yet sent the demand soaring.

In 1943, a new chapter in the history of drugs opened in the Sandoz Chemical Works in Basle, Switzerland. A chemist named Albert Hofmann had synthesized a substance called lysergic acid diethylamide – LSD for short. On April 16, he began to feel dizzy, and went home. Like Humphry Davy and Friedrich Sertürner before him, he experienced strange and marvellous sensations – dazzling images and colours, a kind of delirium. He had breathed in only 100 micrograms of LSD – enough to induce 'visions'.

Hallucinogens
After the war, American psychologists began to experiment with the new 'Hallucinogens' – including a closely related drug, mescalin. It seemed harmless and nonaddictive, and the writer Aldous Huxley, who tried it in 1953, recommended that it should become as freely available as tobacco or alcohol, since it was less harmful than either.

When the young generation of hippies discovered how easy it was to manufacture, LSD became almost as freely available as alcohol. Only then was it recognized that, even if LSD is not addictive, it *is* liable to create psychosis, and lead to violence. In just over a decade, LSD has become as popular among the younger generation in the United States as opium was in China 150 years ago.

Under the Nixon administration, the budget of the Narcotics Bureau has been increased from $78 million to over $500 million, and new drug laws have made it possible for a 'pusher' to go to jail for life. The immediate effects, however, were counterproductive: they clogged the courts with a backlog of cases, and pushed up the price of heroin.

The world was as far away as ever from the solution of its drugs problem.

DUAL PERSONALITY

There is a popular misconception that the word 'schizophrenia' means 'split personality'. This is not so; it means a loss of contact with reality. The schizophrenic feels as if he is separated from reality by an invisible glass wall. On the other hand, all psychologists recognize that there *is* such a phenomenon as 'dual personality', although there is some disagreement about its cause. A genuine dual personality is a rarity.

Dr. Pritchard, the Victorian poisoner, has been called 'the benevolent monster'; but this was *not* because he was a Jekyll and Hyde. He was a weakling, a braggart and a liar, whose chief desire was to be famous; he poisoned his wife – and her mother – because he was tired of being married and wanted to be free to pursue his affairs with servant girls. Those two eminent burglars, Deacon Brodie and Charlie Peace, are altogether closer to the authentic dual personality, for while they burgled by night, they genuinely wanted to be respectable – and respected – citizens by day.

As Robert Louis Stevenson recognized in his story of Jekyll and Hyde, the man with a split personality is to be pitied. Stevenson wrote the book in 1886, before psychologists had the basic concepts for understanding the workings of the 'divided man'. These were provided by Sigmund Freud, with his recognition that the subconscious mind is an enormous hidden realm, containing impulses and desires that may be foreign to the conscious personality. Freud also formulated the classic theory of 'suppression', whereby some 'illicit' desire or thought may be instantly thrust into the depths of the subconscious – only to fester there, like a splinter, until it erupts in the form of mental illness or some unexplainable voilence. In Freud's view, most of these 'suppressions' are sexual, although there are others – for example, death wishes directed against people who are close to us, and whom we may consciously love and respect.

Suppressed desire

The German sexologist Dr. Magnus Hirschfeld cites a typical example of the sudden eruption of suppressed desire. The patient was a 35-year-old doctor, who had been subject to fits of epilepsy and of sleepwalking since childhood. The doctor was treating a 13-year-old schoolgirl for eczema, which covered her whole body. Hirschfeld writes:

'He sat on the settee, drawing the child's head down to him; during this act, her whole body approached his and induced in him sexual excitement accompanied by an erection. He now pressed the child close to himself. Of the rest of his actions, the defendant has no clear recollections. When he came to himself, he was sitting on the settee, with the child, now in tears, standing between his legs.' During this blackout, the doctor had made the child turn with her back to him, then inserted his penis between her closed thighs, and moved it back and forth until he induced an orgasm. The account ends: 'His mind did not clear until he reached his flat.'

Of course, it is possible that the doctor invented the story of the blackout. But it is just as likely that it is genuine. His fits of sleepwalking indicate that he had an unusually active subconscious mind. Epilepsy is a convulsive seizure due to electrical discharge of the brain; when the 'discharge' occurs, the subject usually becomes unconscious, but may writhe in convulsions, foam at the mouth, or even attempt violence against another person.

Sexual excitement

Dr. Grey Walter has cited a case of a man who, whenever he went to the cinema, had to fight off a strong impulse to strangle the person sitting next to him. On one occasion, he 'came to' with his hands around his neighbour's throat. It was discovered that these seizures – epileptic in nature – were caused by the rate of flicker of the film. It is quite conceivable that, in the case of the doctor cited by Hirschfeld, his sexual excitement 'triggered' a seizure; in a semi-somnambulistic state, he committed the offence against the child, then 'woke up' – although he was still only partly conscious.

The 'Sydney Mutilator', William Macdonald – discussed in the chapter on homosexual killers – described his murder of a man he had casually picked up. He woke up in the middle of the night and picked up a knife. 'As I stood looking at him, with the knife grasped firmly in my hand, a mad rage came over me. I knelt down and stabbed him in the neck . . . I struck down at him again and again. During the stabbing, I accidentally struck my own hand, and then I lost count of how many times I thrust the knife into his body. Even after I knew he was dead, I kept on plunging the knife into him.'

This description certainly suggests that Macdonald had some form of seizure, not unlike that of the man in the cinema. Many criminal activities are associated with a brain wave known as the theta rhythm. These waves were first noticed in young children, and they became pronounced when the child experienced emotions of pleasure or pain.

Theta rhythms could be easily evoked in a small child by offering a sweet and then snatching it away. In adults, these rhythms play a very small part – except in aggressive psychopaths. Grey Walter comments about this sudden murderous violence towards other people, or animals: 'These destructive or murderous episodes were often almost or completely unmotivated by ordinary standards.'

This is not, of course, to suggest that psychopathic violence – like Macdonald's – is *caused* in some way by theta waves, as an epileptic attack is caused by an electrical discharge. Possibly the theta waves appear when the psychopath induces a certain state of mind in himself: Macdonald had decided to kill the man before he went to sleep, and the 'blind rage' came over him after he had picked up the knife. He had somehow *triggered* the attack in the way that a normal person can trigger sexual excitement by directing the thoughts towards sex.

But all this – like the discoveries about the amygdaloid nucleus in the brain, the source of our aggressive instincts – suggests that many violent killers may be suffering from some *physical* imbalance of the same kind that makes some people abnormally active and others sluggish and dull. And it could be connected with the kind of hormone activity that turns some women into nymphomaniacs and some men into 'satyrs'.

This speculation is suggested by the fact that so many 'Jekyll and Hyde' crimes *are* sexual. A quiet young Sunday school superintendent named Theodore Durrant, genuinely devoted to the local Baptist Church in San Francisco, invites a pretty girl into the church, strangles her, drags her to the belfry and rapes her, then leaves the body neatly laid out with a block under the head. Ten days later he takes another girl into the church library, has intercourse with her – apparently with her agreement – but still murders her and leaves her body behind a door.

Overpowering urge

It is senseless; if he is simply a sex maniac why doesn't he lure the girls to some remote spot? And why doesn't he try to hide the bodies? Obviously, he is taken over by a 'second self' – like Ed Gein, the kind little baby sitter of Wisconsin who was overcome twice a year by the overpowering urge to dig up female corpses, violate them, and make waistcoast of their skins . . . .

The Jekyll and Hyde syndrome can also be seen clearly in the case of the Chicago murderer William Heirens, only 18 years old at the time of his arrest. Heirens had been sent to various correctional institutions for burglary. The motive was sexual – he broke in to steal women's underwear, and when he was finally caught, the attic of his house was found to be full of stolen panties. He soon reached the stage where actually climbing in through an open window could induce sexual excitement, and even orgasm.

On October 1, 1945, the 16-year-old Heirens – already a powerfully built, good-looking boy – broke into the apartment of a nurse, and when she interrupted him, struck her with an iron bar and tied her to a chair. He then left and went back to his classes at the University of Chicago, where he was known as a brilliant student. The police found fingerprints, and wondered whether the sturdy youth could have been responsible for an unsolved murder that had taken place the previous June. A 43-year-old divorcee, Josephine Ross, had been found in bed in her North Side apartment, her throat cut and with many stab wounds; it looked as if she had been attacked by a burglar.

Then, on December 10, 1945, a maid entered the sixth-floor apartment in the Pine Crest Residential Hotel and discovered a body draped over the bath tub. It was Frances Brown, and she had been shot and stabbed. Apparently she had walked naked out of the bathroom and bumped into a burglar. Above the bed someone had scrawled in lipstick: 'For God's sake catch me before I kill more. I cannot control myself.'

The odd thing was that the killer had dragged the body to the bath and washed off the bloodstains. Just as the blood had been washed off the body of Mrs. Ross with wet towels. The detective in charge of the case warned his men: 'He will kill again unless we catch him.'

A month later, on January 7, 1946, the parents of six-year-old Suzanne Degnan went to her bedroom and found she was missing from her bed. A ransom note demanded $20,000, and ordered, 'Burn this for her safety.' Police searched the area, and

Suzanne's head was found in a sewer. In other local sewers, police found more parts of her body. The killer had carried her down a ladder, into a nearby basement, and there strangled and dismembered her. He had then carefully washed the pieces of the body before disposing of them.

The murders ceased for several months. On June 26, 1946, a janitor reported a young burglar in an empty apartment on the North side; then he and another tenant tried to tackle the youth as he ran away. The man fired shots at them, but with the help of the police was finally overpowered. This was William Heirens, and at police headquarters he explained that the murders were committed by a man called George. However, he admitted, he and George were simply aspects of the same personality.

Violent explosion

'George' periodically took over. On one occasion, Heirens had locked his clothes in the washroom and thrown the key inside so he would be unable to go out on a burgling expedition; but 'George' was too strong; he crawled along the house gutter to get the key, and went out. He explained that his tension during a burglary was so great that if anyone interrupted him, he exploded into violence. Heirens was sentenced to three consecutive life terms in prison.

Was Heirens a true 'Jekyll and Hyde', or was George merely an invention? Both could be true. George was a fantasy that Heirens invented to explain his own dual personality. It is impossible to know precisely how much control he had over this criminal alter-ego. In one of the most famous cases of dual personality, an American housewife named Eve was periodically 'taken over' by a brash, sexy, empty-headed female who loved a good time. Thigpen and Cleckley, describing the case in their book *The Three Faces of Eve*, call the two 'personalities' Eve White and Eve Black. When 'Eve White' was taken over, she simply lost consciousness, and had no idea of what 'Eve Black' did in her absence from her own body.

Dr. Morton Prince had described an equally baffling case of the late 1890s: a girl named Christine Beauchamp who, under hypnosis, became a totally different personality. The new personality called herself 'Sally', and apparently had a completely separate existence from Christine. Christine would wake up from a kind of amnesia – once in a strange city – and have to find out what Sally had been doing in her absence. This case was further complicated by the emergence of a third, totally distinct,

personality who loathed 'Sally'; the three 'women' spent most of
their time struggling for possession of Christine's body. Both
Christine and 'Eve' were eventually cured through hypnosis and
other treatment.

Now Heirens may have 'invented' George. But why did he
write 'For God's sake catch me before I kill more' over Frances
Brown's bed? Why did he leave fingerprints in several of the
apartments, as if in a frenzied or semi-dazed state? It is impossible to doubt that, in some sense, he *was* two people.

Many Jekyll and Hyde murders have been the result of brain
injury or physical degeneration. The Chinaman Lock Ah Tam
was known as a kindly, reasonable businessman until a drunken
sailor struck him on the head with a billiard cue, knocking him
senseless; after that he became subject to sudden fits of blind
rage, which ended, in 1925, with the murder of most of his
family.

William Hepper was an artist and an ex. B.B.C. translator,
whose behaviour became unpredictable after a car accicent in
which he received head injuries. Hepper's wife – from whom he
was separated – was a friend of the parents of an 11-year-old
girl, Margaret Spevick, and when the child broke her arm in
February 1954 the parents were persuaded to allow him to take
Margaret to Hove, Sussex, to stay in his flat, where, he claimed,
there was a resident nurse.

Unfinished portrait
They knew Hepper as a reliable elderly man – he was 63 – and
apparently felt no misgivings. Four days later, Mrs. Spevick
went to Brighton to see her daughter, arranging to meet her at
the station; but neither Margaret nor Hepper were there. She
went on to the flat in Western Avenue, Hove, and there found
the strangled and raped body of her daughter on a divan;
nearby, on an easel, there was an unfinished portrait of her.

Hepper was eventually caught in a hotel in Irun, on the
Spanish frontier. The defence at his trial argued that he was
suffering from hallucinations and loss of memory, and it *was*
clear that this normally serious, balanced man was periodically
subject to violent personality changes. But the jury found him
guilty, and he was executed.

Undoubtedly, one of the most curious cases of a Jekyll and
Hyde personality of recent years is that of the Jersey rapist,
Edward Paisnel. Just before midnight on Saturday, July 10,
1971, two Jersey policemen were sitting in their patrol car at a

traffic light when another car hurtled across the road in front of them against the amber light. They decided to give chase to the car, which was heading towards St. Helier: they suspected it might have been stolen for a joyride by local youths. The driver ignored their signals to stop, struck an oncoming car a glancing blow, and roared off at 70 miles an hour. He began weaving from side to side to prevent the police from overtaking. Finally, after a chase of many miles, he turned into a private road, ran through a fence and across a garden, and into a field of tomatoes. The occupant leapt out and ran; one of the policemen brought him down with a rugger tackle.

At the police station they discovered that the man – who was middle-aged – had rows of nails, their points outward, sewn to the lapels of his jacket. In his pockets they found a wig, a rubber face mask, and adhesive tape. The police realized suddenly that they had at last caught the man who had been committing rape on the island for many years – perhaps as many as 14.

He was Edward John Louis Paisnel. Back at his home – a farmhouse called Maison du Soleil – they discovered a secret room behind a bookcase; it contained a raffia cross, more masks, coats with nails, and black magic paraphernalia. When asked about this, Paisnel replied: 'My master would laugh very long and loud about this.' His 'master' was the devil, and it later turned out that Paisnel was obsessed by Gilles de Rais, burned in 1440 for the murders of more than 50 children.

Peculiar rape pattern

The pattern of the crimes had been peculiar. In November 1957, three women had been attacked by a man with a knife, and one was sexually assaulted. In April 1958, a man threw a rope round the neck of a girl, dragged her into a field and raped her. In October 1958, a girl was dragged from a cottage and raped. The attacks ceased until 1960, and police hoped they had stopped. But then, in January 1960, they took an altogether more alarming turn. A 10-year-old girl woke up to find a man in her bedroom. He warned her that if she cried out he would shoot both her parents. He then sexually assaulted her in her own bed, and left by the window, driving off in her father's car. When she told her brothers the next morning, they were inclined to believe that she had dreamed it all – a feature that recurred in some of the later cases.

A month later, a man entered the bedroom of a 12-year-old boy, made him go out with him to a field, and committed a sexual assault. The rapist then took the boy back to the house and back to his bedroom. This was perhaps the oddest feature of all. Why should he risk being caught? It seemed that, once he had committed his assault, the rapist became apologetic.

For the next 11 years, Jersey became an island of terror. Householders had bolts and bars put on windows. In March 1960 a 24-year-old air hostess, waiting at a bus stop, was dragged into a field and raped. On April 27, a woman whose husband was in hospital heard a noise in the middle of the night and found a man in her kitchen. The woman's 14-year-old daughter came downstairs, and a rope was thrown around her throat. She was dragged out to a nearby field and raped, then allowed to go home.

In this, as in many succeeding attacks, it became clear that the rapist had studied the house, and knew how to achieve his object with the minimum of risk. He often wore the terrifying rubber mask. Usually, the children were too frightened to scream; the man would commit a sexual assault and then courteously escort them back to their bedrooms. In some cases, penetration was minimal – he was evidently worried about hurting his victims – but at least one girl became pregnant. When 11-year-old Joy Norton was found stabbed to death in September 1965, it was feared that the rapist had at last turned to murder; but it was discovered that she had been sexually abused over a period of years, and her elder brother was charged with her murder.

And so the rape and assaults continued, usually at the rate of one or two a year, until Paisnel was caught. One man who was generally suspected of the assaults had been so ostracized that he had been forced to leave the island. Altogether, Paisnel was charged with seven sexual assaults, including rape and sodomy. Found guilty, he was sentenced to 30 years' imprisonment. But what baffled all those who knew him was that the kind Edward Paisnel, the man who genuinely loved children, and often played Father Christmas at parties, should also be the rapist who had terrorized the island.

Was Paisnel genuinely a devil-worshipper? The question is perhaps irrelevant. The Jekyll and Hyde personality is one of the great mysteries of psychology. But at least, thanks to Freud, Jung and other psychologists, we now know more than Dr. Prince knew about Christine Beauchamp. If present-day advances continue, it is hopeful that Mr. Hyde will be banished from the soul, and the beneficent Dr. Jekyll will be in control.

FAMILIES OF DEATH

One of the most bizarre cases in criminal history is also the earliest British murder case of which there is a detailed record. And the details are so incredible that they sound like the plot of a horror film. Anyone who knows the highlands of Scotland realizes that there is something frightening about those great tracts of bleak hillside and boggy valleys – a touch of the emptiness of the Sahara Desert. In the year 1400, the whole of Scotland was like this, from John O'Groats to the border. 'Glasgow' means 'dark glen', and it was little more than that; even the city of Edinburgh, later the seat of the royal family, was hardly larger than a modern country town.

Reign of terror
It was in the reign of James I of Scotland that the people of Galloway were subjected to a reign of terror. Travellers were vanishing – so many of them that the natives at first suspected packs of wolves. But there were no wolves – in that bleak country they would have starved to death. And even wolves would have left behind some sign of their presence – bloodstained clothing, or the bones of a horse. There were no such signs; the travellers had simply vanished.

Alarmed by the situation, the king sent his officers to investigate the natives. Several suspicious looking tramps were arrested, and hanged just to be on the safe side. A number of inn-keepers fell under suspicion, and were also executed. But the 'vanishings' went on. They continued for so many years that some people reached the conclusion there were supernatural forces at work – werewolves, or perhaps the Devil himself.

One day, a man and his wife were returning from a village fair, both riding on the same horse. Suddenly, a wild looking man leapt out of the bushes at the side of the road, and seized the horse's bridle. The horseman was well armed; he pulled out his pistol, and fired. There was a yell, and suddenly the horse seemed to be surrounded by savages. The man drew his cutlass and slashed at them, spurring his steed. His wife screamed as she was pulled off from behind him. One of the creatures slashed her throat with a knife. The man was dragged to the ground. And, at that moment, rescue belatedly arrived.

A crowd of about 30 people, travelling from the same fair, came round the corner. What they saw stunned them. The woman's clothes had been torn off, and someone had disembowelled her. Others were tearing at her flesh, and apparently eating it. It was like watching a pack of hunting dogs tearing a deer to pieces. The husband was still holding off other attackers with his cutlass. Someone gave a shout. Within seconds, the cannibals had vanished at incredible speed.

The woman was dead, but her husband — and the horse — were alive, the first living creatures to survive an attack from the human wolves in 25 years. It now became clear why travellers had vanished without trace. The wife's body had already been dragged a considerable distance off the road. If any traveller had passed by the spot 24 hours later, he would have noticed nothing — for by that time the bloodstains would have been indistinguishable from the brown grass and heather.

The news was carried immediately to the king in Edinburgh. Within four days, he was in Galloway, with a troop of 400 men. They went to the place on the road where the woman had been killed. There were plenty of rocks and thickets where the murderers could have hidden to waylay travellers. They then set out across the moorland, in the direction taken by the fleeing murderers.

In a short time, they arrived at the seashore. The scene was dominated by tall cliffs, and below them the sea pounded on the rocks. They waited until the tide went out, then rode along the beach, looking for any sign of habitation. There seemed to be nothing; they noticed some caves, but none of them big enough to shelter a large gang. Discouraged, they turned and went back.

Sickening smell

At this moment, however, two of the hunting dogs began barking at a small crack in the cliff face. Someone clambered up to examine it; it hardly seemed wide enough to admit a human being. But the dogs had now gone inside, and were still barking and howling with excitement — as if they had sighted their quarry. The king sent some men to the nearest village for torches, while a few of his soldiers ventured into the rocky cleft, and called out that it seemed to go deep into the cliff. Finally, the torches arrived. Led by the almost hysterical dogs, the men squeezed through the crack, and followed the winding, narrow way. A sickening smell came from inside.

Quite suddenly, the tunnel opened out into a cave. In its recesses, they could see crouching human figures, dazzled by the torchlight. In the corners, there were piles of money and jewels. And hanging from the ceiling, objects that were easily recognizable as parts of human beings – arms, legs, torsos.

Cornered in their den, the wild creatures were prepared to fight; but they were quickly overcome by the men in armour. The soldiers counted their prisoners and discovered that a family of 48 beings was crowded into the cave. It became clear why the cave dwellers had flung themselves on the murdered woman with such ravenous appetite. They were cannibals, and the unappetizing lumps of flesh were part of their larder. They ate it raw. It must have seemed a luxury for them to be able to eat fresh meat.

The soldiers buried the limbs and torsos in the sand. The savages were taken to the Tolbooth in Edinburgh (which is still standing), then to Leith. By this time it had been established that the head of the family was a man named Sawney Bean, who had been born in East Lothian, not far from Edinburgh. As a youth, he had run away with a woman, and for 25 years they had been living in the same cave. The woman had been fertile, giving him eight sons and six daughters: these, in turn, had produced eighteen grandsons and fourteen granddaughters.

Leith was their place of execution. There was no trial, 'It being thought needless to try creatures who were even professed enemies to mankind,' recorded the chronicler, John Nicholson, of Kirkcudbright. The barbarity with which the Beans were executed was typical of the period; the men's hands and feet were chopped off and they were left to bleed to death. The womenfolk, having been made to watch this, were then burned alive in three fires. 'They all in general died without the least sign of repentance,' wrote Nicholson, 'but continued cursing and vending the most dreadful imprecations to the very last gasp of life.'

In executing them without trial, the king recognized that they were wild beasts; it is a pity he could not have ordered them to be killed as cleanly as such. Civilized culture is only skin deep, and there are well authenticated cases of human babies who have been brought up by wild animals; there have been several such instances recorded in India. In one of the most remarkable, a 'wolf-child' was captured by hunters at the age of two, and taken back to civilization.

Carnivorous species

Like Kipling's Mowgli, he had been brought up by wolves since babyhood – presumably his parents were killed by them, and the baby acquired the smell of the animals, which would be enough to protect him. But the child remained a wolf for the rest of his short life. No amount of civilized training could make him behave like a human being.

There is a central lesson to be learned from the Sawney Bean family; it applies to all 'murderous families' – which explains why they are so rare in the history of crime. When people reach the extremes of desperation, they turn away from human society, and in so doing place a gap between themselves and the rest of humanity. They look upon other human beings as a farmer looks on his sheep and pigs – as a *different species*. It makes no difference whether they do this instinctively, as the Beans did, or intellectually, as Charles Manson's followers did. In a fundamental sense, they cease to be human.

It is shocking to read about Sawney Bean's family disembowelling a woman and eating her flesh in front of her husband. But it is no worse than what Manson's followers did to actress Sharon Tate and the LaBiancas. It is definitely not 'sadism', any more than the Jewish butcher is sadistic when he cuts the throat of a *kosher* animal and drains off its blood. It is basically the attitude of one carnivorous species to another. The same is true of the Bender family. They were not murderers so much as butchers.

There is a paradox in the idea of a family banding together to commit murder. Members of a family feel close to one another. They are aware of one another as human beings. In that case, they are found to be aware of their neighbours as human beings. Unless they feel desperate – fighting with their backs to the wall against the rest of society – they are unlikely to combine together for purposes of slaughter. Families like the Beans, the Benders, the Mansons, are a million-to-one chance accidents. In almost every case, the reasons for the accident are completely different. But they can be roughly classified into three groups: sadism, gain, and resentment.

Apart from the Beans, British criminal history has two cases of murderous families which fall into the first classification, sadism.

They both occurred at the same time, and in the same place: London in the mid-eighteenth century. Elizabeth Brownrigg was a midwife who treated her servant girls – supplied to her from the Foundling Hospital – with such barbarity that one of them died from the beatings. She and her husband and son were tried for the offence, and Mrs. Brownrigg died on the gallows, to the howling of an indignant mob.

Badly beaten

A few months later the London crowds had an even more sensational case to gloat over, when a mother and her daughter, both called Sarah Metyard, were tried for murder of two servant girls. Like the Brownriggs, the Metyards were given to sadistic ill-treatment of their hirelings. The mother was a milliner who lived in Bruton Street, and in 1758, five girls were handed over to her from various foundling hospitals; these included a sickly child called Anne Naylor and her sister.

Anne worked badly, and was beaten and half-starved. She tried to run away twice, and Sarah Metyard decided to tame her by cruelty. The girl was badly beaten, then made to stand upright, with her hands tied behind her back to a door handle so she couldn't sit down. After three days without food, she was allowed to crawl into bed – whereupon she expired of exhaustion. The other girls were told to go and wake her: when they said she wouldn't move, the younger Sarah Metyard, a teenager, flung herself on the body and beat it with a shoe. She soon realized that the child was dead.

For a while, the two women panicked. They decided that the best plan was to conceal the body. They locked the attic door – where the child lay – and told the other girls that Anne had run away again. That seemed to satisfy them – all except the younger sister, who had noticed that Anne's shoes and clothes were still in her room. During the next two months, she voiced her suspicions. The Metyards, who were already half insane with worry about the decomposing body behind the attic door, decided she had to die too.

They duly strangled her and hid the body. After this, they set about the gruesome task of disposing of Anne's remains, chopping them up, and wrapping the members in two bundles. An attempt to burn one of the hands made so much smell that they took the corpse out into the street, and tossed it over a wall on to the grate of a sewer. The watchman found it there next day, and the local coroner was called to look at the pieces. Since they were so decomposed, he gave it as his opinion that the body had been dug up from a churchyard. The pieces were buried, and no one suspected the Metyards. Presumably they disposed of the second body more efficiently – it was never found.

Psychological question

Four years went by and young Sarah Metyard ceased to be her mother's favourite. All the evidence indicates that Mrs. Metyard was a violent, foul-mouthed old woman who felt the world had treated her badly. A lodger called Mr. Rooker felt sorry for the daughter, and invited her to come and be his servant. The girl accepted, in spite of her mother's objections; within a short time, she was Mr. Rooker's mistress. Her mother was enraged; she called at Mr. Rooker's house every day and screamed abuse through the front door. He tried moving out to the western suburb of Ealing; but the old lady traced him, and continued to make a nuisance of herself.

One day, he let her into the house, hoping to cajole her into a less hostile mood; but she flew straight at her daughter and beat her. Angry words passed – some of which puzzled Mr. Rooker. When they had got rid of the old lady, he asked Sarah what she meant about 'killing'. Sarah told him everything. Mr. Rooker decided this was the ideal way of getting his revenge on the mother. He assumed the daughter would not be brought to trial, since she was still under age. He was mistaken. The Brownrigg scandal had made the officers of the law sensitive. And both Metyards had taken part in the disposal of the body. They were tried together, and executed at Tyburn in July 1768, one year after Elizabeth Brownrigg.

It is a psychological question of great interest whether crimes like these should be labelled sadistic. The motive behind them seems to be less a desire to inflict pain than a need to inflict 'just' punishment; probably Mrs. Metyard, like Mrs. Brownrigg, would have been outraged if anyone had accused her of *enjoying* hurting Anne Naylor. The same is certainly true of America's worst case of calculated ill-treatment, the Ocey Snead affair, which involved three highly respectable sisters.

The sisters were Caroline, Mary, and Virginia Wardlaw, daughters of a Supreme Court Justice of South Carolina. Virginia, the clever one of the family, became head of Montgomery Female College in 1900. Her two sisters lived nearby. Caroline was married to a Colonel Martin, and had a daughter named Ocey, a quiet, gentle girl; Mary, separated from her husband, had two sons, John and Fletcher. One day, John ran away with a pretty student from his aunt's college. He was pursued and dragged back. Two days later, there were screams from the Wardlaw house on the campus: John was found writhing on the ground, his clothing burning. He died shortly afterwards, and the coroner agreed that the death was suicide. But his mother benefited by an insurance policy worth $12,000.

Starvation

There was much local gossip about the incident, and the sisters decided to separate. Mrs. Martin went to New York with Ocey and was joined there by her husband. One day, the landlady heard groans; she burst open the door, and found Colonel Martin writhing on the floor, and Ocey – filthy and in rags – on a bed in the corner of the room. Colonel Martin died shortly afterwards; his death was assumed to be from natural causes – and the widow benefited from a policy for $10,000.

Virginia Wardlaw had now changed her job; she was principal of a women's college at Murfreesboro, Tennessee – where the other two sisters joined her. The women seemed to be dominated by a pathological meanness. They proceeded to starve Ocey to death. A doctor who called was shocked by the filth and bareness of the house. Another doctor quickly diagnosed Ocey's complaint as starvation, and threatened to get the police. The sisters told him that it was none of his business – Ocey was now married to her cousin Fletcher. This turned out to be true. But the doctor still caused trouble, and the three sisters – who now habitually wore black – left the college hastily.

With the benefit of normal food. Ocey immediately revealed that she was no invalid – indeed, she blossomed and became pregnant. But then the three deadly sisters descended again. Fletcher was completely under his mother's thumb, and allowed himself to be sent to Canada. Once more, the sisters began to starve Ocey to death. When the baby was born, they immediately handed it over to a foundling hospital, telling Ocey it was dead. And on November 29, 1909, at a house in East Orange, New Jersey, the police were called into another 'suicide'.

Ocey had drowned in her bathtub, in a few inches of water. As soon as the police discovered that she had been insured for $32,000, they arrested the 'sisters in black'. Virginia Wardlaw starved herself to death in jail. Ocey's mother was sentenced to seven years in prison, although the prosecution declared she was insane. The third sister was found not guilty. In jail, it soon became clear that Mrs. Martin *was* insane; she died in an asylum in 1913.

No account of family murder would be complete without a mention of the strange case of Russell Colvin, which took place in New England in 1812. Two brothers, Stephen and Jesse Boorn, hated their brother-in-law Colvin, not only because they suspected that their father meant to leave him his farm, but because he made excessive sexual demands on their sister Sally. Some time later, as they were clearing a field of rocks, Colvin and the brothers began to quarrel. Colvin's son ran back to the farm in a panic. Later, his uncles told him that his father had 'run away up the mountain', and threatened to kill him if he mentioned the quarrel.

Seven years after this, in 1819, Old Amis Boorn, the uncle of the brothers, had a dream in which Russell Colvin appeared and told him he had been murdered, and his body buried near the farmhouse (which had meanwhile been burned). Charred bones were found in a field; the brothers were arrested, and confessed to the murder. They were sentenced to hang. Then, to everyone's amazement, Russell Colvin turned up again. He *had* gone off up the mountain. No one has ever answered the question of why the brothers made such a circumstantial confession; it remains one of the greatest psychological puzzles in the history of crime.

In today's society the phenomenon of the lethal family – the family that stays together slays together – is not likely to occur. With the increase of social communications, and the 'shrinking' of the world, it is no longer so possible for families to hide in hills and backwoods – or in city tenements even – without their presence being known to the authorities.

Once they are officially on record their murderous activities (if indeed they plan any) are severely circumscribed. They have become part of the human family in general, and are guarded against turning on their kind.

FEMALE MURDERERS

The psychology of women who kill is one of the most fascinating subjects in the whole field of criminology, for, on the whole, women are not inclined to crimes of violence. At present, women form a negligible percentage of all criminals – well under 10%.

It *is* true that crimes of violence among adolescent girls – mostly from slum areas – more than doubled in the first three years of the 1970s, but there is no sign of a general rise. And, in spite of overcrowding in the big cities – which always produces a rise in the crime rate – it seems unlikely that female crime will ever become a serious social problem.

The reason is obvious; woman's basic instinct is for a home and security, and someone who values security will think twice about doing anything to jeopardize it. Man, with his more restless desires, his wider sense of purpose, is more likely to take risks, including crime.

What about the women who *do* commit crimes – particularly the most serious crime of all, murder? The first noticeable thing in considering a cross-section of such women is that so many of them are sexually unattractive, often downright ugly. There *are* cases of pretty criminals – Marie de Brinvilliers, Ruth Ellis, Sharon Kinne – but they are rarities. Most murderesses are physically unattractive, highly dominant, and highly sexed. And this immediately explains why they take to crime, for *all* crime springs out of frustration – from the drunken husband who batters the baby to the company director who embezzles millions.

A dominant woman may be very happy if she can find an even more dominant male to live with, as the researches of Abraham Maslow showed, but highly dominant women find it very difficult to find the right male – it is literally a chance in a million. If she is beautiful, she may continue to search and experiment until she finds 'Mr. Right'. If she is ugly, or

175

middle-aged, or both, her chances are minimal; she may then express her resentment against society through crime.

This pattern is visible in the careers of most female poisoners. Mrs. Merrifield, Nurse Waddingham, Nannie Doss, Mrs. Major, were all dominant and unattractive. Psychologists have suggested that administering poison may even have been a kind of sexual substitute to these women, but this point is difficult to verify.

For example, how can anyone fully understand the motives of Rhonda Belle Martin, the waitress of Montgomery, Alabama, whose career of crime extended over three decades? In 1970, doctors were puzzled by the illness that had paralyzed Ronald Martin from the waist downwards; extensive tests in the Veterans' Hospital, Biloxi, Mississippi, revealed that the trouble was arsenic poisoning. His wife, Rhonda Belle, was several years his senior, and had been, at one time, his step-mother.

Casual ruthlessness
Rhonda had been married to his father, Claude Martin, who had died in 1951, with symptoms that resembled his son's. Claude's body was exhumed, and found to be full of arsenic. The police now became suspicious of a number of deaths that had occurred in Rhonda's family circle, starting in 1934, when her four-year-old daughter had died. Her first husband, George Garrett, died in 1937; four more children subsequently died, and her mother died in 1944.

Confronted with this evidence, Rhonda Belle confessed that she had poisoned them all with ant-poison, bought at the local grocery store. Her career bears remarkable resemblance to that of her fellow countrywoman Nannie Doss; but this does not help us to understand why either of them poisoned husbands, children and relatives.

Many women who kill do so out of a brutality which is due to a harsh and difficult background. In 1969, tipped off by an anonymous letter, gendarmes in the little French village of Pierre-les-Nemours called at the home of André Lelièvre and his 41-year-old wife, Yvette. They had five children – but in the garden, police found the corpses of seven new-born babies. The Lelièvres had decided they could afford no more children after number five, but they were too lazy – or ignorant – to investigate the possibilities of birth control. So after each baby was born, it was drowned in the bath like a kitten, after which the husband buried it in the garden. A photograph of the couple shows them as stocky peasant types.

Even more characteristic of this type of casual murder is a case that came to light in Hungary in 1929. A medical student from Budapest, walking along the banks of the river Tisza, near the village of Nagzrev, discovered the corpse of a man that had been washed ashore. A brief examination convinced him that the man had not drowned, but had been dead when thrown into the water. An autopsy revealed that the man had been poisoned.

Two widows

The police now began to investigate in the nearby villages of Nagzrev and Tiszakurt, and heard rumours of many more mysterious deaths. As a result of these rumours, the bodies of two men, Josef Nararasz and Michael Szabo, were exhumed; both were found to have died of arsenic poisoning. The men had been nursed during their final illness by two local midwives, Susanne Olah – who became known as the White Witch of Nagzrev – and Frau Fazekas, both widows.

These women were arrested; so were some women who were rumoured to have been their 'clients'. One of these latter confessed to having bought arsenic from Frau Fazekas to poison her husband, his brother and another man. The police began to suspect that they were dealing with mass murder on an unprecedented scale. Frau Fazekas proved to be hard, cunning and immovable; after hours of questioning, the police allowed her to go.

She fell into their trap, immediately rushing around to various 'clients', warning them to be on their guard. When the police called on her later, and she realized what she had done, she seized a cup of poisoned water and drank it; she died a few hours later.

The police worked on Susie Olah, and on the other 'clients' of Frau Fazekas, and one old woman, Juliana Lipka, confessed that she had killed seven people in the past 20 years. The first had been her brutal and drunken husband – who had enraged her by selling some of their land to pay off debts. This embittered her grasping peasant soul; she took immense pleasure in watching his agonies as he died slowly from the arsenic that had been soaked out of fly papers.

As the case dragged on, woman after woman confessed to murder – more than 50 of them. The story was incredible and sordid. Susie Olah was a 'witch', and those who availed themselves of her arsenic to get rid of unwanted husbands or children, believed that her charms would ensure immunity from the law. A whole community of peasant women had allowed murder and witchcraft to become a way of life. Life in these primitive villages on the great Hungarian plain was harsh and dull; hatred came easily.

Dozens and dozens of victims were exhumed. The trial of the 'Angel Makers' – the name given to them by the Hungarian press – was probably the biggest peace-time murder trial on record, from the point of view of the number of defendants – and of victims. Many of the women – mostly those responsible for manufacturing and selling the poison – were sentenced to death, others to various terms of imprisonment. And yet, strangely enough, the case has now been largely forgotten, even in Hungary.

Strands of hair

It is even conceivable that murder may be hereditary – or at least, the tendency to violence that leads to murder. In January, 1956, 20-year-old Hurbie Fairris died in the electric chair at Oklahoma State Prison for the murder of Detective Bennie Cravatt, whom he shot in the course of a robbery. Fairris's mother was brought from a Texas jail to see her son before his execution; she was serving a term for the murder of her fourth husband; she had killed the previous two as well, during the course of quarrels – so the verdict was of second degree murder. Fairris's brother was serving a 10-year term for burglary. His uncle, Ray Hamilton, a close associate of Bonnie and Clyde, had died in the electric chair in 1934.

It is arguable that this is a case of bad environment rather than heredity – Fairris commented that he'd been in death row 'longer than I've ever stayed in one place before'. But he certainly had courage; when asked if he had anything to say before being strapped in the chair, he tapped his foot rhythmically, saying: 'What is there to say, daddy-o? Let's get on with it.' Would Fairris have killed if he had not become accustomed to violence in his home life? It is doubtful.

True female criminals – that is to say, women who choose crime as a career – are rare, but not unknown. The name of Anna Hoffner would certainly be better known to students if her trial had not occurred in the middle of the Nazi period, when German newspapers were encouraged to devote their space to other things than crime. When an elderly shoemaker named Wilhelm Hayn was found stabbed and shot to death in his Dortmund basement, police found one interesting clue at the scene of the crime – a few strands of long auburn hair.

Hayn had been shot by a type of revolver issued to stormtroopers and police: this was embarrassing. In 1938, no policeman was anxious to be forced to arrest young Nazis — particularly if the affair turned out to have homosexual overtones. But Kriminalkommissar Manus's investigations soon revealed another possibility. Although Wilhelm Hayn was unknown to the Dortmund police, he was well known to a certain section of the underworld — as a fence, a receiver of stolen goods.

There were a number of fingerprints in the bedroom, but none of them was known to the police, and this suggested that *if* these prints belonged to Hayn's clients, they were too young to have police records. An interesting picture was begining to emerge — a gang of young men, and a redheaded woman. Manus heard rumours from the Dortmund underworld of such a gang, but could find no further information.

However, he ordered his men to keep watch for a young redhead hanging around the haunts of known criminals, and one day a constable noticed a young and pretty redhead waiting outside a cinema. She looked nervous. The policeman watched unobtrusively from the shadows — perhaps having nothing better to do. He saw a young man pass the girl, and go into the cinema. A few moments later, the girl also bought a ticket and went in. This was definitely suspicious. If she was simply out for the evening, why didn't she go in sooner?

Sharp stiletto

The officer rang headquarters, and a plain clothes man came to relieve him. When the cinema emptied the redheaded girl and the young man came out together. They were followed to a café, where they were joined by two other young men. Later, the redhead and her escort went to an address in a residential area; the man came out alone, carrying a briefcase. Then he realized he was being followed, and ran, hurling the briefcase over a wall. The detective retrieved it; it contained a piece of stolen gold plate whose description had been circulated to the police earlier.

A check on the woman's apartment revealed that her name was Anna Hoffner. But she had disappeared. However, the police had more luck in tracing the origin of the briefcase. They not only found the shop where it had been sold — to a young man who answered the description of their fugitive — but the shopkeeper also recalled that he had sold the same man a sharp stiletto, of the type that had been used to stab the shoemaker. He described the man as having bushy hair and a red tie.

Some time later, the police were called to a bar, where a
drunken young man was brandishing a knife; he wore a bright
green tie. He was arrested and taken to the cells to sleep it off,
then questioned about the death of the shoemaker; eventually,
the youth confessed. The beautiful Anna was the leader of the
gang. He had been her lover, but now she had another. Hayn
had been killed because Anna discovered he had been cheating
the gang.

The suspect mentioned the name of another gang member,
Hans Greil, who was located, and followed. That night, in a
restaurant, he was joined by the redheaded girl. Both were
arrested. The final irony of the case was that Hans Greil was the
son of the district Chief of Police, and had used his father's gun
to kill the shoemaker. The Chief of Police resigned, although he
was in no way to blame. The members of the gang were not
executed – they were under age; instead, all were sentenced to
long terms in prison. Unfortunately, no further details of Anna
Hoffner's remarkable criminal career are available.

Attractive woman

Anna maintained her leadership of the gang by distributing
sexual favours. The same is true of Marta Romero, arrested in
Mexico in 1972. The police of Mexico City had many
complaints from men who had been robbed in their apartments
by a gang consisting of three young men and a young woman.
The girl was clearly the leader, but her dark eyes seemed to be
glazed with drugs.

Then, one evening, police heard that a robbery was taking
place in the vestibule of an apartment building. They moved
quickly, and found three young men and a girl – who was armed
with a .38 revolver. The robbers surrendered quietly. All were
under the influence of drugs. The men were two brothers named
Gonzalez and a youth called Guttierrez. They protested that they
disliked the idea of crime anyway, but Marta, who was the
mistress of all three – and slept with them in the same bed –
threatened to withdraw their sex unless they took part in
robberies.

Fantastic case

Most of these robberies brought in fairly small sums of money –
at most a few hundred dollars, as well as T.V. sets and similar
booty; their aim was to get money to buy drugs. Marta admitted
that she had taken to petty crime at an early age; her father had

abandoned her after the death of her mother. Since then, her life had been a continuous pattern of robbery, drugs and sex – she appeared to be a nymphomaniac. This is consistent with Maslow's finding that highly dominant women tend to be promiscuous. The gang were all imprisoned.

Women who plan murders carefully for gain are mostly the product of the crimewriter's imagination; they seldom appear in real courtrooms. Sharon Kinne is an interesting exception, and her case is certainly fantastic enough to be pure invention. On March 19, 1960, a policeman was called to the home of James A. Kinne, an electronics engineer who lived between Kansas City and Independence, Mo. He found James Kinne dead on the bed, shot in the back of the head.

His pretty 19-year-old wife, Sharon, was in hysterics; their 2-year-old daughter looked puzzled and frightened. When police finally managed to get a statement out of Sharon, it was to the effect that the child had gone into the bedroom with her husband's revolver, and somehow shot her sleeping father. Tests on the gun indicated that it *could* be true; and friends testified that the child had been known to play with the gun.

A coroner decided that James Kinne's death was an accident, and the pretty widow received a large insurance payment, part of which she spent on a Ford Thunderbird. The salesman was a handsome young man named Jones. He introduced Sharon to his wife, Patriçia. Sharon found him very attractive. On May 26, 1960, Patricia failed to return home from work. Two members of her car pool who had dropped her off mentioned that she had climbed into a Ford Thunderbird with a brown-haired woman.

The following evening, Sharon, out on a date with a young man, suggested that they might look around motels and bars for the missing Patricia. At 11.30 that night, as they drove down a lover's lane in Jackson County, they saw a body in the headlights. It was the missing Patricia Jones. Police discovered that she had been shot four times with a .22.

When police discovered the chain of coincidences – that the victim's husband had sold the Thunderbird to Sharon Kinne, that Patricia had last been seen getting into a Thunderbird, that Sharon had found the body – they were more than intrigued, and Sharon was arrested. When they also discovered that she owned a .22 revolver it began to look as if they had a strong case – except that they were unable to find the weapon. Nevertheless, she went on trial. Things looked black – and then an odd incident saved her.

The previous owner of the .22 was traced; he had traded the gun in for another. He remembered firing bullets from it into a certain tree. The bullets were dug out and tested. They were *not* from the .22 that had killed Patricia Jones. The witness admitted he could have made a mistake — he owned several guns. But Sharon was acquitted. She was promptly put on trial again, this time for the murder of her husband, and when one witness testified that Sharon had offered him $1,000 to murder her husband, the case suddenly went against her. She was found guilty of murder.

But in prison, she continued to insist on her innocence. Fourteen months later, the verdict was quashed, and she was put on trial again. On a technicality connected with a juror, the judge stopped the trial. Sharon's fourth trial began. The jury disagreed and Sharon remained free.

At which point she made the mistake of deciding to go to Mexico. In a bar in Mexico City on September 18, 1964, she met a middle-aged man named Francisco Ordonez, and allowed him to accompany her back to her motel room. Not long after, there were shots. The motel owner rushed to investigate, and saw Sharon emerge from the room, gun in hand; when the owner tried to stop her, she shot him. He was still struggling with her when the police arrived, and the .22 revolver in her hand proved to be the one that killed Patricia Jones.

However, Sharon had already stood trial for that murder, and could not be tried again, under the rule of double jeopardy. But she *could* be tried for killing Ordonez — who, she said, had accompanied her to her room because she felt unwell — she had been drinking heavily — then tried to rape her. In October 1965, a judge declined to accept that the crime had been in defence of her honour, and sentenced her to 10 years in jail. She appealed — and the court decided that 10 years was not enough, and added another three. She should have let well alone.

FORGERY

Generally speaking, swindlers and forgers are the cleverest of all criminals. They are the very reverse of murderers, who are childish and self-defeating in their destructiveness – so much so that it is not surprising that one third of them commit suicide. From Macbeth to the Boston Strangler, they give the impression of being caught in a physical and mental trap. Forgers, however, have the scope and comparative freedom of gamblers. They are playing for high stakes, and sometimes they win and spend the rest of their lives in comfort. When they lose, it is possible for even the most law-abiding citizen to feel a twinge of sportsman-like sympathy.

Natural gift

At the top of this list of swashbuckling swindlers stands the name of Jim the Penman. In the Victorian age, every British schoolboy – and many in the United States – knew about him. Nowadays, little is remembered except his nickname. His real name was James Townsend Saward, and he deserves to be immortalized as one of the most successful professional criminals of all time. For nearly a quarter of a century he pursued a successful career of forgery; and if it had not been for the stupidity of an accomplice, he might have ended his career a rich man.

Jim Saward was an intelligent, educated man, with a natural gift for imitating handwriting. He could have made a success in almost any profession, and indeed, he made a considerable success in his chosen profession – the law. But it was from swindling – particularly the art of forgery – that he derived real satisfaction.

He was called to the bar in 1840, and by that time, he had already thought long and deep on the art of forgery. It was obvious to him that the usual method – forging somebody's signature and taking the cheque to the bank – was highly dangerous. Even if the clerk handed over your money, he might remember your face.

The real trick was to cover your tracks so thoroughly that there was no chance of the forgery ever being traced back to you. The plan Saward devised was elaborate, and very nearly fool-proof. The first move was to get hold of blank cheques. That wasn't too difficult; burglars and pickpockets often found cheques among their loot, and they usually threw them away.

Through an accomplice, he circulated a rumour in the under-world that someone might be willing to pay well for stolen cheques – either blank or used. If he could also get used cheques, so much the better: he had a signature to imitate.

'Chain of command'

The next question was how to cash the forgery. Saward handed the forged cheque to an accomplice named Anderson. Anderson duly passed it on to another accomplice named Atwell. Atwell then advertized for an errand boy and messenger, and sent him to the bank with the cheque. Atwell followed the messenger and Anderson followed Atwell, to make sure he handed over the money.

Usually, there was no problem, and the bank parted with the cash. By the time the forgery was discovered, the culprits were untraceable. Even if the bank became suspicious, and arrested the messenger boy, there was nothing he could tell them. Atwell always took the precaution of disguising himself with a false beard and moustache when he engaged the messenger.

It was this elaborate 'chain of command' that ensured the success of Jim the Penman for so many years. His identity was known only to his closest associates. No one dreamed that the brilliant advocate, James Townsend Saward, with chambers in the Temple, London, was one of the most successful criminals of the age. Like Conan Doyle's Professor Moriarty, he was a Napoleon of Crime.

By modern standards, his embezzlements were not large (although it must be remembered that a pound in those days would support a poor family in comfort for a week). The cheques were seldom for more than a few hundred pounds, and his real pleasure came from the employment of his skill and cunning.

For example, on one occasion, a burglar sold him two cheques stolen from a solicitor named Turner. Saward needed a signature of the solicitor to copy. So he sent Atwell to Turner, asking him to collect a £30 debt. The solicitor wrote an 'or else . . .' letter, demanding the money. But even with this letter in his hands, Saward was unwilling to forge the cheque.

Out of luck

Even in those days, people guarded against forgery by using a special signature on a cheque. What he wanted was one of the solicitor's signed cheques. The debtor paid the £30, of course – he was another accomplice. Then, to Saward's annoyance, the solicitor paid the £30, minus his commission, in cash. Saward tried again. This time, the solicitor was asked to collect a debt of £103 15s 6d. Because it was an odd sum, the solicitor voluntarily paid by cheque. Saward had the signature he needed, and the solicitor was soon poorer by £400.

Inevitably, there came a day when luck ceased to favour the master forger. One cashier at a Lombard Street bank became suspicious when the messenger asked for £1000 in the form of five £100 notes, eight £50 notes, and the rest in gold. He peered very closely at the bill of exchange, and decided it was forged. The innocent messenger was seized: but an accomplice who had been waiting outside the bank was able to warn Saward, and the gang escaped as usual.

A few failures of this sort convinced Saward to try a wider field – the provinces. It was a bad decision. To begin with, the gang was short of funds, and Saward was feeling harassed – always a bad state of mind for a confidence swindler; it seems to induce bad luck.

They decided to work the usual trick in the east coast town of Yarmouth – get solicitors to collect 'debts', then forge their signatures on cheques. An accomplice named Hardwicke opened a bank account in London with £250, using the false name of Whitney; the money was then transferred to Yarmouth. In Yarmouth, Hardwicke visited various solicitors, using another false name – Ralph.

Compromising letter

In due course, he ran short of money and went to the bank. It was only then that he realized he had forgotten to request the bank to pay out the cash to a man by the name of Ralph . . . The bank, naturally, refused to pay Mr. Whitney's money to Mr. Ralph; and Ralph was in no position to tell them that he *was* Whitney. Anxiously he wrote to Saward for instructions.

If Saward had not been harassed and impatient, he would have realized that the best plan was to forget the money, for the bank was already suspicious. Instead, he wrote 'Ralph' a detailed and compromising letter, instructing him to return to London and start all over again.

By the time it reached Yarmouth, the bank had already told the police of their suspicions, and the police were questioning 'Ralph' and Atwell. The letter arrived while they were in custody, and was promptly opened by the police.

The men in Yarmouth confessed, and saved themselves by turning Queen's Evidence. Jim the Penman, and his accomplice Anderson, however, went on trial in March 1857, and were sentenced to transportation for life.

Saward was lucky. Until 1837 – by which time he had already commenced operations – forgery was punishable by death. The penalty had not always been so savage. To begin with, the chief offenders in the Middle Ages were priests – the only class who could write – and they usually claimed 'benefit of the clergy' and escaped with a light punishment.

In the time of Queen Elizabeth I, a forger could be fined, put in the pillory, have his nostrils slit, and lose his ears. But until there were banknotes, the forger's opportunities were obviously limited. There had been bank notes in Lombardy (Italy) as long ago as the twelfth century (hence Lombard Street, London's banking centre), but it wasn't until 1694 that they made their appearance in England.

Hotel and prison

They were called 'Accountable Notes' or 'Running Cash Notes', and since they were handwritten, they invited forgery – the first one was detected a mere two weeks after they were first issued, on July 31, 1694. It was for £100, and the four culprits were heavily fined and placed in the pillory.

Since the gains could be so enormous, and the crime so easy to commit – the criminal only needed a pen and a piece of paper – the bankers became alarmed. As a result, forgery was made punishable by death in 1697.

In one classic case of the eighteenth century, the new law was used to hang a villain who had been evading justice for years. The notorious James Bolland was, oddly enough, an officer of the law – an office he procured by the simple expedient of paying for it. This meant he could arrest people for debt, and take them to jail in his own good time.

He hired a dockside house in Southwark, in London, had bars put in the windows, and ran it as a cross between a hotel and a prison, where debtors with money to spare could eat and sleep in comfort. This was perfectly legal; but Bolland's hotel was really a clip joint, where his prisoners were parted from their money by every known means – Bolland was an expert card sharp – and then hurried into the less comfortable atmosphere of Newgate Prison as soon as they were penniless.

For years Bolland continued his career of fraud and extortion with great success.

Then he made his slip. He was holding a post-dated 'note of hand' (basically a cheque or IOU) for £100, and he asked an acquaintance to cash it – at a small discount. Like any cheque, it had to be endorsed, so Bolland wrote his name on it. His friend protested; he intended to cash the note with a third person, and Bolland was so notorious that this name would make it hard to negotiate. Obligingly, Bolland erased his name, and wrote 'Banks' instead.

In doing so, he had technically committed forgery – although no fraud was involved because the note was perfectly good. Unfortunately for Bolland, the man who originally wrote the IOU went bankrupt. The man who had cashed it – a Mr. Cardineaux – demanded his money.

As usual, the slippery Bolland tried to evade his responsibility; he looked at the IOU, said that his name wasn't 'Banks'.

But Cardineaux mentioned the transaction to an officer of the law. The authorities had been waiting for a long time for an excuse to get Bolland behind bars. He was arrested, tried for forgery, and executed in March 1772.

That was not the only time the forgery laws were 'stretched' to secure a conviction. In September 1803, a confidence trickster named John Hadfield was executed for what really amounted to seduction of a pretty waitress. Hadfield was a gambler who liked to pose as the Hon. Augustus Hope.

The wronged beauty

In 1802, he arrived in the English Lake District – which had been made popular by the poems of Wordsworth and Coleridge – and did his best to lure a rich heiress into marriage. He signed the name 'Hon. Augustus Hope' on various bills – but swindling was not part of his plan; he only wanted to get the lady.

Her father became suspicious, so the 'Honourable Augustus' went off and married (bigamously) the pretty daughter of an innkeeper at Buttermere, Mary Robinson. The girl was already something of a minor celebrity because she had been the subject of a well-known poem called 'Sally of Buttermere'. Just as she thought she'd acquired a rich husband, the Hon. Augustus was arrested as a fraud. He succeeded in escaping, and during the months he was on the run, the story of the wronged beauty of Buttermere caught the imagination of the English people.

Hadfield was finally caught, and tried for forgery — when, in fact, his crime was that of bigamy.

The only case of forgery to achieve a place in the *Notable British Trials* series is also one of the most tragic. Henry Fauntleroy was a brilliant young businessman who started his career, in 1800, as a clerk in his father's bank in Berners Street, London. Times were bad, and when his father died in 1807, Fauntleroy realized that they were on the edge of bankruptcy.

He applied all his energy and intelligence to remaining solvent, and inspired so much confidence that the bank was soon attracting crowds of investors. But things were not as good as they looked; the war with Napoleon was strangling trade. Fauntleroy was juggling the books — selling stocks and shares belonging to his depositors whenever he required money, and quickly replacing them when they were needed.

All this demanded a certain amount of forgery of depositors' signatures. Like all gamblers, Fauntleroy pinned his hopes on eventually making a fortune that would wipe out all his debts. But as the 'debts' rose to £400,000, it became more difficult to cook the books.

In 1824, when he was 40, the crash came. Fauntleroy was the executor of many wills. In the case of the will of a Lieutenant-Colonel Bellis, the other executors wanted to hand over their responsibilities to the Court of Chancery, and were puzzled when Fauntleroy hysterically disagreed with this.

They went to the Bank of England one day, and discovered that most of Colonel Bellis's stocks and shares had been sold, and the proceeds transferred to Fauntleroy's bank. The banker was duly found guilty, and was executed on November 30, 1824.

One man and his dog

One of the most successful — and improbable — forgers of this fresh breed was a mild little American named Edward Mueller. Outwardly he appeared to lack the quirky, devious, and off-centre mind so essential to the forger and his work. To his friends and neighbours in New York City he was a nice old man who had led a peaceful and uneventful life as the superintendent of an East Side apartment block.

He retired from legitimate work in 1937 and then set about making money in the literal sense. A widower with a married daughter living away from him, he spent most of his time alone with his dog in his tiny apartment on 96th Street. After a unsuccessful venture as a junk dealer, he bought an antiquated printing press and installed it in one of his rooms. He already possessed an old stand camera, and he spent his few remaining dollars on chemicals and supplies. Now he was ready to manufacture his first one-dollar bill.

He photographed a genuine bill, made a plate of it, and – using the wrong sort of paper and incorrect shades of ink – turned out some sample bills. They were crude and they were clumsy. But Mueller wasn't worried about that. He knew from experience that no one bothered to examine a one-dollar bill closely: a five, yes; a ten, certainly – but not a one. So providing he spent them wisely, he figured that his crime would not be discovered – or at least not traced back to him.

Petty offence

Each day he took his dog for a walk along 96th Street and stopped at a store, a bar, or a tobacco kiosk to make a purchase. He was an extremely careful shopper. If an item cost, say, four dollars, he would pay for it with three real notes – and one of his own. That way he never passed more than one counterfeit bill at a time. And when he had exhausted the possibilities of shopping on his home street, he went further afield – still getting rid of a 'Mueller dollar' everywhere he went and with everything he bought.

Before long the dud bills were taken by their new and angry owners to the police. Puzzled by the apparent pettiness of the offence – after all, what was the point of forging one-dollar bills so obviously and so badly? – the police did not at first regard the affair very seriously. They warned local shopkeepers and bank tellers to be on the lookout for the bills, and then got on with the more serious business of the day – such as hunting down murderers and armed robbers.

By the end of 1938, however, some 6,000 forged bills had been circulated – and the source showed no sign of drying up. Working quietly at home – flashing his camera and turning his press – Mueller continued to make the notes even when his printing plates became dirty and ridiculously worn. By then the money would have fooled no one – except perhaps a child – who looked more than casually at it. But no one did so and Mueller spent the next ten years 'slaving over a hot press'.

Methodically, unhurriedly, never losing his confidence or his patience, he continued with the 'hobby' that lent interest to his old age. He was also – although he did not suspect it – the subject of a large scale police investigation into the manufacture and disposal of the notes. As the officers got nowhere – there were no leads, no clues, no underworld informers – James Maloney, chief of the New York branch of the American Secret Service, took over the case.

Before long he, too, had to admit that he was baffled and bamboozled. If the forgeries were the work of one man, then the man was an idiot and an incompetent. His dollar bills were nothing more than a bad joke – and only bigger idiots would be taken in by them. If it was the work of a gang, then it was an extremely secretive and discreet one. Also it was perversely clever, trying to kid the authorities that its members were not professional crooks and forgers.

Edward Mueller might have gone on until death, making and distributing his bills at no more than one or two a day. Then came disaster. One afternoon while out exercising his dog (and, incidentally, making a couple of one dollar purchases), fire broke out in his apartment. The fire brigade was called and his rooms forced into.

In an attempt to save his humble possessions, firemen threw everything salvageable out of the window – including some printing plates and some half-burnt pieces of paper. The paper was picked up by an inquisitive boy whose father handed it to the police. The charred scraps were, in fact, forged bills – and when Mueller returned home he found a group of detectives waiting for him.

'Master' forger

They were as surprised as he was, and could hardly believe that here was the person they had been seeking for the last ten years. The scourge of the Secret Service! The pest of the police force! Mueller was arrested, taken to court, and sentenced to nine months' imprisonment for his career as a 'master' forger. On his release he went to live with his daughter and son-in-law. He was allowed to take his dog with him – but his camera and printing press were kept from him for good.

GALLOWS CHEATS

Right up until the last moment, even as he mounted the steps to the gallows, he insisted his innocence. Someone else had murdered his employer – an elderly spinster – and his conviction was a nightmare mistake. But now it was all too late. Within a few minutes John Lee's protestations would be cut off by death.

The Rev. John Pitkin, the prison chaplain, intoned the ritual prayers for Lee's eternal soul. Lee's arms were strapped to his side and a white hood was pulled down over his head and face. The hangman secured the noose around his neck, moved him to the centre of the trap – and pulled the lethal lever. Nothing happened. The executioner jerked the lever again and again. Still Lee stood waiting for death.

That was the first stage of the 'miracle in triplicate' which was witnessed at Exeter, England, on February 23, 1885 – a miracle which was to win Lee a very special place in the ranks of those who have escaped the gallows.

Lee, aged 19, had been condemned for the killing of Ellen Keyse, once a maid of honour to Queen Victoria, who had employed him as a footman. She was an austere and wealthy woman who insisted that her servants attended daily prayer sessions. During the night of November 14–15, 1884, she went down to the pantry, where she was found dead early next morning by one of the maids. Her head had been battered and her throat cut with a knife Lee had been using. Lee slept in a ground floor room adjoining the pantry.

The maid said she had been awakened by the smell of smoke and had found the body saturated in oil and surrounded by burning papers. All the evidence on which Lee was arrested – and eventually found guilty – was purely circumstantial. The prosecution suggested that his motive was anger over Miss Keyse's meanness. His wage was four shillings a week – but she had reduced it as punishment for some trivial offence.

There was fierce controversy in Britain over his death sentence. But that did not save him from mounting the newly constructed scaffold on that February morning. There was Berry, the executioner, slamming the lever back and forth. Two warders started crashing their heavy boots down on the yard-square trap, but it still did not budge. The chaplain said afterwards: 'During all those terrible moments John Lee stood firm, erect and unmoved, save for the jerks he felt from the violent stamping of the feet, to push down the trap door.'

After six minutes of feverish suspense, the prison governor signalled for Lee to be removed. The bolts were examined by a carpenter and found to be working perfectly. The carpenter then shaved away the edges of the trap to ensure that it could not stick. A weight corresponding to that of Lee's body was placed on the trap, which opened immediately the lever was pulled.

Lee, whose legs were also secured, was lifted back into position. Once again the Rev. Pitkin recited the last words. Berry pulled the lever. Lee still stood there. Berry tried frantically, but the trap would not budge. Once more, Lee was lifted clear. Twenty minutes passed while carpenters planed away more wood, and while a different engineer oiled the hinges, greased the bolts, and checked the lever. More tests were made; each time the flap fell with a crash.

Chaplain's horror

Lee was lifted back a third time. The chaplain, distraught with horror, was shaking as he hurried through the words of prayer. Later the chaplain said: 'The lever was pulled again and again. A great noise was heard, which sounded like the falling of the drop. But to my horror, when I turned my eyes to the scaffold, I saw the poor convict standing upon the drop as I had seen him twice before. I refused to stay any longer.'

Lee was taken back to his cell, and within hours he was reprieved. At his trial he had said: 'The Lord will never permit me to be executed.' After his triple escape he wrote: 'It was the Lord's hand which would not let the law take away my life . . .' He spent 22 years in prison. After he was set free he married and emigrated to America, where he died in 1933.

Other people have escaped the gallows in even more remarkable ways. Miss Jessie Dobson, when she was Recorder of Britain's Royal College of Surgeons in 1951, stated in the respected medical journal *The Lancet* that 'the procedure employed in judicial hanging has been, and maybe still is, an uncertain means of causing instantaneous death'. She described how the bodies of 36 criminals were dissected after hanging, and how pathologists found that in 10 of them the heart was still beating. In two cases the heart beats continued for five hours; in one case they continued for more than seven hours.

She cited examples of complete recovery after 'execution'. One of them involved a woman who, in 1650, hanged for half an hour at Oxford gaol. After she had been cut down, Sir William Petty, Professor of Anatomy at the university, and other doctors arranged to start a dissection. 'Perceiving signs of life, they administered cordials, and the woman lived for a further nine years, during which time she married and had three children.'

In 1728 a woman was hanged in Edinburgh, and her body was taken away in a cart by relatives. 'The jolting of the vehicle over the rough roads was apparently sufficient stimulus to restore her, and by the time it had gone six miles she was "almost well". She was still living in 1753.'

These escapes, like that of Lee, were regarded by many as evidence of Divine intervention – as proof that the people concerned were innocent in the eyes of God. And that led criminologists to the heart of one of the central arguments which, through the generations, has been put forward by opponents of capital punishment. If it is subsequently discovered that a man has wrongly been committed to prison, he can be released and compensated with cash. But there is no reprieve from the grave. So how many innocent people have paid that final terrible price because of some failing in the legal system? How many men and women who, after being locked in the death cell, have been exonerated?

Thomas Harris, landlord of the Rising Sun Inn on the York–Newcastle road, was executed for murder in 1819. Later it was established that the killer had been a barman at the inn, the chief witness for the prosecution. Harris's posthumous pardon did him little good.

One of the most controversial cases in modern times involved the mass murderer John Christie, the monster of London's Rillington Place. In March, 1950, a young man called Timothy Evans went to the gallows for the murder of his young daughter. A second charge of murdering his wife had not been heard by the court. Evans, a simple soul, had protested that his wife had been murdered by the 'other man' living in the house.

Years later the bodies of six women were found in the house, and the 'other man' – Christie – confessed that he had killed them. This led, in February, 1955, to an amazing statement in the House of Commons from Mr. Chuter Ede who, as Home Secretary, had refused a reprieve for Evans. He said:

'I was the Home Secretary who wrote on Evans's papers – "The law must take its course." I think that the Evans case shows, in spite of all that has been done since, that a mistake was possible – and in the form of which a verdict was given in a particular case a mistake was made. I hope no future Home Secretary, in office or after he has left office, will ever have to feel that – although he did his best, although none would wish to accuse him of being either careless or inefficient – in fact, he sent a man who was not guilty, as charged, to the gallows.'

The arguments about the execution of Evans continue until this day. What about the innocent people who have survived the death cell? William Habron, 18, was just one of many. In 1876 he was sentenced to death for the murder of a London police-man. However, purely because of his youth, he was reprieved. Three years later, while Habron was serving his life sentence, the notorious criminal Charles Peace – by then convicted of another murder – confessed to the crime of which Habron had been found guilty. The young man received a pardon and £800 compensation.

If Habron had been just a few months older – as old as 19-year-old Derek William Bentley, whose execution raised an uproar in 1953 – another irrevocable mistake would have been made. The circumstances of the Bentley case were extraordinary. He and 16 year old Christopher Craig had been found guilty of murdering a policeman in Croydon – although Craig had actually fired the lethal gun. The law said that no murderer under the age of 18 could be hanged, so Craig was given a prison term and is now free. Bentley was sentenced to death by Lord Goddard, the Lord Chief Justice – although his had been a very secondary role.

Supreme penalty

Men like Lord Goddard were staunch believers in the correctness of capital punishment, and two years before he sentenced Bentley he told a Royal Commission that too many murderers were being reprieved. He was also firmly against raising the hanging age from 18 to 21 because 'it might be an encouragement to other young men'. 'I think it right that, prima facie, the supreme crime should carry the supreme penalty,' he said.

Had Lord Goddard been the man making the final decision, people like Oscar Slater would have been legally killed for crimes which they did not commit. In Glasgow, in 1909, Oscar Slater was sentenced to death for the murder of an elderly woman. He was reprieved. After he had served 19 years in prison it was established that he was completely innocent – and he was given £6,000 compensation. Once more, the more vengeance-happy members of the public were denied the 'thrill' of a hanging.

Executions have always attracted ghouls and the morbidly curious – particularly in those days when they were treated as family entertainment. The last public guillotining in France took place on June 17, 1939, when a large crowd at Versailles watched the beheading of the murderer Eugen Weidmann. The last public hanging in Britain took place on May 26, 1868, outside Newgate Prison, London, and hundreds of children were in the audience.

The condemned man was an Irish political agitator called Michael Barrett, who had been convicted of having committed a murder while trying to blow up Clerkenwell Prison. The executioner – William Calcraft – did well out of the perquisites of his job. He used to sell the clothing of notorious criminals to Madam Tussaud's waxworks show in London – as well as selling pieces of rope to souvenir-hunters.

Hard-liners such as Lord Goddard insisted that capital punishment was essential because of its deterrent value, and because it was an expression of society's abhorrence of crime. 'It is undoubtedly a deterrent, and all police experience shows that,' he said. 'I think there is a real fear among the criminal classes of capital punishment, and that is why it is not considered among professional burglars that it is desirable to carry weapons.' On the question of 'irresistible impulse' Lord Goddard said that was a defence which might be put forward by every woman shoplifter. He relished the story of the prisoner who pleaded kleptomania and was told by the judge: 'That is just the disease I am here to cure.'

Hanging 'too good'

Men like Professor Terence Morris, however, one of Britain's leading criminologists, forced the country to abolish capital punishment for every crime except that of treason. And for treason a man could be beheaded in Britain up until 1973 – if hanging was considered too good for him. Professor Morris says:

'So many factors are not considered by the hangers and the floggers and the others who howl for more severe punishments.

They should, for a start, stop assuming that criminals – and I'm thinking particularly of youngsters – rationally calculate the penalties. In some degree or another, most people who commit premeditated violence are unbalanced. They also tend to lack the capacity to anticipate punishment – or to recollect it. The real criminal also has a great deal of the gambler in his make-up, and he tends to take the view that it will not happen to him – at least, not this time.'

A classic example of this attitude was seen on November 10, 1960, when two young men were hanged in London. Norman Harris, 23, went to the scaffold at Pentonville Prison, while his friend, Francis 'Flossie' Forsyth, 18, was executed a few miles away at Wandsworth Prison. At about 8.0 a.m. – an hour before the death time – a discharged prisoner came through the gate at Wandsworth and said that Forsyth could be heard all over the prison screaming: 'I don't want to die. I don't want to die!' Both men had been found guilty of kicking another man to death.

News of the double hanging was heard on a car radio by 20-year-old Victor John Terry of Chiswick, London – another small-time criminal who had been a teenage acquaintance of 'Flossie' Forsyth. Almost exactly an hour after Forsyth died, Terry walked into a bank in Worthing, Sussex – and shot a bank guard in the head. His defence against the charge of murder was that he believed himself to be a reincarnation of the legendary American gangster, Legs Diamond. He stated to a psychiatrist: 'When a person dies his mind leaves him and goes into another body. My mind was from Legs Diamond.'

In other words it was not Victor John Terry who had decided to carry a gun on that bank raid – it was the long-dead Legs Diamond. Diamond had issued the orders to the body of Terry – and Terry's trigger finger had done no more than respond to instructions from beyond the grave.

A third-rater

It would not be unusual for Terry to have had an interest in or an obsession with Legs Diamond. Third-raters often identify themselves with big-timers in the same walk of life – rather like a small-time repertory player daydreaming himself into an Olivier or a Brando. In Terry's case the alleged hallucination would probably have been aggravated by the fact that he had habitually taken drugs. None of that, however, saved him from dying on the same scaffold as Forsyth.

Lord Goddard – who argued strenuously for the hypocritically macabre ceremony of the Black Cap, which was initially worn as a sign of mourning for the condemned man – would have regarded the stories of Terry and Forsyth as powerful evidence for the retention of capital punishment. He also scorned 'sentimentalists' who suggested that women should not be executed and said:

'I do not understand that point of view, especially in these days when equality of the sexes is emphasized in every way. Some of the most shocking cases of murder have been committed by women.'

Women, however, have finished on the gallows for crimes far less serious than murder – crimes which, in some cases, they almost certainly did not commit. Mary Squires, who almost died because of a corset she did *not* steal, provides just one chilling example. Her story is an important one, for it underlines the appalling dangers of such an irrevocable punishment.

An 18-year-old girl called Elizabeth Canning mysteriously disappeared in the Houndsditch area of London on New Year's Day, 1753. She was considered to be extremely respectable, and her baffled family organized an intensive search for her. All in vain. Then, late one evening – exactly four weeks after she had vanished – she arrived home. She was filthy, hungry, and exhausted. The clothes she had been wearing were gone, and she was dressed in an old petticoat and shirt, covered with a bathrobe.

Where had she been? Her story was tearful and confused. Two men had seized her in a dark street, ripped away most of her clothing, and forced her to walk for 'miles and miles' until they had reached a bawdy house. There were three women in the kitchen of the house, and they had become extremely angry when she refused their invitation to work for them. One of them had taken a knife and slashed through the laces of her stays – before bundling her upstairs and locking her in a hayloft. There she had lived for a month on bread and water – which she had conveniently found there – until she succeeded in loosening a wallboard and escaped. Then, in her half-starved state, she had walked some 10 miles home.

Who were these women? Where was this house? Elizabeth could not remember. The ordeal had wiped such details from her memory. Why had she not sought help or refreshment on the way home? Because all she could think of was getting to the safety of home as quickly as possible. From which direction had she come? Through her hysterical sobbing she told them – as far as she could remember. One of the neighbours questioning her, a young man called Robert Scarratt, recalled that there was a house which might well fit her scanty description – owned by a woman called Susannah Wells. Elizabeth Canning immediately seized upon the name. Yes, she was certain. It was about Susannah Wells she had heard while in captivity.

The following morning, at the insistence of her family and friends, she told the whole strange story to an alderman. A warrant was issued for the arrest of Susannah Wells. A posse of law officers and family friends then escorted Elizabeth Canning to the house, where they found five women and three men. She was asked to point out those who had robbed her of her stays. Ignoring Mrs. Wells, she indicated the heavily cloaked figure of an old gypsy woman who was smoking a pipe. That old woman over there by the fire. She was the one.'

The gypsy, Mary Squires, threw back her cloak and revealed the frightening deformities of her face. Her nose was grotesquely big and misshapen; because of a glandular imbalance, her lower lip was swollen to the size of a hose pipe. Her skin was scarred with scrofulous tumours. This was a face straight out of a nightmare, a face which surely no one could ever forget. Yet Elizabeth Canning had never before mentioned that there had been anything unusual about it.

Mary Squires screamed and protested that she had never seen the girl before, but she and all the others in the house were taken to prison. Public opinion was hopelessly biased against them. They were gypsies and people of low morals. Besides, a woman with such an evil face would obviously be capable of any crime.

Mary Squires insisted that she had been more than 100 miles away in Dorset on January 1. But one of the house prostitutes – a girl with the unlikely name of Virtue Hall – tried to save herself by going back on her original denials and turning King's evidence. Now she was testifying that Elizabeth Canning's story was true. That clinched the fate of Mary Squires. She was sentenced to be hanged at Tyburn Tree. Susannah Wells, for harbouring and protecting a thief, was to be branded on the hand with the letter 'T'.

The sheriff's men, anticipating the sentence, were ready with their irons. The mob howled with delight as the metal seared into Susannah Wells's flesh. But the Lord Mayor of London, Sir Crispe Gascoyne, intervened before the hanging of Mary Squires. He was uneasy about the whole affair and petitioned the King for a postponement – until further inquiries could be made.

Telling the truth

For 15 months Mary Squires stayed in prison while investigators scoured the West of England for witnesses who could support her alibi. Then it became obvious that Mary Squires had been telling the truth. Even more important, other evidence showed conclusively that Elizabeth Canning had lied about her entire disappearance – and had never been to Mrs. Wells's house before that day when she had gone there with the posse.

There was talk that she had left home for those four weeks to have a baby in secret, and had invented the story of abduction. But that was never proved, and – even after her conviction for perjury in the spring of 1754 – she refused to tell the truth about her lost month. Elizabeth Canning was sentenced to transportation for seven years to 'His Majesty's Plantations in America'. In November, 1756, she married a man called John Treat at Wethersfield, Connecticut – and it was there that she died in 1773.

It is alarming to reflect on how many people must have been punished – some suffering the 'ultimate deterrent' – because the world breeds liars like Elizabeth Canning. On the other hand, innumerable murderers have escaped the gallows because courts have decided that their crimes were so horrifically bizarre that they must have been conceived in madness.

That was the category into which 18-year-old Ernest Walker, a footman in a house in London's fashionable Lowndes Square, was placed. His motive for murder – which, to his twisted mind, seemed completely logical – ranks as one of the most macabre on record. He wanted to die so that he could be reunited on 'the other side' with the mother he had adored. But he was terrified by the prospect of going alone to the grave. He wanted a companion in death.

In April, 1922, he began making his plans with the elaborate thoroughness of a small-minded person determined to make a spectacular gesture – a gesture which would show the world how important and clever he really was. For in Walker there was that curious mixture of callousness and childish conceit which is found so often in killers. He wrote down his scheme on a sheet of paper torn from an exercise book, detailing every action in the manner of the items on a shopping list. At this stage he did not know who his victim would be – but that, after all, was a trivial detail. On that dark journey into death anyone would do as a companion.

He decided that when he had the house to himself he would

telephone the District Messenger Company in nearby Sloane Street and get them to send him a boy. This was his timetable for murder.

'1 – Ring up Sloane Street messenger office for boy. 2 – Wait at front door. 3 – Invite him in. 4 – Bring him downstairs. 5 – Ask him to sit down. 6 – Hit him on the head. 7 – Put him in the safe. 8 – Keep him tied up. 9 – At 10.30, torture. 10 – Prepare for end. 11 – Sit down, turn gas on. 12 – Put gas light out. 13 – Sit down, shut window.'

One Saturday – when the other servants had the evening off, and Walker's employer was in Ireland – a 14-year-old boy called Raymond Davis died according to the dictates of the timetable, and of Walker's lunatic mind. But the boy died alone, for Walker avoided that last journey. By the time Walker reached item 13 his conceit had melted into cowardice, and he bolted from the house. His earlier determination to win posthumous respect was emphasized by a letter he had written to the butler, headed 'The Fatal Day'. The letter read:

'. . . I brought him to the pantry and hit him on the head with a coal-hammer. So simple! Then I tied him up and killed him. I killed him, not the gas. Then I sat down and turned the gas full on. I am as sane as ever I was, only I cannot live without my dear mother. I didn't half give it to that damned boy. I made him squeak. Give my love to Dad and all my friends.'

However, as he fled from his blood drenched 'death companion' he had forgotten his visions of fame. The sadism had drained from him; in its place was stark terror. He wanted to get away – as far away as possible. He took a train from Charing Cross station to Tonbridge in Kent. As the miles increased between him and the boy's body, his fear became tinged with elation.

Godlike power

He, he told himself, Ernest Walker, had done what the ordinary, dull, humdrum, little man could never do. He had demonstrated his power of life or death over another person – and that was a Godlike power which put him on a higher plane. But those people he passed in the Tonbridge streets, they did not even know, they had no idea of what a superior man he was. He wanted them to know. He wanted them to be amazed by his greatness – so he stopped a patrolling policeman and told him all about it.

At the Old Bailey he was found guilty but insane. In 1937, only 15 years later, the medical authorities considered it safe to discharge him from Broadmoor hospital. The man who had yearned for death – and who had murdered in his desperation to reach it – was set free to start a new life.

He, and others before and since his time, had avoided the executioner, and cheated the gallows or the electric chair. But Walker and the rest – the ones who were actually guilty – had not escaped all punishment. Shakespeare rightly said that conscience makes cowards of all men. But it does more than that; it turns them into their own hangmen, with the memory of the murders they committed the rope around their necks.

GANGSTERS

On the evening of July 22, 1934, people began to emerge from the Biograph Cinema, on Chicago's West Side. The plain clothes police who were standing around the entrance were tense with anxiety. They were hoping to arrest John Dillinger, America's Public Enemy Number One; they knew he'd gone into the cinema with a brothel madame – who had tipped them off – and another woman. What scared them was that some of the women and children in the crowd might get shot if Dillinger went for his gun. They had reason to worry; last time the Federal agents cornered Dillinger, in a Wisconsin farmhouse, they got so nervous they opened fire on a car full of innocent people, and killed several; Dillinger escaped.

Now, as Melvin Purvis and his agents waited outside the movie theatre, a police car suddenly drew up. The cinema cashier had noticed the plain clothes cops, assumed they were planning to stage a robbery, and rang the local police station. A Federal agent rushed up to the car, showed his identification, and ordered the police to move on fast. A few minutes later, John Dillinger walked out of the cinema with the two women, one of them wearing a bright red dress, so the police could identify her. To Purvis's relief, Dillinger pushed clear of the crowd, and started along an empty stretch of pavement. Purvis yelled: 'Stick 'em up, John, you're surrounded.' Dillinger went for his gun; dozens of shots sounded, and he crumpled to the pavement.

Most criminologists agree that the death of Dillinger was the end of an era. Capone had been in jail since 1932; prohibition had been repealed in 1933. There were still a few notorious gangsters at large – for example, 'Creepy' Karpis and Ma Barker's gang – but never again would the hunt for a gangster produce the nationwide excitement provoked by Dillinger.

It was the notorious Volstead Act – better known as Prohibition – that plunged the United States into its greatest period of lawlessness, starting of January 16, 1920. The puritans and bigots who persuaded the United States Senate to ban all alcoholic drinks thought they were inaugurating 'an era of clear thinking and clean living'; in fact, they were allowing organized crime a stranglehold on the U.S.

The Irish and Italian gangs of New York City and Chicago seized their chance to move into the big time. It was the era of Dion O'Banion, Johnny Torrio, Al Capone, Joe Masseria, Salvatore Maranzano, Vito Genovese. On February 14, 1929, six Capone gangsters, disguised as policemen, walked into the garage, two of them lined seven men up against the wall, and mowed them down with sub-machine gun fire.

The 'St. Valentine's Day Massacre' shocked the world; suddenly, the U.S. wanted to be rid of its gangsters. A tough but intelligent Sicilian named Charles Luciano – known as 'Lucky' – organized the killing of many of the old-style gangsters. He then called a meeting of the survivors, and warned them that the public was sick of gang warfare. In future, he said, there would be a policy of co-operation. Their common enemy was the law; their common prey was the public. A few of the older mobsters – such as Dutch Schultz – preferred to carry on in the old way. After Schultz had eliminated his chief rival, Legs Diamond, he himself was shot down as he sat in a restaurant in Newark, New Jersey, in October 1935. After that, America was more securely than ever in the grip of the mobsters – but the average American knew nothing about it.

Murder incorporated

Quietly and efficiently, Luciano organized 'Murder Incorporated', a pool of professional killers who committed murder only when the gang bosses decided someone was stepping out of line. Instead of booze, this new syndicate – sometimes known as the Mafia, sometimes as 'Cosa Nostra' ('Our Thing') – dealt in narcotics, gambling, prostitution, extortion, labour racketeering, and anything else that made money.

The general public became intrigued by its existence in November 1957, when the New York State Police stumbled on a business conference of more than 60 top racketeers near the village of Apalachin. All at once, 'Murder Incorporated' was world news. There was a national scandal, and a special commission to investigate crime, headed by Senator Kefauver, produced amazing revelations of mass corruption. A top mem-

ber of the Mafia, Joe Valachi, decided to talk, in exchange for
police protection. Some of the more notorious gangsters, including Luciano, were deported. A book about the Mafia, written in
1959, ends with a chapter entitled: 'Twilight of the Villains?' The
years since then have shown that the answer is: definitely not.

Soon after the immense success of Mario Puzo's Cosa Nostra
novel *The Godfather* in 1971, there were further outbreaks of
gang warfare in New York City. Gangleader Joe Colombo was
shot and critically wounded at a rally in Central Park; the rival
gangster responsible for this shooting, Joe Gallo, was himself
murdered as he celebrated his birthday in April 1972; in between
these shootings there were a dozen other Mafia executions. Now,
forty years after the death of John Dillinger, America is still firmly
in the hands of its 'mobs'. Capone and Luciano have been
replaced by another Mafia leader; but there is always a 'Godfather' ready to step into the shoes of his predecessor.

Will this ever change? An unprejudiced look at history suggests
that the answer is: probably not. If prostitution is the world's
oldest profession, then gangsterism is probably the second oldest.
Moreover, scientific investigation suggests that this is more than
just plain wickedness; it is a deep rooted animal instinct. An
instinct that is activated and intensified by conditions of overcrowding – not only in present-day communities and cities, but in
the living areas of long ago.

This gives an interesting insight into the beginnings of crime –
and of gangs. It is known that most of man's earliest cities, some
of which sprang up 5000 years B.C., contained overcrowded
slums. This may sound strange; after all, the world of those days
had a tiny population. So why didn't the people spread themselves out more? The answer is simple. Men built cities for mutual
protection; they preferred to be huddled together. Moreover,
these cities were often in river valleys where there was a limited
amount of space to expand. The result was inevitable – crime on a
large scale. To people from quiet country villages, the wickedness
of the cities must have seemed terrifying – as is instanced in the
Bible, with its stories of Sodom and Gomorrah, and those godless
cities of Mesopotamia that were destroyed by the Flood (which
actually took place about 4000 B.C.). The city, therefore, literally
created crime – at least, large-scale crime. And, unfortunately, the
pestilence soon overflowed into the surrounding countryside;
travellers were robbed and murdered; small villages were overrun
by robber bands who killed the men, raped the women, and
burned the houses.

It can thus be said with some confidence, that the first gangsters appeared soon after the first cities. But at this point, an important distinction must be made. There are two distinct kinds of gangster which, for convenience, can be labelled the bandit and the 'true gangster'. Bandit obviously means the same as gangster (since a gang is a band); but their motivations are different. To put it simply, the gangster tends to be crueller and more vicious than the bandit. The bandit lives in rural areas; he has space. He may have taken to crime for a variety of reasons; but one of these is *not* overcrowding. He prefers to be a member of a band because being a loner in wide open spaces is a demoralizing business. (Criminal loners often commit far more atrocious crimes than 'bandits', because boredom and solitude make them lose their sense of identity.)

Emotional damage

Apart from his criminal activities, the bandit may be a normal human being with normal human emotions. On the other hand, the man who becomes a gangster because of the pressures of an overcrowded slum, has often suffered permanent emotional damage. To begin with, as already noted, overcrowding produces bad mothers and brutal fathers. The true gangster is the product of the slum, and he sees the world as a place to be plundered – if he can get away with it.

The city of Hong Kong offers some gruesome examples of this dating from recent years. Trapped between the sea and steep hills, Hong Kong is one of the most overcrowded cities in the world, and its murder rate has always been high. After World War II, the population quickly rocketed from half a million to more than two and a half million. Consequently, there was a terrifying wave of gang murders – murders so atrocious that the police speak of them as the work of 'horror cults'.

In 1958, there were more than 900 murders – five times the American murder rate, and 150 times the English. These 'horror cults' are, in fact, Chinese 'tongs', or 'Triad Societies'. (The earliest tongs were called 'Three Harmonies Societies'.) Like their American counterpart, the Mafia, they operate prostitution, drugs rackets, protection, and extortion. But their methods of ensuring obedience depend upon terrorism.

For example, in 1958, a rich merchant named Ko Sun Wei, together with four of his family, were horribly murdered in his house in Kowloon. The victims were staked out, with their arms and legs spreadeagled. Three women – the merchant's two daughters and his daughter in law – were raped repeatedly, then tortured to death with knives. One woman was still alive when the police arrived, but was unable to speak – her tongue had been cut out.

These were only five among 350 murders that took place in Hong Kong in September 1958. Sergeant Arthur Ogilvie, of the Hong Kong Police, who gives these figures, also mentions that during the riots of 1956, Triad Societies took the opportunity to pillage more than $25,000,000 worth of goods. With a figure of this size involved, it can be seen that crime in modern Hong Kong is an even bigger business than it was in the Chicago of the 1920s. The interesting point here is the verification of observations about overcrowding. It produces true gangsters – men who are adepts in cruelty and violence, because they are unable to experience ordinary human emotions.

Bearing in mind this important distinction, it can be seen that many of the famous criminals and gang leaders of the past 200 years have been bandits rather than gangsters. For example, Australia's most famous criminal, Ned Kelly, was definitely a bandit. Kelly, the son of an Irish farmer and former convict, became Australia's public enemy Number One when he killed three constables at Stringybark Creek in 1877.

From then on, he lived the traditional life of the bandit on the run, moving around the countryside with his gang – which included his brother Dan – and robbing banks. He made himself head and body armour, weighing 97 lb, and was wearing it when the police finally ambushed his gang in Glenrowan. He was only 24 when he was executed in 1880. Asked why he had decided to confront the police at Glenrowan, Kelly made a reply that was to be echoed by many American gangsters of the Bonny and Clyde era: 'A man gets tired of being hunted like a dog . . . I wanted to see the thing end.'

The most significant feature about Kelly is that he was a man who thought he had a grievance against the law – and in this he resembles many of the famous 'bandits', from Billy the Kid to John Dillinger. Whether the grievance is real or not is beside the point; but it starts the bandit off on the road that leads to the gallows, or the final bloody shoot-out with the police.

Most wanted man
The story of South Africa's most famous 'gangster' may be taken as typifying the pattern. William Foster was born in 1886, and his family moved to Johannesburg in 1900. While still under

20, William decided to seek his fortune in German South West Africa. Plodding around in the desert one day, he met two companions who were driving a pack of donkeys. He joined them – and a few miles farther on, all three were arrested and charged with stealing the donkeys. The young men claimed they had found the donkeys wandering in the desert, and were driving them back to the nearest village. William lost his temper with the officious German magistrate. As a result of this, he was sentenced to a month in prison, while his companions were allowed to go free. The injustice of this infuriated him. When he came out of jail, he was aggressive and inclined to drink too much. A series of minor offences led to further prison sentences – and a thoroughly resentful William Foster was ready to become a 'complete' criminal.

He fell in love, and wanted money to marry. His first major crime, therefore, was a well-planned robbery of a jeweller. He and two accomplices ran into bad luck and an efficient police force, and each received 12 years' hard labour. Foster's girlfriend Peggy married him while he was in jail, awaiting trial. Nine months later, Foster escaped. In a bank robbery a few months later, two clerks were killed, and Foster's career as a 'hunted dog' began. Like Kelly, he had an amazing ability to shoot his way out of tight corners; and, as the deaths piled up, he became South Africa's most wanted man.

Committed suicide

Whenever possible, his wife – who now had a baby daughter – joined him. The tragic end came in September 1914, when Foster and two companions were cornered in a cave in the Kensington Ridge. One of the men committed suicide. Foster's parents, his sisters, and his wife Peggy were then sent for. They agreed to try and persuade him to give himself up, and bravely entered the cave. The parents and sisters came out, with Foster's baby daughter. Then three shots rang out. Peggy had decided to die with her husband.

In the United States, the gangster era began long before Prohibition. New York was America's first major city, and as early as 1790 it had slums that were as foul and miserable as any in the world. In the hundred or so rooms of the Old Brewery, human beings were packed like rats, and murders averaged one a night. When the district was demolished in 1852, the builders filled numerous sacks with human bones and remains. There were many tough and colourfully-named gangs: the Dead Rabbits, the Roach Guards, the Shirt Tails, the Plug Uglies (which referred to their huge plug or top hats). Then, during the 1840s, Tammany Hall politicians discovered that gangsters could be useful allies, threatening rivals and drumming up votes. And it was from this period that the real history of American gangster-dom began.

At the time, most of the gangsters were Irish – and, oddly enough, Chinese. The Chinese were accustomed to their 'Triad Societies' at home. When they came to settle in America – mostly on the West Coast – they naturally formed themselves again into 'tongs' for mutual protection.

The Chinese were also among the first to practise gang assassination. In 1897, a rich Chinese gangster, Little Pete – owner of several gambling houses – was sitting in a barber's chair in San Francisco. He had made the mistake of sending his bodyguard out to find the result of a horse race. Two men who had been trailing him for months, awaiting their opportunity, came in and literally filled him full of lead. The killers were never caught. A similar scene was to be repeated half a century later when, in October 1957, Albert Anastasia, one of Murder Incorp-orated's assassins, was shot in a Manhattan hotel barber's shop.

Black Hand Gang
In the early years of the century, most of America's most formidable gangsters, were Chinese. By comparison, the Irish were relatively amateurish and badly organized. But another racial group was slowly achieving ascendancy – the Italians. Fleeing from the poverty of their homeland – and from its chronic political troubles – they also had their tradition of secret societies. The word 'Mafia' originally described a Sicilian out-law who had taken to the hills, covered with low scrub (mafia), to hide from justice (either at the hands of the police, or of the family of someone he had killed).

The Mafia came to New Orleans – under the name of 'the Black Hand' – in the 1880's. Almost without exception, mafiosi preyed upon their fellow citizens, who, in turn, were too terrified to appeal to the police of their adopted country. Similarly, the Irish gangsters tended to prey upon their fellow Irish, and the Chinese on the Chinese.

Escape from slums
As the century progressed, the Chinese slowly lost their reputa-tion as gangsters – perhaps because many of them succeeded,

through hard work and intelligence, in escaping from the slums – and the Irish, and their bitter rivals the Italians, took over. Then came the double-edged sword of Prohibition. Chicago's crime industry was run by men like the O'Donnell brothers, and the flamboyant Dion O'Banion, who was quoted as saying angrily: 'To hell with them Sicilians!'

On November 10, 1924, three men walked into O'Banion's flower store, and unceremoniously gunned him down. The man who arranged the murder commented ironically: 'O'Banion's head got away from under his hat.' His name was Al Capone. The United States had entered its third and most lethal era of gangsterdom. It is still in the midst of it.

GENTLEMEN CROOKS

Although it has been somewhat obscured by inverted snobbery, the urge to 'become a gentleman' remains one of the most powerful motivations in most civilized societies. Half a century ago it was open and unconcealed. Anyone who enjoys records of old music hall songs knows how many of them are about a man pretending to be a 'toff' – like Burlington Bertie, who demonstrates his gentility by walking down the Strand with his gloves on then walking down again with them off.

And the literature of this period is also frankly dominated by class feeling. Oscar Wilde belonged to the 'upper classes' by right – his father being a knight – yet he was still fascinated by the aristocracy. So, in a different way, was that sturdily working-class writer D. H. Lawrence, who, after his marriage to a German aristocrat, took care to mention casually in all his letters that her father was a 'Von'.

Dream of heaven

It is easy enough to understand the nineteenth-century reason for this fascination. Thousands of poor people literally froze and starved to death every winter; so the thought of the security of wealth, of winters on the Riviera or large country houses, was like a dream of heaven. In our present-day welfare society no one starves to death; and it might therefore be expected that the interest in the aristocracy would gradually fade away.

It has done nothing of the sort. When a human being has satisfied his – or her – desire for a home, for sexual security and a family, the next 'level of need' to emerge is the craving for self-respect, the desire to be *looked up to* by other people. This need is as universal as the sexual urge. Consequently everybody feels a certain admiration – or envy – for those who are above him in the 'self-esteem hierarchy'; it is as fundamental as the interest we feel in Don Juan and Casanova, or in the famous 'scarlet women' of history.

So it makes no real difference that we are living in an altogether more affluent society than that of our great grandfathers. It still remains a fundamental human daydream to be born in a position that *automatically* confers respect. One of the early 'Blondie' cartoons showed a uniformed hall porter addressing Dagwood as 'sir', and Dagwood is so drunk with delight and self-importance that he walks round and round in the revolving door. We laugh at this; but James Thurber's Walter Mitty, who has fantasies about being a great surgeon, a fighter pilot, a ship's captain, is a universal symbol.

This explains why the 'gentleman crook' is such a familiar figure in the police courts. It is not so much because crooks find the role of gentleman an effective disguise as that the craving to be a gentleman drives them to crime. Some 'gentleman crooks' actually achieve their ambition, and are accepted as gentlemen in 'high society'. This is what happened to Casanova, who was born the son of a poor actor. His charm, his ready wit, and his skill as a confidence man carried him into the society of kings and lords, who accepted him as a man of culture and intelligence.

The same was true of another remarkable impostor of the late eighteenth century, the 'Count Saint-Germain', who set out to be a 'man of mystery'. He liked people to believe that he was many hundreds of years old, making casual reference to historical events – like the Crucifixion – as if he had been present. Saint-Germain also claimed that he never ate, and would sit at the dinner tables of the rich with only a glass of water in front of him.

He was widely believed to have magical powers. However, he did not take in all his contemporaries, and one of them, Count Warnstedt, described him as 'the completest fool, charlatan, rattle-pate, windbag and swindler'. Saint-Germain undoubtedly *was* something of an inventive genius, particularly in the field of textiles, so he cannot be dismissed as a gentleman crook. The same is true of another of his remarkable contemporaries, Cagliostro, the founder of a secret order of freemasons; although there can be no doubt that he *was* a windbag and a pretender, he also possessed a certain amount of genuine 'occult' knowledge, as well as being a brilliant doctor.

These men, then, are genial impostors rather than gentleman crooks; but they make fascinating studies for the criminologist because the basic motivation is the same. The 'real thing' is always of a lower order. Most 'gentleman crooks' lack the polish and intelligence of a Casanova or Saint-Germain. As a typical example we may consider the case of Vidocq and the gentleman crooks, recounted by the famous criminal-turned-detective in his memoirs.

The story begins one night in 1817, when a butcher named Fontaine set out from his home in Courtille, near Paris, to buy cattle at the Corbeil market. Fontaine was a stupid man who was given to boasting, and, like many such individuals, he was highly susceptible to flattery from his 'betters'. In a *bistro* near Essone he began to talk to two well-dressed and rather well-spoken travellers.

They seemed to be gentlemen, and Fontaine tried to impress them by talking about the amount of money he made in his business. Time went past, and he suddenly realized that it was late afternoon. His new acquaintances pressed him to stay overnight; but Fontaine was a stubborn man; he wanted to sleep at Corbeil, to be up early for the market. One of the 'gentlemen' now suggested to the other that perhaps they ought to go with him, since it was their direction too; and besides, three of them would be a deterrent to highwaymen.

Tremendous blow

They seemed so polite and well-mannered that Fontaine had no suspicions. They set off walking, stopped for another glass of wine a few miles along the road, then continued to walk after dark. One of the men had a limp. When they came to a narrow lane the man with the limp said it was a short cut to Corbeil; Fontaine followed him without suspicion. Suddenly he felt a tremendous blow on the back of the head and fell to his knees. The other 'gentleman" pulled a knife and began stabbing him. Fontaine fought back with his stick, but after receiving 28 stab wounds, he fainted from loss of blood.

When he woke up, his money was gone. His groans attracted a passer-by, and he was taken to a hospital. Recovery was slow, but Fontaine was tough; besides, he was determined to have his own back on his treacherous 'gentlemen' acquaintances. Vidocq, the detective, talked to him in hospital, then proceeded immediately to the scene of the crime. There were footprints in the mud, and Vidocq had casts made of these. He also found two buttons in the mud – and some fragments of a letter. Fontaine had torn off part of a pocket from one of his assailants, and the letter fragments must have fallen out.

The words read: 'Monsieur Rao, Wine Merchant, bar ...
Roche, Cli ...' The paper was similar to that used for court
summonses. Vidocq decided that the full address should read:
Monsieur Raoul, barriere Rochechouart, Clignancourt – a suburb of Paris. Raoul had an underworld reputation as a smuggler,
ran a sleazy bar, and was, compared to most crooks something
of a 'gentleman'.

Vidocq had the bar watched. His agent finally saw a fairly
well-dressed man with a limp, and followed him home. Vidocq
was informed, and kept watch on the house. When the limping
man came out, Vidocq recognized him as a crook named Court;
Vidocq had arrested him years previously for robbery with
violence. Now Vidocq was sure he was on the right trail. He got
a warrant, gained entry to Court's room by claiming to be
Raoul, and arrested him. But Court's room contained no
evidence to connect him with the attack on Fontaine.

Vidocq spent the next day in Raoul's bar. Raoul was not
there, and the man behind the counter would only give him the
information that Raoul was in his room in Montmartre. Hours
later the bar-owner returned. Vidocq now tried bluff. He
introduced himself, and told Raoul that he was suspected of
holding revolutionary meetings on his premises, and of possessing inflammatory literature. Raoul indignantly denied having
democratic tendencies, and told Vidocq he could search the
house. Vidocq's men did just that, but found nothing. 'How
about your place in Montmartre?' said Vidocq. 'You can search
that too,' Raoul said sullenly.

Vidocq called two cabs, and he and his men drove to
Montmartre, where Raoul led them to a house. Vidocq was
fairly certain that he would find nothing obviously incriminating
– Raoul looked too unworried. All the same, he *did* find what he
was looking for – the police court summons with a corner
missing – the corner which had contained Raoul's name and
address, and which had been at the scene of the crime.

Raoul's nerve broke, and he tried to snatch a pistol; Vidocq's
men grabbed him and took him to prison. There, Vidocq had
Court and Raoul brought face to face, and proceeded to play
them off against one another. When he saw that Court was
obviously shaken, he played his master card – the fact that the
butcher Fontaine was still alive, in spite of his 28 knife wounds,
and fractured skull. Court was taken to a cell on his own, and
eventually signed a confession. Then Vidocq went back to
Raoul. But Raoul was altogether tougher and denied everything.

He had a good business in Clignancourt, he said; why should he play the gentleman crook and waylay travellers? Vidocq went back to Court and said: 'All right, he's confessed. Would you like to talk to him?' Court nodded, and Vidocq had them brought together. Court immediately said: 'Good, I'm glad you've confessed too. We may as well get it over.' Raoul swore – but signed a statement.

The cunning Vidocq had not finished. He pretended that, now the case was cleared up, there were no hard feelings, and treated the two men to a good supper with several bottles of wine. They ended by involving another regular accomplice, and Vidocq was able to arrest him the next day.

Touch of coarseness

Raoul and Court may be taken as thoroughly representative of the class of the 'gentleman crook'. Most of them are very perceptibly *not* gentlemen; there is a touch of coarseness that would instantly give them away to any real gentleman.

Of course there have been exceptions: for example, 'Count' Victor Lustig, the con-man who actually sold the Eiffel Tower, and whose impeccable manners reminded many of his victims of the film star Adolphe Menjou. Gerald Chapman, the 'Count of Gramercy Park', the man who, on the proceeds of a bank robbery, set up as an English gentleman of leisure in New York and fooled a large part of New York society. However, such men are exceptions. Criminals like Raoul and Court are the rule.

In the year 1899 a journalist named Edward William Hornung published *The Amateur Cracksman*, whose hero was Raffles, the gentleman burglar. The book was an immediate and enormous success, and was followed by four further Raffles books. Ironically, Hornung was the brother-in-law of Conan Doyle, the creator of Sherlock Holmes, and for many years the popularity of Raffles equalled that of the great detective. It is interesting to consider why Raffles made such an appeal to respectable Edwardian England.

He has been to a public school and university, and plays cricket for a gentleman's amateur eleven; unfortunately, he lacks the money to maintain himself in the society to which he is accustomed; his old school-fag Bunny is in the same state. So the two of them make a living by committing burglary. Naturally, most of their victims are the kind of people that excite no particular sympathy or pity in the average man – jewellers, wealthy bankers and the like.

What Hornung implies is that Raffles is simply a bold and daring man, who has chosen a life of adventure on the edge of society. Besides, he finally expiates his life of crime by dying bravely for his country ... It is an interesting piece of 'double-think', and indicative of the curious immaturity of the average upperclass Englishman at the turn of the century. Raffles's life of crime is merely an extension of schoolboy pranks – or so we are supposed to feel.

But, in fact, Raffles is like no gentleman crook who ever existed. For Hornung, with his inadequate knowledge of criminal psychology, missed out the essential element: the Walter Mittyish daydreams, the tendency to fantasize, and the capacity for self-deception. The gentleman crook is usually out to deceive himself as well as other people.

Twinkling eyes

Consider the astonishing career of Italian born Carlo Ponzi, one of the great financial swindlers of the twentieth century. Ponzi came to American from Italy as a boy immigrant, certain that he would make his fortune in the land of opportunity. In fact his only asset was a mercurial vitality and a preposterous optimism. He began his career as a waiter, but the little man with twinkling eyes was so inclined to chatter to his customers that he quickly lost the job. He went to Montreal, worked at a series of menial jobs, and made enough money to buy himself elegant clothes and a malacca cane – which became something of a trade mark. He longed to be taken for a gentleman. He began his career of crime by swindling Italian immigrants of money, which he promised to send to their relations in Italy, and he soon went to prison.

He came to Boston just after the First World War, married a pretty girl called Rose, and became manager of her father's wholesale grocery business. His business acumen was not equal to his optimism, and the father-in-law was soon ruined. Ponzi then became a clerk at $16 a week. One day he saw a postal reply coupon in one of the firms letters. He discovered, to his astonishment, that this coupon could be bought for one cent abroad, and exchanged in America for five cents-worth of stamps. It was the post office's way of encouraging business.

Instantly Ponzi saw marvellous possibilities: borrow $5,000, spend it on coupons, exchange the coupons for $25,000 worth of stamps, sell the stamps at a cut rate. He bought a few dollars worth of coupons, and tried to exchange them; but the post office told him it was illegal to do it in such quantities; they weren't trying to give away money.

Ponzi, however, saw that he was at last within reach of the fortune and position he had always dreamed of. He went to various friends and persuaded them to invest in his scheme. *He* had a method of getting around the postal regulations. And he hinted that the Rockefeller fortune was based on the same trick. They lent him money. Three months later he paid them back 50 per cent, which he said, was pure interest. 'Re-invest it,' he said. 'You can't lose.' They took his advice, so did their friends. Ponzi soon had enough money to float the Financial Exchange Company, and he was taking $3,000 a day. One enthusiastic admirer shouted: 'You are the greatest Italian in history.' Ponzi said modestly: 'No, no – Columbus was greater.'

There was method in his madness. He was, of course, repaying the 'interest' out of the money he took in; but he reasoned that if he could make enough money he would be able to invest in legitimate business, exercise his business genius – which neither he nor anyone else doubted for a moment – and soon become a millionaire. He actually bought shares in the Hanover Trust Company, and purchased the J.P. Poole Company. He bought his wife Rose a vast mansion.

He might have succeeded, but for one mistake. He called in a real financial expert to act as his public relations man. When William McMasters realized that this financial empire was built on sand, and that Ponzi's 'genius' was largely optimism and sheer ignorance, he whispered a word in the ear of the state authorities. The bubble burst. Ponzi had taken twenty million dollars, paid back three-quarters of it, and spent the other five million: he went to prison for 10 years for fraud and grand larceny.

Poverty stricken
When he came out he decided that he would return to Italy and offer his genius to Mussolini, who seemed to be a man after his own heart. Mussolini thought so too, at first, until it dawned on him that Ponzi's chief asset was his colossal ego and his boundless – and unfounded – optimism. So he was dismissed, and died – poverty stricken – in Rio de Janeiro in 1949.

Carlo Ponzi is the Italian-American version of the gentleman crook. The English version tends to wear old school ties, speak with a drawling accent, and call people 'old boy' – the sex-killer Neville Heath is a typical representative. So was the crook known as Anthony St. George, who arrived in the riverside village of Send, near Woking, in 1924. He lived in an enormous punt that had been converted into a houseboat.

He was tall, athletic and good looking, and he seemed to have plenty of money. He was soon extremely popular at the village inn, for he was obviously a man of 'independent means', and it was rumoured that he was the son of a peer. He ate and drank well, and had no difficulty acquiring half a dozen mistresses.

The police were worried about a series of spectacular burglaries in the area, which then – as now – was popular with retired businessmen. One day, before dawn, Police Constable Elkins was called by a householder named Lucas, who had interrupted a burglar. The burglar had only taken a pair of shoes. There was one clue – a fragment of yellow paper that looked as if it had come from a match book. Elkins put it in his pocket. On his way home, in the dawn, he met Anthony St. George on a bicycle, and asked him where he had been. St. George said he had spent the night with a local girl, but declined to reveal her identity.

Got a Match?

Elkins didn't like his story, and went to the house-boat later in the day. While talking to St. George, he took out a cigarette, and asked casually: 'Got a match?' St. George handed him a yellow matchbox. A small piece of the flap was missing. Elkins took this out of his pocket, and tried it. 'Seems a good fit,' he said. St. George said plaintively: 'That's not very sporting.' But he 'went quietly'.

Ex-chief Superintendent Fred Cherill, describing St. George in his memoirs, remarks that he was a crook who had an obsession with the aristocracy. His real name was Arthur Hazel, and he had been born in Liverpool in 1894. He had never been to a public school or university. Until 1914 he was in and out of jail for petty theft. Then he went into the Coldstream Guards, became a sergeant-major, and became obsessed with the idea of being a gentleman. He felt he *ought* to have been an officer – and this was the identity he adopted.

Until 1940 St. George was in and out of prison for burglary – always of big mansions and titled families, as though this was his way of 'identifying' with them; stealing gold cufflinks or jewelled pendants gave him the same pleasure that some sex maniacs get from stealing women's underwear. Yet he always made the same absurd mistake: he never wore gloves, and again and again his fingerprints sent him to gaol. Could it be that he *wanted* to leave his 'signature' in the homes of the aristocracy? It is possible to conceive a democratic society without gentleman crooks; but perhaps one has to admit that, in many ways, such a society would be duller.

GREED

The real greed-murder is, strangely enough, the rarest of all murders. Because to be *that* greedy is basically a pathological condition. For the psychologist, the greed murderers are among the most fascinating of all types of killer.

The case of Frau Loewenstein-Marek, who was born around 1904, is a prime example of this illness. Martha Loewenstein was a dazzlingly beautiful young girl who worked in a dress shop in Vienna, and whose background was miserably poor. She was foundling, who had been adopted and brought up in the slums of Vienna. When she went to work in the dress shop, she was so efficient, and carried herself so well, that the woman who owned the shop presented her with smart dresses.

One day in the early 1920's, she met a rich man who lived alone in a villa in the nearby city of Mödling. He was so impressed by Martha's charm and firmness of character that he invited her to become his ward. Suddenly, the life of poverty was behind her; Cinderella was adored and spoiled by her elderly Prince Charming.

Yet there were drawbacks. She would have preferred a younger admirer, and this explained why she experienced fits of depression and irritability. Her kindly benefactor, Moritz Fritsch, cheered her up by telling her that he intended to leave her the house and a part of his fortune. A year later, at the age of 74, Fritsch died peacefully. His ex-wife was infuriated to learn that he had left the house to a girl who had been his ward for less than five years; but her son persuaded her against having the body exhumed.

Fraulein Loewenstein soon married a handsome engineer, Emil Marek, with whom she had been carrying on a secret affair before Fritsch's death. Cinderella should have lived happily ever after. Unfortunately, there were problems. Although young and handsome, Emil had not yet established himself in a career; and the money left by her benefactor proved to be less than she had expected. At this point, Martha and Emil Marek concocted a plot that must be unique in the annals of crime. Emil took out an insurance policy for $30,000 against disablement or accident – which was easy enough for an obviously healthy young man.

A week later, they went into the garden, and Emil started to cut down a tree. After this, he sat down, closed his eyes, and allowed Martha to hack off his leg with the razor-sharp axe. Then she went back into the house. Emil cried out, Martha and the servants rushed out, and found him bleeding to death. Martha 'conscientiously' applied tourniquets and Emil was then rushed to hospital.

Preposterous scheme

It was a preposterous – to say nothing of painful – scheme. For how does a man accidentally chop off his leg below the knee while swinging an axe? Naturally, the doctors – and the police – were curious. Close examination of the amputated stump revealed that it had taken three separate blows to sever it, and the Mareks were accused of fraud. Martha promptly made things worse by trying to bribe an orderly to testify that he had seen a doctor tampering with the wound.

The Mareks then appeared in the dock, but the magistrates were unconvinced by the medical evidence – or perhaps they thought Emil Marek had suffered enough. The case against the couple was dismissed, and the insurance company settled for a relatively small sum – by dropping hints that they were thinking of having Moritz Fritsch's body exhumed. For some reason, Frau Marek did not like the idea.

It was the beginning of a long run of bad luck for the Mareks. An attempt to set up a radio business in Algiers was a failure. An ambitious engineering scheme – that might have made Emil's fortune – fell through because of the scandal of the trial – which followed them to North Africa. When the Marek's returned to Vienna, they had two children, and were so poor that Martha had to sell vegetables in a street market. Not long after, Emil Marek died in a charity ward of 'tuberculosis', and a month later their small daughter, Ingeborg, also passed away.

Free of such 'encumbrances', Martha's luck turned. She moved into the home of an elderly relative, Susanne Loewenstein, and cooked for her. Before long, Frau Loewenstein died, leaving the house and her money to Martha. But Martha still hadn't learned how to live modestly and without attracting attention.

She was extravagant, spent the money, and then took in a few selected lodgers. These included an insurance agent, and an elderly lady named Kittenberger, together with her son. The insurance agent arranged to insure Frau Kittenberger for $1000, with Martha as the beneficiary. Soon Frau Kittenberger conveniently died.

The insurance money did not last for long, and once again, Martha resorted to fraud. She arranged for a removal firm to call one night, and take her paintings and tapestries into storage. She then reported them stolen, and claimed the insurance. The detective sent to question her – Ignatz Peters – had also been on the earlier 'amputation' case. Suspicious from the start, he checked around the city's removal firms, and quickly found the one that had stored Martha's valuables.

For a second time, Martha was arrested and charged with fraud. The announcement of her arrest led Frau Kittenberger's son to approach the police and assert that his mother had died of poison. Ignatz Peters immediately went to work. Four corpses were exhumed: Emil Marek, their daughter Ingeborg; Frau Loewenstein, and Frau Kittenberger. All were found to have been poisoned with thallium, a rare metallic chemical element discovered in 1861.

Then Peters recalled that Martha had a second child, a son. He traced him to where he was boarded out in a poor district of Vienna. He was also suffering from thallium poisoning – although the symptoms looked like tuberculosis. His mother had been paying him visits and bringing him food. The boy was hurried to hospital, and his life was saved.

Martha Marek, accused and found guilty of four murders, was duly sentenced to death. This was in December 1938, when Hitler had reintroduced beheading as a means of execution. The headsman was more efficient than Martha had been. He accomplished his task with one clean swing of the axe.

Peculiar character

Beyond all doubt, Martha Marek was sane; no one ever suggested otherwise. Yet what can be said of a woman who can poison both her children, and who poisoned one of her victims – Frau Kittenberger – for a mere $1,000? She was clearly an obsessional character of a very peculiar type. Her greed and obsession with money was almost a physical disability, like colour blindness.

The case records reveal nothing about Martha Marek's psychological problems; but a significant amount can be deduced from her history. She was a bastard, brought up by a foster mother, whom

Ignatz Peters described as 'fat and vulgar'. Her later development strongly suggests that she did not receive affection in her early years. It is now a well-known fact that the first months of a child's life are of vital importance. Baby animals who are deprived of parental affection during this period become *incapable of giving affection* later. It is as if something inside them has starved to death. The same happens to human beings.

It can be inferred that Martha Loewenstein was affection-starved during this important period. Added to that, she certainly belonged to the group of 'high dominance females' who, in order to achieve sexual satisfaction, need to settle with a man who is even more dominant.

Martha Loewenstein married a man who was undoubtedly of merely moderate dominance. *She* dominated him – for it is impossible to imagine a high-dominance male allowing his wife to chop off his leg merely to collect a thousand dollars. He would have suggested insuring *her* and chopping off *her* leg.

After five years as the ward – and probably mistress – of an old man, she wanted a passionate and violent young lover. Emil Marek failed to satisfy her, physically or psychologically. So she killed him, and administered poison to the two children of the union.

It is tempting to say that the basic motivation of the crimes was her dread of poverty – something to be sympathized with. But if that was really her basic motivation, she would have carefully conserved the money Moritz Fritsch left her – and the later legacy from Susanne Loewenstein. In fact, it is clear that she was thoroughly spoilt and undisciplined. Instead of being grateful to Fritsch when she became his ward, she indulged in tantrums and black moods that would have led a less patient man to throw her out.

Frau Marek became a killer through an unusual combination of character traits: high dominance, inability to feel, with its inevitable self-centredness, and pure – or impure – greed. Strictly speaking, this does not constitute insanity. Yet today alcoholism is recognized as a kind of disease, even though it is agreed that the alcoholic is not insane. Martha Marek was suffering from a compulsion similar to alcoholism, if more complicated. Her curious mixture of compulsions can be seen, in varying degrees, in all greed-criminals, whether they are killers, or only robbers or swindlers.

One thing is clear: the greed criminal is suffering from a kind of violent, unquenchable thirst, similar to that of the alcoholic.

The result is that the crimes of the greed criminal have a weird air of irrationality.

It can be seen that most of the greed killers were also swindlers and confidence tricksters. But here again, there is a distinctly irrational element. The ordinary confidence swindler — like 'Count' Victor Lustig, the man who, in 1925, 'sold' the Eiffel Tower to a group of scrap metal tycoons — has a touch of bravado and humour about him; and a man with a sense of humour is basically sane. But the greed criminal is slightly paranoid; he has delusions of grandeur, and he lies to impress people.

This is true of the most spectacular mass murderer of modern times, the Frenchman Dr. Marcel Petiot. The greed crimes for which Petiot was executed began, strictly speaking, in 1941, and by the time they terminated, in 1944, he had killed at least 63 people. But Petiot had prepared for murder with a career of petty theft.

Born in Auxerre in 1897, he stole from classmates at school, and later from letter boxes. After a brief career in the army — from which he managed to get himself discharged as mentally unstable — Petiot qualified as a doctor at the age of 24. There is a strong possibility that he was a sadist. As a child, he had a reputation for amputating the tails of cats with scissors; women patients whom he 'treated' after hours in his surgery were heard to cry out in pain.

In 1928, by virtue of his persistent canvassing, he was appointed mayor of Villeneuve. Shortly afterwards his house-keeper became pregnant and then vanished. Two years later another woman patient was killed and robbed. Petiot was suspected, but his chief accuser — who was also one of his patients — died suddenly, and Petiot signed the death certificate. In spite of being mayor, he was in trouble several times for absurd petty crimes — robbing a gasmeter, stealing from a bookshop. He also trafficked in drugs.

It was the war that gave Petiot his opportunity to rise above petty crime. A Jew named Joachim Gubsinov wanted to escape to England with his wife and children, and Petiot offered him an 'escape route' in return for a large sum of money. Gubsinov duly raised two million francs on his fur business, and called with his wife and children at Petiot's lonely house in the Rue Lesueur. Petiot gave them lethal injections, claiming that they were a protection against typhoid. Then he went into the next room, and through a secret window, watched the Gubsinovs die.

Overstoked fire

Petiot lived – with his family – in the Rue Caumartin. The house in the Rue Lesueur was his execution chamber. But one day in March 1944, he overstoked the fire that consumed the bodies. The house went up in flames and a fireman who burst into the basement rushed out, shouting: 'The place is full of bodies!' Petiot, who came up in time to see what was happening, accosted a police officer and whispered: 'I am a member of the Resistance. Those bodies are the remains of traitors against France.' The police believed him and let him go. By the time they realized – from identification papers found in the house – that the victims were mostly Jews, Petiot was nowhere to be found.

But his vanity was his undoing. In October of 1944 – after the liberation of Paris – he wrote a letter to a newspaper claiming that he had been framed by the Gestapo, and that he was an officer in the Resistance. The handwriting was checked against that of Resistance officers, and Petiot was discovered to be hiding under an alias of Captain Henri Valéry; he had been in the Free French Forces for six weeks. He was guillotined on May 26, 1946.

It is true that Petiot's case was complicated by sadism; nevertheless, he is a typical example of the greed killer. There was the usual inability to form meaningful human relationships (his wife was a pale, docile girl, 15 years his junior, whom he married to silence gossip about his affairs and sexual perversions), the curious tendency to petty crime – as if he was unable to resist any opportunity to steal – and the vanity that made him so determined to become mayor. Above all, there was the decision to use murder – and not his talents as a doctor – to gain riches and rewards.

Criminal instinct

One of the world's strangest greed killers was another Frenchman – a young homosexual named Jean Baptiste Troppmann, who was obsessed by the idea of gaining money without legitimately working for it. Unlike most greed killers, he was never accused of the usual petty crimes; but the criminal instinct was certainly there. He was a student of poisons, and developed one that he claimed was undetectable. When he was 20, in 1869, he met a rich provincial businessman, Jean Kinck, and decided that this was his key to wealth.

An early attempt to con his new friend into parting with money was a failure. But Kinck was finally taken in by a story about deposits of precious metals near the mountains of the Upper Rhine. He set out with Troppmann, and was poisoned over a meal – his body being hidden in a heap of stones.

Troppmann then persuaded Madame Kinck to send him a cheque for 5500 francs. The local postmaster in Alsace, however, refused to cash it, and Troppmann decided that his only way of obtaining the wealth he needed – so that he would emigrate to America – was to slaughter all eight members of the Kinck family – including the youngest of the children.

He therefore arranged a meeting in Paris with Madame Kinck, and all her sons and daughters. He then lured them to the open countryside, where he brutally and sadistically stabbed them to death. His next move was to flee to Le Havre, where luck was against him. A policeman mistook him for a sneakthief, and when he tried to arrest him, Troppmann leapt into the harbour. The Kinck family papers were found on him. He was executed – fighting frenziedly – in January 1870, still under 21 years of age.

As far as the homicidal-cum-sexual greed criminal is concerned, France has an unenviable lead over Britain, other European countries, and the United States. Her most enigmatic greed killer, however, was a German: Jerome Weidmann. This case began in 1937 when Jean Belin – the Paris-based police officer who had arrested the French Bluebeard, Landru – was investigating the disappearance of a young American dancer, Jean de Koven. She had last been seen with a good-looking and apparently rich young man known as 'Bobby'.

On September 8, Belin learned that a hired car driver named Gouffy was found shot in the back of the head on the Orléans road. He, too, had driven off with a good-looking young man who appeared to be rich. Shortly afterwards, the naked body of a dead man named Leblond was found in the back of a car at Neuilly. He also had last been seen with a good-looking young man.

On November 20, 1937, an estate agent, a M. Lesobre, was found in the cellar of a house with a bullet in the back of his neck. His secretary's description of the young man with whom he had left the office suggested that this was the same killer. Apparently the man chose his victims for the little money they carried with them.

The police were searching for the murderer when Belin next heard about the disappearance of a young man named Frommer. He had been friendly with a foreigner called Sauerbrey, who lived in a house in the St. Cloud forest near Paris. Two detectives called on Sauerbrey, who invited them into the house. Suddenly he turned round with a gun in his hand, and began shooting. His aim was poor. He only grazed one of the policemen, and the other knocked him out with a hammer.

When gendarmes searched the grounds, they found the corpse of Jean de Koven under a foot of earth. She had been killed for her traveller's cheques; there was no evidence of sexual assault. Frommer's body was then found in the cellar; he had been shot in the back of his head. Sauerbrey subsequently said that his real name was Jerome Weidmann and admitted to being the notorious 'mass killer'. After his confession, Weidmann repented, publicly and noisily, and went to his death without flinching.

Mad recklessness

His basic motivation, however, remains a mystery. Why should he have killed so casually for such absurd sums of money – at most, a few hundred francs? The evidence suggests that he killed out of a kind of boredom, as boys pull the wings off flies.

All this explains why greed killers, and greed robbers in general, are the subject of inexhaustible interest to the criminologist – as unpredictable and exceptional as man-eating tigers, but far more difficult to understand. The only thing that is clear is that all of them suffer from a form of schizophrenia.

Whether the target is a train – stopped and robbed of the valuables it carries – a bank with rich deposits, or a lonely and frustrated widow, there is one element present in the greed criminal's behaviour and mentality. He – or she – does not countenance the possibility of failure or of being caught. In that alone lies madness, recklessness, and the greatest aid to the police in the tracking down of the offender, and his ultimate imprisonment or execution.

GUN DEATHS

When you consider that firearms were invented in the fourteenth century, it seems strange that it has taken so long for the gun to achieve its present pre-eminence as a murder weapon. The pistol – probably invented around 1450 in Pistoia in Italy – is certainly one of the quickest and most efficient methods of taking life – its chief disadvantages being that it is noisier than the knife, and a great deal less discreet than poison. This undoubtedly explains why the entry of the firearm into criminal history was relatively late and unspectacular. The Middlesex County Records for the year 1602 contain the following entry:

'On the highway at Howneslow, Co. Middx, Francis Kimber (a Gentleman of London) assaulted Wm. Peverell with a certain instrument called a pistol, which he, the said Francis, with his right hand pointed at the said William's beast and put him into great fear and terror.'

No further information is given, but it is clear that the writer was not at all familiar with the properties of pistols.

Pistols certainly came as a boon to highwaymen, who, prior to the 16th century, used swords and knives as their only weapons of intimidation. James Shaw, a highwayman, who was armed only with a sword: 'robbed several coaches and single passengers, and that with very great inhumanity, which was natural, he said, from his method of attacking . . .' Shaw got the victim to hand over his wallet by holding a sword to his throat, solving the problem of pursuit by hamstringing the victim's horse, or slashing the muscles at the back of his victim's knees.

By 1720 – the year in which Shaw was executed – England had been engulfed by a crime wave. The pistol had revolutionized the art of robbery. In one three-week period there were 25 major highway robberies around London, and people in coaches and sedan chairs were robbed in broad daylight in crowded streets.

227

The law tried to halt the epidemic with sheer barbarity; the gallows at Tyburn were in use from morning till night, and even women and children were executed for stealing a few pence.

Old methods
When someone asked a notoriously strict judge, Sir Francis Page, after his health, the old man quavered jocularly: 'Oh, I keep hanging on, hanging on.' But it made no difference; the crime wave continued until it was finally halted by the creation of an efficient police force more than half a century later.

Yet in spite of the highway robbers, surprisingly few murders were committed with guns. Most people preferred to stick to the old methods – knives, hatchets and bludgeons. Dick Turpin, the famous highwayman, committed a murder – his only one – with a pistol: but that was of a man trying to arrest him. And ten years later, a party of smugglers added a curious episode to the history of firearms in one of the most gruesome murder cases.

A Customs officer named Galley, travelling in company with a shoemaker named Chater, made the mistake of stopping for a drink in the Hampshire village of Rowland's Castle. As soon as the word got around that there was a Customs officer at the inn, the local smugglers moved in. Galley was tortured with a pair of spurs, his testicles were squeezed until he fainted, and then he was whipped to death.

Mistrust
Chater was also tortured, but no one was willing to take on the responsibility of killing him. Finally, someone suggested that they should put a loaded gun to his head, tie a long string to the trigger, and that all fourteen of the smugglers should pull the trigger. If they had gone through with it, it would have raised an interesting point of law: whether fourteen men can all be convicted for the same murder. But they decided against it; instead, they threw Chater down a well – alive – and buried him with stones. By that time, half the smugglers had got tired of the whole thing and gone home; so only seven were eventually tried and executed for the murders.

The mistrust of firearms persisted even into the nineteenth century. The two most widely publicized crimes of the 1820s were William Corder's murder of Maria Marten in the Red Barn, and the murder of William Weare by Thurtell and Hunt. Corder shot his ex-mistress, Maria Marten, with a pistol, and although (as he confessed) 'she fell and died in an instant', he then stabbed her several times with a carving knife. When Thurtell and Hunt — two 'sporting gentlemen' — murdered the crooked bookmaker, William Weare, in 1823, they began by discharging a pistol in his face. The bullet glanced off Weare's cheekbone, and the wounded man ran away. Thurtell flung him to the ground and cut his throat with a penknife, then jammed the pistol against his head with such force that it smashed the skull, filling the barrel with blood and brains.

When Thurtell was executed in 1824 (Hunt escaped with a sentence of transportation), street hawkers were selling a poem that does not mention the pistol:

'They cut his throat from ear to ear
His head they battered in.
His name was Mr. William Weare —
He lived in Lyons Inn.'

If criminals were unhappy about the use of firearms, the police disliked them even more. If a man was killed with a knife or a bludgeon, the murder weapon could be produced in court and the jury convinced that it had inflicted the wounds; but a gun was a different matter. The bullet might have been knocked out of shape against a bone, and in any case, it was almost impossible to prove which gun had fired it.

Fortunately, there were a few men who took a less defeatist attitude. One of these was Dr. Joseph Bell, the man who inspired Conan Doyle with the idea of Sherlock Holmes. On August 10th, 1893, an ex-army tutor named A.J. Monson went out shooting with his employer's son, a youth called Cecil Hambrough.

As Cecil was climbing over a dyke, there was a shot and he fell dead. Monson claimed that the boy's gun had exploded accidentally. But when it was discovered that Monson had insured Hambrough's life, he was arrested and charged with murder. The key factor was whether Hambrough really had accidentally shot himself at close range or whether Monson had shot him from a few feet away. According to Monson, Cecil had been carrying the gun over his shoulder, and had stumbled and blown off the back of his head.

Dr. Bell brooded on the question. Shotguns are notoriously unpredictable weapons. Finally, Bell took a twelvebore shotgun to the morgue in Edinburgh, and fired it into the skull of a corpse. What he observed enabled him to say confidently in court that Cecil Hambrough could *not* have been shot with his own gun; he was shot from a distance of between six and nine feet from behind.

Bell's evidence should have hanged Monson, but the defence managed to confuse the issue with such a mass of financial evidence that Monson was acquitted on a Scottish verdict of 'Not Proven'. Nevertheless, Dr. Bell had proved that, where guns are concerned, no pathologist needs to acknowledge defeat.

At the time Dr. Bell was firing shotguns at cadavers in Edinburgh, another firearms expert ran a gun shop near Charing Cross station; his name was Ted Churchill, his shop was conveniently close to Scotland Yard, and he was often summoned there to give his opinion in cases involving guns. When Ted Churchill wanted to find out how far the bullets from a certain gun would damage a human skull, he tested the gun by firing at a sheep's head. And it was Ted Churchill's evidence that hammered the last nail into the coffin of a swindler and murderer called Samuel Herbert Dougal.

Dougal was what the sensational press would now call a sex maniac. His libidinous appetite was truly extraordinary – on one occasion, he had seduced a mother *and* her three daughters. His career in the army had been reasonably successful, although two wives had died under somewhat suspicious circumstances. After his discharge, however, Dougal found it difficult to continue to live in the manner he preferred; seduction cost money.

He tried his hand at forgery, was caught, and served a prison sentence. Then he had the good fortune to meet a middle-aged spinster named Camille Holland, who soon allowed herself to be seduced. Miss Holland was rich. In 1899, Dougal and 'Mrs. Dougal' moved into rooms in Saffron Walden while Dougal carried out negotiations to buy a property called Moat Farm near Clavering – with Miss Holland's money. The landlady took a great liking to the sweet, gentle-mannered 'Mrs. Dougal'; then her lodgers moved into Moat Farm, and she saw no more of the lady.

Identical crack

At Moat Farm, Dougal was now living alone – although he had a succession of young female visitors. Four years went by, and then in March 1903, a police officer called to question Dougal about the missing Camille Holland. Dougal explained that he had never married Miss Holland because he was in the process of divorcing his previous wife. Miss Holland, he said, had left him for another man in 1899, not long after moving into Moat Farm.

The police found the story unlikely; they knew that Dougal had made determined attempts to seduce a servant girl shortly after moving into the farm, and there had been quarrels between husband and 'wife'. The police began digging in the garden, and they continued digging, in spite of Dougal's threats to sue the Chief Constable for damaging his crops. The moats that gave the farm its name were drained, but no body was found in the black mud.

Then the police heard about a ditch that had been filled in on Dougal's instructions. They found the man who had superintended the work, and dug where he suggested. Soon the police were looking down at the badly decomposed body of Miss Holland. The pathologist's report showed that she had died from a gunshot wound in the side of the head. A bootmaker identified the boots on the corpse as having been made for Miss Holland. Now it was up to Ted Churchill.

No revolver had been found, but there were a number of .32 calibre bullets found at the farm. Churchill fired some of these bullets into sheep's heads. In court, he was able to demonstrate not only that the bullet found in Miss Holland's skull was a somewhat distorted .32, but that it must have been fired by someone sitting beside her – probably in a car. He had been able to produce a crack in the sheep's skull practically identical with that in the head of Camille Holland.

Throughout the trial, Dougal had been cheerful and ironically polite; but as Churchill gave his evidence, his *sang froid* disappeared. He recognized this was the end – and indeed it was; he was executed on July 8, 1903. As the trap was about to open, the chaplain whispered urgently: 'Guilty or Not Guilty?', and from the hood that covered Dougal's head came a muffled reply: 'Guilty.'

Hooded man

The man who, more than any other, was responsible for turning ballistics into a science was not Ted Churchill, but his nephew, Robert Churchill, who took over the family gun shop in 1910. The affair that first brought him to public notice was the case of the 'Hooded Man'.

In the early hours of October 9, 1912, Inspector Arthur Walls, of the Eastbourne police, saw a burglar crouching on the portico of a house in South Cliff Avenue, and called to him to come down. Instead, the burglar fired two shots, and Walls fell dead. Not long afterwards, the police discovered the identity of the killer: he was George Mackay, alias John Williams, a petty crook.

Mackay was betrayed by a 'friend', Edgar Powers, who was in love with the burglar's beautiful mistress, Florence Seymour. At the instigation of the police, Powers persuaded the girl to lead him to the revolver with which Walls had been killed – she had helped Mackay bury it on the beach.

Churchill's task was to try and prove that the bullet that had killed Walls had been fired from this revolver. At that time, there was no sure way of proving that a particular bullet had been fired from a certain gun – more than ten years were to pass before this became possible with the comparison microscope. But Churchill devised a way of showing the jury that the rifling on the bullet corresponded closely to the rifling inside the barrel of the gun.

He poured wax into the gun and made a 'cast' of the inside of the barrel. In court, he produced enlarged photographs of the bullet, and of the wax cast; the jury could see how closely they corresponded. Mackay, known in the press as 'The Hooded Man', because the police kept him hooded on his journeys to court – they were still searching for witnesses to identify him – was convicted of the murder, and hanged in January 1913. Before he died, he was allowed to kiss his newly-born child. He placed a piece of prison bread in the baby's mouth, saying: 'Now no one can say your father never gave you anything.'

It was in June 1914 that a young Bosnian called Gavrilo Princip fired the two shots that led to the outbreak of the First World War. Archduke Ferdinand of Austria was visiting Sarajevo with his duchess. Serbian patriots wanted to register their protest about the Austrian occupation of Bosnia. Shortly after 10 a.m. on June 28, 1914, a bomb was thrown at the Archduke's carriage, but it missed, wounding several spectators instead. An hour later, the Archduke left the town hall, and remarked to his wife: 'I've got a feeling there may be more bombs around.'

He was mistaken; the weapon that Gavrilo Princip concealed in his pocket was a Browning revolver with six shots in it. The car approached Princip – and then turned off into another street: modern history hung in the balance. Then someone shouted that the car had taken the wrong turn; the route had been revised. It backed, and proceeded past the young Bosnian – who drew his revolver, and fired twice at close range. One shot killed the Archduke, and the other, his wife.

Princip was seized, but the decisive tragedy of modern history had taken place, and the rest followed inevitably – Austria's declaration of war on Serbia, Russian mobilization, the Kaiser's declaration of war on Russia . . .

Social parasite

Those two revolver shots also launched the world into a new epoch: the age of guns. The 1914 war was the first time that vast numbers of men actually handled guns. Before the war, most guns were owned by farmers or sportsmen; now everybody learned how to use them. An early Spencer Tracy film called *They Gave Him a Gun* put its finger on what happened: the servicemen came back from Europe, and found a new world that had already forgotten the war and the men who fought in it.

There were no jobs for the returning heroes; life was hard. So many of them decided to make use of what they had learned in the army, and suddenly, the police were faced with the greatest crime wave since 1720. But this time it was not just in England, but in America, France, Italy, Germany . . . The petty criminal who had never stolen anything larger than a watch discovered that it was just as easy to walk into a bank and point a gun at the cashier.

And the Americans, with an innocence and optimism that now seem stunning, decided to reform their country by banning all alcoholic liquor, and thereby produced an entirely new breed of social parasite called the mobster; fifty years later, in spite of numerous Acts of Congress and Commissions of Enquiry, America is still as securely in the mobsters' hands as it was in Al Capone's.

In most of the countries of the world, the authorities have achieved some sort of control by banning the sale of guns to private citizens. In America, financial interests – known as the 'gun lobby' – continue to prevent a measure that would probably cut the crime rate by 75%.

America's gun problem is not so much social as psychological. The past 25 years have seen an alarming increase in mass murders committed with guns, and the majority of such cases have taken place in America. On December 30, 1950, a young psychopath named William Cook stopped a car driven by Carl Mosser; Mosser's wife, three young children and family dog were also in the car. Cook brandished a gun, and made the Mosser family drive around Texas for 72 hours; then, when the wife and children became hysterical, he killed them all.

On September 6, 1949, a 28-year-old ex-G.I. named Howard Unruh walked out of his house in Camden, New Jersey, carrying a German Luger pistol, and, in the next twelve minutes, killed thirteen people at random. Captured after a siege of his home, Unruh declared: 'I'd have killed a thousand if I'd had enough ammunition.'

In January 1958, Charles Starkweather took his girlfriend Caril Fugate on a murder rampage across Nebraska, and had shot and killed ten people – mostly strangers – before he was captured a couple of days later. In Lathrup Village, Michigan, in August 1968, a family of six called Robison were all 'executed' by an unknown killer with a .22 revolver.

In October 1970, John Linley Frazier 'executed' the family of Dr. Victor Ohta at his home near Santa Cruz, California, and threw the five bodies into the swimming pool. On November 7, 1973, a family of nine – four adults, three teenagers and two young children – were all shot through the head by unknown killers at their home near Victor, California . . .

It would be possible to list dozens – even hundreds – of such cases that have taken place in America – the only English parallel is the case of psychopath, Peter Manuel, who killed two families with a gun in late 1956 and early 1957 – but one more will suffice. On November 15, 1959, two ex-convicts named Perry Smith and Richard Hickock broke into the home of the Clutter family near Holcomb, Kansas, and slaughtered all four in the course of robbery.

In 1966, Truman Capote's reconstruction of the crime, *In Cold Blood*, broke best-selling records in America, although it failed to achieve the same success in other countries. Obviously, Capote had touched on some strange, dark nerve in the American psyche. If we understood this, we should understand something important about the mysterious lure of gun violence in America. That lure can only be quashed by outlawing the gun.

HEADLESS CORPSES

As the Duke of Monmouth was about to kneel and place his head on the block, he held out his hand to the notorious executioner, Jack Ketch. 'Here are six guineas for you. Pray do your business well. Don't serve me as you served Lord Russell.'

He had reason to be nervous. When Ketch had beheaded Lord William Russell – for his part in the Rye House Plot to kidnap Charles II – he had completely bungled the job. After several violent swipes with the axe, Russell was still twitching, and his neck was unsevered. Monmouth, now being executed for his rebellion against James II, was understandably anxious to die less bloodily.

He turned to a servant, and handed him a purse containing more guineas. 'Give him that if he does his work well.' Then he felt the edge of the axe, and said, sighing: 'I fear it is not sharp enough.' Ketch was unnerved by all this coolness. He raised the axe, then threw it down, shouting: 'I can't do it.' The sheriff had to threaten him with dire penalties before he could be persuaded to make another attempt.

The crowd gave a groan

Looking pale and ill, he raised the axe above his head, and brought it down. The crowd gave a groan, and Monmouth jerked with agony; but his head stayed on his shoulders. Now thoroughly demoralized, Ketch made three more attempts, but there was no strength in the blows. The neck was only lacerated. Finally, he threw down the hatchet, pulled out a knife, and sawed the head off. The servant holding the purse pocketed it and walked away. Meanwhile, the crowd booed and threw things.

It was no sinecure, being an executioner in those days. Ketch usually hanged his clients; but he wasn't very good at that either, and most of the condemned men died by slow strangulation. It was preferable, however, to being butchered with a blunt axe, and even when the headman *was* efficient, it was tiring work. In 1746, Jack Thrift had to behead two Jacobite rebels, Lord Kilmarnock and Lord Balmerino. He severed Kilmarnock's head with one clean blow, but it took him three swings of the axe to decapitate Balmerino. There were many officers of the law who felt that somebody ought to devise a swift and infallible method for taking a man's life.

Half a century later, it became an urgent necessity. France rebelled against its rulers. The Bastille was stormed, and its defenders massacred, the king fled and was recaptured: the Terror began. The enemies of the new regime had to be killed by the hundred – by the thousand. How could it be done? The solution was found by a gentle, kindly man, well-known for his good works: Dr. Joseph Ignace Guillotin.

Dr. Guillotin was a freemason – in fact, one of the founders of freemasonry in France. The freemasons are a benevolent secret society, devoted to the improvement of mankind; but the Church regarded them as wicked atheists. And it was for this reason more than for anything else that Dr. Guillotin found himself in the Constituent Assembly, with an influential voice in the new revolutionary government of France.

Now this gentle humanitarian was horrified at some of the bloodshed he had seen. He loathed those barbarous and primitive instruments of execution, the wheel and the gibbet. He was sickened by the sight of a man swinging from a gallows all day, while the crowd underneath drank beer and made merry. Guillotin foresaw the mass executions that were coming, and he brooded on how they might be made painless and swift: a moral lesson rather than a sadistic spectacle. Some kind of 'machine' was needed. He consulted the public executioner, Charles Henri Sanson, and they looked over various old prints and engravings.

As early as 1555, the Italians had invented a beheading machine, in which a heavy axe blade was placed between two upright posts, so that it could be hauled up to the top with a rope, then allowed to fall down the groove on to the neck of a man kneeling underneath. These 'sliding axes' had also been tried in Germany, in Persia – even in Scotland. But they'd never really caught on. The blade often got stuck in the groove, or the rope caught. The old manual method was simpler and more reliable.

An agonizing eternity

And now occurred one of those supreme ironies of history. The man who solved the problem was none other than the king himself, Louis the Sixteenth. It was shortly before the flight that cost him his life, and precipitated the Terror. The Assembly had asked Dr. Antoine Louis, the king's physician, to look into Dr. Guillotin's plan. Dr. Guillotin was asked to call on Dr. Louis at the Tuileries Palace, and he took Sanson, the executioner, with him.

As the three men were engaged in examining the sketches of the machine, a stranger knocked and entered. It was the king, dressed in ordinary clothes. He asked Dr. Louis what he thought of the machine, and looked at the drawing. Then he shook his head. 'That curved blade wouldn't suit every kind of neck.' The king picked up a pencil. 'What you need is something more like *this*.' He drew a straight, sloping line on the underside of the axe blade. Guillotin looked at the drawing. 'Yes, of course, you're right . . .' A few weeks later, the first guillotine was tried out on three corpses. The king had been right: a curved blade failed to decapitate one of the corpses, but the sloping blade worked perfectly on the other two. Two years later, the king was decapitated by the machine he had helped perfect.

For the next two years – until the Terror ended with the execution of Robespierre in 1794 – the guillotine thudded with horrible, mechanical persistence, and thousands of heads rolled into the basket. As to the good Dr. Guillotin, he continued his humanitarian work. He was one of the earliest pioneers of smallpox vaccination, and his work on the extermination of smallpox undoubtedly saved more lives in Europe than his guillotine destroyed. But when he died, in 1814, he already knew that it would not be his medical discoveries that would immortalize his name, but that triangular blade, with all its association of horror . . .

This raises the interesting question: *why* is it that decapitation strikes us as so sickening and gruesome? Guillotin was right: as a method of execution, it is certainly more humane than hanging, electrocution or the gas chamber. Hanging is only about 95% certain; a slight miscalculation in the placing of the rope, and the condemned man strangles to death. Men in the gas chamber have been known to hold their breath for minutes before breathing in the cyanide gas. And the criminologist Nigel Morland, who once stepped on a highly charged electric grid, is on record as saying that the last seconds of an electrocuted man must seem to be an agonizing eternity.

Only the guillotine has never failed to carry out its work with perfect swiftness and efficiency. Yet Guillotin is remembered as a monster, because the idea of decapitation touches some deep chord of horror in the human psyche. It may be because the loss of the head is so final; men can lose an arm or leg and still survive; not the head. Or could it be, perhaps, because our earliest ancestors cut off the heads of their enemies in battle, and often ate the brains? Is the twinge of horror due to some deep racial memory?

Whatever the reason, there can be no doubt that crimes involving beheading always seem more cruel and brutal than other types of crime. And this is absurd. For sheer vicious cruelty, slow poison is probably the most inhuman method of killing. Then there are the murderers who get pleasure from the fear of their victims – like José Marcellino, Mexico's 'lover's lane killer', captured in 1973, who admitted: 'I liked it so much, to see the males squirm, and the women frightened and crying, that I'd make my threats last a long time . . . I enjoyed the fear of death in their eyes.'

By comparison, murderers like Crippen and Patrick Mahon seem decent and sane. Yet it is Crippen and Mahon whose cases are endlessly rehashed by crime journalists under titles like: 'Horror of of the headless corpse.' Still, no matter what the general public may feel about them, Crippen and Mahon are of scant interest to the professional criminologist. He is concerned with the motivations behind a crime, and it hardly matters to him *what* the killer does to dispose of the body. On the other hand, he finds a criminal like Patrick Byrne, the Birmingham Y.W.C.A. killer, of altogether greater interest.

There is no need to ask why Byrne killed Stephanie Baird – that is perfectly obvious. He was drunk, and he wanted sex. When he had strangled her into unconsciousness, he undressed her and raped her. All that is straightforward, if horrible; but why did he then cut off her head, and commit further sexual acts on the body? Why did he, even then, go out and try to kill another girl by hitting her with a stone? Why did he write a note saying: 'This was the thing I thought would never come.'

In the course of his confession, Byrne said one thing that provides a key to his strange personality. He said he wanted to terrorize all the women in the hostel 'to get my own back on them for causing my nervous tension through sex'. This is a curious statement. Even the most stupid man must see that women are not to *blame* for making him sexually excited. A cat may as well blame mice for making it feel hungry.

But Byrne was not trying to be logical; he was trying to explain, in his own fumbling way, what dark forces had suddenly mastered him when he found himself in a room with an unconscious girl. He also admitted to a psychiatrist that he had been indulging for years in daydreams in which he cut up girls with a circular saw. This brings us altogether closer to the heart of the problem, for what we can see so clearly, in Byrne's case, is that when he made his way into the Y.W.C.A. that December afternoon, it was not simply a girl he wanted – ordinary sexual intercourse. It was somehow *all* women, all the women in the world. He was expressing one of the savage, basic frustrations of man.

Craving for gratification

In 1930, Freud published a book called *Civilization and Its Discontents*, in which he advanced a disturbing – and profoundly pessimistic – theory. He suggested that man is not made for civilization, or civilization for man. Man is a carnivorous animal, and his basic instincts are violent and aggressive. Whether we like it or not, it is 'natural' for him to go on a raiding party to another village, kill the men, and then drag off the women for his own pleasure, as natural as it is considered for a tiger to eat antelopes.

But this human tiger was also intelligent and gregarious. He learned to live with other human beings in communities, and to create civilization. Every step he has taken into civilization has been a violation of his basic instincts. Culture is another name for suppression of these instincts. The great basic conflict of all human existence, says Freud, is the conflict between the individual's craving for personal gratification and the claims of society. So how *can* man be happy? Unhappiness is a basic part of his condition . . .

Less pessimistic psychologists, like Abraham Maslow, have pointed out that this is a one-sided view. Happiness does *not* mean unlimited self-indulgence. The history of crime and violence reveals to us that the men who *could* indulge themselves without self-discipline – Caligula, Ivan the Terrible, Vlad the Impaler – were not particularly happy men. Long-term happiness must involve self-discipline. Nowadays, there are very few reputable thinkers who take Freud's argument about civilization seriously.

Nevertheless, without fully intending it, Freud *had* expressed the basic psychology of psychopathic killers like Patrick Byrne, Jack the Ripper, Peter Kürten. These *are* men who feel that Man and Civilization were simply not made for one another. Consider, for example, the nature of the male sexual drive. Unlike most women, man is not basically 'faithful'. Particularly when young and virile, the average man would be perfectly happy to sleep with a different girl every night; even healthy men have their sexual fantasies.

Avenging sexual tensions

Surely, where sex is concerned, civilization is *intended* to torment males, as you might torment a caged tiger by poking it with a stick? Taking it a step further, is a man to blame if he seizes his opportunity to grab a girl and pull her into a dark alleyway . . .? *This* is what Byrne meant when he talked about 'getting his own back on women for causing my sexual tensions', and he was almost paraphrasing Sigmund Freud.

But why the decapitation? This is also easy to explain. Once a man is possessed by this urgency – like a fox in a chicken farm – he is subjected to endless twinges of desire, like electric shocks. He compensates for an increasing feeling of frustration and inferiority with daydreams in which he dominates the girl completely; and the longer the fantasies continue, the more violent they are likely to become.

Charles Melquist, arrested in 1958 for the sex-murder and decapitation of 15-year-old Bonnie Leigh Scott, near Chicago, admitted to years of fantasizing about naked women, and of tossing them into huge grinding machines. When such a man finally finds himself with his hands around the throat of an unconscious girl, sexual intercourse is not enough. It seems an anticlimax. His overheated desires crave some stronger satisfaction, some ultimate act of violation and possession. And here, the basic human revulsion at the idea of decapitation rises up from the subconscious – the ultimate act of aggression. . . .

What is equally significant is that both Byrne and Melquist were horrified by what they had done. Byrne said he was glad the police had found him; the murder had tormented him for the past two months; Melquist also made his confession in a long, relieved babble, and admitted that he had been unable to sleep after the murder. Not only is their act of violence no solution to the cravings that produced it: the killer recognizes that he is *further than ever* from a solution. Many killers of this type commit suicide.

The pattern can be clearly seen in the case of Jack the Ripper. The early victims – Mary Anne Nicholls, Annie Chapman, Catherine Eddowes – were mutilated in the area of the genitals, indicating that the Ripper's basic obsession was with the woman's sexual function – perhaps with the womb. The last murder took place indoors; this time, the killer had unlimited time at his disposal, and the victim – Mary Kelly – was not only disembowelled but almost decapitated. Then the murders ceased, and all the evidence suggests that the Ripper committed suicide.

The novelist Zola based a novel on the Ripper crimes – *La Bête Humaine* – the human beast. This goes to the heart of the problem. Such a man has decided to become the solitary hunter in search of prey, rather than a responsible human being. In doing so, he has retreated from society as deliberately as if he had decided to become a Trappist monk. But men like Byrne, Melquist or the Ripper lack the qualifications for becoming hermits; they *need* society. Hence the conflicting whirlpool of urges that may end in suicide.

'Mad butcher'

The case that most clearly demonstrates the complex morbid psychology of 'the human beast' took place in Cleveland, Ohio, in the mid-1930s: the curious unsolved case of the Butcher of Kingsbury Run. Between 1935 and 1938, the 'Mad Butcher' killed at least a dozen people, hacking the bodies into small pieces, and removing the heads – several of which were never found.

On September 23, 1935, two decapitated bodies were found in the area of Kingsbury Run and East 45th Street, a slum area. Both had been mutilated with a knife; both were men – one, a 28-year-old medical orderly, the other, a 40-year-old vagrant, who was never identified. The fact that both victims were male suggested that the killer was homosexual, and a sadistic pervert. But when, four months later, the headless body of a 42-year-old prostitute was found not far from Kingsbury Run, the police became less sure that they were looking for a homosexual; the woman's body had been hacked as if in a frenzy, and the head was never found.

At intervals during 1936, three more victims were found in the area; all were men, all were headless, and in one case, the head was never found. The killer was obviously possessed by some kind of frenzy; some of the bodies were little more than a pile of mangled pieces.

On February 23, 1937, the victim was again a woman – headless, and in pieces. In June, the dismembered body of a 30-year-old Negro woman was found in a burlap bag under the

Lorain-Carnegie Bridge. The ninth victim, a man, was found in July; he had been decapitated and the body hacked in pieces. The head was never found. And in 1938, there were victims; a dismembered and headless woman was found on April 8, and on August 17, the 'Mad Butcher' (as the press called him) committed another double murder, a man and a woman. In each of these cases, the killer decapitated the victim, and in six of them, the heads were never found.

The man who was then in charge of Cleveland's police department was Eliott Ness – hero of T.V.'s 'Untouchables'. Ness recognized that the usual methods of detection were of doubtful value here. But he realized that the mad killer was finding most of his victims among prostitutes and down-and-outs. The latter congregated in a shanty-town area in the centre of the city, near the market. One night in August, Ness raided the place, forced its inhabitants to leave, and burnt it down. This had the desired effect of depriving the killer of his victims; there were no more murders.

Ness also reasoned that the 'Mad Butcher' must be of a certain type. He must be big and powerful to overpower his victims. He must own a car, to transport the bodies. He must live alone, and in some quiet area – perhaps an unfrequented *cul de sac* – in order not to arouse the curiosity of his neighbours. And in order to fit this pattern, he must be rich, or at least well off.

Ness's team made painstaking enquiries in Cleveland society and, according to Oscar Fraley, chronicler of the 'Untouchables', soon found a suspect who fitted. He was physically huge, homosexual, sullen and paranoid, and well-to-do. Ness had the man brought in for questioning, and for months played a cat and mouse game with him. The man, confident he was cleverer than the police, almost admitted the murders, and dared Ness to find evidence.

And, finally, while Ness was still searching, he had himself committed to a mental home, where he died a year later. Ness never doubted that this was the torso killer.

Ness's suspect was an intelligent, literate man; he may well have read Freud's *Civilization and Its Discontents*. If so, he could have added a final footnote; that the man who lives as a beast of prey will almost certainly die as one alone and unmourned by his fellow creatures.

HIGH SOCIETY MURDER

The woman's body lay at the foot of a flight of stairs; the angle at which the head was twisted made it clear that the neck was broken. Her name was Amy Robsart, and she was the 28-year-old wife of Robert Dudley, later the Earl of Leicester. It happened on September 8, 1560, and for the past four centuries historians have argued as to whether it was murder – and whether, if so, Queen Elizabeth I of England planned it.

Robert Dudley, Master of the Queen's Horse, was tall and good-looking (his portraits make him look rather like Errol Flynn). When Elizabeth became queen in 1558, they were both 25 years old. She fell in love with him, and her infatuation was so obvious that the country was alive with lewd rumours – such as the 'fact' that she had borne one of his children. Whether or not the rumours were true, Elizabeth certainly considered marrying the courtier.

Grave accident

However, he was already married to the daughter of Sir John Robsart, a wealthy Norfolk landowner. Since Dudley spent most of his time in London, and the Queen spent most of hers at home near Oxford, the 'sweethearts' saw little of one another. Elizabeth apart, Dudley was not much liked. A Spanish envoy described him as 'the worst young fellow I have ever encountered. He is heartless, spiritless, treacherous and violent.'

On September 4, 1560, Queen Elizabeth told a foreign envoy that Amy Robsart was dead. The odd thing about this is that Amy was still alive and in the best of health – she died four days later. On the day of her death she allowed the servants to attend a local fair, and was alone in her home, Cumnor Place, Oxford. When the servants returned that evening they found that a 'grave accident' had taken place.

The news was sent to Dudley, who was at Windsor, only 30

miles away. He might have been expected to rush straight home. Instead, he sent his cousin, with instructions to empanel a jury of 'discreet and substantial men' to conduct an inquest. The actual evidence presented at the time has vanished, but the verdict was 'accidental death'.

If Elizabeth meant to marry her favourite, she had reckoned without the storm of rumour and suspicion that was inevitable after such a convenient happening. Public opinion against her was too strong; Dudley never became Prince Consort. In an attempt to discover evidence that the Queen was an accessory to murder, the historian J.A. Froude studied the letters of the Spanish ambassador in Madrid. It was he who discovered that the Queen had 'anticipated' Amy's death. A year before that, the same ambassador was telling his king that Dudley planned to poison his wife.

Seven years after Amy's death, her half-brother stated, in an indiscreet moment, that he had covered up the murder of his sister for the sake of Dudley. Questioned about this, he quickly withdrew his statement, merely saying that he had never been satisfied with the inquest verdict. Interestingly enough, Dudley had obtained an excellent sinecure for Amy's half-brother in 1564, four years after the accident.

The historian A.L. Rowse states positively that Amy was dying of cancer when she fell downstairs. It is true that the Spanish ambassador states in another letter that Amy had a cancer of the breast – this was 18 months before her death. But *if* she died of cancer, surely her husband would have taken care to make the verdict as public as possible? It would have been perfect way of silencing all rumours. When all the evidence is weighed, it must be admitted that the balance of probability is in favour of the view that Robert Dudley had his wife murdered, with the connivance – or at least the knowledge – of Queen Elizabeth.

Homosexual experience
Half a century after the death of Amy Robsart, England was rocked by the scandal of another death in high society. But on this occasion, the murderers were brought to justice – rather to the surprise of the British public. Elizabeth's successor, James I, was on the throne, an ungainly man, who slobbered as he talked. He was also a homosexual.

In 1606, the King was watching a tournament when a handsome young man fell off his horse and broke his leg. James immediately took a close interest in the invalid, whose name was Robert Carr. In fact, Carr had also had considerable homosexual experience; at the age of 11, he had been seduced by the poet and essayist Sir Thomas Overbury (whose *Characters* is a classic of English literature). Overbury had no objection at all when Carr became the King's lover; he had his own ambitions. He was appointed Carr's secretary, and within two years he was knighted.

At this point, the tall and virile Carr fell in love with a teenage beauty, Frances Howard. Aged only 15, she was already married to the Earl of Essex; but he was abroad, and she was still a virgin. Since Carr was illiterate, Overbury did his wooing for him, writing his love letters. These were so effective that she soon yielded her virginity to Carr. Before long, her husband came home from abroad but by then she was so infatuated with Carr that she refused to allow him his marital rights – even though they slept naked in the same bed. Finally, the Earl was persuaded to grant her a divorce.

For some perverse reason her projected marriage to Carr filled Overbury with bitter jealousy. It seems possible that he and Carr were still lovers, and that the wedding would put an end to it. He quarrelled so violently with the young man that the King stepped in and offered Overbury a diplomatic post abroad. Carr, acting on the advice of Frances Howard, persuaded Overbury to refuse. As Carr expected, the King lost his temper, and ordered Overbury to be thrown into the Tower of London to teach him manners. This was what Carr and his mistress wanted. Overbury was now at their mercy. Sir Gervase Elwes, a friend of Frances's, was made Governor of the Tower, Carr bought poison, and his manservant, Weston, administered it to the prisoner in small doses. On September 15, 1613, Overbury died.

Carr and Frances Howard were then married, and Carr continued to be the King's favourite – his wife had the sense not to be jealous. But Carr was stupid, spoiled, and got into the habit of making scenes. Even the infatuated James began to tire of him. Then, two years later, the chemist's assistant who had prepared the poison died, but confessed to his 'awful crime' on his deathbed. The King had to be told, and he appointed Sir Edward Coke to investigate the affair.

As a result, Sir Gervase Elwes (who had known about the murder), the servant Weston, and the chemist who had supplied the poison, were all hanged at Tyburn. Carr was fairly certain he would escape, convinced that the King was too fond of him to allow him even to be tried. When it became clear that he *would* be tried – together with Frances – he threatened to announce in open court that he and the King had been lovers for nearly ten years.

Famous beauty

The result was that when he appeared in Westminster Hall, two men stood behind him with a cloak, ready to throw it over his head if he tried to say anything against the King. Both Carr and his wife were sentenced to death. But the King kept his word that Carr should not be executed. The poisoners spent six years in the Tower of London, then they were allowed to retire to their country estate. Frances Howard died of a cancer of the womb at 39. Carr lived on into old age; when he visited the King a few years later, James broke down and cried on his shoulder.

In general, the English have an excellent record for behaving impartially towards offenders from high society; a remarkable number of Lords have stood trial on capital charges. In fact, one of them, Lord Mohun (pronounced *moon*), was tried for murder on two occasions.

In December 1691, when he was 16 years old, he agreed to help one of his drinking companions, Captain Richard Hill, to kidnap a famous London beauty, the Drury Lane actress, Mrs. Bracegirdle. (She was actually 'Miss', but all actresses were given the courtesy title 'Mrs'.) The plan was to drag her into a coach as she left the theatre, and then to take her to a house where she could safely be raped. The actress's mother was with her, and clung on tightly, screaming, until the watch came to help them. Whereupon, Lord Mohun, with admirable presence of mind, apologized for the disgraceful conduct of his unruly friend, begged everyone's pardon, and offered to escort the ladies home.

Superb swordsman

They refused angrily, but Mohun and Captain Hill followed them all the same, and began to make a disturbance in the street outside the house. They were still shouting, and drinking wine from bottles, when an actor named Mountford had the misfortune to walk past on his way home. Hill was convinced that Mountford was Mrs. Bracegirdle's lover; his appearance on the scene seemed to confirm this. The captain drew his sword, and before Mountford could defend himself, ran him through. Hill then fled, and Mohun was arrested.

The nobleman was fortunate; before Mountford died, he gasped out that Mohun had offered him no violence. So when Mohun was tried in front of a jury of his peers – the right of every English Lord – he was only charged with 'maliciously abetting' the murder. Mohun's defence was that he was waiting outside Mrs. Bracegirdle's house to apologize to her. His peers believed him and he was acquitted. Hill was never caught.

Eight years later, however, Mohun again stood at the bar of the House of Lords. There had been a wild party in London, ending in violent quarrels. Mohun and two companions challenged three other men to a duel. All six went off to St. Martins in the Fields, proceeded to fight, and a Captain Coote was mortally wounded. Once again, Mohun was acquitted; but he was warned that if he didn't 'amend his ways' he could expect less leniency next time. To everyone's amazement, the notorious frequenter of brothels and taverns did just that, and for the next 12 years lived a blameless life, punctuated by a few brilliant speeches in the House of Lords.

But in November 1712, his dark fatality caught up with him. He sued the Duke of Hamilton for debt, and the enraged Duke challenged him to fight. Mohun, a superb swordsman, ran his opponent through, then lowered his guard and called on him to give up. The Duke rallied long enough for him to run his sword into the 37-year-old Mohun's stomach, whereupon both of them expired – so saving their peers the embarassment of yet another trial.

The last nobleman to be executed in England was Lawrence, Lord Ferrers. Ferrers was a quarrelsome brute with a tendency to violence. On one occasion, when his horse had been beaten in a race, he thrashed his groom into unconsciousness. Another time, when a delivery of oysters was found to be bad, he ordered a servant to swear the barrel had been changed on the way. When the servant refused to perjure himself, Ferrers stabbed him in the breast, then smashed him into unconsciousness with a candlestick. After that he kicked the poor servant in the groin so brutally that the man was lamed for life.

At the age of 32 – in 1752 – Ferrers married, and then treated his wife with unremitting cruelty. He injured her seriously by kicking her senseless one day, and after six years of such behaviour she understandably left him. Ferrer's steward, John Johnson, was then put in charge of the household. Pathologically suspicious, Ferrers soon became convinced that Johnson was plotting against him. Two years later, in 1760, his insane suspicions came to a head; he sent for the steward, and demanded to see the accounts.

When Johnson produced them, Ferrers began to scream that they were falsified. The old man denied it. Ferrers ordered him to get on his knees and beg pardon; when the steward refused, he drew a pistol, and shot him. Johnson collapsed and died a few hours later. The doctor who had attended the dying steward then summoned men to help him seize Ferrers. The nobleman tried to escape through the garden, but was captured. All the fight seemed to die out of him, and he was in a state of apathy when he was taken to the nearby Leicester Jail, in Leicestershire.

Robber barons

Doubtless he expected that his fellow peers would find reason for acquitting him of the capital charge. But his previous insane rages had made him widely detested, and he was sentenced to death. His execution at Tyburn – on May 5, 1760 – drew a record crowd.

It was five years after the execution of Ferrers at Tyburn that Lord Byron (the great-uncle of the poet Lord Byron) stood trial in the House of Lords on a murder charge. He had got into a quarrel with a friend, a Mr. Chaworth, after a heavy drinking session in a tavern. Byron haughtily invited Chaworth into the next room, drew his sword, and ordered Chaworth to defend himself. Chaworth was killed after a few minutes' fighting.

The House of Lords obligingly found Byron guilty of man-slaughter, which would probably have entailed a sentence of a few years. Byron, however, claimed 'benefit of clergy' – an old law which ordained that a clergyman could only be tried by an ecclesiastical court, but later extended to anyone who could read and write – and was allowed to go free. It is an interesting footnote to the affair that the poet Lord Byron fell in love with the great-niece of the murdered Mr. Chaworth, Mary Chaworth – but she preferred to marry another man.

In the United States 'high society' crime was a relative latecomer. If men of honour quarrelled, they fought duels and no one thought of charging the winner with murder. It was not until the late nineteenth century, with the go-getters and robber barons, that there was a significant change in the pattern. It was the year 1872 that gave America its first chance to gloat over a real society murder. The killer was a 'gentleman', the victim most emphatically was not – which may explain why Jim Fisk was murdered in a public place rather than challenged to a duel.

Fisk epitomized the American dream of the poor boy who made good. The son of a Vermont door-to-door peddler, he had perceived the flaws in his father's business methods by the time he was 14. His ideas about change and improvement soon put him on the way to being a rich young man. A Boston hardware store noted the quantity of goods the youngster ordered, and asked him to come and work for them.

Fisk was a wildly successful salesman – hearty, generous, expansive. During the Civil War, he unloaded vast stores of hardware on the army. After the war he went to New York, met a robber baron called Daniel Drew, and, with another freebooter named Jay Gould, succeeded in stealing the Erie railroad from Drew – one of the great piratical exploits of American commerce.

Plump beauty

New Yorkers loved Fisk's flamboyance, showmanship and extravagance, and called him 'Jubilee Jim'. He loved opera – so he bought the Grand Opera House, a typically grandiose gesture. He fell in love with Josie Mansfield, a plump beauty who decorated the fringe of the acting profession. Although married, Fisk built Josie a magnificent house in the heart of the theatre district and staffed it with an army of flunkies. Josie tended to get bored when her lover was out seeing to deals. But she consoled herself by trying to spend the money as fast as Jim made it.

Then one night Fisk made the social mistake that was to cost him his life. He took his patrician friend Ned Stokes along to have supper with Josie. Stokes was a magnificently handsome man; Josie felt under no moral obligation to be faithful to Jim, since he kept several chorus girls in apartments. So, feeling no pangs of guilt or conscience, she and Ned became lovers. Some time after this the two men quarrelled. Stokes started a libel suit against Jubilee Jim because of certain intemperate expressions about their business deals that Jim had let fall to journalists.

The newspapers were not slow to discover that Josie had deserted Fisk for Stokes, and the story was the delight of New York. Fisk countersued, alleging that Josie and Stokes were trying to blackmail him. On January 6, 1872, Stokes spent a trying morning in court, being roasted at the hands of Fisk's attorney. Eating lunch back at Delmonico's, he learned that the Grand Jury had indicted him for blackmail. In a fury, he rushed to his hotel to get a Colt revolver, then went to the Grand

Central Hotel on lower Broadway, where Fisk was going to pay a call that afternoon.

Fisk arrived carrying a gold-headed cane and dressed in a red-lined military cloak and top hat. As he started to mount the stairs, Stokes stepped out from the head of the staircase and said: 'I've got you at last . . .' Fisk had time to shout 'Will anybody help me?' before he was shot down. He died with a bullet in his bowels. Stokes was tried for murder, but the jury disagreed. At a second trial he was sentenced to hang. At a third trial, a technicality enabled him to escape with six years for manslaughter. He died a few years after his release from Sing Sing.

Death in high society is always news – more so than in most other cases of violent or bloody happenings. In addition to the usual titillations of sex and brutality, there is the glamorous element of men and women – the slayers or the slain – who were either born high up the social scale, or got there by means of their looks, personality, or talent. It is a unique and infallible combination.

HIRED KILLERS

'I started killing people for pure pleasure when I was eight years old. Then I learned that you could get good money for killing, and so I set myself up in business . . .' The speaker was a 22-year-old Mexican, Zosimo Montesino, whose murder record certainly exceeded a hundred and fifty. His first victim had been a 'witch' who had betwitched his parents by giving them a strange brew.

Twelve years later, Zosimo and his chief lieutenants, two brothers named Alcocer, set up an ambush outside the town of Tepalcingo; they had been hired by a local farmer to murder Mendoza Omana, a politician. Mendoza happened to be accompanied by his wife and 3-year-old son; but that made no difference. All three were cut down with shotguns and the father and son killed outright, while the sobbing mother, lying beside the body of her boy, begged two peasants passing by to help her. 'We cannot interfere,' they said, and walked off.

Casual brutality

Nearly seven weeks later, the killers were arrested in a shanty town shack on the outskirts of Mexico City. They took their capture very lightly, treating it as something of a joke, and Zosimo casually admitted to his hundred and fifty or so contract killings, at prices ranging from £3 to £150. A week later, he alleged that the confession had been obtained from him by torture. 'I haven't really killed more than half a dozen people, and that was mostly in self-defence.'

Most of us find such casual brutality incomprehensible. It seems more frightening than the more familiar type of murder – the crime of passion or greed or anger. At least these have *personal* motives. To murder a stranger for money seems more depraved. Surely the existence of such monsters is a sign of some profound sickness in our civilization?

251

Not necessarily. It is a mistake to try to judge Zosimo Montesino in terms that would apply to the average citizen of London or New York. Mexico itself is a weird social paradox. It has the highest murder rate in the world; murder actually accounts for more deaths than disease; yet up to a few years ago it also had one of the lowest rates of juvenile delinquency in the world. In rural areas, the families were very close-knit; a Mexican teenager will put his arm around his mother in public without embarrassment.

On the other hand, because there is so much poverty, life is cheap. It is only in affluent societies that people treat illness and death as a catastrophe. All such societies have high murder rates – it is true of most tropical countries. And nowadays, as Mexico becomes more urbanized – and prosperous – the rate of juvenile delinquency also climbs steadily. It is hardly surprising that Mexico seems to be caught in a spiral of crime.

The theories of the anthropologist Ruth Benedict enable us to understand what is happening. Among American Indians, she observed societies in which there was a high level of kindness and co-operation; she called these 'high-synergy societies'; other tribes were naturally mean and self-centred, and she called these 'low-synergy societies'. Mexico is in process of transition from a high- to a low-synergy society. This does *not* mean that it will one day be wholly composed of mean and self-centred people. Civilization may cause a lot of problems; but it also produces a lot of people who care about their fellow human beings. So there *is* reason for optimism.

Most societies *start* as high-synergy societies – when they are primitive – and then they drift towards low-synergy, as they become more sophisticated and civilized. As they slowly become *more* civilized, there is a movement back towards high-synergy, and this appears to be a kind of social law. But when a civilization drifts from high- to low-synergy, it is the poor who feel the effects first – one cheerfully callous student of sociology compared the process to the rats that die first in a plague. *This* explains the existence of people like Zosimo Montesino. It is clear from his confessions that he felt he was living in a wholly vicious and murderous society, where it was a case of kill or be killed.

He told the police: 'I don't know why you're making such a fuss about me. I know people who have killed more. For example, the police captain Cosme Maldonado. He was a real mass murderer.' Zosimo then described at some length how he and one of his gang finally shot Maldonado. 'It took 13 bullets to do it, because he was so fat.'

Was Maldonado such a mass killer as Zosimo represented him to be? Probably. In the Argentine capital, Buenos Aires, a few years ago, the police got so sick of the crime wave that a special execution squad was formed; they rounded up known gangsters, took them for a 'ride', and dumped their bullet-riddled bodies where they would attract attention and serve as a warning to other criminals. Typically, this 'rough justice squad' got so out of hand that it had to be suppressed by the police themselves. The moral is a familiar one: in countries with a soaring crime rate and a high level of poverty, where the police are underpaid, they themselves are forced to out-do the criminals in brutality. So Zosimo may not have been exaggerating when he called the Mexican police captain a worse killer than himself. But all this adds up to a low-synergy society, where two farm workers can watch a mother and child cut down by shotgun blasts, and walk away saying: 'It is nothing to do with us.'

If Zosimo is by no means the rule among Mexican criminals, neither is he the exception. Martin Rivera Benitez, nicknamed 'Big Soul' in the state of Hidalgo, told police in 1972: 'I cannot count the number of people I have killed for money. My fame spread so far that I often had a long waiting list. In order to prove that the job had been done properly, I would cut off the head and show it to the man who had hired me.'

In his mortuary in the woods near Jazatipan, twelve headless corpses were found, but these are probably only a small proportion of the people Benitez killed between 1969 and 1972; police believe the victims total more than fifty. 'I didn't see anything wrong in killing for money,' said Benitez. 'If I hadn't done it, somebody else would. And it was better paid than working as a farm labourer.' The comment brings to mind the remark of Reggie Kray, the London gangster, to his biographer John Pearson: that in the society in which they were born, crime was the *only* way to get out of the social rut in which you were stuck.

Another vital aspect of the psychology of the hired killer emerges in the case of Nestor Mencias Alarcon, the 26-year-old youth who killed Isabel Garcia and her 9-year-old daughter Elvira with a machete. Alarcon claimed he was ordered to commit the murder by his employer, Senora Martinez Anguilar, who was jealous of a long-standing love affair between her husband and the victim. After paying a witch doctor £50–1,000 pesos – to bewitch Isabel out of her involvement, the impatient

Senora Anguilar ordered Alarcon to kill her – or so Alarcon alleged. Alarcon was paid £55 – 'That's a lot of money for a man like me,' he said.

Senora Garcia's 9-year-old daughter was with her mother, the killer liked her 'because she was a nice polite little girl'. But as the child saw her mother hacked to death with a machete, she fought with Alarcon and was also killed. The murderers, like so many others in Mexico, might have gone unpunished if, said Alarcon, his employer had paid up. But Senora Anguilar lost her temper when Alarcon admitted to killing the child, and called him a sadist. She refused to pay, and Alarcon made the mistake of going on the run, so that he became an automatic suspect.

The police had been convinced that Isabel and her daughter had been killed in a rape attempt. As soon as Alarcon was picked up, he confessed everything, implicating his employer. What is significant here is that Alarcon claimed he felt obliged to obey his employer's orders simply *because* she was his employer – his social superior.

Criminal mentality

A psychologist who was asked to explain the hired killing of Olga Duncan by Luis Moya and Gus Baldonado pointed out that the killers were Mexicans of poor family, and that they found it easy to obey the orders of a white woman whom they felt to be their social superior. In other words, they felt *absolved* of the crime of murder, in the way that the soldiers at My Lai felt absolved because they were ordered to massacre Vietnamese civilians by a superior officer. Soldiers in war generally feel no guilt about killing; dispossessed persons of a 'socially inferior' group often feel they are at war with the non-synergic society that surrounds them.

The Mother Duncan case also raises the interesting issue of the psychology of the person who hires the killer. Elizabeth Duncan had the typical criminal mentality, the outlook that can be seen in murderers like Neville Heath, Marcel Petiot, and George Smith, the 'Brides in the Bath' killer; she was a plausible confidence trickster who could become so involved in her own lies that she came to believe them true.

She was also an example of a rarer phenomenon: the female counterpart of A.E. Van Vogt's 'right man' – the man with such a paranoid obsession with being 'in the right' that he will commit any violence rather than admit that he might be wrong.

Mother Duncan was a 'right woman'. When she set her mind

on something, it seemed to her that it was one of the laws of nature that she should get it — a religious 'right man' would say that it was the 'will of God'. In her eyes, a woman who had married her son against her wishes had *no right* to be alive. It is tempting to declare that she was insane — and if the definition of insanity is to be out of touch with reality, she was. But if she was insane, it was by her own will, her own decision. She *wanted* to believe that her wishes were the will of nature, and she had always lived in such a way that she had got away with it.

The same may well be true of the principal figure in one of the most brutal cases of hired killing in America in recent years. The man behind the crime was a good-looking, smooth young lawyer named Joe Peel, who was a municipal judge at West Palm Beach, Florida. Peel was a 'go-getter' whose ambition was to become governor. In 1949, at the age of 32, he seemed well on the way to achieving his ambition. He was well-liked, a member of the social set, and the owner of a number of thriving enterprises such as night clubs. He also found vice profitable, but his neighbours knew nothing about this.

It was in 1949 that Peel met an ex-convict named Floyd Holzapfel. Holzapfel was also good looking and charming, and his criminal record was not too serious — a few incompetent gas station stickups, for which he had served terms in jail. Holzapfel was weak rather than wicked, with a feeling that fate had always dealt him a losing hand, and a strong desire to be liked and accepted.

The chief obstacle to Peel's plans for political eminence was another judge, Curtis Chillingworth, who had had occasion to rebuke Peel for legal double-dealing. Peel had good reason to suspect that the judge had learned about his rackets, and that he could not expect to remain a member of the Florida bench for much longer. To Peel's logical and ruthless mind, the answer was to murder Judge Chillingworth. When he explained the situation to his new right-hand man, Holzapfel was scared, and also shocked.

Social respect
He was basically an easygoing, good-natured man, but his position as Peel's chief lieutenant also gave him the kind of standing and social respect that he had never had before. He allowed himself to be persuaded, but he stipulated that he needed an accomplice. Peel suggested a negro called Bobby Lincoln, who was involved in his rackets. Lincoln was also a

non-violent man, with no criminal record, but when a judge asked him a favour, he felt bound to agree.

On June 14, 1955, Holzapfel and Bobby Lincoln went in a boat to the beach below Judge Chillingworth's house. They expected him to be alone that night — his attractive wife was supposed to be with relatives. Unfortunately for Mrs. Chillingworth, she had changed her plans.

The hired killers knocked on the door, and the unsuspecting judge opened it in his pyjamas. Holzapfel asked if there was anyone else in the house; the judge called his wife. Holzapfel and Lincoln tied their hands with tape, and forced them into the boat. At one point, Mrs. Chillingworth screamed, and was silenced with a heavy blow from the gun butt.

Undercover man

Once at sea, they put weights around Mrs. Chillingworth's waist. Her husband said: 'Remember, I love you,' and she answered: 'I love you, too'; then they tossed her overboard. She sank immediately, without screaming. At this point, the judge managed to fling himself overboard, and began to swim with his feet. He was moving away from the boat when Holzapfel began battering him with a rifle butt. Then the anchor rope was looped around Chillingworth's neck, and the anchor tossed overboard. The corpses were never recovered.

But in killing a man as distinguished as Judge Chillingworth, Joe Peel had over-reached himself. Police began an intensive investigation into his disappearance; it was a long job, and in the meantime, Holzapfel had a chance to commit another murder. This was of a crook named Lew Harvey, suspected of being an informer. Harvey was also forced into a boat, shot in the back of the head, and dumped in the canal with a block of concrete attached to his legs.

A few days later, the body floated to the surface. On the night he was 'taken for a ride', Harvey had felt nervous, and had given his wife the number of the car in which Holzapfel and Lincoln collected him. The police soon traced the car to Holzapfel; they now had a strong suspicion that this was how Judge Chillingworth had disappeared, and that Peel and Holzapfel were the men behind it.

An acquaintance of Peel's, an insurance salesman named Jim Yenzer, was hired by the police to act as an undercover man. Yenzer's inside information had soon got Holzapfel into so much trouble that he was sent to trial for an attempt to hijack arms from a group of Cuban revolutionaries. He was finally set free; but his faith in Peel's friendship – and his generosity – had been heavily eroded; Holzapfel began to mutter threats. Peel now approached the police informer Jim Yenzer, and offered him $2,000 to murder Holzapfel. Yenzer agreed, but kept putting it off. Since the police were now paying constant attention to Holzapfel's affairs, his boss persuaded him to flee to Rio de Janeiro, with a promise to support him indefinitely. Shortly thereafter, Yenzer also went to Rio de Janeiro, commissioned by Peel to murder the hired killer of Judge Chillingworth – and by the police to try to get a confession out of Holzapfel.

He did not succeed immediately, but he *did* succeed in persuading Holzapfel it was safe to return to Florida, and during a two-day drinking session in a motel in Melbourne, Florida, Yenzer and another undercover agent finally got Holzapfel to describe the murder of the Chillingworths in detail, while other police agents listened in the next room with a tape recorder. It had taken five years of unremitting police work. As a result, Holzapfel was sentenced to die – although sentence was not carried out – and Joe Peel and Bobby Lincoln each received life imprisonment.

What emerges very clearly from the study of hired killers is that money is seldom the basic motive. In 1973, an American publisher brought out a book called *Killer*, the anonymous autobiography of a 'hit man', who is identified on the title page only as 'Joey'. According to Joey, he has thirty-eight 'hits' to his credit, and rates as one of America's top hired killers. Born in the Bronx, Joey became involved in the rackets from childhood. At the age of 16, he was asked if he would kill a man. He accepted the job, and shot the man in the back of the head in the street.

'Then the realization came to me that I was a made individual. I was a force to be reckoned with. A lot of people who had looked at me as being a snot-nosed wise-ass kid would now be speaking of me in different tones. The job paid $5,000.' It is significant that he mentions the money last.

What is more important is the feeling of 'being somebody'. Joey's autobiography may or may not be authentic – an anonymous book is bound to be open to doubt – but there can be no doubt that these blood-chilling pages are an accurate reflection of the psychology of the hired killer. The money is only secondary, even in mob-killings.

All of which makes it clear that it is inaccurate to speak of 'hired killers'; it would be more exact to speak of 'cat's-paw killers'. In the great majority of cases, the true psychological motivation is to be found in one man's dominance over another. The murders committed by the Charles Manson family are an archetypal example of 'cat's-paw' murders, and the Manson case also raises one of the basic legal problems of the cat's-paw murder. Manson's defence – and the defence that his supporters have been making ever since – is that he did *not* order Tex Watson, Susan Atkins and the others to commit murder. They may have thought he did, but that does not make him guilty. In Manson's case, it is almost impossible to believe that he was not closely involved, because his 'family' committed at least three sets of murders, but in a more recent case, there is room for doubt.

On the night of February 19, 1972, the home of Black Power leader Abdul Malik – also known as Michael X – burned down near Port-of-Spain, Trinidad. Police investigating what looked like a case of arson discovered the corpse of a man buried in the garden. It was Joseph Skerrit, a 25-year-old barber and disciple of Michael X. Further digging finally revealed the body of Gail Ann Benson, the pretty 27-year-old daughter of a British Member of Parliament. She had been stabbed 7 times, and buried alive.

Gail Benson, it soon transpired, had been the mistress of another of Michael X's close associates. Hakim Jamal. It was believed that she had disapproved of Michael X's influence over her lover, and had tried to cause a rupture between the two men. This, said the police, was the motive for her murder. Skerrit was murdered because he happened to witness it. Jamal was also subsequently murdered by Black Power members in the U.S.A.

Disturbing possibility

Michael X escaped to Guyana, in South America, but was arrested there on March 1, 1972. In Trinidad, three 'lieutenants' were arrested and accused of the actual murder. Of these, Edward Chadee and Stanley Abbott were found guilty, whereas the third, Adolphus Parmassar, turned Queen's evidence, and thus escaped conviction. It was his evidence that really convicted Michael X, who was sentenced to death as the man who gave the orders, although he claimed to have been at home at the time of the murders.

And it must be admitted that, on present evidence, there is no clear proof that Michael X ordered the executions. He was hanged on 16th May 1975; his lawyers were given no time to appeal.

The cat's-paw killer is a social phenomenon, the product of a painfully evolving society. If Ruth Benedict is correct, world civilization will one day become a unified high-synergy society. When that happens, the hired killer will be no more than a relic of the savage past.

HOMOSEXUAL MURDER

When we consider that homosexuality, like murder, has been known since the dawn of civilization, it seems strange that it is only in the past hundred years or so that the two have come together. Dean Corll, the Houston mass murderer, is certainly the worst example of a homosexual killer known to criminal history, although Troppmann, Haarmann and Macdonald may be regarded as rivals. Before Troppmann, who was executed in 1870, the homosexual murderer was almost unknown – or possibly the subject was regarded as so taboo that no one would dare to mention it in any case.

Nowadays, moral attitudes have come the full circle; homosexuality is accepted almost as fully as it was in ancient Greece or Rome. It is true that there is still a large proportion of the population in all western countries that regards it as wicked, or at least 'unnatural', but certainly most intelligent people now regard homosexuality as no odder than being born left-handed or colour blind.

Medically speaking, it is certainly among the most baffling of the sexual anomalies or deviations – it is now unfashionable to refer to it as a 'perversion'. The heterosexual, or 'normal', person finds it almost impossible to imagine how anyone could feel sexually attracted to a member of their own sex – and from the biological point of view, this is no doubt just as well. But no one has been able to explain precisely *why* some men are solely attracted by other men, and why some women experience feelings of desire only to a member of their own sex.

Fear of incest
Freud took the view that homosexuality is the result of 'incest fear'. That is to say, if a boy has no father, or a weak or generally despicable father, he may project all his love on to his mother, until the feeling for her becomes unhealthily powerful. Then, out

of a subconscious fear of incest, he excludes women from his sex life – because they all remind him of his mother – and turns to men.

This view certainly seems to fit the known facts. A large proportion of homosexual men *are* fixated on their mothers. And it is rare for a boy with a strong father, whom he admires, to become homosexual. On the other hand, there is no evidence that a boy who is emotionally fixated on his mother experiences a powerful subconscious fear of incest; on the contrary, many homosexuals kiss and caress their mothers in a manner that suggests they find nothing repellent in the idea of incest.

Freud admits that many perfectly normal sons fantasize about making love to their mothers, and that many normal daughters base their notion of an ideal lover on their fathers. The modern Reichian psychologist Robert Ollendorff takes the view that homosexuality may be formed because the sexual desires of a young child are unusually powerful, and because female objects of adoration are simply unavailable – as is obviously the case in English public schools.

On the other hand, there is an equally strong body of informed opinion that believes that homosexuality is an inborn condition, like hermaphroditism – where a man or woman also possesses some of the sexual characteristics of the opposite sex, so that a man may have breasts, or a woman a rudimentary penis and scrotum.

Whatever the reason, the 'moral turpitude' theory was long ago exploded. It may be true that a proportion of homosexuals live with a promiscuity that would be unacceptable to most middle-class people; but this is partly biological – homosexual couples cannot be bound together by children – and partly social – because most homosexuals still feel themselves to be social outlaws to some extent. In many cities – Los Angeles, for example – there are whole communities of homosexuals, in which the 'couples' are as stable as any husband and wife. This could be the pattern of the future.

The attitude towards homosexuality fluctuates from age to age. Leonardo da Vinci and Michelangelo seem to have experienced no social ostracism because they were homosexual. Christopher Marlowe, the Elizabethan playwright, who was murdered, not only paraded his homosexuality openly, but risked the severe penalties for blasphemy when he stated that Jesus's love of men was physical and not spiritual; but he remained a hero to his cultured contemporaries.

By the nineteenth century all that had changed. There was a cult of masculinity and Oscar Wilde spoke of homosexuality as 'the love that dare not speak its name'. The fact that Lord Byron liked Greek boys as much as Italian girls was a well-kept secret until recent years. The self-pity of Tchaikovsky's music is due in part to his sense of being a social outcast because he loved men. The poet A.E. Housman – the author of *A Shropshire Lad* – wrote a poem about a man who is condemned because of 'the colour of his hair' – a euphemism for his homosexuality.

A few men dared to defend it openly; the German Ulrichs wrote a series of pamphlets in praise of homosexuality – but under a pseudonym; Edward Carpenter – Bernard Shaw's friend – declared in print that it was a deeper and nobler form of love than the male-female variety. But most homosexuals kept quiet about it, or even married and maintained a social façade of normality, often at psychological cost to themselves and their families.

This seems to have been the atmosphere that led Jean Baptiste Troppmann to commit his atrocious murders in 1869. The Russian novelist Turgenev, who was opposed to capital punishment, has a moving article describing Troppmann's execution in his *Literary Reminiscences*. He emphasizes his youth, the slender, youthful neck and child-like gaze, and implies that it is barbarous that such things should happen in a civilized country. But when one reads of Troppmann's murders, it is difficult to agree.

Pools of blood

A young workman, intelligent, proud and rather secretive, he decided to make his fortune and go to America. He lured a businessman named Kinck to Bollwiller, in Alsace, poisoned him – like Graham Young, he was obsessed by poisons – and then buried the body under some stones. After this, he lured Kinck's family from Alsace to Pantin Common, near Paris, stopped the cab in the middle of the common, and then stabbed and hacked to death the pregnant Madame Kinck and five young children, close to place where he had already murdered their eldest son. The seven bodies were found the next day, buried under a thin layer of earth – a workman noticed pools of blood under a tree. The pathetic grave contained dolls and children's toys, and the family had been hacked with a spade. The two-year-old had been disembowelled. There were also signs of a sadistic attack on the boy's body.

In Le Havre, a gendarme went to ask Troppmann a question, and Troppmann fled and jumped into the harbour. It was not until they fished him out that the police realized they had caught the Pantin mass-murderer. At first he tried to put the blame on Kinck, then, when Kinck's body was found, insisted he had accomplices in the murders.

Troppmann is a strange psychological study. He was the youngest of a large, poverty-stricken family, adored by his mother, not much liked by his brothers. His father, a bitter, over-worked man, was an inventor who had seen others reap the reward for his invention of an appliance used in weaving; he was, in fact, ineffectual. Troppmann himself was an 'outsider' at school, and when he went to work at 14, the other workmen made his life hard. His brother Edward was one of his chief tormentors, and one day, without warning, Troppmann struck him violently in the face with a hammer. From then on, he was left alone.

He achieved a brief popularity when he saved a workman's life by tearing his hand out of some machinery, but it didn't last. He hated his poverty, and dreamed of making himself — and his mother — rich. In many ways he deserves sympathy; he was intelligent, sensitive, too good for his poverty-stricken background. His response was to develop a blind hatred of the 'world', and a determination to be rich at all costs. The savagery with which he hacked the Kinck family reveals that he felt no bond of human sympathy with them, and detested their 'normality'.

Men of genius

And this 'Troppmann syndrome' can be found in a large number of homosexual murders. It seems highly probable, then, that the same causes are at work: the sense of being an 'outsider', the hatred of people who seem to be happy and comfortable in the world. Anyone who has known cultured homosexuals will know that many of them have an irritating tendency to insist that all the greatest men of genius were homosexuals — Plato, Michelangelo, Shakespeare — although most historians agree that he was not — Tchaikovsky, and so on. Like militant Negro movements in America, homosexuals often respond to the feeling of rejection by insisting that they form a kind of élite — the 'gay' equivalent of 'Black is beautiful'. When this overbalances into violence, it is like a volcanic upsurge of hatreds and resentments.

It is difficult to know how to begin to understand the motives of Fritz Haarmann, the 'butcher of Hanover', who, at the end of the First World War, made a living out of picking up youths at the station with an offer of a night's lodging, killing them and then selling their bodies for meat. He may have been egged on by his lover, Hans Grans, a petty thief and pimp, and there can be no doubt that both committed sexual attacks on the youths.

Haarmann is believed to have killed more than 50 victims, so he probably qualifies as the world's record holder for mass-murder. A cheerful, fat little man, he was gay and irresponsible at his trial, and seemed to be liked by the police officers; even his insistence that he killed his victims by biting them through the throat did not seem to decrease his popularity. In prison, before he was beheaded, Haarmann produced a confession explaining that he took enormous pleasure in sexual perversion and torture: in this respect, he seems to resemble Dean Corll.

The case of the Cleveland torso killer, who dismembered and decapitated a dozen victims – mostly men – in the mid-1930s has already been discussed in the chapter on Headless Corpses. Although he was never caught, circumstantial evidence makes it certain that he was homosexual. And the strange case of the homosexual mutilator who terrorized Sydney, Australia, in the early 1960s provides some interesting parallels with the crimes of the Cleveland murderer. Like the mad butcher of Kingsbury Run, he preyed on deadbeats and down-and-outs.

Bloodstained

The history of the case begins on July 4, 1961, when an old man discovered a bloodstained corpse behind the dressing sheds of the Sydney Domain Baths. Forensic examination revealed that the man, identified as Alfred Greenfield, had been stabbed 30 times. The killer had hacked off his genitals, and seemed to have made an attempt to cut off the head. Five months later, on November 20, another body was found in a public toilet at Moore Park, a suburb of Sydney.

The same mutilations and stabbings revealed that the killer was a sadist who had wielded the knife in a frenzy. The presence of the body in a toilet suggested that the victim and his killer had gone in together for sexual purposes. The dead man was identified as William Cobbin.

The police launched an enormous manhunt for the Mutilator – as the papers were soon calling him; but it was impossible to patrol all the areas where the killer might strike. It happened again four months later; this time the victim was still alive when he was found; he was Frank Maclean, about 30 years old, and he had lost too much blood to be able to talk. He died soon after he was found in Little Bourke Street, Darlinghurst, not far from Moore Park.

On November 19, 1962, the deputy health inspector of the council visited a house at 71 Burwood Road, Concord, to investigate a smell the neighbours had complained about. Underneath the building, at the back, they found another mutilated body. A cleaning mark in the sleeve of the coat gave the police a lead, but checking it was a long business. The house – which was a shop – had been purchased in October 1962 by a man named William Macdonald, who had not been seen since early November.

It looked, then, as if the murdered man was probably Macdonald. But doubts arose when the postal authorities reported that one of their employees, a man named Allan Brennan, had also not been seen for some time, and that he had given his address as 71 Burwood Road. Perhaps the dead man was Brennan? It was under this name that the corpse was buried.

But when the police traced the shop that had cleaned the jacket, they came up with yet another name – Patrick Hackett. This raised an interesting question in the minds of some of the detectives on the case. For in the house, together with a bloodstained pillow, they had found two paperback books, one on Jack the Ripper, the other a novel called *Ritual in the Dark* by Colin Wilson, dealing with a homosexual mass-murderer. Clearly, these were part of the library of either William Macdonald or Allan Brennan.

Identikit pictures

Then, on Monday, April 22, 1963, came the break in the case. A workman strolling along George Street suddenly recognized a man who was walking past him: it was Allan Brennan, who was supposed to be dead. He told the police, and a hunt for Brennan began immediately. Identikit pictures were circulated. Two weeks later, two clerks at the Spencer Street Railroad Station, Melbourne, thought they recognized Brennan. He was working as a station assistant. The police were informed.

The man's birth certificate bore the name David Allan, but the police had no doubt this was the killer they wanted. They took 'Allan' in for questioning, and he soon admitted that he was the former tenant of Burwood Road, and that his name was really

William Macdonald. Like the English sex murderer Christie, his great mistake had been to leave a corpse behind on his own premises, then flee. In his room in Melbourne, police found a copy of *An Encyclopedia of Murder* by Colin Wilson and Pat Pitman. Asked why he wanted to read such rubbish, Macdonald replied: 'It's the only thing I get any pleasure from.'

Macdonald alleged that he had been sexually assaulted by an army corporal when he was 15 years old – this was in England. And ever since that time he had been tormented by a compulsive desire to kill. He had picked up his last victim, Patrick Hackett, at the People's Palace Hotel, when Hackett was drunk, and invited him back to the house for a drink. His intention was to kill him. In the middle of the night, when Hackett was asleep on the floor, Macdonald got out of bed, got a knife, and began stabbing him 'in a blind rage', as he said.

He cut his own hand badly, and had to go to a hopsital to have it stitched, claiming he had cut himself on a breadknife. Yet the compulsion to kill remained as strong as ever. A few weeks later he went out looking for another victim in Sydney, and went to the suburb of Redfern, hoping to murder a Russian acquaintance. Luckily, the man was not at home. 'Brennan' then decided to move to Melbourne. Three psychiatrists decided that he was a paranoid schizophrenic; he was found not guilty on grounds of insanity, and committed for life to the Morriset Mental Home.

Toadstools and fungi
Macdonald and the Cleveland killer preyed on tramps and deadbeats. Some homosexual killers have been tramps themselves: for example, Adolf Seefeld, executed in Germany in 1936, at the age of 65. He had been killing boys since 1908, and a curious feature of the crimes was that he used a poison he concocted from toadstools and fungi, and that the victims were all found in an attitude of repose, with no obvious sign of sexual assault. He confessed to a dozen murders of boys between the ages of 4 and 11 – two of them on the same day in October 1934. Carl Panzram, the mass-murderer, was also a tramp and 'deadbeat', and many of his murders were apparently committed purely for the pleasure of killing.

Murders committed by female homosexuals are relatively rare, but there is one case that certainly ranks in horror with any of those discussed above. On May 11, 1961, a schoolteacher driving through Peter Skene Ogden Park, Oregon, looked down into Crooked River Canyon and saw what she thought to be two dolls. A ranger went to investigate and found them to be the bodies of two children, a girl of four and a boy of six. The genitals of both had been mutilated with a knife, and the girl had been alive when thrown into the canyon.

The publicity led to a phone call from a woman in Eugene, West Oregon, who said they could be the children of a neighbour, Gertrude Jackson, who had lived in the area with a mannish young woman named Jeannace Freeman. They had left the area in a red Mercury car two days before the bodies were found. Her description of the car was so accurate that the police soon found it in a used car lot in Oakland, California; the dealer had the address of the woman who had sold it – Gertrude Jackson.

The women had left the apartment, but the police arrested them when they returned to pick up some clothes. Gertrude Jackson, aged 33, immediately confessed to the murder of her two children. Her husband had left her, and she had been seduced by 21-year-old Jeannace Freeman. 'Jeannace was the boss. Her word was law. She wanted me to walk around the house naked all the time, but I couldn't do it in front of the children.' It was again a relationship of total dominance, like so many that have led to murder.

Bullied and ill-treated

Jeannace, a tough-looking, delinquent girl, admitted: 'I'm the butch.' She had hated men ever since, as a four-year-old child, she had been raped by a young boy who had been left in charge of her while her mother went shopping. The relation with Gertrude Jackson was ideal: Gertrude was a low-dominance female who adored being bullied and ill-treated. The only trouble was the children; Jeannace apparently had no difficulty persuading Gertrude that they would have to die.

On May 10, at Crooked River Canyon, Gertrude had gone for a walk while Jeannace strangled the boy Larry, then mutilated his genitals with a knife. When Gertrude came back, she helped Jeannace undress the four-year-old girl, mutilate her genitals, then toss her over the cliff, still alive. Mrs. Jackson pointed to blood on Jeannace's hand; Jeannace said 'Yum yum' and licked it off; they then kissed and hugged in the car. Both women were sentenced to life imprisonment.

The sheer violence and brutality of such murders is a puzzling feature which is still not fully understood. But it should not be taken as an argument that homosexuals are more violent or cruel than other people; in fact, considering the large number of homosexuals, statistics show that, as a group, they are less violent than the rest of the population.

From the criminologist's point of view, it will be interesting to see whether, as homosexuality becomes more socially acceptable, this sadistic and violent feature of so many homosexual murders will diminish. At present, all the evidence suggests that it will.

HOUSES OF DEATH

The late Professor Francis Camps did not look in the least like a crime doctor. A cheerful, untidy man in baggy clothes, he might have been a farmer or auctioneer. He was, in fact, one of the most brilliant of English pathologists since the great Sir Bernard Spilsbury. On March 24, 1953, he became involved in an investigation into a death house murder case that received wider publicity than any criminal affair since Jack the Ripper.

Late that afternoon, he was contacted by the Criminal Investigation Department of Notting Hill Police Station in West London. They had received a five word message: 'Woman's body found in cupboard.' Camps packed his murder bag, and joined the murder squad detectives at a squalid, grimy-looking house at the end of a cul-de-sac. Its address, 10 Rillington Place, became as familiar to the British public as 10 Downing Street.

Earlier that evening the current tenant, Beresford Brown, had been tapping the wall at the end of the kitchen, looking for a place to put up brackets for a radio set. The wall sounded so hollow that he pulled off a strip of paper, and found a cupboard door with a corner missing. He shone a torch through the hole, and saw the naked back of a woman.

Well preserved

When Camps arrived, the police had stripped the remaining paper from the door, and opened it. The seated woman was not quite naked. She was wearing a suspender belt and brassiere, and also a jacket and pullover. These had been pulled up so that a strip of blanket could be tied to her brassiere, then fixed to the wall to prevent her falling forward. When the police removed the body, they spotted another victim, shrouded in a blanket and propped against the wall. They took it out, and came across a third body, also standing upright and wrapped in a blanket.

When the corpses were laid out in the next room, they proved to be those of three young women, all in their mid-twenties. A further search of the house revealed yet another corpse under the dining-room floor – this time of a woman in her fifties. She was soon identified as a previous tenant of the flat, Mrs. Ethel Christie. Her husband, John Christie, had left the place only three days earlier.

The corpses in the cupboard were remarkably well preserved; a constant steam of air had started to 'mummify' them. Camps took vaginal swabs, and quickly established that the motive for the murders had been sexual; the girls had each had intercourse shortly before or after death.

But where was Christie? A nationwide alert went out for him. Surkov, head of the Russian writers' union, who was on a visit to England at the time, remarked contemptuously that the capitalist press seemed more interested in the bodies of women found in a cupboard than in political realities. But this was hardly fair. A mass murderer was apparently at liberty, and he might kill again. Camps recalled that there had been two other murders in the same house four years earlier – Mrs. Beryl Evans and her daughter Geraldine. The husband, Timothy Evans, had confessed to the crimes and been hanged. At one point, however, he had accused Christie of being the killer. No one had taken his accusation seriously, either in the police station or at the trial.

Now, as the police combed the death house, they discovered a human femur propping up the fence in the garden; digging uncovered two more skeletons – both female. Camps examined the other bodies at the nearby Kensington mortuary. The three bodies from the cupboard showed signs of carbon monoxide poisoning – coal gas – and they had been strangled.

The murder hunt for Christie ended a week later, when he was recognized by a policeman as he stood on Putney Bridge. He made no attempt to escape. He was a tall, thin, bald-headed man in his fifties. He seemed exhausted and confused; but he confessed to the murders.

When Camps examined Christie's shoes, he made a curious discovery; there were definite traces of semen on them. Christie had not only raped his victims; he had also masturbated as he stood above them. The enigma of Christie's mind began to fascinate Camps as much as the forensic details that emerged from his examination. And, as detectives slowly uncovered the evidence of Christie's past, he began to gain some insight into the motivations of this middle-aged, quietly-spoken monster.

The police investigation showed that Christie had committed

eight various murders between 1943 and 1953 – including, most probably, that of the baby, Geraldine Evans. He had lured women to the house when his wife was away, killed and sexually assaulted them, and then concealed the bodies – except in the case of Mrs. Evans. He had disposed of his wife in December 1952, and followed this by a three-month 'murder spree', slaughtering the women whose bodies were found in the cupboard.

Traumatic experience

Many sex murderers are subnormal men, who slay without considering the consequences of their acts. But Christie was a man who gave an impression of intelligence and control. He had appeared as a witness in the trial of Timothy Evans, and had been complimented by the judge on the clarity of his evidence. What had driven such a man to an orgy of killing, for which he was almost certain to be hanged?

Little by little, Camps pieced together the evidence of the strange life of John Reginald Halliday Christie. He had been born in Yorkshire in 1898, the son of a harsh, stern father, a carpenter. Christie was a born 'loser' – weak, myopic, always ill. He was inclined to pilfering, and was usually caught; his father beat him brutally on these occasions. When he lost a job as a clerk through petty theft, his father threw him out of the house.

At some time during his teens, he had a traumatic sexual experience. He took a girl out to lover's lane, and she led him on to have intercourse; at the crucial moment, his nerve broke, and he failed. The girl repeated the story, and he became known in the area as 'Reggie-No-Dick', or 'Can't-Do-It Christie'. During the 1914 war he was mustard-gassed and blown up. How far he suffered a real disability is not known; but it encouraged his lifelong tendency to hypochondria. Periodically, he suffered from blindness and loss of voice due to hysteria.

At 22, he was married to Ethel, but it was two years before he was able to have sexual intercourse with her – the hysterical fear of failure remained. They had no children. Then, in 1934, he was knocked down by a car and suffered head injuries. Due to his handicaps, he earned low wages as an unskilled clerk. Yet he had a tendency to boast and show off. At one point he even became a member of the Halifax (Yorkshire) Conservative Association, and encouraged the rumour that he had been a rich man when he married, but had lost his money.

In 1939 he became a war reserve policeman. It was what he had always wanted – authority. But he abused it by acting as a petty tyrant, taking pleasure in issuing summonses for minor blackout offences. He was still a constable in 1943 when he invited a woman called Ruth Fuerst back to his London home. But he was incapable of sex with a fully-conscious woman, even if she was willing. So he devised a way to render his 'girl friends' unconscious. He claimed that he had an ideal remedy for catarrh and various nasal ailments – a mixture of Friar's Balsam and other ingredients, mixed with boiling water.

Sense of peace

The bowl, had to be covered with a cloth, to prevent the steam escaping and the patient had to breathe in the vapour. Christie then connected a rubber tube up to the gas tap, and allowed the gas to bubble through the hot liquid. When the girl was dizzy or unconscious, he carried her to the bedroom, raped her, and then strangled her.

When he had satisfied his desires – in a kind of frenzy that came from years of frustration – he knew he had to kill the girl, to prevent her from charging him. In this way, he killed Ruth Fuerst in 1943, and Muriel Eady – a friend of his wife's – in 1944 (also during his wife's absence). In 1949, his neighbour Timothy Evans who lived in the flat above, confided in Christie that his wife was pregnant again, and that he wanted to procure an abortion.

Christie immediately claimed that he was an expert abortionist, and agreed to do it one morning when Evans was at work. It seems fairly certain that when Christie saw Beryl Evans half-naked, he lost control of himself, beat her unconscious, and raped her. After this, he killed her and the baby Geraldine.

Perhaps the strangest feature of the murder is that Christie then somehow persuaded Timothy Evans that his wife had died during the abortion, and that he, Evans, would be blamed unless he fled. Evans did so and the police assumed he was the murderer. When caught he proved to be mentally subnormal, and later, after questioning, readily confessed. No one will ever know what went on in Evan's mind when he discovered that Beryl and Geraldine had been strangled.

In 1952, Christie's violent urges again reached a climax; but his wife was there to prevent him realizing them. In December, he strangled her and buried her body under the floor. Then, early in January, he invited Rita Nelson, a prostitute, to the house. He went through his usual procedure of persuading her to inhale gas, then raped and strangled her. In all probability, he kept the body around for several days before putting it in the cupboard. A few days later, he raped and strangled another prostitute, Kathleen Maloney.

During these murders, he was like a starving man eating his fill for the first time; in a confession he later described the enormous sense of peace that came over him afterwards. But the danger of being caught was growing keener. Ethel's relatives were getting worried; Christie had no job; he had sold his furniture. He was going to pieces. There was one more victim, Hectorina McLennan, the mistress of an out-of-work Irishman. Christie had allowed them to sleep in the flat overnight, then he lured the woman back the next day and killed her. His final act in the death house was to pack the bodies of his victims in a cupboard and cover it with wallpaper.

Mummified body

Christie was executed for his crimes on July 15, 1953. Nineteen years later No. 10 Rillington Place was demolished together with the rest of the street (whose name had, by then, been changed to Ruston Close to discourage sightseers); it is now a truck park. But in the far corner of the park one can still see the outer walls and floor that once belonged to Britain's most notorious death house.

In his posthumously published book, *Camps on Crime*, Francis Camps has described another case of a body-in-a-cupboard, which was investigated by his friend Dr. Gerald Evans of Rhyl, North Wales. In May 1960, a widow of 65 named Sarah Harvey was taken into hospital for observation; during her absence, her son decided to redecorate her house, 35 West Kinmel Street. On the landing there was a large wooden cupboard that had been locked for many years. Mr. Harvey opened this, and recoiled. On the floor there was a hunched shape covered with a sheet; a discoloured human foot grotesquely protruded from one corner of it.

The police were at once called, together with Dr. Evans. When the rotting cloth was cautiously pulled from the body, they saw a brown, mummified body, whose skin was as hard as granite. It seemed to be a woman. The mummy was placed in glycerine, to soften it, and then examined. There was a mark around the neck which could have been due to a ligature, and there were fragments of a stocking stuck to it.

In hospital, Mrs. Harvey explained that the corpse was that of an old lady named Frances Knight, who had come to live with her in 1940. One night, she said, Mrs. Knight died in pain. Mrs. Harvey then panicked and pushed her body into the cupboard. She continued to collect £2 a week – due to Mrs. Knight as a result of a court order – for the next 20 years.

The presence of the stocking gave rise to suspicions of murder, and Mrs. Harvey was put on trial. The defence pointed out that many working class people have a custom of curing sore throats by wrapping an unwashed sock or stocking round the neck. Mrs. Knight could have done this, and accidentally strangled herself; or perhaps she had died of natural causes, and the neck had swelled after death, producing the mark on the flesh. The court gave Mrs. Harvey the benefit of the doubt. The trial was stopped after three days; but she *was* found guilty of obtaining £2 a week for 20 years under false pretences, and sentenced to 15 months in prison.

The Christie case and the Rhyl mummy case make it clear why 'murder houses' are so rare. It is true, of course, that many murders are committed in houses; but it is only under exceptional circumstances that the body is then kept in the house. It is not a wise thing to do, as Crippen discovered to his cost when he buried Belle Elmore in the cellar. When a man is suspected of murder, his house is the first place the police search. The consequence is that although horror stories are full of houses with corpses hidden under the floorboards and behind the walls, it very seldom happens in practice.

Really professional murderers understand the importance of disposing of the body as far as possible from home. The result is that not only were no bodies ever found at Landru's murder house in Gambais, but no bloodstains or other evidence was found either. Even the 'calcined bones' reported by *The Times* proved to be an unfounded rumour.

H.H. Holmes, the master of 'murder castle' in Chicago, discovered the most ingenious way of disposing of the bodies of his 20 or so victims. He hired a workman to strip off the skin, claiming that the people had died 'normally' and that their corpses were intended for a medical school.

The village of Cinkota, near Budapest, can claim to possess a genuine death house, at 17 Rákóczi Street. Its owner had gone to the war in 1914, and was never to be seen again. In May 1916, the house was put up for sale by the local authorities, to pay for its back taxes. It was bought by a blacksmith, Istvan Molnar. Molnar became curious about seven large tin drums concealed behind a pile of old metal in the workshop. A few days later he forced one open – and recoiled when confronted by the naked corpse of a woman. The other barrels also proved to contain female corpses.

Detective Geza Bialokurszky, in charge of the case, found it baffling. He looked through the files of more than 400 missing women before he found one who seemed to fit. She was a 36-year-old cook called Anna Novak, and her ex-employer was still resentful because she had left without giving notice. Her trunk was in the attic, and in it the detective found his first clue: a newspaper advertisement: 'Young man seeks female companion for walking tour in Alps; marriage possible.'

It gave a P.O. Box No. 717. A search of Budapest newspapers revealed that advertisements involving Box 717 had appeared 20 times in two years. The box was apparently owned by Mr. Elemer Nagy, but the address was – 17 Rákóczi Street, Cinkota. Nagy's handwriting was reproduced in newspapers, and a lady came forward to say that it was the handwriting of her fiancé, Bela Kiss; she had last received a postcard from him in 1914.

Baby sitter

Kiss had apparently been killed in battle. The police obtained a photograph from his regiment, and showed it around Budapest's red light district. They discovered that Kiss was a man of boundless sexual appetite – in fact, a satyr. He was well dressed, a 'gentleman', and he paid well for his sexual pleasures. It was his physical drive which led him into the business of lady-killing; his advertisements lured spinsters with savings into his death house home. They ended up in metal drums, and their savings were spent on prostitutes. Kiss was never traced. He may have been killed in battle. One rumour has it that he changed identities with a dead soldier, killed in battle, and later emigrated to America.

In the United States the town of Plainfield, Wisconsin, also possesses a death house with a history as lurid as that of 10 Rillington Place or 17 Rákóczi Street, the residence of a gentle, quiet man named Ed Gein, whose obvious inoffensiveness made him a favourite baby sitter in the area. One afternoon in November 1957, a deputy sheriff, Frank Worden, called at the Gein farm. Worden's mother, who kept a grocery store in the area, had disappeared, leaving a pool of blood on the floor and a cash register showing that her last customer had been the mild-mannered Ed.

When Worden found that the farmhouse was empty, he looked into the woodshed – and saw the corpse of his mother, naked and headless, hanging upside down from the ceiling. The body had been 'dressed' like a carcass in a butcher's shop. He re-entered the farm and in the dining-room discovered a woman's heart in a dish; Mrs. Worden's head and intestines were in a box nearby. Gein, out at supper with a neighbour, was quickly arrested. He admitted committing the murder, but claimed he had been in a daze at the time.

Sexual passions

Detectives made a full-scale search of the farmhouse – which was indescribably filthy and untidy – and found no less than ten skins flayed from human heads, and a box containing noses. Human skin had been used to repair leather armchairs, and even to make a belt. Gein had been living on his own at the farmhouse since 1945 and from his admissions, the police constructed an incredible story. His mother had been violently religious, convinced that God was about to destroy the world because women wore lipstick. She instilled into Gein a highly ambivalent hatred of 'scarlet women'. Gein's father died in 1940, his only brother in 1942. Old Mrs. Gein suffered a stroke in 1944, and Gein nursed her until she died a year later.

Then, alone in the house, he began to suffer from tormenting sexual passions. In 1942, he had called at a neighbour's house, and seen a woman wearing shorts; that night, a man had broken into the house, and asked the woman's son where his mother was. The intruder fled, but the boy thought he had recognized Gein. Not long after his mother's death, Gein saw an announcement in a newspaper that a woman was being buried. That night, he drove to the graveyard, dug up the body, put it in his truck, then replaced the coffin and buried it carefully.

Waistcoat

Back at home, he at last had a woman to share his bed. 'It gave me a lot of satisfaction,' he explained. He found the corpse so sexually exciting that he ate part of the body, and made a waistcoat of the skin, so he could wear it next to his body.

At Christmas 1957, Gein was found insane, and confined for life in the Waupan State Hospital.

So the death houses – 'castles', apartments, farms – stay where and sometimes as they are until they are renovated or razed. People lived in the buildings, in the bedrooms and lounges in which the murders were committed, frequently without knowing the previous bloody history of their homes. The death houses keep their secrets to themselves. Their walls may have ears, but they do not have tongues.

HUSBAND KILLERS

Women who murder their husbands are far rarer than husbands who murder their wives. Why should that be so? The obvious answer is that women are less violent then men. Indeed, a woman is unlikely to experience the same degree of hostility towards her husband unless she is more dominant than he is, or he is thoroughly unsatisfying in bed. This theory is the key to most of the famous cases of husband murder. As recently as 300 years ago, the English regarded husband murder as such a 'horrible and unnatural' crime that they punished it by burning the lethal wives alive.

Alice Arden

A case that occurred in 1551 became the subject of one of the most popular of early Elizabethan plays, the anonymous *Arden of Faversham*. The lady concerned was Alice Arden, sister of Sir Thomas North, who translated *Plutarch's Lives*. Alice married a Kentish gentleman, Thomas Arden, the mayor of Faversham. It seems likely that Arden desired her for her family connections rather than because he was in love with her; all the evidence shows that he was more interested in money than sex.

After a few dull years of married life, Alice met a tailor named Morsby, and became his mistress. Her husband knew about it and didn't care; in fact, he even invited Morsby to come and stay in the house while he was away on business trips. Morsby was perfectly satisfied with this arrangement, but Alice wasn't. With a woman's natural instinct for tidiness, she didn't want to be one man's wife and another's mistress; she may also have found it annoying to satisfy her husband's sexual demands when he came home. At all events, she persuaded Morsby, against his will, that her husband had to die.

Morsby was not the aggressive type, so he approached a man named Greene, who had been defrauded of his land by Thomas

278

Arden, and asked him to help. Greene, in turn, hired two assassins. As killers, the men were obvious and crude. They simply walked into Arden's house one evening while he was eating his supper, and stabbed and throttled him. Morsby then finished him off by hitting him with a flat iron. After that, they dragged the body to a nearby field. The killers had failed to notice it was snowing when they arrived to kill Arden. The next day, peace officers had no difficulty tracing the footprints and bloodstains across the field, back to Arden's house.

The murder of a husband by his wife was considered so wicked and scandalous that it was gradually discussed all over England. Alice, her lover, one of the assassins, and two servants who had helped drag the body, were all arrested, tried and found guilty. Morsby's sister was also charged with complicity.

Alice Arden was then burned alive at Canterbury on March 14, 1551; so was the maidservant, 'crying out on hir mistresse that had brought hir to this ende'. Morsby and his sister were hanged at Smithfield in London, a manservant was hung in chains at Faversham, and the assassin who was caught was burned alive. Six lives were taken for that of a worthless miser who connived at his wife's infidelity. It was a sign of the horror inspired by husband murder among the Elizabethans.

Catherine Hayes

Two centuries later, another case created an even greater sensation, and became the subject of innumerable pamphlets and broadsheets. The wife was Catherine Hayes – born Catherine Hall, in Birmingham, England. All accounts of the case make it clear that she was a highly dominant female, with a powerful sexual appetite. She was only 15 when an army officer persuaded her to leave home; before long she had become the mistress of the entire officers' mess.

After this exploit, she found a job as a servant with a farmer named Hayes. The farmer's son, John Hayes, fell in love with her, and they were secretly married. Young Hayes was a carpenter – a quiet, easygoing man, dominated by his highly attractive wife – whose descriptions make her sound like an eighteenth-century Gina Lollobrigida. After six years of country life, Catherine was so bored that she insisted they move to London. There Hayes became a successful coal merchant and moneylender.

Despite, or because of this Catherine claimed that he was unbearably mean. Their marriage deteriorated steadily. At 35,

Catherine felt she had been cheated out of life. One day, a young man named Thomas Billings came to their house. Catherine declared he was a relative, and insisted that he stay. She lost no time in becoming his mistress.

Before long another Warwickshire friend, Thomas Wood, arrived; Catherine quickly added him to her collection. Then in the midst of an orgy with her two lovers, she suddenly felt that it was intolerable to have such a mean – if easily fooled – husband. John Hayes was a fairly rich man for those days, and a tempting prey. Catherine persuaded her lovers to help her kill him, with a promise of sharing part of his fortune.

Accordingly, on March 1, 1725, the two men challenged Hayes to a drinking match. When he agreed, they sent for several bottles of wine, and Hayes downed six pints of it without considering its potency; the others drank beer. Finally, Hayes staggered off to bed in the next room. Billings came in with a hatchet, and hit him a tremendous blow on the back of the head. The dying man struggled so violently that a neighbour from below came up to investigate. Catherine explained they had noisy guests, and promised to keep them quiet.

The room was drenched in blood – it was over the bed, the floor, the walls. The young men were thoroughly sickened and unnerved by the sight. And it was their dominant mistress who had to give the orders for the body's disposal. She made them saw off the head with a carving knife, holding it over a bucket to catch the blood. Then the two men went off with the head – concealed under a coat – while Catherine talked in a loud voice for the benefit of the neighbour – pretending that her husband had been suddenly called away on business.

The murderers hurried down to the river Thames – and discovered the tide was out. Finally, after discussing various alternatives, they tossed the head from the end of a dock, where it landed on the mud. Then they went back to the house, and helped Catherine clean up the blood. Meanwhile, a man had seen them throw 'something strange-looking' into the river. He went to investigate, and found the head. He reported his grisly discovery and the parish officers came to inspect it. Distressed by the mud which 'disfigured' it, they ordered that it should be washed, the hair combed, and then that it should be set up on a stake in St. Margaret's churchyard in Westminster. A young apprentice who saw it rushed to tell Catherine that the features resembled those of her husband. But she told him angrily that he could get into trouble spreading 'false reports'.

In the meantime, the killers had hacked the body into manageable pieces, put most of them into a trunk, and thrown it into a pond in Marylebone Fields. In spite of the rumours about her husband's disappearance, Catherine Hayes behaved with remarkable coolness. She changed her lodgings, taking her two lovers – *and* the curious neighbour – with her; and she went to collect her husband's debts.

The head in the churchyard, however, had created too much suspicion for the whole affair to be forgotten. Eventually, a Justice of the Peace called at her lodgings to make inquiries, and came across her in bed with Billings. Together with the neighbour, the lovers were arrested. Catherine was then shown the head – which had been pickled in spirits. Instead of being revolted, she seized it in her hands, crying: 'It is my dear husband', and kissed it violently. After that, she fainted.

But her histrionics were of no avail. When Wood – who had been in the country – was arrested, his nerve broke and he confessed. At their trial, Wood and Billings were sentenced to be hanged, and Catherine to be burned alive. She screamed all the way back to the prison. Of the two men, only Billings was hanged – Wood, fortunately for him perhaps, died of a fever in jail.

Catherine's end was as horrible as the one she had inflicted upon her husband. She was due to be strangled before she was burned. However, someone lit the fire too soon, and the hangman jumped back as the flames seared his wrists. Logs of wood were then hurled at the screaming woman to try to knock her unconscious, but without success. It took three hours for her body to be reduced to ashes.

After Catherine Hayes, most cases of husband killing could be anticlimactic. But, in fact, the Florence Bravo case has inspired even more literature, including two full length studies and a novel. It took place in 1876; and if the Catherine Hayes case is typical of the brutal eighteenth century, then the Bravo affair is quintessentially Victorian.

Florence Bravo

It happened in the Priory, Balham, south London, where Charles Bravo, a 30-year-old barrister, lived with his newly-married wife Florence. She was an attractive girl, who had been a widow for four years when Bravo married her in December 1875. Her first husband, Captain Alexander Lewis Ricardo, of the Grenadier Guards, had died of alcoholism, leaving Florence a welcome –

and, she thought, well-earned £40,000.

When Charles Bravo proposed to her, he was aware that she was the mistress of a middle-aged doctor called James Manby Gully, who had tended her when her first marriage was breaking up. Charles's sexual past had not been entirely blameless, so the lovers agreed to put all thoughts of jealousy from their minds. Charles was undoubtedly in love with her, and just as undoubtedly attracted by her money.

As she soon discovered, he could be overbearing and bad-tempered; but Florence wasn't the type to be bullied. She had a mind of her own – and a tendency to drink rather too heavily. She ran the Priory – an imposing Gothic pile – with the help of a widow named Mrs. Cox. To begin with, the marriage seemed happy – even though Florence had two miscarriages in four months, and Bravo suffered from fits of retrospective fury about Gully, and once even struck her.

On Friday, April 21, 1876, Charles Bravo ate a good supper of whiting, roast lamb, and anchovy eggs on toast, washing it down with burgundy. Florence and Mrs. Cox drank most of two bottles of sherry between them. At ten that night loud groans came from Bravo's bedroom; he had been seized with severe abdominal pains, and began vomiting. He vomited for three days, until he died.

Sir William Gully, Queen Victoria's physician (who was suspected by some twentieth-century criminologists of being Jack the Ripper), saw him before he died, and gave his opinion that Bravo was suffering from some irritant poison. A post-mortem confirmed this – there were signs of antimony poisoning. At this point, Mrs. Cox declared that Bravo had told her: 'I have taken poison. Don't tell Florence.'

An open verdict was returned at the inquest. But the newspapers smelled scandal, and openly hinted that Florence had killed her husband. Another inquest was held, prompted by Charles's brother Joseph, who was out to get a verdict of wilful murder – which would lead to Florence's arrest.

This time, the Dr. Gully scandal came into open court – doing Gully a great deal of professional damage. Added to this a dismissed servant of the Bravos' testified that he had once bought tartar emetic for the doctor. But again, the jury decided that there was not enough evidence to charge anyone – although they agreed that it *was* a case of murder. So Florence was exculpated, and she died of alcoholism two years later in Southsea.

Ever since then, students of crime have argued about the case. The most popular theory, obviously, is that Florence did it. An inquest on the body of her first husband — conducted after the Bravo inquest — showed traces of antimony in *his* organs. However, Ricardo had by then been separated from Florence for months.

It seems possible that his violent attacks of vomiting were not due to alcoholism, but to slow poisoning with antimony. But why should Florence kill her husband? Possibly because he insisted on his marital rights, and she was terrified of further miscarriages; possibly because she came to realize that he was interested only in her money.

In *How Charles Bravo Died*, author Yseult Bridges suggests that Bravo accidentally took the poison with which he had been dosing Florence. Crime novelist Agatha Christie believes that Dr. Gully did it, or helped Florence do it. Many other writers believe Mrs. Cox was the culprit. Bravo disliked her, and is known to have wanted to get rid of her. The Priory has now been turned into working-class flats, and has a reputation for being haunted; but no one has ever produced a satisfactory explanation of the mystery of Bravo's death.

The two classic cases of husband murder in the twentieth century — Ruth Snyder and Edith Thompson — show this same pattern of the dominant woman. Since 'Granite Woman' Snyder died in 1928, the United States has added at least one more classic to the list: Cora McKown of Virginia.

Cora McKown

On January 8, 1969, the police of Chesapeake, Virginia, learned of the disappearance of Tim McKown, an ex-marine, recently back from Vietnam. His wife Cora explained that he had vanished after a quarrel two days before. She mentioned coyly that her husband had been in the habit of 'trying to excite her' by beating her with a leather belt before sex, and she pulled up her miniskirt to show bruises on her thighs. The police then broadcast inquiries about the missing man, with no result.

Cora — a beautiful 22-year-old with a sultry mouth — kept in touch with their investigations, and reported one day that she had just received a monthly statement from a credit card firm, showing that someone had signed her husband's name to garage bills. The bills included the numbers of two cars; the owners were traced, and were baffled. They still had their cars, and they denied signing the bills in Tim McKown's name.

A short while later, in March, a man noticed something floating in the Elizabeth River at Portsmouth, Virginia. The moment he recognized a human foot sticking out from the bundle, he called the police. It proved to be a headless and handless corpse, wrapped in a plaid quilt. Death was due to stab wounds in the chest. One of the policemen who was working on the disappearance of Tim McKown realized that the corpse had been found opposite a house where he had conducted inquiries about McKown's credit card.

He had talked there to a young housewife named Judy Clere. The same investigator had since heard rumours that a dark, good-looking man had been calling on Cora McKown. His description matched that of Henry Clere, Judy's husband. Clere had a criminal record, and was now on bail for theft and impersonating a police officer.

It was at this point that Cora McKown appeared, asking to see the quilt in which the corpse had been wrapped. When it was shown to her, she declared that it looked exactly like a quilt she had been given for a wedding present. She was taken to see the corpse, and confirmed the police suspicion that it was her husband when she mentioned that he had had a mole on his left thigh. A chunk of flesh from the left thigh had been hacked away.

In spite of her attempts to behave like an innocent person, Cora was the obvious suspect. For if her husband's body had been mutilated to disguise his identity, the murderer must have been someone who had a forceful motive for doing this – someone who knew him. When the police confronted her with Henry Clere, she broke down and admitted to the murder of her husband.

Confessions

In her first confession, she claimed that she alone had stabbed Tim, after a quarrel. Then, she continued emotionally, she had dragged his body into his car, and driven it into the river at the waterfront. However, she refused to sign this confession, and made another, in which she alleged that it was Clere who had murdered her husband – without any cooperation on her part.

Cora was the first to be brought to trial, in August 1969. She repeated her story about Tim being a sexual sadist. However, some of her admissions at the trial firmly indicated that she had masochistic tendencies. Asked whether she had had intercourse with other men beside Clere, she explained demurely that she had been raped by four different men – three of them friends of her husband. She also admitted to having had an affair with an insurance man, who had sold her a $10,000 policy on her husband's life.

The jury found her guilty of murder, and she was sentenced to life imprisonment – a minimum of 15 years. Three months later, at the trial of Henry Clere, she admitted in court that her husband beat her with a belt because 'he knew it excited me'.

The prosecuting attorney pointed out that she had talked about how much she hated the beatings during the course of her own trial; Cora explained that 'None of that is real to me any more.' Her lover was then sentenced to die in the electric chair.

But it would be inaccurate to imply that *all* husband killers have a touch of nymphomania. Study of the case histories shows that they fall into two well-defined groups: the young and highly sexed women, and the drab, middle-aged matrons who, for various reasons, are disenchanted with marriage.

Beatrice Pace

In this latter category was Mrs. Beatrice Pace of Gloucestershire, England, the wife of a shepherd who beat her. When Harry Pace died of arsenic poisoning in January 1928, she was charged with his murder. The defence contended that Pace died accidentally, by getting sheep-dip (which contains arsenic) on his moustache. The prosecution pointed out that this hardly accounted for the ten grains of arsenic found in his stomach.

Nevertheless, the judge agreed with the defence's submission that there was no case to go before the jury, and the trial was stopped. There was strong sympathy for Mrs. Pace, who had obviously lived a life of misery with a man whose fits of violence could be terrifying.

Helen Bartlett

Mrs. Helen Bartlett also fits into this second group. Widowed in 1940, she met Alfred Babin in Buffalo, N.Y., and married him during the war. Babin was a heavy drinker. One day in 1956, Mrs. Babin called the police; her husband was lying face down in his bath, dead. She declared that he had drunk a full quart of whisky before taking a bath, and analysis of his stomach showed this to be true. Mrs. Babin benefited to the extent of $69,000 insurance. Not long afterwards, she met a 69-year-old patient at the Veterans Hospital where she worked – Wright Bartlett, who had a 100 per cent war disability pension.

The couple married in 1959, and the new Mrs. Bartlett proposed taking a long honeymoon in Florida and Texas. It was after they had left in her car that an insurance company had the ghost of a suspicion; she had insured Bartlett for $10,000, then tried to take out a second insurance on him.

Investigators checked with other companies, and quickly discovered that Wright Bartlett was now insured for a total of $110,000. The police began a frantic but fruitless search for the honeymooners. A few months later, however, they returned of their own accord to Buffalo. Bartlett was looking sick and half-starved – the result, he said, of eating sandwiches on their travels instead of hot meals.

Hazardous business

At first, Mrs. Bartlett indignantly denied that she had intended to kill him – or had killed anyone else. Then, under long police questioning, she suddenly broke down, and admitted that she had held Alfred Babin's head under water until he had drowned.

At the best of times marriage – making what the novelist Henry Fielding called 'that monstrous animal a husband and wife' – is a hazardous business which can bring grief and unhappiness to either or both partners. Rarely, however, does the mismatching end in murder – whether of the husband *or* the wife.

When it does, the publicity it receives makes it seem an everyday, almost commonplace crime. It is not, and because it is not its occurrences must be taken as the exception. Most unhappily married people do not poison their husbands or butcher their wives. They divorce each other, and live to risk marriage – and the miseries that can go with it – again.

IMPOSTERS

'We impostors, sir, are unaccountable people.' The speaker was a large, shambling man, Ferdinand Waldo Demara, whose exploits had been on the front page of every American newspaper. At the beginning of the Korean war, he had presented himself at a Royal Canadian Navy recruiting office, and introduced himself as Dr. Joseph Cyr, anxious to serve his country. His medical knowledge was nonexistent; nevertheless, as a lieutenant-surgeon, he served in the battle zone, tended wounded men, and actually performed surgical operations – successful ones.

When a Chief Medical Officer noticed that he was poor at diagnosis, he maintained his imposture by putting all the cases he couldn't diagnose in a special quarantine room in the bowels of the ship – where his chief never saw them or knew of their existence. By pumping penicillin into his patients, he got through his six-month career in the navy without killing any of them.

It sounds like the average man's idea of hell, a kind of sick comedy dragged to agonizing lengths. So why did Demara do it? Not out of any desire for gain; but because he had a craving to *be* somebody, to be saluted and respected. He knew the imposture had to end, that he had to go back to being just plain Ferd Demara, with no qualifications. That didn't matter. The craving of the ego was too strong; he cared for the future about as much as a sex maniac contemplating rape.

Frustrated artists

The true impostor – a man like Ferd Demara – must be clearly distinguished from the swindler or confidence man, who is simply out to make a comfortable living by 'taking in suckers'. It is true that there are borderline cases – for example, the Rumanian adventurer George Manalescu, whose flamboyant career was the inspiration for Maurice LeBlanc's Arsène Lupin, the gentleman-burglar turned crime-fighter; and novelist Thomas Mann's confidence man, Felix Krull.

As 'Prince Lahavary', Manalescu breezed through the European salons and grand hotels of the late nineteenth century, leaving a trail of broken hearts and empty jewel cases. The fact remains that Manalescu adopted his career for the money and the sex rather than for the ego-satisfaction it provided. The same goes for the extraordinary 'Count' Victor Lustig, the man who 'sold' the Eiffel Tower to a group of Parisian scrap merchants.

On the other hand, the true impostor – men like George Psalmanazar, Stanley Weyman, Ferdinand Demara – are frustrated artists, whose deceits are almost a form of creativity; if they happen to make money through the imposture, it is purely a byproduct.

The first great impostor on historical record seems to be the ninth-century Pope, John VIII. According to the historian Platina – who was the Vatican librarian – Pope John was actually a woman called Joanna, who spent most of her life disguised as a man. Her story has been told in a book called *Pope Joan*, by the Greek novelist Emmanuel Royidis – who was excommunicated for his pains.

According to Royidis, Joanna was born at Metz, in France, where her mother – a peasant girl named Judith – happened to be staying with her current lover. It was after this that Judith was raped by two Saxon archers and then gave birth to Joanna. A wandering English monk – who had earlier been castrated by savage German tribesmen – met the couple and offered to become Joanna's 'father'. On Judith's death, he trained his adopted daughter to be a kind of 'quiz kid'. Her memory was phenomenal. The monk would take her to a castle and invite the Father Confessor there to examine the girl in any branch of human knowledge, from theology to cookery.

Forbidden lovers

When her father died, Joanna decided that her future lay in the Church. The trouble was that nuns were expected to be seen and not heard. So Joanna decided to be a monk. This was after she had met a Holy Father called Frumentius, helped him to copy out the Epistles of St. Paul and become his mistress.

The forbidden lovers travelled around Europe, staying in monasteries. Joanna's brilliance in theological disputation made her welcome everywhere. She studied for a while in Athens, then went on to Rome where 'she met with few that could equal, much less go beyond her, in knowledge of the Scriptures'.

As 'Father John', she became a member of the Papal household, an instructor in theology at the school of St. Martino. Two years later, when Pope Leo IV died (855 A.D.), she had enough influence and support to become the newly-elected pope, John VIII.

Voluminous robes

During the next two years, she crowned the Emperor Louis, ordained fourteen bishops, built five churches, wrote three books, and added an article to the Creed. Then she fell in love with a young monk – whose business was to sleep next to the papal bedchamber – and seduced him. As a result, she became pregnant. This was not too difficult to conceal – the Papal robes were voluminous. However, her love life and her pregnancy caused her to neglect her ecclesiastical duties to such an extent that her enemies began to plan her overthrow.

A plague of locusts increased her problems, and the people became restive. Then, as she was leading a procession to the Lateran Church – to pray for the end of the plague – she collapsed, gave birth to the baby, and died shortly afterwards. She had then been pope for three years. Pope Nicholas I was appointed in her place, and ecclesiastical historians tried so conscientiously to wipe out her memory that the next Pope John, who should have been John IX, was given the title John VIII.

Patron saint

According to the Church, the story of Pope Joan is just an amusing – if embarrassing – legend. But it persisted throughout the Middle Ages, and Platina recorded it in his *Lives of the Popes*. There is certainly a short gap between the death of Leo IV and the accession of Benedict II in 855. Royidis, although he wrote his book in semi-fictional form, insists upon its basic accuracy, and quotes an impressive list of medieval authorities for it.

Even so, the Church still denies her existence. If she existed, then she was undoubtedly the greatest impostor of all time: one might say, the patron saint of impostors.

Another intriguing historical mystery surrounds another Joan – Joan of Arc. Burned at the stake in May 1431, she seems to have reappeared a few years later, and married a nobleman named Robert des Armoises. At first sight, this sounds like another of the typical legends about famous people who have touched the public imagination. But the documentary evidence is very impressive indeed: so much so that author Anatole France devotes the last two chapters of his Life of the Maid to it.

Five years after the Maid had been burned at the stake, a girl claiming to be Joan appeared in a village near Metz. She was about the right age – 25. Joan's two young brothers went to see her, and immediately recognized her as their sister. In the same year, the town councillors of Rouen received a letter from Joan announcing her survival. Her former herald was sent to identify her, and agreed that she *was* Joan. It is a historical fact that the memorial services which had been held for her since her death were discontinued in 1436.

Secret

According to a court chamberlain named De Boisy, a girl who claimed to be the Maid came to the court of Charles VII – whom Joan had crowned king – and proved her identity to the king by telling him a secret that only he and Joan of Arc knew. This girl, however, later confessed to being an impostor called Jeanne la Féronne, and begged forgiveness for the deception. Which would seem to dispose of the legend of the survival of the Maid of Orléans. Except that her family – not only her brothers – continued to accept her as the true Joan.

The account books of the town of Orléans show that Jeanne des Armoises was given a civic reception on account of 'the good she did to the said town during the siege of 1429'. Since this happened a mere ten years after the siege, it seems inconceivable that a false Joan could have deceived her old comrades in arms as to her identity. Finally, the scholar Albert Bayet – who discovered the marriage certificate of Joan and Robert des Armoises in a lawyer's archives in 1907 – declared that the signature 'Jehane' was identical with the signature of a letter written to the citizens of Rheims in the year before the Maid's 'death' at the stake.

Pure fiction

Either Jeanne la Féronne was a brilliant impostor – who could deceive Joan's own relatives and comrades in arms – or the real Joan was quietly spirited away from prison in 1431, and some unfortunate substitute burned in her place. But it now seems unlikely that the truth will ever be known.

With the career of George Psalmanazar, impostordom moves out of the realms of historical conjecture into those of well-attested fact. Born in Gascony in 1679, Psalmanazar – who took his name from the Assyrian king, Shalmaneser – was an adventurer, like his contemporary, Casanova. It may have been his small stature and sallow complexion that gave him the idea of posing as a Japanese who had been converted to Christianity. He was about 20 when he visited Rome, and discovered that his pose as a Japanese convert opened the doors of the pious rich and kept his stomach filled.

He then went to London, and introduced himself to the Bishop of London – who was so impressed by him that he paid him to translate the catechism into Japanese. Needless to say, Psalmanazar did not speak a word of Japanese. But he translated it into some kind of gobbledegook, and since Japan was still virtually an unknown realm, no one was in a position to contradict him. To make the deception more foolproof, he explained that he was actually a native of Formosa. In 1704, at the age of 25, he wrote his *Historical and Geographical Description of Formosa*, which was pure fiction. He was introduced to royalty, and the Bishop of London sent him to Oxford to teach the Formosan language to would-be missionaries at Christ Church.

Religious conversion

Psalmanazar burned a candle in his window all night to give the impression he was studying. He met a great many scholars and notables, including Hans Sloane, secretary of the Royal Society, Lord Pembroke, and the Prussian minister, and fooled them all. It was the astronomer Halley who was his downfall. Halley asked him simple scientific questions – such as how long the twilight lasted in Formosa, and the sun's position at noon.

Psalmanazar's replies convinced Halley he was an imposter. The impression gradually spread, and the Gascon suddenly found himself in obscurity again. He might have vanished silently from public knowledge, like so many of his kind. But at this point he was suddenly overtaken by yet another religious conversion. This was around 1712. Whether it was genuine no one will ever know; but it certainly served its purpose. In an age when volumes of sermons were best-sellers, the repentant Psalmanazar was almost as great an attraction as the former convert from the distant East.

He made a living by hack journalism, and held court at a public house in Old Street, London, where his pious discourse attracted many celebrities – including the young Samuel Johnson, who later said that Psalmanazar was the 'best man' he had ever known.

Clearly, what Psalmanazar wanted – and what he got – was a reputation, and a way of making a living. This is something that must be borne in mind when discussing impostors. The world is a difficult place; neither money nor fame comes easily to most. For every pop singer who makes a fortune overnight, there are a few thousand hard-working men of talent who achieve it only after years of training and effort. But it is always the pop singers and their like who impress the general public – these and the impostors.

The impostor may be a man of real talent, as Psalmanazar obviously was. (To begin with, he was an excellent linguist.) But he lacks the one-track mind that carries so many men of talent to final success. He feels that he ought to have been *born* rich and successful. In fact, he almost certainly possesses the qualities necessary for success – imagination and ambition. But he makes the fatal mistake of trying to achieve his aim by deception. And so, as far as lasting success goes, he has presented the wrong face.

Harmless joke

This was vividly demonstrated by one of the most remarkable of modern impostors. Stanley Weyman – who is the subject of an excellent book by the American writer St. Clair McKelway. 'Weyman' was born Stephen Jacob Weinberg in Brooklyn in 1890. A typical example of his imagination and enterprise is the way he introduced Princess Fatima of Afghanistan to President Harding. One morning in July 1921, Weinberg – or Weyman, as he preferred to call himself – read in his morning paper that Princess Fatima had come to New York with her family, hoping to meet the President. However, various problems of diplomatic protocol stood in the way.

In a flash of audacious inspiration, Weyman decided to effect the introduction himself. He dressed himself up in a naval uniform, and went to the Princess's hotel, the Waldorf Astoria. A few days later, an assistant Secretary of State got a call from 'Rodney S. Wyman', the State Department Naval Liaison Officer telling him that Princess Fatima was agreeable to meeting President Harding in a couple of days. (There was, in fact, no such thing as a Naval Liaison Officer of the State Department.)

Weyman telephoned the White House and made an appointment – the officials there assuming it had been made by the State Department. He then marched up to the front door with Princess Fatima and her entourage, and performed the introductions. It was as simple as that. Weyman profited from his deception to the sum of a few hundred dollars – given him by the Princess for 'expenses' incurred in the Washington trip. It was one of the few occasions when he made money from his impostures.

The subsequent exposure of this piece of enterprise cost Weyman a fine of one dollar, and two years in jail – a sad ending to an affair that seems to be essentially a harmless joke. However, it was typical of Weyman's lifelong bad luck. His exploits may qualify as a kind of creative art, but he never received the kind of reward that society bestows on some of its creative artists. In a way, he was profoundly stupid.

But what *motivated* him to spend his life involved in a series of deceptions? Weyman was a bright and intelligent young man, and his father was a fairly successful estate broker. His trouble was that he was *too* ambitious. He wanted to become a diplomat, a doctor, and a lawyer. His father, a self-made man, thought this was too ambitious; he wanted the boy to show he was capable of making good in some ordinary business, and then go on to university or medical school.

The young Weyman went to work for a real estate firm, conceived marvellous plans for its improvement, and tried hard to persuade his bosses to let him put them into practice. His employers proved too cautious, however, so he left. He then worked for a professional photographer, had a misunderstanding, and walked out, taking an expensive camera. He became thoroughly frustrated about his father's understandable refusal to send him to Princeton until he had showed himself capable of sticking at a job.

Great success
One day, therefore, he made a typical gesture. He sent out dozens of invitation cards to celebrities and public notables, asking them to attend a banquet at the St. George Hotel, Brooklyn, in honour of the new United States Consul General to Algiers, Clifford Weinberg. The banquet – charged to his father – was a great success. Weyman basked in the congratulations of the celebrities present.

A judge who was present invited him to sit with him on the bench next day, and Weyman graciously accepted. While he was sitting there, a photographer was called in to take a picture of the judge and the Consul General. It turned out to be Weyman's former employer, who indignantly denounced the 'Consul', and accused him of stealing an expensive camera from his store.

Compulsive urge
Weyman admitted the charge, and ruefully confessed that the banquet had been intended as a gesture to force his father to send him to Princeton. It didn't work. His father paid the $400 bill –

grimly – and also the bail to keep his son out of prison. But Weyman got probation for the theft of the camera, and spent six months in a psychiatric hospital.

It seems likely that if Weyman had persisted in his ambition to become a doctor at all costs, he would have succeeded. Instead he went into journalism as a cub reporter. That might have been acceptable, too, if he had continued to report to his probation officer. But his pride revolted at the idea. He was arrested, and spent eight months in reformatories. When he was released, the newspaper refused to give him his job back.

He worked for a time as a freelance journalist, but continued to go back to jail for violation of parole. The urge to playact became more compulsive, although it was harmless enough. He married when he was 30. He and his wife would then dress up in their best evening clothes, go to an expensive restaurant, and let it be known that the Consul General from Algiers was there. The attention of the waiters and the manager would be balm to his soul. He would pay his bill and go home – his ego temporarily satisfied.

Hysterical women

At times, however, the longing to 'be somebody' would become unbearable when he read about some celebrity in a newspaper. In 1926, shortly after the death of Rudolph Valentino, Weyman heard that the film star Pola Negri – who claimed to be engaged to Valentino – was in New York. He called on her at her hotel, introduced himself as an old friend of 'Rudi's', and said that he had decided to be Miss Negri's personal physician while she was in New York.

She liked him and invited him to move into the spare bedroom of her hotel suite. For a few weeks, he was a 'man of importance', giving interviews to columnists, acting as P.R.O. for Valentino's manager, and playing a leading part in the organization of the actor's showpiece funeral – which, needless to say, drew hordes of hysterical women.

When reporters recognized him as an impostor, and denounced him, Miss Negri declined to throw him out. She said that whether he was a real doctor or not, he was the best medical man *she'd* ever had. Since Weyman had committed no offence, no criminal charges resulted from this escapade.

Useless action

In August 1960, Weyman was working as a night clerk in a Yonkers hotel when two gunmen tried to snatch the cashbox.

Unarmed though he was, Weyman apparently tried to attack them. His body was later found on the floor in front of the reception desk; the cash box was still intact. It was a brave, useless action, and some psychologists might say it was a form of suicide – or the gesture of a man who was willing to risk his life for a brief burst of fame and glory.

The final verdict on him – as on so many other impostors – is that he was a living version of James Thurber's Walter Mitty: a dreamer who could never learn the trick of harnessing his fantasies to reality. So he became not only a pest and a menace to other people, but also a self-destructive danger to himself.

INHERITANCE CRIME

Pieces of Martha Sheward were scattered somewhat untidily around the outskirts of the city of Norwich, in the east of England. A mongrel dog, hunting for a rabbit, pulled one of her hands from under a hedge. A farm labourer found another part of her in an overgrown ditch. Medical experts decided that this mystery woman they were starting to jigsaw together must have been aged between 16 and 26 – although it was eventually established that she was really 55.

A few months later, towards the end of 1851, a constable tapped at the front door of a notorious local drunk – a third-rate and impecunious tailor called William Sheward – and asked some disturbing questions.

'Where is your wife?' he demanded.

'She's gone away,' said Sheward. 'I've no idea where she is now.'

That matched the story he had told all the neighbours and which they had implicitly believed.

Obsession

The Shewards had rowed violently and publicly over money. Martha was desperately worried that they never had enough. Sheward, a genial optimist, always insisted that one day – somehow – their luck would change. Then they could set up a splendid business and have no more problems. But Martha went on fretting – nagging him and threatening to leave. One evening, befuddled with drink and provoked by her tongue, he silenced her with a pair of tailoring shears.

Now he was eyeing the constable warily. 'She said she was going to London, but I don't really know. Anyway, why do you want her?'

'There's no need to look so worried – she hasn't done anything wrong. She's inherited some money, that's all. Three hundred pounds. But, of course, she's got to claim it. . .'

Sheward suddenly realized he had murdered his wife a few months too soon. That inheritance would have been enough for them to have bought the business he had always wanted. The bits of body found around the city were never connected with the disappearance of Martha Sheward because the surgeons had been so wrong in assessing the victim's age. So Sheward was never even suspected of being a killer – and, if it hadn't been for that inheritance, he would probably never have been brought to justice.

For 18 years he brooded on his loss, tormented by thoughts of how different his life could have been. These thoughts became such an obsession that he convinced himself that he had been the victim of a singularly cruel trick of fate. Finally, he walked into a London police station to unburden himself of the whole sad story. The authorities were unsympathetic, and on April 20, 1869, he was hanged in Norwich Castle. The story of the unclaimed legacy had been a major part of the case for the prosecution.

Indecent haste

A second Mrs. Sheward, married by him during those 18 years of remorse, was left with two young sons. She had become a wife and a widow because of the almost-forgotten murder of a woman she had never known.

But she was far luckier as a second wife than Mrs. Anna Sutherland, the wealthy and hard-drinking owner of three of the most fashionable bordellos in Newark. Only a few years after Sheward's execution Mrs. Sutherland made the most tragic mistake of her life – by agreeing to marry a dashing young doctor called Robert W. Buchanan.

Dr. Buchanan, who was born in Nova-Scotia, amazed his friends in Greenwich Village with the announcement that he had divorced his beautiful young wife. They had always considered the Buchanans to be an idyllically happy couple who adored their small, adopted daughter. However, the doctor explained that the happiness had been little more than a veneer, and that his flighty wife had run away with another man.

So he was left alone to look after the child. But Dr. Buchanan was a surprisingly resilient man and, with almost indecent haste it seemed, he started to console himself with company in the saloons and in the bawdy houses. Soon he was boasting that an older woman called Anna Sutherland, who ran three of the best bawdy houses, was showing a flatteringly unprofessional interest in him. Fortunately, she did not seem to have a jealous or possessive nature. So, while treating her as a rather special friend, he continued to avail himself of the services of her girls.

He became her personal physician and her principal confidant, and it seemed quite normal for her one evening to invite him and a pair of his drinking companions to witness her last will. The main clause in it did seem a little odd. All her property – worth nearly $60,000 – was to go to any husband she might have at the time of her death.

Two days later, although she was more than 15 years older than himself, Buchanan married her in secret. Anna moved into his home in West 11th Street and, almost immediately, started showing the most unreasonable resentment over him visiting her old houses. She held the view – quite ridiculous in Buchanan's eyes – that he should spend his nights with her. Her attitude so concerned him that he started telling his friends how he longed to be rid of her.

Morphine

It was not long before Anna was taken seriously ill. Buchanan tended her himself and, towards the end, called in a series of reputable physicians to help him. These physicians eventually certified that she died of natural causes – not even suspecting that those 'causes' had been helped by doses of morphine mixed with atropine.

Less than three weeks after the funeral Buchanan, wealthier than he had ever been before, remarried his first wife. But an old friend of Anna's – a man who claimed he had helped her build her immoral business and so deserved a hunk of her money – forced an exhumation.

In the 1890s many people in high places, whatever their private morals, were quick publicly to condemn loose living in others. The doctor's patronage of the bordellos was, in many eyes, enough to brand him as an evil man. And the results of the autopsy confirmed that view. He had little time to enjoy his inheritance before his life came to an end in the electric chair.

Doctor's wives, through all the history of crime, seem to have been in particular danger. Indeed, one of the most fiendish killings-for-cash enterprises was planned by a medical man – Dr. Edward William Pritchard of Sauchiehall Street, Glasgow. In 1865 he murdered two women – his mother-in-law and his wife – so that he could inherit what was then a small fortune of

£1600. He did it with a callous deliberation, and then crowned it with an obscenely theatrical gesture which demonstrated his talents as a ham actor.

Pritchard was a fine-looking man from a good family. He was unquestionably devoted to his five children, the eldest of whom was only 13 when he murdered their mother. He was also a notorious rake. Women patients suffering from minor complaints were examined far more intimately than most doctors would have considered necessary and servant girls in his home did not last long unless they consented to him joining them in their beds.

Spice of vice

But, even if they did share sheets with him, their future employment was by no means guaranteed — for Pritchard considered variety to be the spice of vice. His activities as a sexual enthusiast undermined his interest in his work and, as a result, his finances suffered. That was why it was so imperative for him to secure that legacy.

His reputation was one of the popular subjects of gossips in the Sauchiehall Street district. An indication of that came two years before he embarked on his inheritance-by-murder scheme — when there was a horrifying incident at the house he was then occupying in nearby Berkeley Street.

On May 5, 1863 — while his wife and one of the two girl servants were conveniently away on a visit — the other girl servant died in a mysterious fire which devastated her attic bedroom. There was a swirl of monstrous allegations and whispers. The girl had been pregnant by Pritchard. Her bedroom door had been bolted from the outside. She had been dumped in there, drugged, by Pritchard. Then, to stop her blabbing — or presenting him with a sixth child — he had started the blaze. The insurance company at first refused to pay him any compensation, but was eventually forced to by threat of legal proceedings.

Ugly noises

This, then, was the man who had married Mary Jane Taylor, the daughter of a retired Edinburgh silk and lace merchant called Michael Taylor. His mother-in-law had never approved of him, and she arranged for much of her personal money to go direct to her daughter. That meant that Pritchard, in order to get hold of the money, had to kill Mrs. Taylor and then his wife — in that order. He was overdrawn at the bank and creditors were beginning to make ugly noises. The time for action had arrived.

At first he started feeding poison to his wife. Nothing too severe. Just enough to make her ill and keep her in bed. Then he encouraged his mother-in-law to stay with them for a while to help look after her daugher. Mrs. Pritchard began to improve, but the mother-in-law, inexplicably, became more and more sick. Both invalids were being nursed by a housemaid called Mary MacLeod who – after Pritchard had thoughtfully aborted a baby she had been expecting by him – was a most loyal member of the household.

Although she was only 15 she cheerfully coped with all the tempers and disconcerting habits of old Mrs. Taylor. And she did have a number of those disconcerting habits – such as bursting unannounced into Pritchard's consulting room when he was giving Mary an enthusiastic kiss.

As Mrs. Taylor began to sink further, Pritchard called in another medical man – a Dr. Paterson – for a second opinion. Paterson considered she was in a state of 'narcoticism', but, for reasons best known to himself, took no action and never saw her again. He was later asked to sign the death certificate but refused and sent a note to the Registrar:

Mustard poultice

'I am surprised that I am called to certify the cause of death in this case. I only saw the person for a very short period before her death. She seemed to be under some narcotic; but Dr. Pritchard, who was present from the first moment of the illness until death occurred (and this happened in his own house) may certify the cause. The death was certainly sudden, unexpected, and to me mysterious.'

The Registrar, perplexed by this lack of co-operation, asked Pritchard to certify the cause of death. He did so – citing apoplexy following upon paralysis.

One down and one to go. Barely three weeks later the final hurdle between him and the legacy was cleared. The cook was startled by the insistent ringing of the bell connected with Mrs. Pritchard's bedroom, and was puzzled that apparently no one else could hear it. She found Pritchard in his consulting room – where he was being ardently consoled by Mary MacLeod – and the three of them hurried to see Mrs. Pritchard. Within hours she was dead.

Pritchard demonstrated his grief by shouting to the body, 'Come back, come back, my dear Mary Jane.' Then he applied a mustard poultice to her in a theatrical attempt to restore her to life. And, after the poultice had gone cold, he announced that she had died from gastric fever.

Arrangements were made, in deference to the wishes of her family, for her to be buried in her mother's grave at Edinburgh. As the coffin was being carried from his house, Pritchard asked the undertakers to unscrew the lid so that the servants might have one last look at their mistress. Then he rained kisses upon the mouth of the woman whom he had so recently murdered, swearing his passionate and unswerving love.

However, an anonymous person wrote to the Procurator Fiscal, drawing attention to 'very suspicious' circumstances surrounding the double bereavement of Dr. Pritchard. Before he had time to make use of his inheritance Pritchard was arrested. On July 29, 1865, nearly 100,000 spectators crushed into Jail Square to see him die. This was to be the last public hanging in Scotland.

Exactly ten years after Pritchard's death another man, equally hungry for money, was in the process of being married. He, too, was interested exclusively in inheriting money, and his actions during the following two years marked him as a particularly sadistic killer.

Grotesque animal

Lewis Staunton, a 24-year-old auctioneer's clerk, found there was one irresistible attraction about a 36-year-old woman called Harriet Richardson. She was, by any standards, quite exceptionally ugly – dumpy and bovine, with a skin like sun-parched leather. Her mother, who did love her, had tried unsuccessfully to get her certified as a lunatic. But Harriet was rich. In fact, she was worth more than £4000.

Staunton decided that, in order to inherit such a sum, he was prepared to tolerate Harriet with all her faults – particularly as he had long-term plans for employing his mistress in the household as the 'maid'. On June 16, 1875, they were married – against the wishes of Mrs. Richardson – and set up home in south London. His mistress soon moved in with them and, once he had given up his job in the auctioneer's office, the three lived comfortably enough on Harriet's money.

But Harriet, an imbecile and filthy in her personal habits, was very much in the way. Staunton therefore arranged for her to 'take a rest' at his brother Patrick's lonely country home near Bromley in Kent. Soon afterwards he and his mistress – a girl named Alice Rhodes who was now calling herself Mrs. Staunton

– moved into a 20-acre farm near Bromley. Harriet's money was naturally providing the rent of £70 a year. And, now that her legacy had been virtually weaned from her, the time for her death was drawing close.

Harriet's accommodation in Patrick Staunton's home was a dark and filthy attic. The door was kept permanently locked to prevent her escaping. The only window was boarded to ensure that people outside could never catch a glimpse of the fast-deteriorating prisoner. Her main food was scraps from the downstairs table. They would be served in a bowl, rather like a dog dish, and she would scoop them into her mouth with her hands. Sometimes, for a day or two, there were no left-overs – and that meant there was nothing for Harriet.

No one ever spoke to her, and in time she lost the ability to articulate. She was reduced to making strange grunting and snorting noises and her clothes and body became revoltingly dirty. She was no longer a woman, no longer a human being. She was a grotesque and shambling animal – no longer, in her permanent darkness, comprehending whether it was day or night. And downstairs the people sharing her inheritance waited for her to die.

There was, however, a streak of caution in the Staunton brothers. They recognized that it might be dangerous if she died in the house, for that might lead to an investigation into the way she had been treated. So they decided that she must be moved somewhere else. In April 1877 they took her to a boarding house in Forbes Road, Penge, in south London, and explained to the landlady that she was basically healthy, but needed help and 'persuasion' to make her eat.

Harriet, they said, was Staunton's mother. Staunton's mistress Alice, and Patrick Staunton's wife Elizabeth, shared a room with her while the two men moved into a nearby hotel. On Friday the thirteenth Harriet was in a starvation-induced stupor and sinking fast. At 1.30 in the afternoon she died.

Black and hideous

If Staunton had then followed the example of Dr. Pritchard, and made some display of grief over his bereavement, he would probably never have been brought to justice. But he showed absolutely no emotion. The death certificate was signed by a Dr. Longrigg and, within an hour of Harriet dying, Staunton had paid a local undertaker to bury her on the following Monday. Then, having given instructions to a nurse to lay out the body, he and the other three returned to his home near Bromley. They had no intention of attending the funeral of such a wretched and unimportant creature as Harriet.

Their callous attitude – coupled with the nurse's horror at the emaciated and verminous state of Harriet's body – set people talking. And one of the neighbours in Forbes Road chanced to know Harriet's mother, Mrs. Richardson. She could not be certain that this was really Mrs. Richardson's daughter but she had a 'feeling'. . .

Mrs. Richardson was called and, on police instructions, the funeral was stopped. A post-mortem examination showed that Harriet had suffered protracted undernourishment and criminal neglect. Her weight was only five stone – about half of what it should have been. The implications were inescapable.

On September 19 the Staunton brothers and their two women were in court on a charge of murder. The judge who pronounced the death sentence on the four of them described their conspiracy as 'so black and hideous that I believe in all the records of crime it would be difficult to find its parallel'.

Three days before the date set for the execution the Home Secretary intervened. Alice Rhodes was given a free pardon. The Staunton brothers and Mrs. Staunton had their sentences commuted to penal servitude for life. And Mrs. Richardson was left with the realization that her mentally-crippled daughter would still have been alive . . . if only she had never come into that inheritance.

Saucy drawings

All of the men considered so far found that inheritances slithered from their grasp, that crime did not pay. In Britain today there is one man who is very conscious of the fact that crime could prove disastrously expensive for him – because of the conditions of a will under which he stands to inherit a fortune in 1992.

Peter Ascher, born in 1944, was abandoned as a baby on the steps of a home run by a Catholic Rescue Service in south London. Two years later he was adopted by a middle-aged couple, Mr. and Mrs. Joseph Ascher, who had no children of their own. Mrs. Ascher died when the boy was four, and a few years later Mr. Ascher – who had made a fortune in a picture-postcard business, specializing in the saucy seaside drawings of artist Donald McGill – also died.

A few weeks before his death Mr. Ascher made a will leaving his shares – which, it has been estimated, will soon be worth more than £40,000 – to Peter Ascher. There was, however, one important condition: Ascher was not to get the money until he was aged 48 – and if by then he had gone to prison for two years or more he would not get it at all. All of it would go to an orphanage.

Real danger
In February 1965 Peter Ascher was jailed for 15 months after admitting receiving a stolen cheque book and passing worthless cheques. It was his eighth conviction. The Recorder at Poole, Dorset, told him: 'I do not believe your offences justify a sentence of two years. It would be wrong, therefore, to sentence you to a term of imprisonment which would deprive you of the money.'

Five months later the Court of Criminal Appeal changed the sentence and substituted a three-year probation order. Then, in April 1967, Ascher was again apprehensively standing before the Recorder of Poole because of breaches of a probation order. This time, he knew, there was a real danger of him losing his inheritance. He sighed with relief when the sentence was announced – nine months in prison.

Old Mr. Ascher, apparently, worded his will carefully with the intention of doing the best he possibly could for his adopted son – who, for some reason, he feared would run foul of the law. Many other men have used their wills as a means of sending reproaches from the grave.

Horrified fury
Stefan Wojtczaks, whose will was filed for probate in New York in March 1954, left his wife two dollars 'for good rope to hang herself for all the misery she caused me during my lifetime'. That was double the sum left in 1922 to each of his five children under the American will of Park Benjamin, father-in-law of the operatic tenor, Caruso. Each of them was to get one dollar 'because of their long-continued and persistent undutiful and unfilial conduct towards myself . . . I have had only ingratitude and no help in supporting the many heavy burdens I have had to bear.'

The Countess of Stafford, in 1719, listened in horrified fury as she heard herself described in her husband's will as 'the worst of women, who is guilty of all ills, whom I have unfortunately married'. He left her 'five and forty brass halfpence which will buy her a pullet for her supper'.

Another husband, Sydney Dickenson, did leave his wife a fortune and still could not resist a final scathing dig: 'The only happy times I ever enjoyed were when my wife sulked, but, as she was nearly always sulking, my married life might be considered happy. Because of this I am inclined to forget the revulsion the contemplation of her face caused me.'

Remarkable event

There were no snide comments in the will which provided Thérèse Humbert with her fortune of more than $6 million. Not the slightest suspicion of criticism. That was hardly surprising, for she inherited through the last will and testament of a man who was never even born. And Thérèse's shrewd manipulation of the greedy and the gullible made her the unrivalled Queen of Inheritors.

She was born into a poor country family in Toulouse, France, about 1860 and, while still a child, she had to work as a washerwoman. She married into a wealthy local family, the Humberts, and her lawyer father-in-law became the country's Minister of Justice. Shortly after her marriage, according to her story, there came a remarkable event which was to change the whole of her life.

One afternoon she was travelling alone on the Ceinture Railway when she alleged she heard groans coming from the next compartment. She climbed along the outside footboard to that compartment and there found an old man in great agony. She unfastened his collar and made him as comfortable as possible.

When the train arrived in Paris he was sufficiently recovered to leave the station without further help. But, she claimed, before doing so, he told her that he was an American millionaire called Robert Henry Crawford — and he made a note of her name and address.

Soon afterwards she received a copy of the old man's will — showing that he had left her his fortune. However, a second will then turned up — in which the mysterious Mr. Crawford stated that his money was to be divided into three. A third was to go to each of his nephews, Henry and Robert Crawford, and the remaining third was to go to Thérèse's sister Maria. However, under the terms of this second will the three legatees were to pay Thérèse some $40,000 a year out of the interest.

A dupe

An extraordinary agreement was then made between the Crawford nephews — who also existed only in Madame Humbert's mind – and Thérèse. All the securities constituting the inheritance should be locked in a safe at Thérèse's home until agreement was reached on how they were to be divided.

So with a man as eminent as Thérèse's father-in-law – the Minister of Justice – confirming that she had inherited a vast fortune, it was hardly surprising that Paris believed the story implicitly. It was never established if the Minister was a party to the fraud, or if he was merely a dupe – but his role was invaluable.

Lawyers and bankers were eager to provide the wealthy Thérèse with heavy loans, at high rates of interest, which would be repaid when the safe was opened and the matter settled. She always paid the interest promptly out of money raised by more loans. For 20 fantastic years she kept the story going. During all that time, with the safe kept under armed guard, she managed to acquire between $6 million and $9 million – all from people who were convinced they would eventually make a huge profit.

Countless letters

To keep the incredible charade on the boil she instituted a series of court actions against herself. Even the courts who heard them thought they were being brought by the Crawford nephews. These imaginary Crawfords fought, through counsel, time and again in the courts. They lost cases against Thérèse and they won them. They appealed and were appealed against. They wrote countless letters of instructions to leading lawyers – although, in fact, these letters were really written by Thérèse's brother. And all the legal bills were footed by Thérèse.

Trouser button

The publicity which the court hearings attracted – despite the fact that the Crawfords were never actually seen – convinced the world of the authenticity of the contents of the now famous safe. Then the bubble burst. A series of sceptical articles were printed in the newspaper Le Matin and, almost immediately, large numbers of Thérèse's creditors became worried and demanded the return of their money. A judge ordered that the safe be opened. It was found to contain a copper coin and a trouser button. Nothing else.

Thérèse and her husband were each sentenced to five years' solitary confinement. Other members of the family who had taken part in the inheritance conspiracy also went to prison. But the father-in-law who had been so invaluable was already dead.

When she was released from prison in September 1906, Thérèse still insisted that the Crawford millions did exist and was rightfully her property. 'I was prepared at the trial to justify my position when suddenly I saw in court the son of Henry Crawford,' she said. 'He made a sign to me to keep silent. I decided to suffer even imprisonment rather than speak out.'

Old proverb

Some years later, when she was living in penury on the outskirts of Paris, she did at last receive a legacy. Her only surviving relative, a brother, left her all his money – so far from being a fortune, it was only a little over $30.

An American lawyer, conversant with Thérèse's case – and with those involving other inheritance frauds – summed such legatees up when he said cynically: 'To expand on the old proverb – where there's a will there's a way. A way to try to make money illegally!'

INTOLERANCE

On March 20, 1911, the hacked body of 13-year-old Andrei Yushchinsky was found in a cave near Kiev in Russia. He had been stabbed 47 times. Andrei had been missing for the past eight days, ever since he had decided to play truant from school on March 12. To begin with, it seemed likely that this was a sex crime. The body was only half-clothed, and there were traces of semen on a rag found in his pocket. When Andrei was buried a man walked among the mourners distributing mimeographed leaflets that began:

'Orthodox Christians! The Jews have tortured Andryusha Yushchinsky to death! Every year, before their Passover, they torture to death several dozen Christian children to get blood to mix with their *matzos*. . . If your children are dear to you, beat up every Jew. . .'

The man who distributed the leaflets was arrested for disorderly conduct; he was a member of a right-wing group called The Union of True Russians and of the Double Headed Eagle (the symbol of Czarist Russia). One of the leaders of the Union was a brilliant but mentally unbalanced student of 19, Vladimir Golubev. Golubev organized meetings to protest about the arrest of an 'honest patriot'; two weeks later, the arrested man was released.

This curious accusation – that the Jews use Christian blood to make Passover *matzos* – was not invented by the Union. It had been repeated against the Jews for many centuries. However, it started as an accusation levelled at early Christians by the Romans, and was used to justify the slaughter of Christians in the arena by lions and gladiators. As the Christian church became powerful, the Blood Accusation vanished – to reappear a thousand years later, as antisemitic propaganda.

Pogroms

As waves of plague rolled over Europe, in the eleventh and twelfth centuries, it was the Jews who were blamed for the disasters. They were accused of poisoning the wells, and thousands of them were massacred. The Hebrews were internationally hated to begin with, because they were the 'murderers of Christ', then later on because they were forced to make their living out of moneylending (all other forms of trade being closed to them by law). Driven out of the Mediterranean world by progroms, then out of France, England, and Germany, many thousands of them settled in Poland and Russia.

Their pride and independence made them unpopular there also. They insisted on speaking their own Germanic dialect (which became 'Yiddish'); they were clannish, and inclined to religious bigotry. The Christian authorities retaliated by making them live in communities outside the towns and villages, which were often surrounded by a paling or stockade – hence the term 'beyond the pale'. In the civilized countries of western Europe, rich Hebrews gradually became accepted in society; but in Russia, all Jews continued to be outcasts.

It wasn't simply the Russian liking for persecution that told against the Jews. In Poland, they were harried by the Roman Catholics; but when, in 1648, a Cossack chieftain named Bogdan Kmelnitsky, invaded Poland, he concentrated on slaughtering noblemen, Catholic priests, *and* Jews. He had reason to hate noblemen; a Polish aristocrat had flayed his small son alive; he had reason to hate the Catholics; they had oppressed the Cossacks for centuries. But why Jews?

Antisemitism

As a rationalization Kmelnitsky used the glib 'enemies of Christ' excuse. He made a speciality of cutting Jewish women and babies in half, and later hanged a trio consisting of a priest, a jew, and a dog. Significantly enough, Bogdan Kmelnitsky is now a folk hero in the Soviet Union.

In 1881, a Russian anarchist blew the Czar Alexander II to pieces with a bomb. The savagely right-wing minister Pobydonostsev immediately ordered stern measures against all anarchists ... and Jews. Again why Jews? Because whenever the Russian people began to feel rebellious about their rulers, there was no better way of diverting their attention than encouraging them to slaughter the hated Hebrews. Twenty thousand Jews were thrown out of Moscow, and there were bloody pogroms in Odessa and Kiev.

This is why, in 1911, the Russian authorities were quick to bow to the wishes of the Union of True Russians, and release the man who had been distributing vicious antisemitic propaganda. All over Russia, the right-wing press demanded that the Jewish murderers of Andrei Yushchinsky be caught and punished.

As it happened, the police were relatively certain who had murdered Andrei. One of Andrei's best friends was a boy called Zhenya Cheberyak. And his mother, Vera Cheberyak, was a notorious local character. A woman with a violent sex urge, her tastes ran to young men in their teens. She had blinded one of her lovers with sulphuric acid. Yet he was so besotted with her that he pleaded for her when she was tried for the offence, and secured her acquittal. Among other things, Vera was a receiver of stolen goods. She had made handsome profits during the great Kiev pogroms of 1905, when the populace stormed through the Jewish quarter, breaking into shops and carrying away everything they could pile on to handcarts.

Stolen goods

At this point, one of the policemen on the case, Detective Krasovsky, came across some interesting information. On the day of Andrei's disappearance, the boy had walked across to Lukyanovka, where his friend Zhenya lived, and they had gone out to play with a third boy. The youngsters got into a quarrel, and Zhenya said: 'If you don't give me your switch, I'll tell your mother you played truant today,' at which Andrei replied: 'If you do, I'll tell that your house is full of stolen goods.' Zhenya and the other boy ran home, and the boy heard someone – possibly Mrs. Cheberyak – say: 'He must be put out of the way at once. . . .'

The threat of exposure was an obvious motive for the murder, and Vera was arrested. Meanwhile, however, the Union of True Russians had found an even better suspect: a Jewish workman called Mendel Beiliss, who was employed at a brickworks not far from where the body had been found. Four months after the murder, a lamplighter called Shaklovsky came forward to say that he had seen Andrei, Zhenya, and a third boy playing together on the day of the killing. Then, equally unexpectedly, the lamplighter's wife declared that her husband had told her he had seen Mendel Beiliss dragging Andrei's corpse through a hole in the fence. The lamplighter himself denied telling her this, but admitted that he had mentioned Beiliss's name to the police because Beiliss had once accused him of stealing wood. However, now that a Jewish suspect had been introduced, no one really cared about these finer points.

Trial a fiasco

The situation was further complicated when young Zhenya died of dysentery. When it was obvious that he was mortally ill, his mother insisted on dragging him out of the hospital and back home, in spite of protests from the doctors. Was she afraid of what he might say on his deathbed? Whatever her motive, Mendel Beiliss was duly arrested and charged with murder.

In fact, it took two years to gather enough 'evidence' to bring him to trial. And the trial, when it did finally take place, in October 1913, was something of a fiasco for the prosecution. The jury had to make up its mind on two charges: 'That on March 12, 1911 . . . in one of the buildings of the Jewish surgical hospital . . . Andrei Yushchinsky was gagged, and wounds inflicted on him. . . and that when he had lost five glasses of blood, other wounds were inflicted on him. . .totalling 47, and leading to his death.' The second: that Mendel Beiliss was the man who overpowered Andrei and dragged him off to the hospital.

Centrally, the evidence for the prosecution rested on Vera Cheberyak, and her nine-year-old daughter Ludmilla, now the only one of her three children still alive. They insisted that Zhenya had seen Beiliss carrying off Andrei Yushchinsky – in fact, Ludmilla said *she* had been there too. This left the prosecution the problem of explaining why it had taken Vera nine months after the murder to bring forward this vital piece of information. An old derelict known as 'the wolf woman', who had earlier told the police she had also seen the seizing of Andrei, denied everything in court, and practically admitted that she had said what she had been told to say.

Perjury

The prosecuting lawyers therefore decided to admit that Vera was a nymphomaniac and a criminal – since the defence would undoubtedly make this clear. Vera didn't like being described in open court as depraved and vicious, and tried to help her case by asking one of the child witnesses to say he also saw Beiliss carrying off Andryusha. She was overheard, and her attempt at getting a witness to perjure himself came out in court. As to the semen-stained cloth in the boy's pocket, a witness identified it as coming from a pillowslip in Vera's apartment – where more semen stains were found.

But perhaps the prosecution's worst piece of luck was an antisemitic priest, Father Justin Pranaitis, who was called in as an expert on Jewish religious ritual – and ritual murder. Not only was he an obvious crank, it was soon clear to the Jewish people in court that he knew nothing whatever about their religion. The defence unmasked him by asking him to define a series of elementary words – words that every Jewish child would know – and then by firing the question: 'When did Baba Bathra live and what did she do?' Baba Bathra is a tractate of the *Talmud*, so the question would be the equivalent of asking: 'Who lives at the Gettysburg address?' When Pranaitis answered 'I don't know' to every question, it was blazingly apparent, even to the non-Jews, that he was a fake.

Obviously innocent

Yet the horror of the situation was that although everyone could see Beiliss was innocent, this was no guarantee that he wouldn't be declared guilty. When the jury returned, the judge asked whether it had found that Andrei Yushchinsky had been taken to the Jewish hospital and drained of blood. The foreman replied: 'Yes, it has been proved.' Beiliss's face became ashen. The judge asked: 'Is the accused found guilty of conspiring with others to kill the child?' The foreman answered: 'No, not guilty.' For a moment, everyone in the court wondered if they had misheard. Then there were cheers and waving of handkerchiefs, and Beiliss burst into tears of relief.

Ambiguous verdict

Yet the verdict was obviously ambiguous. The Jews *did* murder Andrei to mix matzos with his blood – in which case, Beiliss was most probably – if not certainly – guilty. World liberalism was not slow to point the moral: that in Russia, a jury is afraid to do its duty honestly. The Beiliss case was a godsend to the leftwing press in Russia too; Vladimir Nabokov, father of the 'Lolita' novelist, had some brave things to say about Russian justice which would certainly have landed him in jail under any other circumstances. The underground left also made the most of the case, their propaganda insisting that in a Socialist Russia, the persecution of racial minorities would cease – a claim not borne out by the later series of Communist regimes.

The Jews have certainly been one of the most persecuted groups in world history; but there are plenty of other groups that share that doubtful distinction, including Negroes, Catholics, and Protestants. In Spain, the activities of the Inquisition were directed mainly against Jews who had been converted to

Christianity for social reasons, but continued their Jewish religious worship in secret. The most infamous case of this being the theologian, Tomás de Torquemada and the Jews he burned alive in *autos da fé* (acts of faith – a euphemism for burning at the stake).

Protestants tortured

By comparison, little was broadcast about the atrocities against Protestants in Holland at the same time. Philip II of Spain was a Catholic fanatic who decided to eradicate Protestantism in the Netherlands by killing every member of the offending religion: that is to say, the whole population. An impossible task: but he set about it with the same determination that Hitler showed about the 'final solution' – the Nazi dictator's wholesale slaughter of the Jews.

In the first few years of Philip's reign, tens of thousands of Dutch Protestants were tortured and burned. But it was not until 1567, when he appointed the Duke of Alva to 'subdue' the Netherlands, that his 'final solution' gathered impetus. The Duke's task was to kill three million people. Another well-nigh impossible task in the days before gas chambers and atom bombs; but he did his best – or worst.

18,600 executions

He felt that the most practical – and justifiable – way of doing his duty was to make the Protestants repent by torture. In Holy Week 1668, 800 heretics were to be executed. To prevent them from talking to one another, their tongues were forced through an iron ring, then the tips were seared off with a red hot poker, so the swelling would keep the ring from slipping. They were then burned alive. In Antwerp, after abandoning these time-wasting refinements, the Spaniards managed to kill 8000 heretics at one session. When the Duke of Alva finally left Holland, he reckoned that he personally had ordered 18,600 executions – a record for its day.

Philip's Dutch pogrom, however, brought about his downfall. Queen Elizabeth of England was opposed to the idea of the Spaniards being in total control of the Netherlands, and she encouraged rebellion. Accordingly, Philip sent the Great Armada against her in 1588. Its defeat broke the back of Spanish power in Europe. In Holland, the news of the defeat of the Armada was greeted with even more joy than in England – and throughout Europe Protestants were jubilant at the downfall of the 'bestial' Spaniards.

Religious bigotry

But Elizabeth herself had a black record in the history of genocide and religious bigotry. It was she who decided that the Irish were a menace to English public safety, and sent in her soldiers to 'pacify' them. For the next century, the Irish were massacred on a grand scale – for example, 2000 of them at the siege of Drogheda in 1649. The Irish Catholics, in their turn, massacred thousands of Protestants – mostly English families who had been sent to colonize Northern Ireland. It was the slaughter of Protestants (the number varies from 300,000 to a mere 4000) in 1641 that led Cromwell to 'discipline' the Irish in 1649. Now, more than three centuries later, the slaughter of Protestant by Catholic and Catholic by Protestant continues; there is no sign of an end to the intolerance.

American Indians

The United States also has a bad record for religious and political intolerance. There have been mass persecutions of several religious and racial groups; a notable example being the American Indians. Some 90 per cent were slaughtered by the whites during the struggle to settle and extend their frontiers westward into America. Also, thousands of European Jews who fled from the pogroms of Russia and Poland quickly discovered they were mistaken to suppose that America had no antisemitism. In 1913, the year of the Blood Accusation trial, the United States had its own equivalent of the Beiliss case – and the comparison is not favourable to the Land of the Free. Leo Frank was sentenced to die, not because he was guilty of rape and murder, but because he was a Jew.

Leo Frank was the manager of a pencil factory in Atlanta, Georgia. On Saturday, April 26, he was alone in his office when a pretty 14-year-old girl, Mary Phagan, came to collect her wages. When she left his office, she vanished – until her body was found, 23 hours later, in the basement. A string was tied around her throat so tightly that it disappeared into the flesh; her dress had been pulled up above her waist; it was obvious that she had been sexually assaulted. Two badly-spelt notes beside her body described her murderer: a 'long, tall sleam black Negro did buy his slef'.

In the American South, they had their own equivalent of the Blood Accusation. It was the belief that Jews were encouraged by their rabbis to 'pollute' as many Christian girls as possible. This twisted thinking made Frank the obvious suspect, and he was arrested. The evidence, however, all pointed in another direction – to the Negro janitor, Jim Conley. He had been in the building on the Saturday, sleeping off a drunk. When the police asked him if he had written the notes, Conley swore he couldn't write, Frank immediately contradicted this, whereupon Conley admitted that he was the writer, but had been so at Frank's direction.

Lynched

The trial lasted 30 days, and there was so much mob violence and talk of lynching that Frank was not even allowed in court to hear the verdict: that he was to die on June 22, 1915. With admirable courage, the Governor commuted the sentence to life imprisonment. But this did not save Frank. Two months later, a crowd of prosperous looking men marched to the Georgia penitentiary and forced their way in; impressed by their air of authority, the guards made little resistance. Frank was taken from his cell, driven back 125 miles to the suburbs of Atlanta, and lynched. His killers then posed beneath the swinging body, looking grim but self-satisfied.

The Leo Frank trial was virtually ignored by the world's press. But sixteen years later another case of racial intolerance in America made international headlines. The accused were nine Negro youths, whose ages ranged between 13 and 21. They became known as the 'Scottsboro Boys', and were also noted for the fact that one of them was almost blind, another suffered from a venereal disease, and four were mentally subnormal. Their story again raised serious doubts about the quality of American justice.

Scottsboro Boys

On March 25, 1931, the group of young Negroes had stowed away on a goods train travelling from Chatanooga to Memphis. They got into a quarrel with a group of white stowaways, which included two prostitutes, Ruby Bates and Victoria Price. There was a fight, and when the train slowed down, the white youths – together with some other Negroes who had become involved – jumped off, leaving the nine 'Scottsboro Boys' on board with the white girls. The white youths then rang the authorities and claimed they had been beaten up by Negroes.

At the next stop, Paint Rock, police officers came on the train, and the Negroes were taken on to Scottsboro, Alabama. The fact that there were white girls involved led the police to put an altogether more sinister interpretation on the affair; Bates and Price were medically examined, and were said to have been raped.

Howling mob

With mobs howling outside the courthouse for vengeance, the boys were tried, and all but the two youngest sentenced to death. But the publicity brought nationwide scandal – particularly when Ruby Bates later admitted that the rape had never taken place. A second trial was ordered, by which time world liberal opinion was marshalled on behalf of the accused Negroes. To demonstrate their contempt for such 'do-gooders' the Southern jury again found the boys guilty. The judge, James Horton, showed remarkable courage by rejecting this verdict, and declaring that he could see no evidence for their guilt. A third trial also led to no definite result.

Finally, the Southerners made a 'deal'. If the Northerners would stop their campaign, only five of the nine would be found guilty, and they would be released within a year. The campaigners agreed. Whereupon, the Southerners went back on their word; it was only in 1950 that the last Scottsboro Boy was released.

It is always the oddball, the outsider, the religious or political 'freak' who is discriminated against by those seeking to persecute. In order to have a world free of prejudice, bigotry, and intolerance it would be necessary for all people to share the same views, tastes, beliefs and opinions. As this is as impossible as it is undesirable, it seems that intolerance – and all the suffering, misery, and hatred it engenders – will be an integral part of society until society itself – in some Utopian future – changes its basic, inbuilt structure.

JUSTICE DELAYED

'January 2, 1588. Executed: George Hörnlein of Bruck, Jobst Knau of Bamberg, a potter, both of them murderers and robbers. Two years ago, Hönlein and a companion attacked a carrier on the Remareuth, stabbed him four times, so that he died, and took 32 florins. Six weeks ago, he and Knau were consorting with a whore. She bore a male child in the house, where Knau baptized it, then cut off its hand while alive. Then a companion called Schwartz tossed the child in the air, so that it fell upon the table, and said: 'How the devil whines', then cut its throat and buried it in the garden . . . The two murderers were led out on a tumbrel. Both their arms were twice nipped with red hot tongs, and then their right arms and legs broken; lastly, they were executed on the wheel.'

Public executioner

This sickening and hair-raising account comes from the diary of Franz Schmidt, the public executioner of Nuremberg from 1573 until 1617. 'Broken on the wheel' meant that the men were stretched out on a wheel, then their limbs smashed with a sharp-edged bar, so they were almost literally hacked to pieces. Schmidt's diary is one of the most horrible documents in criminal literature: both on account of the crimes described, and the punishments inflicted: criminals were tortured, burned, hanged, and beheaded.

But perhaps the most sobering fact that emerges from Schmidt's diary is that many people who were imprisoned without real cause – for being aliens, or destitute, or vagrants – spent their lives in the airless and lightless dungeons of the Nuremberg jail. Conditions were so appalling that even when they were released, they were often broken in health or insane. Prisoners were supposed to pay the jailor for their keep; if they had no money, they had to promise to pay later. And if they had no

317

means of paying, they might spend years in the wettest and coldest cells until they died. In medieval Nuremberg, a quick execution could be preferable to the normal, endless delay of justice.

It is a point worth bearing in mind when dealing with 'justice delayed'. Liberals refer to the treatment of Caryl Chessman as barbarous; but at least Chessman received ample legal advice, and was publicly tried. In the twentieth century, justice may be delayed for a long time, but it finally arrives. However, it is only in fairly recent times that there was any real concern over justice and its application. Even in the days of Charles Dickens, a man could be imprisoned in London's Fleet prison for his debts, and spend the next ten years there, with no means of earning the money to pay them off. Justice delayed was the rule, not the exception, in earlier centuries.

Naturally, the records of such cases are scarce; nobody cared enough to write about them. But one of them is still famous in France, because the victims were championed by a man with a powerful sense of justice – Voltaire. His indignation was sharpened by an event that took place when he was already a famous playwright and philosopher. His acid wit had offended a nobleman, the Chevalier de Rohan. One day, when Voltaire was eating dinner with a duke, a messenger arrived saying someone wanted to speak to him. He went to the door – and was dragged out by ruffians, who beat him black and blue, while the Chevalier looked on and encouraged them.

Ready for vengeance

Voltaire was enraged; he took lessons in fencing, and prepared for vengeance. Rohan whispered a word in the ear of a royal minister – and Voltaire was thrown into the Bastille, and released only on condition that he left France. Thirty-six years later, in 1761, Voltaire became involved in another case of apparent injustice when a young man was found dead in a house in Toulouse; he was 28-year-old Marc Antoine Calas, and he had a rope mark round his neck, and a bruise under the ear. The Calas family, in whose house the death took place, were Protestants – very much a minority in Roman Catholic France. Marc Antoine Calas was intending to become a Catholic, and his father was opposed to it.

Immediately, everyone jumped to the conclusion that Marc had been murdered to prevent him renouncing his Protestantism. France was shocked and enraged. Although all the evidence pointed to suicide, and the dead man was known to be of a romantic and melancholy disposition – and torn by conflicts about his religion – the father was accused of his murder.

M. Calas's defence was that his son had killed himself in a unique way – by opening two doors of a storehouse, balancing a rolling-pin across them, and hanging himself with a rope from this rolling-pin. According to the father, Marc was already dead when his distressed relatives found him. Their first thought was of the disgrace of a suicide in the family. So Marc was carefully taken down, and the rope and rolling-pin were hidden. A sort of tie was placed round the dead man's neck, to hide the rope mark – Calas stupidly hoped that his death would be regarded as being due to apoplexy. The doctor who removed the silk tie remarked that Marc Antoine had been strangled. When the cellar of the Calas house was searched later, the investigators discovered a ring in the ceiling from which a man could have been hanged.

Calas was duly tried and sentenced to death. His limbs were broken on the wheel, then he was strangled. It was widely expected that the rest of the family would receive a similar fate; but the law was comparatively lenient. The daughters were placed in a convent; the mother and sons went into exile. At this point Voltaire became interested in the case. He proceeded to ask questions. His conclusion was that Marc Antoine had lost a great deal of money at cards that day, and had hanged himself out of remorse and fear. He was a big man, the biggest in the family; his 62-year-old father was, by comparison, frail. How could Jean Calas possibly have overpowered and hanged his son?

Voltaire's one-man campaign was successful. Protestant churches all over Europe subscribed money for the Calas family. In March 1764, the royal Councillors met at Versailles, and in a four-hour sitting, decided to ask the Parliament of Toulouse to explain why Jean Calas had been executed. A year later, it was decided that Calas had been wrongfully executed, and that the rest of the family were innocent. Their property was restored. Voltaire remarked with satisfaction that it was 'the finest fifth act the theatre can give us'. After a delay of four years, justice had triumphed.

Violent quarrel

Or had it? In the 1920's, a French writer, Marc Chassaigne, re-examined the evidence, as well as Voltaire's brilliant defence of Calas. He concluded that in all probability Calas had murdered his son, after a violent quarrel, with the help of Marc Antoine's brothers. Servants heard shrieks, and a cry of 'murder' not long before the body was discovered. Experiments with the storeroom doors and the rolling-pin showed that it was almost impossible for a man to have hanged himself as Jean Calas described. He believes that Calas and several members of his family were guilty. If he is correct, this is perhaps the longest case of 'justice delayed' on record.

Whether or not Voltaire was mistaken, he inspired other men of conscience to crusade for justice. When, in 1898, the novelist Emile Zola called upon all his powers of invective to defend Captain Alfred Dreyfus, he almost certainly had Voltaire's example in mind. The 'Dreyfus Affair' was one of the most popular *causes célèbres* of all time. In 1894, a document was discovered, addressed to the German military attaché in Paris, listing secret French papers that the writer was willing to supply to the Germans. Suspicion fell on Dreyfus, an army officer, who was also a Jew and an Alsatian – both despised minorities. Because the handwriting on the document resembled Dreyfus's he was sentenced to life imprisonment on Devil's Island in 1894.

While there he never ceased to protest his innocence. He had been in prison for almost two years when a French cleaner who worked for the German embassy in Paris found a letter – torn up in a wastepaper basket – mentioning a certain Commandant Esterhazy. The woman was also in the employ of French Intelligence, investigated Esterhazy, and found that he was dissolute, a gambler – and that his handwriting was very similar to Dreyfus's. Yet the case was still so hot that the authorities ignored this new evidence.

The famous criminologist Bertillon, whose handwriting expertise had condemned Dreyfus, affirmed without hesitation that Esterhazy's handwriting was identical with Dreyfus's. On the strength of that, Dreyfus's brother started an outcry which was taken up by the French newspapers. Suddenly, all France was split by passionate argument about the affair.

As in the Calas case, it was the Roman Catholics who continued to believe Dreyfus guilty. Left-wingers and anticlericals declared him innocent. In an attempt to settle the controversy, Major Esterhazy was tried by a military court, and acquitted. The Catholics and reactionaries accused anyone who defended Dreyfus of being 'bought by Jewish gold'. On hearing this the renowned novelist Emile Zola, regarded by many as a muckraker and pornographer, hurled himself into the case with some passionate pro-Dreyfus articles. Then he produced a bombshell of an article called, *J'Accuse* – an attack upon the authorities and justice of the day. The mobs yelled 'Death to Zola' and smashed the windows of the statesman Georges Clemenceau, another Dreyfusard.

Devil's Island

Zola's accusations of chicanery were so violent that he was put on trial, and sentenced to a year's imprisonment. He then fled to England, where he continued to work for Dreyfus. At this point, the French resorted to the old English problem-solving method – compromise. Dreyfus was brought back from Devil's Island and retried. The court found him guilty, but with 'extenuating circumstances', for which he was pardoned. Dreyfus's name was still tarnished so the fight went on. A retrial took place in 1899, and seven years after that the Supreme Court of Appeals at last cleared Dreyfus. He was readmitted to the Army, given the Legion of Honour, and promoted.

Zola and his faith in justice had triumphed. Because of their involvement in the affair, half the army chiefs of staff had been sacked or demoted. Yet many Frenchmen continued to believe in Dreyfus's guilt and did so until 1930, when the publication of the papers of the German military attaché, Schwartzkoppen, proved conclusively that it *was* Esterhazy who had betrayed his country.

Dreyfus died five years later. It had taken 36 years to finally establish his innocence.

Compared with the Dreyfus case (usually known simply as *L'Affaire*), all other cases of 'justice delayed' seem anticlimactic. Yet the criminal records of both Britain and the United States can show examples just as disturbing in their implications. In one of these, the creator of Sherlock Holmes, Sir Arthur Conan Doyle, played a similar leading role to that of Zola in the Dreyfus scandal.

The case in question occurred in 1903, and involved a kind of Jack the Ripper who confined his sadistic attention to animals. The unknown maniac operated near the village of Great Wyrley, in Staffordshire. He would creep up to animals in the night – horses, cows, sheep – and disembowel them with a very sharp knife. Like the more infamous Ripper, he also wrote jeering letters to the police, urging them to try and catch him. He then threatened to use his knife on little girls in the district.

Small nervous man

The vicar of Great Wyrley at the time was a Persian, the Rev. Shapurji Edalji. And the locals were suspicious of foreigners.

Neither did they much like his eldest son, 27-year-old George Edalji, a Birmingham solicitor who lived at home; he was a small, nervous man with bulging eyes. Ten years earlier, when George was at school, there had been an ugly campaign of hoaxes directed against his father; respectable people received obscene letters signed 'Shapuri Edalji'. George Edalji had been suspected of these hoaxes at the time. Now, because he was a 'foreigner', he was again suspected of being the culprit.

Accordingly, the police searched his room, and found some cut-throat razors, and boots with mud on them. Some of his clothes were taken away, and packed in the same bundle as a strip of the hide of a mutilated pony; not surprisingly, they were found to be covered with horse hairs later. George Edalji was tried, and sentenced to seven years penal servitude. He was released after three years, but found it impossible to get work. He than appealed to Conan Doyle. As soon as Doyle met him, he noted Edalji's short-sighted, bulging eyes; such a man would never have been able to see in the dark to mutilate animals.

Doyle applied the methods of his own Sherlock Holmes. He read the anonymous letters, and deduced that they were written by a youth with sadistic leanings, who had a grudge against the headmaster of Edalji's old school, and who subsequently became a sailor. (The letters referred to going to sea; and this would also explain the time gap between the two sets of outrages.) He soon traced a boy who had been expelled from the school, who loved ripping railway cushions with a sharp knife, and who indulged in forgery.

Doyle duly sent a long report to the Home Office. A committee examined it, and decided that Edalji was not guilty of cattle maiming. But, they said, he *had* written the anonymous letters. In a rage, Conan Doyle wrote a series of forceful articles in the *Daily Telegraph*. He submitted the anonymous letters to an expert who had testified in the Dreyfus case, and who verified that they were the work of the sadistic schoolboy. However, unlike Dreyfus, Edalji was never completely exonerated, and the real criminal was never brought to trial.

Women swindled

Another case in which Doyle took a keen interest had a more satisfactory outcome. In 1895, a Norwegian mining engineer named Adolph Beck was walking down Victoria Street in London, when a woman named Madame Meissonier thought she recognized him as a man who had swindled her. Beck was arrested, and the police soon established, to their own satisfaction, that he was a petty swindler named Wilhelm Meyer, alias John Smith, who often preyed on women, and who had gone to jail in 1887. All Beck's protestations of innocence were useless. Other swindled women declared he was the culprit, and he was sent to prison for seven years. Two years later, the Home Office checked a list of 'John Smith's' characteristics and discovered that Smith was circumcised. Beck wasn't. Instead, the judge on the case stubbornly decided that there was no cause for interference; Beck remained a prisoner.

In 1901, after his release, his bad luck again caught up with him. There had been more frauds on women; Beck was again arrested for the crimes of 'John Smith'. He made a dramatic appeal to the press to help establish his innocence – an appeal that aroused the interest of many notable figures, including Conan Doyle. But this time, fate intervened on Beck's behalf. After his arrests, the frauds on women continued, and were so similar in nature to those of which Beck was accused that even the police realized something was wrong.

Then, while Beck was being tried, the actual culprit was arrested while pawning some of his ill-gotten gains – Wilhelm Meyer, alias John Smith, alias Turner and Thomas. Meyer and Beck proved to be incredibly alike – although Meyer's face was coarser; even their handwriting was similar. Beck was granted a pardon, and awarded £6000 compensation. He later married a younger woman and died peacefully in 1948.

Court of Appeal

It was largely due to his case, and that of George Edalji, that a Court of Criminal Appeal was finally set up in England. But it remains a disgrace to British justice that Beck remained in prison until 1901, although his innocence had been fully established three years earlier.

The classic case of 'justice delayed' in the United States began in 1923, in Waukegan, Illinois. The Ku Klux Klan were active in the area as they wanted to keep Waukegan all white. Police were often involved in framing Negroes on bootlegging charges. A 30-year-old Negro named Jim Montgomery, a property owner, tried to stir his fellow black men to resistance. In turn, the Klan decided to 'put him away'. The method chosen was simple but effective. A semi-imbecile white woman of 62, Mamie Snow, was bribed to go to the police and allege that Montgomery had raped her. His protests of innocence were ignored. After a trial lasting a mere 12 minutes, he was sentenced to life imprisonment.

He looked honest

Oddly enough, the other prisoners believed his story that he had been framed – perhaps because he had the look of an honest man. But he had been in jail for 20 years before one brave individual decided to investigate the rumours. In 1944 a lawyer named Louis Kutner listened to Montgomery's story, and embarked on the near-impossible task of proving him innocent. First, he looked up the medical evidence – and discovered there was none. No doctor had been called to assert that Mamie Snow had been raped. Mamie Snow herself was long dead. Yet a doctor *must* have examined her. She had been sent to Victory Memorial Hospital in Waukegan to be examined for rape.

Kutner next visited the hospital and asked to see the records. He was curtly refused. He persisted quietly, and after many attempts, managed to persuade a young night receptionist to let him into the basement where the records were kept. It took him eight nights to finally locate the relevant document. Then he discovered that the doctor who had examined Mamie Snow, John E. Walter, had found no evidence for rape.

Why, Kutner wondered, had he not testified in the Negro's defence? Discovering that Dr. Walter was still alive, Kutner called on him, and finally forced him to talk about the case by threatening to throw him out of the window. Walter admitted that the Klan had warned him to keep quiet. And after all, Montgomery was only a 'nigger'. Kutner then located the nurse who had assisted Walter in the examination. She agreed that Mamie Snow had been a virgin when Walter examined her.

Kutner needed one more piece of evidence – proof that the Klan had framed Montgomery. He got this by burgling the Waukegan office of the Ku Klux Klan. It took several hours, even with a squad of helpers, to turn up the document that gave details of the plot against Montgomery. At last, he had what he wanted. With this evidence, he was allowed to investigate police records of the case – which revealed that, on the day after Montgomery's arrest, Mamie Snow had failed to identify him in jail.

The petition for Montgomery's release on a writ of *habeas corpus* was heard on June 27, 1947. Dr. Walter testified in court that the prosecutor himself had been involved in the plot. Two months later, on August 10, 1947, Montgomery – now, a white-haired man of 54 – was granted a pardon. He was given $10, the sum usually granted to discharged prisoners. And that was all he ever did receive, although Kutner pressed for $150,000 compensation. The tax authorities declined to allow Kutner's claim for $5000 allowance for the time he had spent on the case – over two years. They felt that the cause of justice for a Negro was not important enough to justify such a hefty claim.

Truth in action

In the words of the nineteenth-century British prime minister, Benjamin Disraeli, 'Justice is truth in action.' That, however, is the ideal. In reality, the legal systems of both Britain and the United States have all too often shown that the action can sometimes be a long time in coming. And that when it does arrive, it can be more of an approximation to the truth than truth pure and simple.

KIDNAPPERS

It was not until the second half of the nineteenth century that professional criminals thought of seizing a human hostage and holding him for ransom. In the days when crooks lived in slums, and the rich resided in great houses or country estates, criminals seldom had a chance to encounter the children of the rich. Then came the age of industry and factories. Men acquired fortunes overnight, and many evildoers brooded on how to separate them from their wealth.

It was in the United States, where the rich and the poor rub shoulders, that the first notable modern case of kidnapping occurred. It was conceived in the summer of 1874 when two men made a habit of driving past the home of Christian Ross, a once moderately successful Philadelphia grocer who had recently become bankrupt. The men stopped and spoke to Charley Ross, aged four, and Walter Ross, aged six, as the children played innocently on the sidewalk. On July 1 the children asked their new friends to buy them fireworks for the Fourth of July celebrations. The men agreed and invited the youngsters to hop into the buggy. A few streets away, they gave Walter 25 cents and sent him to a nearby shop. When the little boy returned, the buggy had vanished, and his brother Charley with it.

The howling Walter was then taken home by a neighbour, and Christian Ross hurried to the police. Everyone was baffled. Why, they asked, should anyone steal a four-year-old baby?

The mystery was solved two days later when the Rosses received a scrawled and badly spelled letter; it said 'you wil hav two pay us befor you git him', but did not mention any sum. Such a thing had never been heard of in North America before. Indignation swept the country. Thousands of police joined in the search for 'little Charley Ross'. No one bothered about search warrants as they burst into any premises that might conceal the missing child. On July 6, Ross received a letter asking for

$20,000, and threatening to kill the child if the hunt was not called off. He was told to insert an advertisement in the *Philadelphia Ledger* saying he was ready to negotiate. Instead, he tried to drag out the correspondence, hoping that the kidnappers would provide a clue to their whereabouts.

The men expressed their impatience at his tactics, and he countered by stating publicly that he was 'damned if he would compound a felony.' His wife, however, was so shattered by the ordeal of waiting that he changed his mind, and agreed to pay $20,000 which he had managed to borrow. Ross went to an appointed rendezvous, but no one appeared to collect the money. So month after month dragged by. There were more appointments, more correspondence, but still no sign of the missing child. The grim story ended six months later, on December 14, 1874, when a burglar alarm sounded in the home of a rich New Yorker, Holmes Van Brunt; it meant that burglars had broken into the summer residence belonging to his brother, next door.

Dying confession

Van Brunt and three other men duly crept up to the house with shotguns, and waited. When, an hour later, the burglars came out, Van Brunt ordered them to halt. Instead, they started shooting. The Van Brunt party fired back with their shotguns, and both burglars fell. One of them gasped out a dying confession: his name was Joseph Douglass, and he and his companion, William Mosher, had kidnapped Charley Ross. The boy would be returned alive and well within a few days. . .Then Douglass died.

The confession was undoubtedly genuine, for the police already knew that Douglass and Mosher were the men they wanted: another crook had informed on them. But no sign of flaxen-haired Charley Ross was ever found. A third man named William Westervelt was tried as an accomplice, and sentenced to seven years' imprisonment, although there was no real evidence against him – a sign of how much frustrated anger had been aroused by the kidnapping.

The age of kidnapping had arrived; but fortunately for parents and relatives it got off to a slow start. This was partly due to the death of poor Charley Ross, for in February 1875, the Legislature of Pennsylvania passed a law defining kidnapping, setting the penalty at a maximum of 25 years' solitary confinement and a fine of $100,000. It is a measure of how much horror was excited by the Ross affair. There is also a certain irony in it. The word kidnapping was originally coined in England about two hundred years earlier, and the kids who were 'nabbed' were usually sent to America as cheap labour on the tobacco plantations; now America was forced to enact the first law against the crime.

At about the time of the Charley Ross kidnapping, a country on the other side of the globe was being forced to give serious thought to the question of how to stamp it out. In Greece, as in Corsica and Sicily, kidnapping was a long-established custom, and brigandage was looked upon as an almost respectable occupation.

Complete amnesty

In 1870, however, the whole system backfired, and nearly caused the occupation of Greece by England. On April 11, Lord Muncaster, an Irish peer, together with his wife and a distinguished party of tourists, set out to see the ancient battlefield at Marathon – the site of the Athenians' victory over the Persians, around 490 B.C. A group of soldiers warned them about brigands and started to escort them back to Athens; but the soldiers were too slow, and the carriages rushed on ahead. A band of brigands, led by the notorious Arvanitákis brothers, swooped down and seized them, then forced them to run at top speed over rough countryside. Negotiations with the authorities followed, and the females – including a six-year-old girl – were released, together with Lord Muncaster. Four men, including an Italian nobleman, Count Alberto de Boÿl, remained as hostages. The ransom demanded was £50,000. Alternatively, the brigands sought a complete amnesty. Previous hauls had made them rich; they wanted to be able to return to society.

When he heard of the outrage, King George of Greece was so upset that he offered to hand himself over to the brigands as a hostage. For the next ten days, however, negotiations dragged inconclusively on. The Greek government categorically refused to grant an amnesty. But Takos Arvanitákis, the brigand chief, said there had to be one – otherwise the prisoners would be killed. Troops drew up near the ravine where he held the four prisoners, while negotiators tried to persuade the brigands to take the ransom and withdraw over the Turkish border. Then something went wrong. The troops, unable to resist taking a potshot, opened fire. The brigands fled towards the village of Dilessi, and on the way, the four captives were callously murdered. Seven brigands, including one of the leaders, were killed; six more were captured. Takos and seven others escaped into Turkey.

Invasion threat

The furore that followed was tremendous. England burst into roars of rage. The British said that if Greece couldn't cope with her own brigands, England should invade the country and do it for them. The Russians promptly stated that, in the event of hostilities, they would go to war to help Greece. 'Investigating commissions' were set up; dozens of men who had helped the brigands were rounded up. Fifty eventually went on trial, but most were released. The 'Dilessi murders', as they were known, became the scandal of Europe, and Greece lost face badly in the eyes of the world. The government was brought down. One of the brigands was extradited from Turkey and beheaded. Takos himself was finally shot two years after the killings. And in Greece, at least, kidnapping ceased to be a more-or-less acceptable custom.

In the United States, on the other hand, its popularity was growing. In June 1907, in the Italian district of New Orleans, seven-year-old Walter Lamana went off trustingly with a man who offered him his hand. His father soon received a demand for $6000, and it gradually became clear that the kidnappers were the Mafia, or 'Black Hand'. The organization already ran the Italian part of New Orleans as Al Capone was to run Chicago 20 years later. The publicity aroused by the kidnapping led many Italians to admit that they had been paying 'protection money' for years. One of the gang was arrested – Frank Gendusa. Under questioning, he admitted to being involved in the kidnapping, but said he didn't know where the child was. Other members of the gang were then taken into custody. One of them, Ignazio Campisciano, was captured by a posse, who used a time-honoured method to induce him to talk: they bound his hands, put a noose round his neck, and pulled it tight over the branch of a tree. Campisciano broke down, and led them to a dirty swamp, where wrapped in a blanket, was the body of the missing boy. The child had kept crying for his mother, he said, and one of the men had strangled it. (In fact, Walter had been killed with a hatchet blow.)

Four of the kidnappers went on trial, including Tony Costa, who had actually abducted the youngster. They were found 'Guilty without capital punishment', and for a while, it looked as if the angry crowds of New Orleans would take justice into their own hands and lynch them – as they had done in 1890, when nine members of the Mafia were acquitted of the murder of the Chief of Police, and were subsequently dragged from their cells and killed by a mob. But the crowd was persuaded to disperse quietly.

The trial of two other accomplices – Nicolina and Leonardo Gebbia – had to be postponed for another four months because public feeling ran so high. The Gebbias were both found guilty; Leonardo was hanged, and his sister sentenced to life imprisonment. The man who actually killed Walter Lamana was never caught. But at least his crime had one beneficial result: the power of the Black Hand in New Orleans was crushed and broken.

Major undertaking

It was slowly becoming clear, to the police and the general public, that the surest way of dealing with kidnappers – and of lessening the danger to their hostages – was to pay the ransom, then let the police take up the trail. The value of this method was proved in 1909, in Sharon, Pennsylvania. On March 18, a man drove up to the local school and explained that he had been sent to collect Billy Whitla, the eight-year-old son of a wealthy attorney; his father needed him immediately at the office. The boy was allowed to go and that afternoon Mr. Whitla received a ransom note demanding $10,000. No doubt recalling the Ross case, Whitla declined to co-operate with the police. He delivered the ransom according to instructions, and his son was safely returned. Skilful police work, aided by luck, located the room where the boy had been held by a man and a woman. Detailed descriptions of them led to the arrest of James H. Boyle and his wife within six days of the kidnapping. Both were sentenced to life imprisonment.

But it was in the 1920's, the Bootleg era, that kidnapping became a major criminal undertaking in the United States. Possibly the Sicilian gangsters recalled how lucrative such activities had been in their homeland. For these gang-snatches, children were no longer the automatically chosen victims. The gangsters realized it was just as easy to kidnap a rich business man – and it aroused less public indignation.

Machine-Gun Kelly

Even when it became a crime punishable by death, the crooks didn't seem to be deterred. One of the classic police investigations into such a 'snatch' occurred in 1933. The millionaire

Charles F. Urschel was sitting on the porch of his home in Oklahoma City, playing cards with his wife and another couple. Suddenly, two men with Tommy guns appeared. When Urschel and his friend refused to say which was Urschel, they were both bundled into a car and driven away. A few hours later, the friend reappeared; he had been released by the kidnappers when they established his identity. Edgar Hoover, Director of the F.B.I., personally took charge of the investigation.

Urschel, so he told the agents, was driven for 12 hours, then taken to a house, where he was blindfolded. He was made to write a ransom note. Then, for the next eight days, he was kept tied up in a dark room. But he kept his wits about him, and noted that aeroplanes flew overhead at 9.45 every morning and 5.45 every afternoon – all except Sunday, when a heavy storm apparently prevented the 5.45 from passing that way. The following day, he was driven a further distance, then put down at a railroad station and released. His ransom of $200,000 had been paid.

The aeroplanes were the only clue the authorities had to go on. Hoover's men studied hundreds of airline schedules. Since the drive had taken about 12 hours, they assumed that the hideaway must be within about three hundred miles of Oklahoma city. Next, after hours of painstaking research, they located an air route that crossed a certain point in Texas at 9.45 each morning and 5.45 each afternoon. They were even able to verify that on the Sunday, a heavy storm had caused the plane to turn off its usual route. The town in question was called Paradise. And in Paradise, they discovered, lived the mother of Kathryn Kelly, wife of a gangster named Machine-Gun George Kelly, who was prominent on their list of suspects for the kidnapping.

Posing as state surveyors, F.B.I. men then called at the house. One of them asked for a drink of water. It tasted bitter with minerals, just as Urschel had described it. A few days later, the F.B.I. swooped at dawn, and found Harvey Bailey – identified as the second kidnapper – with a Tommy gun at his side. Another accomplice, Albert Bates, was traced when he got into a fight in Denver, Colorado; the money the police found on him was from the kidnap ransom – the bill numbers of which had all been noted. For a few months, Machine-Gun Kelly became the latest Public Enemy Number One. He even wrote letters threatening to kill Urschel.

Then, in October, a girl in Memphis, Tennessee, confided to a schoolfriend that her 'parents' were not actually her parents; they had 'borrowed' her. A policeman who heard this story from his child made cautious investigations. There was another dawn raid, and as the armed policemen burst into his bedroom, Machine-Gun Kelly threw up his hands and yelled 'Don't shoot, G-men!' It was the first time Hoover's men had been called G-men, meaning Government men, and the name stuck. As for Kelly, he died 21 years later in Leavenworth Penitentiary.

Lindbergh laws

Before the snatching of aviator Charles A. Lindbergh's son in 1932, America's most famous – and horrible – kidnapping case was that of 'The Fox'. This was the signature on the ransom note sent to Perry Parker, father of 12-year-old Marian Parker. Parker was a Los Angeles banker; and Marian had been abducted from her school one day in December 1928. During the next few days, Parker received more letters, signed 'The Fox' or 'Fate', and it was clear that the sender had a sadistic desire to make the parents suffer. Finally, Parker kept his rendezvous with the kidnapper; he could see Marian sitting stiffly beside him in the car. He handed over the money, and the man drove off, promising to let Marian out at the end of the street.

When Parker reached her, she was dead; her legs had been hacked off, and her eyes propped open with wire. Her legs were found in a nearby park. But the shirt in which they were wrapped gave the police the vital clue; it led them to 20-year-old Edward Hickman, who said he wanted the $1500 ransom money to go to college. He also had a grudge against Parker, whom he considered responsible for a prison sentence he had received for forgery. Hickman proved to be an almost manic egoist, revelling in the publicity. He was hanged in San Quentin jail in 1928.

After carpenter Bruno Hauptmann's execution for the murder of the Lindbergh baby, in 1935, the kidnapping 'boom' came to an end. As a result of the case, laws known as the 'Little Lindbergh Laws' came into operation in various states. These made it a capital offence to commit kidnapping – even if it did not involve a removal across state lines – if any physical harm came to the victim. In New York State, some time later, a man was convicted of kidnapping for forcing a young girl – whom he subsequently molested – to accompany him from the street and onto the roof of a nearby building. Even the sending of a ransom note could mean a maximum penalty in a federal court of twenty years' imprisonment, or a fine of $5000, or both.

In 1960 Australia had its first child kidnapping case. Eight-year-old Graeme Thorne was the son of a travelling salesman of Sydney; his parents had recently won $100,000 in a lottery. Graeme's corpse was found near a beach a month after his disappearance, and scientific examination of the rug in which the body was wrapped finally led the police to the house where he had been taken – and eventually to Leslie Stephen Bradley, a married man with three children, who was arrested on board a ship bound for England.

Symbolic damages
England's first kidnapping case occurred in December 1969, when Mrs. Muriel McKay, wife of a senior Fleet Street newspaper executive, disappeared from her home in Wimbledon, South London. Nine years earlier in France, however, another snatch had taken place which gained almost as many world-wide headlines as the McKay story. Little Eric Peugeot, aged four, the son of the Paris automobile millionaire, Raymond Peugeot, was taken from the playground of a fashionable golf club on the outskirts of the city.

His captors – Raymond Rolland and Pierre Larcher – were two small-time crooks who wanted money in order to indulge their taste for nightclubs and blondes. They demanded $35,000 from the Peugeot family – a mere trifle to M. Peugeot, who handed over the ransom himself. Fortunately for him and his wife, the kidnappers kept their word and Eric was returned a short while later unharmed. It was not until October 1962, however, that Rolland and Larcher – who had been captured living it up in a ski resort chalet with a Danish beauty queen and a striptease dancer – were put on trial.

They were each sentenced to the maximum sentence under French law of 20 years' imprisonment. And the Peugeots – who had recovered some $10,000 of the ransom money – were awarded the symbolic sum of one franc damages. A small price, some people thought, for the agony and torment they had suffered. But the truth is that no parent – or lover, or friend, or relative – can ever be adequately compensated for the distress they undergo in such circumstances. One franc or a million, it does not erase the memory of the event. Especially if, as is usually the case, the kidnapping ends in the physical death of the victim, and the mental death of his family.

KILLER COUPLES

The Jack the Ripper murders – which terrorized the East End of London in the fall of 1888 – had the effect of making little black bags unpopular. Several people who thought they had seen the murderer mentioned that he carried such an object – presumably with his ripping knife in it. As a result, doctors were attacked by mobs in the district, and forced to show the contents of their receptacles; little black bags never regained their popularity.

Similarly, when Maria Manning was executed outside Horsemonger Lane Jail in 1849, she had an immediate and wide-ranging effect on Victorian fashions. Until that time, black satin was the favourite Sunday wear of Victorian ladies of all classes. Mrs. Manning wore it on the scaffold; suddenly, black satin was out of fashion.

Maria Manning was born Maria de Roux – a pretty, vivacious girl who always had a string of male admirers in tow. Brought up in Switzerland, she came to England as a maid to Lady Blantyre. On the boat to Boulogne, she met a good-looking Irishman named Patrick O'Connor, who was immediately attracted to her. O'Connor had been something of an adventurer, but he had finally settled down as a Customs Officer. Maria found him fascinating – but she had enough experience to know that his intentions towards her were strictly dishonourable.

They renewed their acquaintanceship when she returned to England, and she may have become his mistress. But she also became friendly with another bachelor who appeared equally desirable – Frederick Manning. Manning was only a railway guard; but when he told her he expected to inherit property from his mother, she decided to accept his proposal. They were married in London, then moved to Taunton, Somerset, where they purchased the White Hart Inn – with Maria's money.

Infatuated

Manning, apparently, was a petty crook. When a mail train was robbed of $4000, he came under suspicion, and was discharged. This could have been an injustice; but a few months later, there was another train robbery, and this time both the Mannings were arrested – together with two confederates named Nightingale and Poole. They were finally released for lack of proof, although Nightingale and Poole were each sentenced to 15 years' transportation.

The scandal ruined the couple's business in Taunton; they returned to London and opened a beershop in the Hackney Road. There O'Connor made his reappearance – much to Frederick Manning's disgust. Mrs. Manning felt that her marriage had been a mistake; one day, when her husband was out, she closed the shop and ran away with O'Connor. Manning traced them – through the cabman who had taken them to lodgings in Bermondsey, south London.

The three of them then reached an 'arrangement'. The Mannings set up home together in a small house in the district, and O'Connor made a habit of dropping in when the husband was not at home. Manning knew what was happening, but he was too infatuated with his wife to provoke her into leaving him again. Besides, he had discovered that O'Connor had a considerable fortune – at least $20,000. And O'Connor was so much in love with the red-headed ex-ladies' maid that he had made a will in her favour.

Manning was no fool; he knew it was unlikely that his wife would ever receive the money. O'Connor was in good health. In effect he was paying his mistress with a postdated cheque. In turn, Mrs. Manning suspected that O'Connor was getting tired of her. When he declined her invitation to come and lodge in their house, she decided to kill him. On July 28, a crowbar was delivered to the premises, and on August 8, Frederick Manning bought a spade. The following night O'Connor was invited to dinner. He was never seen alive again.

Miles apart

Three days later, friends of O'Connor called to ask the Mannings if they had seen him. Mrs. Manning said she hadn't set eyes on him since the previous Tuesday. Two more days passed, and then some of O'Connor's relatives reported his disappearance to the police. A constable called at the Mannings' house, but it was locked. He forced his way in, and found the

place in confusion. There was no sign of the man and wife. Their
suspicions aroused, the police decided to make a second and
more thorough search. This time, an observant officer noticed
that one of the flagstones in the kitchen had new mortar round
its edges. They levered it up – and found O'Connor's corpse,
buried in quicklime.

When the Mannings were finally caught, they were several
hundred miles apart – Frederick in the Channel Isles. Maria in
Edinburgh. Only then was the whole remarkable story revealed.
O'Connor had been sitting at a table in the back of the house,
drinking, when Mrs. Manning shot him through the head with a
pistol. Later, when Manning came in, he said to his wife: 'I
found O'Connor moaning in the kitchen. I never liked him
much, and battered in his head with a ripping chisel.'

They duly buried O'Connor under the kitchen floor, and set
about getting possession of his money. Mrs. Manning went to
her former lover's lodging – where she had been on a number of
occasions – and asked to be allowed to wait in his room. There
she helped herself to shares and bonds worth several thousands
of pounds, and two gold watches.

The next day, she went back again, looking for some foreign
securities she knew he possessed, but couldn't find these. Irri-
tated, she made her husband sell some of the shares for £110.
Then she sent him off to sell the furniture. When he returned, he
found that his wife had left him – with the bonds.

Stolen bonds

Mrs. Manning went to Euston railway station, where she left her
cases, then took a train to Edinburgh. Manning stayed in the
house for two more days before he fled to St. Helier, in Jersey –
where his swaggering demeanour and bullying manner made
him disliked. There he met two men who had known him before,
and his nerve broke again; he took lodgings in a remote cottage,
and began to consume large quantities of brandy. With everyone
on the island gossiping about him, the police had no difficulty in
tracing him.

Finding Mrs. Manning was just as easy. The cabman who
took her to Euston mentioned her trunks. These were found in
the left luggage – labelled 'Smith' – and a clerk recollected
selling her a ticket to Edinburgh. But by that time, she was
already under arrest. She had tried to sell some of the stolen
bonds, and the brokers – who had been notified about them –
sent for the police.

In court, the Mannings tried to put the blame on one another, but it did them no good. Manning was undoubtedly telling the truth when he said that Mrs. Manning had planned the crime. Mrs. Manning screamed, 'Base and shameful England!' when she was sentenced to death, and had to be dragged out of the dock. Her husband merely bowed to the judge as he heard himself condemned. He tried to see his wife again while they were awaiting execution. But she would only do so if he made a confession clearing her of the murder.

Gentle sex

The case of the Mannings excited such widespread attention because it was so rare for an alleged husband and wife to be involved in a murder. Among the poorer classes, it was understandable. Twenty years earlier, Burke and Hare, the Scottish 'bodysnatchers', were accused of murdering a number of women and selling their bodies to a medical school. At the time their 'wives' were charged with them, as active accomplices. But Burke and Hare were products of the Edinburgh slums; they killed as an animal might kill: to eat.

However, the cold-blooded killing of a lover by a husband and wife struck the Victorians as sheer inexcusable wickedness. They may have consoled themselves with the reflection that Mrs. Manning was a Continental, and that Continentals were notoriously immoral. What really upset them was that Mrs. Manning was obviously the instigator of the crime, and according to their conventions, women were the 'gentle sex', the ministering angels. They had their place in society, and they had to be kept in it, whether they liked it or not. Another 50 years passed before women began to agitate for the vote. The result, in criminological terms, would have justified the Victorians' worst fears.

Slum house

In the twentieth century, killer couples have become a commonplace: Bywaters and Thompson, Snyder and Gray, Brady and Hindley, Bonnie and Clyde, Fernandez and Beck. In the Manson family murders, the girls played as much part in the torture-killings as the men. Even so, 'killer couples' have remained rare in Europe, where old tradition remains strong.

In 1927, however, a couple named Nourric murdered a bank messenger who had been asked to call at their house in a suburb of Paris to collect money. When Leon Després disappeared, the French police constructed a list of 35 addresses at which he was due to call. He had visited the first 20 – then vanished. The twenty-first address proved to be a house in a slum, and the police soon established that its occupiers – the Nourrics and a relative, Duquenne – had a bad name.

A neighbour testified to seeing Nourric and his brother-in-law pushing a heavily loaded handcart in the direction of the river on the morning after the disappearance of the bank messenger. Two months later, the messenger's body was found in the river by a bargeman. The hands were trussed with cord, and the head – badly battered – covered with part of a woman's underskirt. The Nourrics were immediately arrested. In their house, detectives found the other half of the underskirt, and lengths of cord identical with that which bound the corpse. Bloodstains on the cart finally clinched the case against the family – all three of whom were sentenced to life imprisonment.

This case, in fact, was a throw-back to the age of Burke and Hare: a crime committed by desperately poor people, without the intelligence to destroy the evidence that could convict them – and with the wife playing the lesser role.

Comic variations

In the United States, the pattern has been completely different. As often as not, it has been the woman who has either played a leading part in the crime or, at least, accepted her full share of the responsibility. In 1922, for instance – the year the Bywaters and Thompson murder was making the headlines in England – America produced its own classic triangle case, with comic variations.

On the night of August 22 neighbours of the Oesterreich family in Los Angeles heard gunshots and screams. The police found Mrs. Walburga Oesterreich in hysterics, and her husband dead upon the floor. Questioned, she said they had returned from an evening out to find an intruder in the house. Her husband had grappled with him, and been shot.

Fred, a 60-year-old sewing-machine factory owner, proved to be a millionaire. While his wife was winding up his business affairs, the police became increasing sceptical of her story; finally, they arrested her on suspicion. Mrs. Oesterreich sent for her lawyer, and told him that her ne'er-do-well 'half brother' was living in the attic at her home; would he go along and legally evict him?

The lawyer duly went to the house, climbed the stairs, and tapped on a trapdoor in Walburga's bedroom ceiling. There was a short wait, then out stepped a small, shy-looking man, who identified himself as Otto Sanhuber. Inspired by the lawyer's friendly manner, Sanhuber poured out the true version of Fred Oesterreich's death – and the incredible account of a 19-year-old love affair, in which he had lived in the attic of the Oesterreich's house, emerging to raid the icebox and make love to Walburga.

The story began in 1903, when Walburga was 36. Her 41-year-old husband was a drunk, and unpleasant with it. One day Otto – then a 17-year-old mechanic – called at the Oesterreich home to repair Walburga's sewing machine. They were attracted to each other, and he soon became her lover. Fred suspected that his wife was 'seeing someone', and had her followed by a private detective. Mrs. Oesterreich found out about this, and in a fury threatened to leave her husband – who quickly gave way and apologized. However, Walburga knew that her lover would have to stop his visits altogether. Either that, or he must move into the house for good.

Vanishing whisky

Delighted by the idea, she suggested it to him. The youngster – who lived alone and was without a family – had no reason to refuse. One morning when Fred was at business, he moved into the attic – and he stayed there for 17 years. Occasionally, Fred heard noises coming from overhead, his wife told him it was rats, or that he was imagining things. He complained about the rate at which his whisky and cigars were vanishing; she explained he forgot how much he smoked when he was drunk.

On the evening of the murder, Fred had come home unexpectedly early, when Otto was in another room. He started a violent quarrel with his wife, and Otto – who just happened to be holding a gun – decided to intervene. The weapon went off accidentally, he said, and he then fired three more shots into Fred Oesterreich's body 'out of nervousness'. Walburga's lawyer decided to abet a felony. He told Sanhuber to get out of town. The case against his client collapsed, and Walburga was set free.

Future pattern

Seven years passed by – during which time Walburga Oesterreich and her lawyer were on intimate terms. Then her counsel suddenly went to the police, and said he was afraid Walburga meant to kill him. To avert that possibility, he wanted to 'clear his conscience' as to the death of Fred Oesterreich. As soon as he'd told his story, Otto Sanhuber – who was now married –

was arrested. He and Walburga went on trial for the murder of her 'drunken brute' of a husband. In court, Otto repudiated his confession, saying the police had forced it out of him. He was found guilty of manslaughter, and since there was a statute of limitation on prosecutions for manslaughter – of three years – he was automatically acquitted.

The District Attorney brooded on the charges against Walburga, and then finally decided to drop them. So, unlike the tragic Bywaters and Thompson affair, the case of the lover in the attic ended with everybody living happily ever after . . . except for the slaughtered Mr. Oesterreich.

Cases like this, in which the wife and her lover conspire to kill the husband, seem to belong to a past era – to the classic crime novels of James M. Cain, whose *The Postman Always Rings Twice* and *Double Indemnity* portrayed how killer couples operated in America in the mid-1930s and early-40s. This does not stop the pattern being repeated; but it has ceased to be typical. On the other hand, the Bonnie and Clyde team established a pattern for the future: the tough guy and his moll, travelling around the country and living outside society.

But at least – obnoxious as they were – the couple only killed in the course of robbery. In some of the more recent cases, the killing has become frighteningly random and casual, as typified, for example, in the murder rampage of Charles Starkweather and Caril Fugate in 1958.

Frozen body

On January 21 of that year, Robert Von Busch, of Lincoln, Nebraska, had a premonition that there was something wrong at the home of his in-laws, the Bartletts. He went to the house, and found it empty. Then he looked in the chicken coop – and saw the body of Marion Bartlett lying frozen on the ground. He had been stabbed and shot. The police soon found the bodies of his wife, Valda, also stabbed and mutilated, and their two-year-old daughter, Betty Jean – whose throat had been slashed.

The other member of the family, Caril Ann Fugate, was missing. For the past two days she had been refusing to admit visitors to the house, claiming everyone had 'flu. Now the police discovered that Caril had left a few hours before her mother's body was found. She had driven off with her 19-year-old boyfriend, Charles Starkweather. Caril was 14.

Starkweather was bow-legged, pigeon-toed, and short sighted; he wore thick glasses that made his eyes seem small. He had left home a few months before, after a quarrel with his father, and had since then been thrown out of his lodgings for not paying his rent. Caril Ann's parents were known to disapprove of his association with their daughter. Accordingly, the police put out an immediate alert.

Two days later, someone reported seeing Starkweather's car outside a farm belonging to August Meyer. The car proved to be bogged down in the mud. Troops surrounded the farmhouse and burst in. They found only one dead body – that of the 70-year-old farmer, shot through the head at close range.

Pool of blood

Only a few hours passed before another farmer – who was helping in a search for another missing couple – saw a pool of blood near the steps leading down to an old storm cellar. At the bottom of the steps he found the two people he was looking for: Carol King, 16, and Robert Jensen, 17. Both were dead. Most of Carol's clothes had been torn off; she had been the victim of an unnatural sexual attack. Cartridge cases scattered nearby made it clear that these were victims numbers five and six of Caril and Starkweather.

Soon afterwards, three more corpses were found. A Lincoln businessman, Lauer Ward, had failed to arrive at his office that morning. His partner called at the Ward home; there was no reply to his ring, but Ward's car was missing. The police found the body of Ward lying inside the door, stabbed and shot. His wife and their housekeeper were upstairs. The women's hands had been tied, then they had been stabbed and mutilated with a knife. Starkweather's score was now up to nine.

Nervous tension

Within hours, a Wyoming farmer had a terrifying close escape while driving home. He stopped on the road when he noticed two cars, apparently broken down. When he went closer, he saw a bullet-riddled body in the front of one of them, and a crying girl in the back. Then Starkweather suddenly appeared and ordered him to help him release the handbrake of one of the cars. The farmer took a risk when Starkweather's gun was pointed away, and attacked him.

Another car then came on the scene. Starkweather took the opportunity to wrench himself free, and drove off at high speed. Caril Fugate rushed to the arms of the man who got out of the newly-arrived vehicle, screaming: 'Help me, he's going to kill me.' Before long, a police car saw Starkweather behind the wheel of a Packard, and gave chase. One of the pursuing officers fired his carbine and shattered Starkweather's windscreen. Abruptly Starkweather brought his car to a halt. He was weeping with nervous tension. 'I got cut by the glass,' he whimpered.

'You've killed ten people,' said the arresting policeman. 'Eleven,' Starkweather corrected – and confessed to the killing of a gas station attendant in the previous year. He had murdered the Barletts, he said, because he went to the house to talk to Caril Ann's mother, and got into a quarrel with her. 'She slapped me. . .I shot them both. Then I cut them up a little.' He killed the child to stop her crying. Caril then insisted that she had been forced to accompany her lover on his murder rampage; a jury disbelieved her and sent her to prison. Starkweather was sentenced to die in the electric chair.

A man and a woman teamed together for the mutual destruction of a third are one of the deadliest combinations known to crime. Between them they have a strike force of physical strength, deceit, resolution, sex appeal, boldness, and amorality. Few can – or have been able to – stand up against them and live. Fortunately, however, the killer couples do not remain united for long. After their first coup, their first murder, they almost invariably begin to distrust one another, to quarrel, and then resort to betrayal.

There is no more unpleasant – if ironic – courtroom sight than when the couple turn on each other, accusing, protesting, saying anything in an attempt to save their own life at the expense of their partner's.

LADY-KILLERS

The three doctors called in to pronounce upon Henri Désiré Landru's mental condition were agreed upon one thing: the man, despite the ten women he was said to have murdered, was not mad. The first medical expert, Dr. Vallon, faced the crowded court at the lady-killer's trial and stated:

'I already had to examine the accused in 1904, when he was being charged with obtaining money by false pretences. I found him then in a state bordering on the psychopathic, but he was not mad. Perhaps he was on the borderline, but not beyond it. I find now that Landru is perfectly lucid, perfectly conscious of what he is doing. He is quick and alert in his mind. He is easy and facile in repartee. In short, he must be considered responsible for the acts of which he is accused.'

The second doctor, Roques de Fursac, added: 'There is no trace of obsession. In examining Landru's personality, we have found him to be normal in every way.' While Dr. Roubinovich said: 'We were struck by his subtlety and presence of mind. His psychology is what might be called that of the "transportee". Transportation is always before his eyes as a nightmare which threatens him . . . The transportee has to live, and his past means that he cannot be choosy about the means he employs to keep himself alive. He will use any means to avoid being caught and sentenced afresh, to avoid transportation. Landru was in this position in 1914.'

Lack of feeling

Landru – whose criminal and sexual career had been under police surveillance for some twenty years – was jubilant when he heard this. 'The crimes of which I am accused could only be explained by the most pronounced insanity.' he asserted. 'The doctors say I am sane – therefore I am innocent.'

Said to be 'completely lacking in moral responsibility',

343

Landru displayed an ambivalent attitude towards women, whom he courted like any other men and later killed with a brutal lack of feeling that branded him as a monster without humanity or heart.

If murderers derived their interest, like butterflies, from their rarity value, then Landru would belong to the rarest and strangest of species, the lady-killer. A surprising statement, perhaps, if you consider that over fifty per cent of all murder victims are women. But this is because the commonest type of murder is the family quarrel, in which the husband kills his wife in a fit of rage or jealousy. Much lower on the list – but still providing a high proportion of the crime figures – is the sex murder. The sex killer had the mentality of a hungry fox; women are chickens, who are protected from him by a screen of social conventions; like a fox, he waits for his opportunity to slip under the wire and help himself.

Landru, however, was not a sex killer in this sense. On the contrary, he belongs to the very small group of killers who chose to make a poor living (Landru 'earned' about £100 [$250] a victim) by the destruction of gullible women. He was possessed by a strange, morbid compulsion – the same compulsion we can see in the case of the French 'werewolf', Martin Dumollard; of George Joseph Smith, the British Brides in the Bath murderer; of H.H. Holmes, the American mass-killer; of the wife poisoner George Chapman; of the Hungarian Bluebeard Bela Kiss – perhaps even in the case of Jack the Ripper himself.

Killer of children

In order to understand the nature of this compulsion the question must be asked: Why are these lady-killers called 'Bluebeards'? The original Bluebeard, the 15th-century Marshal of France, Gilles de Rais, who fought beside Joan of Arc, was not a killer of women, but of children. Noted because of his glossy blue-black beard, he was a sexual pervert, and also thought he could use the children's blood in the making of gold. But it was the French writer of fairy stories, Charles Perrault, who created the popular version of Bluebeard the lady-killer in the late seventeenth century. One of his more macabre stories tells how a young girl, Fatima, marries the rich landowner Bluebeard, and one day looks into a secret room – to find there the bodies of his previous wives. Although Perrault wrote the tale from the Gallic viewpoint, many countries have similar legends of wife-killers – Cornwall has a story of a giant called Bolster who killed his wives each year by throwing rocks at them. The folk-imagination understands these dark male compulsions to destroy women – and also the woman's half-frightened, half-fascinated attitude towards it, which in some cases leads her to invite assault and violence upon herself.

A modern crime

The strange thing is that all the known cases of real-life Bluebeards are fairly modern. Of the hundreds of criminal cases contained in such compilations as *Lives of the Most Remarkable Criminals* (1735), *The Newgate Calendar* (1774), and even Camden Pelham's *Chronicles of Crime* published as late as 1886, there are no 'lady-killers'. Highwaymen, pirates, cut-throats, housebreakers galore; but no lady-killers. Why should this be? If folk-legend had been obsessed by Bluebeards for centuries, why, up until then, should there have been no real-life Bluebeards?

The work of the psychologist Abraham Maslow suggests a fascinating explanation which, if correct, throws an entirely new light on this question, and on the history of crime. Maslow's basic theory, first published in 1942, is known as 'the hierarchy of needs' or values. It was intended as a counterblast to Dr. Sigmund Freud's theory that man's basic needs are sexual – not to mention Karl Marx's theory that his basic needs are economic, and Alfred Adler's theory that the basic human urge is the Will to Power.

Maslow pointed out that if a man is starving he has *no* other strong urge except the urge to eat, and he cannot imagine any higher bliss than having large and regular meals. But as soon as he achieves regular meals, he begins to brood on security – the need for a roof over his head. If he achieves this, he now begins to think about sex – not just rape, but a mate to settle down with. And when a man has got a home, a good job, and a happy family, what is the next thing he wants? Respect and admiration, to be accepted socially, to be liked – and if possible envied – by his neighbours. This is the stage at which men join rotary clubs, and wives form coffee groups and worry about keeping up with the Joneses. At this stage, the urge for *self-esteem* becomes paramount, and this explains the penchant of some killers – Heath is a classic example – for dressing-up as heroes and officers.

Once all these needs are satisfied, what then? According to Maslow, the highest level of all can emerge: the creative urge –

what, in more old-fashioned days, we would have called his 'spiritual drives'. But this is not restricted to the emotional and egotistical need to write symphonies, compose plays in blank verse, or build cathedrals. Anybody who wants to do a job *well*, just for the sheer pleasure of it, is expressing the creative urge. From this it can be seen that Maslow's hierarchy of needs is a kind of ladder. If you are stuck on the bottom rung, then Marx's materialistic theories will strike you as true. If you are stuck on the next rung, it will be clear that the psychoanalyst Freud was right when he said there is nother more important than sex. On the next rung, the Austrian analyst Adler's Will to Power – and self-esteem – will seem the profoundest truth about human nature. All are partly right; none is wholly right.

Food and territory

Maslow's theory is borne out by the history of crime. In primitive societies, food and 'territory' are the most important things, and if a man commits a murder, it is likely to be for one of these two reasons or drives. Until a hundred years ago, for instance, most people in Europe and America were living at mere subsistence level. These were the conditions under which Burke and Hare, the two Edinburgh body-snatchers, committed their murders in 1828, and it is not surprising that they killed human beings for the sake of the few pounds paid by Dr. Knox of the medical school for the corpses. *This* is basically the reason that *The Newgate Calendar* is so full of footpads and burglars and highwaymen. And why there are so few rapists. Society was still stuck on the bottom rung of Maslow's ladder.

The Victorian age rolled on; the tide of prosperity spread slowly across Europe. Most of the famous British Victorian murders were still for gain; but the age of middle-class murder had arrived, bringing in the domestic dramas of such killers as Constance Kent who butchered her four-year-old half-brother, mass-poisoner William Palmer, wife-poisoner Dr. Edward Pritchard, Madeleine Smith, the Scottish girl who disposed of an unwanted and awkward lover. Then, in 1888, the savage and apparently motiveless murders of five London East End prostitutes, by the unknown killer nicknamed Jack the Ripper, signalled the beginning of a new age – the age of sex crime. Society, by virtue of its progress and growth, had reached the next rung of Maslow's ladder. By the 1940s, sex crime, once the rarest of all reasons for murder, had become commonplace. It still is; but already, the next age has begun – the age of what could be called 'the self-esteem murder'. Why did the London gangster-brothers Ronnie and Reggie Kray commit murders in front of a crowd of witnesses? The answer sounds astonishing: to *impress* the London underworld. The element of pride, of self-esteem, becomes increasingly common among murderers, whatever the motive appears to be. Multiple sex killer John Reginald Halliday Christie loved exerting his authority as an English war reserve constable; Heath posed as 'Group Captain Rupert Brooke'; Arthur Hosein – kidnapper of Mrs. McKay, wife of an executive of the London *Sun* – set himself up as a 'gentleman farmer'; Charles Manson saw himself as leader of a world revolution. Typical of this new trend in murder is the statement of 18-year-old Robert Smith, who made five women and two children lie on the floor of an Arizona beauty parlour and shot them all in the back of the head: 'I wanted to get known – to get myself a name,' he stated afterwards.

There is one major consolation in all this. If society can get past the stage of the self-esteem killer, the murder rate should drop steeply. The next rung up the ladder is the purely creative stage, and creativity and murder are usually incompatible. Whether that stage will ever be reached in our overcrowded world is a matter for speculation; but if Maslow's theory is correct, there is ground for hope.

Masked inadequacies

As for Landru – the prototype and most quoted example of the 20th-century lady-killer – a brief examination of his adult sexual career reveals that he is a typical self-esteem killer. His Paris childhood certainly provides no hint of his subsequent 'anti-women' activities. He was a sunny, good-natured child, liked by everyone, and adored by his parents (as his name – Désiré – hints). His father was an ordinary workman – a stoker. When Landru left school, he went to work in an architect's office – and his old friends immediately noticed the change. He became 'stuck up', and he lost no opportunity to mention that he was a white collar office worker. He had achieved middle-class status – which, in the French provincial society of the 1890s, meant considerably more than it would today. For the rest of his life, Landru played this part of the member of the professional classes: he posed as lawyer, doctor, engineer, businessman, accountant – anything that boosted his ego, masked his inadequacies, and made him feel 'talented' and a 'gentleman'.

Unfortunately for Landru and his future victims, society had no special place for the intelligent but mercurial young man. In the army – where he did military service – his record was excellent. Then he returned to civilian life, married the cousin he had got pregnant, and faced the task of making a career for himself and providing security for his family. But the prospect of a lifetime in an office bored him, and he was too unstable to stay in any one job for long. Attempts to launch his own businesses invariably failed. His natural charm and alertness suggested petty fraud and false pretences as a means of tiding his wife and four children over bleak periods. And it was with the enthusiasm of someone who has finally found his niche that he turned to crime – a more exciting, more 'creative', way of living than office work. Experience showed him that elderly widows were particularly gullible, and eager to give him the keys to their hearts and deposit boxes. Being a confidence trickster – especially such a well-loved and successful one – appealed to his vanity, to his intelligence, even to his artistic impulse (for, as Thomas Mann, the German Nobel Prize-winner pointed out in his novel *Felix Krull – Confidence Man*, the confidence trickster has a touch of the artist about him). Inevitably there were periods in gaol; and when, in 1912 (when Landru was 43) his father committed suicide, overwhelmed by his son's disgrace, the con-man entered a new phase of his career. He determined to throw all scruples to the wind and make an audacious career of murder.

It is a curious fact that – with one borderline exception – the life-styles of all the best known lady-killers resemble Landru's in certain basic respects.

Johann Hoch, born in Strasbourg in 1860, was intended for the ministry, but left Germany – for undisclosed reasons – and went to the United States. There he advertised in German language papers for widows without children, 'object, matrimony'. This technique was very like Landru's. He represented himself as a wealthy businessman or a man with a respectable position in a commercial company. He married the woman – if necessary – parted her from her money, and decamped. Unlike Landru, he appeared to prefer poison when it came to despatching his brides. He was married some thirteen times – unlucky number as far as his 'wives' were concerned – and poisoned six of his brides. He was executed in Chicago in 1906.

Carefree scale
H.H. Holmes, perhaps the most remarkable American criminal of the 19th-century was also born in 1860, the son of a postmaster. Determined to rise in the world, he studied medi-

cine, then became a swindler. His first known murder was of a store-owner, a Mrs. Holden, in Chicago. Holmes duly became owner of the store. He then built a house, riddled with secret passages, and proceeded to murder women on a large and carefree scale. The motive was not sexual, for most of the girls had been his mistress for some time before they 'vanished'. At least eight women disappeared after entering his 'murder castle', and he later schemed with a man named Pitezel to swindle an insurance company. In the end – as often happened with Holmes' friends – Pitezel and three of his children were killed. Mrs. Pitezel was also on the murder list, but Holmes was arrested before he could eliminate her. In all, he confessed to 27 murders.

George Chapman – actually a Pole called Klosovski – was executed in 1903, having been found guilty of poisoning three wives. Chapman's English was poor, and the early part of his life was spent abroad, so altogether less is known about him than about other notable lady-killers. Son of a carpenter, he spent much of his life trying to 'better himself', setting up in various businesses, including those of barber and publican. (He was in Whitechapel in London's East End at the time of the Ripper murders, and has been suspected of being the Ripper.) There is no evidence that he was ever involved in swindling and the motive for the poisonings has variously been put down to sexual lust, craving for security and money, and sadism.

George Joseph Smith, the infamous 'Brides in the Bath' murderer was a Londoner, born in 1872. He was in and out of reformatories and gaols from the age of nine. After a two year sentence for receiving stolen goods, he embarked on the career of a swindler of widows and unmarried females. He married and deserted an unspecified number of women before deciding to drown Bessie Munday in 1912. When his third 'wife' drowned in her bath, a newspaper report aroused the suspicions of a relative of a previous victim. Protesting his innocence to the end Smith was executed in 1915.

Frederick Deeming, born in England about 1853, was a confidence swindler who specialised in cheating jewellers by pretending to be the manager of a diamond mine. For reasons of gain, he also posed as a millionaire, and as 'Sir Wilfred Lawson' and 'Lord Dunn'. He was a braggart and a remarkably inventive liar. In 1891, he murdered his wife and four children, and buried the bodies under the floor in a rented house. He then went to Australia with a new wife, who was soon murdered and buried

under another floor. Posing as Baron Swanston, he had persuaded another girl, an heiress, to marry him when the discovery
of his second wife's body led to his arrest. Three houses in which
he had previously lived in South Africa also proved to have girls
buried under the floors. He declared that the ghost of his dead
mother urged him to murder women. Despite this 'defence', he
was executed in 1892.

Bela Kiss, an amateur astrologer and Hungary's most spectacular lady-killer, claimed a total of at least twenty-four victims.
When he joined the army in 1916, the new tenant of his house
opened seven petrol drums and found them to contain bodies of
women preserved in alcohol. Kiss proved to be well known in the
red light district of Budapest – a man of immense physical
strength and boundless sexual appetite. He had advertized for
ladies to share his rural seclusion in Cinkota; the ladies vanished,
and their valuables provided Kiss with more funds for excursions
to the city brothels. By the time his victims were discovered, the
authorities had been notified of his death in action during the First
World War. Later stories, however, told of him enlisting in the
French Foreign Legion under the name of Hofmann, and of being
spotted by a New York Homicide Squad detective emerging from
the subway station in Times Square.

One other thing that the lady-killers – the men who mask their
loathing of women with love – have in common is the so-called
'hypnotic power' which they have wielded over their victims. This
again can be explained by the way in which they carefully chose as
their 'wives' women who wanted – needed – to be subjected to the
power of a 'superior' man. These eager and willing victims – the
'murderees' – cannot wait to meet a man who is going to mistreat
them, both physically and emotionally, and then strip them of
their pride, their dignity, their money and their possessions.
Without such women – who seem to draw their killers towards
them – the Landrus and other Bluebeards would have no one to
abuse, take advantage of and fleece. Their 'hypnotism' – George
Joseph Smith was reputed to have 'eyes that could make a girl do
anything' – would go for nothing simply because there would be
no one on whom they could successfully practice. Every Landru
has to have a Madame Cuchet – his first widow victim – and but
for her, and those like her, he would be no more than another
eccentric possessed with 'strange' ideas about the sexes and the
roles played by men and women in the marriage game.

Lady-killers are to be abhorred, and their victims pitied. But
compulsion can be a two-way process: the compulsion to kill and

to be killed. Lock up the lady-killers by all means, but also educate their 'wives', teach them to beware of men like Smith, men like Landru, who are too smooth, too polite, too charming – and, underneath it all, too deadly.

LEFT-LUGGAGE MURDERS

G.K. Chesterton suggested that the ideal place for a secret society to meet would be an open balcony overlooking a public square. The same kind of wild logic seems to inspire those murderers who use trunks for the disposal of the corpse. The ideal solution to the murderer's problem would be to make the body disappear into thin air; next on the list, to hide it where it could never be found. Putting it in a trunk, where it is sure to be discovered, is no way to conceal a murder.

The policeman and the pathologist, on the other hand, are bound to experience a certain satisfaction when a killer chooses this method of disposal. It gives them a sporting chance. For unless the murderer has the coolness and foresight of a master chess player, he is almost certain to have left a dozen clues that will eventually reveal his identity.

This was the view held by the Chief Constable of Brighton when, on June 17, 1934, he was called to the Brighton left-luggage office to examine the nude torso of a woman that had been found in a plywood trunk. Railway clerks could recall nothing about the man who had deposited the trunk there on Derby Day – June 6th – the busiest day of the year. But there seemed to be an abundance of clues.

Sir Bernard Spilsbury examined the remains. They were of a young woman in her early twenties. The head, arms and legs had been removed; but the torso suggested that the girl belonged to the middle or upper classes. She had a good figure, with no slack flesh, and the muscles were well developed, suggesting plenty of exercise. The golden brown of the skin also indicated that she spent much of her time in a warmer climate than England. At the time of death, she had been four months pregnant.

Important clues

An alert sent out to all other cloak-rooms in England led to the discovery of the legs in a case at King's Cross station in London. Each had been severed at the thigh and the knee, and they confirmed the view that the girl had been athletic and well-proportioned. The conclusion that the trunk had been left by a man was reached by weighing it; only a strong man could have lifted it without help.

There were two important clues. On a sheet of brown paper – in which the body had been wrapped – there was the word 'ford'. It looked as if it was the second half of a place name, like Guilford or Watford. In the trunk, there were two newspapers. The copies of the *Daily Mail* dated May 31st and June 2nd were of an edition that was circulated only within fifty miles of London. When a porter recalled helping a man to carry the trunk on Derby Day, it began to look as though a solution was near.

Secret affair

For the man had travelled on the train from Dartford to Brighton. A girl who had travelled in the same third class compartment was able to give a rough description of him. But of the five cheap day return tickets that had been issued on that day, not all could be traced, and the police eliminated all those they were able to contact.   Although the police were able to trace the makers of the trunk and suitcase, they were unable to give any useful information as to where or to whom these had been sold. No shop owners came forward with any recollections of either piece having been bought from their shop in the weeks leading up to Derby Day. So here the trail petered out.

Spilsbury estimated that the girl had been dead since May 30, a week before it was left at the station. The man obviously had plenty of spare time, as well as a home where he could conceal a body for a week without fear of discovery. That again suggested a man of leisure. The fact that it had taken him a week to dispose of the body indicated that the crime was not premeditated. And so the police could reconstruct most of the story. A well-to-do man, strong and athletic, has a secret love affair with a girl of his own class. He lives in Dartford, which is on the south-eastern edge of London, part of the 'stockbroker belt'.

She gets pregnant; on May 30, she calls on him to ask him what he intends to do about it. There is a quarrel, perhaps a fight, and he hits her on the head with some heavy instrument – the head was never found, but the body bore no marks of violence – or perhaps fell on top of her against a piece of furniture. Her death shocks him; he spends several days thinking on what to do with the body, then decides to dismember it, and deposit the trunk at Brighton. He travels on a third class day return, so as not to attract attention. And, in all probability, he leaves the country as soon as he has disposed of the body.

Careful searches

Sherlock Holmes would have had no difficulty solving the problem. He would have ordered a check on all ports, to establish which resident of Dartford had left the country immediately after Derby Day. He would have investigated the sports clubs in the Dartford area, and the riding stables. And the murderer would probably have been arrested boarding the *train bleu* to Cannes. . .

The British police had less luck. Careful searches of left-luggage offices revealed the corpses of three children and much stolen property, but no further clue to the Brighton trunk murderer. And from that day to this, the crime has remained unsolved. This can be attributed to luck rather than careful planning. But the case remains the interesting exception that proves the rule: that a trunk is the worst possible place to hide a body.

Wishful thinking

A study of the history of trunk murderers suggests that in many cases, the murderer has a subconscious desire to be caught. It can certainly be argued that the act of hiding a body in a trunk bears an interesting resemblance to the ostrich's attempt to hide by burying its head in the sand. In short, this is an example of Jean Paul Sartre's psychology of 'magic' – wishful thinking – that we have already encountered in the case of passion-killers. This can be seen clearly in one of the earliest cases of trunk murder in England: that of Arthur Devereux. It is a story of weakness, self-deception and wishful thinking that would have appealed to Stendhal, whose *Scarlet and Black* is based upon just such a true-life murderer.

One warm summer day in 1898, a pretty girl named Beatrice Gregory was strolling in Alexandra Park, Hastings, when she fell into conversation with a polite and neatly dressed young man. His name was Arthur Devereux, and he was a chemist's assistant. Beatrice was on holiday with her mother, and the holiday atmosphere no doubt made her more susceptible to romance; she saw Arther Devereux every evening for the remainder of her holiday. Her mother liked him too. Arthur Devereux was 'different' – imaginative and ambitious. When he talked about the future, it seemed marvellous and exciting, and she longed to share it. When he proposed, she accepted at once.

Pretty and feminine

Mrs. Gregory was less than happy about the engagement. There was something of the born loser about her, and she was afraid it had rubbed off on her daughter. She found it hard to believe that the future could be as glorious as Arthur painted it. And after a few months of marriage, Beatrice began to share her mother's misgivings. The truth was that, emotionally, Arthur was something of a child. He had wanted her because she was pretty and feminine; it never struck him that there is a practical side to marriage. He found the penny-pinching of married life on a chemist's assistant's wages less romantic than he had expected. He became gloomy and preoccupied.

Then a son was born. It made things more difficult for Arthur; yet oddly enough, he didn't seem to mind. He adored his son, whom they named Stanley. For a while, it looked as if the marriage was going to be a success after all. Then fate intervened, and Beatrice discovered she was again pregnant. The news plunged Arthur into depression. He spent more time than ever cuddling and playing with his son. When his wife produced him twin boys, Lawrence and Evelyn, it seemed the last straw. His affections were already fully engaged; he had no interest in the new arrivals.

Morphine bottle

During the course of the next two years, the Devereuxs moved to a flat in Kilburn, north-west London. Beatrice was now undernourished. Arthur was still working as a chemist's assistant, but the wages were poor. He was an embittered man who felt that his wife had trapped him, and he daydreamed of how easy life would be without Beatrice and the twins. One day in 1905, he decided to do something about it.

The murder was carefully planned. First, he asked the landlord if, when the tenants in the flat below moved out, he could take over the extra flat. Then he brought home a large tin trunk. A few days later, on January 29, 1905, he brought home a bottle of morphine, and somehow induced his wife to swallow most of its contents – perhaps leading her to believe it was medicine for her cough. Both she and the twins were dead by the next morning. Devereux placed them in the trunk, arranged for it to be taken to a warehouse in Harrow, then moved – with Stanley – to another part of London.

Mrs. Gregory called at the Kilburn flat, and found it empty. She succeeded in getting a letter forwarded to Arthur, but his reply was strangely non-committal. He said that he had sent Beatrice on holiday, and that he would prefer that her mother should try not to contact her. Mrs. Gregory's intuitions warned her of the worst. She heard about the furniture van, traced it to the depository in Harrow, and finally succeeded in getting an order authorizing her to open the trunk.

Twenty-four hours later, with the story of the discovery of the three corpses in all the newspapers, a worried Arthur Devereux prepared to move on again. This time, he went to Coventry, where he found another job with a chemist. Inspector Pollard, the man in charge of the case, had little difficulty in finding him; it was simply a matter of making a nation-wide check on chemists who had recently hired a new assistant with a 6-year-old son. When Pollard called to arrest him, Devereux blurted out: 'You're making a mistake. I don't know anything about a tin trunk.' Pollard had not mentioned it.

Fantasy world

At the Old Bailey, Devereux's defence was that his wife had killed herself and the twins, and that he had lost his nerve and concealed the body in the trunk. But there was one fact that undermined his story. On January 22, 1905, he had replied to an advertisement for a job at Hull, with a telegram: 'Will a widower with one child, aged six, suit?' But at that time, Beatrice and the twins were still alive. On August 15, 1905, Arthur Devereux was hanged at Pentonville prison.

An alienist – which is what psychiatrists were called in those days – had found Arthur Devereux to be sane, but it is difficult to agree with this conclusion. Is it sanity to live completely in a world of fantasy, and to commit a murder without the slightest chance of escaping the penalty? Devereux adored his son; did it not strike him that, in killing his wife, he was risking leaving his son an orphan?

He knew his mother-in-law well enough to know that she would never rest until she had traced her daughter; and he must also have realized that a trunk containing three corpses will soon begin to attract attention by its smell. If he had been sane, he would have taken Stanley and simply left his wife. But he wanted Beatrice to vanish, to disappear like the lady in a conjuror's cabinet. Wishful thinking, to that extent, is surely a form of insanity?

Sexual charms

The Monte Carlo trunk murder, which took place two years after Devereux's execution, raises the same questions in an even more acute form. The killer was an adventuress called Maria Vere Goold, who had assumed the title 'Lady Vere Goold'. Her husband, an alcoholic and weak-minded Irishman, *was* in line for a baronetcy; but his wife was anticipating.

Maria's career had been even more remarkable than that of her fellow countrywoman, Maria Manning, hanged in 1849 for the murder of her lover. Both were hard, calculating women, who used their sexual charms unscrupulously. Maria Goold — born Girodin — had lost two husbands in suspicious circumstances when she met her third husband, Vere Goold, in London. Goold had little money, but that didn't worry the adventuress; she was used to living on credit and borrowed money.

Mumbled answers

In their first year of marriage, Vere Goold exhausted the patience — and the purses — of all his close relatives. In Monte Carlo, in the early months of 1907, they tried gambling with what was left of their money, and lost it. Various dishonest expedients — like obtaining a ring from a jeweller 'on approval', and then pawning it — kept them going a little longer, until Maria succeeded in making the acquaintance of a rich old Swedish lady, Madame Levin, who was impressed by the aristocratic Vere Goolds. But she proved to be tight-fisted with money. She lent Maria forty pounds, but declined to part with any more. In fact, she pressed relentlessly for its return.

On Sunday August 4, 1907, 'Lady' Vere Goold invited Madame Levin out to the Villa Menesimy, where they were living in considerable poverty. And as the old lady sat talking to 'Sir Vere Goold', whose mumbled answers suggested he was drunk again, Maria crept up on her from behind, and dealt her a crashing blow with a heavy poker. Mrs. Levin collapsed, Maria produced a knife, and drove it into her tormentor's throat. Then she proceeded to hack off the head and limbs of the victim, and to pack them into a large trunk. A niece who was staying with them returned later that evening and found the place covered with blood. Maria explained that her husband had had a fit, and vomited blood.

It is not clear what Maria had in mind. They left Monte Carlo for Marseilles that evening, taking the trunk with them. In Marseilles, the trunk was labelled 'Charing Cross, London', and a luggage clerk was instructed to dispatch it, while Maria and Sir Vere Goold retired to a nearby hotel for breakfast and a sleep.

Cold contempt

The clerk, a man named Pons, observed blood oozing from the trunk. The August heat was also causing it to smell unpleasantly. He went to their hotel, and asked them what was in it. Maria explained haughtily that it was poultry, and ordered him to send it off immediately. Instead, Pons called at the police station, where an Inspector told him that the Vere Goolds could not be allowed to leave Marseilles until the contents of the trunk had been examined by the police.

Pons returned to the hotel, and found Maria and her husband about to leave. He asked them to accompany him to the police station. With cold contempt, Maria agreed. She took along a carpet bag that had accompanied them to the hotel. In the cab, her façade collapsed, and she suddenly offered Pons ten thousand francs to let her go. He remained immovable. An hour later, the police had found the torso of Madame Levin in the trunk, and her head and legs in the carpet bag.

It was so obvious that Maria was the guilty party that it was she who was sentenced to death, while her husband received life imprisonment. The death sentence was not carried out. While she was in prison in Cayenne, Maria died of typhoid fever. Her husband, deprived of alcohol and drugs, committed suicide. Yet in retrospect, it seems that Maria also subconsciously committed suicide.

Copious bloodstains

What could she gain from the death of Madame Levin? What was to prevent her flitting quietly out of Monte Carlo by night, as she had flitted from so many other cities? Or had a lifetime of crime and calculation finally loosened her hold on reality, as the murder suggests? Once again, the trunk is seen as the symbol of human inadequacy and self-deception.

As to the interesting question of who invented the trunk murder, there is no agreement among historians of crime. Possibly the honour belongs to a Herr Bletry, an innkeeper of Hegersheim, Germany. When the corpse of a woman was found in a yellow trunk at the Hegersheim left-luggage office, some time in the mid-1870s, the sheet in which the body was wrapped was quickly traced back to Herr Bletry's establishment.

If Bletry was the killer, he was singularly fortunate. Local gossip alleged that the corpse was that of his former housekeeper and mistress, Adèle Brouart, who had vanished some time before. Finally, it was positively identified as that of Adèle Brouart by various witnesses. But while Bletry was preparing to stand trial for his life, Adèle Brouart walked into the police station . . . The case collapsed, and the police were too discouraged to start all over again. If they had, Bletry would surely have been found guilty.

He tried to explain copious bloodstains in his kitchen with a story of a bleeding nose. The police were fairly certain that the trunk belonged to Bletry's present housekeeper, Franziska Lallemend, but because the other evidence seemed so strong, they had neglected to pursue this line of enquiry. Finally, a strange woman had been seen to arrive at the Inn, and had not been seen subsequently. The motive for the crime was probably robbery; but since Bletry was allowed to go free, we shall never know.

A book called *Supernature* by the zoologist Lyall Watson mentions a curious fact that may be of interest to trunk murderers of the future. A Frenchman named Bovis, who was exploring the pharaoh's chamber in the Great Pyramid of Cheops, observed that although it seemed damp, the body of a cat, and various other litter, was apparently undecayed. It struck M. Bovis that perhaps the *shape* of the pyramid might account for this. He made an accurate scale model of the pyramid, and put a dead cat in it.

Cosmic energy

The body mummified instead of decaying. Dr. Watson claims to have tested this himself with a home-made cardboard pyramid (made of four isosceles triangles with the proportion base to sides of 15.7 to 14.94). A dead mouse placed in the pyramid mummified, whereas a mouse placed in a shoe box decayed – and stank – in the normal manner. Even more strange, razor blades left in such a pyramid remain sharp even after much use – a Czech firm has patented the Cheops Pyramid Sharpener.

Dr. Watson's theory is that the pyramid acts as some kind of a greenhouse to cosmic energy, which dehydrates organic matter, and somehow affects the crystalline structure at the edge of a razor blade. So in theory, a trunk shaped like a scale-model of the Great Pyramid should preserve bodies indefinitely – even if dismembered – and prevent smell. On the other hand, it is true that the shape might arouse curiosity in railway cloakrooms. No modification is likely to alter the fact that the trunk is one of the least efficient means of disposing of human remains.

LETHAL LAWYERS

It is an amusing paradox that many of the qualities required by a good lawyer are those that are required by a good criminal: enterprise, coolness, and the courage to take risks. All three are demonstrated in the famous Earl Rogers story of the Gun Trick. Earl Rogers was one of America's greatest – and in some ways most lethal – criminal lawyers. He was a vain man, a bad loser, and a heavy drinker. But he also had the quality of a real-life Perry Mason.

It was on a hot August day around the turn of the century that three men sat around a table in a gambling joint in Catalina Island, California, playing poker. One of them was a professional gambler named Yeager, also known as the Louisville Sport. The other two young men were business partners, Al Boyd and Harry Johnson. They proposed to buy a cigar store together – mostly with Boyd's capital – but the way this game was going, they'd soon have no capital left. Johnson wanted to cut their losses and quit; Boyd, a compulsive gambler, wanted to continue playing, convinced he could win back everything he'd lost. But the point eventually came where he had nothing left but his gold watch.

Suddenly, there was the sound of two shots. Yeager's hat jumped off his head and rolled across the room, and the Louisville Sport slumped across the table. An ace that he had just dealt off the bottom of the pack lay in front of him, stained with the blood that ran from the hole in his forehead. Harry Johnson rushed to the door, holding a gun. 'He shot him. My God, he shot him!' he cried, handing the bartender the gun, which was still smoking. Sitting at the table, his partner looked drunk and bewildered.

Two hits
Later, Al Boyd appeared in court, charged with the murder of the Louisville Sport. The chief witness against him was his partner, Harry Johnson. Johnson was young and blond, and he looked

361

honest and reliable. The jury liked him. But Earl Rogers was convinced that Harry Johnson had shot the gambler.

Questioned by his lawyer, McComas, Johnson told the story of the gambling session. Al Boyd had lost everything but his watch. He begged the gambler to advance him $100 on the watch, so that he could continue gambling. Yeager said the watch wasn't worth two bits, and laughed at him. In a rage, Boyd pulled his gun and shot Yeager. Then he threw the gun down. Johnson picked it up and ran to the door . . .

Doublecrossing

Under further examination, Johnson admitted that he had an arrangement with the Louisville Sport. He would get a percentage of his friend's losses as a payment for steering him into the game. This admission worried Earl Rogers. If it was true, it meant that Johnson had no conceivable motive for shooting the gambler. He was going to get his cut anyway. Rogers grilled Johnson as to why he hadn't told about this 'arrangement' at the preliminary hearing. Johnson flushed and said he was ashamed of what people would think.

Rogers pointed out to the jury that this open-faced young man had been doublecrossing his closest friend, but he could tell they weren't too indignant about this: California was a rough place, and business was business.

It was clear that Johnson was unworried by the tactics of the defence lawyer. He answered all questions promptly and in a clear voice. Apparently without much hope. Rogers took him slowly and carefully over the events of those last few minutes. The bloodstained table was in court; so were the three chairs at which they had been sitting, and the gambler's hat, with two bullet-holes in it. Rogers made Johnson sit in the chair he had occupied at the time of the murder – to the left of Boyd – and describe again how Boyd had held out his watch towards the Louisville Sport and begged for a hundred dollars.

Yell of fear

'And then what happened?' he demanded. Came the answer: 'Boyd pulled his gun and shot him, quick as a flash.' Rogers pounced. 'How could he pull his gun "quick as a flash" if he already held his watch in his right hand? Show me how he did it.' Johnson became nervous and unsure. He repeated his story – how the gambler had fallen, dead, how Boyd had tossed the gun under his chair. 'But if Boyd tossed the gun under your chair, he must have had to turn towards you, with the gun in his right hand. For a moment, the gun must have been pointing *at* you. What did you do?' 'Nothing,' replied Johnson. 'I just sat there.'

As he heard this statement. Rogers' hand darted into his pocket, and came out holding a gun. He pointed the weapon straight at Johnson's stomach. With a yell of fear, Johnson jumped backwards, the chair fell over. The court was in uproar; several officers tried to grab Rogers, under the impression that he really intended to shoot the witness. Rogers looked slightly astonished at the commotion. When it died down, he explained smoothly that he was only trying to show the jury that Johnson's story was unlikely. No man would sit still as another man swung a gun on him, even for a fraction of a second.

Double-think

The jury took the point, and Johnson was now badly rattled. Rogers continued the cross-examination. 'What did you do then? You handed the gun to the bartender? Then what did you do?' 'I went to the washroom,' said Johnson. Question: 'To wash the powder burns off your hands?' Johnson stammered confusedly: 'Did I? Did I?' In effect, he had confessed to the murder. At least, that was how the jury saw it. Boyd was found not guilty. Johnson vanished, saving the District Attorney the trouble of charging him with murder.

This was the first time 'the gun trick' had ever been used in a court of law; later, Rogers used a number of variations of it. He knew it was a risk – that he might not only lose the case, but face a citation for contempt of court. But such 'trivialities' never bothered him. He had the instinct of a gambler, and he enjoyed taking risks.

Rogers possessed another quality in common with the professional crook: what George '1984' Orwell called 'the art of double-think'. It can be seen in the case of his defence of a clumsy murderer called Mootry, who had killed a man in a drunken brawl. In a moving speech, Rogers told the jury: 'You cannot convict a man like Mootry on the word of a pimp, a prostitute, and a policeman.' Mootry was acquitted. As he came up to Rogers, his hand extended, Rogers snapped: 'Get away from me, you slimy pimp. You're as guilty as hell.' Rogers argued that it was his job to get his client acquitted, whether he believed in his innocence or not. This ability to live by two contrasting kinds of morality can also be found in most professional crooks: the need to convince himself that, although he may be breaking the laws of society, he is not breaking his own moral code. Under the circumstances, it is not surprising that most lawyers who have committed a crime usually manage to persuade themselves of their innocence.

Impetuous type

This is illustrated by the case of John Barbot, whose trial in the year 1753 is described in a rare pamphlet, printed shortly after his execution. John Barbot was a young lawyer, son of a wealthy father, who 'sowed his wild oats' soon after qualifying for the Bar, and left his father to clear up an enormous pile of debts. In 1749 his father packed off the crestfallen young man to the island of St. Christopher (now St. Kitts) in the West Indies. Barbot was a likeable, if impetuous type. He soon made friends with a man of his own age, Dr. James Webbe, who helped him to find contacts in the town of Basseterre. It was a slow, difficult business; but Barbot enjoyed life in the islands, the warm climate, the Negro slaves, the cheap rum. After three years there, he was established as a professional man with a good practice and a small fortune of about £800.

Mere fraction

In the autumn of 1752 some of Dr. Webbe's creditors distrained for debt. Webbe owned an estate called Bridgwaters, on the island of Nevis; this was seized and offered for sale. Webbe was frantic; he was afraid the estate would be sold for a mere fraction of its value by his creditors. With the help of John Barbot, he tried to get the sale deferred, but it was no good. It came up for sale in November. Webbe hoped it would fetch at least £4500, but not many people *had* that much money. He and Barbot agreed gloomily that it might go for as little as £2000. Then Barbot had an idea. He could raise £800; in land sales, it was customary to pay a third deposit, and the rest within three months. His £800 meant that he could bid up to £2400. Then it would be a question of persuading his father in England to let him have the remainder of the cash.

Angry words

The next morning, he and Webbe attended the sale. The creditors were being represented by a solicitor called Matthew Mills, an old inhabitant of the island, who was universally liked. Barbot and his client immediately encountered a setback. The conditions of the sale were read aloud: one third of the money on deposit, and the remainder to be paid within a month. If it wasn't paid, the deposit was to be forfeit. This was bad news; it would take at least a month for a letter reach England. Barbot stood up and indignantly objected; the conditions were unreasonable and illegal. There were some angry words, and Matthew Mills accused him of trying to waste time, and of 'boy's play'. Barbot roared indignantly that he expected to be treated 'like a gentleman', and Mills said he considered that he had done so.

Then the bidding began. The sum went up to just over £2000. Next, to the general amazement, John Barbot joined in, and offered £2200. Everyone in the room knew he didn't possess that kind of money. There were more heated words, but it was finally agreed that Barbot could have the estate if he paid the deposit and signed the contract.

Barbot was so upset that his hand shook when he tried to write out an undertaking to pay the remainder within a month. He asked the marshal's attorney, Cottle, to write it out for him. When the attorney handed over the paper, Barbot could hardly believe his good luck. Either by accident or design, Cottle had made the bill payable within *three* months. However, just as he was about to sign, Matthew Mills looked over his shoulder, and indignantly pointed out that he was being given too much time to pay. More heated words followed, and Mills called him an impertinent fellow. Barbot lost the argument, and the contract was changed again.

Outside, in a fury, Barbot went up to Mills and asked him what he meant by being so rude. Mills, although usually known as a peaceable man, was still angry. He told Barbot that if he wanted 'satisfaction', he knew where to find him. Duelling was forbidden, but the law was not strictly observed. If two men intended to fight, they kept the duel a secret, so that if one of them was left dead the other had a chance of escaping the law.

Rendezvous

Barbot brooded on his wrongs. It looked as if he was going to lose all the money he had managed to save. He decided to take up the offer of 'satisfaction'. He wrote to Mills, asking for an opportunity to 'rendezvous with pistols'. After some discussion, they agreed to meet on a beach at Frigate's Bay, St. Christopher, early one Sunday morning. By way of providing himself with an alibi, Barbot stayed with Dr. Webbe on the island of Nevis that week-end. This meant that he had to hire a canoe and some

Negro rowers to take him across to St. Kitts. He left the doctor's house soon after midnight on November 26, 1752. A rainstorm soaked him to the skin, but he found his way to the beach, located the canoe, and was rowed across to Frigate's Bay. Mills rode up, and they saluted one another.

For what happened next we have to take the word of John Barbot. He claimed they placed themselves on either side of the road, raised their pistols, and then, at a signal, fired. At least, Barbot fired. Mills groaned: 'You have killed me,' and sank down to the ground. He died within a few minutes. By that time, Barbot was out at sea again, and Mill's Negro boy had run to the nearest house to bring someone to his master. The canoe was seen by a passing boat – the occupants of which recognized Barbot – and he was also spotted as he stepped ashore on the island of Nevis. Later that same day he was arrested.

It was at this stage that Barbot, quite incomprehensibly, insisted that he knew nothing of the death of Matthew Mills. He knew that Negroes could not be called on to give evidence in court. Therefore, all the evidence against him was circumstantial. A week before the duel he had been heard to say that either he or someone else would soon be dead. The day before the duel he had been practising shooting pistols at a barrel in Dr. Webbe's garden. Various people had seen him – from a distance – after the death of Mills. But all this did not *prove* he was the man who killed him . . . or so Barbot decided.

Legal skulduggery

It was an utterly gauche defence. Most people present in the court were hard-headed settlers who had achieved a position in the community through the puritan ethic of work and commonsense. They *knew* Barbot was guilty, and if he had pleaded that Mills was killed in a fair fight, there might have been at least a 50 per cent chance they would have acquitted him. But they couldn't countenance this legal skulduggery and talk about 'circumstantial evidence'.

Barbot's defence exposed him to another danger. The prosecution called a doctor who alleged that the bullet wound – in Mill's right side – proved that Mills was not in 'a posture of defence' when he received it. The prosecution also said that Mill's pistols were not ready to fire. In other words, they were suggesting that Barbot shot him without even waiting for him to prime his pistols. That would be coldblooded murder. Barbot should have countered this. He could at least have pointed out that a wound in a man's right side *is* consistent with a 'posture of defence' – if Mills had his own pistol held out at arm's length, with his right side turned towards Barbot.

Moving speech

Instead Barbot called various witnesses to try to prove that he was not the man who had been seen leaving Frigate's Bay. The jury would not accept this, found him guilty, and the judge sentenced him to death. Now, when it was too late, the lawyer decided to tell the whole truth. He made a long statement in which he told the story of the quarrel and the duel. But it made no difference. He was executed at Basseterre on January 20, 1752, after delivering a moving speech of repentance on the gallows. He confessed that it was his hot temper that had brought him to his 'sad predicament'. But he was wrong. It was his lawyer's capacity for 'double-think' which had lethally backfired on him.

England has had only two notable murder cases involving members of the legal profession. One was of Major Herbert Armstrong – the other, which took place a year earlier, in 1920, was of the lawyer Harold Greenwood, and it ended in his acquittal. Greenwood was a Yorkshireman, who came to Kidwelly, in Carmarthenshire, Wales, in 1898. He was a bluff, cheerful man, but the local Welsh didn't like him much. There were rumours that, for a married man, he was too interested in the opposite sex. But his wife, Mabel, was well-liked in the area.

Beautiful pink

In her forties, Mrs. Greenwood began to suffer from fainting attacks. The doctor diagnosed a weak heart, complicated by the usual emotional upheavals of 'change of life'. However, Mabel Greenwood continued to attend various local functions, women's meetings, and so on. During the second week in June 1919 many people thought she looked pale and ill. On the evening of Saturday, June 14, a friend thought she looked 'a beautiful pink' – an unusual colour for the usually pale Mrs. Greenwood.

Bilious attack

After lunch the following day, Mrs. Greenwood began suffering from diarrhoea. The doctor sent her a bismuth medicine for stomach trouble. However, she became worse as the evening went on. A nurse who had been sent for advised Greenwood to fetch the doctor, but he said he was unwilling to wake him. The nurse finally went herself. Mrs. Greenwood died in the agonies of a bilious attack in the early hours of Monday morning. Dr. Griffiths certified that the death was due to heart disease. She was buried in the local church.

The town was immediately full of rumours; both the nurse and the vicar were suspicious of the circumstances of Mrs. Greenwood's death. And when, four months later, Greenwood married 31-year-old Gladys Jones, daughter of the proprietor of the *Llanelly Mercury*, the police finally decided to take action. When they informed Greenwood that the body of his wife was to be exhumed, he replied cheerfully: 'Just the thing.' But when he was told that the inquest proved that Mrs. Greenwood had died of arsenic poisoning, his only comment was: 'Oh dear!'

Contradictory evidence

He was brought to trial in June 1920, defended by Marshall Hall. The prosecution alleged that he had put arsenic weed killer into the Burgundy which his wife had drunk with the Sunday lunch. From the beginning, the evidence was contradictory. The housekeeper said that no one else had touched the wine, but Greenwood's daughter Irene said she had drunk it at both lunch and supper. The parlourmaid stated that Greenwood had spent half-an-hour before lunch alone in the china pantry; Irene Greenwood testified that her father was outside cleaning the car at this time.

The defence suggested that *if* Mrs. Greenwood had died of arsenic poisoning, it was possible that Dr. Griffiths had put it in the medicine in mistake for bismuth. Another doctor gave evidence that the amount of arsenic found in the body – a quarter of a grain – was not enough to cause death; people can have as much as two and a half grains in the body without ill effect. He thought that the doctor's tablets had contained too much morphia, and that this had killed her. The doctor, who earlier had agreed that the tablets contained morphia, now insisted they had contained opium.

In all the confusion, it was clear that Greenwood could not be found guilty. The jury's verdict was that, while they were satisfied that Mabel Greenwood had absorbed a dose of arsenic just before her death, it was by no means certain that it had been the *cause* of death.

Unmerited publicity

The day after his acquittal Greenwood gave a lunch for the reporters who had covered the trial, and joked about the absence of

Burgundy from the table. But public opinion still accused him of administering small doses of poison to his wife. His practice declined, and he died eight years later, living in a Herefordshire village under the name of Pilkington, his health completely broken. Whether or not he murdered his wife, there can be no doubt that the gossiping tongues of Kidwelly killed Harold Greenwood.

The fact is that, among the professions, lawyers are among the least likely to turn killer – and that when they do their crimes receive an almost unmerited amount of publicity and criticism. Perhaps they know the ins and outs of the law too well to commit murder. For every murderer who 'gets away with it', there are dozens who don't, and who are either imprisoned for life or executed. As Charles Dickens once said, 'The law is an ass' – but not when it comes to protecting the lives, freedom, and reputations of those who make their income from it.

LIBEL

The attractive girl who stood in the witness-box described how she had called at the consulting rooms of the famous surgeon, and how he had asked her if he could look at a scar on her throat. 'He fastened his hand somewhat roughly between the ribbon that was on my neck and my throat. 'I said: "Oh, you are suffocating me," and he said: "Yes, I will, I can't help it. . ."' Then she lost consciousness.

The famous advocate, Isaac Butt, asked her: 'Are you now able to state whether in that interval of unconsciousness. . .your person was violated?' Dropping her head, the girl whispered: 'Yes.' Butt wanted to make sure the jury got the point. 'And was it?' Again she whispered: 'Yes.' And as the court broke into a buzz of excitement the judge adjourned for the day.

The girl's name was Moll Travers, daughter of a professor of Trinity College, Dublin, and the doctor who was accused of throttling her into unconsciousness and then deflowering her was the famous surgeon, Sir William Wilde. The reader might be forgiven for assuming he was on trial for rape. In fact, he was not on trial at all; it was his wife who was being tried for libel — for writing an angry letter to the girl's father, accusing her of trying to blackmail her husband.

This is the disappointing thing about libel trials. There is something absurdly trivial about most of them. We find great criminal trials exciting because they usually involve a confrontation of good and evil. Libel trials seldom involve anything more exciting than stupidity and malice. The Wilde scandal was no exception. Sir William Wilde may have been one of Ireland's most eminent eye surgeons, but he was not much liked.

To begin with, he looked peculiar, with bulging eyes, a sensual mouth and a receding chin — photographs give him a certain resemblance to Groucho Marx as Dr. Hugo Z. Hackenbush. His skin looked greasy and unwashed: there was a joke in Dublin:

'Why are Sir William Wilde's nails so black?', and the answer: 'Because he scratched himself.' A more scurrilous story alleged that he had taken out a patient's eyes in the course of an operation and put them on a table; while he was looking for some surgical instrument, the cat jumped on the table and ate them.

In spite of his unprepossessing appearance, Wilde had vitality, humour and tremendous drive – all characteristics that are admired by young women, and in the days when he was steadily establishing himself as Ireland's finest ear and eye surgeon he had many mistresses, and fathered a considerable illegitimate progeny. One of these mistresses was a young girl whom he cured of deafness – May Josephine Travers, the daughter of a professor of law at Trinity. She also bore him a child. But Wilde felt no more inclination to marry her than any of the other girls he slept with. Besides, he already had a wife.

Intellectual equals

In the year 1848 a young girl had made a stir throughout Ireland. Her name was Jane Francesca Elgee, and her patriotic verses, published under the name of 'Speranza' – hope – had already made her famous, when she interrupted the trial of a newspaper editor with a shout of: 'I alone am the culprit. I wrote the offending articles.' As a result, the editor of *The Nation* was acquitted on a charge of printing seditious libels. When Sir William Wilde met the tall, strikingly handsome girl not long after the trial, he knew that he had at last met a woman who was his intellectual equal. They were married in 1851, and had two children, one of whom, Oscar Fingall O'Flahertie Wills Wilde, would become famous as the author of *The Importance of Being Earnest*.

Now, whether or not Wilde had really taken Molly Travers' virginity when she was under chloroform – as she alleged – she was certainly infatuated with her seducer, and bitterly angry when he broke with her. She brooded on getting her own back, and soon thought of a way. When Wilde gave a lecture at the Metropolitan Hall, small boys in the foyer gave away copies of a pamphlet entitled: 'Florence Boyle Price'. The pamphlet told the story of how an innocent young girl had gone to the surgery of a certain 'Dr. Quilp' – obviously Wilde – and had been chloroformed by him, then ravished. The pamphlet added insult to injury by claiming to be written by 'Speranza'. The real author, of course, was Moll Travers.

The affair was the talk of Dublin; but the Wildes had the sense to ignore it. If they had continued to do so all would have been well. But when, a few weeks later, Lady Wilde found an urchin selling the penny pamphlet in her own hallway, she indignantly snatched one and carried it off. The neurotic Miss Travers immediately summoned Sir William and Lady Wilde to court for non-payment of the penny. Neither had to appear, and presumably they paid the penny. But Lady Wilde now made the mistake of writing an angry letter to Professor Travers about the 'disreputable conduct' of his daughter. This was all Moll Travers needed. She immediately had Lady Wilde served with a writ for libel, claiming £2000 damages.

The case was heard in December 1864, and Miss Travers got what she wanted – the fullest publicity for her affair with Sir William Wilde. Her advocate, Serjeant Armstrong, told the story of the 'rape' again; this time it was not chloroform that subdued her but strangulation. The result was the same. The serjeant explained sadly that 'she went in a maid, that out a maid never departed more'.

The story was probably a neurotic invention. The flat truth was that Wilde was a philanderer and had seduced his patient because she was a 'pushover'. He had been seen a great deal with her in public, and she often came to his house. Wilde's wife was indifferent to the affair; she had already developed an illness that made her hands and feet swell to elephantine proportions, and had a number of eccentricities, such as staying in bed and receiving all visitors – even on the sunniest days – with the curtains drawn and the room lit by candles.

Bedroom scene

One day Moll Travers tried to visit Lady Wilde in her bedroom and was indignantly ejected. From then on, Sir William began to lose interest in her. Finally, at his wife's instigation, he refused to see her. Then the trouble began.

It was an absurd trial and should have gone in Lady Wilde's favour. Her letter to Professor Travers was not libellous, but both she and her husband made errors of judgment that seriously alienated the jury. Lady Wilde was asked why she had not replied to a letter from Miss Travers telling of her husband's attempt at rape. She replied coldly: 'I took no interest in the matter' – giving the impression she was snobbish and heartless.

And Sir William Wilde made things worse by deciding not to appear in the witness-box to rebut the charges. The jury felt this was cowardly, and may have been angry at being cheated of more scandal. They ended by awarding Moll Travers a farthing in damages, but decided that Lady Wilde should pay the costs – several thousand pounds. A Dublin story insists that Sir William Wilde crossed the court and slapped a penny in front of Miss Travers, saying: 'There's the price of your virtue. Now give me my change.'

But, strangely enough, the verdict broke Wilde. He lost all his old fire. Although only 49 at the time of his trial, he seemed to become an old man. He lacked fighting spirit – a failing shared by his son Oscar. Oscar's downfall also occurred through a libel case, although on this occasion Wilde was the plaintiff, and the defendant was the Marquess of Queensberry, the father of Lord Alfred Douglas, who had accused Wilde of homosexual misconduct with his son. Wilde was guilty of this, and was unwise to have brought the case.

The law is an ass

Queensberry turned the tables on him by simply proving that Wilde *was* a homosexual. This is a point worth noting about the law of libel: and one of those typical paradoxes that makes a character in Dickens say 'the law is an ass'. A libel or slander is not made less libellous by the fact that it happens to be true; on the other hand, if a defendant can prove in court that his libel was true, he has a very good chance of being acquitted.

It would be wrong to give the impression that all libel cases have been trivial. Some of the early ones have been concerned with vital liberties, and one of them gave us a number of great novels, including *Robinson Crusoe* and *Moll Flanders*. This was the trial, in 1703, of a rather dubious political journalist named Daniel Foe, who had changed his surname to Defoe.

Despite the fact that he became a great novelist, Defoe was not a particularly edifying character. He began his career as a writer of pamphlets. When the unpopular William of Orange came to the English throne Defoe saw his opportunity and wrote a series of pamphlets praising and defending the Dutch king. As a consequence he was awarded a government post and became – accordingly to his own account – a close friend of the king's.

But when William died in 1702 Defoe landed himself in hot water. He had been born into a family of 'Dissenters' – that is to say, people who did not agree either with Protestants or Catholics. The Dissenters were much disliked in that age of religious controversy, although William of Orange had allowed them to take public office provided they were willing to attend a Church of England service.

However, after William's death, a group of extreme reactionaries began to advocate harsher measures against Dissenters – that they should be banned from public office. These reactionaries were known as 'high fliers' because they were so rigid about their principles. Defoe rather agreed with them that Dissenters should not be allowed to take public office – largely because he thought that any Dissenter who would attend the Church of England must be a coward and weakling anyway.

By way of livening things up, he wrote a satirical pamphlet called *The Shortest Way with Dissenters*, arguing that they should all be banished or hanged. He was guying the reactionary cause by taking it to an extreme. But the result was unfortunate, for many of the 'high fliers' took the pamphlet seriously, and one clergyman said he valued it above all books except the Bible.

The Dissenters were naturally deeply disturbed, imagining that a pogrom against them was about to break out. When it turned out that Defoe was the author of the tract, and that it was intended to be a satire, the high fliers were enraged. Parliament issued a warrant accusing Defoe of libelling the high fliers by making them out to be bloodthirsty maniacs. Defoe went into hiding; but finally he had to give himself up. In July 1703 he was sentenced to stand in the pillory for three days and to be detained 'during the Queen's pleasure'.

Cheered at the pillory

To Defoe's delighted astonishment the scandal made him. Crowds came and cheered him at the pillory – he was lucky; unpopular criminals were sometimes stoned to death. He was then sent to Newgate prison for a year and was regarded as a national hero and martyr. He launched his first newspaper in jail, and it was an instant success, and his meetings with thieves and prostitutes gave him the basic material for novels like *Moll Flanders*, *Captain Singleton* and *Colonel Jack*. It turned him from a dishonest journalist into a great novelist.

In America, just over 30 years later, a similar case had equally important results, and is regarded as a milestone in the history of civil liberties. The 'villain' of this piece was William S. Cosby, who had been appointed by the King of England to the post of Governor of the Crown Colony of New York. Cosby was utterly corrupt; in fact he had lately been removed from his post of Governor of Minorca for misappropriation of funds, only to have this new plum offered him by the government.

It was Cosby's belief that he was there to make as much money as possible from his sinecure. His predecessor in New York died in 1731; Cosby spent 13 months getting to America, having a final fling in Europe. When he finally arrived in the 'New World' the New York Assembly voted him an excellent salary of £1500 a year – a generous one, considering that it had to come out of the pockets of the taxpayers, and that America was not at that time very thickly populated. The settlers had heard that their new governor was bad-tempered, despotic and greedy; possibly the generous salary was meant to appease him.

If so, it failed. The new governor promptly pointed out that they owed him another £1500 or so in back salary, and he ordered his tax collector, a widely respected Dutchman named Van Dam, to collect it for him. Van Dam firmly declined. Cosby then thought of an ingenious way of laying his hands on the taxpayer's money; he declared that judges of the Supreme Court – of which he himself was one – should have sole authority to hear cases involving finances.

A similar trick had cost Charles the First of England his head, but Cosby got away with it. One judge, Lewis Morris, ruled against him; Cosby promptly sacked him. Two of Morris's ex-associates – James DeLancey and Frederick Philips – were more obliging, and they were appointed to the bench. Cosby now had the State's legal system taped and was prepared to take on all comers.

The first-comer was Lewis Morris. He ran for the Assembly at Eastchester. Cosby tried bribery and trickery to make sure he lost, but it was no good; the citizens elected Morris. Then Morris, together with Van Dam, and a remarkable planter called James Alexander, began to plot Cosby's overthrow.

A young German reporter called John Peter Zenger wrote an article about the Eastchester elections for his paper, the *Weekly Gazette*, describing in detail how Cosby had tried to intimidate voters. His editor not only declined to print it but sacked Zenger. Morris, Van Dam and Alexander immediately offered Zenger the money and support to start up a rival newspaper, *The Weekly Journal*. The first number appeared in November 1733, and it lost no time in making it clear that it considered Cosby to be a parasite and a crook.

The full story of the battle against Cosby is too long to relate in detail. Van Dam and his friends pursued a kind of guerrilla campaign. Scandalous anti-Cosby songs were circulated, and even though Cosby offered £20 reward for the names of the authors, no one came forward. He tried to get grand juries to return an indictment against the 'virulency' of the *Journal's* attacks, but they declined. DeLancey had another try in October 1734, with as little success. Cosby ordered that four issues of the *Journal* were to be burned at the hands of the public hangman, in front of the mayor and corporation; the aldermen refused to attend, and the papers had to be burned by a Negro servant.

Pure dictatorial tyranny

Finally, on November 17, 1734, Zenger was arrested and charged with publishing seditious libels – it should be noted that 'publishing' does not necessarily mean to print; it simply means to make public, even by showing it to a neighbour. A bail of £800 was set, to make sure Zenger could not get out of jail. Since the judge on the case would be DeLancey, Cosby was reasonably certain that there should not be too much difficulty.

James Alexander and his close associate and fellow-conspirator William Smith said they would be Zenger's attorneys. Cosby countered that move by having their names struck off the role of attorneys – although he had no legal right to do so. It was pure dictatorial tyranny. Alexander and Smith decided they had to be more cautious. So they made secret approaches to one of the great attorneys, Andrew Hamilton of Philadelphia. Hamilton was then a man of 59, suffering from gout. His first response to their approach was to name a very high fee; they decided it was worth it, and they proved to be right. Hamilton and Alexander carefully plotted their plan of campaign.

The trial opened on August 4, 1735, by which time poor Zenger had been in jail nearly a year. The Attorney General, Richard Bradley, was hoping to prove that Zenger had published the libels, and had been therefore largely responsible for them. His first intimation that things were not going his way occurred when Andrew Hamilton walked into court. If he had known sooner that Zenger was to be represented by a man as distinguished as Hamilton, Cosby would have found some way of disqualifying him.

But at such short notice it was out of the question, and Hamilton immediately lived up to his reputation by admitting that his client had personally printed the libellous material, but that his allegations were justified by truth. This dismayed Bradley, who had summoned an array of witnesses to prove that Zenger was the printer. Hamilton had taken the wind out of his sails.

Bradley now tried another trick. He declared that, since Zenger had admitted the charges, the jury only had to find him guilty.

Hamilton, calm and magisterial, replied that this was not so: the words themselves had to be found libellous. Bradley cited many cases in which the libel had been found worse *because* true. Hamilton replied gently that he could not agree that just complaints of the people against a bad administration *were* a libel.

Magnificent speech

The judge, DeLancey, obviously agreed with Bradley. After a magnificent final speech from Hamilton, he summed up in a manner that was meant to bully the jurors. He told them that the facts of which Zenger stood accused had been confessed. As to the question of whether they were a libel, they could leave that matter to the court; he was intent on convincing them that their job was simply to bring in a verdict of guilty, and to make it more certain he insisted that the question they had to decide was simply whether John Peter Zenger was guilty of printing and publishing the libels already mentioned.

The jury were only out for a short time and were soon back with their reply: Not Guilty. There was prolonged cheering, which DeLancey tried to silence, without effect. The following day Zenger was discharged. He was regarded as something of a hero by his fellow-citizens and was made public printer of New York City in 1734. As to Crosby, he continued to be governor; but he drew in his horns and was seldom seen in public. The public rebuke was too much even for his thick skin.

There *were* a few more libel trials that had real public significance – notably that of another radical journalist, William Cobbett, in June 1810, for publishing an account of rebellious English militiamen being flogged by German soldiers serving in the British Army. Cobbett, like Defoe, went to prison – and also became a public hero in consequence.

The lesson would seem to be that a libel can be a weapon in the hands of a fighter for truth. But whether used in the service of truth or mere malice, it is always a treacherous and double-edged weapon that is best left in its sheath.

LONELY HEARTS KILLERS

There is a Laurel and Hardy movie, which still gets welcome showings on the TV programmes, in which Oliver answers an advertisement by a widow who wants a husband. The widow turns out to be a homicidal maniac who spends the rest of the film trying to destroy the dynamic duo. The film was based on one of the most infamous – and unpleasant – of all lonely hearts killers, Belle Brynhilde Paulsetter Sorenson Gunness. For, unlike other lonely hearts killers, such as George Joseph Smith and Raymond Fernandez, she did not restrict her activities to strangers; she murdered her own foster daughter, and may have ended by murdering her own children.

Belle Paulsetter was born in Norway in 1859; her father was a travelling conjurer, and she took part in the shows, dancing on a tightrope. When Belle was in her teens, they retired to a small farm. Belle found the life too quiet; so she emigrated to the United States. There she married a Swede named Albert Sorenson.

It would be interesting to know what happened to this marriage, for it is obviously the key to Belle's future career. If it had been happy, Belle Sorenson would never have become a murderess. Obviously it was not happy, for Sorenson died after two years – apparently of a heart attack. He and Belle were living in Chicago at the time, and his relatives demanded an exhumation, asserting that he had been poisoned. But the exhumation never took place, and Belle moved out to Austin, Illinois, with the $8500 she had collected from Sorenson's insurance.

In Austin, her home was burned to the ground. The insurance companies suspected fraud; but there was no proof, and they paid up. Belle moved back to Chicago. It seemed to her that she'd discovered the ideal way of making a living. She bought a confectionery store and, after a while, this also burned down.

Again, the insurance company paid up. Now Belle purchased a farm near La Porte, Indiana, and married again, this time to Peter Gunness, a jolly, good-natured man, much liked by his neighbours. By now, Belle herself had ceased to be the fairylike creature who danced on a tightrope; she weighed over 200 pounds, was muscular, and had the battered face of a Norwegian peasant woman.

The evidence suggests that Belle was a highly-sexed woman. She probably married Peter Gunness for sex, then found that she couldn't tolerate him as a partner. In 1904, Peter died of a broken skull; he had been sitting under a high shelf, Belle explained, and a heavy sausage grinder had fallen upon his head. Fortunately for the widow, his life was insured for $4000.

Belle now had three small children – one, apparently, by Gunness – and an adopted daughter of 14, Jennie Olsen. One day, Jennie disappeared; Belle accounted for her absence by explaining she had gone to Los Angeles to 'complete her education'.

In the meantime, a number of hired men came and went, including, in 1906, a man called Ray Lamphere, who became the hired man, and also Belle's lover. Photographs give him the look of a startled bush baby. It seems clear that their relationship was based upon dominance – *her* dominance. At all events, unlike most of her associations, it lasted. Even so, at about this time Belle began to advertise in matrimonial journals for a husband. 'Comely widow who owns a large farm in one of the finest districts in La Porte County, Indiana, desires to make acquaintance of a gentleman equally well provided, with view of joining fortunes. No replies by letter considered unless sender is willing to follow answer with personal visit.' Another advertisement ended: 'Triflers need not apply.'

One of the non-triflers who applied was named George Anderson. On reaching the farm, he woke up in the middle of the night and found Belle standing over him, holding a candle, with a most 'peculiar look' in her eye. He yelled out in alarm, and she hurried from the room. An instinct of self-preservation made Anderson get dressed and leave.

Next, in May, 1907, an elderly widower named Ole Budsburg, of Iowa, Wisconsin, answered Belle's latest advertisement. He called on her without telling his two sons where he intended to go. He also neglected to tell them that he had negotiated the sale of a mortgage at the La Porte savings bank. Then – understandably enough in Belle's book – he vanished.

Headless body

The suckers, the victims, kept on appearing. In December 1907, Andrew Hegelein, a bachelor from Aberdeen, South Dakota, set out to see Mrs. Gunness. He arrived in January 1908. At the end of two weeks, the hired man Lamphere was mad with jealousy; but he didn't have long to suffer. Hegelein drew $2900 from the local bank. Shortly afterwards, Belle paid it into her own bank, and also discharged several large bills. Hegelein was still alive at the time, and apparently all ready to marry Belle. Then he vanished. Lamphere indiscreetly told a drinking companion: 'Hegelein won't bother me no more.'

It was that remark that aroused local suspicion, and made Belle feel that her luck might be running out. Hegelein's relatives were also making inquiries. On April 28, 1908, the farm went up in smoke. Sheriff Smutzer searched the charred ruins; he found the charred bodies of the three children, aged 11, 9, and 5. And also a headless female body. The rings on the fingers were Belle's. But the body seemed to be that of a much smaller woman than Belle – who weighed 280 pounds at the time of her death. Doubt about the identity of the body vanished when searchers located a jawbone in the ashes; Belle's dental plate was attached, and also a tooth to which the plate had been anchored. That seemed to settle it. Except that a witness claimed to have seen Belle driving out to her farm with a woman on the afternoon before the fire.

On the face of it it looked like murder, and Lamphere was arrested and charged. He had left Belle's employ shortly after the disappearance of Andrew Hegelein. He had been seen near the farm on the night of the fire. Shortly afterwards, Asle Hegelein turned up looking for his brother. He told the sheriff of the matrimonial advertisement that had taken his brother to La Porte, and of a letter from Belle saying: 'My heart beats in wild raptures for you. Come prepared to stay forever.'

High dominance

The men searching the ashes found men's watches, and other bones and human teeth. Asle Hegelein went out to the farm and wandered around. Looking into the bog pen, he had a sudden intuition. He pointed to a rubbish hole in the corner and asked the men to dig there. Within a few hours, they had uncovered four bodies – one Andrew Hegelein's, another Jennie Olsen's. In several cases, limbs had been amputated, Hegelein, it was revealed later, had died of strychnine poisoning. So had the woman whose headless body was found.

The digging now revealed more bodies. Among them were two children, suggesting that one of the prospective husbands had arrived with his family. Eventually, the remains of 14 bodies were uncovered. Most of them were badly decomposed, many mutilated. A few were identified by relatives.

Thomas Lindboe of Chicago had been Belle's hired man in 1905. Henry Gurholdt of Scandinavia had arrived at the farm with $1500; his watch was found near one of the bodies. Olof Svenherud of Christiana, Norway, subsequently of Chicago, was identified by his mother. The remains of John Moo (or Moe) were also tentatively identified. The others never were.

Lamphere finally confessed to setting fire to the farm, but denied committing murder. He was sentenced to jail for arson, and died of tuberculosis in December 1909. After his death, the Rev. E.A. Schnell, the prison minister, made public a confession in which Lamphere admitted chloroforming the Gunness children on the night of the fire, and claiming that a Negress with whom he was living at the time had helped him. He also said he had helped Belle to bury one victim, and seen her chloroform another and kill a third with a hatchet. The American criminologist Melvin Reinhardt, in *Sex Perversions and Sex Crimes*, states definitely that Belle escaped, and later spent some time in a mental hospital.

Did Belle murder her children and then get away? It seems possible. The parent of a schoolfriend of the Gunness children reported one as saying: 'My momma killed my poppa – she hit him with a cleaver.' (That would be Peter Gunness.) The alternative view, that Lamphere chloroformed all the Gunness family before he set fire to the house, sounds incredible. He might murder Belle in a fit of jealousy, but his photographs hardly suggest a man who would also kill children. Besides, he was, by his own admission, living with another woman at the time of the fire.

In that case, would he keep the secret of Belle's escape after his arrest? What is known of Belle Gunness suggests that he would. She was, like so many murderesses, a woman of very high dominance – and therefore, to maintain an emotional and physical balance, needed a high dominance male. Her first husband, Albert Sorenson, failed to satisfy her, and she probably poisoned him. (Murderers seldom change their poison, so it was almost certainly strychnine.) The big, good-natured farmer, Peter Gunness must have seemed a suitable sexual partner. But good nature is precisely what a very high dominance woman finds boring – she needs a strong, slightly sadistic sex partner.

Various writers have speculated on what caused Belle to commit murder; Reinhardt assumes she was probably a sadist. This is doubtful – at least, there is no evidence to suggest it. What is fairly certain is that she was the female equivalent of a sex maniac. If she had been fortunate enough to find the right high-dominance male at the beginning of her career, she would probably have been a normal housewife. Lack of sex turned her sour and mean. She chose males for her victims for the same reason that her Chicago contemporary, H.H. Holmes, chose females; because she had sex on her mind all the time.

It is fairly certain that she slept with all the hired men and all the prospective husbands; then, like a female spider, she killed them. The kind of man she wanted – a ruthless, slightly cruel Casanova – usually doesn't answer matrimonial advertisements, unless he is hoping to gain financially by it.

But the formidable Belle had a certain attachment to Lamphere because she dominated him so completely. This is clear from their relationship: he shared her bed when she was alone, and moved out when a 'husband' turned up – even though he was jealous of the 'husbands'. Why did he move out *after* Hegelein's murder, when he had been so jealous of Hegelein? It could have been because Belle threw him out – but would she be so indiscreet as to dismiss a lover who knew so much about her?

Sexual motif

What seems more likely is that she planned the fire and her disappearance well in advance, realizing that the reckoning was bound to come soon. She sent her lover away as part of the general plan. On the night of the fire, he returned to help her chloroform the children, and decapitate the woman who had already been poisoned with strychnine. (If the dead body *was* Belle's, how did the strychnine get into her stomach?) The plan was probably to join her later on. But he went to jail and died. This seems to be the likeliest explanation of the Belle Gunness mystery. But unless someone can produce evidence that she was alive after the fire, no one will ever know.

This powerful sexual motif appears in all cases of lonely hearts killers, and is particularly clear in a case that took place in Mexico in 1958 – one of the few cases in which the majority of the victims escaped alive. Between August and late September 1958, five women who were taking holidays in the area of Mexico City were beaten, raped, and robbed. The women were mostly over 40, all taking holidays on their own, perhaps hoping that romantic Mexico might provide an exciting companion.

On August 23, a woman from Philadelphia met a tall, rather good-looking man who spoke perfect English. He told her he was an American engineer who had lived in the area for years, and offered to take her to a village where she could buy cheap but excellent local pottery. He called for her at her hotel, and they drove off. A few miles out of town, he pulled off the road, and either forced or persuaded her to drink from a bottle. She blacked out. When she came to, the next morning, she was naked, and she had been raped, beaten, and robbed. She reported the affair to the police, but refused to make any formal complaint, being afraid of the publicity.

Three weeks later, on September 13, another American woman met the same man, and went drinking with him. She also woke up naked on a bed in a cheap hotel, bruised all over, and her jewellery and money missing. Two days later, a Canadian woman met the tall, blue-eyed man, and agreed to go with him to see Indian dances. She drank from a bottle, and woke up the following morning by the roadside – raped, beaten, and robbed. A New York girl who met the same man three days later was luckier; he had taken her to a remote village, and was starting to attack her when a group of men appeared and she escaped.

Photographs

There were two more victims, both of whom died. Anne Karry was a middle-aged schoolteacher from Chicago who had retired to Mexico in 1955. She went out with the same tall stranger. When she was found the next morning by the roadside, she was unconscious and naked. She died on the way to hospital from a vicious beating. Her stomach was found to contain a large quantity of chloral hydrate – 'knock-out drops'. Her landlady described the man she left with as tall, blue-eyed, with a cyst on his neck.

The final victim was Mrs. Harriet Ann Hicks, a 52-year-old American, again on holiday in Mexico City. She was a well-to-do interior decorator. And when she was found, on September 23, on the roadside near Puebla, she also had been partly unclothed, raped, and badly beaten. She had been robbed of about $900 in traveller's checks, and of jewellery. She died on October 3 without regaining consciousness.

But this time, however, the killer had made a mistake. He had allowed Mrs. Hicks to take two photographs of him. The head bellman in her hotel had taken the roll of film, and still had the photographs. They showed a tall, good-looking man with close-cropped hair, in his forties. Prints of the photographs sent to Interpol identified the man as Robert J. Thompson, 49, a wandering engineer, mechanic, aviator, and mining prospector, with several charges of robbery and criminal assault still outstanding against him. Thompson had fled; but traveller's checks belonging to Mrs. Hicks, cashed in various Mexican towns, revealed he was still in the country.

His photograph was shown to all hotels, and in late October, a desk clerk at a Mexico City hotel recognized him as he stood drinking in the bar, and called the police. The victims who had escaped with their lives all identified him as the attacker. In November 1958, the lonely hearts rapist, robber, and killer was sentenced to life imprisonment.

In a case like this, the police are always left wondering: were these his only victims? Does a man suddenly start a career of assaulting women at the age of 49? This is another feature common to lonely hearts cases: that no one can ever be certain of the number of the victims. There is, for example, the puzzling case of Dr. Colin Campbell, who died in the electric chair in New Jersey on April 17, 1930. Now Dr. Campbell was a small, respectable-looking, grey-haired man who lived with his wife in an upper-class neighbourhood in Westfield, N.J. On the morning of February 23, 1929, the smouldering body of a woman was found on a snow-covered road near Cranford, N.J. She had been shot through the top of the head with a .32 revolver. Petrol had been poured on the body. One year earlier, another woman's body had been found in similar circumstances in Morris County; it was identified as that of Margaret Brown, a governess from New York.

Through newspaper publicity, the second body was discovered to be that of Mrs. Mildred Mowry, of Greenville, Pennsylvania, who was in her early forties. Neighbours said that Mrs. Mowry, a widow, had left in February 1928 to go to New York to marry a man named Campbell.

From then on the going was easy. A marriage certificate gave 'Richard Campbell's' address as 3707 Yosemite Street, Baltimore, which did not exist. But at 3705 Yosemite *Avenue*, the residents knew of a Dr. Colin Campbell, of Westfield, N.J.; he was their landlord. Dr. Campbell seemed to be an unlikely murder suspect – a well-to-do married man. But in his pockets, detectives found a .32 revolver. A check with police records revealed that Campbell had served time for forgery and embezzlement, and had a penchant for keeping mistresses — often several at the same time.

He had contacted Mrs. Mowry through a matrimonial agency, and married her when he discovered that her husband had left her a small fortune. But she clung to her money, and made difficulties — which is why Campbell decided to kill her. The other murder — of Margaret Brown — remained unsolved, raising the question: was Mrs. Mowry the first? If not, how many more lonely women preceded her?

There have been other spectacular lonely hearts cases since the end of World War II — but perhaps the most extraordinary of them involved the death of a mother and daughter, who may both have been mistresses of the killer. The daughter, Maria Domenech, was a pretty 28-year-old social worker from New York; her body, clad only in black panties, was found at the bottom of the cliffs of Moher, on the west coast of Ireland, on May 24, 1967.

It took more than a week for the Irish police to identify her, with the aid of Interpol, and by that time her mother, 51-year-old widow, Mrs. Virginia Domenech, had also vanished from her New York home. The trail led the police to Orly Airport, Paris, where Maria had prepared to fly to Ireland on the afternoon of May 22, in company with a man. Careful detective work revealed that they had arrived in Dublin hours later, hired a car, driven across Ireland, and arrived at the cliffs at five in the morning.

Tempestuous affair

There he had knocked her unconscious, taken a large sum in traveller's checks from her pocketbook, and thrown her to the beach below. He then caught a plane from Shannon back to Paris a few hours later. He thought the alibi was perfect; but when the police established his identity as Patrick D'Arcy, an Irish-American who had been having a tempestuous affair with Maria before she left America — as well as showing marked attention to her mother — he realized the gamble had failed. D'Arcy committed suicide in a motel room in Florida a few weeks after the murders. Virginia Domenech's body has never been found.

In a way, the victim of lonely hearts killers are among the most pathetic and pitiful of those who suffer at criminal hands. Naive and trusting — their bodies, their souls calling out for love — they entrust themselves to those whom they believe will end their loneliness, banish their dread of a solitary old age. Only when it is too late do they discover that they have delivered themselves up to men – and women – who prey upon the need for companionship and affection, and then kill their prey – cruelly, heartlessly, without remorse.

MANIC MESSIAHS

The man with the enormous tangled beard raised his arm above his head and cried in a deep voice: 'Bring a curse, O God, on San Fransisco, on Portland, on Corvallis and on Seattle.' With which, he turned and clambered on board the train from Seattle. It was the morning of April 17, 1906. The next day, when he arrived at his destination – Newport, Oregon – his followers met him with the incredible news: San Fransisco had just been torn apart by an earthquake, and was now burning to the ground. 'Yes, I knew that God would respond,' said the prophet quietly.

The man's name was Franz Edmund Creffield. He spoke with a German accent, and in the year 1906 he was 31 years old. He enters the history of false prophets and cranky messiahs in 1903, shortly after he had been thrown out of a Salvation Army group in Corvallis, Oregon. According to the historian Arnold Toynbee, all major prophets follow a cycle of 'withdrawal and return', retreating from society to the solitude of forest or desert, and returning with the Great Message finally crystallized. Franz Creffield was no exception; early in 1903 he vanished into the forests of Oregon. When he emerged, a few months later, he had grown a beard like a briar patch full of birds' nests, and his hair fell over his shoulders. He had also acquired a new name: Joshua the Second.

Like another prophet who was making a reputation at that time – Grigory Efimovich Rasputin, the 'Russian monk' – Franz Creffield held a remarkable fascination for women. There the resemblance seems to end. Rasputin undoubtedly had genuine powers of thaumaturgy, or 'spirit healing', and his diaries reveal that his mystical faith was deep and genuine. Creffield, on the other hand, was a born deceiver. The best that can be said for him is that he was self-deceived.

He preached his mission in Corvallis, and acquired a few dozen followers, male and female. For some reason, the males dropped out; it was their wives and daughters who remained. Joshua's religious faith became more fervent and compelling. Surrounded by adoring women, he would call upon the 'full spirit' to descend on them. They would all sway and chant, clapping rhythmically, and as the excitement became hysterical, Joshua would cry: 'Begone vile clothes,' and start to fling his robes around the room. The women would do the same, some of them modestly stripping down to their shifts, others flinging off every stitch. Then they would all roll on the floor, moaning and crying out.

Inevitably, the men of Corvallis began to feel uneasy, and some of the more respectable wives left. Joshua had announced that he was seeking for a woman who would become the Second Mother of Christ: he, of course, was to be the father. He searched conscientiously; many candidates were rigorously tested, and if the Holy Spirit finally indicated that none was suitable, they at least had the satisfaction of knowing they had been engaged in the Lord's work.

This quest for the Second Mother took place on Kiger Island, in the middle of a river, and throughout the summer the prophet and his followers held prayer meetings by night and danced naked in the woods by day. When the winter came, Joshua moved back into Corvallis, into the home of a man named O.P. Hunt, whose daughter Maude was one of the prophet's warmest admirers. A notice over the door said: 'No Admittance Except on God's Business.'

The prayer meetings finally aroused so much hostility that Joshua was summoned to the courthouse, together with his chief male disciple, Brother Brooks, for a sanity hearing. He was found sane, but advised to leave town. He ignored the suggestion, and went back to the Hunt's house. Then someone began to circulate photographs that had been taken on Kiger Island. They showed naked women – most of them recognizable as Corvallis housewives – romping in the bushes.

On January 4, 1904, a deputation of male citizens called on the prophet, escorted him to the edge of town, tarred and feathered him, and turned him loose. He was found by Mrs. Hunt and her daughter Maude and brought back home; shortly afterwards, he married Maude. But he soon felt the old compulsion to continue with the Lord's work. He went to Portland to visit one of his chief female disciples. One day, the lady's husband found the prophet performing the Lord's work without his trousers on. He took out a warrant for adultery. Joshua's angry father-in-law offered $150 for his capture, but Joshua could not be found.

Immortal

Three months later, a child ran under the Hunt house – which was built clear of the ground – looking for a lost ball. He saw a bearded man dressed in a blanket, and ran out yelling. The police were called, and Joshua was dragged out. It seemed that he had been living under the house since he fled from Portland, supplied with food by his wife and her mother. In court, he admitted adultery with the Portland disciple, but explained that he could not be judged by secular law; after all, Jesus had often broken the Sabbath. He was sentenced to two years in jail, but was released after fifteen months.

His ex-wife Maude, now divorced, was living in Seattle with a brother, Frank, and sister-in-law. Joshua wrote to her, asking her to re-marry him. She agreed, and they were joined again in Seattle. The brother and sister-in-law were deeply impressed by the prophet – so much so that when Joshua ordered them to sell their home and worldly goods, and move with him to a 'Garden of Eden' near Newport, Oregon, they did so without hesitation. It was as he left Seattle that Joshua pronounced the curse that 'caused' the San Francisco earthquake.

Once established in his Eden, facing the Pacific Ocean just south of Waldport, the prophet sent word to former disciples in Corvallis, including a pretty girl named Esther Mitchell. Without hesitation, half the female population of Corvallis left home and streamed towards Eden. One husband rushed after his wife, pausing only to buy a revolver and cartridges.

As he reached the ferryboat across Yaquina Bay, he saw the prophet standing on deck surrounded by disciples; he pointed the revolver, and pulled the trigger five times. Nothing happened. When the outraged husband examined the pistol, he discovered the shop had sold him rimfire cartridges for a centre-fire gun, but the female disciples were not surprised; *they* knew Joshua was immortal.

All the same, the prophet could see that he was courting danger if he remained in Eden during the next week or so. The sensible course would be to allow the husbands to simmer down. As they converged on Eden, Joshua and Maude disappeared. George Mitchell, brother of the prophet's favourite disciple Esther, reasoned that they would probably be making for Seattle again. He tracked them there on May 7, 1906. At eight o'clock that morning, Joshua was looking in the window of Quick's Drug Store in First Avenue, while Maude was weighing herself on a machine. George Mitchell stepped up to the prophet, placed a gun against his ear, and pulled the trigger. Joshua collapsed without even turning his head. Maude flew at Mitchell, screaming. When a policeman came running up, she told him: 'That is my husband Joshua. He will rise in three days.'

But Joshua stayed dead, and Mitchell was tried for his murder. The defence argued that Joshua was 'a degenerate of the worst sort'. The jury agreed, particulaly when Mitchell stated in court that Joshua had taken the virginity of *both* his sisters. George Mitchell was acquitted. His sister Esther listened impassively.

Small revolver

On July 12, 1906, George Mitchell stood at King Street station, waiting to take the train home. His brother Fred saw Esther standing nearby, and asked her to come and speak to George. Esther walked over to the rest of the group, and as they moved towards the ticket barrier drew a small revolver from under the folded coat on her arm. She placed it against George's ear and pulled the trigger. Like Joshua, he collapsed without a word.

Esther Mitchell and Maude Creffield were both held – they admitted planning George's murder together. Maude took strychnine in prison; Esther was tried, but found not guilty by reason of insanity, and was committed to the Washington State Asylum. Three years later she was released, looking very thin and ill, and died at the home of friends shortly afterwards. She was just 20.

The false prophet is not, of course, a modern phenomenon. However, Franz Creffield *is* an interesting example of a typical modern variety. Writers on religious experience concede that it is difficult to draw the line between genuine and false prophets. When *any* human being starts to feel stifled and bored with the quality of everyday experience, he is already experiencing the basic religious urge: the craving for more vitality and a higher quality of life. It expresses itself as a feeling of irritation and contempt for the repetitious dullness that most people accept as 'everyday life'.

Hostile critics

All religions have one thing in common: the belief that man was meant for higher things than 'repetition'. Joshua the Second was possessed by this urge as indisputably as his Biblical ancestor who destroyed the walls of Jericho. As to the over-developed sexual urge that caused so much alarm and envy among the husbands of Corvallis, it must also be admitted that this often co-exists alongside powerful religious urges. A prophet is, by definition, a person of high dominance; and, as Abraham Maslow's researches showed, high dominance is almost invariably accompanied by a strong libido.

Maslow's psychology also suggests the simple way of distinguishing between genuine and false prophets. When a human undergoes genuine psychological development, he or she moves upwards through various levels of need or desire: the need for security, the need for sex and love, the need for self-esteem and for the respect of one's fellow citizens; and then, finally, the need for creative self-expression, for 'self-actualization'.

Only *this* level, Maslow would say, is the genuinely religious level. A truly religious person is driven by higher needs than the craving for sex or admiration, although this is obviously not to say that he must be totally devoid of the need for them. They may continue to exist; but they are no longer his *basic* urges.

When we consider an evangelist like Aimée Semple McPherson, the question of priorities is altogether more difficult. A pretty girl, often referred to as 'the world's most pulchritudinous evangelist', Aimée was the 1920s equivalent of Billy Graham. Her first husband, a missionary, died in China; her second divorced her with the interesting comment that she was a dual personality: overflowing with universal love in the revival tent, but a 'wildcat' in the home.

After a slow start on the east coast, she achieved fame as a preacher in San Diego, California, in 1921. San Diego is America's suicide centre; when Aimée asked the sick and lame to mount the platform, and many of them walked away cured, she achieved overnight fame. She opened an 'Angelus Temple' in Los Angeles in 1923, and her technique was basically Billy Graham's – 'flowers, music, golden trumpets, red robes, angels . . .' – a delightful spectacle conducted with superb showmanship, with an appeal for candidates for instant salvation.

In 1925, Aimée met a radio announcer, Kenneth Ormiston. Their intimacy became a subject of gossip and scandal. On May 18, 1926, she drove to a beach at Venice, Los Angeles – and disappeared. For more than a month ships and aircraft searched for her body. Whispers of her affair with Ormiston reached the newspapers, and it was rumoured that she had not drowned – only fled to some remote love nest. Ormiston had also vanished.

Hysterical pregnancy

On June 1923 Aimée reappeared – knocking on a door in Agua Prieta, New Mexico, and explaining that she had been kidnapped by two men and a woman. Then reporters began digging, and it became clear that Aimée had spent the past month dodging around the western United States with her lover, Ormiston. On September 17 she was charged with a 'conspiracy to obstruct justice'. Finally, the case was dismissed – rumour has it that the public prosecutor accepted $30,000 to drop it – he was afterwards sentenced to jail for corrupt conduct in office – but Aimée's career as a great evangelist was over. A nationwide tour was a flop. She died in 1944 and it looked much like suicide.

On the continent of Europe there is a tendency to dismiss these excesses as typically American; but in fact Europe has been as subject to them as any continent. In 17th-century England, Lodowicke Muggleton was the founder of a sect known as Muggletonians, who preached that God had a human body. A century later, a preacher named Edward Irving called upon the Lord for a miracle; his followers began to speak in strange foreign languages, and spirits informed them that miracles would occur at the end of 40 days. When nothing happened, the sect gradually dissolved. At about the same time, a 'prophetess' named Joanna Southcott gathered thousands of followers when she announced that the new Redeemer would be a woman, and that – predictably – it was herself.

In 1814, at the age of 64, she explained that she was about to give birth to Shiloh, the prince of Peace. When the pregnancy was revealed to be purely hysterical, her followers deserted in droves, and Joanna died in the same year. Joanna Southcott's 'box' was supposed to contain writings and other sacred relics that would save the world and bring the millennium; but when it was secretly opened in 1927 it was found to contain only a lottery ticket and a woman's nightcap.

One of the most remarkable of the preachers of the Spirit of Love was the Rev. Henry James Prince, who became curate of Charlinch, near Bridgwater, Somerset, in the 19th century and was soon drawing enormous crowds with his fiery sermons. He was permanently surrounded by adoring female disciples, and when ugly rumours reached his bishop, he was forbidden to continue preaching. He left the Church of England and began preaching in barns and open fields. One day he announced he was the prophet Elijah, and his followers accepted the revelation without question.

Prince moved to Brighton – then a fashionable resort – and became the most popular preacher of his day. With £30,000 collected from disciples, he bought an estate at Spaxton, near Bridgwater, and turned it into *Agapomene*, or the Abode of Love. Disciples who wished to join him had to sell all they had and contribute it to the community. About 60 followers, mostly women, accepted the invitation.

Unlike his American contemporary, John Humphrey Noyes, Prince did not actually preach Free Love; but he certainly practised it, regarding his female disciples as Brides of the Lord. He himself did not mind being addressed as God, and letters addressed to Our Lord God, Somerset, reached him without difficulty. One day he summoned all his disciples to the billiard room to watch a public act of worship – his intimate union with a Miss Patterson – on the settee.

Private harem

When she became pregnant, Prince told his followers that there would be no birth – just as there was now no death – but when a baby arrived, he had to explain it away as a final despairing act of the Devil. Then lawsuits began to cloud his horizon. In 1860, three female followers sued for the return of nearly £6000, and the revelation of the goings-on in the Abode of Love startled and shocked Victorian England. After the case, Prince's actions became more discreet; but he continued to live happily, surrounded by his private harem, until his death, aged 88, in 1899.

Two years before his death, Prince had acquired an influential disciple: Hugh Smyth-Pigott, another spellbinding preacher. Smyth-Pigott took over the Agapomenite Church at Clapton, a suburb of London, and his sermons were soon producing the same effect as Prince's had done half a century before. On Sunday, September 7, 1902, Smyth-Pigott announced from the pulpit that he had become divine, and that he would shortly walk on water. The next Sunday, 6000 people waited for his arrival, cheering and booing. Showers of stones followed him back home.

Horn of power

Smyth-Pigott decided to move to the Abode of Love, and in 1904 he took up residence, together with his wife and a mistress, who soon bore him a child. When, in 1909, a Bishop's Court found him guilty of 'immorality, uncleanness and wickedness of life', he commented: 'It doesn't matter what they do. I am God', and in the following year a daughter was born to him by another disciple.

He went preaching and gathering more disciples in America and Scandinavia; when he found particularly attractive girls, they were dubbed 'soul brides' and sent back to Spaxton to await his arrival. Smyth-Pigott died in 1927, disappointing the expectations of his followers, who were convinced he was immortal. One woman who had been brought up at the Abode of Love revealed that when the Rev. Prince had died he had handed Smyth-Pigott a 'Horn of Power' and authority to carry on his mission. The exact nature of this horn of power is not known, but the symbolism seems apt.

In 1911, precisely one century after the birth of the Rev. Prince, another Messiah, Francis Pencovic, was born in America. Up to the time of the Second World War, he had a curious and chequered career as a boilermaker, shipyard worker and dishwasher, and had served jail sentences for burglary, larceny, passing dud cheques, not supporting his wife, and sending a threatening letter to Roosevelt.

It was during the war, when he was a conscientious objector, that he organized a cult called The Fountain of the World, followed by the initials WKFL (wisdom, knowledge, faith and love). When he came out of the army he changed his name to Krishna Venta, adopted flowing oriental robes, and explained that he had been born in a valley in Nepal.

He had visited Rome as long ago as A.D. 600 – although, on a more recent visit, the Pope's guards had turned him away – and had been 'teleported' to America in 1932. The cult, with a hundred or so members, settled in Ventura County, California, near Box Canyon. According to Krishna Venta, America would be shaken by a Communist revolution in 1965, and in 1975 he and his 144,000 followers would take over the country.

Tape recording

On December 9, 1958, two disgruntled ex-followers, Ralph Miller and Peter Kamenoff, called on Krishna Venta in his San Fernando Valley retreat, and demanded that he confess that his messianism was basically a cloak for sexual promiscuity – their own wives having been among the Messiah's 'brides'. When Krishna declined to confess, one of the men opened a canvas bag – and a tremendous explosion blew the 'monastery' apart, killing a dozen people and injuring many more. In a pickup truck nearby, police found a tape recording made by the two 'avengers', listing the prophet's misdemeanours, and declaring: 'He isn't Christ, only a man.' The words could serve as the epitaph of manic messiahs in general.

The human capacity for self-delusion is a topic of endless fascination. For centuries, philosophers have discussed the question of where passionate idealism ends and self-delusion begins. The question may be finally unanswerable; but 'messiahs' like Smyth-Pigott, Franz Creffield and Krishna Venta provide fascinating material for the investigation.

MARTYRS

If the definition of a martyr is someone who is willing to suffer and die for a belief, then the family of Harald Alexander undoubtedly qualifies. On the afternoon of December 22, 1970, two police officers and a doctor forced their way into a locked apartment in the Calle Jesus Nazareno, Santa Cruz – the capital of Tenerife in the Canary Islands. The blinds were drawn, but even in the half light it was possible to see that walls, floor and furniture were covered with blood. The detective sergeant pointed to a lump of flesh that had been skewered on a wooden stake. 'My God, what's that?' The doctor peered at it closely, then turned away. 'A human heart'.

What was necessary

There were three dead women in the apartment: two young girls, and an older woman, their mother. All three had been beaten; a bloodstained hammer and other tools lay nearby. The bodies had been hacked open, and the hearts extracted; each of these had been pierced with a wooden stake.

The two men who had committed this slaughter were at present in police custody. They had given themselves up willingly. Harald Alexander was a middle-aged German, who had moved to Tenerife with his family 10 months earlier. He and his 16-year-old son Frank had walked to the apartment of Dr. Walter Trenkler on that afternoon just before Christmas. Their daughter, Sabine, 15, worked there. Harald Alexander asked to see his daughter, and then put his arm round her, and told her in a calm voice that he and Frank had just killed her mother and two sisters.

The girl raised her father's hand fondly to her cheek, and said: 'I'm sure you've done what you thought necessary.' The horrified Dr. Trenkler, who overheard all this, rushed to the telephone, and called the German consul. An hour later, the police had discovered the mutilated bodies of Alexander's wife, Dagmar, 41, his eldest daughter, Marina, 18, and Petra, 15, who was Sabine's twin.

It was ordained

Back at police headquarters it was the son, Frank, who spoke first. He explained that his mother had been giving him a 'strange look' which made him uncomfortable. He picked up a coat-hanger and began to beat her until she fell, unconscious. His father did not interfere; on the contrary, he picked up a heavy spirit level, and began to bludgeon Marina and Petra. None of the three women screamed or made the slightest attempt to escape.

They knew all this was ordained, for their brother Frank was, according to their father, 'the representative of God on earth'. As to Harald Alexander, he explained to the police that when he saw Frank beating his mother with the coat-hanger, he knew that 'the hour of killing had arrived'. 'My son is a prophet,' he said, 'He is inspired by God.'

So the two men carefully battered their womenfolk to death. The women cried, not because they were unwilling to die, but because 'it hurt them to be hit'. When they were dead, father and son took it in turn to complete the work of mutilation. They did this one at a time. First Frank played the organ while his father 'worked', then his father took over while Frank hacked at the naked breasts of his sisters. They then wrote notes, expressing such sentiments as 'to be truly free, you must kill those whom you love more than anything else'.

'A prophet of God'

Clearly, Harald and Frank Alexander were suffering from religious mania; so, apparently, was Sabine, who sobbed when told that she could not go to prison with her father and brother. But how had this come about? The Santa Cruz police contacted the police of Hamburg, the last city of residence of the Alexander family. From them they learned that the family originated in Dresden, but had fled from the Russians. Alexander was the disciple of wheelwright, George Riehle.

One day, many years earlier, Riehle had suddenly become possessed by the conviction that he was a prophet of God, and had become a travelling preacher. Riehle himself was a follower of another 'prophet of God', Jacob Lorber, who, in the first half of the nineteenth century, had founded a religious group known as the Lorber Society, who observed the most rigid ascetic disciplines. Alexander had remained with Riehle until his death, nursing him, and had inherited from him the small organ on which he and his son had played after the massacre of their family.

A doctor who knew them in Hamburg reported that the family had very little contact with the outside world; they seemed to live for one another and for their religion. Neighbours in the Calle Jesus Nazareno said the same thing: since the family moved in, they had lived behind drawn blinds. The only sounds that came from the house were the playing of the organ – presumably a part of interminable religious services. The twins worked for Dr. Trenkler, but the doctor had had no opportunity to get to know them better. They did their work, but remained totally aloof. Presumably they felt that the outside world was hopelessly damned. What did they have in common with the other members of our doomed society?

So when their work was finished they returned home to the darkened apartment and the religious services. They worshipped their brother as a prophet, because their father said he was, and they were perfectly prepared to die when God sent a sign, so their souls could leave behind the dross of this earth and wing their way to heaven.

Father and son were committed to an asylum for the criminally insane. Yet there were doctors in Santa Cruz who doubted whether, in the strict sense of the word, they *were* insane. They had convinced themselves that they were a tiny body of the Elect in a world that was damned, and they had lived out their belief with rigid logic. If *they* were insane, was Hitler also insane for the insistence with which he followed his belief that the Jews were the cause of most of the troubles of the human race? What distinguishes fanaticism and insanity?

Religious possession

This raises one of the most fascinating problems known to psychology: the problem of the human capacity for religious conviction, and the way it can turn men into martyrs. For we are here faced with a strange enigma. When we see moths flying into an electric bulb or candle flame, we do not call them insane. We recognize that this is a natural reflex that compels moths to seek the light. There can be no doubt that human beings experience an equally powerful intensity to seek 'the light' – that is, any form of intensity or strong feeling. They crave for a deep sense of *meaning*.

African natives drum themselves into a kind of trance to the beating of the tom tom; teenagers in discotheques achieve a kind of hypnotic frenzy dancing to stroboscopic lights and deafening music. Crowds scream themselves hoarse listening to a dictator; armies achieve a sense of absolute certainty of purpose as they march to military music. Men hunger for strong conviction as an alcoholic craves strong drink. They long to be 'possessed', and in a state of possession, they are able to kill or be killed.

The history of religious possession can be traced back many thousands of years. For example, we know that well before 1000 B.C. the wild highlanders to the north of Greece, in the land called Thrace, worshipped a god called Dionysus, who took the form of a bull. His worship involved violent orgies, and the sacrifice of an animal – or even a child – by tearing it to pieces. Homer mentions the god as 'raging Dionysus' – but then he knew very little about him.

For it was several centuries after Homer that the god Dionysus came to Greece and swept everything before him. The ancient Greeks were a serious, sober, intelligent people, and their chief god, Apollo, was also serious and severe – the god of form and discipline and virtue. Suddenly – in about the seventh century B.C. – the heathen Dionysus arrived. Under the name of Bacchus, he was the god of wine, and, significantly, he was also the god of sex – one of his symbols was an erect penis with a pair of testicles.

The historian of religion, B.Z. Goldberg, has a remarkable description of a Dionysian festival, beginning with a procession carrying torches, led by musicians and women carry fruit. Men carried wooden penises, while women might carry images of the female sexual organs. In a lonely spot in the woods, the image of Dionysus was taken from its chest. A hog was sacrificed as a burnt offering, and the feast began, with ritualistic drinking of wine.

Dionysian rites
Men and women threw off their clothes. Women provoked men by making lithe, sexual movements of the breasts and pelvis; excited men seized them and thrust into them. Naked bodies writhed on the ground. Women threw themselves into the waters of the bay holding lighted torches, and were convinced that the torches continued to burn. Men plunged after them, and copulated in the sea. Children were grabbed and initiated into the orgy of drunkenness and sex. Finally, as day broke, the exhausted people, staggering and reeling, made their way back to the town, both men and women feeling that they had drained themselves of sexual energy in the worship of their god.

Goldberg's account cannot be substantiated in detail – we have no documents describing such orgies at first hand – but the records we *do* possess suggest that his account may be an understatement rather than an exaggeration. Dionysus could induce madness. King Lycurgus, who opposed him, killed his own son with an axe; King Pentheus, another 'unbeliever', was torn to pieces by his own mother, who was possessed by a Bacchanalian frenzy. Dionysus was not simply the god of total abandonment; he was also the god of dark violence.

This is understandable enough; but what is altogether more baffling is that many of the later forms of Dionysiac religion were rigidly puritanical. There was the Russian sect called the Khlysty, founded by a 'Christ' called Daniel Phillipov. He was a peasant and a deserter from the army, and in the year 1645 he was standing on the hill of Golodina in Vladimir when a god whom he called 'Zebaoth' descended into his body like a flash of lightning, and Daniel Phillipov realized that he had been chosen to be God's representative on earth.

Strange rites

At that time, Russia was split with violent religious dissention, for the Tsar Alexis – who might be compared to England's Henry the Eighth – had made changes in the prayer book and rituals which enraged the 'old believers', who sometimes burnt themselves to death on giant bonfires rather than give way. Daniel Phillipov was crucified twice, and still survived. He preached a stern, ascetic religion, a kind of super-puritanism, and yet the central rite of the Khlysty was a ceremony that sounds very like the Dionysian orgies.

The worshippers, dressed in white robes, danced around a great cauldron of water in some forest grove, chanting rhythmically, flagellating one another with rods. When the Holy Spirit descended, they would begin to chant in strange tongues, and the water in the cauldron would take on a golden colour, and begin to boil of its own accord. Finally, they lost all individual consciousness – and it was at this point, according to their detractors, that they tore off their clothes, and copulated freely, mothers with sons and brothers with sisters.

Religious frenzy

The Khlysty themselves denied that such things happened, but the Orthodox Church was sufficiently convinced to make it a serious offence to belong to the Khlysty. Rasputin, the 'monk' who exercised such a powerful influence on the last of the Tsars and his wife, was reputed to belong to the Khlysty, and legends of his insatiable sexual appetite seem to support this view.

Another Russian sect, the Skoptzy, were even more fanatical. They developed from the Khlysty. A woman called Akulina Ivanovna was worshipped as the Khlysty 'mother of God' round about the year 1770. She 'recognized' a man called Kondrati Selivanov as a reincarnation of Christ – this 'recognition' seems to be a feature of extremist religious sects, as in the case of Harald Alexander and his son.

Selivanov soon became the leader of the Khlysty, and announced new disciplines. All men should be castrated, and all women should have their breasts and outer genital organs amputated. Selivanov led the way by castrating himself with a red-hot iron. It should have been a certain formula for losing all his followers; but, on the contrary, religious fanatics found themselves irresistibly attracted by the idea of self-mutilation. The authorities were worried about this wave of religious frenzy; Selivanov was arrested and placed in a mental home.

Suicide sect

But his followers continued to worship him, and when he was released in 1801 – when Alexander I came to the throne – he had become even more influential. Strangely enough, many of his disciples came from among the wealthy. He claimed to be Tsar Peter the Third – murdered by his wife, Catherine the Great – and castrated or mutilated a hundred men and women with his own hands. Even after his death in 1830, his followers refused to believe that he was dead. Like Jesus, he had only 'withdrawn', and would return to earth on the day that his followers numbered 144,000, and inaugurate the Day of Judgment.

Skoptzy communities continued to flourish. Children born into the sect grew up in the knowledge that they would be mutilated when they reached puberty; according to the great authority on Russian sects, Frederick Conybeare, any who tried to escape by fleeing were hunted down and assassinated. B.Z. Goldberg adds that for some men and women mutilation was only partial; some women could escape with only one nipple. These sometimes became communal prostitutes whose business was to earn money for the common treasury.

Some Russian sects went further than the Skoptzy, and demanded suicide as a religious duty. In the reign of Alexander II, a man named Shodkin founded a suicide sect, and led his followers into a cave, which they proceeded to seal up. Two women became panic stricken and broke out. Shodkin then called upon his followers to kill one another before the police arrived. The children were murdered first, then the women. When the police arrived, Shodkin and two of his acolytes were surrounded by dozens of bleeding corpses.

Self-crucifixion

Normal, rational people are inclined to explain such strange events in terms of the human capacity for self-destruction. But this would be an over-simplification; a man may fall violently in love with a girl – or, at least, feel overwhelming desire – while disliking many things about her. His sexual instincts have fixed upon her, while his reason rejects her. There is often this same ambiguity in religion. Man's reason cannot satisfy his need for food, or his need for exercise. Neither can it satisfy his craving for religion, for some deep, strong belief.

Such beliefs express themselves in symbols. In Christianity, the central symbol is the death of Jesus on the cross. A character in a novel of Dostoevsky says that if he had to choose between truth and salvation on the one hand, and Jesus and damnation on the other, he would unhesitatingly choose Jesus. Sometimes the obsession with the image of the cross may become so great that the worshipper may pray to suffer the wounds of Christ – like St. Francis – or may actually try to crucify himself.

In the early nineteenth century, a shoemaker of Venice named Matthew Lovat, decided to crucify himself in public. Lovat was the son of poor peasants, and his poverty made it impossible for him to carry out his ambition of entering the Church. One day he castrated himself with his shoemaker's knife. After this, he made a wooden cross, carried it into the street, and was in the process of nailing his feet to it when passers-by intervened and stopped him. Lovat went back to his native village of Casale, and this time made more elaborate arrangements for self-crucifixion.

In his third-storey room, he constructed a large cross, with a bracket to support his feet. He also slung a net over this cross to support his weight in case the bracket gave way. Early one morning, he attached the cross by a long rope to a beam of the ceiling, and placed its lower end on the window sill. Then he carefully climbed on to the cross by a long rope to a beam of the ceiling, and placed its lower end on the window sill. Then he carefully climbed on to the cross, and with one violent blow of a mallet drove a nail through both his feet, and into a hole already prepared for it.

Then he used his hands, which were free, to edge the cross out of the window. It slipped, and hung suspended above the street. He had already hammered a nail through the palm of his right hand, and prepared a hole for it in the cross. Now he nailed his left hand to the cross, dropped the hammer, and tried to guide the nail into the hole prepared for it. However, shock had made him too weak, and he hung there, his right hand by his side, until the horrified citizens came and hauled him in again. He was not dead; in fact, he spent the remainder of his life in a mental home.

In this case, we can see with great clarity how the religious compulsion can sometimes gain the intensity of a sexual obsession. The necrophile Sergeant Bertrand would swim an icy stream at night, and dig the ground with his bare hands until they were bleeding, in order to reach the female corpses he craved. Matthew Lovat probably experienced no pain as he nailed himself to the cross, only a kind of intense sexual pleasure, of the same kind that leads certain sexual perverts to hang themselves in women's underwear.

It may seem almost sacriligious to ask where we draw the line between this kind of obsession and a saint's passionate desire for suffering that causes the stigmata of Christ to appear on his hands and feet. The human psyche is full of strange forces, most of which we do not even suspect, and it may be many centuries more before psychologists even begin to understand them.

One of the strangest of all cases of martyrdom is that of a whole South African tribe, the Xosas, in 1857. The Xosas were warriors, who hated British rule. One morning in 1856, a young Xosa girl who went to fetch water at the river became convinced that she had seen strange men. Her uncle also saw them, and recognized among them a brother who had died many years before. These 'spirits of the dead' explained that they had come to help the Xosas destroy the white man; but first they had to eat all their cattle, then destroy their food.

When everything had been destroyed, the dead would rise to help them, the fields would fill with ripe corn, and the day of 'heaven-on-earth' would arrive. More than 100,000 Xosas obeyed, killing their cattle, destroying their corn. The reasonable ones among them were subjected to such intense psychological pressure from the others that they did as they were told – and then died of starvation. When all food stocks had been destroyed, the exhausted Xosas spent the night dancing and rejoicing, convinced that in the morning two blood-red suns would arise, signal that the heavens were about to open.

Only one sun arose. They were stunned. Some thought that perhaps it was the wrong day; they waited another day. Still only one sun arose. Then hordes of weary Xosas dragged themselves towards British territory, looking for food. Of 105,000 Xosas, 68,000 died horribly of slow starvation; the lives of the remainder were only saved by stocks of government food. It was the end of the great power of the Xosas tribe.

Yet although martyrdom seems a form of madness, we must remember that it is men of deep and passionate conviction who have helped the human race to its present place on the evolutionary scale. Without such men there would be no future. In fact, the scriptures may be scientifically accurate when they say the blood of martyrs fertilizes the earth.

MASS MURDERERS

Between June, 1918 and April, 1926 the district of Rudraprayag in northern India was terrorized by a savage killer who despatched his victims by tearing their throats out. He claimed 126 lives. Yet when the man who finally shot him saw the body, he was surprised.

'Here was no fiend, who while watching me through the long night hours had rocked and rolled with silent fiendish laughter at my vain attempts to outwit him, and licked his lips in anticipation of the time, when, finding me off my guard for one brief moment, he would get the opportunity he was waiting for of burying his teeth in my throat.'

The deadly killer was only an old leopard, whose muzzle was grey and whose lips lacked whiskers. Yet over a period of eight years he had brought more terror to Rudraprayag than Jack the Ripper brought to Whitechapel, or Peter Kürten to Düsseldorf. The hunter Jim Corbett ended the reign of terror with a single bullet through the shoulder.

Why is it, then, that we feel no horror when we read of the man-eater? Because, as Jim Corbett said: 'This was the best-hated and most feared animal in all India, whose only crime – not against the laws of nature but against the laws of man – was that he had shed human blood, with no object of terrorizing man, but only in order that he might live.'

Beasts of prey

This goes to the heart of the matter. When killing is performed in this clean, natural way, we feel no horror, because there is no *evil* involved. It is the human capacity for evil, for cruelty, that frightens us. And here we face a strange paradox. The worst modern criminals, from Jack the Ripper to Richard Speck and Dean Corll, *are* beasts of prey, in the most precise sense. They stalk through modern cities like a hungry tiger, completely

405

indifferent to the fear and sufferings of their victims. Their only desire is to satisfy an appetite.

A typical case is that of Jerry Thompson, who was not a mass murderer, but simply a rapist. His one and only murder victim was found on the morning of June 17, 1935, in a ditch in the cemetery at Peoria, Illinois. She was a pretty girl, and her white dress had been pulled up under her armpits; her torn underwear lay nearby. The medical report revealed that she had been raped and strangled. She was identified as 19-year-old Mildred Hallmark, a waitress, who had vanished the evening before, shortly after leaving the cafeteria where she worked. When the police appealed for information, several girls came forward, and disclosed that they had also been raped. The attacker was a good-looking young man who had offered them a lift, then driven them to a quiet place and forced them to submit.

The police decided to make a general appeal through the newspapers, asking for all women who had been attacked to come forward, with a promise of complete anonymity. They hoped that one of these women might be able to give them some clue to the identity of the rapist. The response startled them. More than 50 women came forward, and it became clear that the police were looking for a highly successful sex-maniac.

In many cases he had stopped beside a girl walking along a lonely street and dragged her into the car. If she resisted or screamed, he silenced her with a violent punch on the jaw or in the stomach. He would drive to a lonely place, undress the girl, and commit rape. Then he would take out a camera, and take photographs of her naked, sprawled in obscene positions. He would tell the girl that if she told the police her name would appear in the newspapers, and everyone would know what had happened to her. There are few girls who do not prefer privacy to revenge.

Five days after the discovery of Mildred Hallmark's body the police had the break they needed. A girl named Grace Ellsworth told them that she had been picked up by a clean-cut, well-spoken young man who had offered her a lift. In an empty road, he stopped the car, and tried to kiss her. When she slapped his face, he hit her on the jaw, then beat her up so viciously that she was incapable of resisting as he undressed her. Afterwards, he dragged her into the headlights of the car, took photographs of her with a box camera, and warned her that if she reported him to the police the pictures would be sent to her friends and relatives.

And then, some weeks later, a man had been introduced to her at a dance. She was certain this was the rapist. When she asked him if they hadn't met before, he denied it. But *she* was sure. The man had been introduced to her as Jerry Thompson. The police had no way of tracking down Jerry Thompson. But they suspected that Mildred Hallmark had known her killer. She was a shy girl who would never get into a car with a stranger. They went to her father, who worked in a tractor factory in East Peoria, and asked him if he knew a Jerry Thompson: he did. Thompson worked in the machine shop, and was a neighbour of theirs.

Ripped underwear

Thompson proved to be a handsome young man in his mid-twenties, who was engaged to be married. He flatly denied being the rapist; but Grace Ellsworth picked him out from a line-up, and a lie detector test revealed that he knew more than he would admit about the murder. The detective in charge of the case shocked a confession out of him by throwing Mildred Hallmark's ripped underwear into his lap.

Thompson broke down, he confessed to picking up Mildred, offering her a lift, and taking her to the cemetery. She had resisted, and he had struck her under the chin and throttled her into unconsciousness before tearing off her clothes and raping her in the back seat. Then, he said, he realized she was dead. In his room, police found dozens of photographs of the naked women he had raped, and a diary detailing dozens of rapes that he had committed since he was 16. He was electrocuted on October 15, 1935.

The Thompson case is interesting because we can see that he was living by the 'law of the jungle'. *All* healthy young men, particularly the 'dominant 5%', would like to be able to make love to dozens of pretty girls. No doubt it is partly fear and caution that prevents them from becoming Jerry Thompsons. But it is also, perhaps, a sense of decency; they do not *want* to hurt another human being, any more than they would want to set fire to a haystack or torture a cat. So desire is outweighed by revulsion.

Jerry Thompson was obviously a man of exceptionally strong sexual desires; but his photograph, with its cold eyes and slightly cruel mouth, also reveals that he lacked the human warmth that would have led him to restrain these desires. He may not have been evil or cruel by nature, but after the first few rapes he would begin to *think of himself* as a criminal, a lone beast of prey, and so develop this aspect of his personality.

Thompson's rapes were committed between the mid-1920s and 1935. This was the 'Age of Sex Crime', especially in America. During the Second World War, the rate of sex crime rose steadily – which is to be expected when thousands of men are away from home, deprived of their wives. But it continued to rise after the war. Why? Because men who thought they were coming home to a new world where they would be treated like heroes found themselves in the same old ruthless mechanized civilization, where they were mere cogs in a wheel.

Such a civilization produces the effect which Karl Marx called 'alienation', the feeling of not belonging. The mass murderers of the fifties and sixties were all 'alienated men', 'outsiders': Haigh, Heath, Christie, Richard Speck, Howard Unruh, Charles Manson, Charles Whitman, Ian Brady.

Not all these men were sex criminals; Haigh was motivated by money. Unruh and Whitman and Manson by paranoid hatred of society; but the sense of alienation meant that they had no fellow feeling for their victims. And the Richard Speck case shows something even more disturbing: the alienation turning into cruelty. *Not* sadism; Speck did not actually torture any of his victims; but he took pleasure in terrorizing them.

Speck's orgy of murder came to light at just after 5 a.m. on Thursday, July 14, 1966, when a girl rushed out on to the balcony of a nurses' hostel on the south side of Chicago and began screaming. Two patrolmen who rushed into the building found a nauseating scene. In various rooms there were the naked bodies of eight women. Most of them had been strangled, and also stabbed many times. Their hands had been tied behind them. None of them had been raped, but a perverted sexual attack had been made on one of them, Gloria Davy.

The one survivor, a Philippino girl named Corazon Amurao, told how there had been a knock on her bedroom door sometime after midnight. She opened it, and found herself facing a man who smelt of alcohol and held a gun. He had a pockmarked face and blond hair. This was Richard Speck, a 25-year-old seaman. Speck rounded up six girls into one dormitory bedroom, and tied their hands with sheets that he cut up with a knife. He kept explaining that he needed money to get to New Orleans, and promised not to hurt them.

This indicates that, in spite of his intention of committing murder, he still maintained some 'fellow feeling' for the intended victims. Three more nurses came home late; Speck took their money, and tied them. Finally, Speck took one of the girls out of the room. A few minutes later he took another, and they heard a cry.

Corazon Amurao was a courageous girl, more 'dominant' than the others; she urged them to free themselves and try to 'jump' the man. They replied that he didn't appear to be violent, and that they had better sit still. Miss Amurao decided to roll under a bed, where she hid. The man continued to come in and out for hours. Then all was quiet. When an alarm clock went off at five o'clock, Miss Amurao rolled out from under the bed, crawled on to the balcony, and began to scream for help.

A sultan with his harem

Speck had left fingerprints all over the place, and Corazon Amurao was able to give an exact description of him, even to a tattoo on his arm, with the words 'Born to raise hell'. From the seaman's knots that bound the dead girls, the police guessed that the man was a sailor. There was a labour exchange much used by sailors not far away. The police soon established the identity of the man they were seeking, and half an hour past midnight, on the following Sunday, Speck was taken into the Chicago Cook County Hospital, his wrists slashed in a suicide attempt. The doctor who attended him saw the tattoo, and called the police.

Psychiatrists who examined Speck learned that he had been known at school as a 'sulky loner' who hated his stepfather. He drifted from job to job – labourer, garbage collector, truckdriver and seaman. At the age of 20 he married a 15-year-old girl, and they had a baby daughter, whom he adored. But after five years of fighting, they divorced.

He drank heavily, and took drugs – yellow jackets, red-birds – amytal and seconal drugs that can cause hallucinations. In Dallas, Texas, earlier in 1965, he had attacked a young girl as she was parking her car, holding a carving knife to her throat. Sentenced to 18 months in prison, he was soon released on parole – which he instantly skipped. To drinking companions he was known as a braggart who boasted about all the women he had slept with, but who never seemed to be able to date a girl.

In April, 1966, when Speck had returned to Monmouth, Illinois, where his relatives lived, a barmaid named Mary Pierce vanished from a tavern where Speck drank; her naked body was later found in a hog house behind the tavern. Speck had often asked her for a date. After leaving Monmouth, Speck had worked on Great Lakes ore boats, but had been rushed into hospital for an appendix operation in early May.

He began to date a nurse there; she found him gentle, but full of hatred of society. He talked vengefully of two people in Texas he wanted to kill, and he told someone else that he intended to return to Texas and kill his ex-wife Shirley; significantly, the only Chicago nurse who was sexually assaulted closely resembled his wife. On the day before the murders, he had been drinking heavily in Chicago bars.

Chicago was in the midst of a heat wave, and there were riots when negro children turned on fire hydrants to bathe and police tried to stop them. Towards midnight, drunk and drugged, Speck approached the hostel that he had often passed – the building that was full of young girls. He was like a fox creeping into a chicken house. And the lengths of time he took to kill eight girls suggests that he was enjoying every moment of it: for a few hours he was a sultan with absolute power over a harem of girls.

It was two years after Speck had been sentenced that the police of Salem, Oregon, realized that they were dealing with another sex killer who had claimed several victims. Linda Slawson, of Aloha, vanished in January, 1968; Jan Susan Whitney, 23, had vanished from McMinnville in November, 1968; 16-year-old Stephanie Vilcko, who vanished in July, 1968, was found in March, 1969, on the banks of Gales Creek, her body so decomposed that the cause of death could not be established.

An ordinary transvestite

On April 23, 1969, Linda Salee, 22, vanished when she was out shopping for a birthday present for her boyfriend, and on May 10 a fisherman on the bank of the Long Tom River, near Corvallis, saw a body floating below the surface. It proved to be female, half clothed, without bra or panties, and had been held down by a heavy car-part. It was Linda Salee, and she had been raped and strangled. Not far away, the police found another body, 19-year-old Karen Sprinker, who had vanished on March 27. Her underclothes were also missing; she had been raped and strangled, and was held down by part of a car engine.

In April, a 15-year-old schoolgirl had been grabbed by a man who tried to force her into a car, but she managed to break away. Not long after, two schoolgirls had seen a man dressed in women's clothes in the car park of a big store; the police thought it possible that he was an ordinary transvestite – a man who dresses in women's clothes because he wants to be a woman. However, soon after the finding of the two bodies, the police had a break.

A girl student from Oregon State University told them of a date she had had with a strange man. He had claimed to be a Vietnam veteran, had spent an evening with her in the lounge of her dormitory, and had told her she ought to 'be sad' on account of the girls who had been killed. He seemed a gentle, quietly spoken man, and it was only afterwards that she began to wonder if it was worth telling the police. It was one of hundreds of tips, but they checked it.

It led them to a mild, 30-year-old married electrician and photographer named Jerry Brudos, and they were soon convinced that this man, who made a habit of telephoning girls and claiming to be a Vietnamese veteran, knew something about the murders. He had a police record for stealing women's underwear, and for trying to force two girls to strip by threatening them with a knife. He had been caught near the women's dormitory of the Oregon State University carrying stolen women's clothing, and wearing a bra and panties.

Suspended from the ceiling
The police searched his home, near the State Hospital, to which he had been committed after the sexual charges. Brudos's wife seemed to have no suspicion that her husband had been leading a double life – her time was taken up tending to their two children – but she admitted that he spent much time in the photographer's dark room adjoining the house. In this dark room the police found what they were looking for – photographs of the dead girls.

It became clear that Brudos had kidnapped them, taken them to the studio, and there suspended them from the ceiling by their wrists while he had committed sexual assaults and photographed them. Brudos confessed to killing the four missing girls, though the death of Stephanie Vilcko, the 16-year-old, is still unsolved. He was sentenced to life imprisonment.

Comparing these three cases – Thompson, Speck, Brudos – we immediately note the violence and sadism of the more recent ones. Thompson, a typical killer of the 'Age of Sex Crime', only wanted to possess attractive girls, with or without their consent. Speck and Brudos had a deep, psychopathic hatred of women.

It would not, of course, be true to say that torture murders were unknown in the 'Age of Sex Crime'. One of the grimmest cases on record is that of Donald Fearn, a 23-year-old railway mechanic of Pueblo, Colorado, who in 1942 kidnapped Alice Porter, drove her into the desert to an old adobe church used by the Indians, and whipped and bound her with red-hot wires. He killed her with a hammer after raping her and threw the body into a well; he was executed in the gas chamber.

There was the mysterious 'Moonlight Murderer' of Texarkana, Texas, who in 1946 attacked courting couples, and in two cases killed the man and then spent hours torturing and raping the girl before killing her.

A burnt-out car found near the murder site suggests that the murderer destroyed the evidence – police had tyre tracks of the murderer's car – and then committed suicide by flinging himself under a train. However, crimes like these are solitary examples of sick perversion which stand out from the general pattern of crime as exceptions. The murders of Richard Speck fit all-too-neatly into a pattern of crime that is becoming increasingly familiar in our time.

Seen and not heard
There is a strange sense of *lack of motivation*. We are confronted with patterns of crime that would have baffled criminologists of the old school, like Lombroso or Ivan Bloch. In February, 1968, the bullet-riddled body of August Norry, a landscape gardener, was found on a hill-side in San Mateo County, California. A few months later, a pretty 18-year-old pony-tailed blonde named Penny Bjorkland confessed that she had killed him 'for fun'; he was a stranger who had offered her a lift, and she had suddenly felt the urge to shoot him – for no reason.

In June, 1972, Santa Barbara police arrested a man in connection with a supermarket stick-up. He was 47-year-old Sherman McCrary, and the investigation led police to arrest McCrary's wife Carolyn, his daughter Ginger, his son Danny and his son-in-law Carl Taylor.

And as the police investigated the itinerant family, they came to the conclusion that they had been, jointly, responsible for murdering more than 20 young women, mostly waitresses and shop assistants, who had been abducted and raped over the past two years. The women were apparently aware that their husbands were involved in orgies of robbery and rape, but felt that a housewife should be seen and not heard.

And so the mass murders continue: after Manson, John Linley Frazier, Juan Corona, Herb Mullin, the McCrarys, Edmund

Kemper, Gerry Schaefer, Dean Corll. In all these cases there can be no doubt that the fundamental problem is 'alienation'. Karl Marx would have smiled grimly. But if he was still alive, he would have to admit that *Das Kapital* holds no solution to this most baffling and disturbing problem of our time.

MILITARY MURDERS

In the year 1206 A.D. a powerful and savage army set out to conquer the world. It was led by a man who was known as 'The Wide Ruler' – in Mongolian, 'Genghis Khan'. With his Mongol hordes, he swept across China, and burned Peking to the ground. Then he turned his attention to the vast Persian empire, and conquered that just as easily; his reputation for cruelty was so terrifying that many cities surrendered without resistance. In one town, some inhabitants escaped by lying down among the dead; when Genghis Khan found out, he ordered that all corpses were to be decapitated in future, and the heads arranged in three piles: one each for men, women and children.

On another occasion, an old woman tried to buy her life by promising her captors a large pearl. When they asked where it was, she explained that she had swallowed it, and that they would have to wait until it reappeared by natural processes; instead, the Mongols ripped her body open, and found several pearls inside her. Genghis Khan thereupon ordered that the stomachs of all prisoners should be ripped open.

It was just over seven hundred years later, on June 10, 1942, that German film cameramen set up their cameras in the small village of Lidice, ten miles north-west of Prague. They were there to film its total destruction. The five hundred or so inhabitants of Lidice were made to assemble in the main square; then the men were separated from their families, and the shooting began. Nearly two hundred were thrown into a mass grave. The women and children were sent to concentration camps in Germany and less than a hundred survived. The village itself was burned down, and then blown up with explosives, and the ruins ground to powder. Lidice was destroyed in retaliation for the death of Reinhart Heydrich, deputy chief of the Nazi secret police, who had been killed by a bomb thrown by Czech resistance fighters in Prague.

What have these 'atrocity stories' in common? That both the Mongols and the Nazis were led by a cruel and ruthless leader? No, something even more fundamental than that. They both illustrate the basic attitude of the soldier towards civilians; the attitude of a tiger towards a flock of sheep. This is something that has not changed in the history of the human race, and it remains as true today as four thousand years ago. If we try to dismiss the destruction of Peking and Lidice as 'exceptional' acts of vandalism by barbarians, we shall be evading a basic psychological truth. The psychology of a human being who is a member of an army is fundamentally different from the psychology of the same human being when he is a civilian, and this can be convincingly shown by examining a cross-section of murders committed by soldiers.

From the criminologist's point of view, one of the most interesting things about 'military murders' is that, in nearly all cases, the victims are civilians, *not other soldiers*. There are, of course, rare exceptions, like Sergeant Emmett-Dunne and Lieutenant Hofrichter, and it is also true that in the Vietnam war there were many cases of the murder of officers with hand grenades. (The practice became known as 'fragging', since the officer ended in fragments.) But the soldiers who committed these murders – and often committed suicide afterwards – were usually under the influence of drugs, which intensified their sense of not 'belonging' to the army. In other words, they were killing *as* civilians. They only emphasise the general rule: that for the most part, soldiers do not murder their own kind.

High or low synergy
The reason for this is of great interest to the criminologist, for the light it throws on the general problem of the psychology of crime. It was first clearly stated by the anthropologist Ruth Benedict, who died in 1948. She noticed that primitive peoples tended to fall into two groups: societies that produced 'nice' people, and those that produced 'nasty' people. In the nice tribes, individuals tended to be cooperative, helpful and unselfish towards their neighbours. In the 'nasty' ones – the Chuckchee Indians, the Ojibwa, the Dobwo and Kwakiutl, for instance – it was every man for himself, and the people who possessed money or goods took care to hang on to them. Ruth Benedict called the nice tribes 'high-synergy societies', and the nasty ones, 'low-synergy societies'. Obviously, a low-synergy society has far more crime than a high-synergy society, and the crime tends to be

vicious and cruel; it is a disturbing thought that sadistic crimes are steadily increasing in most civilized societies in the world today.

Military brotherhood

Now there can be no doubt that the army qualifies as high-synergy society. This may sound incredible: a society in which men have to obey orders, whether reasonable or unreasonable, where discipline is rigid and punishment can be arbitrary and harsh? The fact remains that the army is a closed society in which most soldiers feel they *belong*.

The novelist James Jones has a remarkable passage in his best-seller *From Here To Eternity* in which the soldier Prewett, who has been receiving some brutal ill-treatment at the hands of his commanding officer, sits in the canteen drinking beer, and suddenly has an overwhelming feeling of love for the army, feeling *a part of it*. The ill-treatment makes no difference; in a way, it only intensifies that sense of brotherhood. The physical pressures may be greater, but the psychological pressures are altogether lighter when one belongs to any close society or group.

Miles Giffard, the Cornish youth who in 1953 murdered his parents and threw their bodies over a cliff, is a case in point. He had been a problem child all his life, expelled from school, always in some kind of trouble. Yet during his spell of National Service in the navy, all his problems vanished; he became a cheerful, disciplined and *happy* human being. As soon as he became a civilian again, all the old problems and miseries recurred.

At first sight, the implications look frightening. It seems that a society that tries to allow its members the maximum amount of freedom only becomes the breeding ground for psychopaths and habitual criminals. On the other hand, authoritarian societies – like the Austro-Hungarian empire, Hitler's Germany, Stalin's Russia – have a far lower crime rate than democratic societies. And this is not because people are afraid of the authority; it is for the same reason that Giffard became a creditable member of the Royal Navy: because a certain pressure, a certain discipline creates a sense of 'belonging'.

Indifference to civilians

But anyone who thinks this is an argument in favour of authoritarian regimes is mistaken. An army is basically a fighting organization. And when a whole society becomes a kind of army, like Nazi Germany, it directs its aggressive urges outwards, towards the 'civilians' in less disciplined societies. The results are always the same: in Bismarck's Prussia, in Mussolini's Italy, in Tojo's Japan: war. Even Stalin's Russia – a 'pacifist' society – showed the same pattern of hatred and mistrust of the rest of the world, which later expressed itself in brutal violence against the Finns, the Czechs and the Poles. An authoritarian society may bring increased security to those living in it, but it also brings the danger of war.

And this is why the armies of Genghis Khan or Hitler could destroy towns and murder civilians without compunction: *not* because the Mongols or the Nazis were exceptionally vicious, but because moral indifference to the welfare of civilians is a basic fact of the psychology of soldiers. This is true of democratic societies as of authoritarian ones – as the case of the My Lai massacre in Vietnam revealed.

Part of the reason for this is undoubtedly that people 'under orders' will do things that they would normally regard as immoral. It used to be widely believed that a person under hypnotism would wake up if ordered to commit some act that he would normally feel to be wicked. But experiments conducted by scientists like Ludwig Mayer and L.W. Rowland showed this to be untrue. A hypnotized person could be ordered to stab someone – who was actually protected by a sheet of 'invisible' glass – and would try to carry out the order.

Inadequate motive

More recent experiments in America have led to even more disturbing conclusions. The subject of the experiment was given a rheostat – a device for controlling an electric current – which was connected up to someone sitting in a chair. The subject was told that, by pulling the handle, he would administer an electric shock to the person in the chair – shocks ranging from light to extremely severe. There was no electric current; but the subject didn't know this – because the person in the chair groaned or screamed realistically as the handle was pulled. The amazing thing was that ordinary 'decent' people would allow themselves to be *ordered* to administer shocks that they believed were causing great pain, or even a danger to life. A few refused. Irresponsibility is the first step towards the criminal mentality.

The first thing we observe about military murders is their casualness, and an odd feeling of inadequacy about the motive.

Of course, this is true of many murders, civilian as well as military, but it happens too often in military cases to be coincidence. Here are some examples:

In the early hours of the morning of November 13, 1953, Mr. Justice Curran, of Whiteabbey, near Belfast, telephoned the local police to say that his 19-year-old daughter Patricia had not returned home. Desmond Curran, the girl's brother, walked down the drive to look for her and found her lying on her back, covered in blood; she had been stabbed 37 times. After an enormous manhunt, led by Inspector Capstick of Scotland Yard, suspicion came to rest on Iain Hay Gordon, a 20-year-old airman stationed nearby. Gordon had been befriended by Patricia's brother Desmond, and had called at the house on several occasions; but he only knew Patricia slightly.

Motiveless stabbing

Gordon came to the attention of the police when they discovered he had been trying to persuade other airmen to supply him with an alibi for the evening of the murder. Eventually, Gordon confessed to killing Patricia Curran. He claimed that he had met her walking home from the bus at about 5.30, and had asked her for a kiss. After a few kisses, he said, he 'lost control', and began stabbing her. There was also evidence of attempted sexual assault. Gordon was found guilty but insane, and interned 'during Her Majesty's pleasure'.

On the evening of Friday October 9, 1942, a young married woman named Ellen Symes was pushing her child in a pram along a road near Strood in Kent. The four-year-old boy later told police that a soldier had suddenly attacked his mother. Mrs. Symes screamed as a man jumped out of the darkness and stabbed her in the chest; a neighbour who heard the screams ran out to the road, and found her lying on the ground, already dead. There had been no attempt at sexual assault or robbery. At nine the next morning, a policeman saw a soldier near the scene of the crime, and asked him what he was doing away from his unit. The soldier proved to be a deserter, Private Sidney Buckfield, known as Smiler because of his cheerful grin. His comments to the police made it clear that he knew more about the murder than an innocent man should, and the knife with which the murder was committed was subsequently traced to him. At his trial, he was found guilty and sentenced to death, but subsequently reprieved on grounds of insanity, and sent to Broadmoor. No motive for the murder has ever been suggested.

Lonely soldier

Edward Joseph Leonski, a G.I. (whose career has been described in the chapter on Monsters), terrorized the city of Melbourne, Australia in 1942. He strangled and battered three women within a period of a few weeks. But none of the women was raped. Leonski was known as a genial, rather tender-hearted 'mother's boy' who missed his home. He was hanged in November 1942.

From these three cases we can already see a pattern begin to emerge: the lonely soldier, perhaps slightly emotionally unstable, far away from home, feeling bewildered and slightly lost. 'Out there' is a world of anonymous civilians, going about their own business; urges that he would normally repress now struggle to express themselves. The soldier is so 'mixed up' that he would find it impossible to explain why he committed the murder, and indeed the motives themselves are mixed: frustration, a contempt for 'civilians', a sense of unreality. Sometimes, the frustration finds expression in robbery with violence. England has had two cases of this kind, both of which ended in widespread manhunts.

Deserter

On an April morning in 1920, the body of a taxi driver, George Spicer, was found lying beside the road near Andover, Hampshire. He had been shot in the back of the head with a service revolver. Police theorized that Spicer had been asked to drive to a lonely place and been killed, the murderer had driven off in his taxi. Two soldiers who had been driven out to Bulford camp by Spicer on the previous evening mentioned that a man in uniform had asked them for a lift; Spicer had agreed to go back to pick him up later.

Not long afterwards, a policeman in Swansea recognized the missing taxi, a grey Darracq, parked beside the road. There were two soldiers inside; as the policeman ran forward, the car drove away at top speed. A few days later, one of the two soldiers, a man named Fallows, returned to Bulford camp, and admitted that he had been in the car with a deserter named Percy Toplis. Toplis had called at the cookhouse shortly after the murder, and persuaded Fallows – an old friend – to go off with him on a joy ride to sell the car. Fallows said he knew nothing of the murder until he returned to camp of his own accord. He was discharged by the magistrate, and a nationwide manhunt was launched for Toplis, but no trace was found of him for some weeks.

A month after the murder, a Scottish police constable named Grieg was told that a strange man was living in a deserted hut

near the village of Tomintoul in the Highlands. With two other
men, Grieg went into the cottage, found a sleeping man and
shook him awake. The man grabbed for a gun and began
shooting: the constable fell, dying. One of the other men had his
spine shattered. Toplis escaped on a bicycle.

In June, a police constable named Fulton saw a man wearing
an R.A.F. uniform asleep by the roadside near Carlisle. Fulton
woke the man, and during a conversation with him, remarked
that he looked like Toplis; the man grinned and agreed. Back at
home, the constable read the description of Toplis; and decided
that this was the man he had just seen. Fulton set out after him
on his bicycle. This time, Toplis threatened him with a revolver,
but Fulton escaped and rode off to Penrith. A squad of armed
constables in a police car spotted Toplis an hour later. As they
stopped, Toplis drew his revolver, the police opened fire, and the
airman fell to the ground, riddled with bullets.

A case with striking similarities to this one occurred towards
the end of World War II. Karl Hulten, known as 'Ricky', was an
American paratrooper from Boston, stationed in Britain. When
he met a little Welsh dancer named Elizabeth Marina Jones in a
Hammersmith café in October 1944, Hulten told her he was a
Chicago gangster. She was thrilled when he invited her to
become his 'moll'; in fact, Hulten had led a fairly blameless
existence as a bank clerk in Boston.

But within a few hours of his meeting with Elizabeth, Hulten
had turned to crime; he knocked a girl off her bicycle and took
her purse which contained six shillings. The next night, Hulten
and Jones offered a girl a lift in Hulten's army truck, attacked
her with an iron bar, and took five shillings off her. Afterwards
they threw their victim in the river, thinking she was dead, but
she escaped. The next evening, Hulten and Jones stopped a taxi
in Hammersmith. In the Great West Road, they told the driver,
George Heath, to stop, and Hulten killed him by shooting him in
the head. They found £4 in his wallet, and also took his watch;
leaving the corpse in a ditch, they drove off in the taxi. Three
days later, a policeman saw the missing car in Fulham, and
arrested an American soldier who was about to get into it. It was
Hulten. At the trial, both were sentenced to death, but only
Hulten was hanged; Elizabeth Jones was reprieved.

'Blackout ripper'

Other cases could be cited in which the crime was sexual. These
show basically the same pattern as in the Leonski murders: a

young soldier feeling like a fish out of water in a strange city, allowing himself to be overwhelmed by a compulsion to violence. One of the best known of these cases was that of the 'blackout ripper', Gordon Cummins, a 28-year-old R.A.F. cadet, who in February 1942 went on a four day murder spree.

A 42-year-old schoolteacher, Margaret Hamilton, was found strangled in an air raid shelter in Marylebone on February 9, 1942; her handbag was missing, but there had been no sexual assault. The next day, however, Mrs. Evelyn Oatley, an ex-revue actress, was found naked in her Wardour Street flat; her throat had been cut, and her genitals mutilated with a tin opener. Three days later Mrs. Margaret Lowe, 43, was strangled and mutilated with a razor blade in her West End flat. A few hours after her body was found, the body of Mrs. Doris Jouannet was discovered in a Paddington hotel, similarly strangled and mutilated. And only a few hours after this last attack, a young airman dragged a woman into a doorway near Piccadilly and tried to strangle her; when someone approached, he fled, leaving behind his gas mask with his service number on it.

By the time the police had traced this – and discovered its owner to be Gordon Cummins – he had attempted yet another attack in a prostitute's room, and fled when she fought him off. Cummins was executed in June 1942.

Recurring pattern
Seventeen years later, in 1958, the London police were seeking another killer whose methods strikingly resembled those of Cummins. A prostitute named Veronica Murray had been found strangled in her flat in Kilburn, with strange circular marks on her stomach and thighs. During the next year, a number of women were attacked, although they all survived; one was left naked and unconscious, with circular marks on her stomach. A photograph of a cigarette lighter that appeared in the press led to the arrest of 19-year-old Welsh Guardsman Michael Dowdall. Dowdall, diagnosed as a psychopath and sexual pervert, was found guilty of manslaughter, and sentenced to be detained 'during the Queen's pleasure'. The instrument that inflicted the round marks was never discovered.

It takes no great penetration to recognize the recurrence of certain patterns, from the disembowellings ordered by Genghis Khan to the mutilations inflicted by Cummins and Dowdall. Clearly, this is a subject that will be of great importance to criminologists in the future. It could even be the key to that most elusive daydream of mankind: the non-violent society.

MONSTERS

'Because they did not know his identity, they called him the "Monster". It was a fitting epithet, for his crimes were of a diabolical type.' These words from Lord Birkenhead's *Famous Trials* refer to Renwick Williams, a 'Ripper' who terrorized London during the year 1789. And how many murders did this 'monster' commit? None. He was a commonplace sexual pervert who derived satisfaction from slashing women's clothes with a knife. On a few occasions he accosted a girl and asked her to smell a bunch of flowers. The ones who were incautious enough to accept the invitation had a sharp instrument – hidden among the flowers – jabbed into their faces.

An unpleasant character, certainly; but not, by modern standards, a 'monster'. Psychiatrists call such men 'piqueurs' and recognize that they are suffering from sexual frustration and an inferiority complex. The piqueur is usually obsessed with some part of a girl's anatomy – her breasts, buttocks, or thighs. He mingles with a crowd, selects an attractive victim, then gets close enough to jab her with a sharp instrument – often an ice pick. By the time the girl realizes what has happened, he has vanished.

For the modern reader, the most surprising thing is that a piqueur should have caused such terror in London – a terror comparable to that caused by Jack the Ripper a century later. Prostitutes tried to keep their pimp in sight; respectable women went out only with a male escort. Many of the stories about the 'Monster's' exploits were exaggerated; but, in fact, he was a dangerous man. His knife had inflicted deep and painful wounds, and some of the victims had badly scarred faces. London was seized with panic. Crimes springing from sexual abnormality were almost unknown; they couldn't even begin to understand what could drive a man to attack strange girls. The age of Sex Crime lay nearly a century and a half in the future.

Obscene suggestions

Then, in January 1790, the 'Monster' committed the attack that led to his downfall. In St. James's Street there was a tavern run by a man called Porter. His two attractive daughters, Sarah and Anne, were popular barmaids. But on several recent occasions Sarah had been upset when a strange man had sidled up to her in the street and muttered obscene suggestions in her ear.

At 11 o'clock on the night of January 18 the two girls were returning from a ball when Sarah recognized the foul-mouthed stranger on the corner of St. James's Street. He was apparently drunk. He shouted, 'Oh, there you are,' and gave her a blow on the side of the head. Sarah told Anne to run: 'that dreadful wretch is behind us.'

As they reached the door of the tavern he caught up with them, and slashed at their buttocks with a knife. The girls screamed and rushed inside – but not before they had both seen the man's face clearly. Their dresses and underclothes were soaked with blood, and when they undressed, they found they had long slashes on their buttocks – one of them four inches deep.

Six months later, the girls were walking in St. James's Park with their mother and a male friend when the 'Monster' walked past them. He obviously recognized them, for he turned and stared. Anne Porter cried: 'That's him. That's the man who attacked us!' The man with them then hurried after the 'Monster'. He tracked him to a nearby house, banged on the door, and demanded to know the identity of the man who had just gone in. The 'Monster' appeared with apparent astonishment, handed over his visiting card, and asked what all the fuss was about. He even agreed to accompany the young man to the house where the Porters lived. At that Anne and Sarah promptly screamed and fainted.

In spite of his protests, he was arrested, and in due course appeared at the Old Bailey, where crowds flocked to see the infamous Ripper. The judge had to explain to the jury that this was an extremely baffling case, the first of its kind ever heard in England. There was simply no law to deal with a man who slashed ladies' buttocks without apparent motive. On the other hand, there were plenty of laws to deal with damage to property.

So Renwick Williams was charged with damaging the ladies' clothes. The bloodstained dresses and underskirts were produced in court – with ten-inch rents to prove that the 'Monster' had ruined valuable property. Williams was duly sentenced to six years in jail, and ordered to produce £400 as a surety for future good behaviour. After that he disappeared from the criminal scene.

Strangely enough, the next wrongdoer to earn himself the nickname of the 'Monster' was also called Williams; but in his case, he deserved the title. He slaughtered two families with a frenzy that suggests temporary insanity. Thomas De Quincy has described the case – with magnificent suspense, but considerable inaccuracy – in an appendix to his famous essay 'On Murder Considered as One of the Fine Arts'.

Frenzied blows

The scene was the Ratcliffe Highway, in the East End of London, not far from the street where Jack the Ripper would later kill and mutilate six women. The year was 1811. Towards midnight on December 7, Timothy Marr, who kept a hosier's shop, sent out the servant girl to buy oysters. Twenty minutes later, she returned to find the house locked up. There was no reply to her knocks, but she thought she heard stealthy footsteps inside. Neighbours broke in, to find a scene of bloodshed.

The apprentice boy lay at the foot of the stairs, his head beaten to a pulp by frenzied blows that had sprayed his brains on to the ceiling. Behind the counter lay Timothy Marr; his wife Celia was in the doorway, face down; both had their heads battered and their throats cut. In the basement, the baby had been assaulted with the same fury, its throat also slashed. Nothing of value seemed to be missing from the house.

Sledge hammer

The murders caused panic, not only in London, but all over England. Old ladies in remote parts of Wales had heavy bolts put on their doors. Eight days later, the hysteria increased when there was another mass-slaughter within a few hundred yards of the Marrs' house. This time it was a publican called Williamson, who ran the King's Arms. Shortly after 11 p.m. a lodger named John Turner heard the front door slam heavily. Being of a nervous disposition, he sat up in bed and wondered if the unseen murderer had entered the house. He stole slowly downstairs, and saw a man bending over a prostrate body on the floor. In the room beyond, two more bodies lay.

Turner crept back upstairs, knotted some sheets together, and clambered out of the window. As soon as he was safely on the pavement, he began to shout 'Murder, murder!' By the time a crowd had broken in, the killer had escaped out of a back window and scrambled up a muddy bank. Williamson, his wife Elizabeth, and the servant girl, Bridget Harrington, had all been killed in the same violent manner as the Marrs. A 14-year-old girl who had been asleep in a bedroom was unharmed.

The Marrs had been murdered by a kind of sledgehammer called a maul. It was not until after the second mass-murder that this was identified – by initials on its handle – as belonging to a Swedish sailor. The sailor had a perfect alibi, being at sea at the time of the murders; but he had left his tools in a common lodging house, where a man named John Williams now fell under suspicion.

On the morning of the Williamson murders, he had returned to a room he shared with other lodgers, and shouted at them to put out the candle. The next morning, someone noticed that his shoes were muddy, and that he was washing muddy socks. There was blood on his shirt – which Williams explained as the result of a brawl.

A search of the house revealed a pair of heavily bloodstained trousers at the bottom of a privy. The pocket of his coat was also bloodstained, as if it had held a knife, and the knife itself was found hidden in a mouse hole. Williams – a fresh-faced man who didn't look in the least like a murderer – was arrested. But before he could be tried, he hanged himself in jail. His body was buried at a cross-roads near the scene of the murders, and a stake was driven through his 'monstrous' heart.

Deeper understanding

It is understandable why De Quincey and his contemporaries refer to him as Williams the Monster. The murders were ostensibly motiveless – although it seems probable that a small sum of money and a few other objects were taken. But robbery could hardly explain the ferocity of the murders, or the killing of the sleeping baby. Neither was there any apparent connection between the victims and the killer which might justify a theory of revenge-murder. It is not surprising that the Ratcliffe Highway murders obsessed the imagination of the nineteenth century, until they were finally eclipsed by Jack the Ripper, 77 years later.

But although criminologists still have no idea of what turned Williams into a homicidal maniac, they have an altogether deeper understanding of the psychology of 'monsters' in general. One of the most important insights is owed to the work of the Austrian zoologists, Konrad Lorenz. Lorenz did some of his most valuable work with jackdaws. He quickly discovered that, when a jackdaw is first born, it looks around for some object on which to fix its affections. Normally, the nearest object would be the mother. But if there is no mother available, the baby will attach itself to whoever – or whatever – happens to be around. (This is known to zoologists as 'imprinting'.) One baby jackdaw decided that Lorenz was its mother, and expressed its devotion to him in embarrassing ways. For example, it waited until he was dozing with his mouth open, and then deposited a load of chewed-up worms on his tongue.

Remarkably tough

This need for a mother (or father) is so great that a baby peacock has been known to fall in love with a tortoise, and a baby monkey with a stone. But experiments soon showed that if the baby is denied *any* kind of parent-figure during the first weeks of its life, it becomes incapable of affection, and develops into what could be called a psychopath. That is to say, it may learn to become a part of a community, but it never learns the basic rules of give and take.

Most humans enjoy 'giving' because they relish giving pleasure to someone they love or like. The psychopath is 'disconnected'; he doesn't love anybody. He looks coldly at other human beings and calculates what he can get out of them. He can hate, but he doesn't know how to love. Of course, this condition can be produced in perfectly normal people by long periods of emotional strain; but its effect slowly wears off. In the man who is a psychopath through childhood deprivation of affection, it never wears off.

Even so, living creatures are remarkably tough. In a remarkable series of experiments with monkeys, the American Professor Harry Harlow discovered that a newly-born monkey can become passionately attached even to a wire dummy, particularly if the dummy is fitted up with some kind of feeding mechanism that gives milk. The baby will snuggle up to the dummy when it needs comfort. As it gets older, it turns into a fairly normal young monkey, capable of giving affection like any other. Which seems to demonstrate that the mother-substitute doesn't need to *do* anything – just be there.

However, by far the most serious cause of affection-starvation in children is over-crowding. As soon as overcrowding occurs in any animal community, the infant mortality rate soars, and 'psychopathic' babies begin to develop, as an increasing number of babies are actively rejected by mothers who can't cope.

This might seem to raise the question of why there were not far more psychopaths in Thomas De Quincey's London. Surely it was as overcrowded and disease-ridden as many modern cities? But this is not altogether true. London – and Paris and Berlin – may have been overcrowded, but the capital was still a fairly *small* place. Indeed England itself was full of vast open spaces. Moreover, the people who lived in its crowded tenements had deep roots in the community; they were often poor, but they felt they *belonged*.

Symbolic violation

A study conducted among American immigrant communities in the 1930's showed that the first generation of Poles, Croats, etc., were remarkably stable, living in communities with other immigrants from their own country and speaking their own language. It was in the second generation that mental instability began to appear – as the young Pole or Russian Jew found himself torn between two cultures. The rate of mental sickness among Negroes who lived in Harlem – in an all-black community – was far lower than among better off Negroes who moved to partly white neighbourhoods.

All this makes it clear why there were so few psychopaths in the early nineteenth century; why Renwick Williams caused universal panic; why the Ratcliffe Highway murderer became a legend of horror. It is not known what gave Renwick Williams his compulsion to stab women in the buttocks, or what produced John Williams's outbursts of murderous fury. But such people are no longer a mystery. Sexual frustration can take many forms, from stealing ladies' underwear from clothes lines, to jabbing strange women with an ice pick – and they are all clearly forms of substitute rape – a symbolic violation.

Renwick Williams, the 'Ripper', was unmarried. Many witnesses described him as polite and 'gentlemanly', yet he seems to have been only a tailor's assistant. The picture that emerges is of a shy, withdrawn, rather intelligent man, a social misfit, with a fetish about buttocks, and overpowering sexual desires that could burst out – usually when he was drunk – in the form of a longing to slash and rip the object of his obsession.

Foreign seaports

This description also fits John Williams to a remarkable degree. Although only an ordinary sailor, he was better educated than the average seaman, wrote a good hand, and dressed well. Disliked by most men, he was a favourite with women. A fundamentally weak person, he was inclined to bursts of violent rage when drunk. He had probably been drinking heavily before he killed the Marrs and the Williamsons; some deep frustration suddenly exploded into psychopathic violence that left him exhausted and strangely lethargic – but temporarily free of his obsessions. Modern case histories of similar types suggest that he may have committed other murders, perhaps in the slum quarters of foreign seaports.

The modern parallel that suggests itself is the case of Edward Joseph Leonski, the man whose crimes terrorized the city of Melbourne, Australia, in 1942. His first victim was a 40-year-old domestic help, Ivy McLeod. She was found in a shop doorway on May 3, 1942, her clothes ripped to shreds, her face battered and lacerated, her body bruised; she was strangled, but there was no sign of rape.

Yellow mud

A week later, the body of a slim brunette, Pauline Thompson, was found on the steps of an apartment house, the clothes torn and the face unrecognizable. Melbourne suddenly realized that it was harbouring a ripper-type killer, and there was panic. Mrs. Thompson, a policeman's wife, was strangled but not raped.

Scarcely a week had passed when, on May 19, the body of another woman was found lying in the yellow mud near an American army camp. Her clothes had been ripped off and she had been beaten and strangled – but again, not raped. She was Gladys Hosking, a 41-year-old secretary. This time, however, there was a clue. An Australian soldier had seen an American serviceman plastered with yellow mud near the scene of the crime. Police searched the camp, and quickly found a tent with yellow mud on the flap. 'Crime chemist' Alan Dower found it to be identical to the clay in which the body had been found.

Shy manners

The occupant of the tent, Private Joseph Leonski, was a baby-faced, blue-eyed giant, universally liked for his gentleness. The strange thing about him was that when he was drunk, his personality changed completely; he began to talk gloatingly about violence; then, if the mood was on him, he offered to fight anybody in the bar. He was a real-life Jekyll and Hyde. After each killing, he was horrified, and screamed in his sleep. His description of the killing of Gladys Hosking was typical.

He fell into conversation with her as she walked along; his shy manners and appealing face convinced her she had nothing to fear. He had no conscious intention of harming her; he was merely lonely and homesick. He found her voice soothing; when it was time for them to separate, he suddenly experienced an insane desire to 'keep her voice'. The violence took over like an epileptic fit; when it had passed, she was naked and bruised — and dead.

Leonski was hanged quickly — to satisfy Australian public opinion — and little is known about his psychological history. But what *is* on record is revealing. His mother had been a professional weight-lifter from Poland, an immensely dominant woman whose two unhappy marriages had made her bitter. She undoubtedly loved her son; but had she, during those vital early months of his life, treated him as an irrelevant nuisance? She felt she had to be hard and tough to face the world; she had no tenderness to give to a baby. Eddie developed into a gentle, shy boy, with definite artistic leanings. He drew, played the piano, and won prizes at school. But he was always afraid of girls. Almost any snub or rebuke could make him burst into tears. So again, there is the same basic pattern as in the other two 'monsters': the misfit, the 'outsider', not really at home with other men, and burning with frustrations that found total violent release only when drunk.

Repressed hatred

The three murdered women were not the only ones Leonski had attacked; three others came forward to tell of being strangled into unconsciousness by him, and a fourth woman related an attempt to rape her in her apartment. Leonski was a virile male; he wanted a woman badly; but young women scared him. Equally, he didn't know what to *do* with the middle-aged women he killed; the need for sex got mixed up with his repressed hatred of his mother.

It is not true that all 'monsters' are split personalities who kill in a frenzy. Many psychopaths are simply 'cold' — Ian Brady, the Moors murderer, is an example. (Interestingly enough, his mother deserted him almost as soon as he was born.) But in most cases, the basic cause can be traced back to very early childhood.

Perhaps when this psychological trait is something that *every* mother and father knows about and takes steps to prevent, 'monsters' will again become as rare as they were in the days of Renwick Williams.

MOTIVELESS MURDER

A yellow Chevrolet cruises slowly down the street in a quiet Los Angeles suburb. As it passes a lawn on which a four-year-old girl is playing, it slows down. A man leans out of the rear window, and blasts her with a shotgun. A few moments later the child, Joyce Ann Huff, dies in the arms of her sobbing mother. Later, three men are charged with the murder; the one who fired the shot has a long police record. But no motive. Police describe it as a 'thrill killing', like deer stalking or shooting partridge.

In the wilds of Montana, a man dressed as a cowboy rides his horse along a quiet country road. A stranger stops his car to ask him the way. The 'cowboy' pulls out his six-shooter, and shoots him through the head; then he rides on. He is living out a fantasy of being part of the old Wild West.

A bachelor named Norman Smith sits watching TV in a caravan in Florida; the programme is called 'The Sniper', about a man with a psychopathic hatred of women. When it is over, Smith takes his revolver, walks along the road until he finds a lighted window, and a woman watching her television, and shoots her. Smith did not know the woman he killed – Mrs. Hazel Woodard – neither did she know him.

In Cuba, New Mexico, a jeep stops near a woman who stands talking to a neighbour, while two children play nearby. The bearded driver raises his rifle, and shoots the children. Then he drives away, leaving one child dead and the other dying. Trapped by a posse a few hours later, he explains that he had a sudden impulse to do something about the population explosion. They ask if he knew that the mother of one of the dead children had ten other children; he shrugs, and admits that he had never seen any of them before.

In recent years, 'motiveless murder' has become the most typical, and perhaps the most frightening, crime of our time. This is particularly true of the United States, where it has reached epidemic proportions.

Psychologists and criminologists seem baffled by the nature of such crimes. How can one analyze the motive of a motiveless murder? It is easy to talk about a 'generalized resentment against society', but that explains hardly anything. The anarchists of the 1890's had plenty of resentment about society; but they murdered kings and presidents. What can one say of a man who murders perfectly ordinary, innocent people? That he is insane? This explanation fits only a tiny percentage of 'motiveless' killers. The rest are quite definitely sane in the legal sense.

This is an area in which – in the 1960's – a new theory was developed by A.E. Van Vogt which provides some vital clues. Van Vogt is best known as an American writer of science fiction. He is also a brilliant and unorthodox psychologist. There are many psychologists now who believe that his theory about violent men could be one of the most important breakthroughs since Sigmund Freud 'discovered' the unconscious.

Studying newspaper reports of divorce cases, Van Vogt noted an interesting pattern. Many husbands seemed inclined to make unreasonable and almost incredible demands on their wives, and to treat them like slaves. A basic characteristic of such husbands was that *they would never admit they were ever in the wrong*. If the facts were obviously against them, such men would fly into a rage, punch or beat the wife – and sometimes the children – and end by establishing, to their own satisfaction, that they were right all the time. Van Vogt calls such a man the 'right man'.

He cites a typical case of a 'right man'. When a nurse was about to get married, she thought it only fair to tell her husband that she was not a virgin; in fact, she had had affairs with two doctors. The husband-to-be flew into an almost insane frenzy of jealousy, and she thought that was the end of their relation. But the next day, he brought her a document to sign. He would not allow her to read it – he just insisted that, if they were still to get married, she had to sign it. She did so.

Affairs suspected

During their marriage, she was treated as an object. Her husband's job involved much travelling, and she soon came to suspect that he was having affairs with other women. If she ever complained that he stayed away for weeks at a time, he flew into a rage. On the other hand, he was intensely suspicious of his wife, and likely to lose his temper and knock her down at the least provocation.

He would usually be apologetic the next day – but that wouldn't stop him from repeating his 'violence pattern' a couple of days later. Any triviality was enough to set off storms of shouting. Finally, the wife could no longer stand it, and insisted upon a divorce. The husband agreed to this and then set her up in a suburban home – on condition that she did not remarry, and would devote her life to being an ideal mother to their young son.

Van Vogt believes that the paper she signed declared that she admitted to being little more than a whore, and had absolutely no rights as a married woman. If necessary, the husband might produce this paper in court . . . It sounds as if such a man must be close to the verge of insanity, or at least, nervous breakdown. But this proved to be untrue. Many similar husbands were successful businessmen, held in high esteem by their associates, and regarded as 'decent sorts'. It was only their wives – and families – who brought out the element of the tyrant in them.

Van Vogt made an extremely interesting observation about 'right men'. They often desert their wives. *But*, if by some odd chance, the wife deserts them, the result is a severe mental shock. They may go grovelling, begging her to return. If she refuses, they can experience a severe depression that could end in death. Each of the husbands has built a fantasy world on the idea of himself as a kind of monarch, an absolute ruler, within his own household. If this fantasy collapses, it is like removing his linchpin; he disintegrates. But why should that be so?

At this point, it becomes clear that the violent man (an alternative name for the 'right man') has built an entire structure of *self-esteem* on his domination of his wife. In that one respect, he feels like a little god. Most people build their self-esteem on certain achievements, or relationships, or even objects (the family car, the greenhouse, the colour TV).

The nineteenth-century Russian writer Nikolai Gogol has a story called *The Overcoat* in which a humble, rather depressed little clerk gains self-esteem from a new overcoat, and goes insane when it is stolen. Most people have a number of foundations for their self-esteem, so that if one collapses, the damage is not too difficult to repair. The 'right man' is tempted to build everything on one single plank; if it collapses, he feels he is a nobody.

Van Vogt made the interesting comment that he was convinced that many famous dictators have been, or are, 'right men'

– including Hitler, Stalin, and Mao Tse Tung. Hitler's sexual relations certainly seem to confirm this. He chose girls – like Geli Raubal and Eva Braun – who were quiet, domesticated types whose chief function was to adore him. When Geli Raubal committed suicide – to escape his domination – Hitler himself came close to suicide.

When the 'right man' gains a position of power, it is a poor lookout for his country. Totally incapable of self-discipline – completely 'spoilt', like an overindulged child – he always blames his own shortcomings on others. At the least suspicion of opposition, he flies into a paranoid rage and the heads roll.

Executions ordered

It is such displays of emotion which forge the connection between the 'right man' and motiveless murder. To begin with, it stresses that men who have become the victims of their own power mania often order executions on the most inadequate grounds. And they need not even *be* in a rage. In 1861, for example, the English explorer John Hanning Speke was in Africa, hunting for the source of the Nile; in February of the following year he was the guest of the young King Mutesa of Uganda. He presented the King with various guns. The king asked for a demonstration of their power, and sent for four cows – which Speke shot.

The King was delighted. He handed a carbine to an urchin standing nearby. 'See if it will kill a man,' he ordered. The boy ran into an outer courtyard; there was a crash, and he came running back, grinning delightedly. 'Did it work?' asked the monarch. 'Oh yes!' came the reply. He had been supplied with weapons which did not belittle his status, and he demanded no more – and no less.

In primitive societies, the king was often an absolute ruler, who commanded the power of life and death. He regarded this as his absolute *right*. Ivan the Terrible, Czar of Russia in the sixteenth century, would have courtiers tortured or executed for some minor breach of etiquette, which he felt reflected on his dignity.

Thousands tortured

When the 'free city' of Novgorod refused to recognize his sovereignty, he spent five weeks torturing to death its inhabitants, at the rate of thousands a day. He often had children tortured in front of their mothers – and then the mothers were roasted alive. When most of the inhabitants of Wenden, in Livonia, blew themselves up in a castle rather than fall into his hands, he rounded up every remaining inhabitant of the town and tortured them to death. Ivan was a supreme example of a violent man.

But he was not insane; nor were the many other tyrants of history. There is a touch of the 'right man' in everybody. Everybody gets angry with people who oppose and frustrate them; everybody would like to see such people forced to apologize abjectly. In our fantasies, we are all tyrants sometimes. And, from the point of view of human evolution, it is a good thing we are. The will to power is as important to evolution as the sexual urge. A man with a strong will to power is likely to make a good father and provider. And although tyrants like Ivan the Terrible and Stalin may have been bad for their victims, they were very good for the country as a whole, binding it into unity.

Even the sexual urge is built on the will to power. The male desire to enter strange female bodies is a dominance urge – and, when a man and a woman are ideally suited to one another, it is because in the sexual act, the man enjoys playing his dominant role and the woman enjoys playing her submissive role. The key word here is *playing*. Sensible people are flexible and adjustable. They do not take the power game too seriously. They don't *want* to achieve self-esteem at too cheap a price; they are realistic enough to prefer real achievement to the feeling of power that comes from bullying and exercising petty or domestic authority.

In a hierarchy of values, the need for self-esteem comes above the need for sex (and love). When a man has got a secure sexual background, he starts to want the respect and admiration of society, to feel himself a 'somebody'. At the present moment, Western society has evolved to the self-esteem level. This means that more murderers than ever before are motivated by the need for self-esteem.

At the same time, there is more general prosperity now than at any time in history. A few centuries ago, it was only the rich and powerful who had the time or the freedom to indulge their will to power. Nowadays there are millions of people in Europe and America who are, relatively speaking, as well-off as the Ugandan King Mutesa, living in comfortable homes, with money enough to buy a great deal of consideration from society. In these circumstances, the 'spoiltness' that is the chief characteristic of the 'right man' has plenty of room to develop. At first sight, there may not seem to be much in common between King Mutesa and the Chicago thrill killers, Leopold and Loeb. But psychologically speaking, there is a very close resemblance.

The 'right man' is wrapped up in himself; in an odd way, he doesn't really believe that other people are real. So he feels no conscience about treating them as mere objects. Norman Smith, living alone in his caravan in Florida, was almost certainly a 'right man'. But, living alone, he had no one on whom he could impose his will to power. Watching the television programme on the sniper suddenly showed him the way to express it. He could take his revolver, shoot somebody through a window (preferably a woman, so sexual dominance is also involved) – and then, as he came home afterwards, he would feel he was *somebody*.

Shooting a stranger

The same pattern can be seen in all the major cases of 'motiveless murder'. Ian Brady, the British Moors murderer, told his hench-man David Smith that he had committed at least one motiveless killing: that he had stopped his car in a dark street, got out, shot a stranger who was walking along the pavement, then driven off. This was probably fantasy: the police have no record of such a shooting. But it shows the pattern of Brady's thinking.

Ed Sanders' book on the Charles Manson crimes, *The Family*, makes it clear that Manson developed all the characteristics of a 'right man' in the two years before his arrest: the need for absolute, total authority over his followers; the wild rages if anyone expressed doubt: the blinding, manic resentments against anyone who had humiliated him.

At the time Manson's 'family' had embarked on its career of slaughter in Los Angeles, another killer in San Francisco was engaged in a series of motiveless murders. The man who is called 'the Zodiac killer' has never been caught. In December 1968, two teenagers sitting in a station wagon were shot dead.

In July 1969, a man pulled up alongside another couple on the Columbia parkway. He got out of his car, shot them both, then phoned the police, telling them he had also murdered 'those kids last year'. The shot man, Michael Mageau, survived, and confirmed that the killer had shot at him and his girl friend and then walked away. It was after this that San Francisco newspapers began receiving letters signed with the astrological sign of the zodiac, and boasting that the writer would commit more murders.

In September 1969, the killer tied up a couple, then stabbed them both repeatedly; again, the man survived. Two weeks later, the man called Zodiac shot a taxi driver in the back of the head, and strode off; again there was no motive.

Bodies in the pool

On October 19, 1970, not long after the Manson trial had started, the home of a wealthy California eye surgeon was seen to be on fire. In the swimming pool, firemen discovered five corpses: that of the eye surgeon, Victor Ohta, his wife, their two children, and his secretary.

A note found in the doctor's car declared that 'World War Three' had begun; it was signed with names taken from the Tarot cards. The murderer's fingerprints on the car, and on a beer can, led the police to John Linley Frazier, 24, a car mechanic and hippy, separated from his wife.

The evidence showed that Frazier had planned the murders some days in advance, had found Mrs. Ohta alone, and 'executed' her by shooting her in the back of the head. Later, when the secretary, the children, and the doctor returned, he 'executed' them in the same manner.

England's first case of motiveless murder came to light in November 1971, when the police arrested 24-year-old Graham Young, and charged him with the poison-murders of two workmates, and the attempted murder of two more. It was only after he had been sentenced to life imprisonment that newspapers were able to reveal that at the age of 14, Young had been charged with poisoning several members of his family, one of whom – his stepmother – died. The schoolboy-chemist was an admirer of the 'great poisoners'. He was sent to Broadmoor, the institution for the criminally insane.

In the book *Obsessive Poisoner* by Young's sister, the usual typical 'motiveless murder' pattern emerges. He had a craving to be known, to be famous; he regarded himself as highly intelligent, and felt he had no proper outlet in his working class background.

The admirer of Hitler, the man who referred to himself as 'your friendly neighbourhood Frankenstein', began to toy with the idea of committing murder with an almost unknown poison, thallium . . . Observers at his trial noted an odd thing: he seemed to be basking in the limelight, almost as if it were worth a lifetime in jail to be recognized as one of the company of the great poisoners.

Van Vogt's 'right man' theory could be a turning point in criminological science. It provides a new key to the psychology of men like Manson, Frazier, and Graham Young. Whether it can help to prevent motiveless murders is another matter; but to understand *why* they happen will be a major step towards it.

MURDEROUS MILLIONAIRES

It was, oddly enough, a respectable English statesman, Lord Acton, who made the cynical comment: 'All power tends to corrupt, and absolute power tends to corrupt absolutely.' The sentiment sounds so revolutionary that many anarchists to this day believe it was said by Bakunin, or some other rabid anti-authoritarian.

But is is really *true*? Fortunately, from the point of view of the criminologist, no. If it were, the rich and powerful of the world would all be super-criminals. There *have* been plenty of corrupt tyrants in world history – from Tiberius to Hitler and Stalin – but most of them had more than a touch of insanity about their make-up.

Moreover, what Europeans take for horrible cruelty may be just a kind of barbaric indifference to life; a typical example of 'eastern cruelty' can be found in *Severn Pillars of Wisdom* by Lawrence of Arabia. He describes how the Turkish army re-took a certain town from the Bulgarians. All the peasants had fled, so there was no one for the Commander-in-Chief, Enver Pasha, to torment. Finally, someone found a very old man. After baiting him for a while, Enver ordered that he should be tossed into a ship's furnace.

'The old man screamed, but the officers were stronger and the door was slammed to on his jerking body. We turned, feeling sick, to go away, but Enver, his head on one side, listening, halted us. So we listened, till there came a crash within the furnace. He smiled and nodded, saying, "Their heads always pop like that".'

By western standards, Enver was an evil sadist, but are we being accurate when we call him that? The French smuggler, Henry de Monfried, in his classic autobiography *Hashish*, tells of a friend of his who could not resist shooting cats. When he saw a cat dozing in the sun, his rifle went up, there was a crash,

437

and the cat usually dragged itself away to die. Yet Monfried's friend was a compassionate, kindly man, who often went to great lengths to help sick Negroes and Arabs. How do we explain this paradox? Quite simply, Monfied's friend plainly did not regard cats as fellow creatures.

What of some of those great tyrants of history – for example, Caligula and Nero? Are they not evidence of the corrupting influence of power? It is obviously true that being the absolute ruler of the Roman empire turned them into monsters of capricious cruelty. But anyone who has ploughed through the sickening pages of Suetonius's *Lives of the Caesars* will agree that there are hundreds, perhaps thousands, of potential Caligulas walking the streets of our major cities, and that most of them were *born* that way.

Parisian underworld

By way of example, we may cite the appalling case of Georges Rapin, the rich playboy who chose to be a pimp and murderer. Rapin, a suave and rather good-looking young man, was the son of a wealthy engineer. His great compulsion was to be admired and respected; so at school he spent more time boasting and passing around cigarettes than working for his baccalaureate; he left school in his early teens, unregretted by his teachers.

During the next few years, his father tried gently to propel him in the direction of various careers; Georges resisted this firmly until his father gave up the struggle. By the age of 18, in 1962, he was known as a man about town, driving his sports convertible and hanging around the dives and night spots of Pigalle and Montmartre until the first light of dawn. He also committed burglaries for the fun of it, and in 1964 he was arrested. Once again, his father's money allowed him to avoid the consequences of his own actions. The victim of the burglary was reimbursed and the case was dropped.

As a kind of penance, Georges entered the army, but his instability was now so obvious that he was soon thrown out again, on the grounds that he was 'asocial and undesirable'. His parents offered to finance him in business and he chose to run two bars, but did this so casually that they were soon bankrupt. His parents now persuaded him to try a career of their choice, and made him the proprietor of a bookshop. That only convinced him that the thing he detested most in the world was literature.

By this time he knew what he wanted to be – a tough guy, or, as the French say, a *caid*. He had a wide circle of acquaintances in the Parisian underworld. They knew him as 'Bill', a name he preferred. One night, in a bar named the Sans Souci, Bill met a pretty 18-year-old prostitute known simply as Dominique. She came from a village near Rheims, and had been brought to Paris by a Corsican. When her lover — and pimp — ran into trouble through his blue-movie interests, Dominique was taken over by Georges Rapin, who liked to think of himself as 'Bill the Caid'. He had no real need to become a pimp; he had an adequate allowance from his father. But a real *caid* manages girls and lives off their earnings.

Final showdown

Dominique, however, proved to be more trouble than she was worth. It was true that her good looks brought many clients; but she was passionately devoted to gambling and slot machines. Georges beat her up several times, but it seemed to do no good. Then, one day she told him she was getting tired of working as a prostitute, and wanted to retire — perhaps get married and have a family. Georges was outraged. In the Parisian underworld this was unheard of; a prostitute who tried to desert her protector would be scarred so badly that she would be marked for life as a woman of the streets. And Georges had built himself up a reputation as a ruthless thug; he later claimed that he had committed a dozen murders in the 18 months before Dominique's.

One evening in 1969, Georges drove Dominique towards Fontainebleau in his black Dauphine-Gordini. She believed they were on their way to commit a robbery. Georges had told her that she could buy her freedom for 500,000 francs, and she was hoping to obtain this from a single night's work. They stopped in a lonely place. Georges produced his revolver. 'This is it,' and as the girl started to get out of the car, he shot her down. As she lay, groaning, on the road, he stood over her, emptied an oil can on her, then set her on fire. Then he turned the car and drove back to Paris, leaving the girl writhing in the flames.

The body was found the following morning, but the flames had charred it beyond recognition. The shoes, however, were untouched; in her agony, the dying girl had kicked them off. They were fairly new, and of an uncommon design. With slow, patient work, the police traced them to the Parisian shop where they had been bought. The sales girl remembered Dominique. Soon the police were interviewing Georges. He had an alibi; he had spent the night, he said, with his mistress who supported this story.

But in the bathroom, police found bullets of the same calibre as those that had killed the girl. Under slow and persistent questioning, Bill the Tough finally confessed to the murder of Dominique. He went further, and confessed to another dozen gang killings; it seemed that he was determined to make his mark in the Paris underworld.

Physical smell

In fact, no professional *macquereau* could have any respect for a man who, in a burst of outraged self-esteem, had murdered a valuable property like Dominique.

It seems doubtful whether there is any psychologist in the world who would be naïve enough to suggest that Georges Rapin's shortcomings as a human being were due to his father's wealth. We have all met people like Georges Rapin; we all remember the boy at school who was always lying about his sexual experience, or puffing a cigarette behind the lavatory. Georges Rapin was born a waster, and while a harsher environment might have saved him from life imprisonment, it would certainly have failed to turn him into a hardworking, serious member of the community.

The psychological mainspring of the Georges Rapin type is a craving for self-esteem, combined with a lack of the qualities that would make him liked or respected. He spends all his time bidding for admiration with no intention of earning it – to borrow a phrase of Shaw's. Nero was the same; his intimates had to keep assuring him that he was the world's most talented poet, actor, singer and wit; and although he was not a stupid man, the craving to be admired was so enormous that no flattery struck him as outrageous.

We are here once again dealing with the problem of the 'violent man', so brilliantly described by A.E. Van Vogt: the man who will never, *under any circumstances*, admit that he might be in the wrong. The whole rickety structure of his self-esteem depends on this belief. Such a man often treats his wife and family with incredible arrogance and brutality, if he suspects they regard him as less than superhuman.

Paranoid response

On the other hand, Van Vogt points out, if his wife deserts him, he may become seriously ill or even commit suicide; she has *proved* to him that he is not a god. Georges Rapin's violent response to Dominique's threat of desertion suggests that he is a classic example of the 'right man syndrome'.

This is true of most of the cases of 'murderous millionaires' – rich men who kill, or hire someone to do the killing for them. The compulsion that drives them often leads to business success – Rapin might well have become a rich man in his own right if he hadn't committed murder. The success deepens the conviction that they are invincible, incapable of failure, and anyone who poses a threat to this insane self-admiration triggers an avalanche of murderous violence.

For the same reason, any kind of threat to his fortune is likely to produce the same paranoid response. The case of Philip Stansfield provides an illustration. He was the son of Sir James Stansfield, a Scottish baronet of considerable wealth, who owned a fine manor house near Dumfries. Descriptions of Philip's character suggest that he was of the same type as Georges Rapin: lazy, profligate and boastful. Finally, Sir James lost patience, and threatened to disinherit him and settle the estate on his younger brother.

It was this threat that touched the deep spring of violence in Philip Stansfield; he had been looking forward to inheriting the estate, becoming lord of the manor, and being able to do what he liked. In late November, 1687, Philip went home to the house at New Milns, perhaps hoping to persuade his father that he had mended his ways. But a clergyman called John Bell was staying there with his father, and Philip had a particular hatred of clergymen; on one occasion, in church, he had thrown a stone and hit the minister. The minister looked up, and calmly prophesied that whoever had thrown the stone would have more people present at his death than were there in the church.

On the night of November 21, he was in a particularly black mood when he went to bed. Sir James was nervous; he knew his son was capable of violence. In the middle of the night, the clergyman was awakened by loud voices and furious shouts. He later explained that he thought them to be 'evil spirits', and bolted his door. The next morning, Philip Stansfield came to Bell's room, and asked if he had seen his father. The Rev. Bell said no, whereupon Philip went off, saying he was going to look for his father 'upon the banks of the water'. As this seemed an odd comment, the clergyman dressed and hastened downstairs and outside. There he met servants who told him that Sir James's body had just been found floating in a pond in the grounds.

Philip had the body carried indoors; but, to everyone's surprise, refused to let a doctor examine it. Instead, he went into mourning, and ordered an early burial. The neighbours were understandably suspicious. Philip hinted that his father had committed suicide.

Smeared with blood

The Rev. Bell told everybody that he had talked with Sir James throughout the whole evening before his death, and that he had been perfectly cheerful and normal. Finally, an exhumation was ordered. And it was immediately clear that Sir James Stansfield had been throttled with considerable violence.

And now a strange thing happened. Philip Stansfield was one of those who helped to lift his father's body out of its coffin and on to the autopsy bench. As soon as he touched it, the corpse began to bleed, so that Philip's hands were smeared with blood. The explanation may be simply that the body was scratched on some nail sticking up from the edge of the coffin. But in those days it was firmly believed that the corpse of a murdered person would bleed if the murderer touched it. Philip shouted 'Lord help me', and rushed out of the room, confirming the general suspicion.

At this point, two children came forward with damning evidence. They lived in the cottage of a labourer named James Thomson, one of Sir James's servants; it is not clear from the evidence whether Thomson was their father, or whether they were also servants lodging in the same cottage. They had heard Philip Stansfield, James Thomson and a prostitute named Janet Johnston discussing in detail how Sir James could be killed.

In the early hours of the morning, Thomson and Philip left. A long time later, Thomson returned alone. When his wife asked him where he had been, he said that 'the deed was done', and that they had thrown the body into the pond. It seems to have been Thomson who committed the actual murder, while Philip stood guard outside the door.

Philip was tried at Edinburgh and duly hanged – as well as having his hand cut off and his tongue cut out.

Neurotic insecurity

Nearly two centuries later, another crime by a wealthy man touched the imagination of the British public. He was John Tawell, a middle-aged Quaker who had made his fortune in Australia. Tawell had been transported to Australia for forgery as a young man. Having served his sentence, he became a chemist in Sydney. Within a few years he was able to sell his business for £14,000.

He invested this in land, and soon became a property millionaire. He also 'cornered' the whalebone market – in those days, whalebone was in continual demand for corsets, combs and brushes. When he returned to England, he was a very rich man. He had joined the Quakers and habitually wore the Quaker habit.

He bought himself a large house in Berkhamsted, took a pretty servant girl named Sarah Hadler as a mistress, and all seemed to go well. But when Sarah became pregnant, he decided to install her elsewhere, to avoid scandal. In 1845, she was living in a house at Salt Hill, near Slough. She had a second child by Tawell, who visited her regularly and allowed her a pound a week.

Then he decided to marry – a local heiress named Miss Catford. Australia was going through a period of economic depression, and his income from his land had diminished. He was still rich, but the old, neurotic insecurity of the 'right man' suddenly gripped him. He felt that Sarah, whom he no longer loved, was an unnecessary drain on his income. In September 1843, after a visit from Tawell, she suddenly became ill, and was sick for several days; but she recovered.

On New Year's Day 1845, Tawell visited her again, and sent her out for some stout. The two of them drank this; then Sarah clutched her stomach and began to groan and roll on the floor. A next-door neighbour heard the noises and came out to see what was wrong; she saw Tawell fumbling nervously to unlatch the gate. He muttered something to her and rushed off down the road. By the time the doctor arrived, she was dead.

Half an hour later, the Slough police despatched a telegram to Paddington: 'A murder has just been committed at Salt Hill, and the suspected murderer was seen to take a first-class ticket for London by the train which left Slough at 7.42 p.m.' The result was that when Tawell got off the train, he was followed by police; the driver of the omnibus he took to a lodging house in the borough was a policeman in disguise.

He denied having been in Slough, but his denial was hopeless. A post mortem on Sarah Hadler revealed that she had died by poison – prussic acid. The chemist was found who had sold him the poison on the morning of the murder. The defence argued that Sarah could have died from eating too many apple pips, but the jury were unconvinced, and Tawell was hanged on March 28, 1845, after making a full confession to the murder.

Insane jealousy

The case of John Tawell invites comparison with that of another 'murderous millionaire' who made his fortune in Australia: Thomas Ley, who was at one time Minister of Justice in New South Wales. Ley's business methods had been dubious, and he had been suspected of disposing of at least one business rival. Back in England in the early 1930s, he became the lover of Mrs. Maggie Brook, the wife of an ex-colleague; and although their sexual relations ceased after a few years, he continued to regard her with insane jealousy.

In 1946, he became convinced that Mrs. Brook – now 66 – was having a love affair with a young barman, John Mudie. In fact, she had only spoken to him once. On November 28, 1946, Mudie was lured to Ley's house in Beaufort Gardens, Kensington, by a lady who believed that Mudie was a blackmailer, and that Ley wanted to force him to leave the country. Mudie was overpowered, brutally beaten up by Ley, then probably strangled by an accomplice, John Lawrence Smith, a builder's foreman hired by Ley.

Ley and Smith then drove the corpse to a chalk pit near Woldingham, in Surrey, and dumped it there. It was found two days later. When Mudie was identified, the police discovered letters from Ley in his room. Ley and Smith stood trial together, and were sentenced to death. However, Ley was found to be insane, and died within three months of entering Broadmoor. Smith's sentence was commuted to life imprisonment.

The conclusion, then, would seem to be that while most 'murderous millionaires' are violent men – in Van Vogt's sense – few of them furnish evidence of the anarchist contention that it is their power that has corrupted them. Perhaps the last word should be left with Bernard Shaw, who wrote: 'Power does not corrupt men; fools, however, if they get into a position of power, corrupt power.'

OCCULT DETECTION

On a June day in 1943, a young house-painter named Pieter Van der Hurk slipped and fell 30 feet from a ladder. When he woke up in the Zuidwal Hospital in The Hague, he had a severe skull fracture and a broken shoulder. As he opened his eyes, a nurse was holding his wrist, taking his pulse. Suddenly a clear picture came into his head. He said painfully: 'Be careful. I can see you on a train. You may lose a suitcase that belongs to a friend of yours.'

The girl looked at him in amazement. 'As a matter of fact, I *have* just arrived by train, and I *did* leave a friend's suitcase behind in the dining car. How did you know?' But Pieter Van der Hurk had no idea how he 'knew'; the idea had simply come into his head. When the nurse had gone, he turned to another patient and found himself saying: 'You are a bad man.' 'Why?' asked the patient, with some amusement. 'Because when your father died recently he left you a gold watch, and you have already sold it.' The man gasped, 'My God. . . you're right. How did you know?'

Many people were to ask Pieter Van der Hurk – now world-famous as Peter Hurkos, the clairvoyant – that question in the future. And science is still unable to answer it. Hurkos can pick up some common article – a glove or an umbrella – and suddenly 'know' all about the owner. In 1958 Hurkos was asked by the police of Miami, Florida, to sit in the cab of a murdered taxi driver and give his impressions of the killer.

As he sat there, Hurkos described the murder of the driver in detail. Then he went on to describe the killer – tall and thin, and a tattoo on his right arm, a rolling walk like a sailor. His name, Hurkos said, was Smitty, and he had been responsible for another murder in Miami, a naval man shot to death in his apartment. The police were amazed; for there *had* been such a murder recently, but they had not connected it with the cab-driver killing.

'Smitty' sounded an unlikely name, but many Smiths are given that nickname. The police came up with a rogues' gallery picture of a sailor called Charles Smith, and it was identified by a waitress who described a conversation with a drunken sailor who had boasted of killing two men. A 'wanted' notice for Smith went out to police stations all over America; Smith was recognized in New Orleans after a hold-up, and sent back to Miami. He was charged only with the murder of the cabbie, and sentenced to life imprisonment.

Incomprehensible

This raises the absorbing question: how can anyone 'see' things that are not actually present? Hurkos has been 'tested' hundreds of times by parapsychologists. So has the other remarkable Dutch clairvoyant, Gerard Croiset. Both have been found to be genuine, and both have helped solve many murder cases, and yet their powers remain incomprehensible to science.

One of the most convincing theories has been suggested by the American student of parapsychology Alan Vaughan in his book *Patterns of Prophecy*. Vaughan begins by speaking of the concept of 'synchronicity', invented by the psychologist Carl Jung. Synchronicity is another name for 'coincidence that isn't really coincidence'. We have all been amazed by some million-to-one chance: perhaps going to a strange city and bumping into an acquaintance from the other side of the world. Or hearing a word or name for the first time, and then hearing it several more times in the course of the same day.

On these occasions we have a suspicion that 'fate' is taking a hand. Certainly there can be no possible doubt about the reality of 'precognition', knowing something before it happens. There is a machine at the Maimonides Medical Centre in Brooklyn for testing precognition. It flashes a series of five lights in a random manner; each flash comes a split second after an experimenter has pushed a button to try to predict which light will come on next. After a hundred or so tries, most people score precisely what would be expected from chance. But, for some odd reason, a few people can produce scores – consistently – that are a *thousand to one above chance*.

What Alan Vaughan suggests is that if 'synchronicity' is 'a meaningful coincidence without a normal cause', this is the same as saying that it has a *para-normal* cause, a cause that goes beyond what we regard as 'normal'. This sounds rather mystical, but it is not necessarily so. There are millions of 'patterns' that are not obviously visible to the naked eye: the patterns inside the atoms, the patterns of the planets in the solar system.

Is it not possible that human beings also fall into 'types' or patterns, and that therefore, in a sense, they are already carrying their 'fate' around inside them when they are born? This is not to say that *everything* that happens to them is 'predestined'. Perhaps it is only a general pattern, with plenty of room for variation, but this would certainly help to explain, for example, how the 'psychic' Jeanne Dixon was able to state in an interview in *Parade* magazine for May 13, 1956: 'As for the 1960 election, it will be dominated by labour and won by a Democrat. But he will be assassinated or die in office. . .', foretelling the Kennedy murder with frightening accuracy.

Discussions of the precise nature of these powers of prophecy and precognition could go on forever. But one thing seems to be unarguable: we all have the *potential* of suddenly 'knowing' things that we cannot possibly know in the ordinary way. Sometimes it is simply a strong 'hunch'; sometimes a premonition may come in a dream. Sometimes we may actually seem to hear a voice inside the head.

Second sight

One interesting point emerges from the experience of Peter Hurkos. After he left the hospital, he continued to possess 'second sight', but he was completely incapable of returning to his old job as a house-painter: he was no longer able to concentrate. He was like a radio set picking up too many stations at the same time, and he only solved this problem by deciding to use his powers on the music halls. It is possible that we do not usually possess powers of precognition or second-sight because we don't *want* them. They would make everyday life extremely difficult.

And so it seems increasingly likely, as the study of parapsychology is taken up by more and more universities, that our ancestors were not simply revealing ignorant credulity when they believed strange tales about dreams: dreams are one of the methods by which the subconscious mind speaks to us. All modern writers who have discussed the case of Maria Marten and the murder in the Red Barn have asked whether it can be true that the victim's stepmother had a series of dreams in which she saw Maria murdered by her lover William Corder and buried in the Red Barn.

But most primitive people would take it for granted that a dream *could* reveal a murder. The writer Norman Lewis, who spent some time with the Mexican *shaman* – 'medicine man' –

Ramon Medina, described how, in the village of San Andre, Medina 'sensed death', and walked straight up to a house – where the corpse of a murdered man was found concealed in the attic. Lewis adds that everyone in that part of the world, even the Jesuit missionaries, would accept that Medina discovered the corpse by 'extra-sensory perception'. It is simply taken for granted.

The case of Maria Marten is by no means the only one that has been solved by 'extra-sensory perception'; there are dozens more, and many of them are better authenticated than the Red Barn murder.

Thought-reader

The remarkable Booher case, which took place in Canada, was solved by a thought-reader. The Booher family ran a farm at Manville, near Edmonton, Alberta. On July 9, 1928, a multiple murder took place at the ranch. The son, Vernon Booher, contacted the police and notified them that he had found his mother and brother shot dead, and when the police arrived they also found the bodies of two farmhands named Cromby and Rosyk. Cromby was in the bunkhouse, Rosyk in an outhouse, while Mrs. Booher had been killed in her kitchen, and her son Fred in the next room. All had been shot with a .303 rifle. The question of motive was baffling, for nothing had been stolen.

The police soon discovered that the murder weapon belonged to a neighbour named Charles Stephenson; however, Stephenson alleged that it had been stolen from his home the Sunday before the murder.

The local police chief had recently heard about a Viennese 'psychic' called Dr. Maximilien Langsner; he had recently appeared in the newspapers when he had helped the Vancouver police to trace some stolen jewellery by reading the mind of a suspect. Langsner was asked if he would come and help. He attended the inquest on the victims, and when it was over he told the police that the murderer was the man who found the bodies – Vernon Booher. He had also read in Booher's mind precisely where he had hidden the rifle. Langsner led the police to a clump of prairie grass on the Booher farm, and the rifle was found there.

The question was motive. Langsner had to admit that he had not been able to find out why Vernon had killed four people. However, he said, if he could be placed somewhere near Vernon Booher for a short time he should be able to remedy this. Booher had been booked as a material witness and was in the cells in Edmonton. He looked up suspiciously when Langsner sat on a chair outside his cell; but when the little man only sat there, staring into space, he gradually relaxed.

An hour later, without a word, Langsner stood up and went into the police chief. 'I've found out why he did it.' Vernon had wanted to marry the daughter of a local farmer; his mother, something of a martinet, refused her consent. After a violent quarrel in the kitchen, Vernon had seized the rifle and shot her. He had then been forced to kill his brother, in the next room. The hired men might have seen him enter the farmhouse, so he crept up on them and shot them too.

Was there any evidence of this, the chief asked? Well, said Langsner, a little woman in a poke bonnet had seen Vernon sneak out of church on Sunday, at the time the rifle was stolen. It was not difficult to find her; her name was Erna Higgins. When she confronted Vernon with the words 'I saw you leave the church the day Charlie's rifle was stolen', Booher suddenly broke down and confessed to the murders. His description of what had occurred corresponded in detail to what Langsner had said. He was hanged on April 29, 1929. As to Langsner, he remained on the American continent, moving to a small hut in Alaska, near Fairbanks, to continue his research into 'brain waves', and it was there that he died a few years later.

Brain rhythms

Whether the study of 'brain waves' would have given him insight into his own peculiar powers is debatable. Physiologists have identified various brain rhythms — alpha, gamma, theta waves — but none of these seems to have anything to do with thought-transference. Possibly, Langsner was reasoning falsely from his own power to read minds. Both Peter Hurkos and Gerard Croiset have the same power, but they can also 'sense' what has happened to objects — and objects obviously have no thought waves to transmit. What they *may* have is some kind of 'field'.

One writer on parapsychology, Edward Russell, suggests that these may actually be 'thought fields' that have become attached to particular objects, especially if they have been involved in powerful negative emotions – violence, for example. Many years ago, C.J. Lambert produced a remarkable book called *Together We Wandered*, describing how, in 1928, he and his wife set off on a world cruise and bought a statuette of the Japanese god of luck Ho-tei.

Appalling

From then on their bad luck was constant and appalling – mostly in the form of incomprehensible toothaches. When they showed Ho-tei to another couple, the couple were convulsed with toothaches. It suddenly struck Lambert that when Ho-tei was packed in his baggage he had toothache; when the god was transferred to his wife she had toothache. Back in London, he took the statuette to a Japanese art shop.

The manager and an art expert explained that certain 'temple gods' were given 'souls', small papers engraved with magic symbols and hidden inside them. This was one. Obviously Ho-tei's 'soul' was capable of causing toothache to anyone who treated him without due respect – for example, who lugged him around the world packed among shirts. The manager placed the god on a shrine, lit joss sticks in front of it – and Lambert walked out of the shop, leaving his toothache behind.

This is obviously not an explanation of the odd powers of Hurkos and Croiset; only the beginning of a theory. There are many people who would take a totally different view: that such strange happenings may be due to the active intervention of the dead: for example, in the Red Barn murder and the killing of Eric Tombe. Similarly, in the case of the sex murder of 10-year-old Mona Tinsley, the medium Estelle Roberts was able to tell the police that the body had been dumped in a river – many months before it was found in the River Idle. A 44-year-old degenerate named Frederick Nodder was executed for the murder in 1937.

In this case, the medium's prediction did not actually lead to the finding of the body. On the other hand, in October 1956 the South African medium Nelson Palmer was able to lead the police to the naked body of Myrna Joy Aken in a culvert near Durban. The girl had been seen entering a Ford Anglia car, and the police traced this to a radio shop, where the manager was able to tell them that on the day of the murder it had been used by a salesman called Clarence van Buuren, who had since vanished.

Buuren was finally arrested near Pinetown and charged with the sex murder of the girl. He insisted on his innocence to the end, claiming that he had fled only because he knew he had been seen in the girl's company on the day of her death.

He had a considerable past record of crime – forgery, theft, bad cheques – and was in possession of a revolver of the same type that killed Joy Aken. Not long after leading the police to Joy

Aken's body, Nelson Palmer duplicated his feat, leading the police to the body of a doctor who had committed suicide.

No general theory covers all these phenomena; but now that parapsychology is at last being taken seriously by so many researchers, the day cannot be far off when some parapsychological Einstein finally produces a key to this strange world of the 'occult'.

OFFICE CRIMES

The annals of criminology reveal that respectable, middle-class citizens are just as likely to commit premeditated murder as any other class of society. Doctors, lawyers, solicitors, and even clergymen have all been found guilty of murder in the first degree. Yet few, if any, of these homicidal members of the *bourgeoisie* have committed murder at their place of business. There may be an interesting psychological reason for this; perhaps they regard 'the office' as sacred. Or perhaps they are simply deterred by the possibility of interruption by the cleaner. The fact remains that office murders are very rare indeed; and the few that are known present an extraordinary cross-section of method and motive.

In England, the earliest recorded case took place in 1839. At two o'clock in the morning of December 7 flames were seen inside the Newcastle-upon-Tyne Savings Bank. The fire brigade was called, and the fire was soon under control. The police broke in, and went into the office of the clerk, Joseph Millie. He was lying on the floor, and the blow that killed him had been of such violence that his brains were splashed around the room.

In the next office they found the manager, Archibald Bolam, who was also stretched out on the floor, blood streaming from his throat. But the wounds were not deep, and he soon recovered enough to describe what had happened. He had recently received several anonymous letters, threatening his life. One had been pushed under the bank door on the previous day, threatening that he would be attacked at home, and Bolam had decided to go home and see that everything was all right. He had gone back to the bank at seven in the evening, let himself in, and seen the clerk Millie lying down 'as if asleep'. Before he could investigate, someone struck him on the head. It was a man whose face had been blackened. As he tried to rush towards the door he was struck a second time, and collapsed.

The story was suspicious; a man whose brains have been scattered all over the room does not look as if he is asleep. Bolam said he had returned to the office at seven in the evening; even if knocked unconscious, he would have awakened before 2 a.m. What had the robber been doing during all that time? He obviously stayed until after midnight to start the fire. Bolam was asked what he had done with the threatening letters; he claimed he had burned them. The most recent one, he said, had been left on his desk, and the intruder must have taken it.

But there was one simple inconsistency in his story that convinced the police he was lying. He claimed he was lying on his back when he felt the knife against his throat, and then lost consciousness. He woke up, he said, only after the police burst in. But there had been blood *down his shirtfront*. Which suggested that he had inflicted the wounds while sitting up, and then lay down.

Coal was found in the pockets of the dead clerk; evidently somebody had wanted him to burn thoroughly. Why should the black-faced intruder bother? The police searched Bolam's house and found a large sum of money in gold. Bolam was arrested and charged with the murder.

In the England of 1839, carefully premeditated murder was still enough of a rarity to cause nationwide excitement. There was strong feeling against Bolam, particularly in Newcastle, for Millie had been a hard-working man, with four children. His wife had died, and he had looked after the children himself. Like Dicken's Bob Cratchit, he was overworked and underpaid.

Benefit of the doubt

There was so much sympathy that £1000 was raised for the children, and the bank owner also gave them a pension. Feeling against Bolam ran high, so that his trial was delayed until the July Assizes the following year, and although the evidence made it abundantly clear that he had stolen the money and then murdered the clerk and 'staged' the attack and the fire, the jury decided to give him the benefit of the doubt. The judge suggested that Bolam had killed Millie during a quarrel, then attempted to commit suicide. Bolam was sentenced to transportation for life.

The square mile of the City of London might be expected to provide many examples of office murders, but in fact there are none, unless we count a murder that took place in the Lombard Street post office on November 10, 1902. An attractive young girl named Kittie Byron had sent a messenger boy to her lover's

City office, asking him to come immediately to the post office. Her lover, Reginald Baker, was a stockbroker. He arrived at the office while the Lord Mayor's show was going past, and most of the staff were staring out of the window.

An office clerk pointed out to Baker that there was twopence to pay for the messenger boy, but he refused indignantly. Kittie offered him two shillings to pay; he still refused. He turned and started to walk away. In the yard outside he was heard to say: 'No I won't' in a loud voice. Then Kittie rushed at him, raising her muff, and began to strike him. To the clerk it looked as if she was hitting him with the muff. Baker collapsed, stabbed in the back and the chest. He died instantly. A man grabbed the knife from Kittie's hand and she was arrested. She tried to drop to her knees and kiss the dead man.

Kittie Byron aroused a great deal of sympathy at her trial. A pretty girl, 23 years old, she managed to give an impression of wronged innocence. Baker was not her husband; they were living together in rooms in Duke Street. Baker was obviously well-off, and 'upper-class', while Kittie was 'a girl of the people'. Baker drank too much, and when he got drunk he became violent. After a quarrel on November 8 – in which Baker seemed to do most of the shouting – their landlady had given them notice to quit.

A maid overheard Baker telling the landlady that Kittie was not his wife, that she had 'no class', and that she would have to go the next day. The maid hurried to tell Kittie – and so precipitated a murder. On Monday morning, Kittie had bought a knife for 5s. 6d., and then sent the message to Baker's office. Her defence lawyer argued that she intended to try to win Baker back by stabbing herself in front of him. Evidence of premeditation was too strong, and she was sentenced to death, but a public petition to the Home Secretary saved her life; she was reprieved, and spent less than 10 years in jail.

A cast-iron alibi

The City has had its share of attempted murders. One of the oddest occurred in 1925, when a wealthy Armenian merchant, Zarch Avedis Ekisler, was found unconscious in a ransacked office. Serious head injuries had been inflicted with a poker, but although he spent weeks close to death, Ekisler finally recovered, and mentioned the name of a friend as the attacker. The friend was arrested, but when he was brought in front of Ekisler, the merchant said, 'This is not the man.' In fact, it later proved that the friend had a cast-iron alibi. The beating had caused Ekisler's memory to play tricks, and he was never able to recall anything about the attack or his attacker.

In 1903, there was an attempted murder in the Bank of England itself. Just before Christmas of that year a young man walked into the bank and asked to see an official named Kenneth Grahame, who five years later became world famous as the author of the children's classic *The Wind in the Willows*. He carried a roll of paper, tied at one end with white ribbon and at the other end with black. In Grahame's office, he presented the roll; Grahame untied the black ribbon – whereupon the man drew a revolver and fired several shots at him. His aim was poor, and Grahame was only slightly wounded.

The man rushed out, shouting, 'Come on, you cowards and curs', and dodged into another room. A detective inspector on duty at the bank went into the room, ignoring the man's revolver, and tried to pacify him. Then suddenly, the door was hurled open, and a jet of water from the bank firehose hit the gunman full in the chest, making him stagger.

Ribbon of death

At the police station in the Old Jewry he gave his captors a lecture on economics and the injustice of the present distribution of wealth. His name was George Frederick Robinson, and he was an engineer. He explained that he had decided that if Grahame opened the roll by untying the white ribbon, he would spare his life. Grahame chose the black ribbon. At Robinson's trial it was revealed that a dog bite had made him insane, and he was committed to a mental home.

It is possible that there was also a touch of insanity in the extraordinary crook and blackmailer who called himself Von Veltheim, and whose real name was Karl Kutze. Kutze was a huge, handsome German, nearly 6 feet 6 inches tall, and with the perfectly proportioned body of an athlete. He was one of the most remarkable international criminals around at the beginning of this century.

Karl Kutze was born in Brunswick in 1857, and when he was a teenager ran away to sea with money raised on the family silver. He borrowed his alias, Von Veltheim, from a German Captain, whom he served as batman – and eventually robbed and deserted. In 1886, he married an Australian girl. On the boat to England he noticed that a rich passenger was charmed by her; he encouraged her to have an affair with the man, got compromising letters from him, and then blackmailed him for a huge sum of money. Then Kutze moved on to South America – without his wife – and somehow managed to bluff his way into the post of American consul in the state of Santa Marta – he was a man of immense charm, and a brilliant talker.

When Kutze subsequently fled from South America, a large sum of money from the consular fund went with him. The international police stopped looking for him in 1896, when the body of a huge man – trussed in ropes – was fished out of the Thames; Kutze's Australian wife heard about it, insisted on an exhumation and identified the corpse as that of her husband. In fact, 'Von Veltheim' was now in South Africa.

In 1897, the South African millionaire Barney Barnato vanished mysteriously from a ship in mid-ocean. His many businesses passed into the hands of two nephews, Woolf and Solly Joel, and Von Veltheim decided that it was worth trying to dip his hand into the Barnato coffers. He approached the Joel brothers, explaining that he and Barnato had been in 'secret business' – which, included, according to Veltheim, the kidnapping of the Boer president Kruger – and that Barnato owed him £50,000.

The nephews disbelieved him and ordered him to get out. He began to bombard them with violent letters, threatening to kill them unless they paid the money – although he finally reduced his demand to £12,000. Johannesburg in those days was only slightly less chaotic and lawless than the Wild West, so instead of calling in the police, Woolf Joel agreed to meet Veltheim. He changed his mind at the last minute, but Veltheim managed to get into the office.

He shouted: 'If you don't pay me, I'll kill you,' and reached for his gun. Woolf Joel pulled out his own revolver; so did his manager, Mr. Strange. Strange fired first, and missed. Then Von Veltheim fired – and the millionaire fell dead.

He was arrested and tried. In court, he turned on his tremendous charm. His defence pointed out that Strange had fired first, and that his client was only acting in self-defence. The prosecution replied that he was a blackmailer and had threatened both brothers with death. It made no difference; after a nine-day trial, the jury acquitted him, and the South African authorities ordered him out of the country.

Hidden treasure

There were more astonishing adventures: he was arrested at Delegoa Bay and deported to England, where he had several 'wives'; he fled back to South Africa, was imprisoned there, then rescued by British troops fighting the Boers. He moved to Trieste, posed as the son of an Austrian general who knew where Kruger's 'hidden treasure' was buried, and managed to swindle a real general out of £20,000. Using this money, he posed as a wealthy aristocrat, and married a pretty rich girl – then vanished again, taking her money and jewellery.

He married a Greek girl for her dowry of £2000, and during the course of the next few years added two more 'wives' to his collection – he impregnated most of his wives, and left a trail of bastards across the world. But finally, in 1906, he made his major error: he again approached Solly Joel, and tried to blackmail him. The enraged millionaire decided this had to stop, and the machinery of international law ground into action.

Scotland Yard tracked Veltheim to Antwerp – and lost him again when he vanished with the wife of a wealthy merchant. Finally, in 1907, they caught up with him in Paris; it was the end of the career of one of the world's greatest crooks. Back in London, he was charged with blackmailing and threatening to kill Solly Joel; it was a classic trial. Tall, erect, very handsome, Von Veltheim seemed quite confident that he would walk out of the court a free man.

The prosecuting attorney, Charles Gill, proceeded to cut him to ribbons. He pricked Veltheim's lies like balloons. Veltheim fell back on the device of pretending that he couldn't tell everything he knew because of all the famous international figures who would be compromised. Gill questioned him about his relations with Woolf Joel, and then showed him up as a liar by quoting from statements he had made in the court case in 1898. Von Veltheim now stood exposed for what he was – a 'smoothy' who had spent his life cheating and lying. Even so, it seemed likely that he might escape with a light sentence – from two to five years. The court gasped when Mr. Justice Coleridge said: 'Twenty years' penal servitude.'

An unjust verdict

In the strictly legal sense, there can be no doubt the sentence was extreme. The court was sentencing Veltheim for what he was, not for trying to blackmail Solly Joel, and like the judge who later sentenced the Krays, Mr. Justice Coleridge obviously felt that society deserved a long rest from Von Veltheim. After the 1914 war the British government released him from Dartmoor and shipped him back to Hamburg. He died there, in 1932, a poverty-stricken old man.

France's most famous office murder took place on the afternoon of March 16, 1914, when Gaston Calmet, the editor of *Figaro*, agreed to see Madame Caillaux, the wife of the finance minister, who had been the target for some of Calmet's most vitriolic attacks. That morning, President Poincaré had told Joseph Caillaux that he could do nothing to prevent *Figaro* from publishing certain private letters that the minister had written to his present wife while still married to the previous one. Madame Caillaux took a revolver out of her muff and fired at the editor, until he collapsed over his desk. The jury acquitted Madame Caillaux – to the delight of the French public.

America has had no office murder to rival the Caillaux case in sheer scandal value, for Wall Street's most famous office murder was a mere by-product of a far greater catastrophe, the great explosion of 1920. At noon on September 16, 1920, a horse-drawn wagon pulled up opposite the J.P. Morgan building in the heart of New York's financial centre. Whether the two men who drove the wagon remained there is not known, but 57 seconds later a tremendous explosion reduced the wagon to a tiny pile of twisted metal and blew the horse into so many pieces that it vanished completely.

Flying glass victim

Undoubtedly 'office murder' was intended – probably of workers in the office of the millionaire J.P. Morgan, possibly officials of the Federal Subtreasury building, close to the explosion. Since the street was crowded with workers on their way to lunch, loss of life was great – 31 killed, and dozens seriously injured. The only victim who was actually in an office at the time was Thomas Joyce, the chief clerk of the Morgan office, killed by flying glass.

Arthur Carey, Chief of the Homicide Bureau, became convinced that the explosion had been caused by anarchists. Close examination of two horse-shoes – all that remained of the horse – finally led him to the Italian blacksmith who had shod the horse on the morning of the explosion. The blacksmith was terrified of reprisals from the anarchists, but after hours of persuasion he agreed to help the police, if they would guarantee that his name would not be revealed.

They promised, and the blacksmith arranged to come to the police headquarters early the next day and take disguised policemen on a tour of the Italian district in an attempt to pick out the two men. But the next morning, to the fury of the police, a newspaper revealed the identity of the blacksmith, and the terrified man flatly refused to cooperate further. No doubt Chief Cary must have felt like treating the editor as Madame Caillaux treated Calmet. He never found who had 'leaked' the story to the press, and the men who caused the Wall Street explosion were never caught.

Almost 40 years later, in September 1959, the New York police began a massive manhunt for another criminal who chose offices as his field of activity. This man was not a murderer, but a rapist. He operated along Madison Avenue. At the end of the day, as New Yorkers were rushing for the subways, a lightly built Negro would stroll into office buildings and walk casually along the corridors. No one would question him; it was assumed he was a janitor.

He would glance into offices until he found one in which a solitary girl was working at her typewriter. He would go in, close the door quietly behind him, and produce a gun. The girl was made to enter an empty office where there was minimum risk of interruption; then she was made to undress, and was raped. One woman ran, screaming and half undressed, into the street; but her attacker had vanished by the time that police surrounded the buildings. And it was clear that the rapist went out 'hunting' almost every day; in September 1959, 15 girls were assaulted.

The face was familiar
But these victims were able to help a police artist create a composite identikit portrait of the rapist, which was circulated to every police precinct in New York. Patrolman Eugene O'Neill, at the 22nd Street Station, thought he had seen the face somewhere. All day he brooded on it, and then he remembered: it was a young Negro named Henry Iszard, who lived in the Bronx. While the police were in the apartment, questioning Iszard's young wife, another rape was reported – the sixteenth.

And at midnight, as the wife sat in a chair holding her small son, the door opened, and Henry Iszard stepped in – and into the arms of waiting policemen. He was identified by most of the victims. The New York police heaved a sigh of relief. The case of the Madison Avenue office rapist had been solved before it turned into a case of murder. Iszard was sentenced to between 60 and 100 years in prison.

It may seem odd that, since Archibald Bolam killed Joseph Millie in 1839, there have been so few office murders, but it is an oddity for which the police of every large city are grateful.

PARENT KILLERS

According to Freud, the crime of parricide – the murder of parents – is one of mankind's oldest established customs. He theorized that the earliest human beings lived in small hordes, consisting of one powerful male and several females. Naturally, the old male would want all the women to himself, and the only way the younger males could get their share was by rising up and murdering the old man. This, he said, is why man has always been haunted with legends of parricide.

He may have been right; but if so, he failed to explain why ancestor worship is among the oldest of mankind's religions. The ancient Egyptians, Chinese, Japanese, and Hindus worshipped their ancestors as gods, and many African tribes still do. Deep respect for the parents is the basis of Confucian religion – which is still, even in Mao's China, the foundation of morality. Since the earliest times, parricide had been treated as the worst of crimes. Take for example, the grim and bloody story of the Cenci family.

The perfect murder

Francesco Cenci was one of the most vicious reprobates of history. The son of the Treasurer of Pope Pius V, he was the heir to an immense fortune that his father had accumulated by swindling.

Francesco soon discovered that his money gave him immunity. If he wanted to sleep with a beautiful girl, he didn't have to go to the trouble of seducing her; it was easier to have her kidnapped, then rape and sodomize her. When arrested, he simply bought his freedom. Altogether, he paid out over half a million pounds in fines at various times.

Cenci had 12 children by his first wife, and he hated them all. When the eldest two boys died, Cenci remarked that he wouldn't be happy until the others were buried near them. But as his

460

youngest daughter, Beatrice, began to grow up, he found reasons for admiring her more than the others; with her pale skin and auburn hair, she was very beautiful. Cenci was so jealous of her that he transferred her – and his second wife – to a lonely castle near Naples called La Petrella. Francesco now decided to extend his repertoire of crimes to incest.

When a young, rich noble named Guerra – an abbé – made several proposals for Beatrice's hand, her father finally told him the reason for his refusal. 'She is my mistress.' Guerra thought he was lying, and spent three days trying to see Beatrice. Finally, he got his interview – and she admitted that it was true. 'He deserves to die,' said Guerra.

Beatrice, who was disgusted by her father's ill-treatment and avarice, agreed with him. Beatrice's stepmother joined in the plot; so did her brothers Giacomo and Bernardo. It was Giacomo who hired two *sbirri* – a kind of police officer – named Marzio and Olimpio. Marzio was infatuated with Beatrice, and Olimpio had already been her lover – and the keeper of the castle of La Petrella – before Cenci suspected and dismissed him.

On the evening of September 9, 1598, the two women mixed opium with the old man's wine. Always a heavy drinker, Cenci passed out and was carried to his bed. Then the two murderers entered. They took a large nail, hammered it through his eye and into his brain, and drove another nail deep into his throat. The writhing body was then hurled out of the high window, where it caught in the branches of a tree. When it was found the next morning, it was assumed that Cenci had leaned too far off the balcony when he was drunk, and fallen.

It looked like the perfect murder. Except that Cenci's death was a little *too* convenient. A few months after the murder, the wheels of justice began to turn slowly. The court of Naples sent a commissioner to investigate the affair. The only evidence he could find against the plotters was the deposition of a washerwoman, who admitted to washing a bloodstained sheet given to her by Beatrice – who claimed that the blood was menstrual.

Incredible courage

No one really mourned the dead debauchee; but the crime of parricide was too horrible for the authorities to contemplate. If the Cencis were allowed to get away with it, the whole fabric of society might collapse. The court of Naples decided on its favourite means of extorting confessions – torture. The Abbé Guerra heard about these plans, and hired two more *sbirri* to dispose of the murderers. They succeeded in assassinating Olimpio at Terni; but meanwhile Marzio was arrested. Under torture, he confessed. Beatrice, Giacomo, and Bernardo were all arrested. When Marzio saw Beatrice – the woman he still loved – he promptly withdrew his confession.

So the inquisitors thrust the Cencis into the torture chamber. Alexandre Dumas, who tells the story in his *Celebrated Crimes*, goes into gruesome detail. Beatrice was subjected to the *strappado*: that is, she was undressed, her wrists were fastened behind her, and a rope was tied to them. Then she was hauled into the air on a pulley. The effect was to dislocate her shoulders. With incredible courage, she denied everything. Weights were attached to her feet, and every time she fainted, she was lowered to the ground. Then, as soon as she opened her eyes, she was hauled up again. Her brother Bernardo showed less fortitude; he confessed. So did Giacomo, whose flesh had been torn from his body with red hot pincers.

Relatively law-abiding

Appeals were directed to the Pope, Clement VIII. He was sympathetic, and about to grant a reprieve, when news came of another case of parricide: the Marquis of Santa Croce had been stabbed to death by his son Paul. That settled it. Parricide was becoming an epidemic. The death sentences were confirmed. On September 11, 1599 – almost a year to the day after the murder – the Cencis went to the scaffold. Beatrice was the first to be beheaded, and the executioner displayed her head to the crowd. Next came Lucrezia. Giacomo was killed by having his head smashed with a mace. Only Bernardo received a last-minute pardon from the Pope, and a sentence of life imprisonment. (He was freed after a year.) Marzio had already died under torture. Guerra was the one conspirator who managed to escape; he fled from Italy, and was never heard of again.

The grim story has fascinated generations of historians, novelists, and playwrights; the poet Shelley made it the subject of his greatest play. Modern historians are inclined to reject the evidence that Cenci raped his daughter. But whether it is true or not, there can be no doubt that Francesco Cenci was guilty of far worse crimes than the one for which his children were executed.

Compared to the passionate and excitable Italians, the inhabitants of Britain are relatively law-abiding. Yet, surprisingly enough, England has produced a number of classic parricides. The case that invites comparison with the Cenci murder is that of Mary Blandy, executed in 1752 for the murder of her father. Ever since then, writers on crime have argued about whether she was guilty or not.

Mary was the daughter of Francis Blandy, an attorney of Henley-on-Thames. Her father was anxious that she should make a good marriage, and let it be known that she would have a dowry of £10,000 – a vast sum in those days. In fact, Blandy's total fortune was less than half that amount. The suitors came by the dozen, and were all rejected by Mr. Blandy. Time drifted by, and Mary was approaching 30. Then one day, at an aristocratic house, she met the Honourable William Cranstoun.

Gullible girl

He was short and bandy-legged, but his manners appealed to the amiable and placid Mary. One day, Cranstoun confessed that he was in love with her, and added that he was entangled with a mistress who claimed to be his wife. Mary agreed to marry him as soon as this problem was sorted out. This time her father agreed. Cranstoun may have been poor, but he was the son of a Scottish earl. He returned to Henley-on-Thames as a house guest of the Blandys, and his intimacy with Mary ripened.

Then came a setback. One of the captain's relatives wrote to tell Mr. Blandy that the 'mistress' about whom Cranstoun had confessed was actually his wife. There were harsh words; but finally Cranstoun convinced the family that he was unmarried. For the next six months he lived with them, and Mary became his real mistress. Then the abandoned wife took him to a Scottish court, which found the marriage to be legal. This time, Mr. Blandy turned against his prospective son-in-law and told Mary to forget him.

In truth, Mary adored her father, and had always been an obedient daughter. But she was in love with Cranstoun. They continued to correspond, and one day it struck Cranstoun that the answer to his problems would be to remove Mr. Blandy. Accordingly, he hit upon a cunning plan. First, he gave Mary a powder which, he said, would make her father altogether more amiable. Mary put it into her father's tea, and it seemed to work; for a few days, he was less bad-tempered. So when Cranstoun sent her more powder, Mary had no hesitation in putting it in her father's food and drink.

She seems to have been a singularly gullible girl. When she discovered that her lover had another woman in London, she forgave him. When one of the servants drank some of her father's tea, and immediately became ill, she still had no suspicion that Cranstoun's powder was to blame. She introduced the powder into oatmeal soup, and her father became ill as soon as he ate some. The cook tried the soup, and also became ill. The housemaid, Susan, had a small taste, and was sick for two days. Susan took the soup to the local chemist for analysis, and she warned Mr. Blandy that he was being poisoned.

Francis Blandy undoubtedly loved his daughter. He hinted at his suspicion so plainly that she was panic-stricken, and threw the rest of the powder on the kitchen fire. As soon as she left the kitchen, the cook rescued it, and took it to the chemist – who soon pronounced it to be arsenic. Mary drew the net more tightly around her when she wrote her lover a letter, warning him to be careful. She gave it to a clerk to post; he opened it, and handed it to the chemist.

On August 14, 1751, Francis Blandy died. He had told Mary that he thought she had poisoned him, and that he forgave her. When Captain Cranstoun heard of Blandy's death, he fled to France. Mary was arrested and charged with murder.

Love potion
The trial was chiefly of interest because of the detailed scientific evidence of the poisoning. Mary's defence was that she believed the poison to be a love potion to make her father change his mind. In retrospect, this seems to be true: why, otherwise, did she fail to get rid of the incriminating soup and tea? The jury disbelieved her, and she was hanged – asking the executioner not to hang her too high 'for the sake of decency'. Cranstoun died in poverty just over six months later.

There is an interesting sidelight on the case. When she was in prison, Mary Blandy heard about another woman condemned to death; Elizabeth Jeffries had plotted with her lover to murder her uncle. The novelist Horace Walpole wrote in a letter that the motive behind the murder was that the uncle had debauched his niece. Mary and Elizabeth Jeffries entered into a sympathetic correspondence; but before her execution, Elizabeth finally confessed to her part in the crime. Mary was shocked, and wrote her a reproachful letter – which again seems to suggest that she was innocent.

In the present century, one of the most horrifying representatives of parent killers was undoubtedly John Gilbert Graham – who was responsible for the deaths of 43 other people as well as that of his mother. It happened when a DC-6B airliner exploded in mid-air shortly after its takeoff from Denver, Colorado, on November 1, 1955. The wreckage was spread over a five-mile area, and the smell of explosive convinced investigators that the crash had been caused deliberately.

Suicidal impulse

The bomb, it was discovered, had gone off in No. 4 baggage compartment – into which four cases had been loaded at Denver. The passengers who had boarded at Denver were checked. One of them was Mrs. Daisy King, a lady of considerable wealth. Her son, John Graham, a 23-year-old married man with two children, had taken out insurance policies on her life before she left Denver, but had forgotten to sign them. Detectives soon discovered that Graham had a police record for forgery, and his wife mentioned that he had put a 'Christmas package' in his mother's suitcase shortly before she left home.

Under intensive interrogation, John Graham finally admitted that he had made a time bomb with dynamite, and hidden it in his mother's case. He was identified by a man from whom he had bought the timing device. Graham was found guilty, and executed at the Colorado State Penitentiary. He certainly ranks as the most spectacular and hard-hearted of all parricides.

Our own time has seen the emergence of another type of parricide who is both an immature and emotionally disturbed parricide. The central difference is this: that while the criminal-parricide plots his crime with every intention of avoiding its consequences, the psychologically disturbed killer shows a complete lack of realistic foresight, fundamentally driven by a distorted suicidal impulse.

This can be seen in the case of Charles Whitman, the mass-killer of Austin, Texas. On July 31, 1966, Whitman went up to his mother's apartment at midnight, stabbed her, and shot her in the back of the head. In a note he wrote: 'I love my mother with all my heart.' Then he went home to his own apartment, stabbed his sleeping wife three times, and wrapped her naked body in a sheet. After this he continued his note, describing his hatred of his father – whom his mother had left only a few months earlier – ending: 'Life is not worth living.'

This done, he took two rifles, a shotgun and three revolvers up to the observation tower of the University of Texas, and killed the receptionist with a blow from a rifle butt. A few minutes later, some people walked up the stairs. Whitman used the shotgun three times, slaying a 19-year-old youth and his aunt, and seriously wounding the boy's mother. Then, at 11.48 a.m., he began shooting from the top of the clock tower – shooting with a terrifying accuracy. The first victim was a pregnant woman, who collapsed with a bullet in her stomach; a classmate who bent over her was killed instantly. Six more people were shot, and many wounded, within the next half hour.

Police and Texas Rangers who surrounded the bell tower found the angle at which they had to aim impossible. The bullets only struck the walls. A light aircraft was chartered by the police, with a sharpshooter in the passenger seat; but Whitman's deadly fire drove it away. Finally, at 1.24, the police managed to burst into the observation tower, and kill Whitman. An autopsy revealed that he would have died anyway; he had a brain tumour. Sixteen people died as a result of his orgy of destructiveness.

Drug-induced delusions

But perhaps the most typical case of the suicidal parent-killer is that of Miles Giffard, a 26-year-old native of Cornwall. Giffard hated his father, who was clerk of the court to St. Austell magistrates. The two of them were always quarrelling about Giffard's dislike of work. On November 7, 1952, Giffard asked his father if he could borrow the car to drive to London to see his girlfriend; his father refused. That afternoon, while his parents were out, Giffard stayed at home and got drunk on whiskey.

At 7.30 he heard the car returning. He went down to the garage, and beat his father to death with a piece of iron pipe. He then went into the kitchen, and smashed his mother to the ground. When he was sure they were dead, he took the bodies, one by one, in a wheelbarrow, and dumped them over the cliff at the end of the garden. He then got into the car, and drove to London to see his girlfriend.

The bodies were found next day, the car quickly traced, and within 24 hours of killing his parents, Giffard was under arrest. At the trial, his doctor described him as an 'idle little waster'. And in spite of clear evidence that he was schizophrenic, he was sentenced to death and executed. A Cornish jury declined to accept the Freudian explanations of a psychiatrist called by the defence.

In recent years, there has been a marked increase in the number of parricides, particularly in the United States. This is due largely to the increasing use of drugs; in one recent case, a man suffering from drug-induced delusions decapitated his mother, and carefully placed her head on a church altar. Yet the increase is not great enough to support Freud's theory that the majority of people harbour some deep resentment of their parents.

If this was correct, the release of these inhibitions by drugs should have led to a staggering increase in parricide. That this has not occurred suggests that Freud was wrong, and that the Chinese philosopher Confucius was right: most people actually like their parents, and wish them nothing but health, happiness, and long and contented lives.

PERVERTS

The baby-faced, pink-cheeked youth who drove along a quiet road near Coatesville, Pennsylvania, did not look like a killer. But when he set out in his green Ford truck that afternoon of February 11, 1937, he had killing on his mind – and rape.

It was just after 3.30, when the children came out of high school. He passed several girls, but there were always other people around, or other cars on the road. Then he saw, far ahead, a solitary female figure on a lonely stretch of road. Without hesitation, he swerved the truck and struck her, knocking her down. The youth jumped out, picked up the unconscious girl and dumped her in the back.

He drove to a deserted farmhouse and carried the girl inside; there he stripped her and raped her. The schoolgirl seemed to be dead – or so the attacker later claimed. He carried the naked body to the well outside and threw her down it. After that he went home and ate a good dinner. Two days later he returned to the farm with a stick of dynamite, which he threw down the well. The explosion partly covered the body with rubble.

Obsessional neurosis

The police who were confronted with the disappearance of 16-year-old Helen Moyer were at first baffled. They found her shoes and schoolbooks close to the spot where she had been knocked down. The shoes had been split open, and the shattered glass of a headlight suggested that she had been the victim of a hit-and-run driver. But where was she?

When the news of the girl's disappearance became known two people contacted the police. One was a scrapyard worker, and it seemed possible that he had actually seen the 'accident' from a distance. At least, he had seen a green truck swing across the road and hit a telegraph pole. It backed, turned, and hit another pole. Then it had driven off fast.

Helen Moyer's next-door neighbour, a 15-year-old schoolgirl, also came forward. Six days before Helen's disappearance she had accepted a lift from a young man in a green truck; he had a 'baby-face' and wore dirty overalls. He pulled up in a quiet lane and tried to undress her; the girl fought back, and he hit her with a wrench. She had managed to jump out of the truck and run towards a house, and the man drove off.

Police examined the telegraph poles and found flakes of green paint – the same type of paint they had found on Helen's shoes. They began tracing and questioning the owner of every Ford truck in Chester County, and when the Philadelphia police discovered that 20-year-old Alexander Meyer was the owner of a green Ford truck they realized suddenly that this might be their man.

Three years before, Meyer had been sentenced to an indeterminate sentence for firing at two Philadelphia girls with a rifle. He was the son of a well-to-do coal broker from Downington, 12 miles from the place where Helen had disappeared. The medical report from the reformatory said he was a 'constitutional psychopathic inferior, the victim of his own retarded mentality, insensible to pain. . .sadistic and slightly effeminate'.

Meyer was arrested as he was driving his milk truck – the green Ford – and taken in for questioning. At first he denied all knowledge of the girl. Then, when the police pointed out that dents on his truck corroborated the scrap-man's story, and that the paint matched that found on the schoolbooks, he admitted that he *had* knocked Helen down, but said it was an accident. Finally, he told the true story of the attack and the rape, and led the police to the well. There the body was dragged to the surface – minus a leg torn off by the blast. Medical evidence revealed that the girl had been alive when she was thrown in, and that she died by drowning.

Meyer went to the electric chair in April 1937. More than a quarter of a century later the 'Baby-faced Beast' has still not been forgotten in Coatesville.

The horror of the story drives us to ask: why do such things happen, and how can they be prevented? There is no simple answer to either question. Meyer was a 'pervert', like Jack the Ripper, like Peter Kurten, like Harvey Glatman, who indulged his sadistic fantasies by tying up his famale victims and photographing them as they struggled before he finally choked them to death. In psychological terms these men were suffering from 'obsessional neurosis'. One idea dominated their minds to the exclusion of all others.

Most of us have to make a considerable effort to concentrate on a particular subject for more than a fairly short period; we are distracted by things that happen around us. A child may be watching television, but if someone brings him a new toy, he will instantly forget the programme to play with the toy. An older child or a teenager might well finish watching the programme, then examine the toy; it has decided to take one pleasure at a time.

This is sensible – but not entirely desirable, for people who 'take life as it comes', and enjoy the pleasure of the moment spontaneously, are often healthier and happier than more 'sensible' people. An obsessional sense of duty often produces ulcers. We all have to learn to balance our sense of purpose with the ability to just 'open up' and enjoy the present moment. This is something the 'obsessional' cannot do.

An obsessional is *not* necessarily a pervert. Some women are obsessed with cleanliness in the home. Many patients in mental homes wash their hands every time they touch something. Obsession is what happens when the sense of purpose gets wildly out of hand. But if the obsession happens to be sexual, then the community has reason for concern.

Freud's explanation of the obsessional type was that it represented: 'the out-stripping of libidinal development by ego development' – which means simply that a child's 'ego' – his sense of his own importance – grows faster than his 'sense of pleasure' – 'libido' does not refer only to our 'love energies' but to *all* kinds of enjoyment, from playing football to eating an ice cream – but Freud's definition only *describes* the obsessional, without explaining him.

One thing is clear: the pervert is essentially immature. All babies want their own way, and see no reason why they shouldn't have everything they want. If the family background involves a great deal of love and security they soon begin to learn to give – and to give way. They recognize that having their own way in everything would give pain to those they love. So one basic answer to the problem of the obsessional is lack of love in childhood.

Love has the same effect on the personality as sunlight on vegetation: it causes it to grow and ripen. Without love the obsessional sees no need to 'ripen', to try to grow up. Perhaps his parents denied him many things he wanted in childhood, so he harbours a deep feeling of resentment. Later, he feels that society is denying him many things he wants; and so he is prepared to grab it when society is off its guard. The result is behaviour like that of Alexander Meyer, where another human being is treated purely as a dispensable object, like a throwaway handkerchief.

The remorseless ego

In his book *Sex Perversions and Sex Crimes* Dr. Melvin Rheinhardt describes the temperament in two words: the 'remoreseless ego'. The characteristics are always the same: a completely self-enclosed state of mind in which the other person is unreal. The California rapist Harvey Glatman kidnapped models, spent hours — sometimes days — raping them, then killed them.

In 1953 a middle-aged pervert named Carl Folk 'hi-jacked' a trailer containing a man and his wife — Raymond and Betty Allen — tied up the husband, then spent a whole night raping and torturing the wife, who finally died. Folk was so preoccupied that he did not notice the husband's escape, and was startled when Raymond Allen pulled open the door and shot him in the stomach. But it was too late to save Betty Allen. When Raymond Allen shot him, Folk was about to drench the caravan with petrol, to burn the Allens and their baby. He treated them as 'throwaways', whose sole purpose was to provide him with pleasure.

In a sense such perverts are insane. They have allowed their obsession to dominate them until it becomes their sole aim. Yet to call them insane is to evade the central issue. There is undoubtedly an element of *free will* in all this. The pervert *chooses* to be 'insane'.

This can be seen in one of the grimmest cases of 'compulsion' on record, the murder of Alice Porter by Donald Fearn near Pueblo, Colorado, in 1942. Fearn was a 23-year-old railway mechanic, a mild-looking, bespectacled little married man. He was fascinated by stories of the Pueblo Indians and their capacity to bear pain. In an adobe church out in the desert members of an Indian sect called the Penitentes had tortured, and sometimes crucified, one another.

Fearn began to spend a great deal of time in the adobe church, 50 miles outside Pueblo. He was particularly obsessed by the bloodstained altar. No doubt a writer of weird tales, in the H.P. Lovecraft tradition, might suggest that he was 'taken over' by the spirits of the Penitentes. But the explanation is simpler. By brooding on thoughts of torture he brought a flash of intensity into his otherwise dull life, and he dreamed of kidnapping a girl and taking her to the adobe church. 'Ever since I was a young boy I have wanted to torture a beautiful young girl'.

He put his fantasy into practice on April 22, 1942, when his wife was in hospital, having their second baby. Seventeen-year-old Alice Porter, a pretty student nurse, was walking home from evening classes at 9.30 in the evening. Fearn jumped out of his car, pointed a gun at her and ordered her to get in. She screamed, and a nearby resident looked out in time to see a blue car driving away.

Fearn drove Alice Porter to the adobe church and then proceeded to put his sadistic fantasies into practice. He bound her, undressed her, then placed her on the altar and tortured her in a manner that has never been fully reported; it involved binding her with red-hot wires. Fortunately she lost consciousness long before Fearn had finished. Finally, he raped her and, like Meyer, threw her body down a well.

Driving home through a storm, his car bogged down in the mud. He had to find a local farmer to haul it out with his tractor, and then he went back to Pueblo to visit his wife in hospital. The baby had been born the day before. When the police finally searched the adobe church the burnt remains of the girl's clothes and the 'torture kit' convinced them they had found the site of the murder. They soon located her body in the well, the head battered with a hammer.

There were fingerprints on an awl which had obviously been used in the killing, but they were not of any known sexual offender. Routine investigation led police to the farmer who had hauled Fearn's car out of the mud. He told them it was an old Ford sedan. The detective eventually located it in a Pueblo garage. Fearn's fingerprints matched those on the awl. When details of the murder came out, mobs gathered and there was talk of lynching. Fearn was taken away to jail in Canon City for his own safety. On October 22, 1942, he was executed in the gas chamber there.

It is worth making one purely practical point about this case. If Alice Porter had screamed and run it is possible that Fearn might have shot her, but the chances are that he would not have killed her. Rape cases reveal this basic truth: that girls who refuse to allow themselves to be forced into cars escape without harm more often than girls who submit, hoping to 'get it all over quickly'.

As in the case of Alexander Meyer, the girl who fights and tries to escape stands a good chance of survival. This is not invariably true, of course; a girl *may* escape more serious injury if she submits to her attacker. But in innumerable cases involving rapist *killers*, it is the girls who have fought who have lived to identify their attackers; it seems to be partly a question of 'victimology'. The question is not simply how to prevent people like Donald Fearn from becoming possessed by sadistic obsessions but also how to prevent girls like Alice Porter from making it too easy for them.

It is true that cases like the ones described above produce a certain feeling of helplessness: that there is absolutely nothing that doctors or criminologists can do about perverts like Glatman, Meyer and Fearn. But it would be a mistake to allow this feeling to paralyse our sense of balance and logic. To begin with, when we study such cases we begin to see the emergence of an over-all pattern. And to see a pattern is to begin to understand a thing *scientifically*. And that is the first and most difficult step in solving any problem.

For example, we see that men like Harvey Glatman, Peter Kurten, Donald Fearn are not exactly a 'modern' phenomenon. Krafft-Ebing describes the 'girl-stabber of Bozen', a case of 1829 – a young soldier with violently sadistic impulses. 'Gradually, the thought came to him how pleasurable it would be to stab a young girl in the genitals, and take delight in the sight of blood running from the knife'. After several attacks on girls he was arrested.

In 1867, at Alton, in Hampshire, a clerk named Frederick Baker, 'a young man of great respectability', spoke to three small girls who were playing in a meadow and offered one of them, Fanny Adams, a halfpenny to go with him into a hollow. He led her away, crying. Late that evening searchers found the child's head in a hop garden. Other parts of the body were scattered about the garden.

I don't know what I'm doing

After Baker's arrest his diary was found, with an entry: 'Killed a young girl today. It was fine and hot.' He was hanged in December 1867. In 1880 a 4-year-old child named Louise Dreux vanished from her home near the Tuileries, Paris. The following day neighbours reported to the police the foul black smoke that was issuing from the chimney of a retarded 20-year-old youth named Louis Menesclou, who lived on the top floor of the same house.

The police burst in and searched Menesclou; they found the child's forearms in his pockets, and parts of her body half burned in the stove. He admitted luring the child to his room with sweets, where he violated her, then killed her. In his pocket the police found a poem by Menesclou that ended: 'In my blind fury, I don't know what I'm doing.' He admitted sleeping on the corpse on the previous night. He was executed.

In Manhattan, in February 1961, a four-year-old girl named Edith Kiecorius vanished from outside her home; the uncle who had been keeping an eye on her had gone off to buy cigarettes. There was a massive police search. Police finally looked into the recently vacated room of an alcoholic dishwasher, 34-year-old Fred Thompson, and found the child's violated body hidden there. Thompson was caught in Tom's River, New Jersey. He was an electronics expert, but he had been in and out of sanatoriums many times for alcoholism.

These killers all have one thing in common: they are outcasts, men living alone without real social contact. The American psychologist William Glasser has said that before he can start to cure a patient the patient needs to have one real 'contact' with another person; without such a contact there can be no cure. Thompson, Menesclou, Baker, Fearn, Meyer all lacked this contact. They were living in modern civilization like hermits in the desert.

This is the foundation of the problem: Karl Marx's 'alienation'. And this once again suggests immediate grounds for optimism. Marshall McLuhan, the 'communications expert' who is the author of the best-seller *Understanding Media* (1964), has pointed out that the various forms of alienation were the outcome of the invention of printing, and of other mechanical devices – like the wheel and the radio – that became extensions of man and produced a new environment. People felt 'cut off', like a child lost in an engineering factory.

Television is again changing the world into a 'global village'. It is bringing all kinds of people into other people's homes; and the smallness, the lack of definition in a TV picture means that children 'scan' it for meanings in the same simple way that an African tribesman might scan it. They do not 'follow' it, as a literate adult follows a cinema film or reads a novel. So McLuhan believes that some of the basic effects of 'alienation' will wear off; we shall again have a society of non-alienated people who communicate directly with one another.

McLuhan may be over-optimistic, but his ideas suggest that these new mass media – TV, pop records and so on – might be used in some purposeful way to bring people closer together, to educate at a partly unconscious level. His most famous assertion

– that 'the medium is the message' – means that it doesn't matter whether television is showing gangsters shooting each other or Mickey Mouse: it is the medium itself, not what it 'says', that has the really important *subliminal* effect. If this is true it suggests new and interesting approaches to the increasing problem of crime.

It is, admittedly, difficult to see how a McLuhanized criminology could do anything about the real perverts – for example, about a man like the Hungarian Sylvestre Matushka, a 'company director' who needed to see a train crash in order to achieve full sexual satisfaction, and dynamited a number of trains in the early 1930s. On Saturday, September 12, 1931, as the Budapest-Vienna express was crossing a viaduct near Torbagy station, there was a tremendous explosion, and part of the train plunged into the abyss. Twenty-two people were killed. It had been detonated by an electrical device.

One of the 'passengers' who sued the railway company for injuries was Matushka; but when the police began to investigate his background they could find no one on the express who had actually seen him – although he had undoubtedly been at the scene of the explosion. Further investigation revealed that Matushka had bought dynamite. He was arrested, and finally confessed that the Bia-Torbagy explosion was his third attempt on a train.

He had also been responsible for an unsuccessful attempt to derail the Vienna-Passau train near Ansbach on New Year's Day 1931, and for the derailing of the Vienna express near Berlin on August 8, 1931, in which 16 people were injured. Matushka was tried several times, the juries being unable to agree on his sanity. Matushka explained that a spirit called Leo had ordered him to wreck trains. He was finally sentenced to hang; but appeals led to the commutation of the sentence to life imprisonment. The crime writer Paul Tabori has reported that he was subsequently freed by the Russians, and went to work for them as an explosives expert.

It may ultimately be impossible even for the most highly skilled 'social engineering' to eliminate madmen like Matushka. But it *could*, undoubtedly, do a great deal to reduce the 'alienation-level' in our society. In so doing it could not only reduce the number of sadistic perverts, but also have decisive effects in lowering the crime rate. This is an aim well worth the deepest consideration of all criminologists and social workers.

POISONERS

One of the more enduring myths of criminology is that poison is the favourite weapon of the female criminal. All you have to do to disprove that is to glance down a representative list of female killers: Charlotte Corday, Catherine Hayes, Kate Webster, Lizzie Borden, Ruth Snyder, Maria Manning, Ruth Ellis – most of whom used axes or knives. It is true that a similar list could be drawn up to include Lucrezia Borgia, Marie Lafarge, Madeleine Smith, Adelaide Bartlett, but this proves no more than that women have used poison as often as men.

Poison is not the prerogative of either sex. But the very fact there *is* such a myth provides a key to the mentality of the poisoner.

A surprisingly high proportion of poisoners are daydreamers, fantasists – capable of telling splendid, elaborate lies to other people and to themselves. They would shrink from using anything as crude as a knife or a revolver. In short, poisoners usually have a touch of the artistic temperament; and the artistic temperament has more than a touch of the feminine – as Oscar Wilde showed in his essay on the nineteenth-century poisoner Thomas Wainewright, *Pen, Pencil and Poison*.

Weak-willed

Examine the above list of female poisoners, and another interesting aspect becomes apparent. The last four names on it were acquitted, although most students of crime would agree they were probably guilty. Marie Lafarge – a fantasist if ever there was one – was very nearly acquitted. There is something oddly practical about these daydreamers: they get away with it.

And what of the other name on the list – the most notorious poisoner of them all, the woman whose name has become synonymous with evil and murder? Oddly enough, this is another example of myth-making. Poor Lucrezia Borgia almost certainly never killed anybody, and she was anything but a murderess by nature. A gentle, rather weak-willed girl with the temperament of a good housewife, her chief claim to fame is that she was the sister – and mistress – of one of the deadliest men in history, Cesare Borgia. It was Cesare who was the master-poisoner, and who is one of the most interesting examples of the criminal temperament since the Emperor Caligula (A.D. 37–41).

Lucrezia and Cesare Borgia were the bastards of a cardinal and a courtesan. The cardinal, who later became Pope Alexander VI, was Roderigo Borgia. He was rich, powerful, easygoing, and he kept his mistress, Vannozza Cattanei, in style in a *palazzo*. Vannozza bore him five children. Of these Lucrezia, the youngest, was born in 1480. Of the sons, Juan inherited his father's carefree temperament; but from the beginning, Cesare was violent and headstrong. Handsome, charming, vital, and energetic, he had the spoilt child's compulsion to have his own way in everything. He was very definitely a High Dominance Male. And Lucrezia, with her pretty oval face and slightly receding chin, was very much a medium-dominance female.

This is, of course, the classic combination for producing crime – Snyder and Gray, Fernandez and Beck, Brady and Hindley, are all examples of this explosive mixture of the Dominator and the Dominated. Lucrezia seemed made to be dominated, and she adored both her brothers – particularly Cesare. She probably lost her virginity to him before she reached her teens. Cesare was the sort of person who needed frequent sexual conquests – not so much out of sensuality, as a desire to prove his power and potency.

There are plenty of such despots in the history of crime: men who have an insane compulsion to have their way in absolutely everything, and who cannot bear to be crossed in the slightest thing. Most of them, however, have to compromise with reality to some extent. They behave perfectly normally with the world at large, and take out their delusions of grandeur on their wives and families. Cesare Borgia is interesting because he was in a position where he could put his fantasies of god-like power into action.

He set out to sleep with every woman who attracted him – whether it was his own sister, or the wife of his younger brother. When he captured a town, he had 40 of its prettiest virgins sent for him to deflower. When invading Swiss soldiers looted his mother's house, he captured them, and had them tortured to death.

Later he spent some time at the French court where he suffered slights and humiliations. When he returned to Italy, he had most of the servants who had witnessed his humiliations murdered, so they couldn't mention what they had seen. The slightest frustration drove him to murder. His father seemed to prefer his brother Juan to himself. Accordingly Cesare had Juan murdered, and his body thrown into the Tiber. When Lucrezia married Alfonso of Aragon – on her father's orders – Cesare was so frantic with jealousy that he had Alfonso killed. When Cesare called on her at her castle a few months later, Lucrezia, in spite of her grief, welcomed him, and probably slept with him. (Her first child was almost certainly Cesare's.)

Stripped and left

Cesare was an adept in the use of poisons. Some of them could make the victim die a lingering death, making his hair and teeth fall out; others could kill immediately, with all the symptoms of a stroke or heart attack. It is satisfactory to record that his downfall came through poison. Cesare and his father – the Pope – were invited to dine with a cardinal, Adriano de Corneto. They fell violently ill after the banquet. (So did the cardinal – but that was probably political wisdom.) The Pope died. And Cesare, who believed himself invincible and invulnerable, suddenly saw his castle of fantasy collapse.

His troops deserted him. He was made prisoner by a new Pope. He fled to Spain, and was imprisoned for his brother's murder. He escaped and joined a small army belonging to his brother-in-law; in a minor skirmish, he was seriously wounded, stripped and left to die. He was 32 years old, and had been responsible for dozens of murders. His sister Lucrezia married again, became famous for her kindness and piety, and lived happily ever after – or at least for 11 years, until she was 39.

It is ironic that this gentle, affectionate girl should have become known as one of the great poisoners of history, when there is no evidence that she ever harmed anyone except, possibly, herself.

Cesare Borgia dispensed death by many other means beside poison; he also had his enemies strangled, stabbed, and hacked to pieces. Yet in a sense, he remains the archetypal poisoner. His portraits do not show an obviously evil ruffian; they depict a dreamer with an intelligent face. (He loved art, and was a patron of Leonardo and Raphael.) He believed – as did his sister and mother – that he could become the master of Italy, perhaps of the world. It was fantasy; he didn't have the realism of his namesake, Julius Caesar. His military successes were due to the backing of his father as much as to his own good generalship.

Childish act

Everybody, at one stage of their development, would like to impose their will upon the world. Everybody would like to see their enemies humiliated, their loyal friends rewarded. But most of us have to come to terms with a world in which this is not possible. If we learn to adjust well, we become decent, complex, mature human beings. Children don't *want* to adjust. As Freud points out, a child with infinite power would quickly destroy the world in a rage. Criminals are basically people who have failed to come to terms with this reality. Although they know they can't make the world obey their will, they still try to cheat it in minor ways – to steal what it refuses to give.

A man like Cesare Borgia never makes the slightest attempt to come to terms with reality from the beginning. He had two people who adored him – his mother and sister – and one who loved him self-indulgently – his father. So, like a spoilt child, he was allowed to indulge his tantrums all his life. This was a tragedy, for he had the intelligence and vitality to be a great man. But by the time he was 20, tantrums and violence had become such a habit that nothing could cure him. It was also a tragedy for the world that it had to put up with his monomania.

Here, then, is the basic picture of the criminal – but especially of the poisoner. For to kill by poison is perhaps the most *childish* of all criminal acts. It is an attempt to stay on good terms with the world while breaking its laws. At the same time, it is one of the cruellest forms of murder. Anybody who has ever had mild food poisoning knows how bad it can be – vomiting until you are exhausted, and then vomiting again, unable to think because even thinking makes you feel sick.

The poisoner can inflict this because he – or she – has decided to ignore the victim, to pretend he is a mere object with no feelings. Nearly all the famous poisoners have been rather childish personalities – often delightful and charming, but fundamentally children determined to get their own way by stealth.

Lucrezia Borgia was innocent; the woman who *deserves* Lucrezia Borgia's reputation was another pampered aristocrat, Marie, the Marquise de Brinvilliers, executed in 1676. The eldest of five children, she was the daughter of a Councillor of State and Treasurer of France. Like Cesare Borgia, she was eye-catching and charming; and, like Cesare — and like all highly dominant women — she was a sexual experimenter. She later admitted to having had sexual intercourse with her brothers while still a child.

At 21, in 1651, she married Antoine de Brinvilliers, Baron de Nourar, who turned out to be a gambler and a libertine. Eight years later, the Baron met a gambler and charming confidence man named Ste Croix, who soon became Marie's lover. The Baron didn't object to this liaison, but Marie's father did. He had Ste Croix arrested and thrown into the Bastille. There Ste Croix met an expert in poisons named Exili, and became his pupil and disciple. Released from prison after six months, he and Marie decided that the quickest way to lay hands on a fortune was to poison Marie's father.

It was here that Marie revealed the typical 'dissociation' of the poisoner. She visited hospitals, giving poisoned fruit to the invalids, to see whether the poison could be detected at an autopsy. It couldn't — almost no poison *could* be at that date. Then Marie went to stay with her father, and he fell ill. She nursed him with apparent devotion for eight months, until he died. When she had inherited his fortune, she took a series of lovers. She resembled Cesare Borgia in another way: she couldn't bear to be crossed; when a creditor had one of her houses sold to pay a debt, she set it on fire.

Blackmail

The following year, 1667, she devoted to poisoning her two brothers. But her success made her careless. She revealed her plans to her lovers, who were more squeamish than she was. Ste Croix, for example, blackmailed her. Another lover, the tutor of her children, tried to dissuade her from further murders, and so became a prime target himself; he survived several attempts on his life. She now decided to poison her husband, so she could marry Ste Croix. But Ste Croix (wisely) didn't want her. Whenever her husband fell ill, he rapidly administered antidotes.

Finally, Marie met her downfall. Ste Croix died — presumably of natural causes — and Marie's first thought was for the box containing her letters to him — with which he had been blackmailing her. Her concern was not misplaced. When the box was opened, orders for her arrest went out immediately, and one confederate was broken alive on the wheel. She then fled to the Netherlands, entered a convent, and managed to avoid arrest for three years. At last the law caught up with her. Her confessions were so frank and sensational that they had to be printed in Latin. After a trial lasting nearly three months, she went to the block. Her body was burned, and the ashes scattered.

The pattern should by now be clear. Not all poisoners have dominant personalities; but the element of fantasy and daydreaming seems common to most. Perhaps the most celebrated single case in the history of poisoning is that of Marie Lafarge. Marie poisoned her husband with arsenic in 1840, and the case is of interest to criminologists chiefly because it was one of the earliest cases in which forensic toxicology played a major part.

Fake affection

An English chemist, Marsh, had dicovered that if arsenic – or anything containing it – is put into sulphuric acid and zinc added, a gas called arsine is formed. Then, if a narrow jet of this gas is burned and a cold porcelain dish placed in the flame, the arsenic is deposited on the dish. It was this that caused Marie's undoing, and led to her sentence for life imprisonment. But the real fascination of the case is the personality of Marie Lafarge – a spoilt, rather pretty young girl, brought up at an expensive private school with the daughters of aristocrats, but without any large fortune of her own.

She was pleased, therefore, when a coarse farmer and ironmaster, Charles Lafarge, approached her through a matrimonial agency. Although she disliked her suitor, she accepted him because she thought he was a rich landowner, and that she would be able to invite her friends to stay at their château. When she discovered that the château was a decaying house, and the estate was a muddy village, she was at first heartbroken. Then she apparently made up her mind, quite coolly, to escape from the situation by poisoning her husband.

In the months following the marriage – during which she faked affection for Lafarge – she carried out the poisoning with the callousness and deceit of a delinquent child. But several relatives of the doomed man saw her adding a white powder to his food. Even before his death, a medical expert called in to attend to Lafarge said he was dying of poison. Marie was duly arrested; experts on poison clashed at her trial; the case became a *cause célèbre*, splitting France into two factions: her accusers and her sympathizers. For a time, it looked as if she would be acquitted; but the evidence of the great poison-expert Orfila convicted her. She spent ten years in prison – during which she corresponded with her most influential supporter, the novelist Alexandre Dumas – and eventually died of tuberculosis at the age of 36.

This same streak of immaturity and fantasy can be seen in most of the major English poisoning cases, from Dr. Pritchard and Madeleine Smith to Londoner Graham Young, the 'motiveless poisoner' who, in 1972, confessed to administering poison to his father, stepmother, and school friend. One of the most celebrated of English poison mysteries is that of the death of Charles Bravo, who died of antimony poisoning at his house, the Priory, in Balham, South London in 1876. His pretty wife Florence was tried for his murder, but finally acquitted. Yet in all the essentials described above, she had the temperament of a poisoner: the immaturity, the childish desire for her own way, the dreamy, romantic disposition. This does not prove her guilt; but, added to the other evidence, it makes it very likely.

Possibly the oddest thing about poisoners is that there is something in them that keeps them permanently immature, so they never grow up. This can be seen in America's classic poison case, that of Nannie Doss (sometimes known as 'Arsenic Annie') who continued her literally poisonous career over nearly 30 years – and would probably have continued into old age if a doctor's suspicions had not mercifully been aroused.

Coy murderess

This fortunate event took place on October 6, 1954, when a 58-year-old man died in Tulsa, Oklahoma. He had been in hospital shortly before his death, suffering from stomach pains. He recovered and returned home with his wife, 49-year-old Nannie Doss. Nannie made him a large dish of stewed prunes, and he died the next day. His doctor, N.Z. Schwelbein, said he couldn't imagine what had killed Samuel Doss, and that there ought to be an autopsy. Nannie agreed enthusiastically. 'Of *course* there should be. It might kill somebody else. . ."

When the police approached her some time later, and said that her husband's stomach had contained enough arsenic to eliminate ten men, she looked amazed and distressed. 'How could such a thing happen?' she gasped.

Nannie was a plump, bespectacled woman, who had obviously once been pretty; this was clear from the rather coy, soft manner, which seemed to suggest that she was younger and more desirable than she actually was. When asked if she had poisoned her husband, she stared at the police with wide open, innocent eyes, and said in a shocked voice: 'My conscience is clear.'

She talked openly and readily – so much so that the police had difficulty interrupting her. They began to wonder whether it was all a mistake – and then changed their minds when they asked her what she knew about a certain Richard Morton. With her customary wide-eyed frankness, she declared that she had never heard the name. They then showed her four insurance policies, which indicated that Richard Morton had been her previous husband, and that she had benefited by about $1500 from his death.

She giggled coyly. 'Well, I guess I wasn't telling the truth. I *was* married to him.' It took days of patient questioning, of gently bringing her back to the point, to get her to admit that she had poisoned Samuel Doss and Richard Morton.

When news of the case appeared in newspapers across the country, the Tulsa police were suddenly flooded with calls that made them realize they had apprehended a mass murderess. Samuel Doss was apparently husband number five, and four of the five had suffered mysterious deaths. Before Richard Morton, who died early in 1953, there had been Arlie Lanning, who was married to her from 1947 until 1952 – when he passed on of stomach pains – and Frank Harrelson, who died in 1945, the year he married Nannie.

Harrelson's two-year-old grandson had died a few months earlier in the same house; as Harrelson left the funeral he had prophetically remarked: 'I'll be the next.' A young nephew of Arlie Lanning's had also expired in the same house – of 'food poisoning' – just before Lanning's death.

Further investigation revealed that Nannie's mother and two sisters had died with stomach pains when Nannie had been staying with them. Finally, detectives traced Nannie's first husband, George Frazer, whom she had married when she was 15. The union had been unhappy because Nannie had been wildly flirtatious, and had periodically run off with other men. She explained to the officers that she had been searching for her 'dream man' all her life, and that her favourite reading was *True Romances*.

One day, it was revealed, George Frazer had come home to find two of his children dying on the floor. There was no inquest, and shortly afterwards, Nannie went off with another lover – whereupon Frazer divorced her.

Naughty girl

Under questioning, Nannie's manner never changed; she remained smiling and candid, admitting to poisoning four husbands with an apologetic giggle – as if confessing to being a naughty little girl. She indignantly denied murdering anyone except the four husbands, but gave way on this point when her mother's body was exhumed and found to be full of arsenic.

Sentenced to life imprisonment, she died of leukemia in 1965. Even as a convicted murderess, her manner never changed. Apparently nothing could make her admit that being responsible for the deaths of eleven people – four of them children – was at all wicked. Why had she committed murder? Because she was a romantic with a high level of sexual drive; she felt she deserved more of life than boring, ordinary husbands.

Most poisoners – unlike other types of murderers, whose methods are more direct and violent – kill in order to gain emotionally or materially. The wife slowly but lethally disposes of the husband she had grown tired of; the husband, in turn, gets rid of a faded and no longer loved wife, and replaces her with the latest model.

Poison is used by those who have carefully calculated the odds, and who believe they can get away with their crime. When they are caught no one is more surprised and nonplussed than the poisoners themselves – weak, cowardly, and avaricious people, who slay by stealth and are caught by the skill of detectives and doctors.

POLICE CORRUPTION

In January 1728, a play called *The Beggar's Opera* became the rage of London. It was written by John Gay, and presented by a manager called Rich; it made Gay rich and Rich gay. What the audiences found so piquant about it was that it was not about tragic kings and queens, but about thieves, highwaymen, prostitutes, and fences. The villain, Peachum, is a receiver of stolen goods who supplements his income by handing over some of his customers to the law. In essence, it was an amusingly realistic portrayal of crime and corruption in eighteenth-century London.

Only three years earlier, Londoners had crowded to watch the execution of the man who served as the model for Peachum – the 'thieftaker' Jonathan Wild. In fact, Wild may be regarded as the archetype of the crooked cop. He was *not* a cop – officially the British police force didn't come into existence until the end of the eighteenth century – but he was regarded as a valuable ally of the law. Arriving in London about 1710, at the age of 22, Wild quickly made the discovery that the man who makes most out of crime is not the thief, but the man who finances him.

At this time, there was an extraordinary loophole in the law; a receiver of stolen goods could not be prosecuted. Wild set up as a receiver, and soon became so prosperous that he was able to buy an inn. By the time an Act of Parliament changed the law on receivers, he had already devised a way to operate legally. He would approach men who had been robbed, and offer to buy the stolen goods back from the thief, for a small commission. This was so successful that he set up a shop where people who had been burgled could come to inquire about their property.

Jealous friends

For five shillings, Wild would enter their names on his books; a few days later, in exchange for a reward, he would restore the goods. The peace officers – employed by the City of London –

had no objection. Wild was one of their best informers. So long as he helped to send highwaymen and thieves to the gallows at Tyburn, they didn't care what he did.

Wild would probably have died comfortably in his bed if he hadn't overreached himself. He organized some of the robberies himself. Business was so good that he had to store some of the stolen property in warehouses. Jealous confederates finally betrayed him. The law had to act. In May 1725 he was taken to Tyburn – now Marble Arch – in a cart, pelted and jeered at by the mob; there he was hanged on the triangular gallows. It was probably his reputation for betrayal, rather than dishonesty, that prompted the crowd's hostility.

'Wild's system and methods have been copied many times since then, in America and on the Continent, as well as in this country,' wrote a biographer of Jonathan Wild in 1937. This was not quite true. Before you can have large-scale official corruption, you must first have a flourishing crime industry. In the London of Jonathan Wild, the crime rate was very nearly as high as in present-day New York – and for a rather odd reason.

Enormous bribes

In the middle of the seventeenth century, a Dutch professor named Sylvius discovered how to distil a powerful spirit from juniper berries. It was called 'genièvre' – French for juniper – and then shortened to 'gin'. The English had always been beer and wine drinkers; but when William of Orange became king in 1689, Dutch gin began to flow into England. In 1690 an Act of Parliament allowed anyone to brew and sell spirits without a license. Thousands of gin shops opened up; the sign 'Drunk for a penny, dead drunk for twopence, straw free,' became commonplace. The crime rate rocketed, and men like Wild flourished. He was the most notorious 'crooked cop' of his time – but there were dozens of others. Gin, crime, and crooked peace officers went together.

However, it is not quite accurate to talk about 'police corruption'. It is seldom the uniformed man on the beat who gets corrupted. In all the major police scandals – from the 'trial of the detectives' in London in 1877 to the widely publicized Knapp Commission Hearings in New York in 1971 – the culprits have been plain clothes detectives. There was even a certain amount of corruption among the famous 'Bow Street Runners', the forerunners of the modern London police force.

These un-uniformed detectives were known for their high living, and at least two of them left fortunes of over £20,000. That kind of money is not made by honest thief-catching. But the detective has to spend part of his days in contact with crooks, because his job is to obtain information. When he is dealing with small-time crooks, the temptation is small. But the big crook can offer enormous bribes – and his 'success' lends him a certain aura of sophistication and authority that may induce a sense of inferiority in a detective earning less than £2000 a year. As if these pressures are not enough, the detective may be induced to compromise himself, and then be blackmailed.

All three of these factors were at work in the events which led to the London police scandals of 1877. The crooks in this case were two highly successful confidence swindlers named Kurr and Benson. Both had mastered the art of seeming to be rich men. Benson, with an excellent French accent, played the part of an aristocrat; Kurr appeared to be a bluff country gentleman who might have stepped out of the pages of a novel by Anthony Trollope.

Their chosen field was sport. And their method of swindling had a certain classic simplicity and originality. Benson, who was living in luxury at Shanklin, Isle of Wight, under the name of Yonge, wrote a letter to the Comtesse de Goncourt, explaining that he was a brilliantly successful sportsman. As a result, he said, bookmakers always shortened the odds when he backed a horse – knowing it was almost certain to win.

All that he wanted of the Comtesse de Goncourt was that she should act as his agent, and place bets on horses for him. He would send her the money, and when the horse won, she would post him his winnings, upon which he would pay her a 5 per cent commission.

The Comtesse could see no harm in this arrangement. She forwarded the cheque to a bookmaker; in fact, the bookmaker was Benson himself. Soon, she received a cheque for £1000 from the 'bookmaker' – Benson's winnings. She forwarded the cheque to Benson, who promptly sent her £50 for her trouble. Naturally, the Comtesse wanted to invest some of her own money in this apparently foolproof scheme. She gave Benson, and his accomplice Kurr, £10,000 over a short period. She was only one of their victims.

How did Scotland Yard detectives come to be involved with these swindlers? The full story is unknown, but the first one to accept bribes seems to have been Detective Inspector Meiklejohn of the Yard. Meiklejohn was a friend of a man called Druscovitch, who was in charge of the continental branch of the 'fraud squad'. Druscovitch got himself into some extraneous financial trouble, and urgently needed £60. Meiklejohn introduced him to a 'perfect gentleman', who persuaded Druscovitch to accept the £60 as a present. The 'gentleman' was Kurr.

Meiklejohn's boss Clarke was then drawn into the web by the 'aristocratic' Benson. Benson sent him a message, claiming to have information about a gang that Clarke had recently broken up. He explained that he was too crippled to leave his home on the Isle of Wight; could Clarke call on him? (Benson had previously crippled himself in an attempt to commit suicide in jail by setting fire to his mattress.) This was good psychology. Clarke went to the palatial home at Shanklin, and was introduced to the exquisitely dressed gentleman who lay on a couch, and whose handkerchiefs had coronets embroidered upon them.

Benson explained that he was afraid Clarke was about to be blackmailed; rumours were circulating that he had taken bribes from the gang he had recently broken up. Clarke said indignantly that he had never taken bribes. Of course not, Benson agreed silkily. But unfortunately there was a letter that Clarke had written to one of the gang, arranging a secret meeting. Perhaps it *was* all police business, but it certainly read very suspiciously. Finally, Clarke was not so much blackmailed as charmed and dominated.

When a fourth Yard man, Detective Inspector Palmer, was drawn into the circle, the swindlers felt they were ready to face the world. And they very soon had to. Benson decided that it was time for a grand *coup*. He told the trusting Comtesse de Goncourt that he had a superb opportunity to invest £30,000 for her. It would bring a huge return. The Comtesse did not have that much in ready cash, so she consulted her lawyer, a man named Abrahams. Abrahams was instantly suspicious, and checked with Scotland Yard on 'Mr. Yonge of Shanklin'. Druscovitch instantly warned Benson that the Comtesse's lawyer had 'smelled a rat'.

Used notes

The conspirators launched into action. They hadn't expected to be discovered quite so soon. The loot – well over £10,000 – was drawn out of the Bank of England. But in a transaction of that size, the numbers of the notes were known – it would have excited suspicion to ask for the money in old used notes. The police reached the Bank soon after the cash had gone, and Druscovitch was ordered to telegraph the numbers of the notes to all banks in the British Isles.

He conveniently overlooked Scotland – which gave Benson time to get to Glasgow, and change his 'marked money' into £100 notes on the Bank of Clydesdale – which had the advantage of being unnumbered, and the disadvantage of being difficult to change outside Scotland. Duly, the detectives were all given their 'rewards' – Meiklejohn receiving £500. However, he acted stupidly. He changed one of the notes with a wine merchant in Leeds, Yorkshire. The Leeds police soon found out that a Scotland Yard man had cashed a Clydesdale note, and wrote to another of Druscovitch's superiors, Williamson, at the Yard. Druscovitch intercepted the letter and burned it.

The Clydesdale notes were proving to be more trouble than they were worth. Benson went to Rotterdam and cashed one at a hotel; the Dutch police promptly arrested him. Druscovitch informed the other swindler, Kurr, who sent a cable to the Dutch police, signed 'Williamson' (Druscovitch's immediate superior), ordering them to release their captive. They almost did so, but decided to wait for confirmation by letter – which failed to arrive.

Ironically enough, Druscovitch was then sent to Rotterdam to bring Benson back. He was in a gloomy mood; he realized that the net was closing in on him and his confederates. Within a short while, Kurr was also arrested, and he and Benson were tried. Benson got fifteen years, Kurr ten. They then decided that their 'bent cops' had not lived up to their side of the agreement in allowing them to get caught – and in retaliation they denounced them.

The result was the 'trial of the detectives', which shook the English middle class to its foundation. If its members couldn't trust the renowned British bobby, who *could* they trust?

The feeling in favour of the police was so strong that Clarke was actually acquitted. The other three were put inside for two years. The two swindlers were also satisfied; their sentences were reduced by a third. Benson later committed suicide – after a spectacular swindle practised on Adelina Patti, the Spanish-born coloratura who appeared in concerts in New York from 1850 – by jumping from a high gallery in an American prison where he had ended up.

Raw material
The scandal created by the trial of the detectives indicates how strongly the British trust their policemen. And, statistically, they are right to do so. Britain has never suffered from the presence of

major crime – its murder rate is still one of the lowest in the world. Where there are no large pickings to be made from such activities, there is unlikely to be undue police corruption. In the Scotland Yard affair, only Meiklejohn had the makings of a really dishonest official.

In the United States, however, graft has always been so widespread – starting with the local City Halls – that police corruption is accepted with habitual resignation. From the beginning, the United States had the raw material, the wide open spaces, and the vitality that makes for enormous wealth. Violence – together with the opening of the frontiers – was a part of the way of life. In the original Wild West, the distinction between robbers and lawmen was likely to get blurred. In fast-growing towns such as Chicago and San Francisco, the same thing was true; and there it was actively encouraged by the Horatio Alger 'Protestant ethic' of success, which is so basic to American society.

Any society which attaches so much importance to wealth and gain is asking for corruption. One of the first big inquiries into police corruption in New York was in 1893 – inspired by the Rev. Charles Parkhurst, who had discovered that practically every member of the police force had paid 'contributions' to Tammany Hall for the privilege of getting his job.

One police captain had handed out $15,000 for his rank. Where did he get the money? From the keepers of gambling houses and brothels. The police chief, Alexander S. Williams, had shares in a brewery, and forced saloon owners to sell 'his' whiskey on penalty of being raided. Williams was unable to explain how he had managed to afford an estate on Long Island, complete with a yacht (and its own dock) on his police salary. Although no charges were made against him, he resigned a year later.

French connection
Understandably, then, a deep-seated distrust of the law is a part of American life – particularly among oppressed racial and religious minorities. Herbert Asbury, historian of New York gangs, records that in race riots at the turn of the twentieth century – usually started by white youths – the police would join in on the side of the whites, battering the Negroes with their clubs and arresting them.

From 1894 onwards, there have been major investigations into police corruption about every two decades. In New York, the most recent of these was the Knapp Commission of 1971. In spite of the sensational nature of the revelations, the hearings excited little coast-to-coast attention. The final report which came out in December 1972 colourfully divided 'bent cops' into 'meat-eaters' and 'grass-eaters'. Meat-eaters are policemen who 'aggressively misuse their power for personal gain'; the grass-eaters 'simply accept the pay-offs that come their way'. The vast majority of corrupt policemen, said the report, are grass-eaters.

In an area like New York's Harlem, with its illegal gambling, a bent cop could make $1500 a month. If he was transferred to another command, this payment would continue for another two months – giving him time to adjust to his 'lower income'. It could explain how, when the police seized heroin, it was likely to find its way back into the drugs market – and how of $137,000 seized from drug traffickers, $80,000 went into the pockets of the arresting officers. In one police precinct, over 68 pounds of 'French connection' heroin had vanished from the police laboratory – $7 million-worth at current prices then.

The figures poured out regularly, and no one was very shocked or very surprised. Americans had heard it all before. They *expected* their police to behave like that. They might be roused to protest occasionally if the misbehaviour became too public – as when Mayor Daley's Chicago policemen were seen on television beating up anybody who looked like a demonstrator during the Democratic Convention of 1968. But generally speaking the feeling is that the police have got a tough job, and that a little brutality and corruption is inevitable – if not, occasionally, necessary.

There is something to be said for this attitude. England has an average of three murders a week; in 1971, the United States had a murder every *33 minutes*, and the figure shows no sign of declining. With violence on this scale, toughness is regarded as a basic necessity in a policeman or a prison guard. Unless there is some system of public checks, excesses are bound to occur.

When Tom Murton became Superintendent of the Tucker Prison Farm in Arkansas in 1967, he soon discovered that nearly two hundred convicts were listed as having escaped, and had never been caught – a far higher number than would have been expected. Seasoned inmates said openly that there were a hundred or so bodies buried in the prison grounds; men who, for one reason or another, had fallen foul of the 'wardens'.

Murton dug in an area where the ground had sunk, and quickly unearthed three skeletons. For a few weeks, the scandal drew nationwide headlines; then, suddenly, the authorities ordered that there should be no further digging, Murton was dismissed, and the scandal was allowed to simmer.

Dirty hands

Where tensions *have* increased – in racially mixed areas in both the United States and Britain – charges of corruption and brutality against the police have also increased. In September 1973, a Detective Chief Inspector and five of his staff were charged at London's Old Bailey with manufacturing evidence of drug smuggling against a Pakistani family. The police were convinced that the family was guilty, but there was not enough evidence against them. The prosecution alleged the police strengthened the evidence. The father's five-year sentence was later quashed.

The most interesting feature about such a case is that the newspapers scarcely bothered to report it. For the most part, it rated a small paragraph on an inside page. The English public was apparently as blasé about it as the American public was about the New York scandals of 1971.

As long as there is crime, as long as criminals flourish, police officers will be needed to combat the evil. It is inevitable, therefore, that some of the graft, the corruption, will rub off onto them. You cannot put your hand in a sewer without it coming up dirty. In the words of the lyricist W.S. Gilbert, 'The policeman's lot is not a happy one.' It was true when he wrote it some hundred years ago: unhappily it is truer than ever today.

PROTECTION RACKETS

In the year 1880, an English clergyman named Rose was travelling with two Italian companions through Sicily. They were about a mile from the railway station of Lecrera when, quite suddenly, they found themselves surrounded by bearded, rough-looking men who carried knives and carbines. This was the gang of a notorious brigand, Leoni, whose name was feared all over Sicily.

The gang released Rose's companions, who were told to go to the Italian authorities in Palermo and report that the Rev. Rose was being held for a ransom of £5000. The authorities were concerned, but penurious; they reported the incident to the British Consul, and forgot it. A few weeks later they received a parcel containing one of Mr. Rose's ears.

The British government, stirred by the clamour in the newspapers, decided to pay the ransom; but before they had completed the endless formalities the brigands had grown impatient, and sent another ear, together with a note saying that if the ransom still wasn't paid Mr. Rose would be chopped up piecemeal.

The British were now enraged; they paid the £5000 and recovered the earless Mr. Rose; and they also made such threatening noises that the Italian government sent an army into the mountains. There was a bloody battle. Leoni himself was killed, and most of his men captured. The British newspapers congratulated themselves for forcing the inefficient Italians to do something they should have done years ago, and the affair was almost forgotten.

Small and evil-looking
But not entirely. For the most dangerous of the gang had escaped, together with six companions. His name was Giuseppe Esposito, and he was a small, evil-looking man with a cruel

mouth and a low forehead. Friends in Palermo smuggled Esposito on to a ship bound for the United States, and he landed in New York and made his way to New Orleans with a few selected followers. There, under the name of Radzo, he rented a house in Chartres Street, bought himself a boat – probably with his share of the clergyman's ransom – and dredged for oysters. He was so confident that he was a free man in America that he called the boat *Leoni* and flew the bandit's flag from the mast.

But respectability bored Esposito; he had been a bandit for too long to enjoy making money legitimately. There were no mountains here to hide in, but there were plenty of wealthy Italians in New Orleans. Giuseppe Esposito called on some of them, and explained that he needed money to finance a fleet of boats; when they asked what guarantee he could offer in return for a loan, Esposito would casually take out a revolver and cock it, peering down the sights. Then, with slow deliberation, he would pull the trigger. The hammer clicked on an empty chamber. Pretending not to notice the trembling of his startled host, he would say deliberately: 'Protezione' – protection.

It is possible that Giuseppe Esposito was not the originator of this popular euphemism, but he was certainly one of the first of the American 'gangsters' to employ the method. In fact, he got his 'loan' from Italian grocers and restauranteurs who understood the value of Esposito's good will, and he proceeded to organize his local 'Black Hand gang' along the same lines as the great Leoni.

He began by deposing the leader of the local Mafia, Tony Labruzzo, who lacked Esposito's casual ferocity. Then he bought a fleet of boats and ships, and conducted elaborate piracy operations on the Mississippi and in the Gulf of Mexico. With his brigand's instinct for a hide-out, he had huts constructed in the depths of the swamps. He intended to conduct his protection racket along Italian lines: that is, to kidnap anyone who refused to pay, and hold him for ransom – the Italians with their regard for property would only use vandalism as a last resort.

However, Esposito was never to achieve his ambition to become the Leoni of Louisiana. His deposed rival, Tony Labruzzo, told the Italian Consul that Leoni's chief lieutenant was in New Orleans, and the Chief of Police, Thomas Boylan, kept Esposito under surveillance. He learned that two New York detectives, James Mooney and D. Boland, had been hired by the Italian government to find Esposito.

For weeks two of Boylan's best men, the brothers David and

Mike Hennessy, shadowed Esposito, and one day, when they received the word to pick him up, they quickly moved in on their quarry as he walked across Jackson Square, pushed guns into his ribs and rushed him to the police station. It had to be done quickly: the Mafia were capable of storming the jail. Early the next morning Esposito was taken down river, and put on board a ship for New York.

Deported to Italy, he was tried, and sentenced to life imprisonment – in irons. But before he went on trial, Tony Labruzzo, the man who had betrayed him, was already dead, shot down in the street by a Mafiosi. The Black Hand knew that if it was to maintain its stranglehold on the Italian community it had to gain a reputation for absolute ruthlessness and terrible efficiency. The two Hennessy brothers left New Orleans; but Mike was killed in 1886, and David in 1890, both by Mafia gunmen.

Of course, Esposito was not the inventor of 'protection'. It had been known on the border of England and Scotland as far back as the sixteenth century, when bands of wanted men, led by local chieftains, extorted a 'second rent' – or 'mail' – from local farmers by threatening to burn their farms and destroy their crops; this was the origin of the word 'blackmail'.

In Sicily and Corsica – both islands with a violent history – brigands maintained themselves by extorting food and other necessities from the population. But 'protection' was rare for an obvious reason: the wealthy citizens lived in the towns, where they were fairly well protected by the police, and the brigands were in the mountains. In Naples, there was a flourishing secret society called the Camorra, which certainly included 'protection' among its many activities, and in Sicily, the original Mafia was basically an alternative to the police, providing quite genuine protection and other favours for those who paid a certain sum. In its early stages, it was a 'protection racket' only in the same sense as is Securicor.

Dead Rabbits, Plug Uglies
In America, gangs had always abounded; in the early nineteenth century, the New York slums were full of outfits with names like the Dead Rabbits, the Plug Uglies and the Five Points. These specialized in burglary, theft from docks and warehouses, receiving stolen property, intimidation of prostitutes and all the usual extra-legal activities of slum-dwellers with more than the customary share of dominance.

The same was true of San Francisco, Chicago and other fast-growing towns – Los Angeles was, at this time, a tiny and peaceful village with no law enforcement problem. Politicians discovered the use of gangs to bully voters, and by the 1850s, the New York gangs and the Tammany Hall bosses were in close alliance. A man about to enter a polling booth was likely to be stopped by a man with a cosh and asked how he intended to vote. If he mentioned the wrong name, he never got inside; the roughnecks would do the voting instead.

In the 1860s, the Chinese in the goldfields near Marysville, California, organized themselves into secret societies called 'tongs'; the first two were known as the Hop Sings and Suey Sings, and they came into violent conflict when the mistress of a Hop Sing member was stolen by someone from the Suey Sings. The girl was only handed back after many men on both sides had died. The tongs moved to railroad construction camps, then to the larger towns – the chief of which was San Francisco, known for its brothels and gambling houses.

Traffic in girls

The average Chinese in America were a docile and well-behaved people – too docile in many ways, for the whites preyed on them unmercifully. Their two chief necessities were opium – which had been introduced into China by the British – and girls. There was a flourishing traffic in girls, who were glad to get away from the terrible poverty of their own land to the relative luxury of sharing a cellar with 20 other 'slaves'.

The tongs were probably the first largescale protection racket in America, and this was largely because they organized the lives of their fellow citizens in this foreign country, and got them to pay a proportion of their wages. If a Chinaman established himself enough to want to bring his wife to America, the tong demanded a certain payment.

The tongs had a simple way of enforcing their will: murder. Their assassins preferred hatchets – hence the term 'hatchet man' – but also carried a silk rope around the body, like the Thugs of India. Their 'protection' was genuine, like that of the Mafia in Sicily. In San Francisco in 1875, a hatchet man named Ming Long, of the Kwong Dock Tong, came upon Low Sing, a member of the Suey Sing Tong, holding the hand of a pretty 'slave girl' named Kum Ho, and split his skull with a hatchet.

Before he died, Low Sing gasped out the name of his killer to the head of his tong. Formal challenges were sent, and the next day at midnight the deadliest hatchet men of both tongs met in a certain street in Chinatown, and fought earnestly and bloodily until the police – mostly Irish – arrived with their whistles and night-sticks. No one was killed – although some died later. The Suey Sings were held to have won, because they had injured a large number of the enemy.

Payment was made to Low Sing's relatives; Ming Long was formally ejected from the tong, which meant that he was fair game for any hatchet man, and fled to China, where the tongs did not exist. The historian of San Francisco, Herbert Asbury, points out that both the tongs and chop suey were invented by the Chinese in America.

The Italians were the next great wave of immigrants to arrive in New York, fleeing from political troubles at home. The first generation settled down to hard work, running shops, restaurants and small businesses, and eventually many became prosperous. It was then that new arrivals like Giuseppe Esposito began to prey on these more successful countrymen, and the 'protection racket' as we know it today came into being. The rise of the gangs was very slow, and most non-Italian Americans knew very little about them until the year 1890.

A life in chains

After Esposito had been deported back to Italy – and a life in chains – two New Orleans brothers named Charles and Tony Matranga decided that there were better ways of making money than in the saloon business. Inspired by Esposito's efficient take-over of New Orleans crime, they settled down to the business of organizing the gangs, and extorting 'protection' from their fellow Italians.

Many Italians in New Orleans worked in the docks at the fairly reasonable wage of 40 cents an hour. A rich and influential family named Provenzano had a monopoly of the unloading of fruit ships from South America. Charles Matranga approached them, and suggested that, in future, they might like to obtain their dock labour through him. Naturally, the labourers also paid the Matrangas a 'kick back' for their good services.

The Matrangas had discovered what Esposito knew: that a few 'dominant' human beings can always lead a large number of non-dominant ones by the nose. In those days, zoologists knew very little about animal dominance, and had certainly never heard that precisely 5% of any animal group is 'dominant'. Most human beings make the very natural assumption that most other human beings love their independence and will fight for it, and it is true that all animals, including humans, will fight grimly for their own 'territory'.

But it is also true that in any casually chosen group of 20 men, one is a leader, and can impose his will on the other 19. Dictators like Stalin, Hitler and Mussolini owed their power to this biological peculiarity; and so did the Matrangas. If there had been any concerted resistance, no doubt they would have gone back to keeping a saloon and brothel. But their army of labourers handed over 10 per cent of their wages without protest; the Provenzanos paid the Matrangas for their services as a labour exchange, and suddenly the latter were on the road to being rich.

New Orleans masters

One day it struck them that the reason the Provenzanos didn't mind paying them 'protection' was because they were making such an excellent income from the fruit ships they unloaded: after all, the labour force belonged to the Matrangas. So the Matrangas told the Provenzanos that from now on they would cease to act as middle men. Instead, the Matrangas would take over the loading and unloading of the ships. To underline the point, Provenzano managers and foremen were badly beaten up, the Provenzanos gave in to the blackmail, and the Matrangas, still slightly astonished at the ease with which it had all been accomplished, were master of all the Italian casual labour in New Orleans.

But the Matrangas made the mistake of carrying on their war against the Provanzanos; they began to harass their grocery business. In desperation, the Provenzanos hired their own gunmen, and there were clashes in the streets. David Hennessy, one of the brothers who had captured Esposito, knew and liked the Provenzanos. He had an intense dislike of the Matrangas' organization of murder and extortion, which had killed his brother Mike in Houston, Texas, five years after Esposito's arrest.

When he was appointed chief of police, Hennessy decided he would stamp out the Mafia. One morning in 1890, a truckload of Provenzano men were on their way to work at a dock that had still not been taken over by the Matrangas. Suddenly, men with shotguns appeared out of the darkness and began firing indiscriminately. Since they were using buckshot, the darkness made no difference; two men were killed, and many others wounded.

Hennessy decided this was the last straw, and he began collecting evidence of Mafia activity in New Orleans. An anonymous letter warned him that he would be killed if he continued, but he ignored it. He corresponded with the Rome police, asking for names and photographs of some of Esposito's old gang. In April 1890, the Provenzanos retaliated by ambushing Tony Matranga and two of his henchmen. They succeeded in wounding them. Matranga identified two of his assailants as Joe and Pete Provenzano.

The police had no alternative but to arrest them, and their trial was set for October 17. David Hennessy declared publicly that he would appear in the witness stand for the Provenzanos, and make their trial the opportunity to divulge information about the Mafia in New Orleans.

He never reached the court room, for at midnight on October 15, 1890, Hennessy turned into Basin Street, and three men jumped out of a doorway, to riddle him with bullets. The dying man pulled out his own revolver and succeeded in firing four shots at the fleeing assassins; but he died as he reached the hospital.

This was too much – to shoot down a chief of police who was doing his best to stamp out organized crime. It was a direct confrontation between the criminals and the rest of society. Hennessy's investigations had disclosed that, in Sicily, the Mafia was stonger than the police, but it should never happen in America. Feeling against Italians became so intense that they began to be afraid of venturing outdoors during daylight; many were attacked in the street.

Eleven strong suspects

Hennessy's files quickly provided the police with 11 strong suspects. The 11 men were arrested the day after the police chief's murder. One of them was a man called Antone Scaffide. On the day after his arrest, a young man named Duffy walked into the jail and asked to see Scaffide. When the prisoner was brought out, Duffy suddenly produced a revolver and fired. The bullet only wounded Scaffide. Asked why he had done it, Duffy said that if there were more men like him in New Orleans, the Mafia would soon cease to exist. Naturally, his sentence was light.

Twenty-one Italians were eventually arrested, including Charles Matranga, and a 14-year-old boy who was accused of signalling Hennessy's approach to the killers. The law-abiding citizens of New Orleans sighed with relief – it looked as if justice would be done after all. The trial of nine of the Italians, including Matranga, was set for February 1891, but soon the citizens began to suspect that Justice was not going to have it all her own way. The Matrangas could afford expensive lawyers, and a great battery of legal talents was lined up for the defence.

The evidence at the trial was overwhelming. Many witnesses came forward to say they had seen some of the defendants running away from the scene of Hennessy's murder. One defendant broke down and confessed to being present at a meeting of the Mafia when Hennessy's death was decreed. It ought to have been an open and shut case. But halfway through the trial the judge ordered the acquittal of the 14-year-old boy, and also of Charles Matranga. The jury retired; when they returned, their verdict was that four of the accused were not guilty, and that they were unable to agree about three others, including Scaffide. It was obvious that the jurors had been either bribed or intimidated and that the same applied to many of the lawyers on the case.

The flag of Italy

The Italian colony added insult to injury by holding parties in the street to celebrate the acquittal of the nine – which everyone expected to be a prelude to the dismissal of the case against the others. A gang of Sicilians tore down an American flag, trampled it in the mud, and than hung it upside down below the flag of Italy.

For the citizens of New Orleans, that was the final indignity. In the morning newspapers of March 14, advertisements requested 'all good citizens' to attend a mass meeting that evening, and to come 'prepared for action'. It was signed by 61 prominent citizens. That evening, a seething crowd filled Canal Street. The 61 citizens appeared, and some of them spoke briefly from the pedestal of a statue of Henry Clay, declaring that it was necessary for the poeple to take justice into their own hands. The men led the crowd to a gun store and handed out rifles. Then they marched to the prison.

The prison governor locked all prisoners in their cells except the Italians, who were told to find hiding places. The execution squad, led by William Parkerson, a well-known public figure, broke open a wooden door at the back of the prison, stationed armed guards there, then went deliberately through the jail, seeking out 11 Italians who were believed beyond doubt to be guilty of the murder. (Oddly enough, this list did not include Charles Matranga.)

These 11 men were dragged out and killed – nine shot, two

hanged. Then, in good order, the 'avengers' marched out. The mob dispersed quietly. It was the end of Mafia power in New Orleans. There was an attempted revival in 1900 when the 'Black Hand' kidnapped the child Walter Lamana and killed him. But when the gang members were arrested and tried, this second 'rebirth' also came to an end.

Sadly, this was only the beginning of the story of the Mafia and protection rackets. In the 1970s the story is still unfolding and it seems as if organized crime – like the poor – will always be with us.

ROBBER BARONS

Many of the greatest American fortunes – including those enjoyed today by some of the most respected and influential families in the world – were based on terror and corruption. The original Vanderbilt, who began with a borrowed 100 dollars, was so ruthless that he masterminded a war which smashed the government of a foreign country where his interests were threatened. And when his favourite son died, leaving 200 million dollars, the family was so scared that the body might be snatched from the 11-acre mausoleum that they hired a night-guard who was ordered to punch a time-clock every 15 minutes.

The first millionaire Rockefeller, son of an itinerant peddler of patent medicines, was denounced by a Congressional investigation as having attempted 'one of the most gigantic and dangerous conspiracies ever conceived'. He was so hated that, at the peak of his power, he was hanged and burned in effigy. Again, the single-minded greed of the founder of the Astor dynasty – who was one of 12 children fathered by an obscure village butcher in Germany – was largely responsible for a series of murders. He also swelled his fast-growing fortune, which was to establish him as the richest man in America, by trafficking in opium.

In the spectacular hey-day of hell-raising America, when life was cheap and politicians could be bought like pop-corn, these were the men who crushed all opposition and clawed their way to the top. They were the Robber Barons.

John Jacob Astor, born on June 17, 1763, in the small German village of Walldorf, was the first and probably the most remarkable of them all. His descendants are today regarded as the cream of society on both sides of the Atlantic, Royalty is proud to regard them as friends, and, indeed, the Duke of Edinburgh agreed to be godfather to one of the Astor children. Their style of life has become a by-word for elegance, and their influence stretches around the world. Yet this whole amazing dynasty was founded by John Jacob the butcher's son, who arrived in America in 1784 with exactly five English pounds in his pocket.

New York in those days had a population of less than 300,000. What is now downtown New York was open, pleasant country-side with barely a scattering of farms, but the city itself was filthy. Pigs rooted around in the garbage which was strewn across the streets of even the better residential areas, and families got their drinking-water from public pumps at street corners.

But to John Jacob, after the backwater of Walldorf village, this seemed the most exciting place on earth. He could never have guessed then that, thanks to his efforts, his family were later to be described as the 'owners of New York'. He was not afraid of work, no matter how hard or unpleasant, and at first he kept himself by peddling cakes and cookies through the foul-smelling streets. Soon he progressed to a more lucrative and far more odious task – beating the bugs and dust out of furs. For this he was given two dollars a week and his board.

More money

It was not long before his employer was sending him into the wild country north of Albany to trade with the Indians, bartering tobacco, cheap cloth and jewellery for musquash, otter and beaver skins. There were immense dangers, for much of the territory was occupied by hostile Indians, but John Jacob, whatever his faults, certainly did not lack courage.

He was not a man to be content to remain an employee, and realizing the vast profits which could be wrestled from the fur trade, he began trading with the Indians on his own account. Most men in the fur trade at that time hired middle-men to deal with the Indians, for they considered themselves to be gentlemen and that the work was too dirty and dangerous. This was where John Jacob had a great advantage. Having been brought up in the blood and mess of a butcher's shop, he had no illusions about being a gentleman, and he was prepared to do anything if the rewards were high enough.

Other dealers, lacking the tenacity of John Jacob, dropped out of the fur trade because of the obstacles deliberately organized against them by the British. The British, furious over their defeat at the hands of the former colonists, had passed a law which meant that all furs bought in their territory – which included Montreal and most of the frontier posts – had to be sent straight to England before being shipped back to New York.

John Jacob, a genius at buying cheap and selling dear, persevered. His profit margins were reduced by the infuriating double-journey across the Atlantic, but, by persistence and slogging hard work, he became one of the most powerful fur dealers in New York. Then, in 1796, the law was changed. Furs bought in Canada could be sent direct to New York, and within four years – only 16 years after his arrival in America – John Jacob made his first quarter of a million dollars. His empire began to flourish at a tremendous pace. And the more money he acquired, the more he wanted.

All the fur traders were completely unscrupulous in using liquor to swindle the Indians, and John Jacob became the master of the alcoholic bargain. His agents operated their own stills – making the semi-lethal drink at five cents a gallon and selling it to the Indians at 50 cents for a small bottle – and they got the Indians so befuddled that the pelts were virtually being given away. At one stage John Jacob not only got his furs for nothing, but was actually 'owed' vast sums of liquor money by the Indians.

But because of John Jacob – later described as 'a self-invented money-making machine' – hundreds of white men were treated even worse than the Indians. Workmen employed by the traders, who in turn were dependent on John Jacob, were being hired for 100 dollars a year. He considered this far too much, although the work was so arduous that many men died before completing their contract, and insisted that, in future, the rate should be 250 dollars for three whole years. The traders, however, were kept almost permanently in John Jacob's debt because of the astronomical prices charged them for supplies, and sometimes had their workmen murdered just before pay-day, thus reducing the wage-bill.

Bribery was also used as an empire-building tool by the semi-literate John Jacob. He once wrote to President James Monroe: 'It may not *bee* convenient to repay me the *sume* Lend to you nor am I particularly in want of it.' But, instead of the return of his cash, he did expect favours – and he got them. Monroe delegated the authority for dealing with all complaints against John Jacob's company to Governor Lewis Cass of the Michigan Territory. And although there were plenty of complaints, Cass never took any action. A sum of $35,000 was paid to him by John Jacob's company – although the services were never specified.

Crafty deal

It was not long before John Jacob had so much money that he could hardly remember what life was like without it. And it was in all seriousness that he once told a friend: 'A man who has a million dollars is as well off as if he were rich.'

But the really big money came from diversification. He bought a share of a ship, then a whole ship, and finally a splendid fleet of ships. And with these ships he launched a scheme which everyone else considered to be financially suicidal – to open up the Far East as a market for his company's furs. The British East India Company dominated trade in that area, but somehow – and there were rumours that more bribery was involved – John Jacob won their permission to take his vessels into any of their ports.

And those vessels returned to New York with cargoes which were even more valuable – tea, spices and silk. All of this would have made enough profit to satisfy 10 ordinary tycoons; but not John Jacob. On the return voyage his vessels called for food and water at the Hawaiian Islands, where sandalwood was cheap and plentiful. For nearly 20 years, thanks to his initiative, he held the monopoly of the sandalwood trade.

From the Asiatic port of Smyrna, reputed to be the birthplace of Homer, his ships also picked up vast quantities of opium. The fact that people were encouraged to destroy themselves with the drug was of little interest to John Jacob. There was money in the trade, and that was all that mattered.

A typical example of his cunning was seen shortly before the war of 1812, when an embargo imposed by an uneasy government kept all American ships locked in New York harbour. Astor sent a Chinese mandarin, Punqua Wing-chong, to the New York officials with an appeal for him to be allowed to return home for the funeral of his father. The appeal went to the President, who agreed that, in the special circumstances, Punqua Wing-chong could have special dispensation to sail on the ship *Beaver*.

John Jacob's competitors were furious when he started loading the *Beaver* – his own vessel, of course – with a vast consignment of furs. But he pointed out that it would be ridiculous to send a large vessel on such a voyage to carry just one Chinese gentleman – and, anyway, the President had personally approved the sailing. Due to the inflated prices the shortages helped him to charge, the round voyage earned John Jacob nearly $250,000.

However, the vast bulk of John Jacob's fortune came through the soaring values of land in and around New York. One of his first major killings came in 1809. Through a characteristically crafty deal he gained over 51,012 acres of Putnam County. The land had been taken from Roger and Mary Morris during the American Revolution because they were Tories.

Astor discovered that, technically, the government had no legal right to confiscate the land, for the Morrises had held only a lifetime lease on it. After their deaths it was to go to their three children – and it would be illegal for the children to suffer because of their father's political mistakes. Old Mrs. Morris was still alive, but John Jacob ignored her and traced her children to England, where he persuaded them to sell him their eventual rights for about $100,000.

He then waited until the death of Mrs. Morris – who, to his annoyance, lingered to the age of 96 – before revealing his master strategy. Seven hundred families had bought farms on the land from the New York State Government, and John Jacob sent each of them a notice of eviction. They had improved the land and built houses, barns and cottages, but in law they were trespassing on his property. The State had to step in and buy him off – so giving him a fantastic profit.

Another example of the money-spinning art of John Jacob came in 1804, when a neighbour, the politician Aaron Burr, shot his rival Alexander Hamilton in a duel and had to flee the country. It was John Jacob who provided him with enough money to make his escape in return for the lease of a huge tract of land. That land is now Greenwich Village.

Mortgage foreclosures ranked high in his system; that was how he acquired Eden Farm from an impoverished whisky distiller. Relatives of the distiller later disputed the legality of his action, and he bought them off for $9,000. The farm later became Broadway from 42nd to 46th Streets and has been valued at over twenty million dollars.

There was just one bitter disappointment in the life of John Jacob Astor. His first-born son, John Jacob II, was born mentally defective and for some time had to be confined to an institution. But there was another son, William Backhouse Astor, who inherited the bulk of the fortune and who had a flair for making the money grow. A curiously coincidental sequel to this tragedy was seen in the story of the first Vanderbilts.

Cornelius Vanderbilt I – born into a long line of Dutch Van der Bilts who grew vegetables on Staten Island – also named a son after himself. Like John Jacob Astor II, Cornelius Vanderbilt II was also locked away for a while in an asylum; he was an epileptic and a tremendous disappointment to the old man. But, here again, there was another son called William – just as in the Astor family – and it was he who eventually proved as financially astute as his father.

Old Cornelius Vanderbilt, known for most of his life as the Commodore, was born in 1794. And when he died at the age of 83 he left a fortune of $105m. He was a flamboyant six-footer, a hard-living and hard-swearing man with incredible energy. He was almost a fanatic about his diet, and his standard breakfast was a lamb chop, the yolks of three eggs, toast, and a mug of tea into which he carefully counted twelve lumps of sugar. After fathering 12 children by his first wife he eloped with a young girl. He was then 75, but no one was unduly surprised. The Commodore could always be relied on to do the unpredictable.

Invading army

When he was only 16 he persuaded his mother to lend him 100 dollars to buy a two-masted sailing barge in which he could carry produce around New York Bay. She insisted on him earning the loan by ploughing, harrowing and planting eight acres of the family farm within one month. Soon he owned three ferries, and often worked 24 hours without sleep.

A year later came war with Great Britain, and a British fleet was menacing New York. The American commissary general asked for bids to transport supplies to military posts around the harbour. Cornelius Vanderbilt's bid was accepted, and as he was prepared to take risks which frightened off other operators he quickly prospered. In 1849 he secured a charter from the Nicaraguan government for a water route across the isthmus of Panama – using it to transport thousands of 'forty-niners' from New York to California. Like Astor, he too began to diversify and soon established himself as America's first great railroad king.

The Nicaraguan exercise provides one of the best insights into the ruthlessness of the Commodore as a Robber Baron. In May 1853 he took his family on a grand cruise to Russia, England, Germany, France and Italy in his luxury 270-ft-long steam yacht the *North Star*, and while he was away, two of his associates in Nicaragua – Charles Morgan and C.K. Garrison – misused their power of attorney to rob him of his rights there. After his rage had subsided he dictated a letter which gave a clear insight into how he operated. It said: 'Gentlemen, you have undertaken to cheat me. I'll ruin you.'

Shortly afterwards a man called William Walker, from Nashville, Tennessee, arrived in Nicaragua with a small invading army

of Nicaraguan exiles. There was a little fighting before the
country's President was deposed and replaced by one well
disposed to Morgan and Garrison. His friendship, of course, was
encouraged by bribes. But the new President died shortly after
assuming office, and William Walker became President. He, too,
favoured Morgan and Garrison in their fight with the Commodore.

So the Commodore launched his own private war against
Nicaragua. He somehow managed to persuade four neighbouring republics that it was in their mutual interest to organize a
'defensive alliance' against the regime of President William
Walker, and he even arranged the formation of an invading
army. Walker was defeated, and the Commodore, who now
wielded vast influence in Washington, urged that the Marines
ought to be sent to Nicaragua to 'protect American interests'.
They did, and, once again, the Commodore had won. When he
died he left $90m. of his fortune to his son William; by the time
William died, only eight years later, he had transformed that
inheritance to more than $200m.

It is intriguing to note how, with the Robber Barons, the
patterns seem to have repeated themselves. Old John Jacob
Astor, for example, towards the end of his days suffered from
such an acute stomach disorder that he was able to digest only
human milk. A wet nurse had to be found for him. Many years
later the same diet was ordered for another man whose surname
has become a synonym for wealth – John D. Rockefeller.

Rockefeller, born in Richford, New York, in 1839, started his
business career – as Cornelius Vanderbilt had done – with a loan
from his parents. His father William was a glib and unreliable
character who had to disappear from home for a while in 1849
after being charged with raping a servant girl. William earned a
precarious living as a travelling peddler of quack medicines
which could 'cure cancer' and every other ailment from baldness
to ingrowing toenails. However, in 1854 he was sufficiently in
funds to be able to lend John $1,000 – at ten per cent interest.
There was, however, clearly a streak of generosity in old
William, for he did say that if the interest was paid regularly for
three years he would consider the $1,000 a gift.

John, like the original millionaires Astor and Vanderbilt, was
pitiless with himself in his pursuit of money. He worked himself
to the limits. He was also pitiless with others – for he saw success
as being in control of a complete monopoly. By the time he was
38 he controlled 95 per cent of all oil pipe-lines and refineries in

the United States – and behind him was a trail of ruined men. His Standard Oil Company flourished, and one of his major aims was to wipe out all refining competition in Cleveland. By doing a complicated deal with the railroads, he organized a conspiracy which would have smashed the smaller companies out of existence – unless they cooperated with him on his terms.

He was the major customer with the railroads in the area, so with them he could call the tune. Through a corporation called the South Improvement Company he made contracts with three railroads – the Erie, Pennsylvania and the New York Central – under which they agreed to jack up the freight charges for the smaller independents to a prohibitive level. They also agreed to carry Rockefeller's oil at a substantially reduced fee. This would enable him to undercut any company which refused to throw in their lot with him on his terms.

Real piracy

It was all legal – legal piracy of the most blatant kind. Anger flared through the oil business. Rockefeller became the most detested and reviled mogul in American history, and his effigy was hanged and burned. The Pennsylvania legislature was forced to rescind the South Improvement Company's charter, and a hurriedly convened Congressional investigation denounced Rockefeller's efforts as 'one of the most gigantic and dangerous conspiracies ever conceived'.

Seven years before Rockefeller was born another American called Israel Thorndike proved conclusively that in the rough-and-tumble grabbing after riches there was a great deal to be said for real piracy. He never climbed anywhere near the league of the Rockefellers or the Vanderbilts, but he did have the distinction of becoming the first millionaire in New England. He made his money as the captain of a privateer and took many rich prizes. These he invested in the risky manufacturing ventures of Massachusetts and New Hampshire, leaving a phenomenal $1½m. when he died in 1832.

The Rockefeller story might well have been different if a man from Scotland called Andrew Carnegie had been more successful in the great western Pennsylvania oil-rush. For Carnegie, who later went on to control two-thirds of America's steel production, would certainly have been a powerful rival – and it is impossible to speculate on which one would eventually have won domination. However, Carnegie did little more than flirt with the oil business.

Savage battles

Carnegie started his career in the classic American way – as a 14-year-old messenger boy with a telegraph company. He moved on to become a private secretary to a top man in the Pennsylvania Railroad and eventually was appointed superintendent of the Pittsburgh division. With money saved from his railroad salary he bought his way into a company building iron bridges and then joined three others to form the Union Iron Mills.

After two years of the partnership he managed, by shrewd wheeling and dealing, to take control of the Mills. He kept on telling his partners that the business was about to sink and that he was thinking seriously about selling out. Finally, one of them became so worried by Carnegie's gloomy prognostications that he did sell out – not realizing he was selling out to a stooge planted by Carnegie.

An insight into the toughness of his character was provided in April 1892, when he summoned his general manager to his New York mansion and gave him a signed notice which was to be displayed for the benefit of all employees at Carnegie's Homestead Works. It said that, in future, no members of a labour union called the Amalgamated Association of Iron and Steel Workers would be employed – and was intended to pave the way for a wage-slashing campaign planned by Carnegie. Then, having landed the general manager – Mr. Henry Frick – with this unpleasant task, Carnegie hurried off for a holiday in Scotland.

This plan to wipe out the union provoked such a backlash that 300 guards from Pinkerton's National Detective Agency were called to the Homestead Works. Men were maimed and injured in savage gun battles, and more than 40 Pinkerton men were almost torn to pieces. State troops were called in, 163 men were seriously wounded, and fourteen died.

The outrage threw the nation into a turmoil, and most of the wrath fell on Carnegie. He was savagely attacked, not only for having given the orders which sparked the violence but for having hidden away out of the country while Frick did the dirty work.

Union leaders, of course, have often stated that their own jobs have been made easier by the attitudes of men like Carnegie; the more brutal an employer was in his efforts to destroy the power of the unions, the more the men were aware of the need for a powerful union – and the harder they fought for it.

This principle was clearly demonstrated in the Ford company when the management battled so hard to resist the march of the unions in the late 1930s. Henry Ford I – born in July 1863 – was completely different from his grandson Henry Ford II. He was a complex character, a curious mixture of humanitarianism and quite frightening harshness. He considered himself to be a benevolent and generous employer, and he would have been genuinely shocked to learn that he was considered to be ranking high among the most self-centred of the Robber Barons.

Union busting tactics

In 1916 Henry I hired an ex-sailor called Harry Bennett, whose prime job was to act as head of an espionage network which would keep Henry I informed of all the undercurrents in his factories. He formed his own private police force of wrestlers, thugs and college athletes, and it was their duty to beat up anyone who dared to do anything so evil as talk about forming or joining a union; after being beaten up, the victims would then be fired for starting a fight.

In May 1937, the nation was increasingly against union-busting brutality. Leaders of the United Automobile Workers got a permit from the city of Dearborn to distribute handbills in front of the Ford Rouge plant. Bennett and his hoodlums were waiting for them. They grabbed Richard Frankensteen, one of the key union men, and pulled his coat back over his shoulders so that he was unable to defend himself. Then they kicked him in the head, kidneys and testicles. One of Frankensteen's colleagues was dragged down a flight of 36 iron steps and another man had his back broken. Then the thugs turned on the onlookers – kicking women in the stomach, beating up the journalists, and smashing the cameras of newspaper photographers.

Eventually, because of battles over the question of union representation, Fords were found guilty of numerous violations of federal law. The Supreme Court upheld the convictions. After Henry II became president of the company in September 1945 the first thing he did was fire Harry Bennett. An era of terror was finally over, and no one could ever again say that the Ford empire was in the grip of a Robber Baron.

SABOTAGE

It was nearly noon on November 21, 1903, and the superintendent of the Vindicator silver mine, Cripple Creek, Colorado, set out on a routine check of the mine with his shift boss. They walked cautiously; for the past three months there had been constant trouble at the mine; the miners were on strike, the National Guard had been called in, and the night watchman had seen shadowy figures wandering around.

The two men reached the sixth level, and Charles McCormick gripped a handrail to steady himself. The sound of a revolver shot made them both fling themselves backwards; then there was a tremendous roar, and the mine collapsed around them, killing them both. Later, in the wreckage, investigators found the remains of a twisted revolver. Its trigger had been attached to the handrail with a fishing line, so that when anyone grasped the shaky rail, a bullet was fired into a bundle of dynamite sticks.

Union clash

The Cripple Creek mine explosion was one of the first acts of industrial sabotage in American history. But in those days it was not known as sabotage. The word only came into general use after a French railway stike of 1912, when railwaymen cut the shoes (or 'sabots') of the railway lines to wreck trains. But sabotage, or industrial wrecking, had been preached by trade union organizations for more than 50 years; the first recorded instance of it occurred when Sheffield workers destroyed the tools of blacklegs (strike-breakers) in the 1860's.

The Cripple Creek mine explosion was not quite the first piece of industrial sabotage in American history. As early as 1892, there had been a clash between union and non-union miners at the Frisco mine at Gem, Idaho. Fifteen men died in the fight; then the strikers blew up the mine. Again, in 1899, a gang from Burke, Idaho, blew up the Bunker-Hill-Sullivan mine at

Wardner, Idaho. These cases were not, perhaps, 'sabotage' in the modern sense. But an explosion that occurred soon after the Cripple Creek incident *was*. On June 6, 1904, 26 non-union men from a mine at Independence, Colorado, were standing on the platform at a train depot after finishing their day's work. A sudden explosion turned the depot into matchwood, killing 14 of the men and seriously injuring the rest – some were crippled for life.

On November 17, 1904, Fred Bradley, ex-manager of the Bunker-Hill-Sullivan mine walked into the hall of his San Francisco home and lit a cigar; the next moment a discharge blew him straight out of the door. Although seriously injured, he recovered, and the San Francisco gas company subsequently paid him nearly $11,000 in damages, assuming the explosion to be due to a faulty gas main.

On December 30, 1905, Frank Steunenburg, ex-governor of Idaho, opened his garden gate, and was hurled into the air by a blast of dynamite. His wife rushed out to find the snow stained with blood, and her husband unrecognizable – and dying. The police acted quickly. All roads out of the city were closed, and the hotels were searched. They were in luck; the proprietor of the Saratoga Hotel thought that one of his guests had been acting suspiciously; when the police called the next day, the man was still there. In his room, the police found potassium chlorate, and other explosive ingredients. He was a small, cheerful-looking Irishman with a round, red face, and he gave his name as Harry Orchard. Many people at the time recorded the impression that he didn't *want* to get away – that he sought out the notoriety and publicity that he felt were his due. And he got them.

Planted bomb
He confessed to a whole series of crimes. He had personally lighted the fuse that blew up the Bunker-Hill-Sullivan mine; he had planted the dynamite and revolver in the Cripple Creek mine; he had planted the bomb that blew up the railway station at Independence; he had blown up Govenor Steunenburg, *and* Fred Bradley. The explosion that blew Bradley out of his own front door was not gas; it was pure coincidence that it took place as he lit a cigar.

Having got himself arrested. Harry Orchard – whose real name was Albert Horsley – proceeded to wriggle his neck out of the hangman's noose. The first thing he did was to implicate several leaders of the Western Federation of Miners Union, including William Haywood, George Pettibone, and Charles Moyer. He then had a religious 'revelation', and declared himself to be a reformed man who had seen the light. He told reporters smugly that he had believed he was engaged in a class war, but that since God had enlightened him, he realized he had only been seeking revenge. His plan worked; he was sentenced to life imprisonment, and subsequently became a Seventh Day Adventist and a leading preacher in the penitentiary.

But if Orchard's conversion was unworthy of a revolutionary, his methods were an inspiration to labour saboteurs the world over. At the Independence railroad depot, a hundred pounds of dynamite had been placed under the floor. Detonating caps were placed on the dynamite. Above them, attached to a small wheel, was a bottle of sulphuric acid. A long wire fixed to the wheel meant that the acid could be tilted on to the caps at any time. Orchard was several hundred yards away when he tugged the wire that sent the station sky high.

He had got into Fred Bradley's home by becoming the lover of one of his servant girls. He used the same device – sulphuric acid on a kind of windlass. This time, however, the wire was attached to the door, so that the dynamite would explode when the door was opened. The same dynamite and acid-bottle device was used to blow up Mr. Frank Steunenburg.

There is one interesting point about Orchard's long confession. For all its pious expression of repentance for his crimes, it is obvious that he enjoyed every minute of his strange manhunts. He had discovered a new sport that combined the adult's love of hunting with the child's delight in causing loud bangs. It is a characteristic that appears in many saboteurs.

Labour hero

In spite of Orchard's confessions, the accused Union leaders managed to escape largely due to the brilliant efforts of the great advocate, Clarence Darrow. Darrow became the hero of the American labour movement, and Pettibone, Moyer and the rest were regarded as near martyrs. In retrospect, it seems more than likely that the Union leaders *were* accessories. They were fortunate in that America's greatest criminal lawyer chose to defend them.

America suddenly discovered the full meaning of sabotage in World War I. The United States had a high population of immigrant Germans, many of them American citizens. Even before the United States entered the war, in April 1917, it was supplying England with arms and food. And then the explosions began. It was on a hot June evening in 1916 that a guard in the great freight yards of Black Tom – the promontory of New Jersey that faces New York City – was startled to see a fire burning under a railroad wagon loaded with munitions. Then he saw another fire a hundred yards away. He rang the fire alarm, but a quarter of an hour later tremendous explosions sent a column of smoke and fire into the air.

The whole freight yard, full of munitions for the Allies, went off like a giant bomb. The concussion was enough to have destroyed the skyscrapers of Wall Street, but the force of the blast went upwards; only two adults and a child were killed. A landlady subsequently reported that her lodger, a Hungarian named Michael Kristoff, had been pacing his room all night after the explosion groaning 'What have I done?' An American agent actually got an admission of guilt out of Kristoff; then Kristoff disappeared. Ironically, he had been arrested for a civil offence, and put in jail, where he stayed for the duration of the war.

On the other side of the country, in San Francisco, a German reported to the authorities that he had heard of a plot to blow up the Mare Island Navy Yard. Before the authorities could act, the yard erupted in flames and suffered explosions as violent as those at Black Tom. This time 16 children were among the dead.

The solution of the Mare Island explosion came by chance, after the outbreak of war in 1917. Although Mexico was neutral, there was much anti-Americanism there, and the Mexican police made no attempt to harass Germans who were obviously spies. Washington persuaded Paul Altendorf, a colonel in the Mexican army, to act as a counter-spy. In Mexico City bars, Altendorf made the acquaintance of Kurt Jahnke, who was suspected of being an enemy agent. Jahnke was a heavy drinker. One day, in a confiding mood, he told Altendorf that he was the patriotic citizen who had reported the plot to blow up Mare Island to the authorities – and also the man who had then blown it up. He had reported it because he knew that he would then be the last person to be suspected of the explosion.

Jahnke was an explosives expert, who worked in combination with Lothar Witzke, another of Germany's most skilled saboteurs. Altendorf, pretending to be as anti-American as Jahnke, offered his aid in future projects. Jahnke said that Witzke needed help finding his way back across the Mexican border into the United States. Altendorf said that he knew the country intimately and would be glad to help. The consequence was that when Witzke arrived in Nogales, Arizona, he found American Secret Service men waiting to arrest him. He was subsequently sentenced to death, but reprieved and later allowed to return to Germany.

Beautiful spy

The end of the Witzke-Jahnke team was one of the triumphs that helped to put a stop to sabotage in World War I; the other was the capture of the beautiful German spy, Maria von Kretschman. This was due to a fortunate accident: a courier put two letters into the wrong envelopes. On the advice of British Intelligence, American agents were already watching an address on Long Island. A letter was duly intercepted, and the agents were puzzled. The envelope was addressed to a man – one of the German agents they were on the lookout for – but the letter inside was to a woman.

Chemical technicians tested the letter, and found another letter on the back, written in invisible ink. It was about the blowing up of munitions factories and mines. With excitement, the agents realized they had stumbled on a key figure in the sabotage network. But who was she? They traced the courier who had sent the letter – he had put his return address on the envelope – a sailors' lodging-house – but that didn't help much.

The man was simply a go-between who had agreed to post the two letters when he landed in New York. It was he who had removed the letters from their grubby old envelopes and in re-addressing them, put them back in the wrong envelopes. He could even recall the address on the other envelope – but again the agents were frustrated. An old lady who lived there said she sometimes received letters for someone else, but she couldn't give any more information – except that she had once seen the name 'Victoria' on one of them.

That didn't seem much to go on. The agents managed to find another cache of unopened 'Victoria' letters at another *poste restante* address; but again the trail led nowhere. All they proved was that Victoria *was* involved in the series of explosions that were rocking American factories and dockyards every other week. The Secret Service then deployed dozens of agents to watch every person mentioned in the letters. They maintained their surveillance for weeks, and no one did anything suspicious. One weary agent reported to his chief that the young sister of one of the suspects seemed to be very religious – she never missed going to church. His chief looked up sharply. 'In that case, follow her, you fool!'

Prayed briefly

His intuition proved to be correct. The next day, the agent saw the young girl kneel down in St. Patrick's Cathedral in Fifth Avenue, and place a newspaper on the seat; when she left, the newspaper was still there. Another man moved into the pew, prayed briefly, and left carrying the newspaper. The man went to a Long Island hotel, the Nassau, sat in the lounge for a few minutes. Then he walked out, leaving the newspaper behind. A tall beautiful blonde woman in her thirties then sat down and casually picked it up.

A few days later, she was under arrest, the elusive Madame Victoria — whose real name was Maria von Kretschman. Under interrogation, she confessed — and told the agents how she had used religion to aid her activities as a key saboteur. She persuaded Catholic priests to help her in ordering religious statuettes from Zürich, in Switzerland. When the statuettes arrived, they would be full of chemicals vital to the detonating of explosives. The nervous strain had been telling on her; now that she was arrested, she cracked. (She died, a drug addict, a few years later.) With her capture, and the break-up of the Jahnke-Witzke partnership, the United States had eliminated the sabotage ring that had been causing so much damage.

The damage might have been worse if one of Germany's master spies — and saboteurs — had not been hamstrung by jealousy from bureaucrats at home. Franz Rintelen von Kleist — usually known simply as Von Rintelen — got into the United States on a Swiss passport in the month America declared war. His speciality was sabotage.

A German-American, Dr. Schlee, had invented a new incendiary device, no bigger than a fountain pen. It was divided in half by a thin copper wall. One half contained picric acid, the other half, sulphuric acid. When the sulphuric acid ate through the copper, a brilliant, hot flame shot out of the device. It was called a Thermit pencil. Von Rintelen contacted Schlee, arranged for the manufacture of hundreds of Thermit pencils, and passed them on to Irish dock workers who hated the British — and who dropped them into cracks on munition ships about to depart for England.

Soon there were fires at sea, and the British realized that a new master saboteur was at work. Another German inventor named

Fay produced a kind of bomb that would explode as the rudder of a ship moved from side to side; it was attached by a magnet, like a modern limpet mine. The mysterious fires at sea were then supplemented by mysterious explosions that destroyed the ship's rudder.

Von Rintelen's brilliance was his own undoing. Congratulatory messages came from high sources in the Fatherland, and passed through the Washington Embassy. Jealousies and resentments flared. To Von Rintelen's alarm, the men who should have been protecting him began to commit indiscretions; one day, he actually received a letter addressed to him with his correct name (he was under an alias, naturally) and military title. As American agents closed in, he slipped on board a ship. All might have been well; but the ship stopped at Southampton. Although his passport said he was a Swiss citizen, Von Rintelen was questioned. Suddenly, the interrogator tried an old trick; he yelled in German: 'Salute' – and Von Rintelen's heels automatically clicked together.

Greatest saboteur

Even then, he succeeded in escaping from custody, and was finally captured in Leicester. The great British spy chief, Admiral 'Blinker' Hall, took advantage of his resentment about the German Embassy to get him to cooperate with British Intelligence. The man who could have been Germany's top saboteur of World War I was turned into a traitor by the petty envy and jealousy of his superiors.

The greatest saboteur of all time was also a German, although he devoted his life to working for Soviet Russia. Ernst Friedrich Wollweber was born in 1898, the son of a Hamburg miner. He was short, chunky, ugly, and driven by immense energy; later in life, he became an obese dwarf. It may have been some desire to compensate for his unattractive appearance that turned Wollweber into a revolutionary. In 1917, he joined the German navy; inspired by the Russian Revolution, he preached Socialism below decks. It was Wollweber's propaganda that helped stir the German fleet to mutiny in November 1918, and he personally hauled up the Red Flag on the cruiser *Heligoland* at the entrance to the Kiel Canal – the signal for the revolt.

In Bremen, Wollweber led rioters on the Oslebhausen prison, and saw the prisoners set free. He hoped for a swift Communist triumph in Germany – but he was disappointed. Even in defeat, Germany was not ready for revolution. The Weimar Republic was formed in 1919 and Wollweber responded by leading another mutiny on board ship, and took the vessel to Murmansk, as a present for the Soviet regime. As a reward for this, he was appointed by Lenin as chairman of the International Seamen's Union. He sailed round the world, acting as an emissary of Communism in China, Japan, Italy, and the United States.

Undismayed

The Communists were shocked by the ease with which Hitler destroyed the German Communist Party when he came to power in 1933. But Wollweber was typically undismayed. He chose Copenhagen as his headquarters, and settled down to a career as a master saboteur. Ships left Denmark loaded with supplies for the Fascists in the Spanish Civil War. Wollweber's agents mixed TNT with the coal, and many of the ships failed to reach Spanish ports, or had their cargoes destroyed by fire.

One of Wollweber's great triumphs was the destruction of the German troopship *Marion*, which left Denmark for Norway in 1940. A shattering explosion sank the ship, and badly burned corpses floated ashore for weeks afterwards – 4,000 of them. When the Nazis invaded Denmark, Wollweber moved to Sweden. Although he was promptly arrested, he had already succeeded in organizing a sabotage ring there. His agent, Jacob Liebersohn, had recruited two young waitresses, Erika Möller and Gunhild Ahman. They were ideal agents; no one suspected two women. They were responsible for the explosion that destroyed part of the freight yards at Krylbo, in central Sweden, on July 19, 1941 – and detonated truckloads of German shells. There were many more fires and explosions before the counter-espionage branch of the Swedish Statspolisen arrested the two women and their accomplices, and sent them to prison.

The Swedes kept Wollweber in jail until the end of the war, in spite of Nazi demands that he be handed over. As soon as it was clear that the Nazis were losing the war, however, they allowed Wollweber to go to Moscow. There, he was treated as a Soviet hero, and entered Berlin not far behind Marshal Zhukov. Declining important political appointments, he went back to organizing an East German spy ring. He enjoyed undercover work. He may also have felt that a public appointment would restrict his sex life – for he was known as an insatiable satyr.

Again, there were explosions on British and American ships – the fire on the *Queen Elizabeth* in 1953 was almost certainly

Wollweber's work. But that was one of his last achievements in sabotage; in that year, he was appointed Minister of State Security in East Germany. There *was* a point in 1961 when it looked as if Wollweber's luck was at last running out; after a clash with Walter Ulbricht, the Secretary of the East German Communist Party ordered Wollweber's arrest. Wollweber contacted Moscow, and a telegram arrived: 'Let Wollweber alone, he is a friend of mine.' It was signed 'Krushchev'. So Wollweber died a natural death after all, in 1962.

It is the fate of the saboteur to live in an emotional no man's land, with no place that he can openly call his own. His existence – and psychological condition – is one of constant uncertainty, fear, and suspicion. He is like a man who has betrayed his wife *and* the mistress whom he has set in her place. He is his own worst enemy.

SERVANTS WHO MURDER

According to Proudhon, the founder of modern socialism, the relation of master to servant is degrading to both parties. 'No man is good enough to be another man's master,' said the utopian William Morris. Marx elaborated the conception in his revolutionary masterpiece *Das Kapital*: the two classes, master and servant, are locked in a relentless struggle; it can only be resolved when the workers have annihilated their masters.

There is one serious objection to this theory: it happens to be untrue. Every zoologist knows that the 'pecking order' is the foundation of *all* social organization. For example, if the leader of the pack of wild dogs, or a band of apes, is killed or disabled, the two most dominant males will usually fight over the question of who is to be the new leader. They will hurl themselves on one another ferociously, giving the impression that they will fight to the death.

But if, in fact, one of them senses that he is losing the battle, he has a simple method of stopping the fight. He merely turns his back on his opponent and exposes his behind. So powerful is the basic animal instinct that the attacker instantly becomes incapable of further aggression. The gesture of surrender drains off all his fury. It demonstrates that nature's aim is to establish a *basic social order*, not to destroy the weaker. This is true for every member of any tribe or small group: *hierarchy* is one of the deepest animal instincts.

Unclassifiable freaks

This explains why, in primitive societies, rebellion and treason are regarded as the worst of all crimes, and why they were punished so barbarously. It was not simply the tyrant's fear of being overthrown, it was also an instinctive feeling that the relation of a king to his subjects, or a master to his servants, is somehow sacred. It is a ritualized relationship, and even in our democratic age the instinct remains. Every household with a servant is a small social unit, a miniature tribe. It takes some very unusual strain or tension to upset this natural order of things. This is the reason why, in the eyes of the criminologist, nearly all 'murderous menials' are unclassifiable freaks, exceptions to the rule.

Perhaps the most famous and successful of them all was Spartacus, the gladiator who led the revolt against the Romans in 72 B.C. He broke out of a gladiator's school at Capua and took refuge on Mount Vesuvius, where he was joined by other slaves. His army defeated two Roman forces one after the other, until they were 90,000 strong. He fought his way to the Alps and freedom – but his army refused to leave Italy. The Romans managed to split the rebel force in two; then they cut it to pieces. Spartacus died in battle; 6,000 of his followers were taken back to Rome and crucified along the Appian Way. This barbarity was not due to sadism; it was an expression of outraged horror at the thought of slaves rising up against their masters.

In modern history, the most famous slaves' revolt took place in Virginia in 1831; but, unlike Spartacus's rebellion, it was doomed from the beginning. The Negro slave Nat Turner was born in Southampton County, Virginia, in 1800, and from childhood he claimed that he had visions and heard voices. He became a Baptist preacher, held in great esteem among his fellow slaves. In 1828 – when he was 28 years old – Turner had a dream in which a voice told him that 'the last shall be first'.

He took this to mean that the slaves were to become the masters. They began to plan their revolt. It took three years. An eclipse of the sun in February 1831 was taken as a sign from heaven. On the night of August 21, 1831, Turner and seven other blacks entered the house of his master, Joseph Travis, and went into the bedroom. They killed Travis, three other white adults, and a male child, hacking them with tremendous violence with knives and hatchets.

Then Turner sent out word to other slaves in the area to join the revolt, and about 60 joined him. For the next 48 hours the slaves terrorized the area, sweeping through the plantations on horseback, killing every white they found, hunting women and children in the cotton fields, killing or savagely beating Negroes who refused to support them. They were making for the county town, Jerusalem, and stopped on the way at a plantation owned by a man called Parker.

The slaves broke into a wine cellar and got drunk; Turner had to beg them to rejoin him in the sacred crusade against the whites.

Meanwhile, a band of 18 vigilantes had arrived, and fired on the slaves who were waiting at the gates of the plantation. This was the turning point of the revolt. Turner and his half-drunk slaves managed to beat off the attack; but they were on the retreat: they had word that troops had been sent against them.

Mutilated bodies

They attacked another farm, but the owner barricaded himself in, and five of them drove off the small slave army. At this point the slaves panicked and decided to scatter. The militiamen and marines hunted them down in the brush. The Negroes had murdered 24 children, 18 women, and 13 men, and the hatred against them was tremendous; they were killed like vermin, some were drawn and quartered, and their bodies nailed on the doors of slave huts as a warning.

More than 100 slaves died – the additional 40 or so being suspected sympathizers of the original rebels. Finally, Turner himself was captured, two months after the insurrection began, in a cave; his captor was a solitary white man with a shot-gun. In jail he made a confession – William Styron's novel based on it, *The Confessions of Nat Turner*, became a best-seller in 1968 – and was hanged, together with 19 of his associates.

From the point of view of southern Negroes, Turner's revolt was the worst thing that could have happened. There had been a great deal of white sympathy for the slaves – it was eventually to culminate in the Civil War of 30 years later – and there were 'manumission societies' for the purpose of freeing them. All this liberal activity suddenly ceased; stricter slave codes were enacted. The fear and hatred Turner inspired lasted long after the Civil War, and it has left traces down to our own time.

The common factor among menservants who commit murder seems to be a certain emotional instability, often verging on insanity. John Felton, who murdered the Duke of Buckingham, was also, like Nat Turner, a religious fanatic. The Swiss valet Courvoisier, who murdered Lord William Russell, was a highly unstable young man; so was Henry Jacoby, the pantry boy who killed Lady White in 1922. The female of the species, on the other hand, tends to display a certain cold strength of character. Anna Maria Schonleben – known as Anna Zwanziger – may be considered a typical example.

Cold ferocity

Born in Buremberg about 1760, Anna Schonleben was the

daughter of an innkeeper. She was a bright, good-looking girl, fairly well educated for the period. When she married a lawyer, it looked as if she had achieved middle-class respectability; but her husband was an alcoholic, and when he died, he left her only debts. She found the world a hard place, and took refuge — oddly enough — in the recently published best-seller by the young poet Goethe, *The Sorrows of Young Werther*, a book whose gloomy self-pity caused an epidemic of suicides in Germany in the late 1770s.

As she drifted from job to job — as a cook in a circus, a housekeeper, a nursemaid — Anna often contemplated suicide. Finally, she stole a diamond ring from a family in Welmar, where she was serving as a housemaid. Once more she took to the wandering life, until, in Rosendorf, she became housekeeper to an old judge. Now she was on the verge of middle age, her romanticism had soured into a hatred of the world that had treated her so badly. And with a certain cold ferocity she began to plot how she could obtain a secure position in the world.

Jealousy

The judge had money; but he also had a wife from whom he was separated, and if he died, the money would go to her. Anna Schonleben began to write to the estranged wife, talked to the husband about her, and finally brought about a reconciliation. On the day when the wife, Frau Glaser, returned, the house was decked with flowers. A week later, Frau Glaser began to feel ill. Some of their guests were also taken ill after dining with them.

It is not clear whether Anna was experimenting with poison, or whether she resented having to cook for guests; as a grass widower, the old judge had kept to himself. Then, one day, Frau Glaser died with agonizing stomach pains. By this time, the judge was suspicious. In those days there was no way of detecting arsenic in corpses, but his suspicions were so strong that Anna decided to move on. She did it with regret, for it had been her intention to 'make her old age comfortable'.

She found another judge at Sanspareil, a man of 38 named Grohmann, who suffered from gout. For a while, she hoped she had found what she was looking for — a bachelor household in which she could spend the rest of her days; and then she heard that Herr Grohmann was thinking of getting married. Her feelings were complicated by jealousy — she later admitted that she thought of marrying him herself. She intercepted letters, kept a constant watch on her employer — and then decided that he must die. He succumbed to violent internal pains soon after his banns were published, and his doctor assumed it was a natural illness.

Now she was at the change of life, and it seems clear that she became mentally unbalanced. The thrill of poisoning gripped her and became a substitute for the sexual pleasures she still craved. At Grohmann's, she had poisoned the beer of two servants, apparently out of pure malice; they disliked the taste and drank very little, but another servant who drank it nearly died. Anna moved on to become housekeeper to yet another magistrate, a man named Gebhard, whose wife was ill.

The wife rapidly became worse, and disliked the taste of some of the food cooked by the new housekeeper so much that she accused Anna of poisoning her. She soon died, and because she had been ill, there was again no suspicion. Gebhard found Anna likeable and trustworthy; she had a certain air of solid honesty that impressed most people. But when his guests became ill after meals, and he himself noticed a white sediment in the bottom of a glass of brandy, he began to wonder. Finally, he decided that these continual stomach pains were too much of a coincidence and dismissed her.

Darling child

Filled with insane fury, she decided on revenge. On the morning of her departure she caressed the Gebhard baby and gave it a biscuit dipped in milk. Soon after she left, the child became violently ill, and the servants also had to retire to their beds, vomiting. Someone recalled that Anna had changed the salt in the salt box the night before. They had it examined by an apothecary, who had no difficulty in detecting arsenic. The corpses of her three victims were disinterred – Frau Glaser, Frau Gebhard and Herr Grohmann. Arsenic is a preservative and all three were perfectly preserved, suggesting that they had absorbed a large quantity of the poison.

An order for Anna's arrest was issued. Unaware of this, she took a room in Bayreuth for a month and wrote from there to Gebhard, hinting that she was willing to let bygones be bygones and return as his housekeeper. By the time the police arrived, she had moved on to the home of her son-in-law – only to discover that her daughter was in jail for theft, and the son-in-law wanted nothing to do with her. She wrote to Gebhard again from Nuremberg, sending kisses to 'her darling child' – who was still recovering from the poison. The police caught her there, with packets of arsenic in her pockets. It was October 18, 1809.

At her trial before the public prosecutor – whose role is similar to that of the examining magistrate in France – she showed extraordinary cunning and hardness of character. Knowing that it would be impossible to convict her without a confession, she parried all questions, insisting that she knew nothing of poison. With infinite patience, the judge continued interrogating her for six months. Then, one day, he told her dramatically that Frau Glaser's body had been dug up and revealed unmistakable traces of arsenic.

Dirty game

If she had kept her wits about her she might have replied that there was no way of discovering 'unmistakable' traces of arsenic; but she broke down and confessed, then fell in convulsions on the floor. She was executed with the headman's sword in July 1811.

Anna Zwanziger became a poisoner only in later life, when she felt the world was against her. She is typical of a type of criminal whose basic motive is a *sense of defeat*. It could be said that such people have allowed themselves to become 'soiled' by life; they feel the world is a grim and corrupt place. They see life as a dirty game, and they make a conscious decision to 'play it dirty'. The same applies to Courvoisier, the murderer of Lord William Russell.

On the other hand, many 'murderous menials' belong to the same type as Nat Turner: they are young, and a violent sense of injustice drives them to a frenzy of resentment – this is also characteristic of most of the children who kill.

The case of Eliza Fenning, which took place four years after the execution of Anna Zwanziger, is typical. In March 1815, Eliza was 21 years old and had been 'in service' since she was 14. Three weeks after she became cook to the family of Robert Turner of Chancery Lane, London, the mistress of the house threatened to dismiss her because she had been seen going into the bedroom of the menservants in a scanty state of attire. The girl apologized abjectly.

Four weeks later, she offered to make dumplings for the family. This was unusual – the dough was usually bought ready made from the baker; but Mrs. Turner agreed. The dumplings struck them as grey and heavy, but they ate some of them. Soon afterwards, Mrs. Turner, her husband and her father-in-law were all violently sick, and they had to call in a doctor. The next morning the father-in-law went to the kitchen and found the pan in which the dumplings had been cooked. There was a white powder in the bottom, which the family doctor declared to be arsenic.

A packet of arsenic *had* disappeared from a drawer not long before. The queston was: how had it got into the dumplings? Eliza tried to put the blame on the other servants, and her defence pointed out that she had been violently sick, too, after eating from the dumplings. The jury decided that this was probably an attempt to make herself look innocent, and she was sentenced to death. Despite much public sympathy for her, and an appeal for clemency, she was finally hanged, still protesting her innocence.

It has been pointed out that the evidence against her was purely circumstantial, and that the doctor, for example, offered no details of the tests he had conducted to prove that the white powder was arsenic. But a reading of the trial report, contained in *The Newgate Calendar*, suggests that the jury was probably right to find her guilty of poisoning, if not of attempted murder. From her evidence, Mrs. Turner sounds a highly unpleasant bully; Eliza probably intended to make them all severely ill, by way of getting her own back.

Hélène Jegado, the French poisoner who was guillotined in 1851 at Rennes, was probably insane – or, at least, severely deranged. A female servant of a Rennes doctor had died in agony, and the other servants were convinced it was poison. When the police investigated, Hélène Jegado, a heavily built, unattractive woman her fifties, asserted her innocence so violently that the police were suspicious – since no one had accused her.

Superb coolness

A long investigation into her past revealed that during a period of 20 years she and probably poisoned 23 people. It was some strange compulsion, of the same nature as that which drove another habitual poisoner, Graham Young. Like Anna Zwangziger – Hélène Jegado was also a lifelong petty thief.

Kate Webster, England's most notorious 'murderous menial', had been a prostitute as well as a thief when she entered the employ of an elderly widow called Thomas, who lived at 2 Mayfield Cottages, Richmond. Kate was a big-boned, alcoholic Irishwoman of 39. On Sunday, March 2, 1879, Mrs. Thomas returned home from church and found Kate drunk; a violent quarrel followed, and it ended with Mrs. Thomas lying dead on the scullery floor, her skull split open with a hatchet.

Kate then behaved with superb coolness; she dismembered the body, boiled parts in a copper, and burned others on the fire. She tied the remains in brown paper parcels, put them into a wooden box about a foot square, and threw it into the river Thames; the head, hidden in a black bag, was also thrown in from Hammersmith Bridge. Kate then visited friends in Hammersmith, made the acquaintance of a well-to-do publican named Church, and induced him to buy her employer's furniture; Church actually moved into the cottage with her for a few days.

This was a risky period for Kate; she was calling herself Mrs. Thomas – alleging that she was a widow – and Mrs. Thomas's landlady lived next door. The floating box containing parts of the body was found three days after the murder; but by the time the police had heard about Mrs. Thomas's mysterious disappearance – on March 19 – Kate Webster was in Enniscorthy, County Wexford. A few charred human bones were found under the copper in the Richmond cottage.

Spare cash
Kate Webster had made one stupid mistake. A letter addressed to 'Mrs. Thomas' was found and it enabled the police to trace Kate Webster to her Irish home, Killane, where she was arrested. She was hanged on July 29, 1879.

The crime for which 18-year-old Henry Jacoby was hanged was committed in a moment of panic. Jacoby had only been pantry boy in the Spencer Hotel, Portman Street, London, for three weeks when he decided, one night, to see if he could find some spare cash lying around in one of the guests' rooms. He shone a torch around the room of 60-year-old Lady White; when she woke up and screamed, he battered her to death with a hammer, then fled.

Unusually friendly
No one suspected him, but after a week or so he confessed of his own accord. His trial took place in April 1922, and he was sentenced to death. There was a great deal of sympathy for him, particularly when the murderer Ronald True was reprieved. True's family were wealthy, and people said it was a matter of class prejudice. Nevertheless, Jacoby was executed on June 7, 1922.

The French essayist Montaigne once said that few men have been admired by their servants. This may be true; but it is also true that few men have ever been killed by their servants. The most interesting thing about the various cases of murder that have been cited in this article is that there is *no general pattern*.

Every one is an 'exception to the rule'. It is a pity that no one ever pointed this out to Karl Marx; his comments might have been interesting. Marx's own relations with servants were very friendly; so much so, in fact, that he impregnated the family nurse, putting the blame on his friend Engels. Engels only revealed the truth on his death bed. No doubt there is a moral in all this; but it will certainly not be found in the pages of *Das Kapital*.

SLEEP-WALKING SLAYERS

One of the most valuable assets any detective can have is the ability to imagine himself in the position of the criminal he is hunting. 'What would I do if I were in his place?' That is the line of thought which brings success to so many crime investigations. 'If I wanted to rob that bank . . . if I intended to kill that man . . . how would I set about it?'

Many detectives commit the crime, time and time again, inside their own minds. Some become so absorbed that their lives are dominated by their current cases. They mull them over as they drift into the limbo-land of sleep. And, just occasionally, there is a danger of them becoming obsessed.

Robert Ledru, a brilliant murder detective, did become a victim of his own dedication. It began to manipulate his mind – and it transformed him into a Sleep-Walking Slayer.

Courts of law, on both sides of the Atlantic, have returned 'not guilty' verdicts on men and women accused of a wide variety of crimes – although the people concerned admitted the act and were seen committing it. These have involved allegations of dangerous driving . . . shop-lifting . . . money thefts. And of first-degree murder. Charges have been dismissed because the accused have convinced judges and juries that, at the time of the offence, they were fast asleep.

The innocent killer

Ledru provides one of the most dramatic examples of this phenomenon of somnambulistic crime, for he is the only man in recorded history who has tracked himself down as the innocent killer. But, before considering his extraordinary case, let us look at the broad picture of nightmares and sleep-walking crime.

When a man is sleeping the defences of his mind are relaxed; fears and violent emotions which he has suppressed through the day – or which he may not even know exist – are free to roam out of their dark corners. The subconscious, which still bears the imprints of our primeval ancestors, takes control, and the shackles of inhibition and convention are torn away.

That is why so many sleep-walkers display such startlingly uncharacteristic behaviour – why shy and respectable women wander naked through busy streets, and why gentle and compassionate men become savagely brutal killers. Sleep-walking, which usually starts an hour or two after falling asleep, is far more common than many people realize. Britain has half a million sufferers and America has two million. Children are more prone to it than adults, with 5 out of 100 sleep-walking at some time compared with the adult ratio of 2 in every 100.

Killings have been committed by sleep-walking children but, before we get to examples, let us look at a much simpler case – that of two-year-old Craig Welsh. In York, England, he was seen walking in his bare feet between rush-hour cars and lorries on one of the city's busiest streets – wearing just his pyjama top and rubber pants.

Analysis of the sleep-walking state reveals that the sleeper is invariably grappling with some problem. But a child of only two? What sort of inner turmoil could provoke him into somnambulism? The most common reason is that the child wants to escape from some situation which, while appearing trivial to an adult, seems intolerable to him. Possibly he feels he has been scolded or punished unfairly.

In his sleep he dreams of escaping from the unfairness, and so urgent is the need that he really acts out the escape. In Lancashire there was a far more serious case. A seven-year-old boy climbed into the cot of his baby sister and lay on top of her. She was suffocated and the coroner, after hearing that the boy was sleep-walking at the time, recorded a verdict of misadventure.

But what stimulated that misadventure? Unconscious jealousy of the newly-arrived 'intruder'? A burning desire, normally buried in the boy's subconscious, to return to his old place as the pampered baby of the family?

Parents have also been killed by their own innocently sleeping children. Carl Kiger, a successful local-government official in Kentucky, a typical victim, was shot five times by his 16-year-old daughter Jo Ann. On August 16, 1943, Mr. and Mrs. Kiger and their two children – Jo Ann and six-year-old Jerry – went to bed early. Soon after midnight Jo Ann, who had a history of sleep-walking, had a vivid nightmare; a huge madman with wild eyes was easing his way into the house. She saw him creeping up the stairs and she was convinced he was going to murder the rest of the family. It was up to her to save them.

There is a popular but completely false belief that sleep-walkers tend to walk slowly with their arms protectively extended in front of them. In fact, the sleeper usually sits up quietly, gets out of bed and starts to move about in a clumsy and confused way; soon his movements become more co-ordinated and complex and the only clue to his somnambulistic state is the blank expression in his eyes.

This is how Jo Ann Kiger was on that August night. She took two loaded revolvers belonging to her father and first went to the 'rescue' of her little brother; one bullet went into his head, two more went into his body. He never woke.

But the 'nightmare madman' was still amok in the Kiger's once-peaceful suburban house. Jo Ann chased him into her parents' bedroom and blazed away with both guns. Her father died almost immediately. Her mother, 49-year-old Mrs. Jennie Kiger, was shot in the hip. Suddenly Jo Ann woke up – still holding the guns and with the nightmare still lingering in her mind. She stared in horror at the body of her father and said: 'There's a crazy man here who's going to kill all of us.'

She was arrested on a charge of first-degree murder but, because of the sleep-walking defence, was acquitted.

Blemishes on the mind

What *really* caused that tragedy? Our most deeply-rooted motivations, of which we may not even be aware, are a complicated legacy of the past – as it has impinged on us and on our ancestors. Anxieties and irrational dislikes are often buried deeply because they are mental blemishes, 'warts' on the mind, which people are too frightened or too inhibited to consciously recognize.

A man, for instance, may have repeated nightmares in which he is being strangled; this may not be a fear which worries him in the daytime and he may see no reason why it should haunt his nights. But, if it were possible for him to trace all his own history, he might well find that when he was a few days old he had almost suffocated in his cot. The incident has long gone into oblivion but the scar is still etched on his mind.

Legacy of dread

The same applies to the illogical fears and superstitions which we have unconsciously inherited from our long-dead ancestors; this is vividly demonstrated in the Fraser baby-battering case, described in detail in another article.

Our ancestors lived in terror of the beasts that prowled through the night. In their caves and rough huts they knew that death could be stalking them, that they might have to kill or be killed. Fraser, in a small and shabby house in 19th-century Scotland, wrestled through his sleep with that legacy of dread. The adrenalin surged through him in exactly the way it had done through his forebears. He jumped from his bed. He fought the monster and he killed it; and then he found it was his baby.

This common legacy of ours is still there, whether we realize it or not, and it forms a background tapestry to our thoughts; ocasionally we make use of it and then we tend to talk about a 'hunch' or about 'acting on instinct'. The normal conscious mind, one not shadowed by mental sickness, is capable of keeping these mental blemishes in their proper perspective. But during sleep the conscious reasoning process is no longer in command – and so there are tragedies such as the one at the Kiger household.

The Kiger case was a classic demonstration of somnambulism being stimulated by insecurity, a motivation which psychiatrists know is immensely common among children. A child hears his parents quarrelling, perhaps, and hears them threatening to leave each other. This frightens him and the fear permeates his dream; he is going to lose one or maybe both of them, he is going to be robbed of their love and protection.

There does not have to be a row. This pervading sense of insecurity could be fuelled by a chance remark, by a wrongly-interpreted remark even, which festers in the sub-conscious.

Jo Ann Kiger deeply loved her family. The bond was so important to her that she had an obsessive fear that, in some way, she might be robbed of them, and although this fear may not have been in her conscious mind it was firmly lodged in her sub-conscious. She was an intelligent girl, and, if she had been awake on that awful night and had really seen an intruder, she would probably have screamed and raised an alarm; it is most unlikely that she would have tried to tackle him single-handed. But, with reason suspended in her trance-like state, her response was purely emotional. She was going to lose her father, her mother and her brother. She alone was alive to the danger and she alone could save them.

Her brother was the smallest member of the family and so the most vulnerable. That was why her sub-conscious mental blemish took her initially to his room, and that was why he was the first to die. Children are more susceptible to sleep-walking than adults because they react more vigorously to most forms of mental stimulation. They have fewer inhibitions and have not learned the average adult's habit of self-control.

Their lips may tremble

There are ways to recognize potential sleep-walkers, even a day or so before they have set a foot out of bed. They often become quieter or more sullen, their lips may tremble a little or they may have unusual difficulty in pronouncing certain words. These are signs of some problem deep in the mind.

After a sleep-walking session the sufferer's heart usually beats faster than usual and the palms of his hands perspire more than normal. Most sleep-walkers, of course, wander harmlessly around. They may go downstairs or walk along corridors in blocks of flats and then return to their beds without realizing they have ever left them.

Some have killed themselves. One youngster, the son of a professor at Cambridge University, doused his clothing in turpentine and then set fire to himself. Another drank prussic acid. Many have fallen through windows or from great heights. In nearly every part of the world there have been cases of sleepwalkers who have woken up to find themselves in a state of acute embarrassment.

Back in 1954, for instance, there was a housewife who was found doing a Tarzan act, swinging completely naked from the branch of a garden tree. She had to be rescued by her husband and the fire brigade.

Many others find that in their sleep they have innocently broken the law. A 19-year-old apprentice bricklayer was charged with dangerous driving at Chesterfield, Derbyshire, and witnesses described how he was travelling at 60 miles an hour when he crashed into a car. The case was dismissed because the court accepted that he was fast asleep.

At Lymington, Hampshire a 20-year-old girl admitted having taken more than £3 belonging to fellow servants in a large house. She was also found not guilty because she too had been sleep-walking. In February, 1970, a 51-year-old housewife appeared at South West London sessions accused of stealing a case and a calendar from a store. A store detective said that he followed her outside and shouted after but she 'she didn't seem to hear'. Again the defence of somnambulism was accepted.

Psychiatrists agree that these cases of 'innocent dishonesty' again have their roots in our ancestry. Primitive man used to take what he wanted when he wanted it; to him this was absolutely natural. Through the centuries, for the majority of people, that sort of instinct has been repressed, and has become anti-social and unlawful, but the unconscious mind owes no particular allegiance to the laws of modern man.

The full potential horror of sleep-walking, however, is brought home most forcibly by the violent killings and the number of incidents which almost end in a violent killing. At Devon Assizes in February, 1952, consultant psychiatrist Dr. Hugh Scott Forbes emphasized the startling frequency of somnambulistic attacks. Giving evidence in the case of a 34-year-old Royal Navy lieutenant who was charged with attempted wife-murder, he described two cases of somnambulists attacking their wives which, to his personal knowledge, had taken place in the previous eighteen months. One had tried to strangle his wife on two occasions and the other had injured his wife with his fists.

The lieutenant admitted that he had fractured his wife's skull with an axe and that he had woken up to find himself with his hands around her throat. His wife told the court: 'Our married life has always been perfectly happy – always. We have never had a serious quarrel. At no time, apart from that night, has he ever used any kind of violence towards me.'

The defending counsel, Mr. Dingle Foot, asked Dr. Forbes if a man in a state of somnambulism would have any conscious purpose.

The psychiatrist replied: 'No, he is living out a dream. He is not fully in touch with reality. He is incapable of forming any logical purpose.'

Dr. Forbes added that somnambulism was not a mental disease; it existed mostly as an entity in itself, without any other abnormality. It did not cause any form of mental deterioration and it never necessitated certification. It tended to recur. After a retirement of ten minutes the jury returned a verdict of not guilty, and the lieutenant left the court arm-in-arm with his wife.

Some legal experts feel that somnambulism, if it can be established beyond doubt, provides such clear evidence of innocence that it is pointless to put a man through the ordeal of a formal hearing in a criminal court. That was the attitude the authorities adopted towards William Pollard, a 24-year-old chicken farmer of Arkansas after he became a Sleep-Walking Slayer.

Everyone in the district knew that Pollard was an habitual sleep-walker. One typical night, wearing his pyjamas, he loaded his wagon with chickens he intended to sell and started to make the journey to the nearby town of Little Rock; then he woke up, wondering why he was not in bed.

Nobody was very concerned about this type of escapade; his friends thought it was all a bit of a joke. 'Wait till he nods off,' they used to say. 'He always works best when he's asleep.' But in November, 1946, the joke exploded into horror.

Pollard had a nightmare in which he was being attacked by a strange man. He lashed out in self-defence and then awoke. That was all he could remember. Just a short and simple nightmare. But his four-year-old daughter was dead.

Strange and vacant look

Fuller details of that terrible night were given to a coroner's jury by Mrs. Pollard. She had been woken up by noises and had been aghast to see her husband, a strange and vacant look on his face, aimlessly playing a torch over an object on the floor; that object was their daughter Brenda and the back of her head had been crushed. Mrs. Pollard screamed hysterically but the child seemed beyond help.

Pollard had looked at her in a bemused way and shook his head hopelessly; he could not remember. He could not remember if he had dragged the child from her crib or not, he could not remember what he had hit her with or if he had hit her at all; he could not even remember where he had got the torch. All he could remember was the nightmare and how he had lashed out.

When he had collected his senses. Pollard rushed to get his father from next door and the two men took the child to a local hospital; she died within minutes of getting there. The authorities felt that, as Pollard's reputation as a sleep-walker was so well-established, he was not to be held responsible for any crime, so no charges were made.

Some people may feel that the slaying of little Brenda Pollard was no more than a gruesome psychological accident, one of those freaks of behaviour which cannot be explained, and this view might seem to be endorsed by the fact that Pollard was undeniably devoted to the girl. However, there is a strong line of expert opinion which indicates that the cause of the tragedy was Pollard's survival instincts and those to protect his wife and child.

His sub-conscious reacted to the 'nightmare intruder' and immediately propelled his body into action. Fright, in this raw and basic state, leads to one of two things, flight or fight. Pollard, aware of the need to defend his family, chose to fight.

The snatching of the child from the crib, even though he could not consciously remember it, could well have been a desperate attempt to pull her to safety. Then, if she had struggled in his arms, his imagination was almost certainly capable of transforming her into the person who was opposing him. So his daughter could become the enemy who was threatening the safety of the home and who had to be destroyed.

The sleeping strangler

A very different type of unconscious motivation would seem to have been behind the curious strangling of Jean Constable. The way she died, in England in 1961, is described in a separate chapter but here let us consider the psychological battle which must have raged in the mind of her sleeping strangler.

Staff Sergeant Willis Boshears had a marriage which was apparently normal and quite happy; but on New Year's Eve his wife and three young children were away visiting relatives and he was left all alone.

In the early hours of the following morning he was still asleep when he killed a girl who was sharing his bed. As he later explained to the jury: 'There was no quarrel or argument. At no time did I make any overtures or sexual advances to her, nor did I have any desire to kill her or harm her in any way.'

Other evidence seemed to confirm the truth of that statement; so why, then, did Jean Constable die? One of the most probable explanations is that Boshears' sub-conscious mind regarded her as a dangerous intruder. He wanted the company of his wife and this woman beside him had stolen his wife's place; there could be no hope of his wife and children returning to him while this girl was there. So the girl represented a threat to his marriage, and he had to get rid of her.

That may sound as if the killing had undertones of premeditation but this was certainly not the case; the subconscious cannot be indicated of premeditation.

The most bizarre case of a somnambulist killing was the one involving the French detective Robert Ledru. He was a man with a fine record of success which, to a great extent, he owed to his own lively imagination. He specialized in murder and he would try to put himself inside the mind of the criminal; so, in his head, he executed murder after murder, perfecting a small point here, a tiny detail there. He was conscientious, perhaps too conscientious, and in 1888 his long arduous hours brought him a nervous breakdown.

He went to convalesce by the sea at Le Havre and, because the nights were cold, he got into the habit of wearing his socks in bed; one morning, after sleeping for twelve hours, he was perplexed to find that his socks were damp. There seemed no explanation but, then, it was not all that important; he shrugged, put on fresh socks, and forgot the matter.

A chill of recognition

Later that day he received a message from his chief in Paris: the naked body of a man called Andre Monet had been found with a bullet wound on the beach at nearby Sainte Adresse. Ledru's vast experience might prove useful to the local police and, although he was still on leave, would he be interested in helping? Ledru was delighted and, naturally, flattered.

The dead man had been running a small business in Paris and he had apparently gone for a night swim; his clothing was found in a neat pile near the body. As far as could be established, he had no particular enemies and he was not a rich man. So what possible motive could there be? There were two clues to the identity of the killer but the local police did not consider them to be useful.

In the sand, quite near the body, there were distorted footprints which had apparently been left by stockinged feet. Then there was the bullet which, it was established by ballistics experts, had been fired from a Luger. It was so very little to go on; Lugers were such common weapons and, indeed, even Ledru himself had one.

But as Ledru examined the footprints through a magnifying glass he noticed a detail which sent a chill of horror through him; in each footprint there was something missing, the imprint of one toe. Ledru, as the result of an accident, had one toe missing from his right foot.

He pulled off his right shoe and pressed his foot into the sand; then he compared the prints and realized why he had woken with damp socks. His Luger was at his hotel and he found it had a discharged cartridge in the breech.

Robert Ledru had made up murders in his mind just once too often; they were fine and safe when his conscious mind kept his fantasies on a leash and made use of them, but when they percolated through into his unconscious mind they became a grim reality.

He surrendered himself to the authorities, but a court decided that he could not be held responsible. But, because doctors warned that he might kill again while asleep, he had to agree to report nightly to a Paris prison to be locked in. So until he died in his mid-eighties in 1939 he spent his days in freedom but, for the hours of darkness, he always submitted to captivity.

Nightmares in harness

However, no one should imagine that nightmares, in themselves, are dangerous; they can, in fact, be blessings in hideous disguise. Those grotesque fantasy creatures which trespass through your sleep can actually be harnessed rather like cart horses to work for you.

They can, for example, give you advance warning of imminent illnesses. British psychiatrist Dr. J.A. Hadfield reports a typical example. He had a patient who repeatedly had the same frightening dream – that he was paralyzed in the mouth and one arm; months later he did become partially paralyzed in the mouth and in one arm.

This man, Dr. Hadfield concluded, had been suffering mild attacks in his sleep, for the unconscious can pick up tiny symptoms from the body long before they penetrate the conscious mind, and translate them into dream form.

The most important function of nightmares, and dreams in general, is that they release tension. They let us indulge in refreshingly different fantasies, in amazing adventures and even in crimes which real life denies us. Only in the minority of cases is this release function ever likely to develop into tangible physical action. But from that minority come the pitiful ones who, usually unexpectedly, are identified as Sleep-Walking Slayers.

STICK-UP MEN

If you want to understand the hidden mystique of firearms, take a heavy revolver – a toy will do – and heft it in the palm of your hand. It produces an undoubted feeling of satisfaction, of power. You find yourself automatically holding it at arm's length, closing one eye, and pulling the trigger.

The naturalist Raymond Dart suggested that man achieved his present position on the evolutionary scale by his use of weapons: because about three-quarters of a million years ago one of our remote ancestors discovered that the shoulder bone of an antelope could smash the skull of a hyena before he was within range of its teeth. This is certainly plausible, but it still fails to explain the peculiar, potent attraction of *guns*.

On the other hand, if Dart is correct, another interesting hypothesis suggests itself; the gun is a kind of *magic* weapon. You point it at an enemy – even someone twice your size – and he stops in his tracks. It is like a wizard's wand. Now man has always been the weakling of the animal family: less powerful than the ape, less agile than the monkey, less swift than almost any four-footed animal, and without the claws and canines that protect the carnivores.

A strange appeal

Science has never discovered how man survived the great droughts of the Pleistocene Age, when he had to compete with all the other animals for the water holes. And even when he achieved civilization, he remained perpetually in danger from his own kind; marauding tribesmen might sweep down on his village, and undo the work of a lifetime in half an hour, or his cities might be burnt to the ground by pirates. Surely one of the deepest cravings of human nature is to be *invulnerable*, to be able to strike down an enemy by merely pointing at him. The gun satisfies this need, and this is why it has such a strange appeal, even to the most peaceable and kindly of men.

540

All of which helps to explain the otherwise inexplicable fact that, while we all feel the strongest disapproval of burglars, footpads and pickpockets, we have a distinct tendency to make heroes out of equally anti-social thugs like Dick Turpin, Jesse James and John Dillinger: the stick-up men. We don't actually 'approve' of them; yet because they hold the magic wand of sudden death we endow them with a legendary charisma.

Nevertheless, there are good grounds for arguing that the stick-up man is no more than a burglar with psychological problems. A man who commits robbery by pointing a gun at his victim is doubling or trebling his risk of being caught. As a burglar, he stands a chance of entering a house unseen and unheard, and even if he is forced to flee, his chances of being recognized are minimal. The stick-up man on the other hand may wear a mask, but his victim can still distinguish the shape of his face, note his build and height, and memorize his voice.

It is true that if he is robbing a bank, his profits may be many times greater than the burglar's; but the great majority of stick-up men rob petrol stations and shops, and their takings may be less than a week's wages obtained by honest work. In fact, he seems to find this way of stealing money altogether more satisfying than burglary. It involves a confrontation with another human being – perhaps several – pointing a gun, giving orders and being obeyed. It is an ego-boosting exercise, and it produces some of the primitive satisfaction that wild tribesmen experience when they defeat their enemies in battle.

There are many burglars who express their aggression by slashing carpets and furniture in apartments they enter, sometimes even urinating or excreting on the floor. Psychologically speaking such a man is midway between the ordinary, non-aggressive burglar and the stick-up man. He also has a desire to assert himself in the face of a society that considers him a nobody; but the aggression is not quite powerful – or constant – enough to lead him to wave a gun at a bank clerk. He is closer in type to certain sex-offenders who may be mild and inoffensive most of the time, until they feel a sudden compulsion to expose themselves to a child or steal underwear from a clothes line.

But the aggression, the need to express dominance, is only the factor that leads the stick-up man to choose his particular brand of anti-social activity in the first place. He may be compelled to continue because of another factor that criminals are inclined to forget: the problems of a man on the run. The film *Bonnie and Clyde* made this admirably clear. For the young stick-up man, life begins as an adventure; he strolls into stores, strolls out with a handful of dollars, and drives off with one arm around his girlfriend. But a year or so later he is sick of sleeping with a gun under his pillow, looking out for police ambushes, unable to visit old friends or relatives for more than a few hours. His natural aggression is sharpened by a certain desperation and bitterness, and, unconsciously, he may long to be caught. Finally, the desperation may drive him to a kind of suicidal madness, and innocent lives may be endangered.

The career of Frank Dick may be cited as a textbook example of this 'desperation syndrome'. Born in Galveston, Texas, Dick first ran foul of the law in 1949, shortly after his discharge from the U.S. Navy; he was caught trying to rob a chicken coop, and received a few months in jail. Dick was not a brilliant criminal; in fact, he was a bungler who was held in low esteem in the Galveston underworld, and lack of success in his ventures turned him mean.

Captain John Klevenhagen, who arrested Dick on several occasions, is quoted as saying: 'He isn't smart enough to be a good lunch-box burglar, but he'll damn sure hurt you if he gets the chance.' In 1955 a store owner intercepted him as he was making off with the proceeds of a burglary; Dick beat him up. He was caught, and this time it looked as if he faced a long sentence. On the way to the court, Dick attacked the man who was escorting him and escaped.

A tale of two brothels

It was then that he decided to become a stick-up man. He held up the madam of a brothel which he occasionally frequented; when a policeman tried to arrest him a week later, he hit him in the stomach with both hands – held out as if to accept the handcuffs – and ran away. A few days later, police recognized him as he was about to enter another brothel with felonious intent; again, he escaped, this time with a bullet in his leg.

At this point, Dick obviously felt that a return to a safer mode of crime was indicated. He moved to Kansas City, Missouri, and went back to burglary. Here he was caught burgling a lighted store, and sent to prison for a year. The Texas authorities indicated that they would like to interview him; but when Dick was released from jail in 1957, no one tried to stop him from walking away. With a stupidity that seems typical, he returned to Texas, and was arrested in Houston.

Someone put up his bail, but he vanished again. Re-arrested in Lansing, Kansas, he was returned to Texas, and sentenced to prison. He was sent to an open prison at Ferguson, and walked out; re-arrested by Klenvenhagen, he was sent to an escape-proof prison, and remained there until 1969, when he was released on parole. Suspecting that he was still wanted in Kansas, he broke parole and went into hiding, staying with his wife. But his wife was sick of having a husband who was always on the run, and threw him out; Dick decided to go back to crime.

He reasoned that it was time he pulled a big job that would enable him to retire to South America, for this seemed the only way to escape the vicious circle in which he was trapped. Diamonds, he decided, were the answer.

He began to 'case' jewellers in Houston, and his choice fell on Wolfson's, a small exclusive jeweller whose stones were all of high quality. In the guise of a businessman, wearing expensive clothes, he called at the store, and paid down $500 on a diamond ring. He regarded the money as an investment, for in his half dozen visits to the shop, he had noted the position of alarms, the number of employees, and where the safe was kept. He had obtained the money for the clothes and the deposit from smaller hold-ups.

Bullet in the shoulder

In September 1969, he decided he needed more preparation for the 'big job', so he robbed a supermarket of $6,000. The manager ran out after him, shooting, and Dick was hit in the shoulder. The bullet was still there on November 11, when he walked into Wolfson's with a large sack.

From the beginning, the robbery was a failure. Dick pulled a gun, ordered the store owner, his wife and a salesman into the backroom, and shackled them with leg irons from the sack. Then he made Aaron Wolfson open the safe, filled his sack, and went around the display cases, removing the jewellery. At this moment, a man about to enter the store noticed Dick with the gun; he closed the door quietly, and gave the alarm to an unarmed police woman outside. Within minutes, several police cars were on their way to Wolfson's.

Meanwhile, Dick was leaving the store, forcing the male assistant to walk in front of him. A police car stopped; Lieutenant Michna jumped out and ordered him to drop his gun. Instead, Dick pressed it to the head of the assistant, and threatened to kill him instantly unless Michna handed over his pistol; Michna did as he was told. Dick now grabbed Michna as a hostage, and ordered him into the patrol car. Michna pointed out that the street was jammed with cars, and that it would take half an hour before they could get out. Dick recognized the truth of this, and ordered his hostage into Foley's huge department store opposite. Several police followed, but when Dick threatened to kill Michna the patrolmen dropped back.

Dick had apparently decided that Michna was likely to be a difficult hostage; the lieutenant was watching for a chance to jump him. Suddenly, Dick thrust him aside, and grabbed a young woman, Mrs. Elia Narvaez, who was standing behind the wig counter. Michna could see that the gunman was panicking. Dick moved towards the other entrance of the store, dragging the girl with him, his gun against her side; he was obviously hoping to commandeer a car in Main Street.

Several police now followed him and suddenly Dick's nerve seemed to snap; as his finger tightened on the trigger, a detective named Waycott leapt at his gun arm. Dick shot Waycott in the stomach, then turned and deliberately shot Mrs. Narvaez. A bullet fired by a policeman hit Dick in the arm. In the next few seconds, Dick had shot the unarmed Michna in the stomach, and hit another policeman in the shoulder and hand. Then he himself fell to the ground with bullets in both legs and in the back. All Dick's victims recovered. Dick himself received three 45-year terms for shooting the policemen, and another 25 for shooting the young woman. He blamed his wife for forcing him to return to crime.

The case of Frank Dick is worth considering in such detail because it is typical. A hundred similar cases could be cited. The basic motivation for his career of crime was a combination of laziness, aggression and resentment against society. He became a stick-up man when five years of petty crime – and jail sentences – had brought the resentment to the boil. There was one attempt to retreat from the dead-end career of the stick-up man, but instead of giving up crime, Dick merely returned to burglary.

The decision to rob Wolfson's – he actually left the store with a quarter of a million dollar's worth of loot in his sack – at least showed an intelligent assessment of his situation: that one way to break the vicious circle was with a 'big job' that would enable him to retire. When it failed, the desperation boiled over; the shooting of Mrs. Narvaez was an act of rage and disgust.

We can see very clearly that aggression is a central motivation of a man like Frank Dick; but what causes aggression? In recent years, science has made a remarkable discovery about the root of aggression. It springs from a small nucleus, about the size of an almond, in the temporal lobe of the brain. It is called the amygdaloid nucleus, or amygdala, and its role in aggression has been investigated by Professor Kenneth Moyer, of the Carnegie-Mellon University of Pittsburgh. Experimenters studied the behaviour of a tyrannical old male monkey, whose behaviour towards his harem of females was notably violent. When his amygdaloid nucleus was removed, the old monkey became docile and good-tempered. Severing of the nerves leading to the nucleus has been shown to be an effective cure for violent psychopaths.

Screamed abuse

Moyer tried the experiment of stimulating the amygdala of a sweet and kindly old lady with electrodes; she turned on the experimenter and screamed abuse at him. When the current was switched off, she apologized, explaining that she *knew* she had no reason to hate the experimenter, but that the rage had been uncontrollable.

Research in this field is still in its early stages, but certain things are already beginning to emerge. Violent aggression *can* be triggered by brain damage in the area of the amygdala and hypothalamus. This can be seen clearly in the pathetic case of Lock Ah Tam, a Chinese seaman who went into business in Liverpool in the 1890's, and became a rich businessman in a few years. One night in 1918, he got into a fight with a drunken sailor, who struck him on the head with a billiard cue, knocking him unconscious. After this, Lock Ah Tam became subject to fits of sudden violence and screaming rages. In 1925, in a fit of fury, he shot his wife and two daughters, killing all three, and was hanged in 1926.

We should note, however, that Lock Ah Tam's murderous violence was not *entirely* the result of the brain lesion. There is also the question of habit. The brain is basically a kind of computer, and an important part of its work is to learn habits. The real difference between an adult and a child is not a difference in wisdom or maturity, but simply that the adult consists of layer upon layer of habit, which enables him to handle a wide range of situations with confidence.

Anything that deeply affects one's emotions can become a habit. Even quite stupid people can learn to drive a car. Why? Because when you are behind the steering wheel, you know that a false move can send you crashing into a wall; the knowledge touches some deep vital spring, and in no time at all, driving the car has become a matter of habit. The trouble is that *any* strong

emotion can become imprinted in our habit circuits. If something gives you a bad shock when the radio is playing the
National Anthem, you will probably always get a queasy feeling
whenever you hear the National Anthem.

If you happen to be deeply depressed when you are driving
along a certain road, the depression will tend to creep back on
you whenever you drive along the same road, particularly if it is
an unfamiliar road – though if you drive along it every day,
subsequent emotions will gradually 'erase' the earlier impression, just as you can re-record on a magnetic tape.

Once a man like Lock Ah Tam – or Frank Dick – has started
to develop a certain 'amygdaloid response', a tendency to fly into
rages, to generate a feeling of hatred and resentment towards
society, the habit-circuits take over, *strengthening* the response.
Moyer concluded that aggression is triggered by certain chemical
constituents of the blood – like hormones – but these constituents are produced by glands, and the glands produce more or
less hormone as a matter of habit.

In other words, Frank Dick is as much an example of
'conditioning' as one of Dr. Pavlov's dogs, that salivated at the
sound of a bell because it associated it with dinner. The
difference is that Pavlov deliberately conditioned his rats and
dogs. Frank Dick, like thousands of other violent criminals
before him, *conditioned himself.* How? By launching himself
into the vicious circle of robbery with violence. 'Vicious circle' is
here more than a mere figure of speech; it describes precisely the
repetitions that changed Frank Dick from a chicken stealer into a
kind of homicidal maniac.

Now the 'conditioning' theory also suggests a possible solution to this particular problem of criminology. In extreme cases,
the severing of the brain nerves leading to the amygdala is an
obvious possibility. This would have to be done with the
prisoner's consent; but if a man like Dick was offered the choice
of a life sentence, or a five-year sentence plus an operation, there
can be little doubt which he would choose. However, this need
only be considered in extreme cases.

An equally interesting possibility is offered by what has
become known as 'abreaction therapy' – a type of treatment
usually associated with the name of the distinguished psychologist William Sargent.

Emotional collapse
In 1924, the River Neva in Leningrad overflowed its banks, and

the water flooded the laboratory of the psychologist Pavlov, forcing his caged rats and dogs to swim for their lives. A lab assistant saved them when some of them had only an inch of air left in their cages. Some of the animals went into emotional collapse, and when they had recovered, Pavlov noticed an interesting thing. All the conditioned reflexes that he had carefully implanted had been wiped out, like chalk off a blackboard.

Two decades later, William Sargent discovered that this worked just as well on soldiers suffering severe mental strain due to battle fatigue and distress. A strong dose of ether was administered, then the groggy patient was made to re-live the experience. He would experience a kind of emotional orgasm, collapse – and wake up feeling fine. More recently, drugs have been discovered that can 'wipe' the memory tapes without the need for the 're-living' process.

It seems highly probable that such treatment *could* cure men like Frank Dick, victims of their own amygdala. It seems certainly worth trying.

STRANGLERS

The word 'strangler' has a brutal ring: like 'slasher' and 'ripper', it conveys an idea of physical violence, and this is no linguistic accident. In fact, most stranglers have been violent and brutal men. The act of strangling suggests a deliberate savagery.

A man who kills with a gun wants to get it over as quickly as possible, and a man who kills with a knife may be possessed by a vindictive fury, his basic aim being to destroy, to extinguish the spark of life. But the strangler is a man who takes pleasure in close contact with his victim. It takes several minutes to kill someone by strangulation, and during that time the strangler holds the choice of life or death; by simply relaxing his grip, he can allow the victim to breathe again. So strangling is a more wilful and deliberate form of murder than most, and it is never free from a touch of sadism.

It is therefore not surprising that in the great majority of cases, stranglers are motivated by sex. Christie, the rapist of Notting Hill, chose to strangle his victims after he had rendered them unconscious with a coal-gas 'inhaler', and then stripped and assaulted them. It would have been just as simple to have smothered them with a pillow, or even to gas them; he preferred strangulation because it was another form of 'rape'.

Life of murder
Earle Nelson, the 'Gorilla murderer', strangled and outraged 22 women during his incredible career of murder in North America and Canada; the word 'outraged' here has a certain frightful accuracy, since he tore open some of the bodies with his bare hands. Peter Kürten, the Düsseldorf sadist, often grabbed women in dark streets and throttled them until he achieved a sexual climax. If he achieved the climax while the victim was still alive, he left her, and, strangely enough, some girls who went out with him more than once actually allowed him to throttle them

as they had intercourse; Kürten told one who protested: 'That's what love's all about.'

It follows, then, that female killers seldom commit murder by strangulation. The very few known cases involve highly dominant women, and the sexual *motif* is usually present somewhere. There was Nina Housden, who lived near Detroit: a passionate, violent and neurotic woman who was pathologically jealous of her bus-driver husband Charles. In 1947 he left her. Just before Christmas that year, she invited him over for a drink 'for old times' sake', got him drunk, then strangled him with a clothes line.

The next day, she dismembered him and wrapped the parts of the body in newspaper. But from then on, luck was against her. She set out with the parts of the body in the car, intending to dispose of them in the Kentucky Hills. The car broke down in Toledo, Ohio, and the garage proprietor was surprised when the woman said she would wait in the car, even if it took a week to repair.

A garage mechanic looked into one of the evil-smelling parcels on the back seat while Nine slept, and discovered a human leg. She was sentenced to life imprisonment. Then there was Mrs. Stylou Christofi, who strangled her daughter-in-law, stripped her naked, and tried to burn the body on a bonfire in the back yard of her Hampstead home in London. The motive was sexual jealousy of her son's wife, and this is underlined by the stripping of the body.

Pathetic case

Perhaps the most pathetic case of a female strangler was the Scotswoman, Susan Newell, who, in June 1923, strangled the 13-year-old boy who brought her newspapers; her husband had deserted her, and she was living alone. The following morning, together with her 8-year-old daughter, Janet, Mrs. Newell took the body to Glasgow in a go-cart.

As she climbed out of a lorry that had given her a lift, the cart slipped, and a head and foot protruded from the wrapped bundle inside it. A woman who saw this from an upstairs window called the police. Mrs. Newell was found guilty, and in due course hanged. A psychiatrist had declared that she was not insane. It seems probable that the motive for the crime was sexual. Sex-starved women have often been known to approach young boys. He may have struggled or threatened to tell, and she strangled him.

There is no complex Freudian reason for this association of strangling with sex. It is simply that, of all forms of killing, strangulation is the one that most directly expresses resentment. And, as police officers know, there is usually *some* sexual motive concealed in a strangling case, even if it is not at once apparent. For example, when the strangled body of 35-year-old John Mudie was found in a chalk pit near Woldingham in Surrey, the police were at first inclined to believe that the motive was robbery.

Letters in the victim's room led them to Thomas Ley, ex-Minister of Justice for New South Wales, Australia, and to John Smith, a foreman builder who had been hired by Ley to help murder John Mudie. It eventually transpired that Ley had been insanely jealous of Mudie, believing that he was the lover of Ley's ex-mistress, Mrs. Maggie Brook. The belief had no foundation whatever; but when Ley succeeded in luring Mudie to his house in Kensington, he administered a brutal beating, then strangled him.

Even in the case of the death of a woman, the sexual motive may not at once be apparent. When the body of 21-year-old Mary Moonen was found in a driveway in a fashionable quarter of Minneapolis in April 1955, there was at first nothing to suggest a sexual attack. Her red coat, black skirt and white blouse were untorn, and the skirt had been pulled well down over her thighs. Her panties were apparently undisturbed, the autopsy revealed no sexual attack.

A handbag underneath the body contained five dollars, so the motive was clearly not robbery. But Mrs. Moonen had certainly been strangled, and had had intercourse not long before her death. At her home in East 17th Street the police discovered that she was the mother of a 9-month-old daughter, and that she was living with her father, an elderly retired man in poor health. Her husband was in the army, in Korea.

Mystery lover

This offered the police their first real lead, for Matthias Moonen had been overseas for six months. And Mrs. Moonen was found to be three months pregnant. Who, then was her lover? Here they seemed to encounter a dead end. Her father seemed certain that she had no lover. She was a good Catholic, deeply in love with her husband, devoted to the baby. She was a regular churchgoer. It seemed impossible that she could be having a secret affair.

Dentist's pill

The police questioned the victim's sister, Mrs. Donald Newton, a pretty girl in her mid-twenties. At first, she could provide no clue. Then, when the police told her that her sister had mentioned a dental appointment on the day of her murder, Mrs. Newton looked thoughtful. She was able to tell them the name of Mary's dentist: it was Dr. Arnold Asher Axilrod. He was a well-known figure in Minneapolis, having served as mayor during the war, and since then taken an active part in civic affairs.

He *had* been Mrs. Newton's dentist, but she had walked out one day and never gone back. Why? Because Axilrod had given her a pill that had knocked her out for six hours. When she had woken up, he had 'talked suggestively', and on a later occasion he had made a pass at her. But that had not prevented her recommending Axilrod to her sister when she needed a dentist. And the sister knew that Axilrod had given Mary the same 'knock-out pill' on a number of occasions, and had to drive her home afterwards.

When the police called on Mary Moonen's doctor, the case suddenly began to simplify. The doctor told them that Mary claimed Axilrod was the father of the unborn child. He had given her a pill that made her groggy, laid her on the couch and had sexual intercourse with her. Dr. Axilrod, a middle-aged man with dark hair and dark moustache, was brought in for questioning and quickly admitted killing Mary Moonen. He claimed that she had often visited him and accused him of being the father of the child, which he denied.

Wait in car

On the day of the murder she had again accused him of fathering the child. He had asked her to wait for him in his car, then driven off with her. She threatened that she would expose him; then, said Axilrod, he blacked out; and when he came to, he was alone in the car. 'I guess I did it,' said Axilrod, sighing. 'No one else was there.'

The police now discovered that they already had a complaint against Axilrod on file. Three weeks before the murder a 17-year-old schoolgirl had called at his surgery for treatment. He had given her a pill. When she woke up, six hours later, Axilrod was sitting beside her. She had no idea whether any assault had taken place, but she was angry at being kept in his office until the early hours of the morning. Axilrod drove her home, and she had reported the matter by phone.

The police found that Axilrod seemed to prefer female patients – he had few males on his books, and at least 20 women told of being put to sleep with a knock-out pill, and waking many hours later, lying on the couch. Newspapers talked openly of Axilrod's 'love pills' – the laws of libel being less stringent in America than in Europe.

The prosecutor at his trial described him as an amorous philanderer who drugged his pretty victims so they could not resist his sexual advances. The defence confined itself to trying to show that the police had not proved their case against Axilrod: for example, the victim's clothes had not been properly examined, but had been left in a damp morgue for five months. They also called a surprise witness – the victim's brother-in-law, Donald Newton.

Newton was serving a three-month sentence for indecent exposure, and had told a cell-mate that he could crack the case wide open. However, he only added to the confusion; when asked whether he had been at work on the evening of the murder, he replied that he must decline to answer the question 'because it might incriminate me'.

This naturally gave rise to speculation about whether he meant he had some connection with the murder – although, on balance, it seems more likely that he was referring to the crime for which he was serving a sentence. Another witness, a taxi driver, declared that he had seen Mrs. Moonen get out of Axilrod's car and drive off with two men. But the jury remained unconvinced. They found Axilrod guilty of manslaughter, and he was sentenced to between 5 and 20 years in the State prison.

Aggressive impulse

This final ambiguity about the Axilrod case is characteristic of many strangulation murders. When a man seizes a woman by the throat, his intention may only be to silence her; alternatively, he may be expressing some aggressive impulse that intends to stop short of murder. This means that, in many cases, the real solution should perhaps be in the hands of a psychologist rather than a policeman. The following case of Frederick Field may be taken as a typical example.

On October 2, 1931, the almost naked body of a young woman was found in an empty shop in Shaftesbury Avenue, London. She had been strangled. It did not take the police long to identify her as a prostitute, 20-year-old Norah Upchurch, who was well known in the area. Suspicion quickly came to rest on the man who had the keys to the empty shop, an electrician, Frederick Field, who claimed he had given them to a man who wanted to rent the shop.

The police could establish no obvious motive for the crime – why should anyone kill a prostitute for sex? So although both the police and the coroner were convinced Field was lying, a verdict of murder by persons unknown was returned. On the whole, robbery seemed the likeliest motive. In 1933, Field, now in the Royal Air Force, walked into a newspaper office and said he wanted to confess to the murder of Norah Upchurch. It soon became clear that, if Field *was* guilty, his confession was basically false.

For example, he said he had strangled the girl with his hands; but she had been strangled with a belt. It seemed likely that he had confessed to get money out of the newspaper, which had treated his story as an 'exclusive' and talked to him for hours before informing the police. Field went on trial, and now withdrew his confession, saying he made it only because he was 'fed up' and he was having trouble with his wife. The judge instructed the jury to find him Not Guilty.

Prostitute's body

Then, in April 1936, the body of a prostitute was found in her room in Clapham; she had been suffocated. She was identified as Mrs. Beatrice Vilna Sutton; but no one had seen her with her killer. That evening, Frederick Field, who had deserted from his unit, called on a girlfriend and told her mysteriously that she would soon read something interesting in the newspapers. The girl's mother, thinking Field looked insane, telephoned the police.

The deserter was arrested, and at the police station he suddenly confessed to the murder of Mrs. Sutton. His description of her room was circumstantial – and nothing had yet appeared in the newspapers. At his trial, Field tried the same trick as before: repudiating his confession, declaring he had made it because he was 'fed up', but it was obvious that this time he knew too much about the crime to be innocent. The jury found him guilty, and he was sentenced to death. Police suspected that he may have been responsible for the murder of at least four more prostitutes in the Soho area.

The Lucie Berlin murder investigation, which took place in 1904, certainly deserves a high place among epics of forensic detection. Lucie Berlin was a 9-year-old girl, well developed for her age, who lived in a slum tenement in Berlin. On June 11, 1904, a boatman on the River Spree saw a bundle floating in the river and pulled it out. It contained the headless and limbless torso of a child, who was soon identified as Lucie Berlin, who had been missing for two days.

It was definitely a sex murder; the child had been raped, and her parents declared that she had been told repeatedly never to go off with a strange man. This led the investigators to wonder if she had been killed in the slum tenement at 130 Ackerstrasse. They questioned all the other tenants. On the floor above Lucie's parents lived a prostitute named Johanna Liebestruth. A man who was also in her room identified himself as Theodore Berger, and gave another address.

It was only later that the police discovered that Johanna had been in prison for three days – for insulting a client – at the time of the murder, and that Berger, her lover and pimp, had lived in her room during that time. They also learned that Berger was proposing to marry Johanna – which caused some remark among their neighbours, since he had been steadfastly refusing for the past 18 years.

More parcels, containing the missing head, arms and legs, were found in the ship canal. Berger was taken to view these remains, but he continued to insist that he knew nothing about the child's death. Johanna Liebestruth was taken to police headquarters and questioned; she had nothing to hide, and she was even frank about the reason Berger had finally agreed to marry her. On the day Lucie's body had been found, she had come home from gaol and had discovered that a wicker suitcase was missing.

Making love

Berger had admitted that he was responsible; he had taken a prostitute back to the room, and only after love-making had he admitted that he had no money. He gave the woman the suitcase instead. And to placate Johanna for his infidelity, he had agreed to marry her.

The police asked Berger about the suitcase, and he instantly denied knowing anything about it. A few days later, a bargeman handed the case to the police. The stains in the basket proved to be of human blood; so did certain spots on the floor of Johanna Liebestruth's room, and Berger was charged.

What had happened was pieced together at the trial. One day not long before the murder, Lucie had been in Johanna's room, standing on her head, and Berger had noticed how well formed her legs were. When Johanna was in prison, Berger became sex starved. He invited Lucie into the room and attempted indecent assault on her, but she struggled; he strangled her, raped her, then dismembered the body and transported it to the river in the wicker suitcase, which he then threw away. Berger was executed.

It is an interesting reflection that, although the Boston Strangler achieved more notoriety than any murderer since Jack the Ripper, few people can actually remember his name. Crime experts have always found it puzzling that it is the *idea* of strangling that seems to have a morbid fascination for the public, rather than the strangler himself.

SUICIDE

The police are continually being astonished by some of the strange forms of suicide they encounter. Wendel and Svensson's classic study *Crime Detection* has a description of a man who killed himself by placing the blade of a jack knife against his forehead, and then driving it in by beating his head against a tree; it also contains a photograph of the body of an old lady who carefully placed all her furniture in a pile in the middle of the room, lay down on it, and set it on fire.

Taylor's *Medical Jurisprudence* has an even stranger case of a man who burned himself to death by lying down on his mattress and setting it on fire; but as he burned to death, he periodically got up, and made notes about his sensations.

All healthy creatures loathe the thought of death; so we find such cases incomprehensible. We try to dismiss them by saying: 'They were insane' – and we are reassured by the usual coroner's verdict: 'Suicide while the balance of mind was disturbed.' Yet in recent years, criminologists have realized that this simplistic view is false, and that the truth about suicide brings us to the edge of some of the most disturbing and fascinating revelations in the whole field of criminology.

Expressed in crudely simple terms, you could say that most psychologists now accept that murder *is* a form of suicide. At first sight, this seems absurd. Take the case of a bank robber who shoots a policeman in the course of escape, or a rapist who strangles the girl to make sure she cannot identify him. Surely this is a matter of self-preservation rather than 'suicide'?

No. The impulse that makes a man *capable* of murder springs from his indifference to life: *to others' and to his own*. This point is brought out brilliantly in one of the autobiographical sketches of the Russian writer Gorky, describing a murderer called Vassili Merkouloff. The case was described to Gorky by the judge L.N. Sviatoukhin. Merkouloff was a highly intelligent carter; he was also exceptionally powerful physically. One day he caught a man stealing sugar from his cart and hit him. The force of the blow killed the man. Merkouloff was not sentenced to jail for manslaughter; he was sent to a monastery to do penance.

Light bulb

But the thought of how *easily* he had killed the man became an obsession. A kindly priest talked to Merkouloff about the importance of repentance, but it struck the carter as absurd. He only had to give this priest one violent blow, and he would also be dead. . . . One day, after his release, Merkouloff lost his temper with an idiot girl who was importuning him, and struck her with a piece of wood. The blow killed her, and Merkouloff's obsession deepened.

This girl was always falling down or walking into walls, and never seemed to hurt herself; yet one blow had killed her. For this killing, Merkouloff served a term in prison. When he came out, the obsession had become a torment. Merkouloff's new employer, Ivan Kirilich, was a kindly man, cheerful, good-tempered and brave. As in the case of the priest, Merkouloff was haunted by the thought that one blow could destroy this man and all his good qualities, and one day, in a kind of frenzy, he overpowered his employer, tortured him, and then strangled him. He was captured immediately after the crime. Merkouloff committed suicide in prison by strangling himself with his chains.

His 'confession' to the judges makes it clear that he was not insane in the ordinary sense of the word. 'All the time, I kept thinking: "I can kill any man I choose, *and any man can kill me.* . .".' This is what disturbs him so deeply. And, about his first manslaughter: 'A man was walking along the street. I struck him and – no more man. What does it mean? The soul – where is it?' What haunts him is the feeling that if people can die so easily, *then life is meaningless.*

All the religion, all the goodness, all the talk about divine providence and wisdom, fail to disguise the fact that man can be snuffed out as easily as an electric light bulb. Presumably, therefore, he has no more soul than a light bulb . . . But in order to live, human beings have to believe in the future, and in the *value* of what they do and think.

Why did Merkouloff kill his employer? Out of a sort of hope that he would bear the torture unflinchingly, and perhaps refuse to die – proving the power and strength of the human spirit, the reality of the human will? We can see that Merkouloff killed himself for precisely the same reason that he killed Ivan Kirilich: out of a sense that life had lost all meaning.

It is this that explains why so many murderers become suicidal – one third of all murderers commit suicide – and also why they often experience a compulsion to confess. The murder leaves him with a sense of living in a vacuum, cut off from other people and from the meaning of life; confession, even if it brings life imprisonment or death, restores him to his place in human society.

Self-sacrifice

It is impossible to understand the psychology of the murderer without understanding how far all animals are possessed by the herd-instinct. In nature, this is often so powerful that it completely overrules the instinct of self-preservation. A typical example was described by the naturalist Eugene Marais. A troop of baboons lived in a high, inaccessible cave in a cliff. One evening, before they had left their feeding place, a leopard cut off their retreat to the cave, and prepared to attack. Two male baboons edged above it on the cliff; then both dropped on it simultaneously. One bit its spine, the other tore at its throat from below. Within seconds, the leopard had killed both of them – but the baboon at its throat had reached its jugular vein and killed it.

This kind of incredible self-sacrifice is part of the herd instinct. Not killing your own kind is equally a part of this instinct – except, perhaps, in fights to establish dominance or secure a particular female. When men moved together into cities, this old tribal impulse was distorted and weakened. The herd-unity was lost. Murder ceased to be a rarity. But it still affronts something deeply instinctive in human beings – as well, perhaps, as some higher impulse to evolution.

Another vital piece of this puzzle was discovered by the sociologist Emile Durkheim, who wrote a remarkable study on suicide. It was almost a casual observation. After classifying suicides into various types – egoistic (men who feel little or no attachment to society), altruistic (those who commit suicide for the good of society, like Japanese suicide pilots) – he goes on to mention a rather strange type, which he calls the *anomic* or 'unnamed' suicide.

There is something absurd, paradoxical, about this type. For example, we expect the suicide rate to rise during a period of economic depression, when many people are out of work; but it also rises during periods of prosperity, particularly before people have had time to get used to it. Sudden prosperity upsets people just as much as sudden tragedy.

Human beings prefer to live rather narrow, habit-bound lives, like a canal flowing between its banks; if the 'banks' disappear, they experience the same fear, the same sense of meaninglessness, that Merkouloff experienced after his first murder. The response to this meaninglessness is often suicide.

The zoologist C.R. Carpenter observed the same 'dissolution of values' when he had a troop of rhesus monkeys transported by sea to an island. On the ship, it was impossible to establish 'territory'; they were confused and bewildered, and their usual herd-instincts vanished; males allowed other males to rape their wives, and mothers allowed their babies to die of starvation. Once on the island, they immediately established 'territory' and reverted to normal.

In short, the situation that produces 'anomic' suicide can also produce all kinds of anomic action, including murder. In fiction, the man who has explored this situation more deeply than any other is the Russian novelist Dostoevsky. (He was also fascinated by real murders; his *Writer's Diary* is full of notes on contemporary cases.) A high proportion of Dostoevsky's characters commit murder or suicide – because they feel alienated from society. They are in the basic 'anomic' situation; they are 'outsiders'. The most famous of them, Raskolnikov in *Crime and Punishment*, can only escape the burden of his guilt by confession, and by doing penance in Siberia. He has to rediscover his sense of human solidarity.

We can now see the answer to the question raised earlier: in what sense the robber who kills a policeman, or the rapist who kills a girl, is 'suicidal'. The act of murder alienates a man from society, and cuts him off from a sense of meaning. To have reached the mental state in which he can commit murder, he must already feel alienated, cut off from meaning like a diver with a blockage in his air-pipe. The murder can only increase this alienation, pushing him closer to self-destruction.

This also provides an interesting side-light on a phenomenon that has always baffled criminologists: the 'compulsion to confess' – the compulsion that makes innocent people go to the police and confess to murders they never committed. We can now see that these are people who are *already* suffering from alienation, the feeling of meaning-suffocation. Some deep instinct impels them to do what Raskolnikov does: to re-establish contact by 'confessing'. It is an instinctive feeling that the way to escape the meaninglessness is by somehow drawing closer to 'society'. They *want* to confess to something – any-thing; and if they have nothing to confess to, then they will take someone else's crime and confess to that.

Perhaps the most striking illustration of this intimate connection between suicide and murder is to be found in the case of the American mass murderer, Carl Panzram, hanged in September 1930. Panzram was an implacably anti-social type, with close resemblances to Vassili Merkouloff. When he died, at the age of 39, Panzram had spent more than half his life in prisons – although never for murder. He was known as an extremely violent prisoner, and spent much time in 'torture blocks' and solitary confinement.

In 1928, a young Jewish prison guard named Henry Lesser felt sorry for Panzram. One day after Panzram had been brutally beaten for some breach of discipline, Lesser sent him a dollar by a 'trusty'. At first Panzram thought it was a joke; when he realized it wasn't, tears came to his eyes, and he told Lesser that he would write his life story for him.

Biographical notes

It is an interesting exemplification of the theory put forward by the American psychologist William Glasser, that *all* human beings must have at least one person they 'relate' to. Mental illness, says Glasser, occurs, when a person cannot relate to *anybody*. But provided there is at least one person, it can be averted. Panzram, after a life of relating to nobody, suddenly seized this chance – not only of treating Lesser as a friend and an ally, but also of 'justifying' himself to him by means of his confessions.

Panzram's biographical notes are one of the most disturbing and important documents in modern criminology. When Panz-ram was executed – for a murder committed in prison – Lesser tried to get them published; but they were so horrifying and brutally frank that no publisher would take the risk. It was not until 1970, in the wake of such studies as Capote's *In Cold Blood*, that they were finally published, edited by Thomas E. Gaddis and James O. Long, under the title *Killer: a Journal of Murder*.

Panzram's life had been hard and violent. His father, a Minnesota farmer, deserted the family when Carl was a child. At eleven, Panzram burgled the house of a well-to-do neighbour, and was sent to reform school. He was a rebellious boy, and was violently beaten. But he was also dominant and strong-willed, so the beatings only deepened his desire to strike back at society. 'Life being what it is, one dreams of revenge', said the painter Gauguin, and the words could be taken as the motto of Carl Panzram's life.

Untameable

Travelling around the countryside on freight trains, the young Panzram was sexually violated by four hoboes. But the experience only deepened the rage against society, and suggested a new method of expressing his aggressions. Panzram became a lifelong sodomite, and four of his victims were boys, whom he killed after raping. There is a typical passage describing how a brakeman caught Panzram and two other hoboes in a railway truck.

Panzram drew his revolver, and committed sodomy on the man, then forced the other two hoboes to do the same at gunpoint. It was his way of telling society what he thought of it.

From then on, Panzram's life took on the pattern of a man beating his head against a brick wall. He was like some juvenile delinquent whose father beats him black and blue, and who then goes and does something even more outrageous by way of defiance, provoking another beating, and still another act of defiance. . . . In prisons where he spent time for burglary, he was known as one of the most violent and intractable prisoners they had ever known.

He was capable of screaming and beating the door all night, smashing every object in his cell, being punished until he was exhausted and unconscious, and then attacking the guard the moment he had enough strength to sit up. His incredible will-drive had no object except to prove to the 'screws' that he was untameable. There was a brief period when a kindly and sensible prison governor almost 'tamed' him by allowing him freedom and treating him with sympathy. But it was too late; this freedom was an 'anomic' situation that produced a sense of bewilderment and meaninglessness in Panzram; he ran away, was captured, and again thrown into solitary confinement.

He was in his late twenties when he began to kill. He would pick up sailors, take them out to a stolen yacht, commit sodomy on them, kill them with a revolver, and dump their weighted bodies into the sea. 'They are there yet, ten of 'em'. In Africa, he committed his first true sex crime, raping a negro boy of twelve, then beating in his skull. After this, he hired a canoe with six negroes, waited until they were in a remote place, then shot them all in the back, throwing their bodies to the crocodiles, and stealing the canoe. Significantly, he explained that his motive was 'to do people good' — since human life was so vile that to murder somebody was to do them a favour. He liked to describe himself ironically as 'the man who goes around doing people good'. The suicidal attitude already begins to appear — as in his remark: 'I have seen all [the world] and I don't like what I have seen of it. *Now I want to get out of this damned world altogether.*'

In America, Panzram raped and killed three more boys, bringing his murders up to twenty. After five years of robbery, rape, murder, and arson, Panzram was caught as he robbed the express office in Larchmont, New York, and sent to one of America's toughest prisons. Dannemora. 'I hated everybody I saw.' This becomes increasingly the theme of Pamzram's life. Like some stubborn child, he had decided to turn his life into a competition to see whether he could take more beatings than society could hand out; and his attitude had destroyed his potentialities as a human being.

Paranoid fantasies

In Dannemora he leapt from a high gallery, fracturing a leg, which was allowed to heal without proper setting, so that he limped for the rest of his life. He spent his days brooding on schemes of revenge on the whole human race; how to blow up a railway tunnel with a train in it, how to poison a whole city by putting arsenic in the water supply, even how to cause a war beween England and America by blowing up a British battleship in American waters.

It was during a period in jail in Washington DC that Panzram met Henry Lesser, and began to write his autobiography. What is so interesting is that in spite of the paranoid fantasies of universal destruction, he instantly grasped at the chance of getting closer to one human being, to being able to confess everything, to justify himself. Yet, like Vassili Merkouloff, Panzram knew he was, in a sense, already dead.

One day Lesser came into his cell and checked the bars. Panzram said in a low voice: 'Never turn your back on me like that again.'

Lifetime habits

'But you wouldn't hurt me,' Lesser objected. Panzram agreed.

'You're the one man in the world I don't want to kill. But I'm so erratic, I might do anything.'

That is to say that, like Merkouloff, his sense of values had been eaten away by his sense of meaninglessness; he had killed so often that he could not trust himself not to kill on a sudden perverse impulse.

What is so moving, and in a sense, so shocking, about Panzram's diaries is that he is so obviously intelligent. He has a natural gift of self-expression. In his later days in jail, he read the German philosopher Schopenhauer, and his fellow countryman Kant's *Critique of Pure Reason*. Significantly, it was after he met Lesser, and had written most of his life story, that he murdered the foreman of the working party with an iron bar – as if determined not to go on living.

When Lesser held out hopes of a reprieve – perhaps even of getting Panzram freed on parole – Panzram wrote, with cool self-knowledge: 'I would not reform if the front gate was opened right now and I was given a million dollars when I stepped out. I have no desire to do good or be good.' And in another letter he comes even closer to the heart of the matter. 'I could not reform if I wanted to. It has taken me all my life so far, 38 years of it, to reach my present state of mind. In that time I have acquired some habits. It took me a lifetime to form these habits, and I believe it would take more than another lifetime to break myself of these same habits even if I wanted to.'

He set out determinedly to die. He demanded to act as his own advocate in court, and was enraged when this was refused – obviously, he wanted a last chance to 'confess' publicly. After he was sentenced to death, he heard that an anti-capital punishment society was agitating for a reprieve, and wrote them a letter telling them firmly that he didn't want a reprieve and to mind their own business. When he thought he might not be executed, he brooded on suicide. But his wish was granted, and he was hanged on September 5, 1930.

For forty years after his death, Panzram was forgotten. And then, suddenly, he was recognized as one of the most important and interesting figures in twentieth-century crime, comparable to the Düsseldorf sadist Kürten, whom he resembles in many ways. The reason is paradoxical: *not* because his crimes were so appalling – compared with some later killers, they were almost humane – but because Panzram, after a lifetime of destruction, finally turned his intelligence towards its real purpose: the act of creation.

Appalling waste

His letters and autobiography remain a remarkable monument to the indestructibility of human intelligence and honesty. A man with

Panzram's intelligence and determination was intended by nature to *evolve*. Society frustrated him; so his creativity turned to destruction. It was an appalling waste of human potential, and at the same time a proof that such waste can very often produce the urge to self-destruction.

SUPER THIEVES

On October 16, 1906, a humble shoemaker made a laughing stock of the imperial German army. His name was Wilhelm Voigt, and he had spent nearly half of his fifty-seven years in prison. On that cool autumn morning, he was strolling along the streets of Tegel – now a suburb of West Berlin – in the uniform of an army captain. Voigt had no right to the uniform: he had purchased it in a second-hand shop. A troop of soldiers came marching down the street, headed by a sergeant. Voigt stepped in front of them and roared, 'Halt!' He inspected them, twisting his moustache.

Then he told the sergeant that he had business in the town hall at Köpenick – twenty miles away – and ordered the squad to follow him. No one dared question a German officer; they marched smartly behind him all the way to Köpenick. There, the 'captain' presented each of the men with a mark, and told them to fall out for lunch. After that, he lined them up in front of the town hall, ordered three men to guard all entrances, and told the others to accompany him.

He marched into the mayor's office, and told the mayor he was under arrest. He looked so fierce that nobody dared to say a word. Then the captain asked to see the cash box. An underling quickly fetched it. The captain counted the money, glared at the mayor as if to say 'Just as I thought', then announced that he was confiscating it. 'Take him away,' he snapped, pointing to the mayor. The soldiers fell in on either side of the bewildered official, and escorted him out.

Meanwhile, three soldiers were ordered to go and commandeer vehicles. The mayor and the soldiers were installed in two of these, and told to proceed to the police station in Berlin – while the captain climbed into the third. When the soldiers arrived at the police station, the third carriage had vanished, but still no one suspected anything. The mayor was hurried inside, and it was some two hours before anyone realized they had been hoaxed. By then, the captain had vanished with the cash – some 4,000 marks.

News of the hoax travelled over Germany, then throughout the world. Even the Kaiser roared with laughter when he heard about it. 'It could only happen in my Germany,' he said, with a certain satisfaction. But the police and the army were enraged. The bogus captain became Germany's Public Enemy Number One, and a massive manhunt was instituted. A few days later, Voigt was arrested in his room in a Berlin slum. He received four years' hard labour, but was released after twenty months – due to the behind-the-scenes intervention of the Kaiser. For the rest of his life, the shoemaker was something of a hero, frequently posing for photographs in a captain's uniform. And in Germany, the 'Captain from Köpenick' is still a much-admired figure.

Voigt's haul was neither the biggest nor smallest on record; but his robbery was one of the most typical in the annals of crime. For the real robber – the man with a vocation for it – has a touch of the adventurer, and a touch of the comic opera hero about him. He robs for profit, but also for pleasure – for the excitement of the challenge.

Indeed, this was the spirit displayed by the man who deserves credit for the biggest robbery on record. He stole a whole country. Pavel Mihailovich Bermondt-Avalov displayed the spirit of the captain from Köpenick on a grand scale. He demonstrated his powers of bluff in 1917, when he was spying against the Bolsheviks for Germany. On his way through a forest, wearing a Russian officer's uniform, he came across a large ammunition depot. Without hesitation he marched up to the Russian sentry, who raised his rifle and challenged him. 'Idiot, put that down!' shouted Bermondt, 'Get out of my way, you ignorant peasant!'

The soldier was convinced of the man's authenticity; only a Russian officer could be that rude. Bermondt marched into the camp, banged on the door of each billet in turn, and demanded to see the N.C.O. in charge. Then, followed by a line of respectful corporals, he proceeded to make a tour of inspection. In a shed full of artillery shells, he walked out of sight, and used a wrench to set off the timing fuse in front of a shell. He then marched out, towards the camp entrance. He was just passing the sentry when the explosions started – one setting off the other – until the whole camp was destroyed.

Ruthless charge

Carried away by the spirit of sheer audacity, Bermondt next led a small army of mercenaries into the town of Jelgava, in Latvia, and rode down its Red defenders in a magnificent and ruthless cavalry charge. It was this success which sparked in his mind the outline of a daring plan to take over the country. He called on Von der Goltz, the commander of the remnants of the German army, and offered him his own three hundred men. Goltz said gloomily that it wasn't men he needed – he had 30,000 – but money. 'Leave that to me,' said Bermondt, and hurried off to Berlin.

There, as Goltz's representative, he visited various banks who held mortgages on Latvian territory, and pointed out to them that if Latvia fell to the Reds, they would lose their investment. They quickly put a million marks at his disposal, Bermondt then prepared to doublecross Goltz. It was 1919, and in Vienna the Allies were discussing how to partition post-war Europe. Bermondt sent the British delegation a cable warning them that German bankers had sent Goltz a million marks, and that Goltz intended to take over Latvia.

The idea was to alarm the French premier, Georges Clemenceau and the American President, Woodrow Wilson, into having Goltz removed. Next Bermondt returned to Latvia, called on Goltz, and told him that he had managed to raise a quarter of a million marks. Goltz looked at him sourly. 'What about the other three-quarters?' he asked, waving a cable from the German bankers. Bermondt remained nonchalant. 'They are sending that in a day or two,' he shrugged. Goltz was suspicious, but he allowed Bermondt to go – and sent an urgent cable of enquiry to the bankers in Berlin.

Promise of looting

Now it was a race between two telegrams – one from the bankers telling Goltz that Bermondt was trying to swindle him, the other from Allied Headquarters stating that he was being relieved of his command. Unfortunately for Bermondt, the cable about money arrived first. He was being tortured by Goltz's men when the second cable arrived, and Goltz realized he was beaten. Bermondt offered him a quarter of a million marks in exchange for his army – which consisted of mercenaries, not German soldiers. Goltz, therefore, was not committing treason when he took the money, and signed over his army to its new commander. Losing no time, Bermondt then marched his men on the capital of Latvia, Riga – which was held by Bolsheviks. Encouraged by promises of land and looting, the mercenaries fought spiritedly and in October 1919, they took Riga. Bermondt was master of Latvia. He had stolen a country from under the nose of the Allies!

All he needed now was time to entrench himself as the new king of Latvia. He was hoping the Allies would see no reason to dislodge him. That was his major miscalculation. He thought all politicians were crooks; it didn't strike him that Wilson and Clemenceau might object to the idea of Latvia being ruled by a super-thief. The French navy shelled Riga; Allied troops poured into the city. With his army overpowered and helpless, the man who stole a country was forced to abandon his loot and flee for his life. But, like the captain from Köpenick, he moved for the rest of his days in a certain aura of celebrity.

The exploits of Voigt and Bermondt-Avalov draw attention to a point that has never been adequately recognized by criminal psychologists: that there are thieves and super-thieves. Robbery is the commonest of all crimes, and most thieves recognize that they are basically parasites, with no real place in society. The super-thief, however, does not accept anything of the sort. He belongs to the group of 'high-dominance' males. And the high-dominance male is gripped with an instinctive craving for achievement, for *adventure*. In an obscure, perhaps only semi-conscious way, he feels that he deserves to be famous, to be a 'somebody'. What he wants ideally is to lead a life in which he can commit robbery and – as sometimes follows – rape.

The super-thief is a loner. He has qualities that might carry him far as a soldier or businessman. But he doesn't want to co-operate with society. The idea strikes him as boring. The concept of crime, however, produces a strange, almost sexual excitement in him. The Chicago University student and sex murderer, William Heirens, for instance, began as a burglar, breaking into houses to steal women's underwear. He discovered that the act of climbing in through a window could alone induce an orgasm and offered this as a 'defence' before being sentenced, in 1946, to life imprisonment. Police in all countries are familiar with similar cases, in which burglars urinate or defecate in the flats they burgle. This is not, as it might first seem, a mere act of social defiance. The burglar gets his pleasure from taking down his trousers in a strange flat; it is a variation of indecent exposure. Some burglars slash beds – and brassiers and panties – with razor blades. There is a definite element of 'rape' about these robberies, which is the distinctive stamp, or calling-card, of the super-thief as opposed to the 'ordinary' robber.

The super-thief, however, is not always a menace to his contemporaries. When a society is expanding and changing, there can be a place for him. For example, from the time of Queen Elizabeth I onward, the British government actually encouraged piracy. It was called 'privateering', because the ships were hired by private citizens instead of the Royal Navy; but it amounted to the same thing. The privateers were entitled to attack ships belonging to enemies of their country – or anyone who gave those enemies supplies. This provided them with a fairly wide field. If, for some reason, they captured a ship belonging to a friendly nation, there was a simple way of preventing the mistake from getting known: to kill all aboard and sink the vessel.

The Elizabethan hero Sir Francis Drake was, in fact, little better than a pirate, using the war with Spain as an opportunity for robbery and plunder. Since the Spaniards were also in America and the West Indies, this gave free-booters such as Drake a very wide range indeed. The West Indies became a nest of pirates – harbouring such characters as Blackbeard (whose real name was Teach), Henry Morgan, Major Stede Bonnet, Captain England.

Piracy was the ideal way of life for the super-thief. He could rob, cut throats, burn towns and carry off women. He could live out all his childish fantasies of aggression and violence. Many of them did just that, with horrifying sadism. This was why pirates seldom received mercy from the authorities when they were caught – the captain and the entire crew, down to the cabin boy, would swing on the same gallows. Society regarded them as among the most evil kind of vermin.

One of the most powerful expressions of the psychology of the super-thief occurs in the famous drama *The Robbers* by the eighteenth-century German poet Schiller. The hero of the play, Karl Moor, becomes the leader of a robber band because, he says 'only freedom breeds true greatness' – by which he means freedom to commit robbery, arson and rape. *The Robbers* was, admittedly, one of Schiller's earliest – and least mature – works; but it establishes an important point: that even a man as gentle and intelligent as Schiller could believe that in order to be 'truly free', a man ought to be allowed to burn down nunneries and rape the nuns.

Most men can feel a sneaking sympathy with that point of view. It arouses an awareness that the super-thief, like all high dominance criminals, is basically *a man who never grows up*. Children can never understand why they can't have the moon, or why they shouldn't be allowed to walk into a toyshop and help themselves. As they get older, they become more realistic. Their desires mature; so do their methods of achieving these desires. Some men can never throw off the childish, Peter Pan-like feeling that they ought to be allowed to grab whatever they want. If they also happen to be men of high-dominance, then there is a good chance that they will turn into super-thieves.

Statistically speaking, society is bound to contain a certain number of super-thieves. Some of them will be intelligent enough to become successful businessmen. (For example, Gustav Myers' book *The History of the Great American Fortunes* makes it clear that many of the most successful American businessmen were little better than pirates.) The remainder will become 'enemies of society', outsiders who, unable to make money 'legitimately', will turn to theft as naturally as tycoons and executives negotiate contracts, engineer deals, and originate take-over bids.

Another salient fact about super-thieves is that they seldom commit murder. Why? Because they have a strong desire to 'be somebody' in society, and they realize that murder closes the door on social acceptance. The captain from Köpenick spent the rest of his life strutting around in a captain's uniform. Bermondt-Avalov wrote a book about his exploits and became quite a social figure. When the super-thief kills, it is usually because he is cornered, and can see no other way of escape.

In that sense, England's most celebrated super-thief, 'the devil man' Charlie Peace, is an exception to the rule. He was called the devil man because of his ugly, monkey-like face and great jutting jaw; he also spoke as though his tongue was too big for his mouth. But these features seem to have been no impediment to an active love-life. In 1875, when Peace was forty-three, he was living in the Sheffield suburb of Darnoll, working as a frame-maker, and spending his nights in his favourite occupation – burglary. Two doors away lived a pretty, well-built Irishwoman called Katherine Dyson, whose husband was a railway engineer. She became Peace's mistress, but she eventually tired of him and refused to see him. Peace flew into a frenzy at this, and made such a nuisance of himself that the Dysons took out a court order to stop him molesting them. A few months later, the Dysons moved to another part of Sheffield; but Peace traced them so promptly that he called on them as they were unpacking.

His first murder

By this time, he had already committed his first murder. In August, 1876, escaping from the scene of a burglary near Manchester, he was stopped by P.C. Nicholas Cock. Peace shot the officer, but two brothers, John and William Habron, were arrested for the crime, and William was later sentenced to death – although this was subsequently commuted to penal servitude. Peace attended the trial, and immediately after hearing the sentence, he called on the Dysons, quarrelled with Arthur Dyson, and shot him dead. Then he climbed over a garden wall, and vanished for the next two years.

In that time he moved to Peckham, in south London, rented a suburban villa, and became, to all appearances, a respectable Victorian householder, attending church on Sundays, and giving musical evenings at which he recited pathetic ballads and played the fiddle. During this period the police of south London were troubled by a series of daring burglaries. On October 10, 1878, two policemen saw a man acting suspiciously in a back garden in Blackheath. When they challenged him, he produced a gun and fired two shots – deliberately wide – shouting at them to keep away. One policeman was hit in the arm, but the other battered Peace to the ground. It was the end of the career of the devil man. To his credit, he confessed to the murder of P.C. Cock, and William Habron was released. Peace was hanged – for the murder of Arthur Dyson – on February 25, 1879. For some reason, he touched the imagination of the English; there are more legends about him than any other super-thief since Robin Hood.

That is not true of a man who perhaps deserves the title of the greatest super-thief of the twentieth century – although he is the subject of a crime classic, *The Count of Gramercy Park* by Robert Alcorn. Born in Brooklyn about 1890, Gerald Chapman had the typical super-thief's romanticism, the desire to shine in the world. But his career of crime was at first unsuccessful; by the age of 30, he had spent nearly twelve years in jail, on charges of burglary, grand larceny and armed robbery. It was during a seven-year stretch in Auburn, N.Y., that he began to plan a grand *coup* that would make him rich. He may have been inspired by an acquaintance he made in jail – the college-educated Dutch Anderson, who became his faithful accomplice.

In Auburn, Chapman read books, learned about music, and taught himself to speak with an upper-class English accent. When he was released, in 1919, he gravitated to the Wall Street district of New York, since this was where the big money lay. On October 24, 1921, Chapman slipped into the seat of a mail truck, held up the driver, and forced him to drive down a side street. There two more accomplices – Anderson and a man called Charlie Loerber – joined him. They transferred the mail bags – containing more than two and a half million dollars, in cash and bonds – into their car, and drove off. The Leonard Street robbery was the biggest ever committed up to that time.

Then, with thousands of dollars at his disposal, Chapman put into operation the second half of his plan. He rented a large house in fashionable Gramercy Park, in New York. He called himself G. Vincent Colwell, and he and his 'wife' and accomplice Betty, posed as a rich English couple. Their evening parties – with music – were a great success. It was after one of these parties that a rich lady named Van Gedden discovered that she had lost a rope of priceless pearls. But she had no suspicion of Colwell – who presented her with a sapphire brooch by way of commiseration.

A daring escape

Some time after that, the police caught up with him for the Leonard Street job – he was traced through a traveller's cheque – and he was sent to Atlanta penitentiary. From there he made a daring escape with a rope and grappling hook. He was caught twenty-four hours later, and he was shot in the back. In the prison infirmary, he managed to look so sick and feeble that the police allowed a visit from his 'wife'. With the revolver she slipped him, he made another escape. But crime was too alluring. In October, 1924, he was cornered by two policemen while robbing a safe in New Britain, Connecticut, and killed one of the officers in escaping. Captured three months later, he was sentenced to death. His accomplice, Dutch Anderson, murdered an innocent farming couple who had given Chapman up, and was himself shot to death by a policeman soon after.

Whether they realize it or not all thieves – the 'supermen' and the lesser specimens – are reacting against the belief of the renowned French moralist and social reformer, Pierre-Joseph Proudhon that 'property is theft'. By stealing the property – the money, the jewels, the securities – of the rich they are only obeying one of society's basic precepts: that of acquisition. And by violating the wealthy men's wives, daughter and mistresses, they are merely helping themselves to something else which was obtained 'illegally'.

TRAIN MURDERS

On July 25, 1814, a strange contraption with iron wheels groaned and hissed into life, and dragged eight wagonloads of coal along parallel iron tracks. That first railway engine, christened 'Blücher' and affectionately known as Puffing Billy, also dragged its inventor into the limelight of world history.

George Stephenson, the self-educated son of a Northumbrian miner, was not only an inventive genius; he also proved himself an inspired prophet when he told the British House of Commons: 'People will live to see the time when railroads will become the great highways for the King and all his subjects . . .' What he did not foresee was that his great invention was inaugurating a new and fascinating chapter in the history of murder.

Oddly enough, the classic cases of 'murder on the railway' – Müller, Dickman, the Merstham tunnel mystery, the Rock Island express murder – now have a nostalgic fascination for students of crime. We can anticipate the day when railway stations will disappear and give way to airports – as they have already disappeared in many parts of America – and the thought of a steam engine chugging between green fields has all the charm of a pleasant daydream.

A run for his money

England's first train murderer was Franz Müller: Müller may well be the world's first train murderer, for he killed Thomas Briggs in 1864, and it was almost another ten years before Jesse James committed the world's first train robbery and brought a new kind of risk into the lives of railroad passengers. At least Müller had a run for his money. This was not true of England's second train murderer, Percy Mapleton, alias Lefroy, who seems to have been one of those unfortunate young men for whom nothing ever goes right.

573

He had a beaky nose, a low forehead and a receding chin, and his ambition was to make a living as a writer. His short stories were heavily sentimental, and the one he finished in mid-June 1881 was no exception. It was about a music-hall comedian, whose wife, Nellie, leaves him for a life of gaiety and sin, and finally returns, dying 'of cold and want'. Her husband naturally forgives her.

'"At last – Joe – darling husband – goodbye —", and with a sweet and happy smile, Nellie went down with the sun.' Mapleton was a vain young man, and he liked to dress well. Short-story writing was obviously no way to a fortune, so on June 27, 1881, Mapleton took a decision that had been reached by the hero of Dostoevsky's novel *Crime and Punishment*: he would commit one remunerative crime, and use the proceeds to finance a career devoted to the entertainment and betterment of humanity.

He was seen walking up and down the platform of London Bridge Station, peering into carriages. In those days, the corridor train was almost unknown; so once you were in a compartment, you stayed in it till the next station. Mapleton selected a compartment containing an old gentleman who looked rather well-to-do; he was, in fact, a retired merchant named Frederick Gold.

As the train was about to enter Merstham tunnel, between London and Brighton, passengers were startled by the sounds of revolver shots. At Horley, a village on the other side of the tunnel, several people in cottages near the line noticed two men struggling in one of the compartments as the train went by. A few miles farther on, at Balcombe tunnel, a door was heard to slam. When the train arrived at Preston Park, Brighton – where Mr. Gold lived – a young man climbed out, and his appearance attracted the attention of several passengers.

His face was blood-stained, his collar and tie missing, and he looked as if he had been in a fight. When the ticket collector noticed a watch-chain hanging from his boot, he stopped him and asked him his name. The young man said Lefroy. He explained that he had been attacked in Merstham tunnel. According to 'Lefroy', there had been two other people in his compartment: an old gentleman – Mr. Gold – and a rough-looking man of 'rustic appearance'.

In Merstham tunnel, said Lefroy, he had received a violent blow on the head. When he recovered consciousness, the other two passengers had vanished . . . The story was absurd; he was asking them to believe that the robber had first knocked him unconscious, then leapt out of the carriage with Mr. Gold. The ticket collector sent for a policeman, and Lefroy was arrested.

Not long after, the body of Mr. Gold was discovered in Balcombe tunnel – minus his watch and wallet: but his death was due to a violent blow on the head; there were no gunshot wounds. With some dignity, Lefroy asked if he could go to his lodgings to change his clothes. The policemen agreed. Lefroy took them to a ladies' boarding school in Croydon, which, he claimed, was run by his aunts. He asked the police to wait outside; and, amazingly enough, they did. Lefroy vanished inside. Half an hour later, the police realized he was gone; he had walked out by the back entrance.

But Lefroy's appearance was too distinctive for him to remain at large for long. A *Daily Telegraph* artist made a sketch of him according to the description of witnesses – the first identikit picture. When it appeared in the newspaper, a landlady in a cheap Stepney lodging recognized it as a strange young man called Park, who kept his blinds drawn and stayed indoors all day. He had told her he was an engraver and needed quiet to work.

But when the police arrived, Lefroy, whose real name was Percy Mapleton, gave himself up quietly. At his trial he strenuously maintained his innocence. He also asked permission to be tried in a dress suit, convinced that no English jury would sentence a 'gentleman' to hang. He was mistaken. Before his death, he confessed to killing Frederick Gold. He was hanged on November 29, 1881. Oddly enough, the revolver was never found.

The next railway murder was unsolved. At 8.25 on the evening of February 11, 1897, a cleaner who entered a railway carriage at Waterloo Station saw a pair of legs sticking out from under the seat. The compartment was heavily bloodstained, and the body proved to that of 33-year-old Elizabeth Camp, a barmaid from the East End of London. The motive was robbery; she had been carrying a silver-handled umbrella and wearing a rather flashy brooch – actually made of paste diamonds. She had also carried £16 in her handbag – which, like the umbrella and the brooch, was missing. She had been battered to death.

A blood-stained pestle

The compartment she had been travelling in was second class; her sister, who had seen her off at Hounslow Station at 7.42 that

evening, had remarked that third-class compartments were safer
for women; Miss Camp had replied that she preferred the class
of people she met travelling second. Her murderer – who must
have killed her very quickly, since the train halted every few
minutes – was never caught. The only clue, a bloodstained
chemist's pestle found on the line, led nowhere.

In 1901, a Mr. Pearson was shot in a tunnel near Wimbledon;
a third passenger had been present, and the killer, a man named
Parker, was quickly found and executed. But the next British
train murder remains an intriguing mystery. On Sunday, September 24, 1905, at eleven o'clock at night, a gang of workmen
who were about to carry out repairs to Merstham tunnel – the
same tunnel in which Mapleton had attacked Mr. Gold – found
a body lying by the railroad track. It had been badly mutilated
by a train, and closer examination revealed it to be a young
woman. The first assumption was that this was suicide. The head
was smashed, the face unrecognizable, the left leg cut off, and
the arm crushed.

Two facts soon convinced the police this was murder. A gag
had been forced into the woman's mouth; and on the sooty side
of the tunnel there were long marks indicating that she had
jumped – or been thrown – out of a train. She had rebounded
under the wheels of the train. The next day, a young dairy
farmer named Robert Money viewed the body and identified it
as his sister, 22-year-old Mary Sophia Money. Mary was a
book-keeper who worked for a dairy at Clapham and lived on
the premises.

And now the police encountered impenetrable mystery. Mary
had been on duty that Sunday. She had finished her work at
seven o'clock, and told another woman, a Miss Hone, that she
was going for 'a little walk'. Shortly after, she called at a
confectioner's at Clapham Junction and told the man from
whom she bought chocolates that she was going to Victoria. No
other witnesses could be found who saw her after she walked
towards the Victoria train at Clapham Junction.

But now a problem arises. There were only two trains from
which Mary Money could have been pushed, and both of them
ran from London Bridge to Brighton. Before Merstham tunnel,
these trains both stopped at Croydon. So it seems that she went
out from her lodging, claiming that she was going for a short
walk, and had every intention of going to Victoria. Why? Almost
certainly, to meet someone – a man. For some reason she then
went on to London Bridge, or, possibly, Croydon. A guard who

walked along the platform at East Croydon noticed a young man and woman in one compartment – No. 508 – and they looked so 'intimate' that another passenger, for whom he opened the door, went into the next compartment.

At South Croydon, the same guard – who seems to have had the instincts of a Peeping Tom – looked into the compartment again and saw they looked even more 'intimate', having pulled up the arm-rest between them; they also looked guilty and furtive, as if they had been kissing. His description made the girl sound like Mary Money.

Altogether, then, the evidence suggests that Mary Money went off that evening to meet a male acquaintance at Victoria, intending to return to Clapham later the same evening. The man persuades her to get on another train to London Bridge or Croydon. Then he persuades her to take the train to Brighton with him. She is sufficiently infatuated with him to agree. They kiss and cuddle from Croydon to somewhere just before Purley Oaks; then the man gets carried away and tries to rape her. She screams; he forces a gag into her mouth – at which point he either decides to throw her from the train, or she opens the door and jumps.

In August 1912, the British press speculated about another possible solution after a sensational suicide case. A woman ran screaming from a room in a Brighton boarding house. Shortly after, there was a roar of flame, then the sound of shots. Firemen were called, and when they had extinguished the blaze, they found five charred bodies in the room: a man, a woman, and three children. In a vase there were twenty gold sovereigns, and a note saying: 'I am absolutely ruined, so killed all that are dependent on me . . .' It was signed C. R. Mackie, but Mackie was soon identified as Miss Money's brother Robert, the man who had identified her body.

The woman who had run from the room was his mistress; the dead woman was her sister. Robert Money, it seemed, was a weak, vain man and an inveterate liar. He posed as 'Captain Murray' and said his father was a barrister, although he was, in fact, a carpenter. He had lived with one of the sisters in Clapham, and given her two children, then run away with the other and given her a child, too. He married her, but later left her to return to his original mistress.

The circumstances that led him to despair are not clear; all that is known is that he invited wife and mistress – separately – to the room in Brighton, together with the children, then pulled out a revolver and tried to kill them all. The mistress escaped, wounded. Money had time to soak the bodies in petrol, throw a match on it, then shoot himself.

Was he the murderer of his sister? many journalists now asked in print. It seems possible but unlikely. What was his motive? Why should his sister go with him to London Bridge, then take the Brighton train? The tragedy of Robert Money only strengthens the possibility that Mary Money was murdered by a man with whom she was starting a liaison, for it suggests that brother and sister may have shared the same taste for 'forbidden pleasures'. Many leader writers at the time pointed out that railway murders could be stopped quite easily – by doing away with the old type of train in which the compartments are separate, and substituting corridor trains.

Baffling features

As an increasing number of corridor trains came into service, train crimes became rarer, and murders almost ceased – although as recently as the 1960s rapes have taken place in the old type of railway carriage. A case that occurred in 1914 has some of the same baffling features as the murder of Mary Money. On January 9, a boy travelling in a train from Chalk Farm to Broad Street noticed a leg sticking from under the seat.

It proved to be that of a five-year-old boy named Willy Starchfield, who had been strangled. Willy had lived in Chalk Farm with his mother, who was separated from her husband, John Starchfield. He had been missing since the previous afternoon. witnesses said they had seen a boy answering to Willy's description with a man on the previous afternoon, and the inquest brought in a verdict of wilful murder by the father.

But the witnesses were unreliable, and at his trial Starchfield was acquitted. He had no motive to kill his son – unless out of spite against the mother, which was never established. Not long before the murder, John Starchfield had been shot when he tackled a murderous maniac with a revolver, and he was awarded a 'hero's pension' of £1 a week. It has been suggested that someone killed Willy out of 'revenge' for his brave act, but this seems just as unlikely. The murder remains unsolved.

Another English railway murder occurred on March 13, 1929, when a Mrs. East was murdered when she was travelling between Kidbrooke and Eltham. However, the crime aroused little interest, and the murderer was never caught. Neither was the killer of a nurse on a London–Hastings train in January 1920.

America has had many rail murders, but most of them have been connected – as one might expect – with train robbery. The Rock Island Express murder of 1886 had, for a while, an interesting element of mystery. Kellogg Nichols was an Express Messenger, and on March 12, 1886, he was carrying over $22,000 from Chicago to Davenport, Iowa. Somewhere between Joliet and Morris a train hand named Newton Watt gave the alarm afer a masked man had held him up. Investigation of the mail car showed that Kellogg was dead, his brains beaten out.

The safe had been broken open. William A. Pinkerton, son of the famous detective, was called in. His suspicions soon fell on Watt, and on the brakeman, Fred Schwartz, Schwartz's hands were badly scratched, and the dead man had had skin under his nails, indicating that he had fought his attacker. Although no evidence could be found against the two men, Pinkerton was certain of their guilt – they had been several times overheard talking about large sums of money, and they talked of retiring from the railroad.

Finally, Schwartz made his mistake; he fell in love with an attractive young girl, Ella Washam, and married her. Since he already had a wife in Philadelphia, the police now had an excuse to arrest him, and while he was in jail, Pinkerton talked to Ella and got from her an admission that Schwartz claimed he had 'found' a large sum of money. Confronted with her husband, Ella said: 'Please tell them about the money you found . . .' Schwartz now alleged he had found $5,000 in a package under a seat in the train on the day after the murder. A jury did not believe him, and although the evidence was entirely circumstantial, he and Watt were both sentenced to life imprisonment.

Cold-blooded shooting

Perhaps the most spectacular case of train murder in America took place in the autumn of 1922. Three brothers named DeAutremont – Hugh, Roy and Ray – held up the Southern Pacific mail train near tunnel 13 in Oregon. When E.E. Dougherty, the mail clerk, saw a man with a revolver approaching, he slammed the door, whereupon the gunman, Hugh DeAutremont, placed dynamite under the car and blew it apart, killing Dougherty. The driver was ordered to take the train into tunnel 13, but when it failed to move – because of the damaged mail car – both he and the foreman were shot down in cold blood.

When the bandits tried to get into the mail car, dense fumes drove them back, and they eventually fled. An envelope containing Hugh DeAutremont's name and address was found in a discarded pair of overalls near tunnel 13, and launched a manhunt for the brothers which lasted four years; Hugh was captured in the Philippines, where he was serving as a soldier; the twins Ray and Roy were captured in Steubenville, Ohio. All three brothers went to jail for life.

The name of Winnie Judd also deserves to be remembered in connection with railroad crimes, although her murders were not actually committed on a train. It was in October, 1931, at the Southern Pacific station in Los Angeles, that a baggageman noticed the strong smell emanating from two trunks which had been sent from Phoenix, Arizona. Blood was dripping from one. When a young man and woman came to claim the trunks, they were asked to open them; they said they didn't have the keys, and went off to get them.

When they failed to return, the baggageman forced open the trunks – and found the bodies of two women, one dismembered. By now, Mrs. Judd, to whom the trunks were addressed, had vanished. The young man, her brother, had simply been asked to accompany her to the station – although, it appeared, she *had* finally admitted to him that the trunks contained bodies, and asked him to help her throw them in the sea. Her husband, a doctor, knew nothing whatever about the murders.

It transpired that Mrs. Judd had been in Phoenix for her health, and the two victims were her ex-flatmates, Hedwig Samuelson, 23, and Agnes LeRoi, 30. When Mrs. Judd finally gave herself up, after a nationwide hunt, she alleged that they had quarrelled about men freinds, and that Hedwig had tried to kill her with a gun, wounding her in the hand.

She had grabbed the gun, shot Miss Samuelson, then shot Agnes LeRoi when she attacked her, after which she dismembered Hedwig, packed both bodies in the trunks, and sent them by rail to Los Angeles. If Mrs. Judd had left them where they were, she would probably never have been suspected. As it was, she was found guilty but insane, and was not freed until December 1971.

When the train finally gives way to the aeroplane, no doubt we shall read books on train murders with the same nostalgia with which we now read the Sherlock Holmes stories. In the meantime it may be as well to remember that most of them were exceptionally stupid and brutal. Perhaps they deserve to be recalled with interest; but never with regret.

UNDERWORLDS

James Island is a half square mile of territory out in Chesapeake Bay; and, apart from a U.S. quarantine station, its inhabitants are mostly Sika deer. It was in 1956 that a scientist named John Christian went to study the deer. Five of them had been transported from the mainland in 1916; 40 years later they had increased to a herd of 300.

And then, two years after Christian's arrival, a strange thing happened. The deer began dying off at an astounding rate — more than half of them died in three months. By the middle of 1959 there were only about 80 deer on the island. Then the deaths stopped.

What was so puzzling was that there appeared to be no obvious reason for their deaths. They looked healthy and well-fed. Christian had shot a number of deer when he first arrived on the island and made a detailed study of their internal organs. The only obvious difference between these and the more recent deaths was that the animals that died in 1959 and 1960 had enlarged adrenal glands — in some cases nearly twice as big as in the shot deer. The adrenals are the glands that flood the system with the hormone adrenalin when confronted with a crisis.

Christian's observations indicated that the deer had died of stress due to overcrowding. Yet in realistic terms they were not overcrowded: around one to an acre. All the same, that was enough to produce a condition of continual stress that caused haemorrhages of the glands, brain and kidneys. It was nature's way of controlling the population.

Rapists and cannibals
The deer is a non-aggressive animal; its response to overcrowding is to 'give up' and die — one writer on ethology noted that the same thing affected some American prisoners in Korea; they

581

would become dull and lethargic, and die of convulsions; it became known as 'give-up-itis'. In more aggressive species the response to overcrowding is crime – violent and often pointless aggression. The researcher John Calhoun observed that over-crowded rats became rapists and cannibals.

When slum areas of cities become overcrowded a certain proportion of their inhabitants – usually about 5% – develop a king of 'alternative society', a way of life that is based on crime, and which is taken completely for granted as a social norm: an 'underworld' develops.

It is an interesting observation that the 'underworld' of a city seems directly related to its population. Before the 1917 revolution the Russian port of Odessa had a flourishing underworld, and it is described – humorously – in stories by the writer Isaac Babel. By comparison modern Russia has no underworld, and this is only partly due to the totalitarian system, which reduces crime by reducing the freedom of the individual. The basic cause is the fact that, as the Russian population expands, a new city is built in the wilderness to house the overflow.

Russia has well over 200 cities with populations of over 100,000. By American – or even English – standards these are little more than villages. Consider, on the other hand, that New York has a population of more than twelve million, that Hong Kong has more than four million, and Calcutta nearly five million – and that these cities, crammed into a relatively small area, also have the highest crime rates in the world. One statistician calculates that by the end of the present century Calcutta may have as many as sixty million inhabitants – it is currently expanding at the rate of a million every three years. If this actually happens, Calcutta will be one immense seething hotbed of crime.

Anti-climactic

It is necessary to understand all this if we are to understand the frighteningly steady growth of the 'underworld' in the twentieth century. In the 1850s a sociologist named Henry Mayhew undertook an enormous study of the habits of the London poor and produced four big volumes describing them. If we turn to the sections on London's underworld, they seem absurdly anti-climactic compared with modern organized crime.

There are accounts of prostitutes and their 'bullies', pick-pockets, shoplifters and thieves. Types of robbery described include stealing from street stalls, stealing from clotheslines, breaking shop windows, and child-stripping – enticing a child into a dark alleyway and stealing its resaleable clothes. This 'underworld' was run on a strictly amateur basis. The real professionals, it seemed, were the 'fences' who bought the stolen goods.

The last real attempt to organize crime had been made more than a century earlier by the notorious 'thief-taker' Jonathan Wild, who was basically a highly successful fence. Wild had been executed in 1725, in the days when the commonest crime in England was highway robbery. By half-way through the nineteenth century a fairly efficient police force had made the highways safe; besides, the great majority of travellers now went by rail. So crime had contracted again into the heart of the great cities – Glasgow, Liverpool, London.

But it sprang out of poverty rather than from any anti-social resentments. The same was true of most of the great crime cities of the world, including Paris, Berlin and New York. In these cities there was no room for a 'crime explosion', for the police knew most of the habitual criminals.

Sheer cunning

In Paris the Sûreté was even *run* by an ex-convict, Vidocq, and when he began work as a police-informer, around 1809, Paris had a number of gangs of efficient thieves; by sheer cunning and skill, Vidocq broke up most of these. On one occasion he joined the gang run by a man called Constantin, posing as an escaped galley-convict from Toulon; when the gang arrived back from a burglary Vidocq had the police waiting for them.

It was America that gave birth to the first truly organized crime: the Chinese tongs, which originated in the gold fields of California in the 1860s. They were originally intended as protection societies for the Chinese, who were hated by the white Americans, as were the Mexicans. Inevitably they began to live off their own people, and 'protection' took on its modern meaning – extortion. There were plenty of gangs of desperadoes in all the major cities – New York, San Francisco, Chicago – but they usually controlled a small area, perhaps only a single street.

Then in the 1870s the Italians began to create their own secret societies – or, rather, they brought them from Italy. In Italy societies like the Camorra had been formed for the protection of citizens, since the police were underpaid and subject to political pressures.

In America the Camorra became the Black Hand, then the Mafia. It began an organized despoliation of the Italian community. New Orleans was one of its major breeding grounds. After the murder of police chief David Hennessy in 1890, and the subsequent acquittal of the nine accused, the irate citizens rose up, broke into the jail and lynched the malefactors; and for the time being the power of the Mafia in America was broken.

It soon revived, however, this time in New York. In 1902 and 1903 there was a sudden wave of murder in the Italian colonies of New York City. Bodies were found in sacks, barrels and boxes. In many cases the tongues had been slit in two, indicating that this was a gang murder whose aim was to impose silence. The victims had been 'talkers'. The gangs' code of conduct was harsh and brutal; Giuseppe Morello, a Sicilian gang-leader, had his own 18-year-old stepson kidnapped and tortured to death because the boy had let slip some of his stepfather's secrets. Most of Morello's large income came from a counterfeiting ring whose products went out all over the United States.

The downfall of the Morello gang occurred shortly after this. Its most feared members were Morello himself and two lieutenants known as Lupo the Wolf and Petto the Ox. On April 13, 1903, a woman strolling past a lumber pile on the edge of the Italian section of the lower East Side saw a barrel – with an arm and leg protruding from it.

Powerful slash

When the police opened it they found the body of a man whose head had been almost severed with one powerful slash of a razor. The fact that his ears had been pierced suggested that he was a Sicilian. He wore a watch chain but no watch. A detective who saw a photograph of the murdered man recognized him as an 'unknown' who had been seen in the company of the Wolf and the Ox in an Italian restaurant run by Pietro Inzarillo; the detective had been shadowing the Wolf and the Ox.

Good detective work soon led them back to the Italian restaurant. The barrel, with sawdust in the bottom, scattered there to soak up the blood, had contained onion skins and butts of Italian cigars. It was traced through the manufacturer to a wholesale grocer, who had supplied it to Inzarillo's restaurant.

A brilliant Italian operative, Joseph Petronsino, was assigned to the case. he went to Sing Sing to interview a convict named de Priemo, an ex-member of Morello's gang, now serving time for counterfeiting. When de Priemo saw the photograph of the murdered man he wept. It was his brother-in-law, Beneditto Madonia. Mrs. Madonia later identified her husband's body.

JOJO

#

224-19-3693 A

Detectives went to question Lupo at his wine shop, Lupo instantly pulled a stiletto, and was about to plunge it into the throat of a detective when another policeman grabbed his arm and dragged him to the floor. Lupo was arrested; so were Petto the Ox, Morello, Inzarillo and several other suspects. In Morello's house the police found a letter, written to him by Madonia shortly before his death, saying that he was tired of this dangerous work of distributing counterfeit money and intended to return to his family in Buffalo. It was clear he had been killed because he knew too much.

But the inquest on Madonia revealed something of the power of Morello and his Black Hand. Madonia's son was asked to identify his father's watch. There was an ominous shuffling of feet in court, and a man rose to his feet and placed his finger to his lips. Madonia's son stammered and was suddenly unable to swear that the watch was his father's. Mrs. Madonia also seemed to lose her memory when the shuffling began. De Priemo was brought from Sing Sing to testify, and he declared with an air of apparent frankness that he was certain the Ox had *not* killed his brother-in-law because the Ox was one of his oldest friends.

And so all the suspects went free. However, the New York police were determined to get them behind bars. Not long after, Morello and the Wolf were arrested and charged with counterfeiting. And although the evidence seemed thin, a judge sentenced them to 25 and 30 years respectively. Inzarillo was picked up on a charge of altering his citizenship papers and sent to prison for a longer term than the offence warranted. In fact, reading between the lines of the account given by ex-Deputy Inspector Arthur Carey, it looks as though the police stretched the letter of the law to get the killers of Madonia behind bars.

Unknown intruder

Petto the Ox moved to Browntown, Pennsylvania. But in October 1925 he stepped into his back yard and was cut down by five shotgun blasts. Coincidentally, de Priemo, the man who had sworn to get the killer of his brother-in-law, had recently been released from Sing Sing, his term of imprisonment commuted for exemplary conduct. When Inzarillo came out of prison he opened a pastry shop; shortly afterwards he was also killed by an unknown intruder.

It became increasingly clear to the American police – and politicians – that the problem of organized crime started in Italy.

A member of a committee from Congress was told by the police chief of Palermo that Sicily had very little crime. He asked why, and was told seriously: 'Most of our criminals have gone to America.' In 1907 Joseph Petrosino went to Palermo to see what could be done about close co-operation between the Sicilian and American police. On the day of his arrival he was shot down in broad daylight outside the Palazzo Steri, the court of justice, by the head of the Sicilian Mafia, Don Vito. Vito, of course, had an unshakable alibi and was never charged with the murder. That round of the fight had definitely gone to the Mafia.

Ever since the 1870s America had been convulsed by violent labour disputes. In many ways this is understandable. The accounts by Jack London of his own early days as a stoker make it clear that labour was ruthlessly exploited. The American 'success ethic' meant that an employer had no pangs of conscience about keeping a man on a starvation wage, and dismissing him and allowing his wife and children to starve if he could get someone at an even cheaper rate.

The commercial world was a jungle – the title Upton Sinclair gave to his great novel of corruption in the Chicago stockyards. With fighters like Sinclair, Jack London, Clarence Darrow and Eugene Debs, organized labour slowly began to make some headway against the big corporations, although strikes were often long and bloody, and imported strikebreakers were sometimes ambushed and murdered by angry workers.

And as organized labour finally began to establish its right to exist, the thugs moved in. In New York all the major industries were controlled by gangs – the docks, the garment industry, the gambling houses and brothels. The 'protection racket', which had developed in New Orleans in the 1870s, was now a recognized and established business. The gangs fell into three clear groups: the Jews, the Irish and the Italians – the Chinese, who had once been New York's leading racketeers, had long ago been forced into a minor position.

In the autumn of 1912 East Side clothing workers went on strike. At least, most of them did; some were not militantly inclined and continued to work. Labour leaders, who were always hand-in-glove with racketeers, approached a Jewish gangster, Dopey Benney Fein, to send some strong-arm boys over to persuade these recalcitrants to join the strike.

However, the clothing bosses had also bought 'protection' from a couple of gang leaders named Tommy Dyke and Harry Lenny, an ex-prize fighter. It was an absurd situation, with both sides of labour represented by mobsters. Dopey Benney's chief lieutenant was an Irishman named Joe Miller, who, to demonstrate his freedom from racial prejudice, had re-named himself Jew Murphy. Murphy was told to interview Dyke and Lenny and order them to withdraw their protection from the clothing bosses.

One of Dyke's men punched Murphy in the face and threw him out. Murphy swore revenge. A month later, at the opening of the six-day bicycle race at Madison Square Garden, shooting started between the two gangs. Luckily only one Lenny henchman was injured. Commissioner Arthur Woods, who had recently been installed in office, realized that next time the innocent bystanders might not be so lucky.

He proved to be an accurate prophet. Trouble came on the evening of an annual ball given by the Dyke and Lenny gang at Arlington Hall, near St. Marks Place. As Dyke and Lenny were about to swagger up the steps of the hall to meet a respectful reception committee, firing suddenly broke out behind them. They leapt up the steps and into the hall. For the next ten minutes the air was full of bullets. And when the shooting stopped a man lay dead on the pavement. Frederick Strauss, a court official.

No police allowed
Woods was furious. The gangs were going too far. Not long before, he had had to send in whole contingents of police to the Car Barn district on the East River because the Car Barn Gang had put up notices declaring that no police would be allowed in the area. The Car Barn gang had been broken up; now he was determined to do the same for the Dopey Benney Mob and the Dyke and Lenny Association. His first problem was to find out how the Fein mob had managed to get hold of guns.

Most of them were known to the New York police and were likely to be stopped at any hour of the day or night. If they were found in possession of a hidden weapon it usually meant at least a year in jail, so Woods was reasonably sure that they had not gone to Arlington Hall carrying guns. The underworld grapevine brought him his answer: a girl named Annie Britt had carried seven guns in her handbag. She was one of the first 'gun molls' on record.

Woods ordered the arrest of seven members of Fein's gang, including Annie Britt. The trial was a fiasco. Most of the testimony came from gangsters and it conflicted so much that the accused men were acquitted. Nevertheless, police harassment had its effect. During Woods's administration the gangs almost disappeared. Dopey Benney's gang broke up as a consequence of the case. Woods had proved that the police *could* break this new kind of organized crime if they simply harassed enough.

Then America entered the First World War. Many of the gangsters went off to fight, and New York crime dropped. When the soldiers came back home there was a crime wave – there usually is after a war – but the police showed themselves able to cope. For a while it looked as if the pattern of organized crime in America might be broken.

Unfortunately for America there were powerful forces at work in support of crime – forces that believed themselves to be on the side of law and order. The Temperance Movement began in America as long ago as 1770, when a member of a Quaker meeting in Philadelphia protested that he was 'oppressed by the smell of rum' from his fellow Quakers. Rum was one of the most popular medical remedies of the time.

By the 1830s 'Temperance' had become a powerful movement in England as well as America. Dramas like *The Drunkard* and *Seven Nights in a Bar Room* brought in massive crowds in the 1840s and 50s. But England, with its usual genius for compromise, declined to embrace strict Temperance; the Americans, as usual, preferred to do things the hard way. Hot gospel revivals had always been an American speciality; now the Anti-Saloon League, represented at national level by Senator Andrew Volstead, succeeded in declaring all forms of alcoholic liquor illegal in the United States as from January 17, 1920.

Prohibition had arrived – and with it America's last chance, in the twentieth century at least, of beating organized crime. The story of Johnny Torrio, Al Capone, Dutch Schultz and the other gang-leaders of the bootleg era has been told many times. The problem was that they had the average American citizen on their side, that the man in the street thought it was stupid that his democratically elected government should deny him his finger of whisky or gin. In effect Capone and Schultz were *voted* into office by the people. Organized crime gained the stranglehold that it has held ever since. It may yet prove to be the most serious challenge America will have to face in the last quarter of the twentieth century.

UNWANTED LOVERS

The crime writer experiences something very like nostalgia when he looks back on some of the classic cases of unwanted lovers; they seem curiously innocent and straightforward compared to more recent examples. Madeleine Smith, Patrick Mahon, Norman Thorne, all found themselves involved in tiresome entanglements, and brooded on the simple way out. Nowadays, the cases of unwanted lovers are usually complicated by perversion, promiscuity or sheer viciousness.

The Wigwam murder is perhaps the last of the classic cases. It also occupies a distinguished place in the annals of medical detection. On October 7, 1942, two Marines, walking over Hankley Common, Surrey, observed an arm sticking out of a mound of earth. They hurried back to camp to report it. The next day, a group of police officers, accompanied by the noted pathologist Professor Keith Simpson, went to the site with shovels, and proceeded to unearth the body.

It was that of a girl, fully dressed and badly decomposed. It was clear that she had been killed by heavy blows on the head, and since the police had no clue to the girl's identity, Simpson asked for the body to be sent back to his laboratory at Guy's Hospital, London. There it was immersed in a bath of disinfectant. During the next week, Simpson and his secretary spent their tea breaks seated beside the bath, while the famous pathologist dictated notes on the nature of the injuries.

A knife with a hooked tip
This painstaking work paid off. Simpson was able to tell Inspector Fred Greeno, of Scotland Yard, just how the girl had met her death. Her assailant had started to stab her in the top of the head, using a knife with a peculiar hooked tip. She had first tried to ward off the blows, receiving injuries to her right arm and hand, and then had run away, before tripping and falling so

violently that she knocked out several front teeth. Her killer stood over her, and dealt her a tremendous blow with a blunt instrument that killed her instantly, also causing her cheek to strike the ground so violently that it was factured. The man had then dragged her uphill on her right side – there were scratch marks on the right leg – and buried her. It was odd that he had chosen the top of a hill.

Armed with this information, and a rough physical description of the girl and her clothing, Greeno approached the local police. They said it sounded like a description of Joan Pearl Wolfe, regarded as an amateur prostitute. She had apparently run away from home some time in 1941, and had been 'living rough' in the area of an army camp. She had vanished about three weeks before. Oddly enough, she was also a Roman Catholic with strong religious convictions; she was known as the 'wigwam girl'.

The police made a very long and very detailed search of Hankley Common, and one by one they found the clues they needed: Joan Wolfe's identity card, a religious tract, her shoes – and a letter to a Canadian private called August Sangret, telling him that she was pregnant.

Greeno called on Sangret at the nearby army camp. The soldier turned out to be half-Indian. He readily admitted knowing Joan Pearl Wolfe – in fact, to 'sleeping rough' with her in a kind of wigwam construction on the common. With his Red Indian background, he found nothing odd in a girl living in the middle of a common; he claimed that he had not seen her for several weeks – and also, significantly, that his clasp knife had been stolen from near their wigwam a short time before she disappeared.

Bloodstained battle dress

The net closed around him. No one else had a motive for killing Joan Wolfe, but it was established that Sangret had obtained a marriage application form from his commanding officer; this was found near the site of the wigwam. What finally established his guilt was the discovery of a battledress and blanket, both bloodstained, although an attempt had been made to wash them. The battle dress was identified as Sangret's, and bloodstains and hairs were also found on a heavy birch stake near the murder scene.

All the police needed now was the knife with which she had been stabbed. This was discovered in the army camp, by a maintenance man who was investigating a blockage in a waste pipe leading from a washbasin. It proved to be a clasp knife with a hooked point. Then someone recalled that while Sangret was waiting to be interviewed by Greeno, he had asked if he could go to the wash-house.

In court, Sangret showed true Redskin passivity as he listened to the evidence that would cost him his life. It became clear that his was no accidental murder during the course of a quarrel. The initial stab wounds were in the top of the head, so she must have been sitting or stooping; she had run away, but fell over an army trip wire and smashed her teeth. Sangret stood over her, and despatched her with one blow. Simpson produced the skull in court, wired together like a jigsaw puzzle, to demonstrate the savagery of that blow. Then Sangret had wrapped the upper part of the body in a blanket, to avoid leaving a trail of blood, and dragged her to a hilltop to bury her, as his ancestors had always buried their enemies. In spite of a recommendation of mercy, Sangret was hanged at Wandsworth Prison on April 29, 1943.

In certain basic respects, the Wigwam murder is typical of its kind. Sangret was willing to sleep with the bedraggled 'wigwam girl', with her reputation for promiscuity, but not to marry her. Most men have a strong and automatic preference for 'virtue'; they may enjoy sleeping with promiscuous girls, but they prefer to marry virgins. Our permissive society has seen the gradual erosion of this idea; but in the Victorian age no one questioned it. The very fact that a girl *had* 'yielded her virtue' to a man was enough to make him feel a certain basic contempt for her, and society was inclined to agree with him.

The Reverend Anthony Hayden was almost certainly the murderer of Mary Stannard, a 22-year-old maidservant, whose body was found near Rockland, Connecticut, in 1878. Her skull had been fractured, and her throat cut; medical examination revealed arsenic in the stomach. Mary Stannard had once been a servant in the house of the Rev. Anthony Hayden, and had subsequently talked frankly about the clergyman's passionate nature. She had also mentioned that she believed herself to be pregnant – for the second time – and that the Rev. Hayden intended to give her some medicine to induce an abortion.

Hayden was unable to account for his movements on the afternoon of her death – although his wife later insisted that he had spent the afternoon chopping wood. When it was discovered that he had purchased an ounce of arsenic, he was arrested, but there was widespread sympathy for him; after all, he was a minister, and Mary Stannard was a 'fallen woman'. Shortly thereafter, one of his parishioners went to the police with a packet of arsenic, which, he alleged, he had found in Hayden's barn. It contained precisely one ounce.

The police were puzzled, since they had already made a thorough search of the barn; but Hayden's trial was delayed for a year while a Yale professor went to England to analyse samples of the arsenic found in the barn and in the stomach of Mary Stannard. Predictably, a jury found itself unable to agree on Hayden's guilt, and he was released. In nineteenth-century Connecticut, a respectable clergyman was presumed innocent even when proved guilty.

What is so interesting about this case is that it reveals so clearly the basic criminological pattern of the 'unwanted mistress' murder. To begin with, the majority of men who kill unwanted mistresses are Don Juan types, dominant males with a powerful sex-drive. Now, if a Don Juan is handsome and wealthy, he can take his pick of desirable women, particularly those who are pretty and wealthy. If he is neither handsome nor wealthy, he will take whatever he can get, and the girls he will find easiest to get are those whose dominance is altogether lower, and whose 'inferior' social position makes them more easily accessible. So the Rev. Hayden seduces a maidservant who has already had one illegitimate child.

However – and here is the important point – having seduced this social-reject, he feels no further interest in her. As Abraham Maslow's researches into 'dominance' showed, men and women, given a free choice, tend to choose permanent partners *within* their own dominance group. A high-dominance Don Juan soon begins to find a low-dominance female incredibly boring, and if she also threatens his social position – and therefore his craving for 'recognition' and respect – he is likely to brood on ways of getting rid of her.

Insatiable sexual itch

These same basic features can be found in an English case of the Victorian age: the murder of Florence Dennis by James Canham Read. Read was a book-keeper at the Royal Albert Docks in London, earning three pounds a week; he was also married with eight children. This was a pity, for Read had an insatiable sexual itch. He was a good-looking, well-dressed young man, and he devoted most of his spare time to the pursuit of love affairs. One of his mistresses was a married woman, a Mrs. Ayriss; they wrote to one another under assumed names, writing to a small stationer's shop, and Read called on her when her husband was out.

One day, they met on a common; Mrs. Ayriss had brought her sister with her — a pretty, dark-haired girl of nineteen named Florence Dennis. As soon as Read saw her, he felt the familier itch. How he managed to continue seeing her without her sister's knowledge is a matter for conjecture; but soon Florence Dennis also became his mistress. Read was leading an involved sex life at the time, for he was also having an affair with a third woman, who knew him as Mr. Benson, a commercial traveller. He had installed her in a cottage at Mitcham.

It was some time in 1892 when Read met Florence, and their affair continued for the next two years. And in June, 1894, Florence discovered she was pregnant. For a Victorian young lady, this was the end of the world. She wrote Read a letter, and addressed it to him, under his own name, at the Royal Albert Docks. It said: 'Dear Sir, I have left Sheerness [her parent's home] and am staying at Southend, I should like to know what arrangements you have made.'

Read realized that this was a determined young woman, who might become very difficult. He stopped visiting the Mitcham mistress for several weeks, and held clandestine meetings with Florence instead. And on a warm evening in late June, he and Florence walked in the fields near the village of Prittlewell, near Southend — where Mrs. Ayriss lived. In his pocket, Read was carrying a revolver.

At some time between nine and ten, he shot Florence Dennis in the forehead, at close range, then pushed her body into a ditch, and walked quickly away. An old lady saw him, and he asked her the way to Prittlewell. But he seems to have lost his way. After midnight, a man asked a policeman the way to London; the constable noticed his face and later identified him as Canham Read.

Covered up his tracks

But how could Read have expected to get away with the murder? The answer is that he believed he had covered up his tracks. He had sworn the girl to silence — although she had not kept her promise. He had made the appointment to meet her with an unsigned telegram, dropped into a pillar box. He had no idea that Florence's sister *and* her parents knew that she was pregnant by him. On the Monday after the murder, he received a rude shock when a telegram arrived at his place of work, asking about Florence, and signed by Mrs. Ayriss.

He sent back a letter claiming that he had not seen the young person in eighteen months. But he realized his plan had misfired. The only thing was to flee. He helped himself to the money from the office safe, and fled to his mistress in Rose Cottage, Mitcham. The police had little difficulty in tracing him there, and he was arrested. The revolver with which he shot Florence Dennis was never found, but a number of people – including his daughter, his sister, and the mistress from Rose Cottage – all testified that he had possessed such a weapon.

Before the sentence of death, Read made a speech, insisting that it was Mrs. Ayriss he had met secretly on the evening of the murder, and that she had wanted to borrow fifty pounds to procure an abortion for Florence – who had got herself pregnant 'with a soldier from Hounslow'. It was a feeble defence, and did not prevent the judge from passing the sentence.

The murder case on which Theodore Dreiser based his monumental novel *An American Tragedy* has many similar features. Son of Salvation Army preachers who neglected him, Chester Gillette obtained a job in the skirt factory of his uncle, near Cortland, New York. He quickly seduced 18-year-old Grace Brown, who became pregnant. When, in desperation, Grace threatened to tell his uncle, Gillette invited her for a boat trip on Big Moose Lake in the Adirondacks.

On July 11, 1906, they rowed out of sight of other trippers – and Grace was never again seen alive. Her body floated to the surface three days later, the face badly bruised, and the coroner reported that she had been dead – from heavy blows on the head – before she fell into the lake. Gillette was executed at Auburn on March 30, 1908.

Since those far-off days, the pattern has changed considerably. While England and France continued to produce 'unwanted lovers' cases that might have taken place fifty years earlier – the Wigwam murder is an example – American cases have displayed strange and perverse variations.

Joe Ball, a 40-year-old alligator-breeder and owner of the Sociable Inn, near Elmendorf, Texas, was the Don Juan type, who liked to hire pretty waitresses. But his own solution to the problem of what to do with the girls when he grew tired of them was to feed them to his pet alligators. Their pool, surrounded by wire, was in his back garden, and nearby stood a foul-smelling-barrel containing chunks of rotting meat.

In mid-September 1938, Ball's latest mistress, Hazel Brown, disappeared, and her mother telephoned the sheriff of Elmendorf to enquire about her daughter. Ball – a stocky, ugly man – told the police she had left to work 'in Laredo or El Paso'. The sheriff discovered that a large number of waitresses – four in the past two years – had apparently left town just as unobtrusively as Hazel Brown – often leaving behind their clothes. And Hazel Brown had opened a bank account only two days before disappearing, leaving the money untouched. It certainly looked like murder.

Buried on the river bank

Sheriff Klevenhagen reasoned that Ball's feebleminded hired man, Willie Sneed, must be an accessory to the crimes. He and his deputy called on Ball, and told him that Sneed had 'spilled', Ball agreed to go with them, and opened the cash register. He took out a gun, with which he shot himself through the head. Sneed confessed to helping Ball dispose of the bodies – and revealed that two of them, including that of Hazel Brown, were buried on the river bank. Sneed was eventually sentenced to two years in prison as an accessory. The alligators, five of them, were sent to the San Antonio zoo, but they died – perhaps unable to adjust to the change of diet.

In 1965, America was electrified by a case that seemed to indicate new dimensions in juvenile delinquency. It was on November 9 of that year that a 19-year-old youth named Richard Bruns contacted the police in Columbus, Ohio, and told them he had information about several murders that had taken place in Tucson, Arizona. The motive for his decision to talk was fear for the life of his girlfriend, who was still in Tucson. The man he wanted to see behind bars was 23-year-old Charles Schmid, known as Smitty.

The police quickly recognized that this was the break they had been needing for some time. In the past year there had been four disappearances of young girls, with all the indications that these were not ordinary runaways.

On May 31, 1964, the mother of 15-year-old Alleen Rowe returned home from night work to find that her daughter had gone out 'on a date' and had not returned. She was never seen again. Mrs. Rowe mentioned that Alleen had been asked to join a teenage 'sex club' not long before her disappearance, and had told her mother. 'You've got to be in, or you're a nobody.' Oddly enough, the girl's father, living in another part of the country, had a dream in which his daughter was murdered, and rang his ex-wife to tell her about it.

In mid-August, 1965, two daughters of a Tucson doctor vanished; they were Gretchen Fritz, a pretty – if neurotic – 17-year-old, and her 13-year-old sister Wendy. An extensive police search for them met the same dead-end as in the case of Alleen. They mixed a great deal with many teenagers – Tucson is a 'teenagers' town', being close to the campus of the university of Arizona – but no one seemed willing to talk. A few weeks later, on September 8, Sandra Highes, another 15-year-old, failed to return from school, and the police were unable to find any trace of her.

Richard Bruns's revelations led to the immediate arrest of 'Smitty', and to the discovery that many of Tucson's teenagers led sex-lives that would have impressed Casanova. Charles Schmid was five feet three inches tall, and wore boots with high heels to increase his height. His well-to-do parents had given him a house of his own – at the end of their garden – and he used it for orgies. In the subsequent investigation it was revealed that Gretchen Fritz had been his mistress, but that she had become possessive.

On August 16, 1965, Schmid had invited her to his 'pad'. She brought her younger sister with her; but it made no difference; Schmid strangled them both, then dumped their bodies in the desert. A year earlier, he had buried the body of Alleen Rowe nearby; he and two other teenagers – John Saunders and Mary French – had called for her late at night. They took her out to the desert and she left the car with the two males, who apparently intended to initiate her into the 'sex-club' in the quickest way. When she screamed and struggled, she was battered to death with rocks. Schmid then buried her with a shovel he kept in the boot of the car.

The odd thing was that Schmid made no effort to keep the murders secret. Many Tucson teenagers knew that he had killed Alleen Rowe; but they took care not to mention it to their parents. Schmid actually showed Richard Bruns the bodies of the two Fritz girls in the desert, and Bruns later led the police to their skeletons. Alleen Rowe's body was not recovered; neither could the police find any trace of Sandra Highes. Schmid was tried separately, and sentenced to death; but appeals delayed the sentence until the death penalty was abolished.

To murder an unwanted mistress – or lover – indicates an erosion of normal human feeling. But the strange, emotionless brutality of many recent cases – like that of Schmid – suggests that our over-mechanized civilization is adding a new dimension of sickness to the age-old violence.

VICIOUS TRIANGLES

There is one matter on which the professional criminologist and the general public simply do not see eye to eye: the so-called 'eternal triangle'. For the criminologist, most such cases are elementary, if not downright boring. But the general public has a voracious and apparently limitless appetite for them. And who is to say who is right? The 'triangle' murder may be of small psychological interest; but it often contains great drama.

Though it is rare for such a case to appeal equally to both public and criminologist, the murder of Agnes Tufverson achieved this unusual distinction. Her killers were described by Freud as one of the most remarkable examples of sexual perversion he had ever encountered.

'Captain' Ivan Poderjay was not, in fact, a Captain; nor was he, as he declared, a member of Yugoslav Army Intelligence. He was a confidence trickster and professional lady-killer – in every sense of the word.

Born into a poor Serbian family in 1899, Poderjay started his career as a fortune teller in Belgrade, then joined – and quickly deserted – the French Foreign Legion. In 1926, he was cited as co-respondent in a divorce case by a high government official; he subsequently married the ex-wife, got possession of her fortune, and vanished.

Up to the age of 33, Poderjay continued to live off seduction. He was short, plump and losing his hair; but he also had that essential quality of the professional Casanova, the ability to make a woman feel that she was the most fascinating person in the world. He was heartless; but at least his victims escaped with their lives, until, in 1931, he met Marguerite Suzanne Ferrand, a French-woman with a firm mouth and school-mistressy face.

Jackbooted feet
She was a research assistant in the British Museum. As soon as

597

their eyes met, each knew they had found something they had been looking for all their lives, for the 37-year-old Marguerite enjoyed chastizing men; and Ivan enjoyed being chastized. After crouching naked at her jackbooted feet, Ivan realized that he had found the ideal sexual playmate, a woman whose fantasies were as bizarre as his own.

This was another case of a 'catalytic' relationship. If they had never met, Marguerite and Ivan might have pursued their ways harmlessly for the rest of their lives. But together, they entered into a combination as deadly as fire and gunpowder. Marguerite was not shocked to find that Ivan was a confidence man who lived off women; on the contrary, the thought of causing pain to other women caused her deep pleasure. In March, 1932, they were married in London – although Ivan was, in fact, already married to several other 'wives'.

One year later, in the lounge of a cross-channel ferry, Ivan noticed an attractive woman of about 40 – Agnes Tufverson. She was well-dressed, and she looked distinctly sick. Ivan introduced himself as a Captain in the Yugoslav Army, and advised her to get some air on the deck, where he mentioned casually that he was a millionaire and an inventor.

In subsequent weeks, in London, they saw a lot of one another, and Ivan spent a gread deal of money on her – well over £500. But this was not a source of concern to him, for he had persuaded Agnes to allow him to invest $5,000 of her money . . .

Back in New York, Agnes returned to her job as an executive at the Electric Bond and Share Company, and she confided to her best friend that she was to marry a romantic Yugoslav millionaire.

A week later, she received a cable from her 'millionaire', declaring that he had a marvellous opportunity to invest another $5,000 for her, and asking her to wire the money. She decided against it, for she wanted Ivan to come and get her, and that is precisely what he did.

In November 1933, Poderjay arrived at her New York apartment with a huge bunch of flowers, and on December 4 they were married, Ivan explained that it was hardly worth cabling his bankers to send money from London; they would be returning to London in a couple of weeks. In the meantime, they could live on Agnes's money; Agnes agreed.

On December 20 Agnes and Poderjay prepared to leave New York. But instead of sailing as arranged on the *Hamburg*, they returned to their apartment late that night. The next day,

Poderjay told the daily help that his wife had decided to sail on ahead, and that he was following her immediately. Their luggage had gone ahead on the *Hamburg* – all except one huge trunk, which had been delivered to the apartment the day before. Poderjay escorted this trunk to the docks himself, and insisted on staying with it until it was in his cabin on the *Olympic*. He had booked this cabin a week before – a single passage – with instructions that he must have a cabin above the waterline.

No one ever saw Agnes Tufverson again. Some months later, her family began to institute enquiries. These led to the arrest of Ivan and Marguerite Poderjay by the Vienna police, who were astonished to discover that their apartment was filled with instruments of torture and flogging. The police called in Sigmund Freud – the world's most famous psychoanalyst.

Lesbian affair

Freud found the Poderjays fascinating. Marguerite alleged that her true 'personality' was a tyrannical sadist named Count John, although she also had two subsidiary female 'personalities'. Poderjay in turn was physically 'controlled' by a female called Ita, who was the mistress of Count John, and who was having a lesbian affair with one of Marguerite's female personalities; he was also controlled by another two 'spirit' girls who were tortured by Count John.

Poderjay admitted that Agnes had not sailed on the *Hamburg*; he told the police she had run off with another man, on the spur of the moment. Her luggage had arrived in Poderjay's flat at Vienna and was still there. The New York police had no doubts whatever as to what had happened to Agnes. On the day he bought the trunk, Poderjay had also bought 800 razor blades – explaining that they were cheaper in America. He had also bought large quantities of cold cream.

Once on board the *Olympic*, he had spent several days in his cabin. During that time, the police believed, he had carefully shaved the flesh from Agnes's bones until she was only a skeleton. The flesh had fed the fish who follow every liner. The skeleton, greased with cold cream, had also slipped out of the porthole.

Poetic justice

There was no body, and circumstantial evidence was not strong enough to hang Ivan Poderjay. Instead, he was sentenced to five years in prison for bigamy. While he was serving his time, an angry fellow convict, outraged by some bizarre proposition, beat Poderjay so badly that he lost his left eye and eight teeth. It sounds like poetic justice until we reflect that he probably enjoyed it. He returned to Marguerite, moved to Belgrade, and presumably continued to live a multiple sex life with Count John and his harem.

This is surely one of the clearest cases in all psychological literature of the 'catalyst effect' – that is, of two people, who would be harmless alone, inspiring one another to commit murder. Parallel cases – Snyder and Gray, Bywaters and Thompson, Brady and Hindley, Fernandez and Beck – have been discussed in connection with crimes of dominance.

This is only one type of catalyst effect; there is another, equally familiar to criminologists, that is also fraught with explosive possibilities. In this situation, the murderer and the 'catalyst' do not become partners in crime; the 'catalyst' inspires the crime, but takes no part in it. This happens when the 'catalyst' has a particularly yielding and gentle nature, inspiring a frenzy of desire and protectiveness that may explode into violence.

Violent man
It is illustrated perfectly in the relationship between Cesare Borgia and his sister Lucretia. Lucretia, with her gentle face and weak mouth, was a born 'victim'; it was inevitable that she should become her brother's mistress. But from then on, Cesare could not bear the thought of any other man possessing her; one suitor saved his life by fleeing; another became her husband, and was murdered on Cesare's orders.

Borgia was, of course, a 'violent man' in A.E. Von Vogt's sense – a man who would rather commit murder than ever admit that he was in the wrong. On the other hand, Crippen, who was also driven to murder by a 'gentle catalyst', was basically a non-violent man. His wife Cora was dominant, and Crippen accepted her as 'the boss'. His typist, Ethel Le Neve, was completely undominant: gentle, yielding, faithful; half a century after the murder, she told crime-researcher Pat Pitman that she was still in love with Crippen. In her company, Crippen felt like a superman. The result: the murder of Mrs. Crippen, and Crippen's execution in November 1910.

Eyeing a sparrow
The case of Dr. Philip Cross bears some basic resemblances to that of Crippen. A retired army doctor, 62 years of age, he lived

comfortably with his wife and six children at Shandy Hall, near Dripsey, Co. Cork. His wife was 22 years his junior; they had been married 18 years, and it had been, on the whole, a satisfactory marriage. In October 1886, Mrs. Laura Cross engaged a new governess for the children, a 20-year-old girl named Effie Skinner. Effie, like Ethel Le Neve, was the catalyst type: not particularly pretty, but with something soft and yielding about her. As soon as he saw her, the military, rather forbidding Dr. Cross felt like a hawk eyeing a sparrow. For the first time, he realized that his marriage had been merely satisfactory, never ecstatic. It had never provided him with any real outlet for his male dominance.

One day, as Effie stood talking to him about the children, he bent and kissed her. He was afraid she would tell his wife or leave immediately. But she stayed, and his desire to possess her increased. His wife noticed it, and she took what seemed to her the sensible course: she sacked Effie. The girl was shattered, she went to Dublin, and when Dr. Cross visited her there, she finally gave herself to him. Possession did not cool his desire; he wanted to be married to her, living in comfort in Shandy Hall.

Early in May, 1887, Mrs. Cross began to suffer attacks of vomiting. Her husband told her she had a weak heart. She died on June 1st, and was buried three days later. Less than two weeks after this, he married Effie Skinner in London. At first, he decided that they had better keep the marriage a secret and live separately, but when he got back to Dripsey, he discovered the news had preceded him.

There seemed no point keeping Effie in London, so he moved her to Shandy Hall. Inevitably, there was gossip, and the police finally decided to act. Laura Cross was exhumed, and the coroner found 3.2 grains of arsenic in her body, as well as strychnine. There was no trace of heart disease.

State of shock

The police were also able to trace the firm from whom Dr. Cross had bought arsenic 'for sheep dipping'. Tried at the Munster Assizes in Cork, he was found guilty on December 18, 1887, and hanged in the following January. Effie was so shocked by the realization that she had been the cause of the murder that she refused to see him in the condemned cell, and Cross's hair turned white overnight.

Of more recent cases involving the 'innocent catalyst', the one with some of the most dramatic features is certainly that of

Armand Rohart, mayor of Peuplinges, near Calais. In the early hours of May 24, 1967, the mayor of Escalles, near Peuplinges, was awakened by the sound of a motor horn. He found Armand Rohart, one of the district's richest men, collapsed over the wheel of his car.

Rohart seemed to be in a state of shock, and was taken to the Lille hospital. Back at Rohart's farm, his brother Jules mentioned that Rohart and his wife Jacqueline had gone off to the beach for a swim that afternoon, and had not been back since.

A search of the beach revealed Jacqueline's body, dressed in a pink bikini and covered in seaweed. Rohart's story – when he regained consciousness – was that he and Jacqueline – who was 45 – had waded into the sea up to their necks, holding hands, when a great wave had swept them away. Neither could swim. Rohart had struggled ashore, lost consciousness, and wakened after dark on the empty beach . . .

Dairy maids

Why had a middle-aged man and woman decided to go swimming on a chilly May day? Rohart was quite frank with the police. A few years before, he had had a love affair with the 14-year-old nurse of his children, Odile Wissocq, and she had borne him a child. He had sent the girl back to her parents, and ever since then had been trying to make his wife forget his lapse. They had decided to go to the beach because it was on just such a day, many years earlier, that they had made love by the sea . . .

The story sounded convincing. Certainly, Rohart's grief at the funeral seemed genuine. But the post mortem demonstrated that Jacqueline Rohart had not died of drowning; she had no water in her lungs. Further research into Rohart's background revealed that Odile Wissocq had not been his only lapse. For many years, the rich farmer had exercised a kind of *droit de seigneur* on dairy maids and farm girls. But the affair with Odile had been different. She was the sweet, yielding type, and it was not true that Rohart had broken off with her. They had been seen lying together on a blanket long after she had returned to her parents. But recently, Odile had talked of marrying a younger man; she was a girl who needed a protector, and her status as a mistress was wearing on her nerves.

There was still no reason to charge Rohart with murder. Then, on June 14, an ex-legionnaire named Jacob Kerbahay walked into the local police station with a tape recorder, and played the police a conversation in which Rohart asked him to murder

Jacqueline. Kerbahay, who lived in a cottage on Rohart's land, said that Rohart had raised the matter with him earlier. At that point, Rohart's plan was to hide a needle covered with *curare* – the alkaloid used by pygmies on their darts – in her car seat, so it would penetrate her skin as she sat down; she would crash and perhaps break her neck . . .

Perfect plan

Kerbahay didn't like or trust Rohart, so when Rohart called on him again, he decided to tape the conversation for his own protection. Rohart noticed that the tape recorder was turning, but Kerbahay told him he was recording music from the radio, and played it back to prove it – switching to another track.

On Kerbahay's evidence, Rohart was arrested, and the police quickly uncovered the corroborative evidence they needed. On the day before her death, Jacqueline Rohart had been to the hairdresser, and had her hair set in a new style. The fixative would have been washed off if she had been in the sea for any length of time. The body was exhumed, and it was discovered that the fixative was still in place.

Her bloodstream contained a large amount of alcohol, although she normally did not drink, and two weeks after the tragedy two bottles were washed up on the beach, one containing sleeping tablets, the other, traces of ether. Rohart's 'perfect murder' plan now became clear.

He had persuaded her to drink heavily, to celebrate their sentimental excursion to the beach. He had anaesthetized her with ether, then carried her body into the sea to drown her. She had woken up and fought him – he had shown the police scratches on his chest, which, he alleged, were made when Jacqueline tried to cling to him.

He had beaten her unconscious, dragged her ashore, and suffocated her with a car blanket or cushion. She had been dead when he took her back into the sea to 'drown her', so no water went into her lungs. Finally, the police discovered that Rohart had insured his wife's life for a million francs – £100,000 – not long before the murder. Their case was complete. Rohart was sentenced to life imprisonment.

Terribly injured

When a love triangle is complicated by violent Latin tempers, the result is almost inevitably violence. When Dr. Joseph DiFede was found murdered – apparently by a burglar – on December 7,

1961, the New York police sensed that this crime was less straightforward than it looked. The sobbing widow, 35-year-old Jean DiFede, told how she had been awakened by noises coming from her husband's bedroom. She had looked in, and found him dying, terribly injured.

It was the violence of the murder that troubled the police; someone had hit DiFede with a hammer, knocking out one of his eyes, then stabbed him again and again, covering the room with blood. This was surely no burglar, but someone who *hated* DiFede.

It seemed that there might be many people who felt like that. 38-year-old DiFede was not only a highly successful doctor; he was also an incredible lover, who made no secret of his voracious sexual appetite. His temper was so violent that his wife never dared to object; on one occasion he had been heard to boast that he had 15 mistresses.

In the course of a thorough investigation of DiFede's patients, the police interviewed two Italian youths who lived nearby; one of them had only a temporary visa. What puzzled the police was that although neither of them had regular jobs, they lived in a comfortable apartment, and one of them, 19-year-old Armando Cossentino, ran an expensive car.

Eventually, investigation revealed that while the fiery Dr. DiFede was out with other women, Armando was comforting his plump, long-suffering wife, and clearly she was his source of income.

The two youths were subjected to long interrogation. Armando, the stronger character, insisted he knew nothing; but his friend finally broke down, and told how he and Armando had gone to the doctor's house to murder him. Armando was only 19, but he was as hot-tempered and strong-willed as Dr. DiFede, and he felt it was time Jean was freed from her husband's domination.

Cossentino was sentenced to death, later commuted to life imprisonment. Jean DiFede, accused of being an accessory – the actual charge was manslaughter – was also sentenced to life imprisonment.

Cases like these lead to a strange but inevitable conclusion: where a 'love triangle' is concerned, it is a mistake to speak of the 'psychology of the murderer'. What is at issue is the *group* psychology of three people. And as absurd as this sounds, the ultimate responsibility for the murder lies with all three – including the victim.

VICTIMS

The pretty German girl led the man through the hole in the hedge. Between the hedge and the fence behind it there was room for the two of them to lie down. She held out her scarf to the man. 'Tie my wrists. I am your captive princess. Make me know that I belong to you.' When he had tied her, he tugged off her skirt, then her stockings, suspender belt and transparent panties.

As he was unbuckling his trousers, a knife fell from his belt. The girl began to pant. 'Cut me a little. Flick the blade against my flesh.' Then, as he began to make love to her: 'Harder, please. Cut me . . .' She began to whine and moan like an animal. Suddenly, she gasped: 'Now, Kill me. Please kill me . . .' And the man, too excited to disobey, drove the knife into her throat.

'Afterwards, I took her handbag,' said Guido Benedetto Spimpolo, the killer of Marlene Puntschuh, 'I cut it up, and threw the pieces down the lavatory on the train . . .'

His story sounded incredible: he described how, on June 7, 1969, Marlene Puntschuh had picked him up in the Piazza Barberini in Rome, and less than a quarter of an hour later she was begging him to kill her. But a search of her hotel room revealed a diary that left the police no doubt that Spimpolo was telling the truth. Marlene Puntschuh, a bank clerk from Stuttgart, was a masochist who dreamed of being tied up and tortured by virile lovers.

Every year she came on holiday to Italy, looking for muscular, sunburnt men who would help her to act out her strange fantasies; Marlene was the born victim. Guido Spimpolo, the ex-waiter with the body of a giant and muscles of a weight-lifter, was a born conqueror of female hearts; and when their eyes met on the Piazza Barberini, killer and victim instantly recognized one another, and drew together instinctively.

It was in his classic study *The Criminal and the Victim* (1949) that Dr. Hans von Hentig argued that, in many murder cases, the victim may be as responsible as the murderer. But nearly 30 years earlier, in 1920, the novelist Franz Werfel had written a novel called *Not the Murderer, but the Victim is Guilty*. It sounds absurd; but what Von Hertig and Werfel both had in mind was a fact well known to police officers; that people often behave in such a way that they seem to invite violence.

Sexual games

When, for example, we hear about a case of child murder, we are inclined to think in terms of an innocent child lured to its death by a lust-crazed maniac; but in many cases it is the child who invites the adult to play sexual games — and then, perhaps, becomes frightened and begins to struggle; there are clues on record of children who have made a habit of falsely accusing men of exposing themselves.

In the same way, many women who accept lifts from total strangers on dark nights are fully aware of the risk they are running, and may be considered to be playing a kind of Russian roulette with fate. A case in point occurred in Kingsport, Tennessee in August 1970, when a 22-year-old nurse's aide allowed herself to be picked up outside the local supermarket by two men in a car. They parked near a quarry, and one of them, Harley Phillips, ripped off her clothes, and raped her twice.

They drove to a tavern, and the other man went in to get beer and food, but the girl made no attempt to escape from the car. They slept in the open overnight, and Phillips cut her with a knife and talked about killing her. She was raped again. After another day of terror, rape and threats of death, the three spent the night in a barn, and she allowed the other man to have intercourse with her voluntarily — this was the man whose invitation she had accepted in the first place.

After being made to promise solemnly that she would not report Phillips to the law, she was finally allowed to go home. She told the full story to a girlfriend, who immediately called the police, and in 1972 Phillips was sentenced to 18 years in jail. Undoubtedly the girl was the victim of a sadist; but it is equally clear that her ordeal was at least 50% her own fault. A girl who drives off with two strangers cannot be entirely unaware that they have sex on their minds.

This obvious type of 'collaboration' between the victim and the criminal is only one aspect of the complexities of victimology; the relationship may be more subtle. Everyone has known married couples who seem to bring out the worst in one another;

the husband may be an irritable bully, the wife an inefficient whiner whose reaction to her husband's bullying is an attack of self-pity and still more inefficiency. Everything she does makes him worse.

Finally murders

About four-fifths of the murders committed in England are 'family murders', in which victim and killer are related, or at least known to one another, and a large number of these are cases in which the victim-murderer relation already exists.

But there is one aspect of 'victimology' that has so far been totally neglected by the criminologist: the question of the 'born victim': the person who seems to be 'destined' for murder. The reason for its neglect is obvious: to speak of a predestined victim sounds more like crystal-gazing than science, yet this is not necessarily true. We recognize that a woman can be responsible for her own murder if she habitually wears low-cut dresses, behaves in a generally provocative manner, takes off her clothes without drawing the curtains, picks up strangers in bars, and it is surely equally conceivable that a woman's whole *personality pattern* could place her in the high-risk bracket where murder is concerned.

Such born victims are more often women than men, for the obvious reason that a man is less likely to be the victim of a sexual attack. These women often have a pathetic air of accident proneness. It is certainly difficult to analyse such cases in terms of pragmatic psychology, yet you have only to read about them, or even see a photograph, to feel that there *is* such a thing as a born victim, even if they are lucky enough to avoid actually being murdered.

Anyone who has read a biographical sketch of President Kennedy – with his childhood illnesses, his accident proneness, his wartime misadventures – feels that this *was* the type of president to be killed by an assassin's bullet. The same applied to his brother Robert. On the other hand, Lyndon Johnson somehow didn't *look* accident prone; a kind of invulnerability was a part of his total personality.

The same was true of De Gaulle, who was the subject of several assassination attempts, and Hitler survived a bomb blast that went off within a yard of his legs, although other generals in the same room died from it. Yet President Kennedy was killed by a bullet fired by a hopeless marksman from a rifle with inaccurate sights. Moreover, the assassin Oswald's own career shows

him to have been accident *and* failure prone, and his subsequent
death while in police hands underlines it.

It would be easy for speculations of this kind to turn into
absurd hypotheses and preposterous guesses. However, the
psychologist Carl Jung developed a valuable concept called
'synchronicity' which could be defined as 'a coincidence that is
not a coincidence'. Jung himself described, for example, how he
happened to notice that the number on his streetcar ticket was
the same as the number on a ticket for a concert that evening;
and then, to make the coincidence doubly unlikely, someone
gave him the same phone number later the same day.

Since President Kennedy's death, many writers have pointed
out the number of strange similarities between the assassinations
of Lincoln and Kennedy; both were shot in the head from
behind, both succeeded by a southerner called Johnson, both
advised by their secretaries against the visit that led to the
assassination, and so on. There is also the extraordinary fact that
ever since Lincoln, who was elected in 1860, *all* presidents
elected at 20-year intervals have been assassinated or died in
office: Garfield, 1880, McKinley, 1900, Harding, 1920,
Roosevelt, 1940, Kennedy, 1960.

Evil omens

Sceptics may accuse us of credulity for taking notice of 'coincidences'; but, on the other hand, all science has advanced by a
process of observing such matters – for example, comets were
once thought to foretell catastrophe – until someone noticed that
they reappeared *regularly*.

It would certainly be wrong to make too much of this inherent
'victim proneness'; but it would also be stupid to pretend it did
not exist. One of the most obvious cases is the Black Dahlia
affair. Elizabeth Short once remarked to a friend: 'I guess
something sure hexed me, and nothing anybody or anything can
do can help . . .' Yet when one considers her drifting, self-pitying
life, it is also clear that it was partly her own fault.

The 'born victim' is often a person suffering from a *deficiency
of vitality*, who is largely aware that her bad luck *is* her own
fault, yet takes this as simply another form of bad luck, instead
of recognizing that she *could* change it. Such a person often
prefers to live in a world of fantasy and shrinks from facing the
real world: so that the impact, when it finally comes, may be
brutal.

A typical case involving such an 'escapist' victim occurred in

Vancouver in 1949. The body of a woman was found in False Creek on November 9. She had been strangled, beaten, then thrown – unconscious but alive – into the water. Missing panties indicated that the motive was rape. She was identified as Blanche Fisher, an attractive spinster who looked at least 10 years younger than her actual age, 45; she had failed to return home from the cinema the previous evening.

She had been a pretty, shapely woman; why, then, had she been unmarried? Was she having a secret love affair, as she often hinted to her fellow assistants in the store where she worked? Who was the man who, she claimed, had been trying to persuade her into a secret marriage? As detectives investigated her background, they realized they were facing a dead-end, for Blanche Fisher had no secret lover; no man had asked her to marry him. Her only outings were to the church she attended, and to the cinema. She preferred romantic films, and she was an enthusiastic reader of movie-fan magazines. While she lived her quiet, virginal life, she dreamed of excitement, of masterful lovers . . .

Women's panties
A month later police picked up a man who was prowling the streets wearing only a raincoat. He was 34-year-old Frederick Ducharme, who lived on a houseboat. When police went there, they found half a dozen pairs of women's panties on a clothesline, and in the living room Blanche Fisher's shoes and watch. Ducharme finally confessed to her murder, claiming she entered the car willingly, then refused to let him make love to her.

What *is* certain is that he forced her back on to his boat, then beat her, raped her and tortured her with a knife before throwing her overboard. Like the unfortunate 'Black Dahlia', Blanche Fisher had the *mental outlook* of a victim; unlike Marlene Puntschuh, she did not literally beg to be murdered; yet something about her certainly brought out the worst in her killer.

Two other cases afford interesting parallels to the Blanche Fisher and the Dahlia murders. In March 1972 the nude body of a girl was found leaning against a tree near Welles, in Maine. It was covered with more than 200 cigarette burns, had a deformed upper lip, due to a series of healed scars, a cauliflower ear, and a deformed right arm, which had been broken and then allowed to heal without splints.

The girl, later identified as 19-year-old Constance Corcione, had died as a result of choking on her own vomit, and the

injuries indicated that she had been beaten and tortured for
many months before her death. Once she was identified, it was
not difficult to piece together her story. A year before, she had
been a pretty girl. The parallels with the Dahlia, Beth Short, are
interesting; Connie, like Beth, was also born in Cambridge,
Massachusetts, and her father had also deserted her mother,
leaving her to bring up the family.

Connie ran away from home again and again, leaving for the
last time in July 1970 and moving in with the family of a
musician named Richard DiMarzo, in Revere, Mass. DiMarzo
had a wife and children. He was a man of violent temper. It was
he who had apparently beaten and tortured Connie for almost
two years.

On her eighteenth birthday, a family friend had called on
Connie at her home in Lynn, and the girl had pulled down her
slacks and showed enormous bruises all over her thighs and hips.
These had been inflicted by DiMarzo, and the friend threatened
to kill DiMarzo if he ever touched her again: yet it was *after* this
that Connie actually moved in with DiMarzo. Presumably she
was DiMarzo's mistress – medical examination revealed that she
had had sexual intercourse shortly before death, apparently
without force.

The DiMarzos had moved out when the police called at the
house, but in an upstairs room the police found over 200
cigarette butts and other evidence that this was where Connie
had been kept and tortured. Many teenagers had been in and out
of the house duing the period Connie was there; one of them
testified to having heard DiMarzo's 3-year-old daughter saying:
'You beat up Connie, and you even killed her.' DiMarzo had
been seen leaving the house with a four-foot-long carpet bag,
sagging at both ends, which he had put into his car. That was the
last the DiMarzo family saw of Connie.

DiMarzo was already being held on a $15,000 bond on a rape
charge; he was later sentenced to life imprisonment for the first
degree murder of Constance Corcione. But the mystery still
remains: *why* did the girl stay with a man who tortured and beat
her, even if she was a masochist? She can scarcely have enjoyed
having her arm broken, and her lip cut off. This victim
undoubtedly 'collaborated' with her killer.

In June 1972 a pretty Red Indian girl was standing on a
pavement in Phoenix, Arizona, looking for a taxi, when a man in
his mid-fifties suddenly grabbed her and forced her into his car.
After stunning her with a blow, the man, LeRoy Satchel, drove

her to his trailer outside the town. There he gagged and tied her, then cut off her clothes with a pair of scissors. When she fought, he bit her, drawing blood.

Rape and torture
When she woke up, her ankles were chained, and the chain ran over a pulley in the ceiling. For three days the girl remained Satchel's prisoner; between periods of rape and torture she was left upside down, suspended over the bed. A neighbour became suspicious, or may even have seen the suspended body through a window; the police were notified, and called at the trailor.

At first Satchel tried to bluster, but the police soon had him under arrest, and the girl freed. He was found guilty of rape and kidnapping, and sentenced to over 200 years in prison. It was revealed that he had served an eight-year sentence for the 'manslaughter' of another Indian woman, who had been treated in a similar manner, and that, in 1971, he was suspected of the murder of another Indian woman whose body was found buried near his trailer; however, lack of evidence had led to his release.

It would seem that the Indian girl who escaped was *not* the 'victim' type – she might well have died eventually if the police had not arrived. The three days of torture and ill-treatment would have killed most girls; she had courage, and she lived.

A final illustration of the difference between the victim and non-victim can be seen in the case of the rapist Harvey Glatman. Glatman was a 30-year-old TV repairman of Los Angeles; he was also an enthusiastic amateur photographer. On August 1, 1957, a pretty 19-year-old model, Judy Ann Dull, left her apartment in West Hollywood, hired by a slightly built, jug-eared young man who called himself Johnny Glynn and who had told her that he had a 'job' that would only take a couple of hours.

'Glynn' took Judy Dull to his room in Melrose Avenue, Hollywood. She stripped naked and he took two photographs. Then he produced a gun and raped her twice. She promised never to tell anyone and begged him to let her go. 'Glynn' – or Glatman – made her dress, and took several 'bondage' pictures of her with a gag in her mouth, her hands tied and her dress pushed up. Late that night he drove her out to the desert north of Indio, took more flashlight photographs, then strangled her with a rope and buried her in a makeshift grave.

On March 8, 1957, a 24-year-old divorcee, Shirley Bridgeford, went out on a 'blind date' with a man she had met through a lonely hearts club. The man was Glatman; he drove her to the desert near San Diego, raped her, took photographs of her tied up and crying, raped her several times more, then strangled her and left the body covered with brushwood.

On July 23 Glatman called on a 23-year-old Latin girl, Ruth Mercado, another model. He forced his way into her apartment in the Wilshire district of Los Angeles, tied her up, raped her several times and took photographs, then drove her out to the desert near San Diego. He took food and drink along, and spent most of the next day raping the girl and taking photographs of her. Ruth Mercado was altogether less the victim type than Judy Ann Dull or Shirley Bridgeford; when she begged Glatman to let her go, to feed her pet parrot, he was strongly tempted to. 'I liked her.' But finally he decided she had to die, and killed her on the second night.

On October 27 Glatman picked up another model, Lorraine Vigil, a 27-year-old Latin girl, and asked her to come to his apartment to be photographed. She didn't like the look of him, and suggested taking a chaperone, but he dissuaded her. He drove fast out to Santa Ana, turned down a dark side road, then produced a gun. When he tried to tie her, she screamed and struggled. The gun went off, burning her thigh, and Glatman looked dazed, saying: 'I've shot you.' Still struggling, they rolled out of the car. And at this moment a police motorcycle arrived; Harvey Glatman was soon in custody. He admitted the killing of the three girls and on September 18, 1959, was executed in the gas chamber. 'I only want to die,' he had written to the appeal judge.

The victim type
Even the photographs of Glatman's four victims show clearly that Judy Dull and Shirley Bridgeford were 'victim' types, that Ruth Mercado was altogether less of a victim, while Lorraine Vigil was emphatically not the victim type. It is true that this *could* be a matter of chance, due to circumstances, or perhaps to the camera, but, comparing the photograph of Judy Dull with that of Ruth Mercado, it is difficult to believe.

What emerges then, is the interesting suggestion that to be a 'victim' is an attitude of mind, and that the same is true of being a non-victim. (In the celebrated dictum of the British crime writer, F. Tennyson Jesse, women can be put into two clear categories: those who will end by being dismembered and left in a trunk at some baggage office – and those who won't.) In a miserable person, the 'inner pressure' is low; in a happy person, it is high. And low pressure induces accident proneness as certainly as driving on a flat tyre induces punctures.

Eckermann once remarked to the poet Goethe: 'You were born with a silver spoon in your mouth. But supposing you hadn't been born lucky?' Goethe replied contemptuously: 'Do you suppose I would be such a fool as to be born unlucky?' Is it possible that Goethe, with his poet's insight, had glimpsed a truth that is now beginning to reveal itself to the modern criminologist?

VITAL CLUES

Edgar Wallace wrote a novel called *The Clue of the Twisted Candle*, in which an ingenious murderer succeeds in sealing a room by wedging a candle under the heavy latch of the door. As the candle gradually bends in the warmth of the room, the latch – inaccessible from outside – falls into its groove. Wallace was writing in the early days of forensic science, but, even so, his stratagem would have given little trouble to most experienced police officers. To begin with, some of the soft candle wax would inevitably have scraped off on the underside of the heavy latch, and the most stupid detective would have worked out the truth within minutes.

In real life, most 'vital clues' are altogether less obvious. In the two hundred years or so since its beginnings, scientific crime detection has reached a high degree of efficiency. Even so, the kind of brilliant deduction practised by Sherlock Holmes plays little part in the solution of modern crimes. It is a matter of hard work, patience and luck.

We can see all three of these elements in the classic case of the demob suit, recounted by Superintendent Bob Fabian of the Yard. In the summer of 1946, Police Constable Arthur Collins attempted to detain five men who were trying to enter a building in Warwick. He was so badly beaten and kicked that for a time it was feared that he might die. The five men escaped, and the only clue was a small piece of cloth torn from the jacket of one of the men by the constable's wife – who had tried to come to the rescue of her unconscious husband. The Warwick police decided to ask the help of Scotland Yard, and Fabian was put onto the case.

The cloth was photographed, and the photographs sent off to tailors all over England. Then it was exhibited in the window of a local newspaper office. An ex-army officer was able to tell Fabian that it was undoubtedly from a demob suit. Fabian

614

plodded to the nearest Ministry of Supply Depot in Birmingham; there, a check with a register showed that this pattern had been manufactured by a firm in Wellington, Somerset.

The police drove through the night – only to be told, at the factory, that this cloth had been enough for no less than five thousand suits. Moreover, soldiers often sold them to 'wide boys' at the gates of the camp. However, they were able to give Fabian the address of two factories in Birmingham and one in Glasgow who had bought the cloth. Fabian drove back to Birmingham. Neither of the two factories had started using their consignment yet.

Fabian went on to Glasgow. There a supervisor looked at the torn fragment, and was able to tell, from the stitching, the name of the man who had made it into a suit. 'Stitching is as distinct as handwriting,' he said. Finally, the long-shot paid off. The workman looked at the cloth, and was able to recall that the suit was made for an exceptionally tall and broad man – it had had to be specially made, so he remembered it.

Foul well-water

The Ordnance Depot at Branston, near Burton-on-Trent, was able to give Fabian the name of the ex-soldier for whose demob they had ordered the suit, and the police found him at the Birmingham address to which the suit had been posted. When the police constable's wife identified him as her husband's assailant, the big Irishman (6 feet 2½ inches tall) broke down and admitted his part in the robbery. He received four years' penal servitude.

This same quality of incredible patience can be found in a case that certainly ranks among the epics of classic detection. It took place in 1869. During the January of that year, a restaurant owner in the Rue Princesse, Paris, noticed that the water from the well tasted foul. He investigated, and found a parcel floating in the water. When it was opened it proved to contain the lower half of a human leg. The horrified restaurateur sent for the police. A young detective named Gustave Macé was placed in charge of the case. He looked down the well and found another parcel. In it was another leg, encased in a stocking.

Doctors told Macé the legs were almost certainly a woman's. Acting on this assumption, Macé obtained the files of 122 missing women and set about tracing them. It took him months, and finally there were only three left. Shortly after Macé had finally succeeded in tracing these remaining three, the doctors admitted that they could have been wrong. The legs were womanish, but could have belonged to a man. Macé heaved a sigh and started all over again.

He had two leads. On December 22 of the previous year, a policeman had met a man wandering along the Rue de Seine carrying a hamper. Because of the late hour, he asked the man what was in it. The man said he had just arrived in Paris from the country by train; unable to find a cab, he had been forced to walk with his hamper of country products.

He looked so honest that the policeman let him go, but his description – short, round-faced, with a black moustache – led Macé to suspect that this was the same man who had been seen a few days earlier throwing lumps of meat into the River Seine. Someone asked him what he was doing, and he said he was baiting the river because he intended to fish the next day. Since then, large gobbets of meat had been fished out of the river – too big for the average fish to swallow.

The stitches on the parcel in which the first leg had been sewn had a professional look about them. Moreover, why had the murderer chosen the restaurant to dump the leg? It might, of course, be a dissatisfied customer who wanted to spoil the trade. Or it might be someone who had lived in the upstairs part of the house at some time. He asked the concierge if there was a tailor in the house. No. Had there *ever* been one? No. But there had been a tailoress. That sounded a long-shot, but Macé had no other lead. He interviewed the girl, who told him that she often did jobs for other tailors. Did any of them ever visit her at the house? Many of them did, she said: one in particular, M. Voirbo, was very kind and helpful. He often fetched water up from the well for her.

Strange habits

Voirbo was a tailor, and he knew the well: Macé asked the girl if this Voirbo had any special friends. There *was* one old man, she said, a M. Bodasse. She didn't know where he lived, but he had an aunt who lived in the Rue de Nesle. Macé didn't know the aunt's exact address, but compared to tracing a hundred or so missing women it was child's play to locate her and Madame Bodasse was able to tell Macé that her nephew lived in the Rue Dauphine. He was a retired craftsman who had been a tapestry manufacturer. Oddly enough, he hadn't been seen for some weeks now, but that wasn't unlike him. His habits were strange.

The concierge at old Bodasse's apartment startled Macé by telling him Bodasse was at home. She had seen the light in his flat the night before. But he wouldn't answer the door. He was an eccentric. Macé felt he had now discovered the identity of the victim. His guess was confirmed when Madame Bodasse identified the stocking – made of white cotton, with a man's sock sewn on the bottom – as belonging to her nephew. She also thought the legs were his.

As to the mystery man, Pierre Voirbo, he was a police spy, a man who pretended to be a rabid anarchist and attended left-wing meetings – only to make reports to the police. Macé broke into Bodasse's apartment. Everything looked neat, and an eight-day clock was still ticking. Macé decided to have the place watched, and borrowed a couple of men from the secret police. This proved to be a mistake; they knew Voirbo as a colleague, and when they saw him entering the building, they accosted him and asked him why they were supposed to watch him. Macé's quarry was alerted.

But Macé already had much valuable evidence. Bodasse's strong box was empty. But in the back of a watch Macé found a piece of paper with numbers of various securities written on it. Probing Voirbo's background, Macé discovered that, until a few months ago, he had lived in fairly cheap lodgings and had seemed to be poor. Then he had married and moved elsewhere, paying his rent with a five-hundred-franc share that could be cashed by anyone.

Macé hastened to the money-changer. He had kept the counterfoil of the share; the number tallied with one of those in the watch. Macé decided it was time to interview Voirbo. Now began the cat and mouse game. Voirbo was a plump, cheerful young man of 30, and he appeared to be a man of resourcefulness and character. Treating Macé as a friend – since they both worked for the police – he admitted that he had been worried about Bodasse's non-appearance.

He suspected that he might have been killed – in which case the murderer was an alcoholic butcher named Rifer, a petty crook, who had almost certainly been aided by three criminal acquaintances, whom Voirbo also helpfully pointed out. When Macé checked, he discovered that two of the three had perfect alibis: they had been in jail throughout December. And not long after, the alcoholic butcher had a fit of D.T.s and was taken to an asylum.

Macé decided he had to arrest Voirbo. It proved to be a wise decision, for Voirbo had a ticket to Havre in his wallet, and other indications showed he intended to embark for America.

Voirbo seemed surprised and offended. What had he done that Macé should suspect him? They both knew there was no evidence.

Empty strong box

This, unfortunately, was true. Macé went to talk to Voirbo's wife, a quiet girl who obviously knew little of her husband's character and still less of his activities. Macé learned from her that she had brought her husband a dowry of 15,000 francs − about £600. Voirbo had gained the consent of her parents by telling them that he had 10,000 francs in securities; in fact, he had produced them before the wedding, but where were they now? The strong box was empty. Macé searched the house. Finally, in the cellar, he found Bodasses's securities; they had been soldered into a tin box, and suspended in a cask of wine.

Even that did not *prove* Voirbo a murderer. Macé now returned to Voirbo's old flat. A young couple had moved in, but they showed Macé precisely where the table had been when they first arrived. Macé was convinced this was where Bodasse had been killed; the cleaning woman had told him that Voirbo was notoriously untidy; yet on the morning of December 17 − the day after Bodasse was last seen alive − his room had been polished and scrubbed. If Bodasse had been killed at the table, then he had probably also been dismembered there, and his blood must have run on the floor. This was perfectly clean; but it sloped a little towards the bed.

Macé staged his final scene with all the dramatic flair of a fictional detective. Voirbo was taken to his old room in the Rue Mazarin. He seemed calm and indifferent. Macé took a jug of water, poised it over the spot where the table used to stand, and poured it. The water flowed slowly across the floor, and formed a pool under the bed. Voirbo suddenly became restive. Macé sent for a mason, and ordered him to take up the floor tiles under the bed. The dark undersides were found to be coated with dried blood. Suddenly, Voirbo's nerve broke, and he made his confession.

A scoundrel in love

He had been tired of being a scoundrel, a petty crook, he said; he decided he wanted to settle down as a married man. He was in love with a gentle Mademoiselle Rémondé, but it was necessary to impress her parents that he also had money. He begged his friend Bodasse to lend it to him. Bodasse refused, Voirbo decided he had to die.

He invited him to his room for tea, one day after they had dined together. Voirbo moved casually behind him, picked up a flat iron, and struck Bodasse on the head. Later, he dismembered the body and distributed the pieces around Paris, mostly in the river. After meeting the policeman who wanted to look into his basket – which contained bones and flesh – he decided to get rid of the legs by dumping them in the nearby well.

Voirbo was guillotined for the murder of Desiré Bodasse. But for one tiny mistake – sewing the leg into a piece of calico – he would have avoided suspicion. What is more, if he had kept his wits about him, he could have avoided detection even when the underside of the tiles showed traces of blood. He only had to deny that he knew where it came from, or declare that it was animal blood from a joint. In 1869 there was still no way of testing blood to determine whether it came from a man or an animal.

The story of how blood analysis was perfected is one of the great epics of scientific detection. Great scientists like Pasteur and Koch had discovered that if a human body is injected with *dead* germs, the blood will develop a resistance to living forms of the same germs; thus immunization was discovered. Twenty years later, in the 1890s, a German, von Behring, discovered that if a horse is injected with dead diphtheria germs, the serum from its blood – the clear liquid that separates out when blood is allowed to stand – will actually help children who are suffering from diphtheria to recover: the serum develops 'fighting' properties.

Around the turn of the century a chemist named Paul Uhlenhuth discovered that this same serum has even more remarkable properties. If a rabbit is injected with human blood, its blood serum develops a *resistance* to human blood. And if the serum is placed in a test tube, and the tiniest drop of human blood is introduced into it, it turns cloudy. It will not react at all to animal blood.

In 1901, shortly after Uhlenhuth had made this discovery, a travelling carpenter named Ludwig Tessnow was arrested on the Baltic island of Rügen, suspected of a particularly atrocious murder. Two small boys had been found in the woods, hacked and torn to pieces, scattered over a wide area. Three years earlier, Tessnow had been arrested on suspicion of killing two schoolgirls near the village of Lechtingen, near Osnabruck.

He had protested that certain stains on his clothes were of woodstain, not blood, and the police had had to release him for lack of evidence. Now he was questioned about a recently washed suit that showed slight traces of blood. Tessnow said that some of the almost obliterated stains were cattle blood, and that the others were woodstain. When the examining magistrate received the information from Osnabruck, he realized he was dealing with a man possessed of some insane desire to batter living creatures and tear them to pieces. A month before the two boys had been murdered, someone had attacked seven sheep in a field, cut them open and scattered the entrails all over the field. The shepherd had seen the man running away; he now identified Tessnow as the sheep butcher. But Tessnow denied everything.

Human bloodstains

Fortunately, the prosecutor had kept abreast of new developments in legal medicine, and had heard about Uhlenhuth's discovery. He sent Uhlenhuth the bloodstained clothing, and also the stone that had been used to batter the children. Unlenhuth dissolved dozens of small stains in salt water and tested them all. He found 22 human bloodstains and half a dozen stains of sheep's blood. His evidence convicted Tessnow, who was sentenced to death.

Not only would the serum distinguish human blood from animal blood; it would also distinguish different *types* of human blood: the groups A, B, O, and AB. This discovery did not provide sufficient evidence to hang a suspect in Gladbeck, Germany, in 1928, but a jury of sceptical burghers declined to convict on purely scientific evidence. The accused was 20-year-old Karl Hussmann, a dominant and violent student.

In the early hours of March 23, 1928, a youth named Helmut Daube was found dying in the street; his throat had been cut and his genitals slashed off. The police soon discovered that Daube's closest friend was his fellow-student Hussmann; when they went to Hussmann's house, they discovered that his shoes had been recently washed, and showed traces of blood. His clothes were also bloodstained. Hussmann had completely dominated Daube, and the two had been lovers; but recently, Daube had realized that he preferred girls and had tried to break away.

At first Hussmann claimed the blood was that of a cat he had killed, but Uhlenhuth's test quickly revealed that it was human blood. Hussmann then changed his story and said he had had a nosebleed. The forensic laboratory at Bonn demonstrated that this was also impossible, for the blood on the shoes was type A – Daube's group – while Hussmann was type O.

The feeling of the court was that, while they were not convinced of Hussmann's innocence, they were by no means happy about convicting him on what, to them, amounted to purely circumstantial evidence, so Hussmann was acquitted. But the case drew wide attention to the use of testing for blood groups in criminal cases. Since that time, many criminals have been hanged on the evidence of a dried blood-spot on a wooden floor.

On humane grounds, perhaps the jury was right to disregard circumstantial evidence, for there is also the danger of hanging an innocent man. The case of Burton Abbott provides a thought-provoking illustration. Abbott was known to his neighbours in Alameda, California, as a quiet, rather intellectual man. He had never been known to be violent and had no police record.

On July 15, 1955, Abbott's wife was looking through old clothes in the basement when she found a wallet. It contained the identification card of 14-year-old Stephanie Bryan, some photographs, and an unfinished letter dated April 28, 1955. That had been the day when Stephanie had disappeared after coming out of school in Berkeley. She had never been seen since.

Georgia Abbott took the wallet upstairs and asked her husband how it had got there. He seemed as puzzled as she was, and they called the police. The next day, the police dug up Abbott's basement and found Stephanie's schoolbooks and her bra. Abbott pointed out that his garage had recently been used as a polling place, and that dozens of people had been in and out. However, a newsman went up to Abbott's summer cabin on Trinity Mountain with two dogs. The dogs led to a shallow grave. Stephanie Bryan's body was found in it; she had been strangled with her own panties, and the circumstances pointed to sexual assault.

Abbott was arrested and tried. He insisted that he knew nothing whatever about Stephanie or her clothes – and there was certainly no definite evidence to connect him with her disappearance. But the jury convicted him. There were several stays of execution. The last one came just after 11.15 a.m. on March 14, 1947, but it arrived a few minutes too late; the cyanide gas pellets had been dropped under the execution chair at 11.15 precisely. Abbott persisted in denying his guilt to the end, although he is said to have told a doctor: 'I can't admit it. Think of what it would do to my mother.'

All the evidence suggests that Abbott was the killer of Stephanie Bryan. Yet there is an element of doubt: for example, he *could* have been framed by her real killer. The brilliant triumphs of scientific crime detection should never blind us to the fact that the word 'clue' means an *indication*, and that, forensically, there is a vital difference between an indication and a final proof.

WAR CRIMES

The subject of war and war crimes takes us straight to the heart of the mystery that baffles every criminologist: why is man, alone of all creatures, the only one who systematically murders his own kind? For nearly two thousand years Western man has accepted the answer given by the Christian Church: man is a fallen creature, and one result of the Fall was the murder of Abel by his brother Cain.

But in recent years zoologists and students of animal behaviour have suggested an altogether more revolutionary theory: that man achieved his present position as the world's most dominant species *because he is the descendant of a killer ape*. Killing, according to this theory, is so much a part of man's basic personality that he will never be able to throw off the habit. The gloomy conclusion seems to be that civilization will never 'tame' man. In fact, the more highly evolved it becomes, the more man's basic aggression will struggle to burst out.

Looking at the increase in the crime figures, this seems horribly plausible. A mere century ago, America was still a great wilderness, but although there was plenty of casual violence – shootings and stabbings in the course of quarrels – there was very little *premeditated* murder. This is the reason for premeditated murder arousing such widespread fascination and horror – cases like Professor Webster's murder of Dr. Parkman, or England's famous Red Barn murder.

Hidden monster

Now it sometimes looks as if murderers have entered into a kind of competition to see who can commit the most gruesome and sadistic crime. Heath, Haigh and Christie seemed shocking enough in the fifties. Speck, Manson and Ian Brady horrified the sixties. But in the seventies and eighties, the pageant of sadistic mass murder – Dean Corll, the McCrary family, Herb Mullin,

Gerard Schaefer, Edmund Kemper – threatened to hammer our responses into a state of insensibility.

It begins to look very much as if man is protesting against the civilization that is trying to force him to forget his animal past. Each time the hidden monster breaks out, he seems more bloodthirsty than ever.

But before we accept this depressing conclusion, let us take a careful look at how it was reached. As recently as two hundred years ago it was a basic article of Christian faith that man had been created by God 'in his own image', and looking exactly as he does today. Then geologists began digging up ancient bones and fossils that cast doubt on this theory, for some of these primitive bones and skulls were obviously the remains of some kind of human being.

Scientists found a simple way to get around this problem. They agreed that these creatures *were* some form of human being, but they were *not* the ancestor of modern man. No, the world had been through a series of great catastrophes, like the Flood, which had wiped out all life; whereupon Nature had started all over again. So modern man *was* made specially by God after all. In 1859 the whole world was rocked by the publication of a book, *The Origin of Species*, by Charles Darwin, which *proved*, with data, that modern man had evolved from these primitive ape-like creatures.

Mass cannibalism
The Church roared with rage, and declared that it was blasphemy to assert that man had descended from an 'ape', and until recently there were still schools in America's Deep South where it was illegal to teach the theory of evolution. But worse was to come. According to the theories accepted in the first half of this century, *homo sapiens* had evolved because of his intelligence. He started as a gentle, vegetarian creature, like his brother the ape, slowly learned such skills as hunting and agriculture, and so created civilization.

However, in the late 1920s, scientists found an even more primitive form of man at Chou-kou-tien, in China. And there were unmistakable signs of mass cannibalism. They found piles of skulls of Peking Man (or *Sinanthropus*) in a cave, and they all had a hole in them as though cracked open to extract the brain.

There was definite evidence that Peking Man roasted and ate his own type. It began to look as if early man – and Peking Man was nearly 400,000 years old – was not quite the holy innocent

everyone had assumed. Even before the discoveries at Chou-kou-
tien, scientists had heard of an even more primitive form of
ape-man; blasting near Taungs, in South Africa, had uncovered
the skull of a baby. This creature was closer to the ape than
anything discovered earlier, and it apparently dated from around
800,000 years ago – twice as old as Peking Man.

But it was in the late 'forties that the zoologist Raymond Dart
came upon some of the most startling evidence concerning this
South African ape-man. Baboon skulls found near the site had
odd depressions in the skulls. They had been killed with a
weapon – the humerus (shoulder) bone of the antelope.
Southern ape-man – known as *Australopithecus* – had been a
killer. He was closer to the ape than any other form of primitive
man; he was a kind of missing link between ape and man. *And
he had used weapons.*

Dart propounded his startling and alarming theory: not only
was early man a killer, but he had developed his brain as a result
of the need to use weapons. If you are going to hit someone on
the nose, you can swipe out instinctively, and leave it to your
muscles. But if you are going to kill an animal by hitting it on the
head with a club, you need to measure carefully the distance
between the end of your club and the animal's head. It requires a
kind of cold concentration. It was that concentration, said Dart
– in a famous paper of 1949 – that had started the Southern Ape
on the long road of evolution towards modern man.

And this, according to Dart, explains a great deal about the
evolution of the human race. Early man grouped himself into
rough tribes or communities and lived by hunting. Then someone discovered that seeds could be planted and cultivated; man
became an agriculturalist. Between 3000 and 4000 B.C. he
learned to sow wheat and harvest it, and he learned the use of
animals to draw his primitive plough. But as soon as settled
farmers appeared, so did nomads.

Man's old hunting instinct was being turned against his fellow
man. Around 2000 B.C. came the discovery of one of the most
revolutionary of war-weapons: the horse. Certain tribes in
central Asia began breeding the horse – which had always been a
rather small animal, hardly bigger than a large Alsation dog –
into the powerful beast we know today.

These wild men were known in the West as Scythians, and
they were famous for their barbarity. Scythians learned to ride
horses, and this gave them a new mobility. They could swoop on
a village settlement, slaughter half the inhabitants, load up their

winter grain on to spare horses, and be out of sight again in half an hour. Man the warrior was emerging.

As the centuries went by, men developed another kind of horse – the ship, the horse of the sea. The legendary Greek Odysseus – Ulysses – who lived about 1100 B.C. was a pirate who landed near lonely coastal settlements and slaughtered the natives. And by that time, piracy was already an old-established trade. The Trojan War, in which Ulysses took part, was not really caused by the theft of Helen of Troy by Paris; it was an attempt by the Greeks to steal profitable trade routes from the natives of the Dardanelles.

Large-scale crime

This is what war meant in the ancient world – organized murder and robbery. There are, of course, rare exceptions: the Pelopon-nesian War – 431-404 B.C. – was a contest between two powerful rival states, Athens and Sparta, in which the adversaries were more or less equal. This kind of war was more like the fights between animals to decide who shall be leader of the pack; it is a contest chosen by both sides.

But most war was, quite simply, large-scale crime. When we read the Bible story of the fall of Jericho, in which God aided the Israelites by making the walls fall down, we tend to forget that these Israelites were basically a war-like horde who descended on a peaceful agricultural community and took it by force from its rightful owners. It was, in fact, one of the earliest 'war crimes' – Jericho is the oldest city at present known to man, dating back as far as 8000 B.C.

All of this makes it clear that the concept of a 'war crime' is highly ambiguous. Even where two neighbouring states – or countries – fall to quarrelling, it is very hard indeed to allot blame. For example, the increasing violence that has been going on in Northern Ireland since 1969 has it roots in the distant past. The Irish allege, with good reason, that England has been committing crimes against their country for centuries. But on closer examin-ation, things are no longer so clear-cut.

The English landed in Ireland in 1171, invited – oddly enough – by the Pope, and they treated the native Irish much as white Americans treated the Red Indians. So it seems to be the fault of the English? But no . . . for it was these same English, who became 'Irish-ized', who were periodically massacred by their own countrymen in later centuries.

The beginning of the present troubles can be traced back to the landing of the Spaniards and Italians in 1580; from then on, there were a series of incidents, always described as war crimes by the other side, that kept the spirit of hatred alive. The Irish revolted against the English settlers in 1641 and murdered them by the thousand. The English sent Oliver Cromwell to take revenge.

And now it becomes as difficult to discover the rights and wrongs as in any court of law. Irish school textbooks still declare that, at the seige of Drogheda in 1649, Cromwell's men slaughtered nearly 4,000 men, women and children. English historians deny this, citing Cromwell himself, who wrote at the time – in a letter – that only men *in arms* were killed.

Probably we shall never know the truth. According to the English, Cromwell was avenging slaughtered Ulstermen; according to the Irish, he was intent on torture and murder, just as the Nazis were in Warsaw or in Russia. American readers, remembering the story of the brutal mass slayings of white settlers by Red Indians, and Red Indians by white soldiers, will understand how difficult it is to take a simplistic view.

Human tragedy

T.S. Duke's *Celebrated Criminal Cases of America* (1910) contains a hair-raising account of 'The Outrages Committed by the Sioux Indians' between 1852 and 1862, with details of rapes and mutilations that would have convinced any reader that the Sioux deserved mass extermination. Nowadays, civilized opinion has swung the other way; it was the white men who were the criminals; the red man was only trying to defend his own right to live. Yet when we read Duke's account today, we are less concerned with the rights and wrongs than with the unreducible human tragedy:

'The hero of the day was an 11-year-old boy named Martin Eastlick, who carried his fifteen-month-old brother Johnny on his back for fifty miles, but he died shortly afterwards from exposure, over-exertion and lack of nourishment. Mr. Eastlick had been killed and Mrs. Eastlick was lying helpless on the ground from a bullet wound. Her two little boys named Freddie and Frank, aged five and seven respectively, were with her. Two squaws saw them, and catching the children they beat them to death with bludgeons before the helpless mother's eyes. Many other children were only beaten until they were left helpless and then left to die from hunger and exposure.'

Thirty-eight Indians were tried and executed for the massacres. They would have argued that it was unfair to treat the massacre as a 'crime', since they were at war with the white man, and the white man had treated Indian women and children just as brutally. In retrospect we can see that it makes no difference whether it was called an act of war or a crime, for they are synonymous. As soon as we begin to discuss the rights and wrongs of such cases, we are justifying murder – as Charles Manson tried to justify his 'family's' murder of Sharon Tate and the LaBiancas by asserting they were at war with the 'pigs'. The only logical course, it seems, is to recognize that murder is always unjustified, whether it is a criminal act or an act of war.

Legal farce

It was precisely this attitude that led the Western allies to decide to put German 'war criminals' on trial after the Second World War, but the result demonstrated that the problem cannot be solved as simply as that. There are many hidden pitfalls in the argument that war and crime should be treated as identical; in the past, it has always been taken for granted that they are two totally different things.

During the Napoleonic Wars, there was a strong body of opinion, in England and Prussia, in favour of hanging Napoleon. But when it came to the point, sober counsels prevailed and he was sent into exile. During the First World War, there was a powerful 'Hang the Kaiser' movement in England; but again, reason prevailed, and he was sent into exile instead. History agrees that Napoleon and the Kaiser *were* to blame for plunging Europe into war; but the victors chose to regard them as soldiers rather then criminals.

During the Hitler war, none of the Western allies had the least doubt that Hitler should be regarded as a criminal rather than as a military leader: the slaughter of Jews in the Warsaw ghetto, the destruction of Lidice, the existence of Auschwitz and Buchenwald, proved it beyond all doubt. When the end of the war came, Hitler and Goebbels were dead; Himmler committed suicide; Hoess – the commandant of Auschwitz – was executed in Cracow. Of the men on trial at Nuremburg, very few had actually been guilty of 'crimes against humanity', as the indictments made clear.

Goering directed the German air force, Doenitz the U-boats, Raeder the navy, von Schirach led the youth movement, Speer was armaments minister, von Papen a member of the government, Ribbentrop an ambassador, Keitel a general. And Hess was not in Germany for the greater part of the war.

The only defendants against whom it could be alleged that

they had actually taken part in the murder of Jews were Kaltenbrunner, the Gestapo chief, Frank, administrator of Poland, and Frick. Even Streicher and Rosenberg, both rabid anti-Semites, had played no active part in the 'final solution'.

It is to the credit of the court that von Papen, Schacht and Fritzsche – head of Radio Division – were found not guilty, but heavily to its discredit that men like Doenitz, Raeder and Speer were found guilty. If Germany had won the war, then most British and American generals and admirals could have been found guilty on the same grounds. The western allies regarded Nuremberg as the noble administration of justice; historians of the future will probably regard it as a legal farce.

This leaves the interesting problem: what *should* have been done with Hitler, Himmler, and men like Hoess and Eichmann, if they had been taken alive? The simple answer is that the victors in any war have the right – if they choose – to kill their enemies, to prevent them doing further mischief. After all, Napoleon escaped from Elba and forced the British and Prussians to fight him again at Waterloo. If Hitler had been shot, it would have seemed a comparatively clean and honest solution. It is difficulty to apply either adjective to the Nuremberg trials.

Perhaps the case that argues most strongly for a legal definition of 'war crime' is the notorious murder of Polish officers at Katyn Wood. Stalin launched an attack on Poland two weeks after Hitler's troops swept towards Warsaw. Stalin's excuse – later – was that he had to stop Germany taking *all* Poland. Two hundred thousand Polish prisoners were deported to Russia. When Hitler invaded Russia in 1941, Stalin joined the western allies, and since Poland already had a government in exile in London, the question of releasing Polish prisoners arose.

Vast numbers of captured men proved to be missing, notably around 4,000 of Poland's top army officers. At this point, the Germans embarrassed their former allies by asserting in a broadcast that the Russians had deliberately massacred ten thousand Poles at Katyn Wood, near Smolensk. The German troops had found the mass grave when they captured Smolensk in July 1941 . . .

The Russians immediately countered by declaring that *if* there was a mass grave, then the Germans were responsible. The discovery that the 4,143 bodies in the mass grave had been killed by German bullets seemed to lend colour to this accusation – until the Germans pointed out that works in Genschow had supplied quantities of ammunition to Russia.

Investigations that have continued for years since the end of the war suggest definitely that it *was* the Russians who had taken this opportunity to dispose of most of the officer corps of their old hereditary enemy, the Poles. A British television documentary on the murders in 1971 included survivors who were quite positive about Russian responsibility; there were strong attempts by the Russian Embassy to prevent the programme being shown.

There can be no doubt that, according to the Geneva and Hague Conventions, the murder of war prisoners *is* a crime. On the other hand, Soviet communists have always insisted that they make their own rules. A glance at the long article on 'The Laws of War' in *Encyclopaedia Britannica* reveals that moralists and philosophers have been arguing about them since the days of ancient Rome, and that there has never been any general agreement. It seems safe to say that the Katyn Wood murders, like the Nuremberg trials, will remain a matter for moral and legal controversy for centuries.

As to the basic question – of whether man is a killer by deep instinct – there is now a powerful body of opinion in opposition to Dart's fatalism. The psychologist Abraham Maslow, speaking of Freud's theories of sex and aggression, said emphatically that Freud had 'sold human nature short', and an increasing number of psychologists would now agree with Maslow that man has 'higher' as well as 'lower' needs, and that these higher needs are just as instinctive as the basic needs for territory, food and sex. It may be true that man has evolved from a killer ape; but he has shed other simian habits – such as the tail, and a preference for walking on all fours. Science teaches us that it is sensible to learn from the past; but it is dangerous as well as stupid to assume that the future is rigidly conditioned by the past.